# Introduction to Sociology:
## A Collaborative Approach, Third Edition

Rene L. O'Dell • XueMei Hu • Barbara Miller • Beverly Farb

Sally A. Stablein • Kwaku Obosu-Mensah • Sergio Romero • Dara G. John

Liza L. Kuecker • Cheryl Boudreaux • Josh Packard • Steven D. Williams

Bruce D. LeBlanc • John Joe Schlichtman • Chris Biga • Brian G. Moss

Ashbury Publishing
DIVERSITY
INSIDE

Executive Editor: Brenton Roncace

Copy Editors: Cindy Anderson, Margaret Mackenzie, Ruth Paul, Suzan Raney and Bethann Stewart

Book design by Amy Roncace, Brice Roncace and Jade McCoy

Cover photography by Martin Varsavsky

Introduction to Sociology: A Collaborative Approach, Third Edition / Rene L. O'Dell, XueMei Hu, Barbara Miller, Beverly Farb, Sally A. Stablein, Kwaku Obosu-Mensah, Sergio Romero, Dara G. John, Liza L. Kuecker, Cheryl Boudreaux, Josh Packard, Steven D. Williams, Bruce D. LeBlanc, John Joe Schlichtman, Chris Biga, Brian G. Moss

ISBN 978-0-9791538-5-3

Ashbury Publishing LLC, Boise, Idaho
www.ashburypublishing.com

# Contents

# Chapter 9: Inequality and Stratification by Sexual Orientation, Gender and Age 235

# Chapter 10: Families 257

# Chapter 11: Education and Religion 275

# Chapter 12: Politics and the Economy 299

# Editor's Preface

Dear Reader:

Thank you for supporting Ashbury Publishing. Located in beautiful Boise, Idaho, Ashbury Publishing is not a large business. In fact, we currently only have only this title, *Introduction to Sociology*. But what we lack in size we make up for with our drive to provide the highest quality introductory sociology textbook available.

I began this endeavour because I felt that the current textbook market was too homogeneous, controlled by only a few very powerful corporate entities. I wanted to provide something different—something new and hopefully something better—a textbook to stand against the status quo. The book you hold in your hands is the fruition of that dream.

One of the defining characteristics that sets this *Introduction to Sociology* textbook apart from the others is its diverse tapestry of voices. This book was written collaboratively, with each chapter authored by a passionate sociology expert with deep knowledge in his or her area of emphasis. Together these individual voices become a melodious chorus, proving the adage, "The whole is more than the sum of its parts." This approach makes for excellent reading and introduces students to a wide range of thought. In short, I am serious about diversity because I believe in its value. This is why Ashbury Publishing has adopted the slogan "Diversity Inside"—it's how textbooks ought to be done.

A lot of energy goes into making a textbook, and this third edition is no exception. My thanks go out to our copy editors for their dilligent efforts to help make this edition a success, as well as our excellent layout artists, photographers and graphic designers. And, of course, I would be remiss in failing to mention my extreme gratitude to our wonderful team of dedicated authors, without which there would simply be no textbook.

I hope you are both inspired and enriched by this composition of many minds.

Brenton Roncace
Executive Editor
Ashbury Publishing LLC

# Meet the Authors

## Rene L. O'Dell

Chapter 1 An Introduction to Sociology

A student once told Rene, "Sociology is like opening the back of a clock and learning how it ticks." Rene O'Dell took her first sociology course in high school as an elective, and it soon became her favorite class. After graduating, she attended Irvine Valley College in California as a sociology major. Her first passion was social work, helping abused and neglected children. She decided to attend Cal State Fullerton, where she obtained bachelor's and master's degrees in sociology. Her goal was to be a social worker by day and an instructor by night. When presented with the opportunity to teach, she decided to pursue that avenue exclusively—and was right back at the place she started, Irvine Valley College.

Rene says that without the people you love, your dreams are just your own. She has been very blessed to be supported by her loving husband, Patrick, and her family—especially her mother—and her friends.

## XueMei Hu

Chapter 2 Society and Culture
Chapter 4 Social Structure and Social Interaction

Xuemei Hu is a senior professor of sociology at Union County College in New Jersey. She obtained her bachelor's degree in English and American literature and her master's and doctorate degrees in sociology. Her interests of study include social stratification, marriage and family, social problems, racial and ethnic relations, distance learning education, and student learning outcome assessment. Dr. Hu enjoys teaching both on-campus and online courses. She was invited by the League for Innovation in the Community College to attend national conferences and make presentations on online teaching. She was awarded a *Quality Matters Training Certificate* and a *Quality Matters Peer Reviewer Certificate*, which certify the quality of her online courses and components.

In 1997, Dr. Hu was employed by the College of Education at the University of Hawaii (UH) to implement Project CLASS (*Chinese Language Achievement through Sequential Study*), a federally funded program by the U.S. Department of Education. She served as project coordinator and was the UH specialist tasked with introducing the study of Chinese. In her role, she served as liaison; trained and supervised teachers; taught workshops to disseminate the curriculum; wrote annual performance reports to the Department of Education that were published by the Education Resources Information Center; and published a curriculum titled *Mandarin Chinese for Elementary Students*, which includes textbooks, teacher's manuals, and workbooks.

## Barbara Miller
Chapter 3 Socialization

Barbara Miller was born in Tulsa, Oklahoma. She studied piano at a young age, and, at the age of 11, performed as a soloist with the Minneapolis Symphony Orchestra. She also trained in Lake Placid, New York, as a figure skater, winning three national titles and pair skating with Dick Button. She was the alternate member of the 1948 Olympic team. She met her husband of 50 years while skating on a float in the Rose Parade, and teaching ice skating paid for her education.

Educators love learning, and she is no exception. She has gone to law school and nursing school and has kept her emergency medical technician (EMT) license active for 14 years. She loves studying and teaching abroad. In 2009, she spent the spring in Oxford, England, teaching two psychology and two sociology courses. She lives near the Pacific Ocean and enjoys chasing dolphins in a kayak with her grandsons. She has taught at Pasadena City College in California for 41 years and wears two hats—as instructor of psychology and sociology; however, her doctorate is in education. Every year, she says she'll retire, but she loves her job too much to stop.

## Beverly Farb
Chapter 5 Groups and Organizations

Beverly Farb has taught at Everett Community College in Washington for 12 years. She teaches a broad variety of courses, including Introduction to Sociology, Introduction to Psychology, Social Psychology, Criminology, Family, Cross-Cultural Medicine, and Global Studies. Beverly has served as adjunct faculty at Simon Fraser University in British Columbia. She has also worked as a mental health counselor with the homeless. Beverly earned her doctorate in sociology and her master's degrees in marriage and family therapy at the University of Southern California.

## Sally A. Stablein
Chapter 6 Deviance and Social Control

Born in Waverly, Iowa, Sally A. Stablein grew up in Southern California, in the city of Orange. From Orange County, she moved to San Marcos, California, where she attended Palomar Community College and received an associate of arts degree in general studies.

From there, Sally transferred to California State University, San Marcos, and fell in love with sociology. Her passion for the discipline led her to complete a bachelor of arts degree in sociology at CSUSM. Sally's areas of interest and specialty topics include deviant behavior, violence and culture, race and ethnicity, social stratification, and gender.

During her time at CSUSM, Sally decided she wanted to teach sociology. She then went on to obtain her masters of arts in sociology from Humboldt State University in Northern California in 2001. Soon thereafter, she started her first teaching job in Denver in 2002 and taught at several schools in the Denver metro area until she received a full-time position at Red Rocks Community College. She teaches several classes, including Intro to Sociology, Deviant Behavior, Death & Dying, Contemporary Social Issues, Sociology of Gender, Violence & Culture, Sexuality, and Sociology of Religion. She is working on an Environmental Sociology course that she hopes will be offered soon.

## Kwaku Obosu-Mensah
Chapter 7 Social Stratification in the United States and the World

Kwaku Obosu-Mensah was born and raised in Oyoko, a small town in the eastern region of Ghana in Africa. His secondary and higher education landed him in the Ghanaian towns of Nkonya Ahenkro, Hohoe, and Accra. After a stint as a teacher at Osu Presby Secondary School in Accra, he left for Nigeria to work as a high school teacher at St. John's Anglican Grammar School (Ode Lemo, Ogun state) and later at Asabari Grammar School (Saki, Oyo state).

In 1985, he enrolled at the University of Bergen in Norway, and obtained his master's degree in sociology in 1990. His minors were in administration and organization science, methodology of social sciences, and pedagogy.

He then worked as a lecturer at Høgskolen i Bodø (Bodø University College) in Bodø (Norway). In 1992, he enrolled at the University of Toronto to pursue his Ph.D. in sociology. Upon completion of his doctorate in 1998, he worked as a career counselor and a teaching assistant at the University of Toronto before moving to Jackson, Tennessee, to take an assistant professor position at Lane College in 2000. In 2001, he accepted a visiting assistant position at Western Kentucky University, Bowling Green. In 2002, he accepted an assistant professor position at Lorain County Community College in Elyria, Ohio. He has presented papers at more than 50 conferences in Norway, Canada, Germany, and the United States. In addition to courses in sociology, he teaches international studies. At the moment, he is an associate professor at Lorain County Community College.

He has lived in, studied in, or visited 12 countries around the world. His hobbies are soccer, traveling, listening to music, organizing functions, fishing, reading, and discussing international affairs.

## Sergio Romero
Chapter 8 Race and Ethnicity

Sergio Romero is an assistant professor of sociology at Boise State University. He received his Ph.D. in sociology from the University of Oregon in 2004. His scholarship focuses on welfare reform policy networks employing quantitative and qualitative methods.

He has also done research on Latino immigrant labor. He has presented papers at national and international conferences and continues to publish in a variety of sources.

As the director of the Multi-Ethnic Studies Program, Romero revamped the curriculum to prepare majors as community scholars, readying students to live and work in a society that has a growing ethnic and inter-racial population.

## Dara G. John
Chapter 8 Race and Ethnicity

One day Dara G. John was having coffee with her daughter, and she made a comment that included "living my life" in the context. Her daughter responded, "Mother, you don't live your life; you observe it." Dara couldn't see a difference. All of her life she had been interested in why people do the things that they do and why they live the ways that they live. It wasn't until she studied sociology as an undergraduate that she understood that there are people who actually study these things. What a find!

Her undergraduate work involved a dual major in religion and psychology at Central Michigan University. She was then a graduate fellow in the Department of Sociology, Anthropology, and Social Work at CMU. During her years at the university, she learned not only the hows and whys of people's behaviors, but she also learned that she is a feminist at heart and a lover of all things natural. She was "green" before it was a cool and responsible choice.

She has helped families in the Head Start program and has been a counselor for victims of domestic violence and sexual assault. She's also worked as a community event organizer, a public speaker and educator, a cashier, and a Girl Scout field director in charge of programs and volunteer management. She even worked for an auto repair service and scheduled muffler work.

All of these jobs are a part of our society, and to learn what they are and what they involve gives Dara the perspective she needs to help her students see our society and culture more clearly. She now teaches at Central Michigan University and Mid Michigan Community College. She enjoys teaching a variety of courses, but the classes she teaches most consistently are Introduction to Sociology, Social Problems, and the American Family.

## Liza L. Kuecker

Chapter 9 Inequality and Stratification by Sexual Orientation, Gender and Age

Liza L. Kuecker grew up in LaCrosse, Wisconsin, and received a bachelor of science degree in sociology and Spanish from her hometown school, the University of Wisconsin-LaCrosse. She later went on to obtain master's and doctorate degrees in sociology at the University of Oregon. She has experienced a deeply satisfying teaching career, holding faculty positions at the University of South Carolina-Upstate; Montana State University, Billings; and Clark College in Vancouver, Washington. She is currently a professor of sociology at Western New Mexico University and teaches the following courses: Introduction to Sociology, Criminology, Social Psychology, Family, Aging, Research Methods, Sociology of Health, and Rural Sociology. She also supervises student internships in the community and serves as co-advisor to the Native American Club.

Most of Liza's research focuses on the scholarship of teaching and learning. She is now exploring how tribal colleges provide Native American students access to degree programs incorporating culturally centered curriculum; play an active role in cultural preservation/resurgence efforts; and serve as catalysts for environmentally and economically sustainable development on their home reservations. Professionally, she is an active member of the Pacific Sociological Association and was elected to a two-year term representing the Southern Region of the council from 2008 to 2010. In the community, she serves on the board of the Southwest Women's Fiber Arts Collective and is a volunteer certified long-term care ombudsman for the New Mexico Aging and Long-Term Care Services Department.

## Cheryl Boudreaux
Chapter 10 Families

Cheryl Boudreaux teaches in the Sociology Department (Death and Dying, Families in Society, and Love, Sex and Gender) at Grand Valley State University, Allendale, Michigan. Dr. Boudreaux has served two terms as the elected president of the Michigan Sociological Association (MSA) and is an active member of the Society for the Study of Social Problems (SSSP). Dr. Boudreaux is a photographer/sociologist who sees images as a significant part of the social construction of reality. Specializing in the study of transformations of consciousness or worldviews, Dr. Boudreaux's research includes race consciousness, spiritual transformations of consciousness, and changing images of death and dying. Dr. Boudreaux earned a Ph.D. in sociology at Brandeis University, Waltham, Massachusetts, an M.A. at Boston College, Chestnut Hill, Massachusetts, and a B.A. at the University of California San Diego, La Jolla.

Dr. Boudreaux's research and theories of transformation inform her teaching in sociology as well as her advocacy and interest in working toward social justice. She has written and presented papers on marriage and family; images of death, dying and terrorism; and race consciousness in health and illness.

## Josh Packard
Chapter 11 Education and Religion

Josh Packard is an assistant professor of sociology and assistant director of the Survey Research Lab at the University of Northern Colorado in Greeley, Colorado. He earned his Ph.D. in sociology from Vanderbilt University in 2008 and a B.A. in English from Texas Lutheran University in 2000. His book, "The Emerging Church: Religion at the Margins," which examines the organizational dynamics of the Emerging Church, will be published in 2012 by Lynne-Rienner/First Forum press. His research on the impact of racial diversity in college classrooms can be found in The Sociological Quarterly. Along with these interests, he researches the social determinants of health at the neighborhood level from an applied sociology perspective.

## Steven D. Williams
Chapter 12 Politics and the Economy

Steven D. Williams was born in Toronto, Ontario, and raised in the provinces of Saskatchewan and Alberta. After high school, he was convinced he would have a career as either a rock star or a record producer, so he sang in a band in Red Deer, Alberta, and took a recording engineer's course in Chillicothe, Ohio. Shockingly, he became neither rich nor famous. After five years as a night-club disc jockey, he began to notice that some of his friends in college were using words he didn't understand. He started his journey in post-secondary education with no particular goal in mind other than to learn. But an introductory course in sociology changed his life. He was hooked on this way of thinking and seeing the world around him. He completed his bachelor's and master's degrees at the University of Alberta in Edmonton. He received his Ph.D. in sociology from Carleton University in Ottawa in 2000. He took a job at the University of Southern Indiana in Evansville in 2000, teaching introductory sociology, classical and contemporary theory, popular culture, race and ethnicity, and gender studies. He became the director of USI's gender studies program as well as an associate professor, and even paid off his student loans.

With every year of teaching and research, Steven becomes more aware of the ways in which politics and economics intertwine. The institutions he was least interested in as an undergraduate have become integral to the way he now views sociology and the world. The entire planet, after all, is composed of political entities we call nation-states whose primary function is to compete for scarce economic resources. It's sometimes a challenge getting undergraduate students excited about studying these fundamental institutions, but when they realize the direct effects on their lives, there may be no more apt way to demonstrate the "micro-macro link." He remains confident that sociology and rock 'n' roll will save the world.

## Bruce D. LeBlanc
Chapter 13 Health and Population

Bruce D. LeBlanc is a professor and chair of the Sociology and Psychology Department at Black Hawk College, Moline, Illinois. He holds an Ed.D. in post-secondary social sciences from the University of Sarasota, an M.A. in sociology from Idaho State University, an M.A. in transpersonal studies from Atlantic University, and an M.P.A. from the Consortium of the California State University. He is a board-certified sexologist with the American College of Sexologists and a certified sexological instructor/advisor for HIV/AIDS prevention. His research interests focus on marginalized or under-studied social phenomena, including sexuality and the aged, female homosexuality, and the social psychological dimensions of spirituality. Additionally, he is an autocephalous Catholic bishop holding dual affiliations with the Transformational Catholic Church and the Ecumenical Catholic Church. He is currently serving as the president of the Illinois Sociological Association.

## John Joe Schlichtman
Chapter 14 Urban and Environmental Sociology—
Urban Portion

John Joe Schlichtman received his B.S. in finance from the University of Illinois at Urbana-Champaign, and his M.A. and Ph.D. in urban sociology from New York University. His academic interests include urban political economy, globalization, urban change, small cities, homelessness, gentrification, and qualitative methods. Schlichtman's primary research explores the role of cities, especially small cities, in the global context. Another area of Schlichtman's research relates to qualitative research methods, especially the integrity of ethnographic work. His recent research has been published in the *International Journal of Urban and Regional Research*, *City and Community*, and other journals and edited volumes. Schlichtman, a member of the Research Committee 21 on the Sociology of Urban and Regional Development of the International Sociological Association, is involved in efforts to address urban homelessness and is working toward opening a related vein of related research.

## Chris Biga
Chapter 14 Urban and Environmental Sociology—
Environmental Portion

Chris Biga joined the University of North Texas' Department of Sociology in the fall of 2011. He came to UNT from North Dakota State University, where he was an assistant professor of sociology from 2007 to 2011. At UNT, he serves as the department's undergraduate program director and teaches Quantitative Data Collection, Social Statistics, Introduction to Sociology, a Senior Capstone course, Social Problems, Environmental Sociology, Social Psychology, and Sociology of Aging.

His primary research focuses on the intersection of environmental sociology and sociological social psychology; specifically, explaining environmentally significant individual behaviors through self meanings of identities. Currently, Biga is investigating how shared values across identities (environmental, gender, and consumer) influence the occurrence of environmentally significant individual behaviors.

Biga is originally from Omaha, Nebraska. He received his B.A. in sociology and psychology from the

University of Nebraska and his M.A. with an emphasis in environmental sociology from the University of New Orleans . Eager to experience the different cultures and regions of the United States, he next attended Washington State University, where he received his Ph.D. in sociology with a specialization in environmental sociology and social psychology. Biga is a trained bicycle mechanic and worked in the cycling industry for 10 years as he pursued his undergraduate and graduate studies. He is married to Peggy Biga, a molecular comparative nutritional physiologist. They are proud parents of a son, 4½-year-old Avery.

# Brian G. Moss
Chapter 15 Collective Behavior, Social Movements and Social Change

Brian Moss is a sociology instructor at Oakland Community College in Waterford, Michigan. Moss was drawn to the field of sociology after a wide range of professional experiences highlighted the important role of social forces on the lives of at-risk populations. He has provided clinical support to families and children involved in child protective and foster care services, survivors of child abuse and neglect, and families and children needing care in medical facilities. Moss has also worked with parole violators within a Michigan Department of Corrections facility to prepare for re-entry into the community. As the previous director of institutional research for Oakland Community College, he conducted and supervised the creation of formative and process evaluations, needs assessments, economic impact studies, marketing research, and strategic planning studies. Moss has been very active producing qualitative and quantitative research on criminal, health, and educational outcomes.

In addition to these professional experiences, Moss received a bachelor of science degree in psychology from Central Michigan University as well as a master of social work, a graduate certificate in infant mental health and a doctoral degree in sociology from Wayne State University. He has received additional training on advanced statistical and research method techniques at the University of Michigan's Summer Research Institute. Moss has taught a variety of introductory courses and more advanced topics on research methods, statistical analysis, and survey methodology.

# CHAPTER ONE

# An Introduction to Sociology

## Rene L. O'Dell

---

**Chapter Objectives**

At the end of this chapter, students should be able to:

- Explain the sociological imagination, sociological perspective and global perspective and their significance in interpreting people's behaviors.
- Describe the three historical movements that helped shape the formation of sociology as a discipline.
- Identify Auguste Comte, Harriet Martineau, and Herbert Spencer and explain their unique contributions to early sociology.
- Identify and critically analyze the major sociological theories.
- Apply the sociological research perspectives to the analysis of data collection.
- Evaluate various research methods and indicate their strengths and limitations.

---

Once you have read this book, you will never look at people the same way again. Not only is sociology guaranteed to change the way you view yourself and others, it will also help you understand and interact with those of different cultures, beliefs systems, socioeconomic backgrounds and the opposite gender. If you enjoy people watching, this book will teach you methods of understanding people almost to the point of being able to predict human behavior. If you enjoy interacting with people, this book will enlighten you about the ways in which people differ and how communication is helped or hindered in society. This chapter lays the foundation for a thorough understanding of the forces at work in various societies, as it introduces the origin of sociology, sociological theory and sociological research.

# Sociology Defined

Let's start with a simple definition. **Sociology** is *the scientific study of human society and social interaction*. Auguste Comte coined the term in 1838 to describe a new way of thinking about and understanding our social world. The word sociology comes from a combination of the Latin word *socius*, which means "associate," and the Greek-derived suffix "ology" which has come to mean "study." We loosely translate "associate" to mean people in general. Putting the pieces together, we end up with our definition—the study of people (Comte, 1975).

Sociology also includes the study of how people interact with one another, the groups that comprise society, the institutions of society, how institutions and people affect one another, and much more. The goal of the sociologist is to understand the modern society in which we live.

To study sociology, we should use the "sociological imagination." According to C. Wright Mills (1959), the **sociological imagination** is the equivalent of using a pair of lenses to look at a situation in a different light. Another way to say it would be to walk in someone else's shoes in hopes of understanding his or her point of view. We find that our own struggles, which others in society may be experiencing as well, can be viewed in a larger social context. We also come to realize that society influences the way we think, feel, and act.

# Sociological Perspective

To understand phenomena occurring in our social world, we must have tools and techniques that help guide the way we approach a topic. Sociology questions what most people consider common sense or personal choice.

Take, for example, the fact that you are in college getting a higher education. Why is it that you are enrolled in college? Most people will answer that it is because they want to get a good job with a large paycheck. However, enrollment in college actually has little to do with the personal choice of being there. For the most part, people need to have a degree in the field in which they desire to be employed. Society has thus influenced the decision to enroll in college. Therefore, it is very important to keep in mind the first maxim of sociology—things are not always as they seem.

Sociology uses the **sociological perspective** developed by Peter Berger in 1963. First, we are able to see *the general in the particular*. This allows individuals to categorize people based on characteristics they have in common. Categories could include men or women, old or young, rich or poor, the majority or minority, and so on. Once people are grouped into these categories by society, they are treated a particular way. Personal life experiences are also shaped by the various categories in which we are placed (Berger, 1963).

The sociological perspective also allows us to see the *strange in the familiar*. By understanding what falls into certain categories based on what is the same, we are also able to see what is different.

The sociological imagination and perspective provide us with general knowledge for the larger picture of the **sociological paradigm**. This framework allows us to study society using sociological tools, methods, and assumptions in analyzing data and research.

## Global Perspective

It would be naïve to think that our personal actions do not influence other people. No one goes through life without affecting others. For that reason, we must consider others within our own society.

Would it be going too far to say that your actions or beliefs could also reach across the world? With technology and the creation of the Internet, many people are more interconnected now. The Internet allows for communication and contact with individuals with whom we might never have interacted. At the touch of a button, the Internet takes people to destinations around the world.

With that in mind, we should consider the people who comprise not only our own society, but other societies as well. This concept of **global perspective** concerns the impact of our society on others, and also their impact on us. Using a global view allows us to answer questions such as, "How do we as Americans view other nations?" and "How do other nations view Americans?"

Where we live greatly shapes our lives. Have you ever thought about how your life would be different if you were born or raised in another country? What opportunities might you gain or lose? What lan-

## Application: Global Perspective

<u>The impact of our society on other nations, and their impact on us.</u>
*When studying sociology, remember the big picture. We must keep in mind that our culture influences other societies and vice versa.*

McDonald's, Japan

McDonald's, Peru

Source: Courtney Johnson

Source: Ronald Woan

McDonald's is located in more than 100 countries around the world, and you can find a Burger King restaurant in more than 65 countries and U.S. territories (McDonald's, 2011; Burger King, 2011). In Ireland, one noticeable difference is that these two fast-food chains offer fountain drinks, while many restaurants and pubs serve only canned or bottled soda.

On the other hand, we are also able to see the impact of other cultures on our society. For example, if you were to walk into a food court at a mall, you would have many ethnic cuisines from which to choose.

guage would you speak? What viewpoint or beliefs would you have? The country that you live in molds the person you become.

In general, there are two classifications of countries determined by standards of living and wealth: developed and developing. At the top of the list are high-income countries such as the United States, Japan, and Germany, where the wealth is high and so are the standards of living. The countries in this category have been referred to as first-world countries and are now considered developed countries.

At the bottom are low-income countries struggling to develop, where most of the citizens are poor. Most of Africa and parts of Asia fall into this category previously known as third-world countries and now called developing countries. The standard of living in these countries does not meet the most basic needs of food, clothing, and shelter for large portions of the citizens. Other issues include unsafe drinking water and limited access to education.

This categorization does not convey an accurate description of the many societies that comprise the world. What it illustrates is that standards of living are not equal. Keeping a global perspective allows sociologists to study commonalities and differences among the many societies of the world. Societies are more alike than was previously thought. Every society has social problems, but the variation lies in the types of problems and the extent to which they are suffered.

# Origins of Sociology

The field of sociology developed as a response to changes that were drastically transforming society, such as the Industrial Revolution, the formation of cities, and the decline of monarchies as a form of government.

## Technological Advancements

The Industrial Revolution began during the 18th and early 19th centuries in Western Europe. Many people were used to working at home or in small groups where employment was dictated by the individual. For the majority who were farmers, going to work meant opening their back door and tilling their own land. This changed with the arrival of new methods of producing energy, first by water power and later by steam.

With new advancements in the methods of production and the rise of capitalism, people flocked to factories, mills, and mines in search of employment and wages.

## Formation of Cities

Powered by technological innovation, factories became a central focal point and soon cities formed around them. Life in the city was drastically different than rural living. People now interacted with large groups of people at work and in the community, and there was more crime and pollution and less available living space.

## Political Changes

As people earned more money working in factories, they started challenging the Divine Right of Kings for political rule. The focus moved from doing God's will to seeking more individualism.

## Results of Change

Together, these advancements changed the ways people interacted with one another, the types of communities in which they lived, and the rules by which they were governed.

Sociology was formed by the cumulative efforts of Auguste Comte, Karl Marx, Emile Durkheim, and Max Weber as they attempted to understand society's changes. These key intellectuals, along with other voices, will be discussed later in this chapter.

## Sociology as a Science

Auguste Comte (1975) is considered the founder of sociology. He was the first to try to understand society in its modern context instead of imagining an ideal society.

Comte's thinking centered on the notion that Western society developed through three stages. The first, known as the *theological stage,* included the time period through 1350. During this period, people's lives revolved around the notion of God's will. Belief in the divine structured and shaped society.

The *metaphysical stage* was a transition from belief in the divine to natural order. During this stage, the focus was on the natural world rather than the supernatural as had been the case during the theological stage.

The last stage Comte called the *scientific stage.* Many great thinkers arose from this era, such as Isaac Newton, Galileo Galilei and Nicolaus Copernicus. Science was the medium utilized to understand the physical world.

Comte believed the only way to understand social phenomena was to use the methodological approach he called *positivism,* which involved using a scientific approach.

Comte thought that without empirical data, we would not have concrete knowledge. He believed that if we were able to understand society based on scientific research, we would be able to prescribe remedies for change.

Sociology uses the scientific method, which entails conducting research and analyzing results. To be considered a science, however, a discipline must also be founded on well-defined laws. For example, the law of gravity states that if you drop something, it will fall to the ground no matter where you are located on Earth. Sociology, on the other hand, does not have any laws, contrary to Comte's notion. What is true in our society may not be true elsewhere, and what applies to one person certainly does not apply to all people.

Critics use this fact to point out that sociology, along with other social sciences, should not be considered a science. This is why sociology is deemed a "soft science."

## Applications in Sociology

Sociology as an academic discipline was first introduced as a department at the University of Chicago in 1892. Since that time, it has rapidly spread and expanded into an exciting field of study.

Wherever humans live, you can find the issues and aspects studied within the field of sociology. Because sociology deals with human behavior, the topics are vast and broad. Some of the more popular topics include: marriage and family, sex roles and gender, delinquent behavior and crime, race and ethnicity and economics and politics.

## Careers in Sociology

Sociology attracts many people who are interested in a wide array of topics. To be recognized in the field, a person must have an advanced degree such as a master's or a doctorate. Once that degree is obtained, a person is considered a sociologist.

Sociologists work in many fields, often pursuing diverse specialties. Because sociology deals with human behavior of all sorts, it offers a broad base of knowledge for any type of job.

If an individual were to receive a bachelor's degree with sociology as either a major or minor, possible jobs might be in public relations, human resources, sales, advertising, or market research. Knowledge of human behavior in these fields is imperative. If a person wishes to sell products, or attempt to reach people through advertising, knowledge of humans and how they behave is a key component. Without this understanding, a person in sales, advertising or marketing might not be able to connect with their desired customers.

Sociology is also important for anyone interested in a career involving interaction with large groups of diverse people. This would include individuals who want to work in politics or in a nonprofit organization.

A sociology degree is often used as a foundation for higher degrees outside the field of sociology, such as law and medicine. Many universities make sociology courses a requirement to obtain a degree in the medical field. One of the more obvious

## Application: What can I do with a sociology degree?

Here are some famous sociology majors:

| Politics | Entertainment |
| --- | --- |
| Ronald Reagan | Robin Williams |
| Martin Luther King Jr. | Dan Akroyd |
| Jesse Jackson | Regis Philbin |

* Partial list adapted from the website of the American Sociological Association.

reasons is that doctors and other medical professionals interact with people who are in pain or dealing with illness. How can a medical staff member treat patients without some understanding of basic human behaviors?

When an advanced degree in sociology is obtained, the predominate jobs are teaching at the college level and conducting research. Many times, sociologists divide their time between these two occupations.

## Other Social Sciences

Anthropology is the most closely related to sociology. Whereas sociology studies society in its modern context as a whole, anthropology studies various cultures worldwide and some societies that might no longer exist.

Although similar in their methods, each social science analyzes data according to its own theories. Hence, if each were to examine the same situation, each would have its own perspective and analysis.

## Part Two: Sociological Theories

The main goal in studying sociology is to analyze and comprehend the meaning of our social world. To do this, theories must be applied. A **theory** is an integrated set of ideas that connects facts in order to gain an understanding of a specific phenomenon and to illustrate relationships. The purpose of sociological theory is to make generalizations in an attempt to understand human behavior in the modern world. Although there are many sociological theories, this book highlights the three major ones: structural functionalism, social conflict and symbolic interactionism. These theories help guide research and explain social occurrences and may be applied to any research topic.

## Structural Functionalism

The **structural functionalism** approach views society as an intricate structure with many different levels or parts all working in collaboration for stability.

Structural functionalists base their thinking on three major concepts. First, each part provides a function that keeps society working like a well-oiled machine. These different parts include social groups, institutions, and individual interactions, to name just a few. Sociologist Herbert Spencer (1961) compared society to a human body. Within the body are various organs and other parts required to keep the body functioning and healthy. Just like your body needs the brain, heart, and stomach internally, and the arms, legs, and skin externally, society needs many building blocks to function properly, maximizing ability and potential. Even though some people believe certain parts are not needed, structural functionalists would contend that all parts are necessary for the complex system to maintain stability.

Second, structural functionalism seeks to understand the big picture. Society as a whole is composed of many building blocks, such as family, peers, government, religious organizations, and the media, all of which play a role in shaping our lives. Together, these building blocks comprise one functioning entity.

Lastly, as the name suggests, the structural functionalism paradigm seeks to examine society's functions. Robert Merton (1938) expanded on the notion of functions, dividing them into two categories: intended (manifest) and unintended (latent). **Manifest functions** are consequences of a social situation that are intended and expected. In other words, they are the result of the functions that were projected and served their purpose. **Latent functions** are unintended or unexpected consequences of a social situation.

If we apply Merton's principles to schooling, the manifest function is to get an education. A latent function might be that children interact with other peers their age and make friends. So the goal or purpose of schooling is to acquire an education, but as a side benefit, friendships are also formed.

Merton (1938) believed that negative consequences, whether intended or unintended, could also be produced. We call the negative functions *dysfunctions* because they disrupt equilibrium. A dysfunction occurs when an object is not serving its purpose and stability is threatened.

## Application of Theory

Emile Durkheim (1957) was one of the pioneers of the structural-functionalist paradigm. Growing up in France, his research focused on anthropology and sociology. He covered a wide variety of topics over his lifetime—religion, suicide, crime—and provided many insights into the development of sociology as an academic field.

Durkheim, along with other functionalists, believed society was held together by a shared **social consensus** in which almost all members wanted the same outcomes and worked cooperatively to achieve them. Durkheim categorized this consensus into two forms of social cohesion: mechanical solidarity and organic solidarity. **Mechanical solidarity** involves people doing similar work and sharing the same values and beliefs. This type of solidarity is often found in traditional societies that are moderately small and not complex. An example of this would be a farming community in which everyone knows everyone, incomes are tied in some way to farming, and people share the same values and beliefs.

Conversely, in **organic solidarity**, people work in a wide variety of specialized occupations, and thus gain social consensus from their need to rely on one another for goods and services. In a large city, for example, people depend on others to provide them with food, clothes, safety, health care and entertainment, as no one can provide all of that for him or herself in an urban environment.

Throughout Durkheim's research, the theme of society and integration emerged. Durkheim viewed society as a separate entity apart from people, playing a vital part in our lives. Durkheim wanted to investigate why some people committed suicide, while others did not.

In his book *Suicide*, he found that people had higher rates of suicide based on three variables. Individuals were more likely to commit suicide if they were single or widowed or divorced versus married. People also had higher rates of suicide if they were without children. Lastly, individuals had higher likelihood of committing suicide if they practiced Protestant faiths versus Catholicism (Durkheim, 1957).

Durkheim analyzed these findings to show that individuals who were less integrated into society had higher rates of suicide. By integration, Durkheim was referring to connections to social structures. Those people who were more connected were less likely to kill themselves because other individuals, such as their spouses or children, needed them.

Additionally, Durkheim concluded that those people who had abnormally high amounts of social integration would also be more likely to commit suicide. This could be due to the stress of having too many people making demands on them.

# Social Conflict Perspective

The second major school of thought is the **social conflict perspective**, which views society as a compound filled with inequalities regarding the allocation of resources. The social conflict perspective focuses on the big picture. While the structural functionalism approach states that grouping people into categories is beneficial and functional, the social conflict approach highlights those categories as a way to put certain groups of people at a disadvantage. In our society, for example, race, social class, and gender are all areas where you can see inequalities in terms of education, wealth, and power.

Every society has a limited amount of resources which must be divided, in some manner, among its members. While some societies attempt to distribute the resources so that people have similar social standings, that is not the case in the United States. Under the assumption that all people cannot have all the resources or society would crumble, there is a vast difference between those individuals with many privileges versus those with very few.

The social conflict approach is guided by the assumption that there is a constant struggle to gain or keep power. The standard of living for privileged individuals is threatened by those who are not privileged. Dominant groups in society—such as Caucasians, men, the rich, and heterosexuals—must protect their privileges, while ethnic minorities, women, homosexuals, and the poor struggle to gain more for themselves. Going a step further, social conflict theorists state that not only will the dominant group protect its interests, it will also exploit

What are some of the benefits of joining a student club?

# Application: Durkheim's Social Integration

## Example : Completing College

Durkheim theorized that people who do not have ties to society are more likely to commit suicide. His research showed that social integration allows individuals to stay attached to society through social ties.

Expanding on his notion of social integration, many studies have found that students who are attached to their school have a higher chance of completion. McNeal (1995) found that participation in extracurricular activities significantly reduces the dropout rate, even when variables such as gender, race, socioeconomic status, and employment are controlled. Ream and Rumberger (2008) found that student engagement influences relationship networks that contribute to the completion of school. These networks also have the potential to reduce dropout rates. Another study conducted by Mahoney (2000) found that participation in activities was associated with reduced rates of early dropout in both males and females.

What this means is that you are less likely to drop out of school if you have things to do with people you like. Some great ways to get involved include: joining a club, working or living on campus, attending theater or musical productions, attending sporting events, or just getting to know your classmates.

the weak for the benefit of the strong.

Each of the variables of gender, race, and social class are important in understanding the conflict approach. They are sometimes categorized into sub-groupings called *gender conflict or race conflict* approaches.

Social conflict theorists believe that the structure of a society and its institutions perpetuate disparity among its members. Thus, it is the fault of the social system that certain individuals are left disadvantaged. In other words, the structures of society generate and reinforce an imbalance in the arena of social equality. You are able to see evidence of these inequalities in politics, the workplace, and in universities and other educational settings.

Although this viewpoint may appear negative, social conflict theorists are actually seeking social change. By gaining an understanding of the inequalities inherent in society, the goal is to reduce inequality by disbursing resources more equitably. This change may only occur as a result of a revolution where the disadvantaged overthrow the system.

## Application of Theory

Karl Marx (1964), a German who lived in Great Britain, is considered one of the key founders of the social conflict theory. He was a philosopher, political activist, and sociologist who is probably best known for his work *The Communist Manifesto* originally published in 1848.

Marx's philosophy centered on the roles of social class and economics. According to Marx, conflict arose in society due to the structuring of people into social classes. As the opening line of his manifesto states, "The history of all hitherto existing society is the history of class struggles" (Marx & Engels, 2011 p. 19).

Marx believed that people were divided into two social classes or categories: they were either part of the Bourgeoisie or part of the Proletariat. The Bourgeoisie were the owners of the factories and were considered the ruling class. The people in this group had the ability to determine how the factories would operate and how much workers would be paid.

The Proletariat were the workers in the factories and were also described as the subordinate class. The individuals in this category were subjected to the terms set by the Bourgeoisie. These included their working conditions and their pay. Marx believed the Proletariat were enslaved by the Bourgeoisie.

According to Marx (1964), society imposed these two social classes on people. In other words, either a person owned capital and thereby the means of production, or a person owned nothing but his labor, which he had to sell in order to earn money. There were no other options. This created a divide between the two classes of society and contributed to class conflict between owners and workers. All

conflict theorists believe that people battle over scarce resources, and according to Marx, money became the scarce resource and the basis for all class struggle.

During the time that Marx was alive, capitalism was becoming the driving economic force. Marx saw the capitalist system as corrupt because factory owners were the only ones who benefited economically from a good purchasing market.

One way for factory owners to receive more money was to pay workers less. Getting more labor out of the workers, while paying them the least amount of money possible, increased the power of the Bourgeoisie. From this, the Bourgeoisie were able to benefit from increased "labor power," which contributed to their status as part of the ruling class. Workers were powerless against the factory owners who exploited them.

According to Marx, capitalism created an environment that was hostile and competitive as individuals strived for the same privileges. He predicted that the workers would eventually get tired of the poor treatment they received and would overthrow the capitalistic system, resulting in the emergence of a new economic system.

The global revolution that Marx predicted has failed to materialize; even today it is evident that class struggle still exists in society.

# Symbolic Interactionism

The third major theory in sociology is the symbolic interaction approach, which states that society exists due to the everyday interactions of people. Whereas structural functionalists and conflict theorists seek to explore society as a whole, symbolic interactionists stake their claim by focusing on small-scale phenomena. They are interested in individuals and the small groups that comprise a society.

Symbolic interactionism revolves around two basic concepts. First, each society contains symbols or labels from which meanings are derived. Second, the meanings that are attached to items require social interaction. Attaching labels to objects in society creates cohesion among individuals.

Objects themselves do not have inherently embedded meanings. Therefore, the definitions vary by person and by culture. The definitions also change over time, just as the people in society change. Without the interactions of people, objects themselves do not carry any meanings or significance. Symbolic interactionists are interested in the labels we attach to our world, their meanings, and how they change over time.

Herbert Blumer coined the term "symbolic interactionism" in 1969, and he is largely responsible for the development of the theory and its methodologies. Previous theorists, such as Max Weber, George Herbert Mead, and Charles Horton Cooley, are credited with creating the foundation and basic concepts of interaction.

Although not originally associated with this school of thought, Max Weber (1958) is probably the best known symbolic interactionist. Weber, a German, was a political economist and sociologist who studied the sociology of religion and of government. One of his most famous writings is *The Protestant Ethic and the Spirit of Capitalism.*

Whereas Comte was a positivist and believed that science was necessary to evaluate society, Weber was an anti-positivist. Weber believed that to understand society, the focus must be on individuals and their cultural values. To do this, researchers must evaluate the meanings of symbols, their values, and their norms according to the culture.

### Application of Theory

Hand gestures can be found in every society. These symbols have various definitions depending on the culture. In Western society, extending the middle finger while all other fingers form a fist sends a very powerful message. In the United States, this gesture is labeled "flipping the bird," "giving someone the finger," or "flipping someone off."

In another culture, this gesture could be assigned a different meaning or no meaning at all. To have the equivalent effect in another culture, a different gesture might be used. For a symbol to carry any meaning or significance, it must be recognized by the culture. Some symbols have multiple meanings depending on the individual and the context in which they are being used.

## Other Sociological Theories

While sociology is largely shaped by Comte, Durkheim, Marx, and Weber, other theorists should be recognized for their contributions as well. These voices include Jane Addams, Harriet Martineau and W. E. B. Du Bois, to name just a few.

Also, because sociology studies society in its modern context, the discipline is continuously developing and expanding. Since the formation of the discipline, many other theories and theorists have had an impact on the way that we look at our social world.

### Part Three: Sociological Research

As previously stated, sociology is a science; therefore, the conclusions that are drawn are the results of conducting research. As a result, it is important to understand the methods and terminology of research studies. It is through these studies that we gain a better understanding of society.

## Research Perspectives

There are three perspectives on collecting sociological data: scientific, interpretive, and critical. Each of these focuses on different methods and techniques for gathering and analyzing data.

### Scientific Sociological Research

Sociological research is probably the most popular and widely used method of conducting research. This method uses science and empirical data. Sociologists who use this method like to focus on debunking commonly held beliefs. By collecting research, sociologists are able to "prove" or "disprove" what most people would believe is common sense.

For example, most people in the United States would say they married their spouses because they loved them. In fact, people would query a person if he or she gave any other answer to that question. Sociologists who have studied this topic actually find the reason people date and ultimately marry a person has little or nothing to do with love. Shocked or insulted? Don't be. There are many factors that

# Overview: Early Women of Sociology

Harriet Martineau (1802-1876) an English writer and philosopher, is considered the first woman of sociology. One of her contributions to the field was translating Auguste Comte's writing into English, which brought sociology to more people. Martineau focused her studies on women's rights, slavery, the workplace, and factory laws. She also wrote the first text on sociological research in 1838.

Jane Addams (1860-1935) was a social worker in Chicago, Illinois. She cofounded Hull House, a community-based center offering classes for adults and children, an art gallery, and many other facilities. Throughout her life she indirectly provided many insights into the discipline of sociology. She was a friend and colleague to George Herbert Mead and other members of the Chicago School of Sociology.

(Deegan, 1991)

go into deciding whom people date and later marry. Family, peers, religion, social class, race, and government are just a few of the things that influence whom we choose as marital partners.

One might ask a question like, "What role could the government possibly play in whom I choose to marry?" Well, if a woman loved her biological brother, could she marry him? Not in America, where we have laws prohibiting incestual marriage. As a matter of fact, all societies have laws regarding whom a person can marry, based on factors like age, gender, and blood relationship. The government certainly has a say in whom a person can marry. Even though people might give love as their reason to marry, it simply isn't true. There are many social structures that ultimately make our decisions.

## Interpretive Sociological Research

The second method for conducting sociological research is known as interpretive sociology, which focuses on meanings that people attach to their world. An interpretive sociologist would suggest that although science is crucial when collecting data, it is missing the vital ingredient of interpretation. Interpretive sociologists wish to find out not only what people are doing, but the meanings that people attach to their actions.

Interpretive sociologists use different methods of data collection than scientific sociologists. Because they are searching for meanings, they often ask about a respondent's feelings or thoughts. These two things are dismissed in scientific research because they are difficult to measure.

## Critical Sociological Research

Critical sociology focuses on the notion that society is not a natural system with fixed order. In this case, the goal in conducting research would be to change society. Researchers often look for issues within a society and then consider methods for solving those problems. An interpretative sociologist would review the data and consider why the problems exist, while a critical sociologist wouldn't necessarily care about the how or why. This method for collecting "research" is often used by conflict theorists who would like to see a restructuring of society.

# How to Collect Sociological Data

Sociologists collect data and analyze the results just as any other scientist would. They formulate a hypothesis—a tentative statement about how variables are related to each other—collect data, run statistical tests, and analyze results.

## Sample Population

When conducting research, the first item that

sociologists need to decide is which group of people to study and to whom the findings can be applied. A **population** is the entire group of people to be studied. For example, it can be all the people in the United States, males in California, or expectant mothers in the South.

Of course, gathering information from each member of a population would be time-consuming, costly, and virtually impossible, especially if the number of members is in the millions. Because of these factors, sociologists gather data from only a select number of people as a *sub-grouping*, or *sample* population.

## Size of Sub-Grouping

Because researchers are collecting data from only a select number of people, the size of the group becomes very important. Let's say a researcher posed the question, "Who do you believe is the best sociology professor ever?" The results showed that 100 percent of the people asked believed that Professor X was the best. That would be pretty impressive, right? Then, if we looked at the size of the population sampled and found it to be only one person, the results of 100 percent would not be very significant after all. A good sample size can be determined statistically by the number of people who fall into the population being researched.

## Samples and Application of Data

A **sample** is a smaller group of individuals selected from a larger population. The results of a research study can be applied to the entire population only if each person who falls into the population has had an equal opportunity to participate in the study as part of the sample. This would be known as a **random sample**. If a sample is not truly random, the results may be applied only to the people who actually provided the data.

Let's use the previous example. What if the sample was not random, and only the family members and friends of Professor X were surveyed? The results could then be applied only to the people who provided the data: 100 percent of family members and friends of Professor X believe that he is the best sociology professor. Would it be accurate to state that the results reflect the opinion of every student

at the university where Professor X teaches, or all college students in the nation? No, which illustrates why collecting data from a random sample is very important.

Sometimes researchers use **stratified sampling**, which goes beyond a random sample by making sure that the people selected to be in the sample match the proportions of the population being studied. If a population were 60 percent female, for example, researchers using this method would want to make sure that 60 percent of their sample were women.

## Type of Data

There are two types of data that can be collected. Scientific sociologists like to focus on collecting **quantitative data**, or data that can be measured in numbers.

When collecting data, sociologists use questions in which a respondent is limited to answering on a scale. An example of a quantitative question might be, "On a scale of one to five, where five means that you are very happy to be enrolled in college and one means that you are very unhappy, please choose the number that applies to you." Being an optimist and a fan of higher education, I will assume that an individual gives an answer of five. The researcher would then take that answer, along with all the other responses, and compute how happy students are to be enrolled in college, on average. This result is very objective because the respondents had to choose from a limited number of responses.

The second type of data that can be collected is **qualitative data**, or data that can be qualified. This method is widely used among interpretive sociologists who like to understand meanings. Researchers who use this method often use open-ended questions to which respondents are free to give any answer.

Let's change the previous research question into a qualitative format. The question might be, "Please describe how you feel about being enrolled in college and why." By using an open-ended question, respondents have the opportunity to explain their answers instead of simply choosing a number. Results of this kind of research are subjective.

If a respondent gives an answer of three on the

scale of happiness, it is left to the researcher to describe the person's level of happiness. Using the qualitative method, on the other hand, allows the respondent to explain that she is somewhat happy because she is getting her college education, but is somewhat unhappy because she is tired from the demands of working and going to school. Overall, she feels somewhat happy.

Researchers may not be interested in the "why" of an answer; they might only be looking for the "what." Both types of data are useful in different situations, and researchers often use a combination of the two.

## Variables

Once sociologists know whom they wish to gather information from and what type of data to collect, they need to determine the variables. A **variable** is a concept whose values change from case to case. Variables assign numerical scores or category labels; in research, common variables include race, gender, age, social class, marital status, education, and religion. The education of people will vary; some may have less than a high school education, and others will have advanced college degrees. The same goes for gender, where the categories will be male, female, and, possibly, intersex individuals.

Variables can be either dependent or independent. In research, there is only one dependent variable—the variable that changes—while the independent variables are those causing the changes.

As an example, let's use a research question related to drinking among college-age students. We might ask students' age, race, gender, and how frequently they consume alcoholic beverages. The dependent variable is alcohol usage because it is expected to change in relation to other variables. Age, race, and gender would be independent variables. The results might show the amount of drinking will vary depending on the gender of the respondent. Perhaps the researcher learns that males drink more than females. The frequency of alcohol consumption might also change in relation to the age or race of a respondent; thus, how often alcohol is consumed may depend upon age, race, or gender.

A research study may have many variables depending on the topic being studied. For elementary

purposes, there will only be one dependent variable and one or more independent variables in the examples included in this chapter.

## Measurement of Variables

Once the variables for a research study have been determined, researchers must assign them values. **Measurement** is the process of systematically assigning values to concepts for the purpose of research. In other words, the variables must be defined.

Depending on how important a variable is to a study, it can be defined broadly or narrowly. Let's use the same three variables as before: race, gender, and age. Race might be defined as Caucasian, African American, Hispanic, Asian, Middle-Eastern, or other. A researcher would list as many, or as few, race categories as needed to represent the population he or she wished to sample. If the researcher was only interested in comparing African Americans and Caucasians, those might be the only two categories listed for the study.

Definitions of variables must be generally accepted and not far-fetched. As an example, consider a researcher who wants to study children in African American families. Could the researcher define the "child's age" as 0-32 years? This definition would not be acceptable because there aren't many 32-year-olds who would be considered children in our society. Instead, if the researcher defined "child's age" as 0-18 years, most people would accept that definition.

## Importance of Defining Variables

The results of a research study are determined by the variables and how they are manipulated. If a variable isn't given an acceptable definition, the results will be skewed and, therefore, useless. Some variables are more difficult than others to define. For example, the variable of gender is fairly standard, and there are not many choices for the definition. The variable of singlehood, on the other hand, could be quite difficult to define. To determine the status of singlehood, a researcher might have to ask questions like, "Are you currently dating?" or, "When was the last time you went out on a date?"

# Overview: Reliability and Validity

Reliability: Consistency in measurement.

Validity: Accurately measuring what is intended to be measured.

*Review the three targets below. Are the results reliable, valid, neither, or both?*

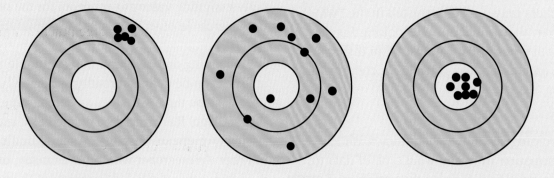

## Reliability and Validity

The process of collecting data and manipulating variables can become valueless if the method of measurement is not reliable. **Reliability** refers to *consistency,* or receiving the same results every time. For example, if a researcher conducted the same study again using the same methods, he or she should receive the same results.

The measurement indicator used for the research study must also be valid or accurate. **Validity** means that the indicator accurately measures what it is intended to measure. If a person who weighed 200 pounds stepped onto a scale, but the scale showed that that person only weighed 100 pounds, then the scale would not be valid; it would not be producing accurate results. To be considered valid, the scale would have to give the measurement of 200 pounds.

Researchers must be careful in the selection of their measurement so that the measurement will be both reliable and valid. Without meeting these two demands, the results of the research will be inadequate.

## Relationships Between Variables

The purpose of conducting sociological research is to determine how variables are related. For example, how much does race influence a person's level of education, or what is the role of social class in the amount of alcohol consumed?

A **correlation** exists when two or more variables change together. This can be either a positive or a negative change. Although variables might change together, this does not necessarily mean that one variable actually causes a change in the other. Instead, correlation refers to the establishment of a relationship between variables.

For example, suppose that as cell phone use increases so does the number of automobile accidents. This may indicate a correlation between the number of cell phone users and the number of automobile accidents. Many people might, therefore, conclude that cell phone users cause more automobile accidents. This conclusion might be true in specific cases, but it cannot be said that cell phone users cause more accidents without further study and analysis. Neither could it be said that a decline in cell phone use would result in a decrease in the number of accidents.

A **spurious correlation** occurs when two variables change together, but the change is being caused by a third variable. For instance, as a person's shoe size goes up so does the frequency of his or her sexual activity. Does this mean that the size of a person's shoe dictates how often he or she will have sex? If researchers were to come across these results, they would have to test other variables to see what is actually causing the change. In this case, the third variable is age. A child's foot is very small, and children do not participate in sexual activity. As they reach adulthood, though, their feet have grown much larger, and sexual activity has also begun.

When manipulating variables, researchers are looking for cause and effect, where a change in one variable causes a change in another. To prove a cause-and-effect relationship, a time line must be established to demonstrate that the cause occurred before the effect.

# Methods of Collecting Data

Once a research question has been established and the variables have been decided, the next step is to figure out how the data will be collected. There are many methods that can be utilized to collect data. Each of the following methods has advantages and disadvantages. It is up to researchers to select a process based on factors such as time, money, topic and data.

## Experiment

One research method is to conduct an **experiment;** this would occur in a controlled environment where the variables could be closely managed. In this type of research there are generally two groups of respondents randomly classified into either an experimental group or a control group. The **experimental group** is the one exposed to independent variables, such as treatments or services. **Control group** participants are not exposed to the variables. The results from the two groups are then compared. This form of research is generally used for clinical research studies.

*Advantages*: Certainly, if the experiment were conducted in a laboratory, unknown conditions would have less chance of interfering with the outcome. A researcher is able to predict obstacles.

*Disadvantages*: Often, experiments conducted in a laboratory lack real-life application because it is difficult to account for all unforeseen variables.

## Survey Research

This method is the most popular and widely used form of data collection. One reason for its popular-

ity is that there are many variations of surveys that can be used. Survey research can be conducted over the phone, in person, or over the Internet. In this case, researchers would create a questionnaire and then administer it in the chosen method. Researchers might also choose to use multiple forms of survey research by starting with one method and following up with a second or third.

*Advantages*: Administering a survey is useful when attempting to reach large numbers of people. It is fairly cost-effective, and people in general are usually willing to answer a few questions. Also, answering a survey over the phone or through the mail allows a participant to remain relatively anonymous. If the subject matter is sensitive, a researcher might get more truthful responses with a phone survey versus an in-person interview.

*Disadvantages*: One of the major drawbacks to this method is that it might take more time to collect the data. Mailed surveys, for example, often do not get returned in a timely manner, if at all. It usually takes hundreds of mailed surveys to receive even one completed questionnaire back. Individuals might throw out the survey as junk mail, or they might intend to complete it but forget or return it too late.

Also, when interviewing individuals, researchers might not get truthful answers because respondents may tend to provide the answers they believe the researchers want, or ones that the respondent decides are more suitable. As an illustration, if a researcher asked a 25-year-old female the number of sexual partners she has had, she might give a lower number (so as not to be viewed as promiscuous) or a higher number (to prove she has had experience).

## Observation

Another method of collecting data is to observe a particular population. This observation takes place in the population's natural setting. For example, if a researcher wanted to see how mothers interact with their children during playtime, perhaps he or she would go to the park and watch mothers and their children. This technique has two components. First, the researcher must write down the group's actions, being both objective and factual. Second, the observations must be analyzed by applying theory. This type of observation is known as **detached observation**, because the researcher observes from a distance without actually getting involved.

A variation of observation involves the researcher joining the group and participating in the activity. **Participant observation** allows a researcher to observe a group's behavior from within the group itself. The people who are being studied may or may not know that they are being observed. Depending on the topic in question, a group might reject an outsider, making research difficult. This method of participant observation is widely used among anthropologists who wish to study various cultures.

*Advantages*: Many things can be learned by studying people in their natural environments. Often, a researcher will receive the most realistic responses by seeing how people interact in real-life situations.

*Disadvantages*: People might behave differently if they know that they are being watched, a phenomenon known as the **Hawthorne effect**. This first came to light in a series of studies on factory workers between 1924 and 1932 (Roethlisberger, Dickson, Wright & Pforzheimer, 1939). Although the change in behavior is generally positive, the results of a research study using this method would not be valid if the changes noted were found to be temporary and unrealistic.

## Secondary Data Analysis

One method of collecting data is to get the data from another source rather than actually gathering it yourself. In this case, researchers are able to tap into databases hosted by other researchers who collected the data. The best example of this is the U.S. Census Bureau. In its database, demographic information has been compiled and made available in one place, allowing researchers to select variables and run statistical analyses.

A variation of this method is *content analysis,* in which a researcher looks at a variety of content, such as marriage, divorce, birth, and death certificates, and police or other public records. This method helps researchers look at patterns of behavior that occur over time. They might also review media such as movies, television shows, advertisements, and magazines. In this case, no respondents

would be physically involved in the study, only their information.

*Advantages*: Conducting research can be costly and time-consuming, and this method is the cheapest and, most likely, the easiest. Because the data are collected from an existing source, it saves the researcher time, allowing him or her to move to the second step, which is analyzing the data.

*Disadvantages*: One major disadvantage of this method is the lack of variables. If researchers did not collect the data themselves, then certain variables in which they are interested might be missing. When conducting their own research, sociologists are able to use any variables and are also able to follow up with respondents if they need more information. If a certain variable does not exist, researchers are not able to get the information. Additionally, a researcher might enjoy collecting data and interacting with respondents.

# Overview of All Methods

Deciding which research method to use when collecting data is entirely up to the researcher. The best methods to use will depend on the topics and the populations being studied.

## ASA Guidelines

Whenever research is collected, scientists are bound by certain ethics and rules that govern their work. This is true for sociology as well. The American Sociological Association (ASA) provides guidelines and specific rules to which sociologists must adhere.

Probably the most important ethic is that researchers are to protect the physical and psychological well being of the respondents. This means the researcher must not purposefully harm the respondent and should also attempt to foresee any potential problems that may arise and take appropriate actions. Researchers should also protect the privacy of the people participating in the study and maintain confidentiality.

Participants will generally sign a consent form that explains the study and the terms and conditions of participation. The consent form will also state that a respondent's personal information will be protected.

Once a study has been conducted, the findings should be published in their entirety. Once in a while, a researcher might uncover results that are disturbing; it would be unethical to just sweep them under the rug by deciding not to disclose that portion of the findings. This extends to sharing techniques and methods with other professionals in the field, should they ask for the information. Conducting research allows for the creation of a body of knowledge. Therefore, professionals should impart their expertise to others to facilitate better understanding of the results and reproduction of the studies.

## Other Areas of Concern

Researchers should also be culturally sensitive to the population they are studying. In seeking information from a certain ethnic group, researchers should be aware of the group's dynamics and lifestyles. Although this isn't an ethical standard provided by the ASA, it is common courtesy to afford such consideration to all respondents.

When conducting research, it is very easy for a person's biases to interfere with the results. Weber suggested that anyone who conducted research should be objective, and assumptions should not be included in the research process (Weber & Shils, 1949). In other words, researchers must suspend all beliefs, assumptions, biases, and prejudices. If a sociologist were to conduct research and relate it to preconceived notions, the results would be tainted and, therefore, invalid. Some common biases relate to gender, race, age or social class.

Most of the time, conducting objective research is a virtually impossible task. Researchers choose the topics and the methods of collecting data, and are also the ones analyzing the results, so the studies are already subject to bias. Therefore, instead of trying to be completely objective themselves, researchers should strive for value-free research, untainted by their own views.

If you were to conduct a sociological research study, what population would you target and why?

## Overview: How to Conduct a Research Study

<u>Choose a Topic/Select your Population</u>: What question would you like to ask, and whom would you like to answer it?

<u>Choose and Define Variables</u>: Consider the group that you are studying when selecting the variables and make sure that the definition is acceptable.

<u>Select a Method of Collecting Data</u>: There are many types of methods to choose from, such as experiments, surveys, observations, or secondary analyses.

<u>Measurement</u>: Make sure that the measurement for analyzing the data is both reliable and valid.

<u>Remember the ASA Guidelines</u>: While conducting the research, keep in mind the rules that govern research, especially those protecting respondents.

<u>Analyze the Results</u>: Look to see how the variables are related and analyze the results by applying theory.

# Summary

This chapter provides a foundation for the study of sociology. The field of sociology is continually growing and expanding through three categories of research: scientific, which focuses on empirical data; interpretive, which strives to understand the meanings people attach to their world; and critical, which works toward the goal of changing society. The origins of sociology lie in the formation of cities, political changes, technological advancements, and the results of change. The viewpoints of the three main schools of thought in sociology introduced in this chapter—structural functionalism, social conflict, and symbolic interactionism—will be discussed throughout this book as they pertain to topics ranging from deviance to social change.

## Review/Discussion Questions

1. What is a theory?
2. What is the difference between organic and mechanical solidarity?
3. Who was Karl Marx?
4. What are some of the methods used by sociologists to collect data?
5. If you were going to conduct sociological research, what would you study, and what method would you use and why?
6. Do you think your behavior would change if you were under constant observation?

## Key Terms

**Class conflict** occurs between the capitalist class and the working class as they struggle for control over scarce resources, such as money.

**Control groups** are those in which participants are not exposed to the variables.

**Correlation** exists when two (or more) variables change together.

**Detached observation** involves a researcher observing behavior from a distance without actually getting involved with the participants.

**Experiments** are controlled environments in which variables can be closely managed.

**Experimental groups** are those exposed to the independent variables, such as participation in a program or use of a medication.

**Global perspective** concerns the impact our society has on other nations, and also the impact of other nations upon our society.

**Hawthorne effect** describes a phenomenon in which people modify their behavior because they know they are being monitored.

**Hypotheses** are tentative statements about how different variables are expected to relate to each other.

**Latent functions** are unintended consequences or results.

**Manifest functions** are intended consequences or results.

**Measurement** is the systematic process of assigning values or labels to concepts for research purposes.

**Mechanical solidarity** is a form of social cohesion in which people do similar work and share the same values and beliefs.

**Organic solidarity** is a form of social cohesion in which people work in a wide variety of specialized occupations and thus gain their social consensus from their need to rely on one another for goods and services.

**Participant observation** allows a researcher to observe a group's behavior from within the group itself.

**Populations** are entire groups of people to be studied.

**Qualitative data** measures intangibles such as people's feelings and can include focus group results, interviews, and observations.

**Quantitative data** is data that can be measured in numbers.

**Random samples** are those in which each person who is part of the population has an equal opportunity to be selected for participation in a study.

**Reliability** refers to consistency, or receiving the same results every time the same study is conducted.

**Samples** are smaller groups of individuals selected from larger populations.

**Social conflict perspective** views society as a compound filled with inequalities in regard to the allocation of resources.

**Social consensus** occurs when nearly all members of a society want to achieve the same goals and work cooperatively to achieve them.

**Sociological imagination** is the process of achieving a better understanding of our own experiences. We do this by discovering our place within society, including our experiences with social institutions and the historical period in which we live.
Putting your self in some one elses shoes

**Sociological paradigms** provide frameworks that allow us to study society and analyze data and research using sociological tools, methods, and theories.

**Sociological perspective** involves being able to see the general in the particular.

**Sociology** is the scientific study of human society and social interaction.

**Spurious correlation** occurs when two variables change together, not because of a causal relationship between the two, but because of a third variable. This result reminds us that correlation does not imply causation.

**Stratified sampling** makes sure that the people randomly selected to be in the sample match the proportions of the population being studied.

**Structural functionalism** views society as an intricate structure, with many levels or parts all working together in collaboration for stability.

**Symbolic interactionism** contends that society exists due to the everyday interactions of people.

**Theories** are integrated sets of propositions that are intended to explain specific phenomena and to show relationships between variables in order to gain understanding.

**Validity** means that indicators used in research, like rating scales, accurately measure the concepts they are intended to measure.

**Variables** are attributes that may change their values under observation. Variables can be assigned numerical scores or category labels.

# Bibliography

Addams, J. (1907). National Protection for Children. <http://pds.lib.harvard.edu/pds/view/2575269?n=1> (2011).

Addams, J. (1990). Twenty Years at Hull-House: With Autobiographical Notes. Urbana, IL: University of Illinois Press.

American Sociological Association (2008). <http://www.asanet.org/> (2008).

Berger, P. (1963). Invitation to Sociology: A Humanistic Perspective. Garden City, NY: Doubleday.

Buchmann, C., & DiPiete, T. (2006). The Growing Female Advantage in College Completion: The Role of Family Background and Academic Achievement. American Sociological Review, 71 (4), 515-541.

Burger King (2011). <http://www.bk.com/en/us/international/index.html> (2011).

Blumer, H. (1969). Symbolic Interaction: Perspective and Method. Englewood Cliffs, NJ: Prentice-Hall.

Comte, A. (1975). Auguste Comte and Positivism: The Essential Writings. New York, NY: Harper & Row.

Cooley, C. H. (1964). Human Nature and the Social Order. New York, NY: Schocken Books.

Deegan, M. J. (1991). Women in Sociology: a Bio-bibliographical Sourcebook. New York, NY: Greenwood Press.

Du Bois, W. E. B. (1989). The Study of Negro Problems. The ANNALS of the American Academy of Political and Social Science.11 (1), 1-23.

Durkheim, E. (1957). Suicide. (J. A. Spaulding & G. Simpson, Trans.). Glencoe, IL: Free Press of Glencoe.

Mahoney, J. L. (2000). School Extracurricular Activity Participating as a Moderator in the Development of Antisocial Patterns. Sociology of Education. 71, (2), 502-516.

Marx, K. (1964). Selected Writings in Sociology and Social Philosophy. (T. B. Bottomore, Trans.). New York, NY: McGraw-Hill.

Marx, K., & Engels, F. (2011). The Communist Manifesto. Seattle, WA: Create Space.

McDonald's (2011). <http://www.mcdonalds.com/us/en/websites.html> (2011).

McNeal, R. B. (1995). Extracurricular Activities and High School Dropouts. Sociology of Education. 68, (1), 62-80.

Mead, G. H (1913). The Social Self. Journal of Philosophy, Psychology and Scientific Methods 10, 374-380.

Merton, R. (1938). Social Structure and Anomie. American Sociological Review, 3 (5), 672-682.

Mill, J. S. (1961). August Comte and Positivism. Ann Arbor, MI: University of Michigan Press.

Mills, C. W. (1959). The Sociological Imagination. New York, NY: Oxford University Press.

Ream, R. K., & Rumberger, R. W. (2008). Student Engagement Peer Social Capital and School Dropouts Among Mexican American and Non-Latino White Student. Child Development. 81, (2), 109-139.

Roethlisberger F. J., Dickson W. J., Wright H. A., Pforzheimer C. H. (1939). Management and the worker : an account of a research program conducted by the Western Electric Company, Hawthorne Works, Chicago. Cambridge, MA: Harvard University Press.

Spencer, H. (1961). The Study of Sociology. Ann Arbor, MI: University of Michigan Press.

Venkatesh, S. (2008). Gang Leader for a Day. New York, NY: Penguin Press.

Weber, M. (1958). The Protestant Ethic and the Spirit of Capitalism. New York, NY: Scribner.

Weber, M., & Shils, E. (1949). Max Weber on the methodology of the social sciences. Glencoe, IL: Free Press.

# CHAPTER TWO
# Society and Culture

## XueMei Hu

---

**Chapter Objectives**
At the end of this chapter, students should be able to:

- Describe the characteristics of hunting and gathering, horticultural and pastoral, agrarian, industrial, and post-industrial societies.
- Differentiate between material culture and nonmaterial culture.
- Explain the six components of nonmaterial culture.
- Apply subculture, counterculture, multiculturalism, high culture and popular culture to the analysis of cultural diversity.
- Differentiate between ethnocentrism and cultural relativism.
- Analyze different sources of cultural change.
- Apply the structural functionalist theory, social conflict theory, and symbolic interactionist theory to the analysis of culture.
- Define the concepts related to society and culture.

---

In Chapter One, you learned that sociology is the study of human society and social interaction. Components of the definition include humans, societies, social interactions, and science. The lenses through which sociologists analyze our world are: concepts such as society and culture; structural concepts such as social institutions; and cultural concepts such as beliefs and values. Sociologists ask: What is society? How did societies change over time? What is culture? What role does culture play in society?

Sociologists use both macro and micro levels of analysis to study human society and social life. *Macrosociology* focuses on broad aspects of society. Conflict theories and functionalist theories use this approach—focusing on large-scale groups and events—to analyze social classes and examine how groups of different social economic status are related. For example, in a macro-level analysis, you as a sociologist would examine how social institutions such as family and school might increase or decrease teenage pregnancies. *Microsociology*, by

---

contrast, focuses on social interaction. For example, microsociology can be used to explain why students might feel comfortable interacting with their professors in the classroom but awkward when meeting them at the store. Both macrosociological and microsociological approaches help us to understand social life in society. Chapter 2 explores society and culture, while social interaction is the focus of Chapter 4.

Culture and society are closely connected because a society possesses the knowledge, beliefs, norms and values that constitute a culture. Without culture, society cannot exist. American culture moves at such a fast pace that we are constantly changing and adapting to new trends and technologies. Society also exists within a culture as a subgroup of a larger populace, and, similarly, culture changes with society. We will now describe and explore the different types of societies in which human beings have lived. Then we will turn to studying components of culture and cultural diversity.

## Society

Societies are made up of people from many different backgrounds. Our differences color the world we live in. In most cultures, people want to build a better life and to live in a safe, secure environment. Some people hope for peace and try to respect each other, while others "stir the pot" and cause trouble.

### What is Society?

**Society** refers to a diverse group of people who share a distinctive culture in a defined geographic location. A society can be a city, a township, a tribe or an association. There are two components of the term *society*: First, society is a group of people bound by such factors as race, ethnicity, gender, social class and age; second, it is a group that shares a mainstream culture with sub-groups that inherit their subcultures from the mainstream.

### Technology in Society

Societies change constantly. In order to understand what life was like at any point in history, one must understand what the society at that time

perceived as normal. Gerhard Lenski, Jean Lenski and Patrick Nolan (1995) describe how societies have changed over the past 10,000 years, emphasizing the role of technology in shaping them. Lenski et al. apply the term *sociocultural evolution* to the changes that occur as a society invents and adopts a new technology. Societies with simple technology can support a small number of people and remain traditional or industrial. But societies with advanced technology can support not only a large population but also higher standards of living.

In fact, society shapes technology as much as technology shapes society. Many historical eras are identified by their dominant technology: The Stone Age, Iron Age, Bronze Age, Industrial Age and Information Age. Where people live and the modes of production they use to provide food are related to subsistence technology. *Subsistence technology* refers to the methods and tools used to acquire basic necessities. Acknowledging that social change occurs through technological innovation and different levels of subsistence technology, social scientists have identified five types of societies: hunting and gathering, horticultural and pastoral, agrarian, industrial, and post-industrial (Lenski, Lenski, & Nolan 1995).

## Evolution of Societies

The earliest fossil remains of modern humans date to more than 100,000 years ago. Early societies were small bands that survived on their hunting and gathering skills. They eventually evolved into large industrial societies with sophisticated technologies. In this section, we will discuss societal stages, followed by a list of large-scale social changes that have occurred in the last 100,000 years.

## Hunting and Gathering Societies

Up until 15,000 years ago, humans took their food directly from the environment, rather than maintaining gardens, fields, or domesticated animals. People in **hunting and gathering societies** used simple subsistence technology to hunt animals and gather vegetation. In much of the world, it would be nearly impossible to live as a hunter or gatherer today; in fact, in the United States it is generally illegal to hunt on public lands except during special hunting seasons. But we still can find a few hunting and gathering societies, such as the Aka and Pygmies of Central Africa, the Bushmen of southwestern Africa, the Aborigines of Australia, the Kaska Indians of northwestern Canada, and the Batek and Semai of Malaysia (Lenski, Lenski, & Nolan, 1995).

## Technology and Simple Tools

For early hunter-gatherer societies, technology consisted of simple tools made of natural materials such as spears, nets, bows and arrows, and traps. Such societies were at the mercy of nature; storms and droughts could destroy their food supply. To survive, hunters and gatherers worked together and shared. They spent most of their time hunting for game and gathering plants to eat. There was no stable food supply and no surplus food.

## Size and Density

Hunting and gathering societies were small by today's standards, usually consisting of fewer than 40 people. Thousands of these societies were scattered about the planet. Population densities were about one person for every two square miles. But a hunting and gathering society needed hundreds of square miles of territory, as it was constantly on the move looking for new food supplies. As a result, there were no permanent settlements (Lenski, Lenski, & Nolan, 1995).

## Social Institutions

Social institutions were primitive and informal. In hunting and gathering societies, kinship—family—was the major institution and also the basic social and economic unit. Food was acquired and distributed through kinship ties. Because hunters and gatherers were nomadic, constantly moving to find new sources of plants or following migrating animals, they did not have residences or households. The family protected its children and taught survival skills. Young children and older people were involved in supplying food; however, most was acquired by the adults of the group.

Divorce in these societies appears to have been quite common. Infanticide (15-50 percent of all live births) and abortion also were not unusual. The economy was primitive; males were hunters, females were gatherers. Except in the Arctic, gathering provided 60 to 80 percent of the food supply. Hunters and gatherers probably worked about 15 hours a week in places where the climate was not extreme (Sloss, 2008). Religion was based on *animism*, the belief that spirits inhabit everything in the world. Politics were somewhat democratic, with decisions reached through discussion and consensus. Some societies did have a chief or headman, but his power was limited.

Education was informal. There were initiations into various stages of life (e.g., adulthood). Art and leisure consisted of music, dancing, and storytelling. Games were based on physical skill and chance. There are no records of these societies having games of strategy (Sloss, 2008). Warfare existed, but it was rare and ritualistic.

## Social Equality

Hunting and gathering societies were relatively egalitarian (Lenski, Lenski, & Nolan, 1995). People or groups had trouble building power bases because they could not accumulate a surplus of food, and there were few resources. Women and men were relatively equal because they were all involved in the supply of food. Private ownership of land was virtually absent. Constant moving made it difficult for people to accumulate much wealth. Those with high status, such as religious leaders, did not receive material rewards since there was no surplus of food.

# Horticultural and Pastoral Societies

Most societies gave up hunting and gathering for three reasons: First, the supply of large game animals as a source of food became depleted because growing human populations with better tools over-hunted them; second, there was an increase in the number of humans without enough available food; and third, there were weather and environmental changes.

About 10,000 years ago, some groups discovered they could cultivate plants. Others found they could tame and breed animals they had hunted, primarily goats, sheep, cattle and camels. As a result, between 13,000 and 7,000 BCE (Before the Common Era), hunting and gathering societies branched into two directions—horticultural and pastoral. Which direction they chose was based on water supply, terrain, and soil quality (Tarrant County College District, 2008).

## Horticultural Societies

The first horticultural societies began in fertile areas of the Middle East. **Horticultural societies used hand tools to raise crops.** They used hoes to work the soil and digging sticks to punch holes in the ground to plant seeds. Horticulturists were able to raise crops in the same areas for longer periods of time, so people settled for a longer time in these areas. Better planting tools allowed horticultural societies to grow food for more people (Lenski, Lenski, & Nolan, 1995).

## Size and Density

Horticulture had the effect of producing larger food supplies, which, in turn, produced larger populations. While hunting and gathering societies rarely had more than 40 people, simple horticultural societies averaged 1,500, with an average density of 13.8 people per square mile. More advanced groups had more than 5,000 people, with an average density of 42.7 per square mile. Horticultural societies were characterized as multi-community because they were linked politically and economically (Sloss, 2008).

## Technology and the Domestication Revolution

The Domestication Revolution represented a fundamental break with the past and changed human history. More dependable food supplies ushered in changes that touched almost every aspect of human life. With more food than was essential for survival, it was no longer necessary for everyone to produce food. Groups developed a division of labor; some people specialized in making jewelry, tools or weapons. This led to a surplus of objects, which stimulated trade. By trading, groups accumulated objects they prized, such as gold, jewelry and utensils. These changes set the stage for social inequality. Still, private ownership of land remained virtually absent.

## Mobility

A few advanced horticultural societies may have had truly permanent settlements, but most moved every few years when the soil gave out and the water source was depleted. Gardens were made by clearing forests using slash-and-burn techniques and then planting crops. As the forest reclaimed the garden, and the soil lost nutrients, people would move on.

**TABLE 2.1** The Domestication Revolution

| | |
|---|---|
| Food supply | Food became more widely and easily available. |
| Large societies | A dependable food supply made large societies possible. |
| Surplus food | For the first time, food surpluses became common. |
| Division of labor | Food surpluses freed workers to make crafts and to specialize. |
| Trade and barter | Surplus food and crafts were traded with others. |
| Accumulation of goods | Some people accumulated more valued goods than others, becoming wealthy. |
| Wars | People had possessions worth fighting over. |
| Slavery | Captives from battles were forced to do less-appealing work. |
| Social inequality | Some people accumulated much over time, while others accumulated less. |
| Hereditary wealth | The wealthy passed their benefits on to their heirs. |
| Concentrated power | Wealth and power became concentrated in the hands of a few. Chiefs, kings, and feudal societies emerged. |

## Social Institutions

The family was still the primary social institution. Some societies had very intricate marriage rules, and marriage itself became an economic activity as an overwhelming number of advanced horticulture societies required the purchase of brides. Female infanticide was also common, especially in warring societies (Sloss, 2008).

Horticulturists created complex systems of tracing family lineage. Education was informal. Religion was often based on ancestor worship. Lenski et al. (1995) believed this was a result of living near the graves of their dead. Females were responsible for cultivation in about 40 percent of the societies and males were responsible in about 30 percent, with men and women sharing responsibility in the rest (Sloss, 2008).

Since there was some food surplus, other full-time occupations arose: priests, artisans, and soldiers. Politics became more complex, and legal codes were developed. There was often a headman or shaman. Recreation included art, music and dancing. Games of physical skill were still common, while games of chance declined, and strategy games were introduced. (Sloss, 2008). Compared with hunting and gathering societies, there were increases in headhunting, cannibalism and human sacrifice. Murder and intergroup violence increased, as did slavery. Warfare became more frequent.

## Social Inequality

Horticultural societies were less egalitarian than hunter-gatherer societies. With the surplus of food, the idea of property rights came into being. People with the greatest material surpluses not only enjoyed economic advantages but also gained higher status and more power. They had the ability to control others. Social inequality emerged, with elites using government power backed by military force.

# Pastoral Societies

Hunter and gatherers living in areas not suited for growing plants, such as mountainous regions with low rainfall, developed into pastoral societies. **Pastoral societies** used technology that supported the domestication and herding of animals for food. These societies first appeared about 12,000 to 15,000 years ago. Most pastoral societies had secondary means of subsistence, usually small-scale horticulture or agriculture. True pastoral societies are rare today (Lenski, Lenski, & Nolan, 1995).

## Size and Density

Pastoral communities were usually small, averaging 72 people, with several dozen communities forming a society with a total population of approximately 6,000 (Sloss, 2008). Domesticating animals and growing plants increased food production and became a more reliable source of food than hunting and gathering. With more food came an increase in population, from dozens of people to hundreds or thousands.

## Mobility

A large majority of these groups (90 percent) remained nomadic, following their animals to fresh grazing lands and water sources. In desert areas, they traveled from water hole to water hole. In mountain areas, they moved up and down the terrain as the weather changed. We can still find societies throughout South America, Africa and Asia that mix horticulture and pastoralism.

## Social Institutions

The family remained the primary social institution. These societies were male-dominated because men controlled the food supply. Religion, education, and politics were relatively informal. Pastoralists believed that one god was directly involved in the well-being of the world, with an active role in human affairs. The religions of Christianity, Islam, and Judaism developed in pastoral societies, with god often likened to a shepherd and humans to domesticated animals such as sheep. Politics were based on a simple form of government backed by military force. Warfare was more frequent than in hunting and gathering societies; most fights were over grazing areas. Slavery was also more common in pastoral societies; in some areas, being a slave was a hereditary status.

## Social Inequality

Pastoral societies were less egalitarian than those of hunter and gatherers. Social status was based on the size of one's herd. These societies had patri-archal customs, and newly married couples were likely to live with the husband's family. Women had few rights because men raised the animals and grew the food crop.

In summary, some families acquired more goods than others in horticultural and pastoral societies. This led to feuds and wars because groups now possessed animals, pastures, croplands, jewelry and other material goods to fight over. War, in turn, opened the door to slavery; winners found it conve-nient to force captives to do their drudge work.

Social inequality remained limited, however, as the surplus itself was limited. As individuals passed on their possessions to their descendants, wealth grew more concentrated, and social inequal-ity became more common. As people learned how to domesticate plants and animals, they produced a food surplus. This resulted in a more complex divi-sion of labor, allowing for trade among groups and the accumulation of material goods. This surplus also resulted in the subordination of females, the development of the state and rule by the elite.

# Agrarian Societies

Another technological revolution occurred in the Middle East about 5,000 years ago, which led to the emergence of agrarian, or agricultural, societies in Mesopotamia and Egypt, and later in China. This period is called the *dawn of civilization*. **Agrarian societies** are based on the technology of animal-drawn plows that supported large-scale cultiva-tion to acquire food. Other breakthroughs included irrigation, writing, numbers, the wheel and the use of metals. Agrarian societies are classified as pre-in-dustrial economic structures, as are the hunter-gath-erer, horticulturist and pastoralist societies. Agricul-tural workers in such societies engaged in primary sector production, which means they attempted to extract raw materials and natural resources from the ground to be consumed or used without much processing (Elwell, 2010).

## Technology

Unlike the hoes and digging sticks of horticul-tural societies, the animal-drawn plow made it pos-sible for farmers to cultivate bigger fields than the garden plots planted by horticulturists. Plows not only could turn and aerate the soil to make it more fertile, they also controlled the weeds that might kill crops. In this way, farmers were able to reap several harvests every year from the same plot of land. With the increase in surplus food and the transportation of goods using animal-powered wagons, populations of agrarian societies expanded. According to Lenski et al. (1995), by about 100 BCE, the agrarian Ro-man Empire contained some seven million people spread over two million square miles. Greater production led to a relatively large division of labor and specialization. Dozens of different occupations arose, including farming, building and metalwork-ing. Money became the standard of exchange, and the barter system—trading one thing for another—was largely abandoned.

## Size and Density

Agrarian societies were larger and denser than previous societies. They could support more than 100,000 people, with densities of more than 100 people per square mile. Modern agrarian societies often had rapidly expanding populations. For the first time, farming allowed people to be born, grow to an adult and die in the same place. These societ-ies were the first to develop cities (Sloss, 2008).

## Social Institutions

Agrarian societies also developed more elaborate and complex institutions, although the family was still primary. The economy was principally com-posed of family-based businesses. For farmers, the farm was the family business. For urban craftsmen and shopkeepers, their shops were family-owned and operated.

Religion was very powerful, providing a ratio-nale for giving surplus items to leaders. In agrarian societies, religion defined loyalty and hard work as moral obligations and reinforced the power of the elites. The gods that originated in horticultural and pastoral societies were still part of the ideology. In simple agrarian societies, gods were seen as being concerned about an individual's moral conduct. As societies advanced, monotheism replaced religions with multiple gods.

Politics was primarily a feudal system based on heredity. Emperors and pharaohs were given absolute power to control political systems, and people had to obey and work for them. Education was expanded as an institution, although only a small number of people had access to it. Elites had time for cultured activities such as the study of philosophy, art and literature. Leisure activities included art, music and dancing. Much of the mass entertainment was raucous and crude; cock fights, gladiatorial combat and public hangings were common. Warfare was constant in agrarian societies. Standing armies fought each other, wiping out earlier types of societies (Lenski, Lenski, & Nolan, 1995).

## Social Inequality

Social inequality was very extreme, with landlords and peasants existing as the two main classes. Landlords owned the land and passed it along through generations of their families. But a large number of people were peasants or slaves who produced the harvests. Peasants signed agreements with landowners to cultivate a parcel of land in exchange for part of the harvest. The landlords became richer and more powerful as they exploited the labor, rent and taxation of the peasants.

Gender inequality also increased in agrarian societies. Since large-scale farming required intensive labor and greater physical strength than in horticultural societies, men became more involved in food production and, thus, were given a position of social dominance. Women might not be included in agrarian tasks and were, instead, left with support tasks such as cooking, caring for children, and weeding. As more men owned land, women's lives grew more restricted and they became a kind of property. Marriage meant the transfer of that "property" from a father's side to a husband's residence. According to Nielsen (1998), men demanded that women practice premarital virginity and marital fidelity so that "legitimate" heirs could be produced to inherit their land and other possessions. Women were engaged in unpaid work in the private sphere inside the home, while men were involved in paid work outside the home, which gave them higher status and social dominance.

# Industrial Societies

The Industrial Revolution began in Britain, then spread to other nations, including the United States. **Industrial societies** are based on technology that mechanizes production to provide goods and services. Industrial technology changed the nature of subsistence production and distribution of goods. In agrarian societies, men and women worked in the home or in the fields. In industrial societies, large-scale agri-businesses replaced family-based farms and ranches. Industrialization brought about changes to the modes of production. New sources of energy—steam, internal combustion and electricity—allowed factories to emerge as the primary means of producing goods. Industrialization attracted agricultural workers seeking employment in factories to process raw materials into finished products.

## Technology and the Industrial Revolution

Industrial societies are characterized by their use of machines rather than animals (or humans). The world's first industrial society developed in England about 280 years ago. Technology-driven changes have been evident in the past century. The invention of the steam engine brought about other inventions and discoveries. Trains, steamships and automobiles came into being. By 1900, railroads crossed the country, steamships traveled the seas, and steel-framed skyscrapers reached higher than any of the cathedrals that had symbolized the agrarian age (Wyatt, 2009).

These changes were followed by automobiles, which created greater mobility and spread out societies. Inventions, such as electric lights allowed people to work around the clock. Electric-powered homes became filled with appliances such as washing machines, air conditioners, refrigerators and stereos. Electric communication began with the telegraph and telephone, to be followed by radio, television and computers. Aircraft shortened traveling times, leading to a "smaller" world.

## Size and Density

Industrial societies were far larger and denser than previous societies, with populations in the millions and densities of hundreds of people per square mile. Population size began to stabilize as birthrates dropped.

## Mobility and Settlements

For the first time, most people lived in urban rather than rural settings (Sloss, 2008). In industrial societies, most people live and work in cities because of job opportunities.

More occupations and jobs were created as new corporations and companies were established. Workers had to have stronger educational backgrounds and mechanical or technical skills. A person's occupation became very important because paid work not only brought income and a place in social networks but also status.

## Social Institutions

Industrialization transformed social institutions and changed family structures. In pre-industrial societies, the family played a multifunctional role by providing food, shelter, jobs, care, socialization and religious worship. Industrialization took over many of these roles as the social institutions of economy, education and politics grew. The economic system tends to be capitalistic, with dominant monopolies. As more and more people pursued education and careers, they postponed marriage or remained single with the help of contraception, which revolutionized sexual mores (Cook, 2005).

Another effect of industrialization was the entry of women into the labor market. Women earned wages and became financially independent. A vast array of living arrangements came into being, including single-by-choice people, single-parent families, childless families, and blended families.

Religion remained a powerful institution. While science took over the primary function of explaining how the natural world works, church membership in the United States increased steadily from 17 percent in the 1700s to more than 63 percent in the 1990s (Sloss, 2008). Education became a major institution. Children were required to receive a formal education, and parents and children could be penal-ized for non-attendance. Warfare remained constant as people around the globe competed for limited resources.

In industrial societies, democracy increased the demand for a greater political voice and also influenced other nations. As the "Four Little Dragons" (Taiwan, Singapore, South Korea and Hong Kong) and NICs (newly industrialized countries) such as Mexico and Brazil became industrialized, many people in these nations increased their demands for political participation.

## Social Inequality

Industrialization had a significant role in raising people's standard of living, but social inequality remained a troubling reality. Due to mass production and industrial technology, they could afford durable goods and enjoy comfortable lives. Improved sanitation and advanced medicine extended life expectancy for all, but elites benefitted from industrial technology the most. In addition, even as more women entered the labor force, the income gap between women and men remained. This division of labor increased the economic and political dominance of men. Similarly, minorities were also discriminated against in the labor market.

# Post-Industrial Societies

Sociologist Daniel Bell (1973) coined the term "post-industrialism." A **post-industrial society**, or postmodern society, is based on computer technology that produces information and supports a service industry. Many countries, such as the United States, have become post-industrial societies with the advent of new information technology.

## Information Technology Society

What characterizes these advanced industrial societies is their reliance on computers and information technologies. Major job categories are involved in creating, organizing or transferring data.

The media play a large role in the world today. News about disasters is reported within seconds. We live in a world where technology enables us to see what is happening globally in real time.

In this new information age, formal education becomes an important social institution; people need to learn information-based skills and obtain degrees for their jobs. Workers also need to have technical skills to use computers.

## Service Sector Economy

Post-industrial societies are associated with service economies based on tertiary-sector production. Tertiary sectors provide services instead of goods. Workers are employed in the fast-food, transportation, banking, letter and package delivery, travel, education, health care, real estate, advertising, sports and entertainment industries.

In 1957, the United States became the first society to have more than half of its working population employed in the service sector. As of 2008, 77.2 percent of the U.S. workforce was part of the service sector, and it is projected that by 2018, that percentage will rise to 78.8 percent (Bureau of Labor Statistics, 2009). Education is the largest employer in the United States, closely followed by health care. Both fields employ more people than the industrial sector (Bureau of Labor Statistics, 2009).

## Consumer Society

Post-industrial societies are also associated with consumerism. With the invention of the credit card, post-industrial societies became cashless, which encouraged people to consume more material goods and services. People are bombarded with commercials that imply status if they buy brand-name products like Porsches, Rolex watches, Louis Vuitton bags, Chanel clothing and other high-end merchandise. Celebrities pitch brands and fashion trends; consumers wanting to live and dress like their idols buy these items.

Post-industrial societies are at the heart of globalization. The emergence of a *global village*, where people around the globe interact and communicate with each other via electronic technologies like cell phones, television, faxes, iPods, email, instant messenger services and the Internet. Although the information revolution originated in wealthy countries, new information technologies spread through the worldwide flow of material goods and information. In this way, societies have become more connected, and a global culture has been advanced. With globalization, companies have become more diverse and transnational. Companies with large global presences include Google, Yahoo, Disney, Coca-Cola and Walmart. Since Walmart opened its first international store in 1991, it has grown tremendously and now has more than 3,000 stores outside the United States (Walmart, 2007).

In sum, societies progress based on their level of technology and their food supply (as shown in Table 2.2). A technologically literate person recognizes the rate of change and accepts the reality that the future will be different from the present. This mindset within a society advances that society forward.

# Culture

The word "culture" comes from the Latin root *colere*, meaning to inhabit, cultivate or honor. **Culture** refers to a particular society's or social group's way of life, encompassing a set of distinctive spiritual, material, intellectual and emotional features of a society or social group. A way of life also includes norms, values, traditions, customs, beliefs, art, literature, lifestyles and sanctions. Culture includes how we live and shapes not only what we think but also how we behave. Additionally, it suggests that societies grow and change from generation to generation.

## Importance of Culture

Culture provides a way of living, thinking, behaving and interpreting the world. It includes the language used to communicate and the types of foods consumed. All cultures have their own customs and celebrations, from bullfighting in Spain to the Festival of the Giants in Puerto Rico.

Globally, there are nearly 7,000 languages, which suggests the existence of just as many cultures. People tend to view their own culture as normal, and may feel uncomfortable when they enter an unfamiliar culture.

**Culture shock** refers to the disorientation people feel when they experience a culture different from their own. The term was introduced in 1958 to describe the anxiety produced when a person moves to

**TABLE 2.2** The Progression of Societies

| Societies | Key Characteristics |
|---|---|
| Hunting and Gathering | First and only type of society until 15,000 years ago. Small (40 people) and nomadic, with little specialization. Religion: animism. Technology: spears. |
| Horticultural / Pastoral | Domestication of plants (gardening) and animals (herding) about 15,000 years ago. Increased population (200-5,000 people). Lacked permanent settlements. Increased specialization and stratification. Slavery common. Increased warfare. Religion: Horticultural societies—ancestor worship; pastoral societies—active god(s). Technology: hoes and digging sticks. |
| Agrarian | Appeared 6,000 years ago. Invention of plow controls weeds and maintains fertility of soil. Population increased (100,000+ people). First permanent settlements (cities). Increased specialization and stratification. Extreme gender and class stratification. Constant warfare. Monetary economies and hereditary political systems. First educational institutions evolved. Religion very powerful, concerned with moral conduct. Technology: animal-drawn plow (natural power or physical labor). |
| Industrial | Appeared 200 years ago. Machine power replaced animal and human power. Population in the millions, with hundreds of people per square mile. Urban living for the majority. Corporate/state capitalism replaced family businesses. Education and science had expanded roles. Increased inter-society trading. Democratic governments emerged. Technology: steam engine and fuel-powered machinery. |
| Post-Industrial | Present day. Service sector became largest employer. Production and control of information became a major activity. Specialization continued to increase. Increased control of environment. Technology: creation, organization, or transfer of information using computers and other forms of high technology. |

a completely new environment (Oberg, 1960). Culture shock expresses a lack of direction, a feeling of being lost and not knowing what is appropriate. People may experience culture shock in the United States if they venture into the Amish countryside in Ohio or into Chinatown in New York. In the military, new recruits experience culture shock when they step off the bus and enter basic training.

Different practices might sound quite surprising to members of other cultures. In the Old West, an Apache warrior would eat the heart of an enemy that had truly tested him so that he could keep some of his foe's spirit and ferocious strength. People in some cultures eat human flesh, such as a son eating a piece of his dead father to increase his own manhood. These people believe that the practice allows them to absorb some of the characteristics of the dead person or to regenerate life after death. In most cultures, cannibalism remains one of the ultimate taboos. If a person grew up eating the dead, though, he would probably learn and accept this cultural practice as normal (Arens, 1979).

## Culture is Learned

We are not born with culture. People learn their traditions by growing up in a society and living together in a community. Children learn how to survive and how to express themselves through agents of socialization such as family members and peers, schools and mass media.

As they get older and learn more, they form a sense of social order and social justice. Culture provides a society's rules of behavior. These rules make us alike or different. Respect for elders, hierarchy of authority and gender roles are examples of shared rules. Some rules of behavior may also be passed down from one generation to the next. The best way to instill values in a child is to set up a role model because children learn by example. If they see tolerance, understanding and respect for other people in their role models, those are the qualities they will learn.

What behaviors are not learned? An *instinct* is an unlearned, biologically determined behavior pattern common to all members of a species that occurs predictably whenever certain environmental conditions exist (Heydenberk & Okrzesik, 2011). The instinctive behavior of humans is attributed to reflexes and drives. A *reflex* is a biologically determined response to a physical stimulus. Examples include sneezing after breathing in pepper or blinking when a speck of dust gets in your eye. *Drives* are biological impulses that satisfy needs like sleep, food, water and sexual gratification. But expressions of these biological characteristics are learned according to culture. For example, we learn to sleep on mattresses with pillows to prop up our heads, or to use a tissue or turn our head away when we are sneezing.

## Culture is Shared

People share customs, traditions and beliefs that they have learned in their communities. Almost all cultures have similar cultural components that people participate in to survive each and every day. Sharing a culture with others makes it possible to interact with people around us. With technological advances and migration, people share different lifestyles as they cross the lines between cultures.

## Culture is Inherited

Culture is passed down from one generation to the next. For example, parents of different cultures are taught to love and care for their children, while children are instructed to respect their parents and love their families. No matter what the culture, the traditions of family are usually upheld. In some cultures, parents put their children through rites of passage. Though these rites may differ from one culture to the next, the tradition of passing culture from parent to child is the same.

Family traditions are demonstrated around the globe. Unlike other species, humans cannot rely on instinct for their survival. They learn culture after they are born—how to express themselves and how to treat people as they want to be treated—and survive because of everything they learn. Many people embrace different cultures, which can bring personal learning experiences and different skills to strengthen teamwork and productivity in the workplace.

# Material and Nonmaterial Culture

## Material Culture

Every culture has its own physical creations and artifacts. **Material culture** refers to the tangible creations that are made and used by members of a society. It includes raw materials and resources such as cotton and potatoes. Through technology, these raw materials are turned into clothing and potato chips.

The material culture of one population may sound strange to another. For example, the Amish value tradition and shun modern technology. Instead of using automobiles, the Amish still use horse-drawn buggies (Nolt, 1992).

Material culture involves our basic needs—food, shelter and clothing. We all need a place to live, clothing to wear and food to sustain life, provide energy and promote growth. But what, how and when we eat differ between cultures.

## Nonmaterial Culture

**Nonmaterial culture** refers to abstract or intangible things that influence our behavior. Food is a universal item of material culture, but the way people eat—a nonmaterial item—varies widely from one culture to the next. People in Japan and China eat with chopsticks, while people in Western countries eat with forks and knives. We may also notice cultural differences in the selection of foods. A pork chop might insult people in Saudi Arabia, while it is likely to please many people in the United States. Nonmaterial culture expresses our beliefs and values, our way of thinking. For example, some people believe in Christianity while others believe in Buddhism, and those beliefs affect their behavior.

## Customs and Rituals

Nonmaterial culture expresses our customs and rituals. In a Middle Eastern arranged marriage, a woman may wed a man she hardly knows. In America, we meet and date one person after another until we find the one we want to marry. In Sudan, there is an egg-breaking ceremony, called *nincak endog*. In this ceremony, the man has an egg broken over his head to pronounce him the master of his home. This concept would probably be foreign to most Westerners (Ubscure, 2011). In many countries, the groom is required to give gifts to the bride's family, but this practice might make women in other cultures feel like possessions.

# Components of Nonmaterial Culture

All cultures include beliefs, values, norms, sanctions, symbols and language because these six components of nonmaterial culture influence our behavior and shape our society (see Chart 2.3).

## Beliefs

Beliefs are a central component of nonmaterial culture. **Beliefs** refer to specific ideas that people adhere to; they represent an acceptance that some ideas are true and others are not. Since achievement is an American core value, many of us believe we are able to reach our goals. Beliefs may be based on cultural influences, trust, faith, scientific research, experience or any combination of these.

## Values

**Values** refer to collective ideas about what is right or wrong, good or bad, desirable or undesirable in a particular culture (Williams, 1970). Values direct our lives because they help people who share a culture to make decisions about how to live. The difference between beliefs and values is that beliefs are specific ideas, while values are abstract standards. Values come in positive and negative pairs— for example, respect/disrespect, success/failure, beautiful/ugly or happy/unhappy.

We use values to justify our behavior. Values provide us with the standards by which we judge behavior or conduct. For instance, people in the United States and Japan value achievement and hard work, but people in the United States value individualism, whereas Japanese people value collectivism. Cultures in higher-income countries value self-expression, while cultures of lower-income countries may be more concerned with survival and tradition.

A consistent value across cultures is success,

though people with different cultural backgrounds have different definitions of success. For some, success is being a millionaire. For others, it is being able to help those who are less fortunate. Success can be having a strong family or enough money to pay the bills. Which category we fall into is primarily determined by our culture.

One similarity shared by all societies is the deep desire to have a sense of belonging, whether it comes from a family, social group or religion. As human beings, we all have the need to love and be loved, to accept and be accepted.

In summary, values determine our preferences, guide our way of thinking and shape our behavior. We create and view cultural values as standards by which we define what is right or wrong. All cultures wish to reproduce their own values through procreation, education or familial ties.

## Core American Values

Because there are so many subcultures in the United States, the impacts of acculturation, assimilation and pluralism make it difficult to identify core American values. Nonetheless, sociologist Robin Williams (1970) identified 10 core values generally shared by the American people. Many other scholars maintain also that the following values are important to people in the United States today.

1. *Achievement and success.* Americans value personal achievement. Individuals are encouraged to compete and to do better than others in school and at work in order to gain wealth, power and prestige. Americans expect people to work hard and "move up the ladder."
2. *Individualism.* Americans advocate individual ability and independent actions. Americans strive to set themselves apart from one another.
3. *Efficiency and practicality.* Americans place great value on efficiency and want to get things done faster. In workplaces, Americans seek out ways to increase efficiency and focus on accomplishing realistic goals.
4. *Science and technology.* Americans develop new technologies and use them, along with science, to control nature and human society. Americans appreciate advances in all fields of

How would your life change if you swapped your car for a horse and buggy?

study and, because of technology and science, America became the world's superpower.

5. *Progress and material comfort*. Americans aim to make continuous improvements and expect rapid social change. Material possessions are considered to be a sign of comfort, and a high level of material comfort includes basic necessities as well as new items of material culture such as luxury cars and the latest electronics.

6. *Morality and humanitarianism*. Americans emphasize volunteer work and the notion of helping others, at home or abroad. Helping others is associated with the idea of morality.

7. *Freedom and liberty*. Americans value individual freedom. People have freedom of speech, freedom of the press and other freedoms that are considered to be basic human rights.

8. *Activity and work*. People who are diligent and hard-working are praised for their successes. Americans view their work as their life and value it because it brings them an income and social status, which result in material comforts and a social network.

9. *Equality*. Americans emphasize having an equal chance to achieve success. Equality of opportunity has significantly pervaded American society. But there is still a discrepancy between legal equality and social inequality. Equality is viewed as equality of opportunity instead of equality of outcome.

10. *Racism and group superiority*. Americans follow mainstream culture and value their own racial and ethnic groups as well. Americans also feel obligated to exert their culture and values on nations that repress fundamental, natural rights that are inherent to all people.

We have called attention to work as a core American value. We value work because it brings us income and status. Workers in the United States put in more hours than anywhere else in the industrialized world. In Europe, workers get an average of four to six weeks of vacation each year, while workers in the United States average two weeks (International Labour Office, 1999).

We have also noted the value Americans place on morality and humanitarianism. According to the U.S. Bureau of Labor Statistics (2011), from September 2009 to September 2010, 26.3 percent, or 62.8 million Americans, volunteered for a nonprofit organization at least once. Looking at the data a little further reveals women volunteered more than men. People aged 35-44 volunteered more often than those in their twenties, and people with college degrees volunteered more than individuals with just a high school diploma.

As culture in the United States grows and changes, it becomes more diverse, making the job of specifying core values more difficult. Five years after Williams created his list, James Henslin (1975) added eight core values: education, religiosity, environmentalism, leisure, self-fulfillment, physical fitness, romantic love and monogamy.

## Value Contradictions

In many ways, cultural values are in harmony, but that is not always the case. **Value contradictions** refer to values that conflict with each other either within or across cultures. For example, the values of racism and group superiority contradict the values of freedom, democracy and equality. Societies regard some groups more highly than others. In the United States, the war against Native Americans and enslaving of Africans are notorious examples. We pursue equality of opportunity, but there is still a discrepancy between legal equality and social inequality in terms of sex and race. For example, we have laws and amendments for equal rights even though men in the same positions as women are often paid more. Although the U.S. government claims to value equal opportunity, it does not allow women to join infantry divisions in the Army and only recently allowed openly gay people to serve.

Different values might bring about different measures of performance. For example, students from some Asian countries value respect for authority. When in the United States, these students may sit quietly in a classroom and be hesitant to speak even though they have differing opinions. The professor might think such a student is not engaged because in America, a good student is expected to ask questions, share personal opinions and even challenge the professor at times.

Value contradictions produce strain, and that can lead to confusion about our beliefs. Some people learn to live with the value contradictions, but others try to fight against and change them.

## Ideal Culture and Real Culture Values

People are expected to act according to stated values and norms, but they sometimes deviate. This means that people's self-reporting of their values sometimes differs from their actual behavior. Sociologists refer to this discrepancy as a gap between ideal culture and real culture. **Ideal culture** refers to the rules of expected behavior that a society has accepted in principle—what people "should" do. **Real culture** refers to the values that are actually practiced by people in a society. For example, a person may claim to be a law-abiding citizen (ideal cultural value) but keep a wallet found on the street (real cultural value). A woman may tell her children drugs are bad (ideal cultural value) yet get high using illegal drugs (real cultural value).

## Norms

**Norms** refer to rules of expected behavior that develop from a society's or group's values. Every society establishes norms, or ways of reflecting the

Source: Emily Bogden

Have you ever done any volunteer work? What did you do and whom did you help?

**CHART 2.3** Six Components of Nonmaterial Culture

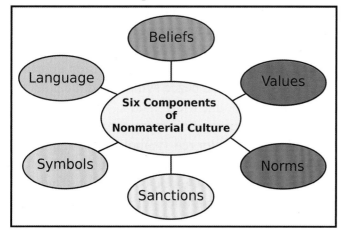

Six Components of Nonmaterial Culture

Beliefs
Language
Values
Symbols
Norms
Sanctions

values of a culture. While values provide standards for behavior, they do not state specifically how we should behave.

Norms reflect the core values of society, specify expected behaviors and clarify what is considered normal or acceptable. It is important to be aware that norms considered acceptable by one culture may be considered rude or inappropriate in another. For instance, in some cultures it is customary to kiss people upon meeting them, whereas that behavior might be considered offensive to another.

*Proscriptive norms* state what behavior is unacceptable, whereas *prescriptive norms* state what is acceptable. Both proscriptive and prescriptive norms apply to all aspects of society, though informal norms are not enforced. Formal norms are typically based on laws and enforced by sanctions.

## Informal Norms

*Informal norms* are unwritten rules of behavior that are understood and shared. People in a group are expected to follow informal norms in order to conform. When an individual follows informal norms, others may respond with informal positive sanctions such as smiles or positive gestures. But if someone violates informal norms, others might apply negative informal sanctions such as frowns or scowls.

**Folkways** refer to everyday customs within a society that may be violated without formal sanctions. Folkways provide unwritten rules of expected behavior but are not considered crucial to social stability. In the United States, examples of folkways include brushing teeth, quietly chewing food or saying thank you for a favor.

Mores are considered more important than folkways but not as important as actual laws. **Mores** refer to strongly held, informally enforced norms with moral overtones. William Graham Sumner (1969) coined the term "mores" (pronounced "mawr-eyz"), which reflect the core values of society and are considered to be crucial to the social order of a society.

We insist on conformity to mores and punish violators with negative sanctions such as gossip, loss of employment or jail because mores are essential to the well-being of a group. A waiter swearing at his customers, for example, is likely to be admonished and could easily be fired.

**Taboos** refer to the most strongly held mores—behaviors that are unacceptable in the cultural norms of that society. Their violation is considered to be extremely offensive. Having sex with one's parent or sibling is an example of a violation of the incest taboo. In American culture, arriving at a funeral in a hot pink mini-dress would be considered a taboo.

## Formal Norms

The norms that are most essential to the stability of society are formalized. *Formal norms* are written down and enforced by formal sanctions. Laws are considered to be essential to the stability of society. Laws are the most common type of formal norms, and violations of laws are punished through sanctions ranging from fines to the death penalty. **Laws** refer to formal norms enacted by legislative bodies. Laws are designed to protect innocent people and punish violators and are divided into two main categories: civil and criminal. *Civil law* covers private disputes between individuals or groups. Individuals who lose lawsuits may have to provide monetary compensation to the winning party. *Criminal law* involves crimes against the public.

It is possible for an event to encompass both types of law. For example, if an individual broke into a car and stole a stereo, that event could be considered both a private and a public wrong. The person whose stereo was stolen would have suffered a private injury and could, therefore, file a civil lawsuit against the wrongdoer for the replacement cost of the stereo. A government prosecutor could also file a criminal case against the perpetrator for the crime of burglary.

In sum, we live in a controlled setting where we follow norms, the basic rules of daily life. Norms promote conformity and are essential to the stability of society. They make our everyday lives orderly.

## Sanctions

Following or breaking the rules of expected behavior prompts a response from society in the form of a reward or a punishment. These are referred to as **sanctions**, the fourth component of nonmaterial culture.

Sanctions function as a system of social controls. *Social control mechanisms* are the means used by society to maintain social order and regulate people's behavior. Sanctions can be either positive or negative. We apply positive sanctions to encourage people to continue an acceptable behavior. Examples include money, awards, career advancement and scholarships.

Negative sanctions are used to discourage people from continuing unacceptable behaviors. Formal sanctions include demotions, fines and jail time. Examples of informal negative sanctions include dirty looks, raised eyebrows and negative gestures.

Human beings are creatures of adaptation and, when exposed to rules of expected behavior, are more likely to follow these shared norms. People who have been to Singapore, for example, find it amazing to see how clean the city is as a result of its culture of severely punishing individuals for littering and defacing property. Tour briefings given to tourists in Singapore stress the importance of not littering, because something as small as spitting gum onto a sidewalk can result in an enormous fine or jail time.

## Symbols

Human beings use their senses to experience the world around them, and they translate their observations and thoughts into symbols. A **symbol** refers to anything that carries a meaning and represents something else. Symbols include written, verbal and nonverbal language like signs and body language.

Symbols help us communicate with each other in

at least two ways. First, they convey the meanings shared by people in a society. In the United States, a yellow ribbon can show support for troops overseas and people may tie them around trees in front of their homes. Some symbols are recognized in many countries, such as the peace symbol and the golden arches that symbolize McDonald's. The Red Cross and Red Crescent symbols represent medical facilities and aid. The color red symbolizes revolution in some communist countries, good luck in China, passion and aggression in the United States and purity in India. White signifies purity in the West but mourning and death in the East.

Symbols can also reflect a person's socioeconomic status. We may judge a person by his job, the way he dresses, the kind of car he drives and the area in which he lives. All cultures make judgments based on such indicators; Americans sometimes appear to be obsessed with dress, a sign of status.

## Language

The final component of nonmaterial culture is language. **Language** refers to an organized system of symbols that people use to communicate with each other. It attaches meanings to actions, as well as to sounds and writing. Not only does it allow people to communicate, it also is the key to transmitting culture to the next generation. Language allows human beings to express themselves. All languages fuse symbols with distinctive emotions.

### Functions of Language

Language is the greatest cultural item on which human activities depend. Without it, cooperation and communication would be very difficult. Johnson O'Connor, founder of the Human Engineering Laboratory, is credited with saying, "If you want to succeed, your vocabulary must equal the average level of your colleagues, but if you want to excel, your vocabulary must surpass that of your colleagues" (Elster, 2000).

People can use both verbal (spoken) and nonverbal (written or gestured) language to express themselves. One of the basic characteristics of human beings is their ability to share experiences, feelings and knowledge. Language is how we express our thoughts and ideas to those around us. We can use our language to persuade others to our way of thinking. Language is the chief vehicle through which we tell others what we think, who we are and what we want to do.

Language also enables us to interact with other people to survive. Research findings by Frederick II, Emperor of the Holy Roman Empire in the 13th century, supported this (Liebreich, 2003). Some newborns were selected to be nurtured as usual, but the use of language (speech, songs and lullabies) was prohibited. All these babies died (Liebreich, 2003). These findings tell us that language helps us to survive in a society. Language is not only a human characteristic but is also a trait of animals. It has been found that animals use sounds, gestures, touch and smell to communicate with each other.

Language lets us transmit culture from one generation to the next. **Cultural transmission** refers to the process through which one generation passes culture to the next. As human beings, we possess the ability to use language to pass on culture, and this separates us from animals.

## Language and Reality

Does language determine reality? In 1929, anthropologist and linguist Edward Sapir and his student Benjamin Whorf observed that the Hopi Indians of the Southwest could not state a word in the past, present or future tense because there were no verb tenses in their language.

From their observations, Sapir and Whorf concluded that people perceive the world and create reality through the cultural lens of their language. Therefore, it is our culture that determines our language, which in turn determines the way that we categorize our thoughts about the world and our experiences in it.

*The Sapir-Whorf hypothesis* suggests that language expresses our thoughts and does more than describe reality. The hypothesis states that people's thoughts are determined by the categories made available by their language. Therefore, the words and grammar of a language organize the world for us (Whorf, 1956).

Other sociologists disagree that language determines reality for the reason that we can shape our view of reality through experiences and other venues. Language may affect our interpretation of reality, but language does not determine reality.

## Gender and Language

Scholars suggest that language and gender are intertwined (Epstein 1988; Holmes & Meyerhoff, 2003). This means that language reflects cultural assumptions about men and women in a society. This is the control function of language. For example, the English language almost seems to ignore what is feminine. Women take the last name of the men they marry. Men attach female pronouns to valued objects—consistent with the concept of possession. Naming a baby perpetuates the *he/she* persona. It is unlikely that a boy will be named Anna or a girl named Tom. Words like "chairman" and "policeman" indicate examples of gender bias.

**TABLE 2.4** Most Widely Spoken Languages

| Language | Approx. Number of Speakers |
|---|---|
| 1. Chinese (Mandarin) | 1,075,000,000 |
| 2. English | 514,000,000 |
| 3. Hindustani[1] | 496,000,000 |
| 4. Spanish | 425,000,000 |
| 5. Russian | 275,000,000 |
| 6. Arabic | 256,000,000 |
| 7. Bengali | 215,000,000 |
| 8. Portuguese | 194,000,000 |
| 9. Malay-Indonesian | 176,000,000 |
| 10. French | 129,000,000 |

*Source: Ethnologue, 13th Edition, and other sources.*
1. Encompasses multiple dialects, including Hindi and Urdu.

# Culture Diversity

Diversity is a powerful word with a meaning that encompasses much more than most people might realize. On any given day, you may come in contact with people of different races, religions, ethnicities, political viewpoints and sexual orientations. The television show *The Real World*, featured on MTV, illustrates diversity in action. It takes seven strangers from across the United States and it is the cast's responsibility to live and work together for six months. Not only does the show depict what it is like for people from all walks of life to live together, but it also shows how they grow together.

## Cultural Diversity: Mosaic Culture

**Cultural diversity** refers the cultural differences that exist within a society as well as across societies. Diversity is the inclusion of people of different races or cultures in a group or organization. It also refers to variations in institutions, traditions, language, customs, rituals, beliefs and values (Kottak & Kozaitis, 2003).

It is important to be aware of the fact that our culture is not the only one in the world. It is equally important to learn how to interact with people who are different from us. If we are not aware of the differences between cultures, there may be times when we offend others unintentionally or are offended ourselves. Understanding cultural diversity helps us to be more conscience of our surroundings and more inclusive of other people.

## Diversity as an Asset

Diversity is important in the business world; a diverse staff can serve as an asset (Walker, 2006). Within the business world, diversity can encompass employees, customers and vendors. In the past, a business could afford to be exclusive and focus on any one culture or group; this is not the case anymore. Businesses that want to reach a diverse client or customer base must embrace the essence of what it means to be diverse.

# Subcultures

**Subculture** refers to distinctive lifestyles and values shared by a category of people within a society. A subculture constitutes a distinctive set of cultural beliefs and behaviors that differ in some significant way from that of the larger society. Thus, subcultures are subgroups of a society's population. This concept has been applied to cultural differences based on gender, age, ethnicity, religion, geography, occupation and social class, and even those subgroups thought to be deviated or marginalized from the larger society. Different groups of people may live or work in one or more subcultures.

For example, if you are a 20-year-old, wealthy male singer with an Italian background, you fall within the subcultures of the upper class, Generation Y, Italian-Americans and entertainers. Video game enthusiasts, traditional Chinese-Americans, Ohio State football fans, the Southern California "beach crowd" and the Old Order Amish all display subculture patterns and lifestyles.

## Ethnic Subculture

People who share lifestyles related to an ethnicity, language or cultural activity may consider themselves to be members of a subculture. Although almost everyone participates in subcultures, they may not have much commitment to them. The United States is made up of many ethnic groups. Examples include British or Anglo Americans (Caucasians), Native Americans, African Americans, Hispanic Americans, Asian Americans and Middle Eastern-Americans.

Some subcultures are concentrated in large communities; people of the same ethnic backgrounds often stick together. In New York City, Korean-Americans, Italian-Americans and Puerto Ricans display distinctive subcultures with different food, music and lifestyles. People in different ethnic subcultures are distributed throughout the United States. For example, Chinese-Americans are the largest segment of the Asian-American population; most live in San Francisco, Los Angeles and New York City. Chinatowns located in these cities represent visible ethnic subcultures, where people speak Mandarin Chinese or Cantonese and follow core values such as respect and loyalty. Chinese language is taught in schools in such communities.

## Age and Subculture

Subcultures can also be examined in terms of age and generations. Take, for example, the traditionalists, baby boomers, Generation X and Generation Y (Hakevich, 2008). Traditionalists value privacy, hard work, formality and respect for authority. Baby boomers value peer competition, challenge, change, success and inclusion. Generation X values entrepreneurial spirit, independence, creativity, access to information, feedback and quality of work life. Generation Y values positive reinforcement, auton-

**TABLE 2.5** Generation Timeline

| 1922-1945 | 1946-1964 | 1965-1980 | 1981-2000 |
|---|---|---|---|
| Veterans, Silent, Traditionalists | Baby Boomers | Generation X, Gen X, Xers | Generation Y, Gen Y, Millennial Echo Boomers |

omy, diversity, money and technology as a tool for multitasking (Assael, 2004).

Generation Y, which includes people born between 1981 and 2000, developed its work characteristics and tendencies from doting parents, structured lives and contact with diverse people. They appear to need to understand why they are performing tasks and how they tie into company goals. People in this group tend to be independent thinkers who speak up without regard to power structure, and they don't thrive well in strict hierarchical work structures. They are adept at using technology and able to quickly learn new technologies. Their informal communication styles include slang derived from texting, reality television and popular music.

## Social Class and Subculture

Different social classes have different jargon, which can create different groups within a society. Family background and culture also play a role in creating divisions. People who grow up in the same country or location will be raised by different families with different communication styles. One family might teach their children manners and how to use proper English. Another might teach their children to use slang and disregard authority figures.

## Negative Results of Subcultures

Cultural differences can set people apart from one another. In the 1990s, a civil war in the former Yugoslavia was triggered by extreme cultural differences. The population of this country used two alphabets, had three main religions and spoke four languages. It was home to five major nationalities divided into six republics influenced by seven surrounding countries. As a result, cultural conflict led to a civil war. These different subcultures helped produce confusion, conflict, and violence (Ljubisic, 2004).

Subcultures may be dominated by another culture. When sociologists study how subculture participants interact with the dominant culture, they limit the scope of inquiry to more visible groups such as ethnic enclaves in large urban areas. Many people view the United States as a *melting pot* where many nationalities blend into a single "American" culture (Gardyn, 2002). Oftentimes we view the dominant or mainstream culture as maintained and favored by the majority, while subcultures are seen as the domain of minority or subordinate groups. With the United States becoming a more multicultural and diverse society, sociologists now prefer to emphasize multiculturalism.

## Countercultures

Members of a subculture are not opposed to the basic principles of the culture that surrounds them but maintain their own distinct identities within the overall cultural norms. **Counterculture** describes a cultural group whose values and norms are opposed to those of the mainstream and dominant culture. A counterculture strongly rejects and rallies against the dominant culture, opposing accepted lifestyles and seeking alternatives. During the 1960s, some young people rebelled against their parents' values. Other examples of countercultures include skinheads, Black Panthers, the Ku Klux Klan and hippies.

## Ethnocentrism and Cultural Relativism

**Ethnocentrism** refers to the tendency to judge other cultures using the standards of one's own. The word combines the Greek word *ethnos*, meaning "nation" or "people," with the English word *center*. A common idiom for ethnocentrism is "tunnel vision." Ethnocentrism expresses the belief that one's own ethnic group or culture is superior to others, and that its norms and standards can be applied in a universal manner to all cultures. The term was first used by the American sociologist William Graham Sumner to describe the view that a person's own culture can be considered central, while other cultures or religious traditions are reduced to less prominent roles (1969). The flip side of ethnocentrism is xenocentrism. *Xenocentrism* refers to a preference for the cultural beliefs of other societies and groups.

## Functions of Ethnocentrism

According to the functionalist perspective, ethnocentrism performs functions that are either positive or negative. The first function is to promote unity, which can help people pursue and achieve group goals. Ethnocentrism may also lead to in-group favoritism like the "promote from within" policies of many organizations, including the government.

The second function of ethnocentrism is to encourage conformity, which promotes order and stability. The third function is to reinforce nationalism. Patriotism is a love of, and loyalty to, one's nation, which is a crucial idea during times of war and economic crisis.

Ethnocentrism serves to maintain a sense of solidarity and allegiance to one's culture by promoting group pride and commitment. Many groups are proud of their heritage and may voice their beliefs to ensure that others are aware of their culture. Reinforcing an ethnocentric view of one's own culture as a means of instilling pride and respect is acceptable when coupled with tolerance and respect for other cultures.

## Dysfunctions of Ethnocentrism

One problem with ethnocentrism is that it may lead to making judgments based on false assumptions about cultural differences. Some people may be so entrenched in their own culture that they refuse to understand and learn about the beliefs of others. When people's cultural differences are discounted, generalizations, stereotypes and biases may surface. We see such biases in groups like the Ku Klux Klan.

If we use our culture as a universal yardstick, we can misjudge other people and cultures. Sometimes people make small judgments that they don't even notice. For example, when we see people in Britain drive on the left side, do we say that they are driving on the *wrong side* of the road? When we see Japanese read from right to left, do we think that Japanese books are *backward*? These judgments can affect how we look at other people and cultures.

Second, ethnocentrism discourages integration. Promoting the view that one's own race or ethnicity is superior to others is simply ignorant. In the past, ethnocentrism was practiced by people and groups, and also governments, that tried to divide and conquer the world for the sole purpose of making other nations assimilate into their way of life. In this way, other cultures could be eradicated.

Third, ethnocentrism accompanies outsider-group hostility, which can lead to intergroup conflict, violence or support for discriminatory behavior. Ethnocentrism is closely related to racism, xenophobia, prejudice, mental closure and authoritarianism. Social scientists have speculated that limited contact with members of outsider groups can lead to stereotyping. Research reveals that a high level of education can reduce ethnocentrism and that, typically, men express ethnocentrism more than women (Hooghe, 2008).

The fourth dysfunction of ethnocentrism is the prevention of beneficial social change. Social scientists in the 19th century operated from an ethnocentric point of view. Anthropologists studied primitive tribes, for example, to illustrate how human civilization had progressed from "savage" customs toward the accomplishments of Western industrial society (Bodley, 1988).

## Cultural Relativism

Cultural relativism is the opposite of ethnocentrism. **Cultural relativism** refers to a tendency to judge another culture by its own standards. For example, when we see Japanese eating raw fish, instead of calling it "disgusting," we could try it ourselves. *Reciprocal inclusivity* suggests that if we reach out and communicate with other people, they will be inclined to reach out to us. Cultural relativism goes hand in hand with cultural diversity and multiculturalism. Just as a salad is made up of many individual ingredients whose parts form a greater whole, the term *salad bowl* is the metaphor of cultural relativism. In a multicultural society, different cultures are described as equal, and a mutual respect for one another's cultures is promoted.

In a multicultural society, we can see that one culture is not superior to any other culture—each is unique and has its own merit. It is important to strike a balance with the cultural focus of ethnocentrism. It is not of value if cultures judge the values and beliefs of another just because its members have different religions, dress, customs or skin colors. These differences do not harm anyone, and if they are viewed as equal, they make it possible for the sharing of knowledge to take place.

When cultures falsely assume something about another culture, a level of hatred can start to build. No culture should have the right to treat other cultures as if they are inferior.

## Multiculturalism

Multiculturalism embraces not only the uniqueness of disparate groups but also the idea of many different groups being part of the same whole. **Multiculturalism** refers to the coexistence of diverse cultures with equal standing in a society. Multiculturalism holds that various groups with different cultures in a society should have equal rights and statuses, rather than living in a hierarchy. It encompasses many cultures without practicing ethnocentrism.

Multiculturalism brings greater value to the United States. Immigrants from different cultural backgrounds enter the country, integrate into the mainstream culture and still maintain their heritage. Since the United States has more diverse groups than any other nation, it would behoove it to embrace the concept of multiculturalism. Multiculturalism represents a sharp change from the past, when a person or group had to adopt the dominant traits of the majority culture.

## High Culture and Popular Culture

In everyday life, we use the concept of culture to indicate different forms of art. If you go to the opera and ballet regularly, people think that you are cultured. Sociologists use the terms "high culture" and "popular culture" to help people understand dif-

Source: Gabiel Saldana

What high culture events have you attended?

ferent forms of culture.

**High culture** refers to cultural patterns that appeal to the upper class or elite of a society. It may include opera, classical music, ballet, live theater and other activities typically enjoyed by members of the elite. In pre-industrial societies, elites did not produce harvests and, therefore, had time for activities such as the study of philosophy, art and literature. High culture usually appeals to the upper classes because they have the leisure time, money, knowledge and education to enjoy these activities.

**Popular culture** refers to cultural patterns that appeal primarily to the middle and working classes and are widespread within a population of a society. Examples include music, movies, reality shows, rock concerts, spectator sports and online social sites.

# A Global Culture

Some scholars argue that all cultures are becoming Westernized or Americanized (Crane & Kawasaki, 2002). The so-called Americanization phenomenon seems to be a consequence of the recent globalization of our world. The process of Westernization is called **cultural imperialism** and refers to the widespread infusion of one culture into the cultures of other societies. Nowadays, we see American icons in almost every country, from McDonald's to Coca-Cola. Our language is also often spoken in nations where other languages are dominant.

Critics argue that cultural imperialism neglects various cross-cultural influences (Gienow-Hecht, 2011). They argue that the spread of popular culture is producing a global culture.

International trade exports a variety of material cultural items from one country to another. Some people would like to curb globalization because they fear losing their own cultures, but it is very difficult to stop. For example, music, movies, food and clothing in the United States reflect African, Asian, Caribbean and Latin influences. It is common to see Americans with tattoos consisting of Japanese Kanji or Chinese characters.

Asianization is the term used to describe the influence of Asian culture on America (Berg, 2008).

Americans are discovering many Asian products, ranging from food and movies to nonmaterial cultural items such as Buddhism, meditation, tai chi, karate and feng shui.

Modern communication systems and the diffusion of information make a global culture possible. Modern technology allows the free flow of information to erase national boundaries.

Global migration brings cultures together to form a global culture. Air travel shortens the distance from one country to another and makes sightseeing, and even relocating, much easier.

# Cultural Change

Culture constantly changes and grows. Our pioneer culture was much different from the one we have now. American culture will continue to change and grow, in part because of immigrants who bring their ideas and cultural items with them. We depend on television, newspapers, radio, the Internet and magazines to stay informed and to learn. These same sources can bring about social change and diversity.

## Cultural Lag

When a change takes place in the material culture of a society, nonmaterial culture must adapt. But not all cultural components adapt at the same pace. According to William Ogburn (1964), technology generated new items of material culture faster than nonmaterial cultures could accept or keep up. Ogburn referred to this inconsistency as cultural lag. **Cultural lag** is a discrepancy between material culture and nonmaterial culture that disrupts one's way of life. Technology plays an important role in adding new cultural items to material culture. An example of cultural lag is how odd it seems to see someone writing a check in a store now that debit cards are so accessible.

## Sources of Culture Change

Social changes are set in motion by discovery, invention and diffusion. Discovery and invention are internal sources that bring about cultural change. Diffusion can be considered an external source of cultural change.

**Invention** is the process of reshaping existing cultural traits into a new form. Technology plays an important role in shaping and adding to the material culture of society. Culture changes because people invent new items. Because Americans value technology and science, they keep inventing new items which, in turn, make cultural change possible. In industrial societies, the invention of the steam engine and fuel-powered machinery stimulated many other changes. Other inventions that have had an impact on cultural change include electricity, household appliances, computers, telephones, cars, automatic weapons, atomic bombs, iPods and iPhones.

The invention of the computer was just an invention, not a change in culture. Cultural change occurred when computers were accepted and adopted by society. The computer is now part of our lives. We use email, Skype, instant messaging and Facebook to communicate. Finally, the computer has changed language patterns and social circles, and provided instant access to information, allowing people to educate themselves. This new technology has shaped our younger generations, creating a divide between them and older generations that will continue to widen if aging generations fail to adapt.

**Discovery** is the process of finding something previously unknown and is the second source of social change. There are several types of discoveries. Archaeological discoveries include dinosaur bones in Canada and the Gobi Desert. Penicillin and vaccines are examples of medical discoveries. Galaxies and extraterrestrial moons are examples of astronomical discoveries. New chemical compounds are examples of scientific discoveries. In terms of mathematical discoveries, the concept of zero was discovered separately by the Babylonians, Mayans, and Hindus (McQuillin, 2004). Modern algebra was based on the theories of French mathematician Évariste Galois.

Some discoveries are accidental. In 1946, Percy Spencer was walking by a magnetron, a device that combines magnetic and electric fields to create short radio waves, and realized that a candy bar in his pocket had melted. He got the idea to place popcorn in front of the magnetron to see what would happen, and it popped. This was the beginning of the microwave oven (Gallawa, 1996).

**Diffusion,** the third cause of cultural change, is the spread of cultural traits from one group to another. Factors such as migration, communication and trade account for diffusion. Generally, cultural traits originate in one area and then spread to a larger expanse of territory. For example, multinational corporations and businesses establish facilities or outlets in foreign countries; thus, the appearance of a Starbucks coffee shop or a Walmart store in another country is a form of diffusion.

# Sociological Perspectives on Culture: Functionalist, Conflict and Interactionist

Sociological perspectives help us appreciate how culture aids us in understanding ourselves and the surrounding world. In the following sections, we will examine culture at the macro level of analysis. A micro-level approach to the personal experience of culture is the focus of Chapter 4.

## Functionalist Theory

The functionalist theory argues that society needs every aspect of culture for survival, emphasizing cultural patterns and their function in a society. The key question posed by this approach is whether every part in society performs its functions and contributes to its smooth operation. The function of culture is to meet human needs. Functionalists tend to believe that shared values are essential for the maintenance of a society, and culture is considered a complex strategy for meeting human needs.

Different cultural traits provide a variety of functions that help maintain society. Cultural values direct our lives, give meaning to what we do and bind people together. In a multicultural society, we are exposed to different cultures and may experience difficulty crossing cultural boundaries and barriers. But we can find many common patterns across such barriers. George Murdock (1945) compared hundreds of cultures and identified dozens of cultural universals. **Cultural universals** refer to traits that people share across cultures. If cultural traits and patterns are found everywhere, they must be useful in society. Families are a cultural universal, functioning everywhere to socialize children and control sexual reproduction. The modern Olympic Games have been bringing cultures together for more than 100 years, illustrating that the drive to compete is something that most cultures share. Music is something that easily crosses cultures, and rock bands such as the Rolling Stones have had sold-out concerts on all continents. Movies are premiered all over the world in different languages. Great literature and famous authors also have works translated around the world. J.K. Rowling's *Harry Potter* books and movies, for example, are enjoyed by millions of people across the globe.

## Conflict Theory

Conflict theory links culture to social inequality. The key question behind this theory is: Who benefits from societal arrangements and why? From the conflict perspective, cultural traits are not equally distributed. Any cultural pattern benefits some at the expense of others. Karl Marx argued that culture is molded by the political and economic systems of a society (Marx, 1964).

For example, the political system in the United States is a democracy, and the economic system is capitalism. Democracy and material comfort have become core values. We have developed our culture through our political and economic structures. Based on our capitalistic culture, much of our lives revolve around earning materialistic rewards and profit. When we adopt the multicultural doctrine, we learn that we can prosper from what diversity has to offer, but we still do it from a business point of view.

At the macro-level, our political and economic systems have shaped our cultural values of democracy and material comfort. In turn, those values allow some people to become wealthier and dominate others, leading to social inequality. For example, rich oil executives can benefit from high gas prices, while others have to struggle to pay the additional costs. This may not seem fair because one small group within the society gets to live in luxury while everyone else pays for it.

Proponents of the conflict approach argue that a "culture of poverty" arises among people who experience extended periods of economic deprivation. Conventional society imposes its norms on people who are adapted to a poor environment and used to that lifestyle. Eventually, when people become educated and aware of the strains of inequality, they will initiate social change. The civil rights movement and the women's movement are two examples of that in the United States.

## Symbolic Interactionist Theory

Both functionalists and conflict theorists focus on macro-level analysis. Symbolic interactionists examine culture on a micro-level and view society as a sum of its social interactions. From this perspective, people create and interpret cultural traits, further changing them as they interact with each other in everyday life situations. Symbols and language allow people to communicate with each other because they provide shared meanings.

According to symbolic interactionalists, our behavior is not determined by values and norms. We negotiate and reinterpret our values and norms in every social situation because each person defines the situation from his or her point of view and responds accordingly.

In this way, we shape reality and modify culture based on our different definitions of reality. Reality is an arena of interwoven potentialities. We may be more controlled by culture than we maintain. For example, with the invention of laptops and cell phones, we may want to slow down but find it difficult because we have become conditioned to be able to get information anytime, anywhere.

Symbolic interactionists also explore how people preserve and change culture through their interactions with those around them. They highlight how we shape culture and, in turn, shape ourselves through our interactions with others.

# Summary

Societies were able to progress based on their food supplies and levels of technology. Society and culture are closely connected. Society exists within a distinctive culture, and culture is the way of life of a particular society or group. There are different cultures, both nationally and globally, and they change constantly. Cultures provide people with alternate ways of seeing, hearing, thinking and interpreting the world. Cultures can be either material or nonmaterial. Material culture refers to the tangible things made by members of a society, while nonmaterial culture includes intangibles such as beliefs, symbols, language, values and norms. Beliefs are the ideas that people feel to be true, and symbols refer to anything that represents something else. Language serves as the primary means of communication among members of a group or society. Every society establishes norms that reflect the values of a culture. Values provide standards for behavior, while norms specify ways of reflecting the values of a culture. The United States is a multicultural society, and as we become more diverse, we experience greater cultural change.

The functionalist theory emphasizes the functions of culture and shows that cultural systems operate to meet human needs. Conflict theory contends that these systems fail to address human needs equally, allowing some members of society to dominate at the expense of others. According to symbolic interactionists, people create, maintain, and change culture through their interactions with others. Functionalist and conflict theorists are interested in a macro-level analysis of culture, while symbolic interactionists focus on the micro-level analysis of social interactions.

## Review/Discussion Questions

1. Can you share any customs or practices from another culture that might shock people in the United States?
2. What are some other examples of value conflicts? What can we do to live with the contradictions or reduce the discrepancies between legal equality and social inequality or equality of outcome?
3. How can we deal with these kinds of value contradictions across cultures in the workplace?
4. Can anybody provide additional examples of discrepancies between people's stated values and their actual behaviors?
5. People are sometimes on the verge of anger as a result of culture differences. What would you think if you heard these questions: "Why do they eat with stupid sticks in Japan?" or "Why do I have to take off my shoes to eat at a Japanese restaurant?"
6. Give three examples of violating school folkways. What are the possible consequences for each type of violation? Give three examples of mores.
7. Certain hand gestures are banned at the Olympic games. What hand gestures mean different things in other places? What happens if some gestures are not welcome in other countries?
8. Can you list three cultural items that were passed on to you from earlier generations? What are three new cultural items that have emerged in your own generation?
9. What are three examples of culture shock that you have experienced in the United States or other countries?
10. Why must we be careful with how ethnocentrism is reinforced in a multicultural society?
11. What might cause people to dislike an entire group of people? Is it possible to change people's attitudes? Are there any theories to explain the existence of prejudice?
12. Is it arrogant when someone says that all people in the United States should speak English? Do you agree or disagree?
13. List six subcultures that are part of your life. Which are the most important to you?

14. Do you think multiculturalism is a good way to strengthen the achievement of diversity, or do you think it draws its share of criticism?
15. In the U.S., Western and Southern businesses and people are casual in their business relationships. In midwestern and eastern states, there is a push for precision and efficiency in business and more formal business relationships. Are these statements true? What is your observation?
16. Do you think we should promote pluralism or multiculturalism? Where do you draw the line to allow a culture to thrive without threatening its dominant values and norms?
17. Can anyone list fads that represent popular culture in the United States and across cultures?

## Key Terms

**Agrarian societies** are based on the technology of animal-drawn plows that support large-scale cultivation to acquire food supplies.

**Beliefs** are specific ideas that people think are true.

**Counterculture** describes a cultural group whose values and norms are opposed to those of the dominant culture.

**Cultural diversity** refers to a variety of cultural differences within a society and across societies.

**Cultural imperialism** refers to the widespread infusion of a society's culture into that of other societies.

**Cultural lag** is a discrepancy between material culture and nonmaterial culture that disrupts an individual's way of life.

**Cultural relativism** refers to the judging of another culture by its own standards.

**Cultural transmission** refers to a process through which one generation passes culture to the next.

**Cultural universals** refer to the culture traits that people share across cultures.

**Culture** refers to a way of life of a particular society or social group.

**Culture shock** refers to the disorientation that people feel when they experience an unfamiliar culture.

**Diffusion** is the spread of cultural traits from one group or society to another.

**Discovery** is the process of knowing and recognizing something previously in existence.

**Ethnocentrism** is the belief that one's culture is superior and other ethnic groups or nations are inferior. All other cultures and societies are judged according to the standards of the society or culture that one belongs to.

**Folkways** refer to everyday customs that may be violated without formal sanctions within a society.

**High culture** refers to cultural patterns that appeal to the upper class or elite of a society.

**Horticultural societies** use hand tools to raise crops in order to acquire food.

**Hunting and gathering societies** use simple subsistence technology to hunt animals and gather vegetation.

**Ideal culture** refers to the rules of expected behavior that people should follow.

**Industrial societies** are based on technology that mechanizes production to provide goods and services.

**Invention** is the process of reshaping existing cultural traits into new forms.

**Language** refers to an organized system of symbols that people use to think and to communicate with each other.

**Laws** refer to formal norms that are enacted by governments and enforced by formal sanctions.

**Material culture** refers to physical or tangible creations that members of a society make and use.

**Mores** refer to strongly held, formally enforced norms with moral overtones.

**Multiculturalism** refers to the coexistence and equal standing of diverse cultures within a society.

**Nonmaterial culture** refers to abstract or intangible things that influence our behavior.

**Norms** refer to established rules of expected behavior that develop out of society or group values.

**Pastoral societies** use technology that supports the domestication of animals in order to acquire food.

**Popular culture** refers to widespread cultural patterns that appeal primarily to the middle and working classes.

**Post-industrial (postmodern) societies** are based on computer technology that produces information and supports service industries.

**Real culture** refers to the values that people actually have.

**Sanctions** refer to rewards for normal behaviors and penalties for abnormal behaviors.

**Societies** are diverse groups of people who share distinctive cultures in defined geographic locations.

**Subculture** refers to distinctive lifestyles and values shared by a category of people within a larger society.

**Symbol** refers to anything that represents an idea.

**Taboos** refer to strongly held mores, the violation of which is considered to be extremely offensive.

**Values** refer to collective ideas about what is right or wrong, good or bad, desirable or undesirable in a particular culture.

**Value contradictions** refer to values that conflict with each other, either within a culture or across cultures.

# Bibliography

Arens, W. (1979). The Man-Eating Myth: Anthropology & Anthropophagy. New York: Oxford University Press.

Assael, H. (2004). Consumer Behavior: a Strategic Approach. New York: Houghton Mifflin.

Bell, D. (1973). The Coming of Post-industrial Society. New York: Basic Books.

Berg, Y. (2008). Asianization—The Influence of Asia on America. < http://www.topics-mag.com/globalization/asianization.htm> (2008).

Bodley, J. H. (1988). Tribal Peoples and Development Issues : A Global Overview. Mountain View, CA: Mayfield Pub. Co.

Bureau of Labor Statistics (2009). The employment projections for 2008–18.<http://www.bls.gov/opub/mlr/2009/11/art1full.pdf.> (2010).

Bureau of Labor Statistics (2011). Volunteering in the United States, 2010. Washington, DC: U.S. Government Printing Office.

Cook, H. (2005). The Long Sexual Revolution: English Women, Sex, and Contraception 1800-1975. Oxford: Oxford University Press.

Crane, D., & Kawasaki, K. (2002). Global Culture: Media, Arts, Policy, and Globalization. London, UK: Psychology Press.

Chapman, G. (2004). The Five Love Languages: How to Express Heartfelt Commitment to Your Mate, Men's Edition. Chicago, IL: Northfield Pub.

Eckert, P., & McConnell-Ginet, S. (2003). Language and Gender. New York: Cambridge University Press.

Elster, C. H. (2000). Verbal Advantage: Ten Easy Steps to a Powerful Vocabulary. Random House Inc.

Elwell, F. (2010). Agrarian Society. <http://www.faculty.rsu.edu/users/f/felwell/www/Ecology/PDFs/Agrarian.pdf> (2011).

Epstein, C. F. (1988). Deceptive distinctions: sex, gender, and the social order. New Haven, CT: Yale University Press.

Gallawa, J. C. (1996). A Brief History of the Microwave Oven. <http://www.gallawa.com/microtech/history.html> (2011).

Gardyn, R. (2002, July/August). The Mating Game. American Demographics, 24(7), 33-37.

Gienow-Hecht, J. (2011). <http://www.americanforeignrelations.com/A-D/Cultural-Imperialism.html> (2012).

Guiness, A. E. (1990). ABC's of the Human Mind: A Family Answer Book. New York: Reader's Digest.

Hakevich, B. A. (2008). Motivational factors of the Traditionalist, Baby Boomer, Generation X, and Generation Y student enrolled in a community college. Ann Arbor, MI: Proquest LLC.

Henslin, J. M. (1975). Introducing Sociology: Understanding Life in Society. New York: Free Press.

Heydenberk, E., & Okrzesik, R. (2011). What is instinct and why is it important? The Human Brain: An Owner's Manual. <http://library.thinkquest.org/C0114820/emotional/instinct.php3> (2011).

Holmes, J., & Meyerhoff, M. (2003). The Handbook of Gender and Language. Blackwell Publishing Ltd.

Hooghe, M. (2008). Ethnocentrism. International Encyclopedia of social sciences. Philadelphia: MacMillan Reference. <www.kuleuven.be/citizenship/_data/ethos.iess/pdf> (2011).

Hoorman, J. J. (2008). The History of Amish and Mennonite Cultures. Ohio State University Extension Agent. <http://www.clark-cty-wi.org/historya&m.htm> (2011).

International Labour Office (1999). Americans work longest hours among industrialized countries, Japanese second longest. Europeans work less time, but register faster productivity gains New ILO statistical volume highlights labour trends worldwide. <http://www.ilo.org/global/about-the-ilo/press-and-media-centre/news/WCMS_071326/lang--en/index.htm> (2011).

Kim, J. H. (1997). Bridge-makers and Cross Bearers. Atlanta, GA: Scholars Press.

Kottak, C. P., & Kozaitis, K. A. (2003). On Being Different: Diversity and Multiculturalism in the North American mainstream. Boston: McGraw-Hill.

Lenski, G., Lenski, J., & Nolan, P. (1995). Human Societies: An Introduction to Macrosociology (7th ed.). New York: McGraw-Hill.

Liebreich, M. (April 20, 2003). Frederick II Hohenstaufen – Scientist. <http://www.liebreich.com/LDC/HTML/HallOfFame/Frederick/Scientist.html> (2011).

Ljubisic, D. (2004). A politics of sorrow: the disintegration of Yugoslavia. Montreal, QC: Black Rose Books.

Marx, K. (1964). Selected Writings in Sociology & Social Philosophy. New York: McGraw-Hill.

McQuillin, K. (January 2004). A Brief History of Zero. <http://www.mediatinker.com/blog/archives/008821.html> (2011).

Murdock, G. P. (1945). The Common Denominator of Cultures. In R. Linton (Ed.), The Science of Man in World Crisis (pp. 123-142). New York: Columbia University Press.

Nielsen, D. A. (1998). Three Faces of God: Society, Religion, and the Categories of Totality in the Philosophy of Emile Durkheim. State University of New York Press.

Nolt, S. M. (1992). A History of the Amish. Intercourse, PA: Good Books.

Oberg, K. (1960). Cultural shock: adjustment to new cultural environments. Practical Anthropology, 7, 177-182.

Ogburn, W. F. (1964). Scientific writings of William Fielding Ogburn. In O. D. Duncan (Ed.), On Culture and Social Change (pp.349-360). Chicago, IL: University of Chicago Press.

Robinson, B. A. (2004). The Amish: History in the US and Canada: 1700 to now. <http://www.religioustolerance.org/amish2.htm.> (2011).

Sloss, S. (2008). Agrarian Societies. <http://homepages.ius.edu/GSLOSS/tth&g.HTM> (2008).

Sloss, S. (2008). Horticultural and Pastoral Societies. <http://homepages.ius.edu/GSLOSS/tth&g.HTM> (2008).

Sloss, S. (2008). Hunting and Gathering Societies. <http://homepages.ius.edu/GSLOSS/tth&g.HTM> (2008).

Sloss, S. (2008). Industrial Societies. <http://homepages.ius.edu/GSLOSS/tth&g.HTM> (2008).

Sloss, S. (2008). Post-industrial Societies. <http://homepages.ius.edu/GSLOSS/tth&g.HTM> (2008).

Smitherman, G. (1986). Talkin and Testifyin: The Language of Black America. Detroit, MI: Wayne State University Press.

Sumner, W. G. (1969). The Forgotten Man and Other Essays. Freeport, NY: Books for Libraries Press.

Tarrant County College District (2008). Horticultural and Pastoral societies. <http://www.tccd.edu/uploadedfi les/employees/2469/courses/SOCI%20201301/Handouts/Ch%20 6%20%20%20Pastoral%20Societies%20%20%20 Horticultural%20Society.doc> (2008).

UBSCURE (2011). How Sudanese Marriages Happen. <http://www.ubscure.com/Art/43115/243/How-Sudanese-Marriages-Happen.html> (2011).

Walker, P. (2006). Productivity through diversity. <http://www.cnn.com/2006/BUSINESS/08/16/execed.diversity/index.html> (2011).

Wal-Mart (2007). Wal-Mart to Open its 3000th International Store. New Wal-Mart Supercenter in Sao Paulo, Brazil features sustainable design, marks a milestone of growth for the company's International Division Retrieved. <http://walmartstores.com/pressroom/news/6924.aspx> (2011).

Whorf, B. L. (1956). Language, Thought, and Reality: Selected Writings. Cambridge, MA: Technology Press of Massachusetts Institute of Technology

Williams, R. M. Jr. (1970). American Society: A Sociological Interpretation (3rd ed.). New York: Knopf.

Wyatt, L. T. (2009). The Industrial Revolution. Westport, CT: Greenwood Press.

# CHAPTER THREE

# Socialization

## Barbara Miller

---

**Chapter Objectives**
At the end of this chapter, students should be able to:

- Explain the three major functions of socialization.
- Understand what happens when an individual fails to be favorably affected by the socialization process.
- Present both sides of the nature/nurture debate and offer examples of each argument.
- Cite examples from Harlow, Cooley, Mead and Freud that illustrate how these researchers influenced their concepts of self.
- Demonstrate how an understanding of Erikson's and Piaget's stages of life affects the development of personality and character.
- Name four agents of socialization and explain how they affect the likelihood of the socialization process working effectively.
- Explain the aging process, retirement to death, and Ross' five stages of dying.

---

his chapter will convince you of the importance of the socialization process by exposing you to a variety of theories, authors, and researchers who have contributed to our understanding of how this process works and how it affects individuals and society.

## Socialization

**Socialization** is a process whereby we internalize our culture's values, beliefs and norms; through this experience we become functioning members of our society. It is a complex, intricate task, and the process lasts a lifetime. It teaches members the skills necessary to satisfy basic human needs and to defend themselves against danger, thus ensuring that society will continue to exist. Socialization also teaches individuals the expected behaviors associated with their

---

cultures and provides ways to ensure that members adhere to their shared way of life by having and enforcing rules and laws (Ferris, Stein, & Meyer, 2008). The importance of the socialization experience can hardly be overstated. It gives us our humanity. We learn socialization through four major processes:

1. Explicit instruction: Teachers, religious leaders, and, especially, parents use this repeatedly.
2. Conditioning: This comes in the form of positive reinforcement, negative reinforcement, or punishment. Positive reinforcement feels pleasant. Negative reinforcement, such as being told not to touch a hot stove, can prevent something bad from happening to us. Punishment is something negative that is done to us. Through all three avenues, the goal is to change behavior (Dodgen & Rapp, 2008).
3. Role modeling: A child watches another person's behavior and begins to act the same way.
4. Innovation: If, through experimentation or change, we come across a behavior pattern that solves a problem, we repeat the pattern.

It is important to note that although natural limits exist on what we *possibly* can accomplish, socialization plays a very large role in determining what we *actually* achieve. Inherited attributes can either grow or wither in the socialization process. Suppose certain infants are born with high levels of **intelligence**, the capacity for mental or intellectual achievement, and of **aptitude**, the capacity to develop physical or social skills, but their parents are physically and mentally abusive. Those inherited traits are likely to fail to reach their full potential. On the other hand, if those same infants were born to parents who were loving and nurturing, those traits would have a better chance to flourish (Thio, 2005).

## Three Functions of Socialization

1. Learning the language of a culture, including body language and other nonverbal forms of language. We enter a network of social relationships while living in the respective culture, learning how to get along with others.
2. Learning the norms of the culture, such as not laughing at a funeral.
3. Determining what we want from life—what is valuable and worth achieving—such as getting a good job, marrying and having children (Dodgen & Rapp, 2008).

Sociologists ask, "Are more people programmed by their genes or by their upbringing? What if we fail to be socialized?"

## Failure to Socialize

There are cases of children who have lived in extreme social isolation. Some were kept in an attic and fed on a pie plate shoved through a crack beneath the door. When found, these children never smiled, talked, or laughed, and most of them died before reaching maturity. Sociologist Kingsley Davis studied several such cases to better understand the relationship between human development and socialization, since there was an opportunity to control one variable—that of nurture (Ferris et al., 2008). The three cases that follow are classic examples.

Anna was born to an unwed mother, a fact that outraged the mother's father. The mother hid Anna in her attic and barely kept her alive. Anna was never touched nor talked to, and never washed; she just lay in her own filth. At age six she was found, unable to walk or talk, lying on the floor with her eyes vacant and face expressionless (Thio, 2005).

Isabella was also born to an unwed mother, one who was a deaf mute; both were kept in a secluded dark room by the mother's father. When discovered, Isabella showed great fear and hostility toward people, and the only sound she could make was a strange croaking (Thio, 2005).

Genie was deprived of normal socialization for many years, kept tied to her potty seat, barely able to move her hands and feet. Her father tied and caged her in a crib, covering her head with a rag. She was beaten if she made any noise, could not stand straight, and had the intelligence of a one-year-old when she was found at the age of 13 (Thio, 2005).

At each stage of life, we acquire new knowledge and learn social skills appropriate for that stage. The socialization process is not a perfect process, nor does it always occur. On any given day, media reports offer numerous indications that there are individuals in our society who have not completely learned our norms. Unfortunately, in the United States and other cultures, there are adults who physically, sexually and psychologically abuse their children and spouses (Curry, Jiobu & Schwirian, 2008). We might say that these people failed to be socialized. What, precisely, is gained by socialization and how does our prolonged adolescent period affect the formation of cultural values and norms?

## The Nature/Nurture Debate

In the 1920s, early sociologists at the University of Chicago spoke of the "tabula rasa" (Durkheim, 1956), which means "empty slate," and implied that every experience in life makes a mark on our slate. By the time we reach adulthood, we are the sum total of the marks on the slate. This narrow view discounted the impact of genes or heredity. Today, *sociobiology* stresses the *nature* side of the long-standing nature versus nurture debate. Edward Wilson, a Harvard professor, coined the term sociobiology in the 1970s and claimed that social behavior was influenced strongly by evolution. Today, sociobiology and evidence from brain studies have given more credence to the importance of nature. According to one sociobiological theory, humans have four basic needs:

1. To acquire objects and experiences;
2. To bond with other humans in long-term relationships involving mutual care and commitment;
3. To learn and to make sense of the world and themselves; and
4. To defend themselves and their loved ones, their beliefs and their resources from harm (Tischler, 2007).

Opponents of sociobiological theories claim that these conjectures are a product of animal studies,

and people's behavior does not always fit conveniently into animal study results (Dodgen & Rapp, 2008). Studies of identical twins, raised separately, have shown us the influence of nurture on social behavior since we are able to control one major variable—that of nature. A question often asked is, "Are racial differences in IQ genetic?" Because there are no black-white pairs of identical twins, we cannot use twin studies to determine the answer to this question. Anthropologists claim that differences in IQ are due to societal advantages, and whites are more likely to be better educated, privileged and advantaged than minorities. How the brain develops is of interest here.

The brain of a fetus lends credence to the theory of sociobiology. The brain is altered by its genes and by its own and its mother's hormones. All brains are feminine unless acted upon by male hormones during two periods—one occurring in *utero* and the other at *puberty*. The hormones are nature, in the sense that they can be altered by drugs taken by the mother. They are also nature in the sense that they are a product of the body's biology (Duffy, 1996). This discovery has gradually altered the views of many psychologists regarding the relationship between *gender* and *education*. An increasing number realize that the competitiveness, mathematical ability, and spatial skills of boys are the product of their biology (genes and hormones), not their family, and that the characteristic reading, verbal, linguistic, and emotional interests of girls are also biological.

Many homosexuals have thought that their sexual preference was biologically predetermined. Studies of identical twins show that if one twin is homosexual, there is a high likelihood that the other will be also, but a non-identical twin has only a one-in-five chance of being homosexual (Duffy, 1996). Some behavior, such as violence, is both nature and nurture. Men are 30 times more likely to commit murder than women of all ages, and no doubt testosterone (nature) makes males more innately aggressive. Yet, young men in Chicago are 30 times as likely to murder as men in England and Wales, which has nothing to do with nature and a lot to do with nurture (Dodgen & Rapp, 2008).

# Theories of Personal Development

As infants develop, they grow not only biologically and emotionally, but socially as well. As infants get older, their personalities begin to show more and more. **Personality** refers to those patterns of thoughts, feelings, and self-concepts that make us distinctive from each another. Along with the development of personality, infants begin to develop a sense of *self*, meaning they become aware of their existence, feelings, and personal and social identities. When infants are born, they do not understand that there is a difference between them and their parents. Later they learn that they are one person, and their parents are separate people. Eventually, they understand that they are small and that their parents are large, and that they are referred to as sons and daughters, while parents are referred to as mothers and fathers (Popenoe, 2000).

## Harry Harlow: Contact Comfort

Few researchers were more significant than Harry Harlow in helping us understand the importance of nurturing a baby. He initially thought that the baby-to-mother attachment occurred chiefly because the mother fed the child, but there were other components at work. His startling findings created a new appreciation of "contact comfort," and today we realize that the nurturing provided by a caregiver is absolutely essential to the life of a child. After World War I, hundreds of babies in orphanages died mysteriously, puzzling those caring for them. When autopsies were performed, no cause of death could be determined; the description of these babies' deaths was that they just "wasted away." The disease was named *marasmus* from the Greek word for "wasting away." Orphanages were apparently so understaffed that nurses only had time to prop up a bottle in each baby's crib and change diapers, infrequently. There was no time to hold a baby or nurture it in any way. Forty years later, Harlow solved the mystery when he discerned that cuddling and holding a baby were essential to the baby's very existence. He also discovered that maternalism *per se* is not instinctual but is a result of learned behavior—another earth-shaking finding (Belsky, 2004).

For example, in his studies of rhesus monkeys, Harlow offered them two "dolls," one made of wire that had a feeding tube attached and another made of soft cloth with no feeding tube. When frightened, the monkeys ran to the soft, cuddly doll rather than to the tube-feeding doll. Before these studies, behaviorists insisted that infants were "attached to the reinforcing stimulus that feeds them" (Belsky, 2004, p. 109). In another study, Harlow took newborn monkeys away from their mothers and raised them in isolation to study the effects. The monkeys who received no nurturing or mothering were abnormal in their behavior. They bit and scratched and were highly aggressive; they would not socialize with other monkeys introduced into their cages. They rocked obsessively and were terrified of trainers and peers. They refused to mate, were inseminated and when they gave birth they refused to mother their offspring—sometimes even killing them. Because these monkeys had never been nurtured, they knew nothing about the experience (Belsky, 2004). Prior to Harlow's studies, maternalism was considered innate and thus automatic. That it is not helps explain why many abused children grow up to abuse their children, a fact supported by research. Now let us explore which experiences socialize us.

## Charles Cooley: Looking-Glass Self

Charles Horton Cooley's **looking-glass self** theory claimed "we are influenced by our perception of what we think others think of us." Cooley felt that the sense of self developed through our imagining the reaction others have to us. There are three steps:

1. We imagine how we look to others (e.g. Are we friendly?);
2. We imagine other people's judgments of us (e.g. Do they find us boring?); and then
3. We experience a feeling about ourselves based on our perceptions of other people's judgments (Ferris et al., 2008).

In effect, other people become a mirror or looking glass for us. In Cooley's view, we are not born with a *self* nor does the *self* emerge merely because of biological maturation. Instead, the *self* is a social product that develops only through interactions

How important do you think physical contact is in a child's development?

Source: Brock Roncace

with other people (Sullivan, 2007). To Cooley, even though our perceptions are not always correct, what we believe is more important in determining our behavior than what is real. W.I. Thomas echoed the same idea when he noted, "If men define situations as real, they are real in their consequences. If we can understand the ways in which people perceive reality, then we can begin to understand their behavior" (Tischler, 2007, p. 78). Normally we strive to behave in ways that are consistent with our perceptions of ourselves. If, for instance, we view ourselves as kind, we will be kind. Thus, the looking glass can be self-reinforcing (Sullivan, 2007).

The *self-concept* provides the foundation for all later socialization. One distinctive feature of human beings, compared to other animals, is that humans are self-aware. As early as age two, we realize that we are unique or different from others. With development comes the awareness that other people have needs, views and perceptions different from our own, and that is the beginning of the *self*. Cooley and Mead did much to help us understand how social experience develops personality. Human beings are unique among animals in part because we are able to put ourselves in another's shoes. We can imagine, for instance, what it would be like to be somebody else or how another person might view us. We are not born with this ability; infants have no sense of themselves as something separate from their surroundings. As Sullivan puts it, "One develops this awareness of *self*, this sense of our own identity, through interaction with other people; the *self-concept*, which is the perception that we all have about who we are—our unique characteristics and attributes—is vital to understanding our nature and worth as human beings" (Sullivan, 2007, p. 77).

## George Herbert Mead: Role Taking

George Herbert Mead developed a theory in which the central figure is the *self*, postulating that the self is that part of an individual's personality composed of self-awareness and self-image. Mead rejected the idea that personality was guided by biological drives, as Freud would assert, or even biological maturation, as Piaget would claim. (More about Freud and Piaget will be covered in later sections.) For Mead, the *self* developed only as the individual interacted with others (Mead, 1934). Without interaction, as in the cases of isolated children, the body grew, but no *self* emerged (Giddens, 2008). Second, Mead asserted that understanding intention required imagining a situation from another person's point of view. Using symbols, we imagine being in another person's shoes and see ourselves as that person does. This capacity lets us anticipate how others will respond to us even before we act. Mead felt that a child learned about the self through *play* and later through *role-taking*. For example, when children play they may pretend to be nurses or firefighters. In doing so, a child assumes the role of that person and judges or imagines life from that point of view.

Mead claimed that there were two parts to the self: the "I" and the "me." The self is both a subject, I, and an object, me. Children are not merely given a self by their parents; they find and construct a self. By age two, they even recognize themselves in the mirror (Giddens, 2008; Rathus, 2000).

Mead used a term—**significant others**—that has endured and is now even used in social circles. We pay more attention to the judgments of some people than we do others; those people whose approval and affection we desire the most are labeled significant others. Parents are a child's first significant others. By age 12, most children have developed an awareness of other people and have gone through three stages as they mature and expand their social world (Mead, 1934). The first is called the *preparatory stage,* in which the child interacts chiefly through imitation, seeking parental approval. In the second, called the *play stage*, the child moves beyond imitating others to act out imagined roles. In the third stage, the *game stage*, children take on the roles of several people at once and readily transfer the games to real-life situations (Mead, 1934; Rathus, 2000). Aside from their parents, children are also influenced by **generalized others**. These people are not necessarily close to the child but still help influence the child's internalization of societal values. Teachers, coaches and church leaders are all examples of generalized others.

## Sigmund Freud: The Unconscious

In 1917, Sigmund Freud felt that to understand human development, we must analyze the symbolic meanings of behavior and the deep inner workings of the mind. The field of psychoanalysis and the interpretation of dreams were his legacies. Freud believed there were three structural elements within the mind:

1. The **id,** which is totally unconscious and consists of biological drives.
2. The **ego,** which is the part that deals with the real world. It operates on the basis of reason and helps to integrate the demands of both the *id* and the *superego* (Ferris et al., 2008).
3. The **superego,** which is the "executive branch" of personality because it uses reason to determine whether something is right or wrong.

The *superego* is likened to our conscience, which keeps us from engaging in socially undesirable behavior. It develops as a result of parental guidance, particularly in the form of rewards and punishments, when we are children. It inhibits the urges of the *id* and encourages the *ego* to find morally acceptable forms of behavior (Freud, 1953). Freud emphasized early experiences and thought that as children grew up, their focus on pleasure and sexual impulses shifted from the mouth to the anus and eventually to the genitals. His five stages of psychosexual development are:

1. Oral
2. Anal
3. Phallic
4. Latent
5. Genital (Santrock, 2007; Ferris et al., 2008).

In the *oral stage* (ages 0-1) infants gain pleasure through the mouth, and feeding and sucking are key activities. Dependency and trust begin in this stage. During the *anal stage* (ages 2-3) the child's focus is on the anus, and toilet training occurs. In the *phallic stage* (ages 3-6) a child's focus is on the genitals. The superego develops and masturbation is common. It was the *phallic stage* that probably received the most attention, especially as it related to gender socialization. At this stage, children recognize the anatomical distinction between the sexes. This is also the time when sexual curiosity is at its peak. Children focus gratification on the clitoris for a girl and the penis for a boy. According to Freud, girls come to believe that the penis, unlike the barely noticeable clitoris, is a symbol of power denied to them. The result is *penis envy*, which culminates in a girl's wish to be a boy (Freud, 1953). She views her mother as inferior because she, too, does not have a penis. The girl's *libido*, or sexual energy, is transferred to the father, who becomes the girl's love object. This experience is called the *Electra complex*. Resolution occurs when the girl's wish for a penis is replaced by the wish for a child. A male child is more desirable than a female because he brings a penis with him. In the *latency stage* (ages 6-11), gender identity develops; boys and girls ignore each other, but sexual needs lurk in the background. In the *genital stage* (adolescent years), puberty kicks in, and the focus is once again on the genitals as boys and girls search for sex and a partner (Santrock, 2007; Ferris et al., 2008).

According to Freud, our adult personality is determined by the way we resolve conflicts between the sources of pleasure at each stage and the demands of reality. In understanding the *self*, Freud believed sexual development had an indelible influence on the individual's identity (Ferris et al., 2008).

Freud's greatest contribution to the understanding of *self* is his belief that just below the surface of the mind exist powerful areas called the subconscious and the *unconscious*. He proposed that *unconscious energy* is the source of conscious thoughts and behavior. For example, one might dislike a co-worker at the office and unconsciously express it by working hard to make the co-worker look lazy.

Freud once said, "Civilization tends to breed discontent in the individual." No normal person wants his or her drives for self-expression, freedom, creativity, or personal eccentricity to be totally suppressed. In other words, if we were completely socialized, we would become extremely unhappy and probably neurotic or psychotic (Thio, 2005).

Critics of Freud point out that his theories were

dominated by sex, that his work focused only on males, and that his studies devalued women (Macionis, 2007). During the span of Freud's career, he became an internationally known figure, even though his research threatened the existing political, social, and moral climate of his times. At that time, sex was not a subject for public discussion. Freud lived and worked under totalitarian and fascist regimes, where independent thinking was discouraged. In 1938 the Nazi invasion forced him to leave Austria, and his sisters were put to death in German concentration camps. Although Freud's ideas generated much controversy, especially in light of the fact they surfaced during the Victorian Era, they had a profound impact on the social sciences, and students will ponder his theories for years to come (Ferris et al., 2008).

## Erik Erikson: Identity Crisis

Erik Erikson helped us understand the factors that influence our human development. Erikson studied with Freud in Vienna and postulated eight stages of human development. He built these on Freud's work but added two important elements. First, he stressed that development is sequential and that a person continues to pass through stages even during adulthood. Second, Erikson paid greater attention to the social and cultural forces at each step of development. Erikson's theory has been called the "single most important theory of adult personality development" (Belsky, 2004, p. 22). His model assumes that:

1. A fixed set of eight life stages exists.
2. These stages unfold over time just as physiology develops over time.
3. At each stage, the person faces a challenge with a positive and negative pole.
4. A healthy personality will achieve the goal of the positive pole and then have the resources to tackle the challenge of the next stage (Novak, 2008).

Each of the eight life stages, called "psychosocial" (instead of Freud's term "psychosexual"), amounts to a crisis brought on by two factors: biological changes and social expectations. At each stage, a person is pulled in opposite directions in order to accommodate, or hopefully resolve, the crisis. In normal development, the individual resolves the conflict somewhere toward the middle of the opposing options. For example, few people are entirely trusting, while very few trust nobody at all. Most of us are able to trust at least some people, thereby forming enduring relationships, while at the same time staying alert to being cheated or misled by those who are unscrupulous (Tischler, 2007). Erikson's eight stages are:

1. Trust vs. mistrust
2. Autonomy vs. shame and doubt
3. Initiative vs. guilt
4. Industry vs. inferiority
5. Identity vs. role confusion
6. Intimacy vs. isolation
7. Generativity vs. self-absorption
8. Integrity vs. despair (Belsky, 2004).

In the first years of life, stage one occurs, involving the crisis of *trust vs. mistrust*. Infancy sets the stage for a lifelong expectation that the world is a good place or not. The second stage (ages 1-4) is labeled *autonomy vs. shame and doubt*, in which a crisis develops if a child is punished too harshly. The third stage (ages 4-5) is *initiative vs. guilt*, during which time preschool children are asked to assume responsibility for their bodies, behavior, toys and pets; if they are irresponsible, they may develop feelings of guilt and anxiety, creating the crisis. Stage four (ages 6-12) is called *industry vs. inferiority*, wherein children are mastering knowledge and intellectual skills; the danger is a child can feel incompetent and inadequate, creating a crisis. Stage five, *identity vs. role confusion*, occurs during adolescence at a time when young people are exploring new roles and career paths, thus producing identity confusion. Stage six (ages 20-30), *intimacy vs. isolation*, occurs as adults form intimate relationships. Intimacy was described by Erikson as "finding oneself yet losing oneself in another" (Santrock, 2007, p. 23). If this effort is unsuccessful, isolation may result. During stage seven (middle age), *generativity vs. self-absorption*, a person becomes more

concerned with others beyond his or her family and focuses attention on how future generations will live. The last stage is *integrity vs. despair* and occurs in old age when we reflect on the past. If we feel remorse and regret, doubt and gloom may produce a crisis of despair (Belsky, 2004). Each of Erikson's stages has a positive pole and a negative pole. In the healthy solution to the crisis of each stage (of primary importance to Erikson), the positive pole dominated, but Erikson emphasized that some exposure or commitment to the negative side is inevitable.

In her book *Passages,* Gail Sheehy (1976) spoke of six predictable stages that occur in our lives, and these are reminiscent of Erikson's stages. Sheehy's stages are presented in the section on *socialization in the later years*. Following Erikson was an equally important cognitive developmentalist, Jean Piaget.

## Jean Piaget: Cognitive Development

Piaget, born in 1894 in Switzerland, published volumes about how children develop. Piaget is probably the best-known developmental psychologist to date; his theories appear in virtually every textbook on child development.

Early in his career he worked with Alfred Binet, a French psychologist who devised the original intelligence test. It was as though Piaget could get into the mind of a child and see precisely how the child viewed the world. He had three children late in life—Laurent, Lucienne and Jacqueline—and was fascinated with every minuscule detail of his children's developmental changes (Miller, 1980). Piaget observed four distinct stages that children experience:

1. Sensorimotor stage
2. Preoperational stage
3. Concrete operational stage
4. Formal operational stage (Rathus, 2000; Santrock, 2007; Belsky, 2004).

In the first stage, *sensorimotor* (ages 0-2), children assimilate or test the outer world through their senses, especially with their mouths. They taste, touch, smell, look, and listen; it's all about the senses (Santrock, 2007). Reality for the infant corresponds to whatever his senses tell him. He learns that objects come in different sizes and colors; some are soft and others prickly. Some taste terrible, others taste wonderful. During this stage, one particularly delightful development occurs— *object permanence.* This is the understanding that objects continue to exist even when they cannot be seen, heard, or touched. If a puppy goes behind a couch he is gone, to an infant. Later on, when we see the infant looking everywhere for the puppy, we know the child has developed object permanence.

The *preoperational stage* (ages 2 to 7) is characterized by the use of language and the ability of the child to use his imagination. Children can attach meanings only to specific experiences and objects, but, lacking abstract concepts, they cannot judge size, weight, or volume. In one of Piaget's best-known experiments, he placed drinking glasses containing equal amounts of water on a table. One glass was tall and skinny, the other short and wide; he then asked children ages five and six if the glasses contained the same amount of water, and they all insisted that the taller glass held more. He then poured the water into a measuring cup, showed them the amount, then poured it back into the original container and asked them the same question. Their answer was still the same, showing that they could not process this concept. However, by the age of seven, they realized that the amount of water is the same—only the container is of a different shape.

The *concrete operational stage* (ages 7 to 11) shows us that children have a realistic understanding of their world. Their thinking is on the same wavelength as adults. Children can manage logic and understand why things happen. While they can reason about concrete objects, they cannot yet think abstractly in a scientific way.

In the last stage (ages 12 and over) children manage the *formal operational stage,* when they can think critically as well as abstractly. They understand cause and effect. When faced with a problem, children at this stage are able to review all of the possible ways of solving it and go through them theoretically in order to reach a solution (Santrock, 2007; Belsky, 2004; Rathus, 2000).

According to Piaget, the first three stages of development are universal, but not everyone reaches the *formal operational stage*; it depends largely on a person's education. Adults of limited educational attainment tend to continue to think in more concrete terms, and they retain a tendency toward egocentrism.

As an educator, Piaget called all teachers *facilitators* and claimed there are no teachers, only learners. He urged parents and educators to allow children to discover the world on their own (Giddens, 2008).

## Abraham Maslow: Hierarchy of Needs

Maslow published his *hierarchy of needs theory* more than 50 years ago, and it is probably the most popular and oft-cited theory about what motivates people to behave the way they do (Maslow, 2008). Maslow's original hierarchy of needs model was developed between 1943 and 1954 and was first widely published in *Motivation and Personality*. He believed we are all motivated by needs. Our most basic needs are inborn, having evolved over tens of thousands of years. Maslow said that needs must be satisfied in a given order; once the needs of one level are met, aims and drives shift to the next level of the hierarchy. If needs are thwarted, it causes stress. Physiological needs must come first. If needs like air, water, food, and sleep are not satisfied, a person's energy must be spent in pursuit of them. Higher needs such as esteem and love will have to wait. The second most important needs to be satisfied concern safety, so that we can be free from the threat of physical and emotional harm. Such needs might include "living in a safe area, medical insurance, job security and financial reserves" (Wood & Wood, 2011, p. 344). In other words, if a person feels endangered, higher needs will not receive much attention. Next are social needs. Social needs are those related to interactions with others and may include the need for belonging and the need for giving and receiving love. Social needs are followed by esteem needs. After feeling a sense of belonging, the need to feel important arises; esteem needs bring self-respect, a sense of accomplishment and recognition. At the top of Maslow's pyramid-shaped hierarchy is self-actualization, which means finding self-fulfillment and realizing one's potential.

Self-actualized people are characterized as being problem-focused, possessing an ongoing freshness and appreciation of life, wanting to achieve maximal personal growth and having "peak experiences" (Maslow, 1987).

Self-actualization is the level that most fascinates students. People at this level have:

1. A keen sense of reality and objective, rather than subjective, judgment.
2. The ability to see problems in terms of challenges and situations requiring solutions, rather than as personal complaints or excuses.
3. A need for privacy and are comfortable being alone.
4. Reliance on their own experiences and judgments. They are independent and don't rely on culture and environment to form opinions and views.
5. Autonomy, and are not susceptible to social pressures. They are nonconformists.
6. A democratic, fair, and non-discriminating sense. They embrace all cultures, races, and individual styles.
7. Social compassion and humanity.
8. An acceptance of others as they are rather than how they want them to be.
9. A sense of comfort with themselves, despite any unconventional tendencies.
10. A few close intimate friends, rather than many surface relationships.
11. A sense of humor directed at oneself or the human condition, rather than at the expense of others.
12. Spontaneity. They are natural and remain true to themselves, despite the wants of others.
13. An excitement and interest in all things, even the most ordinary.
14. Creativity; they are inventive and original.
15. The ability to have peak experiences that leave a lasting impression (Maslow, 1987).

Norwood proposed that Maslow's hierarchy can be used to describe the kinds of information that individuals seek at different levels. For example, those at the lowest level seek *coping information* in order to meet basic needs. People at the safety level need *helping information* in order to be safe and secure. Belongingness creates a need for *enlightening information*. People at the esteem level need *empowering* information so their ego can be developed. People in self-actualization need *edifying* information, which probably includes seeking a "higher power, some power beyond themselves" (Norwood, 2002). In addition to the five-level theory, there are later adaptations of the hierarchy based on Maslow's work. These later models add levels that include *cognitive, aesthetic* and *transcendence* levels of need. For many people, self-actualizing commonly involves each and every one of the newer levels. Thus, the original five-level *hierarchy of needs* model remains a definitive classical representation of human motivation. The later adaptations perhaps serve best to illustrate aspects of self-actualization (Maslow, 1987).

## Lawrence Kohlberg: Theory of Moral Development

Kohlberg was the principal theorist to ask where the concept of moral development comes from. How do we come to judge situations as right or wrong? Sunday school and church might teach children about right and wrong, but not all children go to church. Parents might teach about right and wrong by modeling it, but not all children get their values from their parents. Early researchers were leery of studying moral development because they didn't want to offend religious groups or step on the toes of parents who clearly felt moral development was their job. This is analogous to sex education in schools today; many parents say, "I'll teach my children about sex, thank you" and then don't. Kohlberg believed that it is only during adolescence that we become capable of developing a moral code that guides our lives (Curry et al., 2007). To measure the presence of this moral code, Kohlberg wrote scenarios and asked people to respond to the moral dilemmas presented. Kohlberg discovered that three levels of thought (or six stages of morality) were discernible. Additionally, stage development always moved upward, and the three levels of moral thought—*pre-conventional, conventional* and *post-conventional*—were found in all cultures tested

(Miller, 1980). Each level actually has two stages, but this discussion will be confined to the general levels to avoid confusion.

In the earliest stage, **pre-conventional morality**, people are thought to obey laws chiefly to avoid punishment or to gain some benefit. It is considered good to do something nice for another person, but only if that person would do something nice in return. Even though pre-conventional morality refers chiefly to children's behavior, adults participate in it, too. For example, we might look both ways to see if a policeman is watching before making an illegal turn in our car. Or if we find a $10 bill on the sidewalk, we may look around to make sure no one is watching and put it in our pocket. In the second level, **conventional morality**, people incorporate society's rules and laws into their own value system and behave accordingly. Most adults and adolescents operate in this level (Curry et al., 2007; Miller, 1980). They obey rules not only to win approval or gain rewards, but also because they feel they are doing the right thing. Loyalty becomes an important concept, and some people feel it takes precedence over all other commitments. **Post-conventional morality** is the highest level attainable. At this level, people use broad ethical principles to guide their behavior, such as showing respect for human dignity, equality, and, of late, respect for one's environment—even for the rights of animals and other living creatures. People operating at this level are often instigators of social change and are in the forefront of social movements. One famous post-conventional act was that of Martin Luther King, Jr., in his peaceful protest march in 1963. Followers ignored a court order, and some were arrested and jailed. Dr. King concluded that protesting racial inequality was a higher principle than obeying a court order (Curry et al., 2007).

One criticism of Kohlberg's theory is that he used only boys as subjects for his investigation; another is that very few people ever reach the highest (stage six) post-conventional level. The following story is one of Kohlberg's most widely known dilemmas, and he used it to determine which level a person was operating in:

In Europe, a woman was near death from a special kind of cancer. There was one medicine that a pharmacist in the same town thought might save her. It was a form of radium that the druggist had recently discovered. He was charging 10 times what the drug cost him to make. He paid $200 for the radium and charged $2,000 for a small dose of the drug. The sick woman's husband, Heinz, went to everyone he knew to borrow the money, but he could only get together about $1,000. He told the pharmacist that his wife was dying and asked him to sell it to him at a lower price or let him pay later, but the pharmacist said, "No, I discovered the drug, and I'm going to make money from it." Heinz became desperate, broke into the man's store and stole the drug for his wife (Miller, 1980, p. 35).

If, after reading this, you thought in terms of whether Heinz would be punished for his actions, (i.e., "If Heinz stole the drug, he would go to jail") you would be classified as operating at the *pre-conventional level*. Your concern would focus on the external consequences for Heinz rather than any internalized moral sense. If you're thinking, "Heinz shouldn't steal the drug because that is not law-abiding, and laws must be obeyed," your response would be classified at the *conventional level*. If your concern was, "No matter what society says, Heinz had to steal the drug for his wife because nothing outweighs the universal principle of saving a life," you were at the *post-conventional level* of moral thinking.

When Kohlberg conducted studies with children of different ages, he discovered that at age 13, pre-conventional answers were universal in every culture. By the age of 15, most children around the world were reasoning at the conventional level (Miller, 1980). When Kohlberg described the advances in moral thinking that take place during adolescence, he made an important point: Teenagers are famous for questioning society's rules, for seeing the injustice of the world, and for getting involved in idealistic causes; however, these factors can add to the emotional storm characteristic of the teen years (Belsky, 2004). Gilligan criticized Kohlberg's use of male children in his sample because, according to Gilligan's research, males approach morality from a different perspective than females. "Whereas males define morality in terms of justice, females define morality in terms of responsibility" (Gilligan, 1982, p. 326). Another criticism focused on whether we can depend on an actual link between moral thought and moral behavior.

All societies have value systems that specify what is right or wrong. Today, most people have strong opinions not only about moral and immoral behavior, but also about how moral behavior should be taught and whether it should be taught in school or left to parents and clergy.

## Gender and Socialization

**Gender** refers to learned behavior—how we are characterized as males or females in society. This learning occurs in good part through the socialization process (Sullivan, 2007). Our **gender role** refers to how we are expected to act as males or females, whereas **gender typing** refers to acquiring behavior considered appropriate for one's particular gender. Research has shown that much of our behavior as males and females is a function not of biology, but of learning (Ferris et al., 2008). This finding leads to the distinction that sociologists make between *sex* and *gender*. **Sex** refers to the biological and anatomical differences between females and males. Masculine and feminine, by contrast, are used as gender-specific terms. The way parents treat children reinforces gender. Parents might be rough-and-tumble with a boy. With a girl, they might smile more and hold them closer, for longer periods of time (Dodgen & Rapp, 2008). We will put a female child in long pants, but we would never put a male child in a pink dress. Even height and low birth weight help socialize us by the way our parents react to us. Yet, biologists claim that we are born with tendencies to be introverted or extroverted, hormones give males a push toward greater aggression, and even intelligence is thought to be as much as 70 percent inherited (Dodgen & Rapp, 2008; Sullivan, 2007).

### The Social Learning Theory

Precisely how do children learn their gender roles? According to *social learning theory, conditioning* and *imitation* have significant influence: "People learn by watching others and imitating the ones we emulate" (Belsky, 2004, p. 14). Children are rewarded for behaving in ways that parents consider appropriate for their gender and punished for not doing so; therefore, they eventually conform to society's expectation of gender roles. A boy learns to hide his fears and pain because he has been praised for being brave and scolded for crying. Children also learn by imitation. They tend to imitate their same-sex parent and certain adults because they are powerful role models and people who are able to reward or punish them (Thio, 2005, p. 247). Androgyny, the presence of masculine and feminine characteristics in the same person, is encouraged today because it helps avoid the limiting quality and rigidity of old, stereotypical ways.

Children are given verbal cues from parents about their gender behavior. By age two, children have a pretty good idea of what gender is, and they know if they are a boy or a girl. It is not until age six that children understand that a person's sex does not change, and that sex differences between girls and boys are anatomically based. Many toy stores and catalogs still classify products according to gender (Dodgen & Rapp, 2008). Adults feel the push toward acting in accordance with gender roles, too. Society claims that women are supposed to be shy, easily intimidated, and passive. Men are to be bold, ambitious, and aggressive. Women should pay attention to their appearance, and it's acceptable to be emotional, even to cry easily, but men should hold back emotions and not cry (Thio, 2005). Women need male protection and are expected to be intuitive and unpredictable; men are leaders and expected to be logical, rational and objective. Even though our culture has modified some of these values, certain *gender stereotypes* persist and will continue to affect our opportunities and life events (Thio, 2005).

## Socialization is Reciprocal

Is there a downside to socialization? We wonder if we are just prisoners of socialization, shaped and influenced to such a great extent by others and by society. Are our ideas as individuals unique and

In your opinion, do these two photos violate society's current gender roles?

independent, or is that belief just an illusion? Ferris (2008) suggests it is true that the process of socialization is rather homogenizing, that people are pushed toward conformity to help the culture run smoothly. He asks, "Does this press us toward some sort of lowest common denominator, toward the mainstream? Or is it true that no two people are ever really alike or ever entirely 'finished.' The process by which we become socialized is ongoing; we are not merely passive players, receiving all the influences around us. We are spontaneous, intelligent, and creative, and we exercise free will. We are interpreting, defining, making sense of, and responding to, our social world. That gives us a great deal of personal power in all situations. The socialization process is reciprocal in that we are shaping society at the same time society is shaping us" (Ferris, 2008 pp. 137-138).

## Agents of Socialization

Every society has individuals, groups, and institu-

tions that provide varying amounts of socialization during the life course, and some, like *family*, have a greater impact than others. *Schools, peers,* the *media* and, eventually as an adult, the *work world* are also powerful socializing agents, as are the police and religious leaders. These agents limit our choices by rewarding compliance to rules and punishing noncompliance. Socializing agents also act as role models, serving as especially important reference points for our thoughts and actions (Curry et al., 2007). Humans, however, are not simply passive subjects waiting to be programmed or instructed; individuals come to understand and assume social roles through an ongoing process of social interaction. The impact of any agent is not the same for all people, and no two people experience the same type of socialization because of the influence of other factors such as social class and educational level. **Primary socialization** begins in infancy and childhood and is the most intense period of cultural learning (Giddens, 2008). It is the time when children learn language and the basic behavioral patterns that form the foundation for later learning.

**Secondary socialization** takes place later in childhood and into maturity. In this phase, other agents of socialization take over some of the responsibility from family (Tischler, 2007). **Anticipatory socialization** involves learning the skills and values needed for future roles. This type of socialization begins during adolescence. We prepare for future roles by working part-time jobs, taking certain self-help courses in college, reading books and articles, talking with mentors, and trying out anticipated roles (Giddens, 2008). Three key factors influence the effectiveness of anticipatory socialization:

1. The visibility of the future role.
2. The accuracy with which the future role is presented.
3. The agreement society has about the role.

To the sociologist, **roles** are socially defined expectations associated with a given status. Sometimes we get mixed messages from the culture about what is really expected when we play a given role.

## Daycare

Most American mothers work outside the home or return to work relatively soon after the birth of children. For this reason, we can include daycare and nursery schools as *agents of socialization.* Critics of the *daycare movement* believe that only parents can give children the love, attention and intimate involvement they need to develop into emotionally healthy and socially competent adults (Belsky, 2004). Proponents claim that daycare helps children learn to be independent of "s-mothering" (of which some mothers are guilty) and that research indicates that children exposed to daycare do as well, or better than, children raised exclusively in the home (Sullivan, 2007).

## Family

In the family network, we first learn about intimacy, emotions, and power; we also learn the components of culture and social structure, including language, norms, and values. The family usually protects us and provides us with nourishment and affection. Family also determines such ascribed statuses as racial and ethnic background and influ-ences other statuses, including socioeconomics and religion. These statuses have an impact on how we are raised. For instance, parents from different backgrounds raise their children in different ways and expect different things from them. Working-class parents tend to encourage obedience, conformity, respect, cleanliness, and neatness. Middle-class parents are more likely to encourage curiosity, self-direction, and expressiveness (Sullivan, 2007). Later in life, a strong social support network makes aging experiences easier because within the family, elders can feel useful, loved and accepted (Giddens, 2008).

## Schools

Schools, especially because attendance is mandatory, have a powerful effect in America, not only because they teach intellectual pursuits and job preparedness, but because of something sociologists call the *hidden curriculum.* The hidden curriculum refers to teachings in school that prepare children to accept the requirements of adult life and to fit into the world society provides. Children learn to be quiet and punctual in class, accept and respond to a teacher's authority, and show respect to the principal; these rules are later linked to expectations at work. Riding the school bus, eating lunch in the cafeteria and bringing a note from home when absent all add to the experiential base that children receive from going to school. School provides children with a rich source of new ideas from which to shape their sense of self. When children progress in school, parents tend to accept and respect them, regardless of how successful they are. But often teachers, who replace parents as authority figures in school, are more demanding. Poor performance and low grades bring rebukes and cause a sense of failure, especially with middle-class youth.

Issues such as school prayer, free lunches for the poor, sex education and other controversies reflect changing social values. With so many children coming home to empty houses after school, another issue arises. Researchers are finding that more young people get into trouble with the law because they lack supervision. These so-called "latchkey kids" are deprived of proper socialization by absentee parents and may be exposed to improper socialization by friends who are up to no good. Juvenile crime rates triple after the school-day ends at 3 p.m., and more than 75 percent of first-time sexual encounters take place in the homes of someone whose parents are still at work. Research reveals that, compared to children who have some adult supervision, young people who are home alone are more likely to smoke, drink and use marijuana, as well as get poor grades and have encounters with the police. After-school programs, community education centers, YMCAs and playground supervisors are some of the measures being used to combat the increase in after-school delinquency (Thio, 2005).

## Peer Groups

After family, it is perhaps *peer groups* that have the most powerful impact on one's socialization. Peers are our social equals, our pals, those friends whom we cherish and emulate. The **peer group** is defined as same-aged friends with similar interests and social positions (Sullivan, 2007). Parents may play the most significant role in teaching basic values, but peers have the greatest influence on lifestyle choices, such as length of hair, social activities, and the use of bad language. Davis Elkind's research indicates that "the power of the peer group is in direct proportion to the extent that the adolescent feels ignored by the parents" (Tischler, 2007, p. 123).

The family is eventually supplanted by the peer group as young people spend more and more time in school and at social activities.

## The Media

By the time some young people reach 18, they will have viewed more hours of television than they have spent in school classrooms. Because young children are so impressionable, and because many parents use the television as a baby-sitter, social scientists have become increasingly concerned about the role of television in socialization. The impact of television is greater on males than on females, and it is more substantial on children who are more aggressive to begin with and on children between the ages of eight and 12. Music, such as rap and hip-hop, may contain lyrics that are inconsistent with mainstream cultural values and have a negative effect on the young, as may playing certain video games. These can cause children to become more aggressive, at least in the short term (Thio, 2005). Currently, iPods, cell phones, Xboxes and Facebook raise new concerns about the power of the media to influence our youth. Some believe that the teen years bring turbulence not only from biological and hormonal changes, but also from cultural inconsistencies. Consider that an 18-year-old may face going to war but cannot order a beer. Adolescence is indeed a time of social contradictions, when people are no longer children but are also not yet adults (Macionis, 2007). Researchers are concerned that the public may get socialized by the media into a world that does not exist. However, we do not make decisions in isolation, nor do we simply absorb everything we see or hear. Instead, we usually choose those mediums and messages that suit our own purposes and pay attention to programs that are consistent with our own experiences (Curry et al., 2007; Sullivan, 2007). Sullivan believes the media is a powerful agent of socialization for the young that erodes cultural and family values.

# Adult Socialization

**Adult socialization** is the process by which adults learn new statuses and roles. It differs from primary socialization in two ways. First, adults are much more aware than young people of the processes through which they are being socialized. Some people deliberately invite socialization processes into their lives, pursuing advanced education or changing careers. Others may reject choices that were forced upon them within a **total institution**, such as a prison or psychiatric hospital, where people are cut off from the larger society and forced to follow a strict set of rules. Second, adults have more control over how they want to be socialized and thus can generate more enthusiasm for their own growth. Acquiring a new hobby, traveling to a foreign country, or taking up jogging can provide a way to channel energy and introduce change. Adults, like children, continue their **developmental socialization** process, learning to be more competent in their assumed roles (Tischler, 2007).

*Source: David Hilowitz*

If a person wanted to be a police officer, what occupational socialization steps would there be?

## Work

Work gives purpose and direction to our lives and helps provide for our needs; *work* exists in every culture, but only in industrial societies do we go each day to places of work separate from our homes. In agrarian areas, people farm land close to where they live; therefore, work in these communities is not as clearly distinct from other activities as it is in urban areas. Wilbert Moore studied *occupational socialization* and identified four stages in the process:

1. We must make a career choice and, based on that choice, we have to decide where and how much training we will need.
2. We experience anticipatory socialization, which may last a few weeks or a few years and involves trying out different aspects of the future role.
3. We experience conditioning and commitment when we actually take our job of choice and when we start out very excited about our new duties.

4. The fourth stage is labeled continuous commitment. At this stage, the job becomes an integrated part of our identity (Sullivan, 2007).

The work world requires many adjustments, such as being friendly, but not too friendly, and learning to dress appropriately for a given job. In one example, a young management trainee was rebuked for wearing his keys snapped to his belt. "Janitors wear keys there; executives keep them in their pockets," said his boss. Today, because we live such long lives, we may have a dozen or more jobs and five or six careers during our lifetimes.

Quitting work permanently also necessitates many adjustments. When we're young, maturing means taking on new roles and responsibilities (Tischler, 2007). When we age, the opposite happens, as people leave behind roles that gave them identity, pleasure and prestige. Retirement for some people means restful recreation and leisure time, but for others it can mean lowered self-worth and downright boredom (Giddens, 2008). Some occupations require **resocialization**, which is the process of

80    Introduction to Sociology: A Collaborative Approach • Third Edition

leaving behind old selves and developing new ones; for example, the armed forces use basic training to socialize recruits to accept killing humans as a necessary part of their work. The financial crisis and high unemployment rates we are experiencing today have had a great impact on the necessity of resocialization (Tischler, 2007).

## Socialization in the Later Years

With people living longer, about one person in every eight is over 65 years old, and the elderly now outnumber teenagers. By 2030, the number of seniors will double to 71 million, and almost half of the country's population will be over 40 (Macionis, 2007). The elderly population grew more than ten times in size from 1900 to 2003, going from 3.1 million to 36 million people. Now that baby boomers are retiring, the next two decades will provide a large population whose collective energy, good health, and productivity will likely redefine what it means to be old (Giddens, 2008). Elders who have a healthy sense of self age well. They are less likely to identify themselves as old because they see themselves as being "who they always have been" (Hillier & Barrow, 2007, p. 35). Phyllis Moen believes that we are on the cusp of what she calls "retirement scripts," the set of social expectations that guide perceptions of what is possible during the decades following middle age (1995). Aging poses a number of challenges to every person. These challenges come from at least three sources: social attitudes toward elders, physical decline, and the loss of social roles (Novak, 2008).

## Ageism

**Ageism**, prejudice and discrimination directed against people based on age, is a source of frustration to elders because of the self's sensitivity to the perceptions of others. Robert Butler said that ageism "reflects a deep-seated uneasiness on the part of the young and middle-aged—a personal revulsion to and distaste for growing old, disease, and disability. It also is associated with fear of powerlessness, uselessness and death" (Novak, 2008, p. 3). Older people even try, unsuccessfully, to distance themselves from being old by attempting to stay middle-aged forever. Some refuse to take advantage of reduced fares on buses and discounts in restaurants; they would rather pay more than admit advanced age. Most people feel that "old" is five years older than they are (Novak, 2008). Physical decline is especially challenging for those people who get their self-esteem from playing sports. The loss of social roles can shrink our world, which is why studies recommend playing bridge, joining organizations for seniors, going to church, and seeking friends who have similar values and levels of aging.

## Three Theories on Aging

Three ways for people to adapt to changes as they age are: the *disengagement theory*, the *activity theory*, and the *continuity theory*. Disengagement is a withdrawal from society, consciously or unconsciously, due to the decline of one's strength and energy; it occurs socially as well as physically. The activity theory is almost the opposite of the disengagement theory. This theory suggests that activity leads to the highest satisfaction possible in later life, especially if we find the activities meaningful (Novak, 2008). The continuity theory suggests that our personality does not undergo radical change during the life course. A person who applies successful strategies from the past to current and future challenges helps maintain continuity. Each of these three theories helps us understand how people adapt to change as they age. For instance, perhaps the disengagement theory applies best to people in late old age who have less energy to keep active; they may welcome disengagement and find satisfaction in a less active lifestyle (Novak, 2008).

Gail Sheehy became renowned after her book *Passages* identified six predictable stages in one's life. Those stages are:

1. *Pulling up stakes*, ages 22-28, when we distance ourselves from parents and become our own person. We try to establish intimate relationships.
2. The *trying twenties*, ages 28-33, when we are still trying to separate from our parents, but we reappraise our choices and take another look at our goals in life.
3. *Passages to the thirties*, ages 33-40, when we feel we are established in an adult world and

4. But *I'm unique*, ages 40-45, when we start to question our true course in life, and we have nothing more to prove to our parents. We start to ask if this is the only way to be. It is a period of disillusionment.

5. *Deadline decade*, ages 45-60, when we question our lives, values, and ourselves and wonder if there is time to do everything that we want to accomplish in life. We try to develop other aspects of ourselves and may begin mentoring or caretaking (Sheehy, 1976).

6. *Renewal*, ages 60 and up, when we mellow toward the world and ourselves and become more people-oriented. We begin to look inward rather than focusing on our jobs and other outside stimulations (Dodgen & Rapp, 2008; Sheehy, 1976).

Perhaps we should add a seventh stage now that we are living well past 60, and in it we might refer to changes that take place from 70 to 90 years of age that are similar to those discussed above in the disengagement, activity, and continuity theories.

## Gerontology

College courses that include gerontological studies have added greatly to our understanding of the entire process of aging. (*Geron* in Greek means old person.) These courses contain a sub-section called *geriatrics,* which focuses mainly on diseases of the elderly, such as arthritis, Alzheimer's, and Parkinson's. As people age, their bodies visibly change. Wrinkles appear, hair turns gray or balding occurs, and energy levels decline. Once people reach 50, their bodies begin to break down. Bones become more brittle, and the risk of chronic illnesses such as cancer and heart disease increases. Even sensory abilities such as taste, sight, touch, smell and hearing deteriorate (Macionis, 2007). In some countries, being old lends status and influence because elders control most of the wealth and, subsequently, are shown great respect. At the dinner table, no family member takes a bite of food until the elder member starts. Elders' intelligence is undisputed, and they are thought to have great wisdom from having lived so long. In contrast, an elder's status may be low in this country. Many families feel burdened by elder care, and today families are providing care for as many as four generations at a time—not always gracefully. Women are often overburdened with a job and caring for children, spouses, parents, and grandparents. In the future, wealthy nations will need to use resources wisely to serve a growing elderly population; and elders, in turn, may want to give back because their self-esteem improves when they are contributing to their society (Macionis, 2007). Keeping busy and playing useful roles enhance our health late in life. Our culture can create policies and social opportunities for older people with this in mind.

## Elizabeth Kubler-Ross: Five Stages of Dying

Elizabeth Kubler-Ross described five stages that she observed in virtually all terminally ill patients. These stages are taught to nurses and doctors all over the world because it provides them with a glimpse of what it's like to be dying and helps them be more compassionate. The first stage is *denial*, the second *anger*, then *bargaining*, *depression* and, finally, *acceptance*. In the denial stage, the patient is certain there is a mistake in the diagnosis. "You have the wrong x-rays" is a typical reaction. In the anger stage, complaints and constant criticism of things like wrinkled sheets and bad food are to be expected. Bargaining surfaces when we feel that we are losing all control over our lives. Patients try to make deals with their nurse, their doctor, or God: "I will consent to that last surgery only if you will let me go to my grandson's graduation" or, "God, if you will let me have one more summer at the cottage, I'll leave the church $50,000." The next stage, depression, is difficult to witness, especially for family members who see the fight go out of their loved one. In the acceptance stage, the patient is peaceful and logical. Family members are advised to stop pushing for miraculous treatments and more surgery. Instead, it is recommended that they encourage the writing of a will and ask about special wishes regarding the dispensation of personal items. Burial preferences should also be discussed. At this point, no longer paralyzed by fear and anxiety, people whose lives are ending set out to make the most of the time they have left, and they say their good-byes (Giddens, 2008).

It is useful to distinguish among different age categories of the elderly, such as the *young old* (ages 65-74) the *old old* (ages 75-84), and the *oldest old* (age 85 and older). The *young old* are the people most likely to be economically independent, healthy, active, and engaged. The *oldest-old*, the fastest-growing segment of the elderly population, are the most likely to encounter poor health, financial insecurity, isolation and loneliness; however, these differences are not due solely to aging. The *young old* came of age during the post-World War II period of strong economic growth. They are more likely to be educated, to have had stable employment, and to have acquired wealth in the form of a home, savings, and investments (Novak, 2008). These advantages are much less likely to be enjoyed by the *oldest old*, partly because their education and careers began at an earlier time, when economic conditions were not so favorable (Treas, 1995).

Science and technology have extended our lives, pushing death until later in our old age. A recent study of 1,227 deaths of older people showed an average age of 80 at the time of death; 45 percent of these died in a hospital, 25 percent died in a nursing home, and 30 percent died at home (Novak, 2008). Hospice care has become a viable alternative to the traditional health care methods. The emphasis is on dying with dignity, and people can either go to a hospice or have hospice personnel come to their homes. In 1970, when the United States adopted hospice care, the American Medical Association (AMA) was opposed to it; philosophically, the values of the two groups were at odds. When doctors take the Hippocratic Oath, they declare that everything will be done to keep a patient alive. The goal of hospice care is to keep patients comfortable; if in severe pain, the patient can request an injection of pain medication, and family members can be present day and night. Medicare covers most hospice expenses because they are lower than those incurred during a hospital stay.

Death challenges our values. For example, Oregon allows physician-assisted suicide, but most states do not. Long-term care insurance is heavily advertised and prohibitive in cost. Do we want a

What activities will you be involved in after turning 65?

Source: Woody Hibbard

funeral service or a wake, cremation or a coffin and plot? Have we made adequate financial arrangements for a durable power of attorney or a family limited liability partnership? Should we discuss a do-not-resuscitate order with our doctor? These and other matters occupy our late-in-life thoughts. At least people in our society plan ahead better now than in previous years, and planning ahead is vital to those who are left behind. Most family members will carry out the wishes of the deceased if they know what they are.

Recent research has focused on hundreds of centenarians, and these studies are showing some surprises about the elderly (Cutter, 2008). Centenarians were found to share the same characteristics of healthy aging, with the most important factors being maintaining close relationships with family and friends and possessing a healthy mental and physical lifestyle. One centenarian, Maurice Eisman, offered his advice for long life: "Never stop learning." To demonstrate that these centenarians were in tune with today's culture: Nearly half of all respondents could identify the most recent *American Idol* winner, 19 percent used cell phones and automatic teller machines, and 3 percent had dated someone they met on the Internet (Hitti, 2008). It is projected that by the year 2025, this country will have at least 275,000 centenarians. These and other studies show how growing old is changing with the times (Hitti, 2008).

# Summary

This chapter has presented many aspects of the socialization process and shown it to be a central force in who we are and how we behave. We are indebted to authors and researchers who spent years studying all of the ramifications of socialization so that we could gain a better understanding of how it affects us and our society. After looking at many facets of the socialization process, we can take with us a greater awareness and appreciation of it.

## Review/Discussion Questions

1. What are some agents of socialization?
2. According to Elizabeth Kubler-Ross, what are the five stages of dying?
3. What is pre-conventional morality?
4. Where do you stand on the nature versus nurture debate? Which do you think has the strongest influence on who we are?
5. When you were a child, which occupation did you envision yourself performing when you grew up? How does it match with what you do now?
6. According to Cooley's looking-glass theory, we are all influenced by our perception of what we think others think of us. Do you think this is true? In what ways have you let others people's judgment of you alter your behavior?

## Key Terms

**Adult socialization** is the process by which adults learn new statuses and roles.

**Ageism** is prejudice and discrimination directed against people based on age.

**Anticipatory socialization** involves learning the skills and values needed for future roles.

**Aptitude** is the capacity to develop physical or social skills.

**Conventional morality** is Kohlberg's term for people incorporating society's rules and laws into their own value systems and behaving accordingly.

**Developmental socialization** is the process by which people learn to be more competent in their currently assumed roles.

**Ego** is Freud's term for the part of the personality that deals with the real world on the basis of reason and helps to integrate the demands of both the id and the superego.

**Gender** is the socially and culturally constructed differences between males and females that are found in the meanings, beliefs and practices associated with masculinity and femininity.

**Gender role** refers to how we should act as males or females.

**Gender typing** refers to the acquisition of behavior that is considered appropriate for one's gender.

**Generalized others** are people who are not necessarily close to a child but still help influence the child's internalization of societal values.

**Id** is Freud's term for the part of the personality that is totally unconscious and consists of biological drives.

**Intelligence** is the capacity for mental or intellectual achievement.

**Looking-glass self** is Cooley's theory that we are influenced by our perception of what others think of us and develop our self-image on that basis.

**Peer group** includes a person's same-aged friends who have similar interests and social positions.

**Personality** refers to a person's patterns of thoughts, feelings, and self-concepts that make him or her distinctive from others.

**Post-conventional morality** is the highest level of morality available, according to Kohlberg. At this level, people use broad ethical principles to guide their behavior, such as showing respect for human dignity, equality, and, of late, respect for one's environment—even for the rights of animals and other living creatures.

**Pre-conventional morality** is Kohlberg's term for abiding by the law chiefly to avoid punishment or to gain some benefit.

**Primary socialization** is the period during which children learn language and the basic behavioral patterns that form the foundation for later learning.

**Resocialization** is the process by which people must leave behind their old selves and develop new ones.

**Roles** are socially defined expectations associated with a given status.

**Secondary socialization** takes place later in childhood and into maturity. In this phase, other agents of socialization take over some of the responsibility from family.

**Sex** refers to the biological and anatomical differences between females and males.

**Significant others** are those people who are the closest to and have the strongest influence on a child, and whose approval and affection the child desires most.

**Socialization** is the process whereby we internalize our culture's values, beliefs, and norms. Through this experience, we become functioning members of our society.

**Superego** is Freud's term for the part of the personality that acts as the executive branch because it uses reason and deals with whether something is right or wrong.

**Total institutions** are places where people are cut off from the larger society and forced to follow a strict set of rules.

# Bibliography

Belsky, J. (2004). Experiencing the Life Span: Class Test Version. Boston: W. H. Freeman & Company.

Berk, L. E. (2006). Development Through the Lifespan. Danbury: Allyn & Bacon.

Butler, R. N. (1969). Age-ism: Another form of bigotry. The Gerontologist, 9, 243-246.

Corey, G., & Schneider, M. (2005). I Never Knew I Had a Choice: Explorations in Personal Growth. Belmont, CA: Wad sworth.

Curry, T., Jiobu, R., & Schwirian, K. (2007). Sociology for the Twenty-First Century. Upper Saddle River: Prentice Hall.

Cutter, J. (2008). Living Well to 100. MedicineNet. <http://www.medicinenet.com/script/main/art.asp?articlekey=51451> (2008).

Dodgen, L. I., & Rapp, A. M. (2008). Sociology: Looking through the Window of the World. Dubuque, IA: Kendall/Hunt Pub lisher Co.

Duffy, K. G. (Ed.). (1996). Annual Reports: Psychology (95/96). New York: McGraw-Hill/Dushkin.

Durkheim, E. (1956). Education and Sociology. New York: Free Press.

Ensher, G. L., & Clark, D. A. (2009). Families, Infants, and Young Children at Risk. New York: Paul H. Brookes Co.

Feldman, R. S. (2006). Understanding Psychology. Boston: McGraw-Hill.

Ferris, K., Stein, J., & Meyer, A. E. (2008). The Real World : An Introduction to Sociology. Boston: W. W. Norton & Company.

Freud, S. (1927). A General Introduction to Psychoanalysis. New York: Boni and Liveright.

Freud, S. (1953). A Religious Experience. In J. Strachey (Ed.), Standard edition of the complete psychological works of Sigmund Freud. London, UK: Hogarth Press.

Giddens, A. (2008). Essentials of Sociology (2nd ed.). New York: Norton and Company.

Gilligan, C. (1982). In a Different Voice : Psychological Theory and Women's Development. New York: Harvard University Press.

Hillier, S. M., & Barrow, G. M. (2007). Aging, the Individual, and Society. Belmont, CA: Brooks/Cole.

Hitti, M. (2008). Healthy Tips for Centenarians. WebMD. <http://www.webmd.com/healthy-aging/news/20080729/10-healthy-aging-tips-from-centenarians> (2008).

Kendall, D. E. (2007). Sociology in Our Times : The Essentials. Belmont, CA: Thomson/Wadsworth.

Kubler-Ross, E. (1969). On Death and Dying. New York: MacMillan.

Lawrence, P., & Nohria, N. (2002). Driven : How Human Nature Shapes Our Choices. San Francisco: Jossey-Bass.

Lemert, C. C. (2008). Social Things : An Introduction to the Sociological Life. New York: Rowman & Littlefield, Inc.

Lightfoot, C. (2008). The Development of Children (6th ed.). New York: Worth Publishers.

Lindsey, L. L., & Beach, S. (2000). Sociology: Social Life and Social Issues. Upper Saddle River, NJ: Pearson.

Macionis, J. J. (2007). Society: The Basics. Upper Saddle River, NJ: Pearson Prentice Hall.

Maslow, A. (1987). Motivation and Personality (3rd ed.). New York: Harper and Row.

Maslow, A. (2008). Maslow's Hierarchy of Needs. <http://Chiron.valdosta.edu/whuitt/col/regsys/Maslow.html> (2008).

Mead, G. H. (1934). Mind, self & society from the standpoint of a social behaviorist. Chicago, IL: University of Chicago Press.

Miller, B. (1980). The Contribution of Lawrence Kohlberg to the Study of Moral Development. Unpublished dissertation.

Moen, P. (1995). Gender, Age and the Life Course." Pp. 171–87 in *Handbook of Aging and the Social Sciences,* 4th ed., edited by R.H. Binstock and L. George. San Diego:Academic Press.

National Science Foundation (2010). <http://www.nsf.gov/statistics/seind10/start.htm> (2011).

Norwood, G. (2002). Maslow's Hierarchy of Needs. <http://www.deepermind.com/20maslow.htm> (2002).

Novak, M. (2008). Issues in Aging. Boston: Pearson/Allyn & Bacon.

Popenoe, D. (2000). Sociology. Upper Saddle River, NJ: Prentice Hall.

Rathus, S. A. (2000). Essentials of Psychology. Fort Worth: Harcourt Brace College Publishers.

Rymer, R. (1993). Genie: An Abused Child's Flight from Silence. New York: HarperCollins.

Santrock, J. W. (2007). Child Development (11th ed.). Boston, MA: McGraw-Hill.

Schaefer, R. (2009). Sociology: a brief introduction (8th ed.). New York, NY: McGraw-Hill.

Schaie, K. W., & Abeles, R. P. (Eds.). (2008). Social Structures and Aging Individuals: Continuing Challenges. New York: Springer Publishing.

Sheehy, G. (1976). Passages: predictable crises of life. New York: Dutton.

Sullivan, T. J. (2007). Sociology: concepts and applications in a diverse world (7th ed.). Danbury, CT: Allyn & Bacon.

Thio, A. (2005). Sociology: A Brief Introduction (6th ed.). Boston: Pearson/Allyn & Bacon.

Tischler, H. L. (2007). Introduction to Sociology (9th ed.). Belmont, CA: Wadsworth/Thomson Learning.

Treas, J. (1995). Older Americans in the 1990s and beyond. Population Bulletin, 50 (2).

U. S. Census Bureau (2004). Educational Attainment. <http://www.census.gov> (2008).

Wood, S. E., & Wood, E. G. (2011). World of Psychology, The (7th ed.). New York, NY: Allyn and Bacon.

# CHAPTER FOUR

# Social Structure and Social Interaction

## XueMei Hu

---

**Chapter Objectives**

At the end of this chapter, students should be able to:

- Identify the building blocks of society and ways in which society sets the rules for everyday life.
- Explain the concepts related to status and role.
- Apply role conflict and role strain to the analysis of daily life.
- Evaluate the sociological perspectives on social interactions.
- Apply dramaturgical analysis to the study of everyday life.
- Use examples to illustrate global diversity in nonverbal interaction.
- Explain different types of social interaction.
- Analyze communication barriers and communication differences between women and men.
- Define the concepts related to social structure and social interaction.

---

In society, we structure our behavior through the statuses we occupy and the roles we play. As human beings, we have considerable ability to shape the patterns of social interaction and creatively build reality through such interactions. In this chapter, we will first examine social structure from a macro-level perspective. We will then explore how this structure determines the statuses we hold, the roles we play, and the groups and social institutions to which we belong. Then we will move on to the study of social interaction, through which we build reality.

---

## Building Blocks of Social Structure

To understand human behavior in society, we need to understand **social structure**, which refers to the social relationships that exist within society. Social

---

relationships in a society guide our behavior and provide us with the framework for interacting with others. Our behavior is patterned by social influences and guided by social structure. Human beings rely on this structure to make sense of situations on a daily basis. As an example of social structure, imagine that you are now listening to a lecture by a professor in a classroom. You hold the status of a student and play the role of a student, while your professor occupies the status of an instructor and plays the role of an instructor. There is a relationship between the students in the social group (classmates) and the instructor. Both you and your instructor act according to learned behaviors and attitudes based on your respective statuses within the social structure.

Society uses social structure to set the rules of daily life. Society is cooperation; it is community in action, with females and males of all ages, and all races and ethnicities, interacting within groups and social institutions of a particular society. If there are clear-cut rules to follow, human beings know how to act and react in relation to others. Society is the outcome of conscious and purposeful behavior; it is the complex sum of mutual relations.

The building blocks of society include statuses and roles, groups, and social institutions, as illustrated in Chart 4.1. In every society, people rely on social structure to make sense of their life experiences. The following section provides a macro-level analysis of statuses and roles, examining the ways in which society sets the rules of everyday life.

## Statuses and Roles

### Status

**Status** refers to a social position—characterized by rights, duties and expectations—that is held by a person. Our status guides our behavior in different social situations and is an important part of how we define ourselves. Additionally, our interactions with people are shaped by their statuses. A social position may carry a great deal of prestige, as in the case of a CEO or a lawyer, or little prestige, as in the case of a hotel maid. The status of an ex-convict may be looked down upon. Therefore, status is an indicator of social identity, which helps define our relationships to others.

### Ascribed Status and Achieved Status

People may attain statuses through events over which they have no control, or through effort and choice. An **ascribed status** is a social position that a person receives at birth or assumes involuntarily later in life. We inherit ascribed statuses at birth based on biological factors such as race, ethnicity, gender, and the social class of our parents. Examples of ascribed status include being a son, a Hispanic American, a teenager, a woman or the child of a celebrity. Brad Pitt and Angelina Jolie's twins, for example, are likely to be in the spotlight their entire lives because of their famous parents.

An **achieved status** is a social position that a person earns through personal effort and choices, such as education, occupation, and income. It can also be positive or negative. If you are an honors student, CEO, computer engineer, or professor, you have earned positive achieved status through direct effort. In modern American society, when individuals have been successful in their education and careers, their level of financial security typically changes their status. If a person

**CHART 4.1** Social Structure Framework

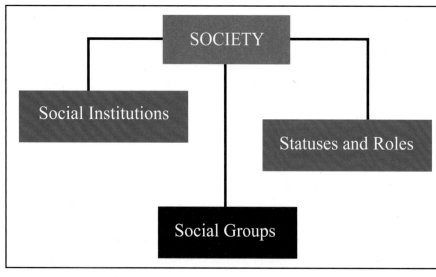

does not make an effort, perhaps dropping out of high school, he or she earns a negative achieved status. Achieved statuses can reveal a great deal about a person's background and values.

Each status provides guidelines for behavior. Like other parts of the social structure, a status sets limits on what we can and cannot do. How we behave in groups is determined by statuses. Everybody occupies multiple statuses in society, some ascribed, some achieved. If asked who you are, you may make a list of your statuses. You might answer, "I am a daughter, a mother, a wife, a student, a woman, an African American, and a store manager."

## Can an Ascribed Status Influence Achieved Status?

Equality is considered an American value, but there is still a discrepancy between legal equality and social equality. Theoretically, it is possible for any person to experience upward social mobility if he or she becomes highly educated, and financially successful through that person's efforts. However, those born into certain conditions and circumstances may be at an advantage or disadvantage to gain certain achieved statuses. People born into wealthy and prominent families often have better opportunities to achieve high levels of education and obtain prime jobs because of their social connections. On the other hand, those born into poor families often have to work harder to separate themselves from the competition to get those same opportunities. Though there are many laws to protect minority groups, ascribed statuses can hinder the attainment of certain achieved statuses.

Similarly, male and female cultures differ, with each having a direct impact on achieved statuses in the workplace. Male culture deters the advancement of women into management positions and contributes to communication gaps. Andrew Agapiou refers to men in the workplace as gatekeepers and believes that men and women are trying to find ways in which they might work together and "comfortably reconcile issues of gender" (Agapiou, 2002, p. 697). Michael Peterson points out that "success for women emphasized values, the corporate culture, and work/family balance" (RTO Online, 2005, p. 1). Peterson continues by drawing a comparison, stat-

ing that, "In contrast, male-oriented culture is based on the assumptions that work is for the purpose of achievement and fortune, and that for a business to be successful it must recognize the importance of achieving results" (RTO Online, 2005, p. 2).

Women's roles have changed significantly since the early 1960s. The Civil Rights Act of 1964 created the Equal Employment Opportunity Commission (EEOC) to enforce laws designed to prevent employment discrimination, extending the act beyond the original grounds of Title VII—race, color, sex, national origin, and religion—to include pregnancy, age (40 and over), and disability. It also extended coverage to governmental entities (U.S. Equal Employment Opportunity Commission, 2002). The EEOC protects the rights of all individuals to be considered for jobs based solely on their abilities, and to have a work environment free from abusive practices.

Other factors can affect a person's achieved statuses. Youth can be an advantage, because many employers believe that younger people will stay with their organizations longer, but it can also be a disadvantage if youth is equated with inexperience. Along the same lines, age can be an advantage if it is considered to be a sign of experience and maturity, but a disadvantage if it is thought to indicate that a person is nearing retirement and may not be as focused on his or her career. Height, weight, personality, race, ethnicity, and many other factors can also come into play when a person wants to achieve a certain status.

## Master Status

Each of us occupies many statuses in life. Among these, one status may matter more than the others. A status that determines a person's overall social position and identity is called a **master status**. A master status overshadows our other statuses, and can be either ascribed or achieved. For example, a high-paying occupation may be a master status for some people since it reflects education, income, and social status.

A master status can have positive and negative consequences. If you are very wealthy, your wealth is likely to become a master status because it cuts across other statuses. When a person suffers from cancer, close friends might avoid him or her because of the illness. Illness or disability can be seen as a master status because others may see people only in those terms. For example, the actor Michael J. Fox has Parkinson's disease, which causes tremors in the body and the muscles to stiffen. The muscle stiffness can make it difficult to accomplish even the simplest of tasks such as getting dressed or walking. To some, Michael J. Fox's master status is that of a person living with Parkinson's disease. To others, his master status is that of a famed actor whose body of work includes the television shows *Family Ties* and *Spin City* and movies such as the *Back to the Future* trilogy, *Teen Wolf* and *Doc Hollywood*, to name only a few (Huse, 2010).

In society, we tend to socialize with people who are similar to us and, thus, our statuses usually match. However, some people also want to socialize with people who are different. **Status inconsistency** occurs when people have a mismatch between their statuses, such as an 18-year-old girl marrying a 60-year-old man. People may feel conflicted about such situations because statuses are characterized by built-in expectations or norms that guide behaviors. Status inconsistency deviates from expected behaviors and can create uncertainty or discomfort.

## Status Set

A **status set** includes all of the statuses that a person occupies at a given time. Our status set defines who we are in society; the multiple roles attached to each status we hold defines what we do. You may simultaneously be a father, computer engineer, and husband, or a daughter, student, part-time store clerk, and grandchild. Over each stage of our life cycle, we gain and lose statuses, and our status set changes. When you are a 2-year-old male toddler, you may be a son to your parents and a younger brother to a sister. As you grow up, you may also become a student or even a filmmaker in a television production class. You may graduate from law school and become a lawyer, in addition to being a son and a brother. If you marry, you also become a husband, and, possibly, a father. You might even become a single person again because of divorce. Therefore, status sets can and do change over the course of our lives.

## Role

Sociologists see roles as essential to our social behaviors. How we behave in society is determined not only by the statuses we occupy, but also by the roles we play. **Roles** refer to socially defined expectations associated with a given status. When we occupy a status, we play a corresponding role. Roles are characterized by behaviors, privileges, rights, and obligations. For example, as you occupy the status of a student, you are expected to play the role of student. This means that you have the right to ask questions and voice your opinions in class, but you are also obligated to attend class, read the material, do the homework, take the tests, and complete any other assignments.

## Role Expectation and Role Performance

Sociologists differentiate between role expectation and role performance. **Role expectation** relates to the expectations required of a role, while **role performance** covers the actual delivery of those expectations. If a woman is a mother, the role expectation attached to that status is that she care and provide for her child. The role performance would be her actual day-to-day mothering activities.

## Role Set

Because each person holds many statuses at any given time, daily life is a mixture of multiple roles. Robert Merton (1957) introduced the term role set. **Role set** refers to a number of roles that can be attached to a single status. If you occupy the statuses of mother, daughter, and manager, each of those statuses is linked to a different role set. First, you occupy the status of a mother. You play a *maternal role* when engaging in child-rearing responsibilities like teaching basic skills and providing economic and emotional support. You also play a *civic role* when driving your children to school and extracurricular activities. In addition, you play a *model role* when you control your behavior to set a good example. In your second status, as a wife, you play a *marital role*, such as being a sexual partner to your husband, and a *domestic role*, such as doing certain chores. Finally, in the status of manager, you play an *administrative role* when you meet with supervisors and complete the payroll on time. You also play a *leadership role* when you make plans, set deadlines, resolve problems, and implement projects.

## Role Conflict and Role Strain

People in modern societies pursue their educational goals and careers in order to make a better living for themselves and their families. As a result, they must to learn how to juggle the responsibilities of their multiple statuses and roles. It is not always easy to maneuver between family, work, and school, and people holding multiple statuses, playing multiple roles, are more likely to be physically and emotionally overburdened. **Work spillover** is the effect that paid and volunteer work can have on individuals and families, absorbing their time and energy and encroaching on their psychological states. On the positive side, family and friends can help alleviate workplace stress. On the negative side, the demands of our home lives may impinge on our concentration, energy, and availability at work.

**Role conflict** refers to conflicting demands that are connected to two or more coexisting statuses. If you are a working mother and part-time student, you may often experience the conflicting demands of work, child care, and school assignments. Because of role conflict, people sometimes postpone marriage or put off having children in order to pursue career success. For example, let's consider an extroverted manager who desires interpersonal closeness appropriate to a workplace. In addition to this role as friend, he or she also needs to act as a boss and manage the staff effectively to achieve organizational goals. Role conflict might occur when this type of manager needs to reprimand an employee that is underperforming, especially if the manager is aware of the personal difficulties the employee may have.

**Role strain** refers to conflicting demands connected to one single status. A college student may hold only that status, but tasks ranging from school work for each course to extracurricular activities may be physically and emotionally draining. Similarly, many single mothers raising children on their own are overburdened financially, physically, and emotionally.

## Role Exit

People often move from one role to another—student to employee, single male to husband, married mom to divorced mom. **Role exit** refers to the process by which people disengage from a role. Ex-husbands, ex-alcoholics, ex-nuns, and ex-doctors

**CHART 4.2** Role Strain and Role Conflict

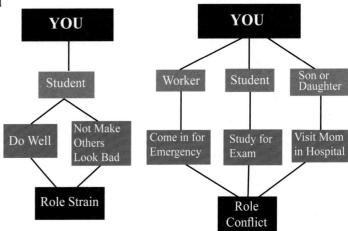

are examples of people who have experienced a role exit. Each "ex" role has common elements. According to Helen Ebaugh, the exit process begins when people come to doubt their ability to continue in a certain role. When they want to disengage from a role that they have been playing, they picture alternative roles and may eventually decide to pursue a new life. Exes move on and build a new image that is still influenced by the past role. An ex-nun may be fearful of wearing makeup and high heels, learning new social skills, and interacting in different social networks. According to Ebaugh's observations, ex-nuns who enter the dating scene after decades in the church are often surprised to learn that sexual norms are very different from those they knew when they were teenagers (1988).

## Groups

Groups are the second major building block of society. In sociology, a **group** refers to a collection of people characterized by more than two people who share frequent interaction, a sense of belonging, and interdependence. Like statuses and roles, the groups to which we belong can become social forces and thus influence our behaviors. When we belong to a group, we are obligated to behave according to the expectations of other group members. In addition, each member of a group occupies a status and is expected to play a corresponding role. In this way, people within a group are interdependent and cooperate in order to build consensus and survive together. The topic of groups will be covered more thoroughly in Chapter 5.

## Social Institutions

Social institutions are the third building block of society. **Social institutions** are organized beliefs, rules and practices established by society to meet its basic needs. Social institutions include family, education, religion, economics, politics, and health care. These social institutions—each with its own groups, statuses, and roles—weave the fabric of society and shape our behaviors. Social institutions will be covered in depth in Chapters 10 through 13.

## Social Interaction

Social interaction is of major importance to sociology because it is the foundation of meaningful relationships in society. We are all social creatures and enjoy interacting. **Social interaction** refers to reciprocal communication between two or more people through symbols, words, and body language. Our daily lives are organized around the repetition of similar patterns of social interaction. Studying these social interactions shows us how people can act together to shape reality and enables us to better understand social institutions and entire societies.

## Sociological Perspectives

Functionalist theory emphasizes supportive interactions, with people treating others as supporters or friends. Conflict theory, in regards to social interaction, emphasizes oppositional interactions, contending that people treat others as competitors or enemies. Symbolic interactionists interpret others' behaviors and act accordingly. Each of these three approaches strives to answer the question of why people do what they do.

**TABLE 4.3** Spotlight on Social Institutions

| Social Institution | Basic Needs | Groups or Organizations | Statuses | Roles |
|---|---|---|---|---|
| Family | Regulate sexual activity, reproduce, socialize children | Kinship | Son, daughter, father, mother, grandparent | Provide food and shelter, respect parents |
| Religion | Explain why we exist and suffer | Church, cult, denomination | Priest, minister, worshipper | Read and adhere to texts |
| Education | Transmit skills and knowledge across generations | School, college, Parent Teacher Association, sports team | Teacher, dean, student, football player | Get good grades, follow teaching ethics |
| Economy | Produce, distribute goods and services | Banks, buying clubs, stores | Employee, boss, buyer, seller | Earn income, pay bills on time |
| Politics | Exercise power, regulate relationships | Political party, congress, government | President, senator, voter, lobbyist | Distribute power equally, vote |
| Health care | Initiate activity to heal the sick and prevent illness | Hospitals, pharmacies, health insurance companies | Doctor, nurse, patient, insurer, pharmacist | Follow work ethics, follow doctor's order |

## Functionalist Perspective: Supportive Interactions

The functionalist perspective on social interaction examines societies, social structures, and social systems primarily on a macro-level. The functionalist perspective emphasizes the way parts of a society are structured to maintain its stability. It looks at a society in a positive manner; all of its parts work together, supporting each other and contributing to the survival of the society. People are viewed as being socially molded, not forced, to perform societal functions. Order in a society, as viewed by a functionalist, is maintained when its members cooperate with one another. Functionalists emphasize social stability.

Emile Durkheim and Talcott Parsons were responsible for the development of the functionalist perspective. The contemporary functionalist perspective on supportive interactions derives its foundation from Durkheim. Supportive interactions are positive ways in which we communicate with others, reinforcing solidarity and unity in groups. One example of positive supports is making each transition positive. Transitions such as greetings and good-byes can be made more positive through rituals that offer a sense of support, such as handshakes, hugs, and enthusiastic words (Mooney, Knox & Schacht, 2000).

Communication plays a crucial role in supportive interactions. One of the most important characteristics of a great communicator is the ability to listen to other people. Learning to actively listen can help us move past our assumptions and overlook distractions. If a speaker feels he or she is not being heard, it has a negative impact on that speaker's ability to communicate effectively in a specific situation. It is essential to interact in a caring and encouraging manner in order to develop positive social skills. If other people experience trouble in a situation, we should provide support and help them work through their difficulties. Even routine interactions can incorporate supportive factors. For instance, non-English speakers may have a hard time keeping up with the pace of our speech, or maybe our mouths are speaking faster than we can think and our words become jumbled. We need to think about how others

process what we are saying in order to make our interactions more supportive.

### Exchange and Cooperation

Supportive interactions are based on exchange and cooperation. Exchange means that two individuals offer each other something to obtain a reward in return. Cooperation means that two or more individuals work together to achieve a common goal. Spontaneous cooperation occurs in an emergency, such as in an auto accident or a house fire.

### Reciprocity

Speakers want to give and receive support in interactions, simultaneously conveying and receiving acceptance and preserving the autonomy of both parties. Previous research on the presence or absence of supportive communication has overlooked how support is conveyed and how some message characteristics accomplish multiple goals. By highlighting these multiple goals, politeness theory integrates previous research on the dilemmas of supportive communication and characteristics of helpful and unhelpful messages. **Politeness theory** is the idea that communicators change and adopt their messages to protect and save the "face" or image of their listeners. The communicator's goal, then, is to get his or her intended message across without insulting, embarrassing, or discomfiting the listener (Brown & Levinson, 1978).

## Conflict Perspective: Oppositional Interactions

The conflict perspective on social interaction also focuses primarily on macro-level analysis of societies, social structures, and social systems. According to the conflict perspective, social behavior is understood in terms of conflict between different groups or individuals. In contrast to the functionalist view of stability, conflict sociologists see societies as being engaged in constant struggle and change.

According to Karl Marx (1964), conflicts between social classes are inevitable because workers are exploited as a result of capitalism. Individuals are perceived as being shaped by power and authority, and order in a society is maintained through social forces. This perspective contends that social inequality exists, with different groups competing for scarce resources. These conflicts lead to social change. The contemporary conflict perspective on social interaction is derived from this foundation, with a focus on oppositional interactions between groups and individuals. This occurs, for example, when a dominant group uses an ethnocentric idea to evaluate another group. Ethnocentrism uses one's own cultural standards or norms as a basis to evaluate another culture. If one group is considered ideal, then all others are judged based on how far they differ from that norm. This can produce some irrelevant comparisons and conclusions, benefitting one culture at the expense of others. This brings up the old insider/outsider debate in which the people on the "inside" make value judgments on practices and procedures that are unique and customary in that society or culture. According to the conflict perspective, there is no value to reinforcing ethnocentrism because there is no group, as a whole, that is superior in intelligence, physical attributes, humanity, religion, or the arts to any other.

## Oppositional Interactions: Competition, Conflict, and Coercion

According to conflict theory, people treat others as competitors, and sometimes even as enemies. In competition, each person or group tries to gain control over limited resources before the others. Conflict in social interactions is inevitable when individuals respond to each other with a different pace or attitude. Even simple words like "soon," "urgent," "shared," "polite," and "respectful" have different meanings for different individuals. Coercion occurs when one person or group forces its will upon another. Usually, a dominant group uses threats or force to get subordinate groups to submit to its ideas.

## Symbolic Interactionist Perspective: Interpreting Interactions

Social interaction is the foundation for all relationships and groups in society. Functionalist and conflict theories provide a macrosociological analysis because they focus on large-scale structures and events. For example, from a macro-level perspective, you as a sociologist would examine how

social institutions such as families and schools have helped to cause teenage pregnancies. By contrast, the symbolic interactionist perspective provides a microsociological overview. Sociologists studying the problem of teenage pregnancy would ask how teenagers are influenced by their daily interactions and their behaviors within small groups. In other words, symbolic interactionists study the small scale in order to understand the large scale.

The origins of this approach can be traced to the Chicago School. George Herbert Mead and Herbert Blumer coined the term *symbolic interactionism*, and Mead is credited with founding the interactionist perspective. Symbolic interactionists study behavior—how people react to their surroundings, including material things, actions, other people, and symbols. Mead was a professor at the University of Chicago, where he focused on the analysis of one-to-one situations and small groups. He paid particular attention to body language, such as a frown or nod, and asked how other group members affected these gestures (Blumer, 1986; Mead & Morris, 1934). The interactionist view of society is that we influence each other through our day-to-day social interactions. Interactionists believe that individuals create their own social world through interactions, and social order is maintained when people share their understanding of everyday behaviors. From this perspective, social change occurs when the positions and communications of the individuals and small groups change.

## Symbolic Interaction: Principles and Shared Definitions

Social interaction is the foundation of meaningful relationships in society. Having a good foundation or structure is the core of our interactions with others. Symbolic interactionists consider society to be the sum of social interactions between people and groups. Symbolic interactionists focus on understanding how people make sense of their everyday social interactions and their world.

## Interpreting Supportive Interactions

The symbolic interactionist perspective focuses on the process of interaction, interpreting people's behaviors and acting accordingly. *Social interaction*

What percentage of your day is spent communicating?

Source: Pedro Ribeiro Simoes

refers to reciprocal communication between two or more people through symbols, words, and body language; it is the process by which we respond to others. This definition involves two components: First, interaction involves supportive interchanges, mutual dealings, and reciprocal results; second, the interaction takes place between two or more people. We expect people to communicate with respect when that is how we communicate with them. If we are being rude to one another, we have a breakdown in communication.

People interpret social interactions and use those perceptions to shape reality. Social interaction occurs when people interact and communicate through the use of symbols. According to the symbolic interactionist perspective, human beings create and use symbols to convey shared meanings. They also know how to interpret the meanings of the symbols to understand social interactions. Symbolic interaction takes place nonverbally in a variety of ways, including facial expression, posture, tone of voice, and gestures like handshakes, bows, and hugs.

*Symbols* refer to anything that represents something else. For example, a four-leaf clover is viewed as a symbol of good luck, and a gift of a freshly baked pie to a new neighbor symbolizes welcome. People interpret social interactions through the shared meanings of such symbols.

## Interpreting Oppositional Interactions

In the business world, you might have noticed a difference in the way people speak to one another depending on their corporate positions. Managers are usually authoritative and direct when speaking to subordinates. Subordinates may exhibit a certain giddiness when speaking to people in a higher position, especially if they are eager to please. People also treat those from other social classes very differently. For example, people of a higher social class sometimes speak very slowly and are condescending toward those of lower classes. Why does this happen, and does it frustrate you? Do you put the blame for this on both parties? Consider a manager and an employee. Is it possible that the manager

Chapter 4: Social Structure and Social Interaction    97

makes the employee feel uncomfortable, while the employee allows the manager to be intimidating?

## Shared Definition of a Situation and Human Behavior

Symbolic interactionists seek to understand human behavior from an individual or cultural viewpoint. Everybody defines a situation differently, and those definitions become the foundation for how everyone behaves.

Let's look at specific scenarios. When you see a woman struggling with a heavy object you quickly come to her aid because you consider yourself to be a helpful person. You have done this on two occasions. In one instance, the lady was very happy after you lent a hand and offered to buy you a cup of coffee. In another instance, you were shocked when you were told to back off. Imagine for a moment that you are a young man. If a 55-year-old woman offers to help with something you are struggling with, how would you define the situation, and how would you react to her and behave? Maybe the woman is offering to help because she has the capabilities to help you, or maybe she always wants to help others from a humanitarian perspective. Do you decline or accept her invitation? If you decline, is it because of pride?

People from different backgrounds will respond to each other in different ways. For example, some people greet others by saying "Good morning," while others hug. The Chinese and Japanese greatly value respect for authority figures and the elderly. According to Japanese folklore, when a worker was forced to criticize his boss in front of his colleagues, he killed himself afterward because of his disrespectful behavior. In traditional societies, if you as a student ask questions in class, it is likely to be considered a challenge, assault, or disrespectful behavior. If you try to correct a Japanese professor's pronunciation, it is also considered disrespectful behavior. In the Hispanic community, many people enjoy a "touchy-feely" culture because they grow up in an affectionate environment. People give hugs and kisses when saying hello or goodbye. When men say hello to women, touching each other—such as patting a shoulder or holding the waist while giving a kiss—is a sign of friendship. However, it

might be considered a sign of sexual harassment in other cultures. People who share meanings about how to interact with each other also understand that there are lines that should not be crossed. Problems are more likely to occur when meanings are not shared.

Different generations do not always share meanings related to social interaction. Members of Generation X would not behave the way their parents did due to different shared meanings. However, we might notice that the older we get, the more we act like our parents as our shared meanings change.

## Consequences of the Definition of a Situation

Symbolic interactionists further contend that the definition of a given situation has consequences, and that it affects social interactions now and in the future. According to symbolic interactionists, our behavior and subjective reality are shaped by our social interactions with others. Sociologists Charles H. Cooley and George Herbert Mead explored how individual personalities are developed by social experience. Every time we engage in a new interaction, we have to define and interpret the situation. In a new encounter, we have to negotiate the situation all over again. We try to make sense of our situations and either derive shared meanings from them or comprehend the outcome (Cooley, 1964; Mead & Morris, 1934).

## Global Diversity in Social Interactions

Race, ethnicity, gender, and social class often influence people's perceptions of shared meanings and how they interact with each other. The way we respond to people has a lot to do with the way we live. In New York City, for example, the lifestyle is fast-paced, and people are often too rushed to have idle conversations. In areas with a slower pace, we find people more prone to converse with strangers.

Interactions within a given society have certain shared meanings across cultures. For example, in the United States, working lunches are the norm and it is not uncommon to discuss business with a meal. Other societies close deals with different norms and shared values.

more social power than another individual or group in a coercive interaction.

**Work spillover** refers to the effect that work has on individuals and families, absorbing their time and energy and impinging on their psychological states.

# Bibliography

Agapiou, A. (2002, November ). "Perceptions of gender roles and attitudes toward work among male and female operatives in the Scottish construction industry." <http://www.informaworld.com/smpp/content~content=a713763888~db=all~order=page> (2008).

Blumer, H. (1986). Symbolic Interactionism. University of California Press.

Bremer, J. (2004). "The "eyes" have it: the fundamentals of eye contact." <http://www.bremercommunications.com/Eye_Contact.htm> (2008).

Chandler, D. (1995). The Transmission Model of Communication. Retrieved on December 14, 2011 from http://www.aber.ac.uk/media/Documents/short/trans.html

CNN.com (2008). "First female four-star U.S. Army general nominated." <http://www.cnn.com/2008/US/06/23/woman.general/index.html> (2008).

Cooley, C. H. (1964). Human Nature and the Social Order. NY: Schocken Books.

Deutsche, F. M., LeBaron, D., & Fryer, M. (1987). What is in a Smile? Psychology of Women Quarterly, vol. 11, 3: pp. 341-352.

Ebaugh, H. R. F. (1988). Becoming an Ex: The Process of Role Exit. Chicago: University of Chicago Press.

ECG (n.d.). "Bridge the gap of language styles: a legacy that holds women back." <http://ecglink.com/library/ps/gap.html> (2008).

Eckert, P. (1989). Jocks & Burnouts: Social Categories and Identity in the High School. New York: Teachers College Press.

Ekman, P. (1985). Telling Lies: Clues to Deceit in the Marketplace, Politics, and Marriage. New York: Norton.

Ekman, P., & Friesen, W. V. (1978). Facial Action Coding System: A Technique for the Measurement of Facial Movement. Palo Alto, CA: Consulting Psychologists Press.

Edgecomb, A. (2008). "Lt. Gen. Ann E. Dunwoody is nominated to receive the 4th star." <http://www.army.mil/-newsreleases/2008/06/23/10287-lt-gen-dunwoody-nominated-to-receive-4th-star/> (2008).

Goffman, E. (1959). The Presentation of Self in Everyday Life. Garden City, NY: Doubleday.

Goffman, E. (1974). The Presentation of Self in Everyday Life. New York: Overlook.

Goldsmith, D. (2008). "Managing Conflicting Goals in Supportive Interaction and Integrative Theoretical Framework." Communication Resource, 19 (2), 264-286. <http://crx.sagepub.com/cgi/content/abstract/19/2/264> (2008).

Hall, E. T. (1966). The Hidden Dimension. Garden City, NY: Doubleday.

Henslin, J. M. (2008). Sociology: A Down-to-Earth Approach. New York: Allyn & Bacon.

Hello and Welcome (2005). "Inclusive communication toward inclusive communication strategy in the city of Edinburgh." (2005). <http://www.inclusivecommunications.co.uk/> (2008).

Huse, J. (2010). Personalizing Parkinson's disease through the journey of Michael J. Fox. The Journal of Nursing Education, 49(12): 719.

Inter Tribal Council of Arizona (2003). "Fort Yuma-Quechan Tribe." <http://www.itcaonline.com/tribes_quechan.html> (2008).

Johnson, C., & Kreger, J. (2008). "Muslim Women in the Workplace Reaching Beyond Stereotypes to understanding." <http://www.diversitycentral.com/learning/cultural_insights.html> (2008).

Kendall, D. E. (2008). Sociology in our times (7th ed.). Belmont, CA: Thomson/Wadsworth.

Marsh, P. E. (1991). Eye to Eye: How People Interact. Salem House Pub.

Marx, K. (1964). Selected Writings in Sociology & Social Philosophy. New York: McGraw-Hill.

Mead, G. H., & Morris, C. W. (1934). Mind, Self & Society from the Standpoint of a Social Behaviorist. The University of Chicago Press: Chicago; IL.

Merton, R. (1957). The Role-set: Problems in Sociological Theory. British Journal of Sociology, 8: 106-20.

Mooney, L. A., Knox, D., & Schacht, C. (2000). Understanding social problems (2nd ed.). Cincinnati, OH: Wadsworth.

Nisbet, R. A. (1970). The Social Bond: An Introduction to the Stud of Sociology. New York: Alfred A. Knopf.

Omi, M., & Winant, H. (1994). Racial Formation in the United States: From the 1960s to the 1990s. New York: Routledge.

Ortony, A. & Turner, T. (1990). What's Basic About Basic Emotions? Psychological Review. 97, 315-331.

Pearson, J. C. (1985). Gender and Communication. Dubuque, IA: W.C. Brown Publishers.

RTO Online (2005). "Is your workplace culture male or female? Answer may affect worker loyalty, health and productivity." <http://www.rtoonline.com/content/Article/Jan05/LuminariStudy013105.asp> (2008).

Schaefer, R. T. (2006). Sociology: A Brief Introduction. Boston, MA: McGraw-Hill.

Schaefer, R. T., & Lamm, R. P. (1998). Sociology (6th ed.). New York: McGraw-Hill.

Shannon, C. E., & Weaver, W. (1949). A Mathematical Model of Communication. Urbana, IL: University of Illinois Press.

Sheikh Nor, M. (2011, January 08). Men, women banned from shaking hands. <http://www.iol.co.za/news/back-page/men-women-banned-from-shaking-hands-1.1009502> (2011).

Simmel, G. (1955). Conflict (K. H. Wolff, Trans.). Glencoe, IL: Free Press.

Tannen, D. (1990). You Just Don't Understand: Women and Men in Conversation. New York: Morrow.

Tannen, D. (1994a). Talking from 9 to 5. New York: William Morrow.

Tannen, D. (1994b). Gender and Discourse. New York: Oxford University Press.

Trevino, S. (2011). Cultural Nonverbal Characteristics. eHow. <http://www.ehow.com/info_8479338_cultural-nonverbal-characteristics.html> (2011).

U.S. Equal Employment Opportunity Commission (2002). Federal Laws Prohibiting Job Discrimination Questions and Answers. <http://www.eeoc.gov/facts/qanda.html> (2008).

Williams, S., & Anderson, B. (n.d.). Defining Genderlects. <http://www.wiu.edu/users/scw105/genderlects.htm> (2008).

# CHAPTER FIVE

# Groups and Organizations

## Beverly Farb

**Chapter Objectives**
At the end of this chapter, students should be able to:

- Identify the sources of group power.
- Compare the benefits and costs of group membership.
- Identify the variables that help individuals resist groups.
- Compare the benefits of diversity and homogeneity.
- Compare the benefits and costs of bureaucracy.
- Identify group dynamics that increase the likelihood of discrimination and violence.
- Identify the variables that help humanize global relationships.

Using the "sociological imagination," we can see that social forces have extraordinary power over individuals (Mills, 1956). Of all social forces, groups exert their power the most directly. This can be either wonderful or terrifying. Have you ever wondered:

(*On the wonderful side*)
- How marriage increases lifespan?
- How social rituals can reduce crime?
- How acquaintances help reduce poverty?
- How local communities can reduce corporate harm?

(*On the terrifying side*)
- Why every major religion in the world has a history of violence, even though they teach peace and universal love?
- How American soldiers, dedicated to defending our nation, could be guilty of torture and abuse?

- Why race and gender continue to affect our available choices in America, land of so-called equal opportunity?
- Why so many people are willing to give up their creativity, freedom, dignity, close relationships, and personal happiness for a job?

Studying the nature and power of groups helps to answer all of these questions and more.

## What Counts as a Group?

A **social group** is more than just a collection of individuals. In a group, there is a sense of shared identity, or "we," that is established through shared interaction. People in a grocery store or at a bus stop are not a true group. Although they share a space and a purpose, they form only a **social aggregate**. But this can change. Imagine this crisis: A bus crashes into a telephone pole as it approaches a stop. Suddenly, the people at the bus stop are transformed into a true group. They interact with energy, perhaps shouting to each other about what to do. They share an identity, too: "We" are now the people who have witnessed this tragedy.

However, a tragedy is not necessary; there is another way that an aggregate can transform into a group. Over time, if the same aggregate continues to assemble, the individuals will begin chatting and getting to know each other. In that case, "we" are the people who wait for this bus at this time of day.

A **social category** is not a true group either. Members of a category share a trait, such as a status (e.g., being a student) or condition (e.g., having cancer). Gender, race, age, and social class are characteristics that form categories, not groups; the people who share such traits do not necessarily interact, nor must they perceive themselves as part of a larger "we."

Others who do not share the same trait often perceive those who do share it as a group, and this is a crucial mistake. This misperception is one of the roots of prejudice. It encourages people to respond to members of a category as if they shared far more than that. Even when a prejudice is positive, such as "Asians succeed in school" or "teenagers have lots

of energy," such expectations tend to place unnecessary limits on social interaction.

Can categories be transformed into groups? Yes, just as with aggregates, a crisis can cause a transformation. For example in 2001, the crisis of a devastating terrorist attack turned the category "New Yorkers" into a group. People were suddenly showing affection to strangers and making sacrifices for each other. Even the criminals in the city were drawn into the social embrace—crime rates dropped significantly for a period of several weeks. Likewise, immediately after the Oklahoma City bombing of 1995, crime rates dropped just as sharply (Kuntzman, 2001).

Another way for categories to change into groups is through political action. For example, Karl Marx noticed that "factory workers" were just a category, a mass of lonely individuals each struggling separately to survive. Marx wanted to make this category into a powerful army. If the workers could only realize that "we" all suffer together because of a common enemy, the capitalist system, then "we" could unite in fulfilling our common destiny to destroy that system.

Other political movements have echoed this idea. Feminist leaders, for example, encourage women to unite, to see themselves as part of a powerful coalition with the strength to overcome the system of male privilege. Such political action has been only partially successful. Not all workers have united, and neither have all women. Instead, much smaller groups have formed, such as workers unions and women's rights organizations.

## Why Do People Join Groups?

Joining groups is a matter of survival. Individuals are far better able to feed, protect, and shelter themselves when they work together. As discussed above, times of crisis remind people of this need for cooperation.

Yet, there are other human needs that drive people toward each other. Emile Durkheim believed that social belonging is necessary for two reasons:

1. Humans need guidance on how to think, act,

and feel. Such guidelines for how to live are called **norms**. Durkheim argued that only social groups can provide norms. Individuals trying to exist alone are hopelessly confused.

2. Humans need to share experiences and feel that they are part of something larger than themselves. Without this kind of bonding, said Durkheim, individuals are unbearably isolated.

In fact, Durkheim believed that confused and isolated individuals are more likely to commit suicide. If he were correct, this would be yet another way that groups are necessary for survival.

Current studies do seem to confirm, over and over again, that people need strong social connections. Deep involvement in a wide variety of strong social networks is correlated with living longer and healthier. A longer and healthier life includes a reduced likelihood of suicide, mental and physical illness. This holds true whether the social network is a religious community, a friendship group, an extended family, or a marriage (Davis, Morris, & Kraus, 1998; Kana'iaupuni, Donato, Thompson-Colon, & Stainback, 2005; Valliant, 2002; Wills & Fegan, 2001). Even a deep attachment to a pet appears to enhance mental and physical health (Allen, Blasovich, & Mendes, 2002; Pachana, Ford, Andrew & Dobson, 2005).

# Where Do Groups Get So Much Power?

At the beginning of this chapter, I said that groups have extraordinary power over individuals. We have discussed how much individuals need groups. Since groups tend to punish and sometimes even cast out members who disappoint them, individuals are highly motivated to meet group expectations. When individuals obey the norms of a group, it is called conformity. How do groups ensure the conformity of their members? Their main tools are: internalized norms, identity control, and the power of division.

## Internalized Norms

Most of the norms we conform to every day are invisible to us; we follow them completely unaware.

For example, we don't imagine that we are conforming when we smile in greeting other people. When such norms are broken, though, we suddenly notice them. A person who consistently fails to smile in greeting soon discovers that social consequences follow, like disapproval, perhaps resentment or suspicion, and withdrawal (for a thorough discussion of this idea, see Garfinkle, 1967).

We tend to be most unaware of norms that are fully internalized. Such social rules have been so completely accepted that our obedience is automatic. When this is so, there is no need for external control.

Authority is one kind of internalized norm. Authority is power that is socially accepted, often so completely that it is not questioned. For example, in a typical college class, students start the first day by helping to establish the teacher's authority. They obey norms when they sit, listen, and write. As the weeks pass, the teacher's authority may be challenged, but likely by only a few. Often the only challenges are quiet absences or privately missed assignments. The conformity level in a college classroom is high, usually without obvious enforcement. This is because each of the participants has internalized the rules of school, including teacher authority, early in life.

The authority of the teacher is *not* a personal trait belonging to that individual. Instead, this power lies in the status and role of the person. A status is a person's position in a social arrangement (e.g., teacher or student), and a role is a set of expectations attached to a status (e.g., grading, lecturing, writing, answering questions). The individuals involved are entirely replaceable. One day, all of the people in the classroom will be dead and gone, but the class will still continue. New members will occupy the old statuses and play the old roles. In this sense, groups can be immortal.

## Identity Control

The fact that most of our conformity is automatic lends groups enormous and effortless power. But equally important, groups have power because they shape individual identity.

A **reference group** is any group that an individual admires enough to use as a standard for his or

How do your primary groups influence your identity?

her own identity. The individual may or may not be a member of the reference group. For example, suppose that I admire the dedication of Mother Teresa and those who worked with her to alleviate poverty. That reference group may inspire me to volunteer at homeless shelters and give to charities. It may even keep me humble to mentally compare my contributions to theirs. Note that a reference group can have a significant influence over an individual's behavior and self-concept, even at a great distance and after some or all of its members have died. In this case, the conformity is managed entirely through the individual's own imagination.

Of course, reference groups can also be much closer to home. In fact, they could actually be a person's primary or secondary groups. **Primary groups**, such as family or friends, are organized around togetherness and assumed to be long-lasting—perhaps eternal. Meanwhile, **secondary groups**, like classmates and co-workers, are organized around a task and assumed to be short-term.

Primary groups have the earliest and deepest hold on our identities. For this reason, they have greater ability to demand conformity than secondary groups. This helps explain why basic values are more effectively taught at home than at school. Business men and women who act with integrity are likely no different than their dishonest peers as far as the number of ethics courses they took in college (Conroy & Emerson, 2004). The difference between them is how pro-social values were taught in their primary groups.

We can see how deeply individual identity is rooted in primary groups by considering "borrowed glory" and "borrowed shame." If a member of my family (primary group) earns an award, my whole family glows in the light of it, shouting "We rock!" But if one of my co-workers (secondary group) earns an award, while I'm happy for him or her, it doesn't have any consequence for my identity. There's no borrowing of the glory. Likewise, imagine if one of my close friends were arrested for a crime. I'd be devastated. In a way, the shame would also rest on me. Meanwhile, if one of my classmates were arrested, maybe I'd simply consider it an interesting story to tell.

Secondary groups can transform into primary groups if they last long enough. For example, when a cohort of students spends several years participating in the same classes, they will begin to experience the dynamics of a primary group. They will imagine their bonds lasting forever and begin to borrow glory and shame. The behavior of each individual will become more dependent on that group. The same can be seen among co-workers who have shared their place of employment for years.

Even though primary groups have superior power, don't underestimate the potential of identity control in secondary groups. Individuals are vulnerable to secondary groups because humans are likely to live up (or down) to social expectations. Obviously, there are exceptions to this kind of rule, but recent research continues to confirm this as a general tendency. (For some examples, see McFarland and Pals, 2005; Nath, Borkowski, Whitman, & Schellenbach, 1991; Sanders, 2002.)

In one classic example, Rosenthal and Jacobson (1968) demonstrated the power of teacher expectations through a series of experiments. The researchers began with a pool of equally intelligent children. They then lied to teachers, pretending that some of the children were especially smart and about to "bloom." By the end of eight months, the academic achievement of the expected bloomers was significantly superior to that of the other students. This occurred despite the fact that none of the students knew they had been labeled one way or the other. It was enough that the expectation existed in the teacher's mind. How could a teacher's private thoughts result in a student's real-life academic achievement? Through the way the teacher responded to the student. Although the teachers in this experiment were not aware of doing so, they answered the supposed bloomers more frequently and thoughtfully than they did the others. The "bloomers" were given more challenges and opportunities.

## The Power of Division

Both sources of group power that we have discussed—internalized norms and identity control—seem to operate largely without the conscious awareness of the people involved. There is another powerful group dynamic that works just as inadvertently: the formation of **in-groups** and **out-groups**.

Any formation of a valued "we" can be called an in-group. Unfortunately, this automatically defines anyone who isn't part of it as "they," the out-group. The more valuable the in-group, the sharper the division between "we" and "they." Naturally, "we" are more immediately relevant to the daily living of each "I" than "they" are. We certainly have more contact and mutual understanding with each other than with anyone outside the group. It is a small step, then, to imagine that we are essentially different from them. Now, add the human tendency toward self-serving bias (for a summary of studies demonstrating such bias, see Aronson, Wilson, & Akert, 2005), and given this self-serving tendency, the belief that "we are essentially different from them" becomes "we are superior to them." Another small step and the members of the out-group are viewed with contempt and suspicion.

Even though such enemies are created unintentionally, the animosity between in-groups and out-groups can have severe consequences.

## Application: The Connection Between Peace-Loving and Violence

At the beginning of the chapter, I asked, "If every major world religion preaches peace and universal love, why does each have a history of violence?" For Americans, it is easy to focus on Muslim and Jewish violence while mostly ignoring the same in Christians. But the Christian crusades of medieval Europe were a bloody campaign to obliterate nonbelievers. In the United States, the racial violence of the Ku Klux Klan was done in the name of Jesus. More recently, the Army of God has been fighting abortion with violent means. About 19 percent of the current hate crimes in the United States are religiously motivated, and more than half of these victimize Jewish Americans (FBI, 2010). Buddhism is often imagined as an exception to this rule, but its followers have not always been peaceful. For example, the Samurai warriors of Japan were devout Buddhists, and in Sri Lanka, the Buddhist Sinhalese and the Hindu Tamil just ended a long civil war.

The puzzling connection between peace-loving religions and violence can be explained by returning to our discussion of the sources of group power. Religion provides individuals with deeply internalized norms, firm identities for each member, and a highly valued in-group. Remember that the very existence of an in-group defines everyone else as an out-group. That basic fact sets the stage for conflict. Even the best intentions of religious people, and the most sincere preaching about peace and love, cannot erase it.

Once powerful in-groups and out-groups are established, is it possible to dissolve them? Social psychologist Sherif and his colleagues ran an experiment to find the answer (Sherif, Harvey, White, Hood & Sherif, 1961). They assembled a collection of unconnected children and divided them randomly into two groups. They then encouraged each of the new groups to form a strong sense of "we" through creating group rituals (e.g., chants and games) and symbols (e.g., a flag and a name). As each in-group developed, animosity toward the other group—the out-group—followed. Although this began automatically, Sherif's research team decided to purposely magnify the effect. They set the groups against each other in competitions and played little tricks, like making sure that half of the available food was spoiled. They succeeded in maximizing inter-group hatred. But the researchers' final goal was to test how inter-group hatred, once created, might be overcome. At first, they tried getting the groups together in shared activities. That didn't help. For example, none of the children were interested in watching a movie because they were too busy taunting and throwing things at each other. What did finally work was setting up a series of emergencies (e.g., the bus broke down, the pipes burst) so that all of the children in both groups were forced to work collectively. Mutual need broke the divide. By the end of the experiment, Sherif boasted, there were best-friend pairs across what used to be enemy lines.

If you were a member of the military, what would your in-groups and out-groups be?

As of this writing, the United States is still at war in Afghanistan. Officially, the conflict is not about religious differences. Yet the animosity between the largely Christian West and the largely Muslim Middle East is certainly fueled by the in-group/out-group dynamic. Could we borrow the wisdom of Sherif's experiment? Could we arrange a mutual need that would break the divide between the United States and its enemies? Social scientists call such a need a **superordinate goal**. Negotiators in the Middle East have been trying for many decades to find one that would unite opposing sides.

The trick in finding a superordinate goal is to expand the definition of "we" to include everyone and join in a common effort. Instead, in the current war against terrorism, definitions of "we" are more solidly exclusive than ever. To conduct a successful war, leaders must strengthen, not dissolve, a nation's sense of "we." That is why former President George W. Bush called Iraq, Iran, and North Korea the "Axis of Evil" (State of the Union Address, 2002). He was making a purposeful connection to WWII when the United States was confident that its fight was righteous against the "Axis" of Italy, Germany, and Japan. Bush's attempt makes perfect sense if the goal is to strengthen a separate "we." But suppose that terrorism is created in the first place by that in-group/out-group dynamic? In that case, we want to solve this problem by going in the opposite direction.

## Conformity: Wonderful or Terrifying?

At the beginning of the chapter, I suggested that the power of groups can be either wonderful or terrifying. Much of that power is achieved through demanding conformity.

### On the Wonderful Side

Conformity can be wonderful: getting good grades in school, obeying the law, maintaining healthy habits, and showing kindness to others. All of these types of conformity are associated with significant benefits for the individual. As we discussed earlier, health and long life are among the rewards that groups can offer.

How can groups provide so much? Part of the answer is through **social ritual**. Social rituals are set behaviors that symbolize a relationship. Such rituals can be complex, such as a wedding ceremony, or simple like a daily hug. The simple, daily rituals are the ones that are associated with positive results for individuals. For example, children who grow up in families with a lot of ritual—like eating sit-down meals, preserving holiday traditions, and following a bedtime routine—are less likely than other children to engage in crime, drug abuse, or early sex (Kiser, Bennet, Heston, & Paavola, 2005; Pollard & Hawkins, 1999).

### On the Terrifying Side

Unfortunately, history has repeatedly shown how conformity can go wrong. The worst example of this is the Holocaust, the slaughtering of millions of people who failed to fit Adolf Hitler's idea of human perfection. Hitler could not have accomplished such an enormous crime by himself. His plan required the conformity of thousands of followers. The rest of the world now sits in judgment, asking, "How could the German people go along with it? How could their soldiers obey such terrible orders?"

Sociology offers a terrifying answer: They did it for the same reasons that anyone goes along with anything. As we discussed earlier, it is normal for individuals to obey authority without thinking, to play familiar roles without complaint, to conform identity to group expectations, and to divide into in-groups and out-groups. Conformity is essential to all human societies, and the people involved in this atrocity were no different than anyone else in the world. It means that the Holocaust might happen anywhere.

A social psychologist named Stanley Milgram tried to prove that Americans can be just as horribly obedient as the Nazi soldiers were (Milgram, 1963). In the 1960s, Milgram did a series of experiments on American college students and community members. He told the experiment volunteers that they must deliver electric shocks to someone they could hear but not see. Milgram explained that the shocks would help the unseen person learn academic information more effectively, since the person would only receive shocks if he answered questions incorrectly. The unseen person was an actor; he didn't actually receive any shocks. But Milgram made the volunteers believe that they were really shocking someone. He had a convincing "shock machine" with blinking lights, lots of electric switches, and bright red danger signs. The unseen actor answered the experimenter's questions wrong on purpose so that the volunteers would have to shock him. As the experiment went on, the actor shouted out in distress, saying something like, "Please don't shock me anymore. It hurts, and I have a heart condition." The volunteers would turn to the experimenter and ask for permission to stop. But the experimenter, who was wearing the white lab coat that symbolizes scientific authority, would say something like, "No, you can't stop. You'll ruin the experiment. You must continue for the sake of science." Sixty-five percent of the volunteers continued to send shocks until the actor no longer responded and was possibly dead. Milgram had found what he wanted: ordinary Americans who would kill an innocent victim because they were told to do it.

The volunteers in Milgram's experiments were not mentally ill, nor were they criminals. In fact, Milgram made sure that all of the volunteers were mentally and socially stable by giving them a series of psychological tests before allowing them to participate. The Nazi soldiers were just ordinary people, too.

Of course, a set of controlled laboratory experiments cannot truly match the social conditions surrounding the Holocaust. Admittedly, Milgram's work can only suggest what might have been involved. Furthermore, Milgram's samples were small, not representative of the whole nation. His studies could not truly yield accurate conclusions about "the average American."

Knowing the limits of this kind of research tempts me to breathe a sigh of relief. I might say to myself, "Americans couldn't really be that obedient, especially not now. People are much less impressed by authority these days." Unfortunately, recent research does not support such an optimistic conclusion about resistance to misused authority.

A new study conducted by psychologist Jerry Burger in 2009 has attempted to replicate Milgram's experiments (Burger, 2009). Because of ethical concerns, the volunteers in Burger's study were not

pressured to continue until the actor pretended possible death. Instead, they were pushed to continue only after the first verbal plea for mercy. Burger reasoned that, since most of the participants in Milgram's study who went that far also continued to the end, this would provide a reasonable comparison. While 82 percent of Milgram's participants continued to deliver shocks after the first plea to stop, 70 percent of Burger's did the same. Although the percentage in the replication study is slightly lower than in the original, this still means that most participants obeyed authority despite substantial personal misgivings.

## Application: Heroes Who Are Villains

At the beginning of the chapter, I asked how American soldiers, dedicated to defending our nation, could be guilty of torture and abuse. I was referring to the scandal at the Abu Ghraib prison in Iraq. At Abu Ghraib, soldiers in the U.S. Army and agents of the C.I.A. extracted confessions from prisoners who were suspected of violent opposition to Iraq's new government. To do so, some of them used torture (e.g., starvation, injury). In some cases, the abuse of prisoners went far beyond what was imagined as useful in gaining confessions (e.g., forced sexual acts, humiliation) (Hersh, 2004).

So far, it has not been proven that any of this activity was officially authorized. But even if the torture was not directly ordered, these incidents are still examples of conformity to social expectations. Besides the obvious group dynamics of conformity, there are two more social conditions at Abu Ghraib that help explain this disturbing set of individual behaviors: *deindividuation* and *dehumanization*.

### Deindividuation: Lost in a Role

**Deindividuation** occurs when a person loses his or her individual identity and effectively "disappears" into a group. Social roles and crowds are the likeliest places to lose someone.

Earlier in our discussion, I mentioned that social roles carry their own power and a tendency to endure, regardless of which individuals might be playing the parts. In a sense, individuals can "disappear" into their roles. When individuals accept roles, they are showing a willingness to allow social norms, rather than personal factors, to determine their behavior. Some roles include harmful behavior, such as that required of a soldier in a war. An individual given such a role becomes far more willing to cause harm than if the behavior was considered a matter of personal choice.

The power of social roles in overwhelming individual conscience was demonstrated in a classic experiment conducted by Philip Zimbardo, a social psychologist like Milgram (Zimbardo, 1972). Zimbardo and his team created a pretend prison, complete with barred windows and bare cots, in the basement of the psychology building at Stanford University. The volunteers in the experiment were randomly assigned to play one of two prison roles: either guard or inmate. Those assigned to be inmates were arrested on schedule by the real Stanford police, handcuffed in front of uninformed neighbors, stripped and deloused, given uniforms, and given prison numbers to replace their names. Those assigned to become prison guards were also given uniforms and a command to keep control of the prisoners. Then Zimbardo settled in to watch what he thought would be a two-week play.

Within just a few days, the volunteers were no longer acting; they were suffering a true loss of individual identity. Some of the guards became sadistic, humiliating and harassing the prisoners. Some of the prisoners became suicidal. Just as Milgram had done, Zimbardo had tested all of the experiment participants to make sure that they were emotionally and socially stable before beginning. Therefore, he was certain that the disintegration of the volunteers was entirely created by the social situation. Zimbardo was delighted; this was just what he wanted to prove. It was a graduate student who challenged him and asked, "What are you doing?" Only then did Zimbardo admit that he was doing harm in the name of science and that he himself had lost his conscience to his social role.

At Abu Ghraib, the soldiers and agents who tortured prisoners in order to extract confessions saw themselves as fulfilling their roles, "just doing our jobs." Their motive was to meet the goals of their organizations. It is unlikely that they would have committed so much violence on their own.

## Deindividuation: Lost in a Crowd

At Abu Ghraib, the abuse of prisoners could not have continued without the silence of many observers who were afraid to intervene. Many did not approve of what was happening, but they did nothing to stop it. Once again, this is a kind of deindividuation, each person refusing to stand out, preferring to remain faceless in a crowd.

Deindividuation explains why so many people will refuse to help an injured stranger on the street. None of the individuals passing by is responsible for doing anything. Even when a group of onlookers is talking to each other about what happened, each person is just "part of the crowd." This is also known as the **bystander effect**. A recent example was caught on a surveillance camera in Connecticut when a 78-year-old male pedestrian was struck by a car. The driver was chasing another driver and didn't even slow down after striking the man. The victim lay paralyzed but still alive while pedestrians and other motorists paused and then left without helping. Finally, a police officer on his way to deal with a different incident came to the man's rescue (Fox News Network, 2008).

If you are ever in trouble in a public place, it is important to break the spell of deindividuation by asking specific individuals for help. Even making eye contact increases the likelihood of getting help. Anything that reminds someone that he or she is an identifiable individual will increase that person's sense of responsibility (Kerr & Bruun, 1983; Latane & Darley, 1968).

## Dehumanization

With deindividuation, there are still individuals in hiding who have personal feelings of empathy for the victims of violence. But with dehumanization, personal empathy is absent. The victims of violence are considered less than fully human and, therefore, are not deserving of full human rights. The victims seem to be part of an extreme out-group, no longer even part of the species. **Dehumanization** is when individuals deprive others of their humanity.

As we discussed, some soldiers at Abu Ghraib were violent toward prisoners because they imagined that their roles required it. Yet, there were some soldiers who went far beyond the demands of the role. They took pleasure in degrading the prisoners and eagerly maximized prisoner suffering.

The U.S. military *does not* purposely teach its soldiers to behave this way. But it *does* train soldiers to dehumanize their opponents. Most soldiers are ordinary people who care. How can caring individuals be trained to kill? By dehumanizing the enemy. Obliterating the enemy must become like winning a computer game. Violence against those who have been dehumanized becomes not only acceptable, but also desirable.

At Abu Ghraib, conformity, deindividuation, and dehumanization were combined. Given this social context, abuse and torture are not surprising.

# Standing Up to Groups

Despite the intense nature of group power, it is possible, after all, for individuals to resist. In some cases, there are social factors that help the individual to do so. Individuals are most likely to stand up to groups successfully when they have at least one ally, self-confidence, high social status, and a smaller group to resist.

## Having an Ally

As it happens, Milgram was once a teaching assistant for another famous researcher of conformity, Solomon Asch. In Asch's experiments, volunteers were shown a straight line and then asked to choose which of three other lines matched the first in length. The correct answer was obvious. Every one of the seven people in the room answered easily. But after a few successes, as they continued to match up lines, six of the seven people began to answer incorrectly. They did this purposely because they were in on the experiment. The seventh person, the only actual subject, was then left to decide whether to report the obvious truth or to conform to the group and report the same wrong answer as everyone else. About 75 percent of the subjects gave in at least once, although it was more typical to give in about one-third of the time (Asch, 1955).

However, in further experiments, Asch discovered that if even one other person in the room would answer truthfully, the subjects were far more likely to do so themselves. Milgram also discovered that his subjects were far likelier to resist conformity when given a positive model who resisted first. Curiously, in Burger's replication of Milgram's study, the presence of a resistant model made no difference. But other recent research continues to confirm the helpfulness of even one ally in resisting the pressure to conform to group errors (Choi & Levine, 2004; De Dreu & West, 2001; Ng & Dyne, 2001).

## Having Self-Confidence

An individual can only successfully resist a group when armed with self-confidence. After Asch's experiments were over, he asked participants why they were sometimes willing to agree with clearly wrong information. Many of them stated that they had begun to doubt their own judgment. Even among the 25 percent of subjects who never gave in, many reported having private doubts about the accuracy of their own perceptions. This is remarkable given the simplicity and clarity of the visual material.

When individuals value a group enough to accept group decisions against their own better judgment, it is called **groupthink**. Social scientists once believed that groupthink was most likely to happen when groups were in crisis and didn't have time to consider alternatives, isolated without outside reality checks, and had high status providing extra faith in the rightness of the group (Janis, 1972). But psychologist Robert Baron (2005) argues that groupthink is far more common and is an ordinary feature of daily life everywhere. According to his investigation, there are two main causes of groupthink:

1. Group members with low self-efficacy are likely to follow the lead of those who are more confident. Such individuals tend to suppress their own, often valid, reservations. **Self-efficacy** is personal confidence that one can accomplish what is desired and manage what is necessary.
2. Group members are likely to spend most of their time and energy talking about the information that everyone already agrees on. For this reason, they often miss unique information that each member could otherwise offer.

## Having High Status

Besides self-confidence, high status is helpful in standing up to groups. As groups form, members automatically and rapidly fall into a hierarchy, with some members having more power and privilege than others. This holds true even in small, temporary groups, like discussion groups in a class. Relative status within the group emerges as members form impressions of each others' likely contributions (Berger, Wagner & Zelditch, 1985; Correll & Ridgeway, 2003).

Members of the group with the lowest status have only their conformity to offer. The highest status members, since their contributions are considered so valuable, earn idiosyncrasy credit (Hollander, 1958). **Idiosyncrasy credit** is group permission for nonconformity. In other words, high status members are allowed to break the rules—at least some rules, sometimes, to some degree. Group members tend to agree on who has such credit and how much (Estrada, Brown & Lee, 1995).

Someone with high status may choose to spend his or her idiosyncrasy credit on helping someone with lower status stand up to the group. This includes allowing newcomers to introduce changes (Lortie-Lussier, 1987). Spending social credit this way is not motivated so much by kindness as by wisdom. Groups are more likely to make successful decisions when they accept dissent and innovation. In turn, the success of the group secures the continuation of idiosyncrasy credit (Hollander, 2004).

## Having a Smaller Group to Face

The smaller the group, the easier it is to stand against it. However, Milgram didn't believe that. In his experiments, conformity was already maximized by the time the group had grown to four members. For that reason, social scientists often cite four as the magic number, though more recent research shows conformity continuing to increase with group size (Walther et al., 2002).

Larger groups become less flexible (Idson, 1990). This is because they must create a formal set of rules to avoid disintegrating. These rules help coordinate efforts and avoid confusion and conflict. But they also add a rigid layer of group expectations,

making conformity that much harder to resist.

As groups grow, it is difficult to stay aware of each member, and attention usually focuses on a smaller subgroup of leaders. Each member who is not a leader is at least one step removed from the decision center. They become dependent on the expertise of the few (Bonner & Baumann, 2008). Once again, the individual who would like to be different has an increasingly difficult task.

# Diversity: An Unappreciated Benefit

Although both groups and individuals are significantly benefited by diversity, both strongly prefer homogeneity. **Diversity** refers to the existence of differences, whether within groups or between groups. The opposite of diversity is **homogeneity**, or sameness.

## The Benefit of Diversity for Groups

Diversity within groups can help members come to more accurate conclusions and solve problems more effectively and creatively. As we were just discussing, when individuals stand up to groups, groups tend to benefit. Dissenters can introduce unexpected information, different points of view, and new strategies. Even when a dissenter is completely wrong, just the fact that someone said or did something different tends to make group members more willing to explore alternatives. This usually results in higher quality group decisions (Brodbeck, Kerschreiter, Mojzisch, Frey, & Schulz-Hardt, 2002; Nemeth & Kwan, 1987).

Groups can also take advantage of diversity by assigning different tasks to different members according to ability and desire. When members specialize, the group can accomplish tasks that are greater, both in number and in complexity.

## The Benefit of Diversity for Individuals

Individuals know that they depend on the help of family and friends, but they often underestimate how much they need acquaintances. For example, a diverse **social network** of acquaintances is essential to most successful job searches. Family and friends cannot know of all the best job opportunities, and strangers would not be motivated to share them. Sociologist Mark Granovetter (1983) called the importance of diverse acquaintances "the strength of weak ties." He and later researchers have documented the benefits that such ties provide:

- Valuable information (not only job opportunities, but news and fresh ideas).
- Increased flexibility and creativity in thinking and behavior.
- Strength in resisting unhealthy conformity to local norms.
- Increased acceptance of dissimilar others (including willingness to racially integrate).
- Involvement in political action.
- Success in establishing small businesses (Ruef, 2002).

## The Preference for Homogeneity

Despite the benefits of diversity, we know from our previous discussion that groups strive to stay homogenous, using all the tools of conformity. Individuals, too, prefer homogeneity. For example, people tend to marry others who are like themselves. Typically, spouses are similar in social class, race, religion, personality, level of attractiveness, I.Q. score, and life experiences (for a summary, see Baumeister & Bushman, 2008, and Hamon & Ingoldsby, 2003). Marriages that cross social lines, such as interfaith and interracial marriages, are often—though not always—at greater risk for divorce (Chan & Smith, 2001; Heaton & Pratt, 1990).

Individuals show the same desire for homogeneity in other kinds of groups, as well. Some examples include work teams, counseling groups, military divisions, and neighborhoods. In all of these, feelings of personal satisfaction and loyalty to the group are enhanced when members are similar to each other (Kemelgor, 2007; Meir, Hadasi, & Noyfeld, 1997; Mouritzen, 2006; Perrone & Sedlacek, 2000).

## Application: Sorry, Not a Small World After All

As strong as weak ties may be, they do have limits. You have probably heard about the "small world" phenomenon. This is the idea that everyone in the world is connected to everyone else within six acquaintance links, or six "degrees." Unfortunately, this is not true, even though some textbooks are still reporting it as a fact.

It was Milgram who introduced the "small world" idea in 1967. He performed experiments in which he asked volunteers to deliver a letter to a complete stranger. Although they had the stranger's name and address, the volunteers were not allowed to simply mail it—they could only pass the letter on to an acquaintance they knew by first name. Then that person must do the same, and so on. Milgram reported that after repeated trials, on average, it took six first-name acquaintances to deliver the letter to the target stranger. Milgram's findings were embraced at once, not only by the American public but by social scientists.

Eventually, psychologist Judith Kleinfeld (2002) pointed out that Milgram's "small world" conclusion could not be true for the following reasons:

- Most of Milgram's letters never reached the target stranger.
- Milgram's original samples were white and well-educated. Such limited samples cannot represent all of America, much less the world.
- Follow-up studies demonstrated that familiar social divisions such as class and race interfered with letter delivery.

Kleinfeld suggested that only some of us enjoy a "small world." High status individuals are well-connected with each other, just like members of a small town. Among such populations, strangers are not far removed from each other. Yet these miniature worlds are isolated pockets relative to the rest of the world.

## Application: Inequality in a Land of Opportunity

At the beginning of the chapter I asked, "If America is the so-called land of equal opportunity, why do race and gender continue to make such a difference?" First, I want to establish that they really do, and then I'll offer four possible explanations.

Below is a chart that shows how race and gender shape the incomes associated with different educational degrees. Even though education is the most powerful tool for upward mobility in the United States, educational degrees do not bring the same financial rewards to everyone.

## Patterns in the Chart

- Within each category: The higher the educational degree, the higher the yearly income. In other words, education is helpful to everyone, to both genders and all races.
- But, when you compare between categories, the inequalities by race and gender are clear. For example, white Americans who have bachelor's degrees make $8,700 more per year than black Americans who also have bachelor's degrees. Males of all races who have bachelor's degrees make $15,687 more per year than females of all races who also have bachelor's degrees. Important: All of the individuals included here have worked full-time, year-round.
- Being a woman is a greater financial disadvantage than being a person of color. That disadvantage increases as degrees advance.
- Asian Americans have some advantage over white Americans when comparing those with advanced degrees. These overall numbers hide the differences between Asian categories. Those who immigrate to the United States with substantial financial resources (e.g., from Japan) are in an entirely different situation than those who immigrate with nearly no resources (e.g., from Burma). Likewise, the overall disadvantage of Hispanic Americans hides some differences. For example, Cuban Americans tend to be wealthier.

**TABLE 5.1** 2010 Median Yearly Income

| | High School/ GED | Associate's Degree | Bachelor's Degree | Master's Degree | Doctoral Degree | Lawyers/ Doctors |
|---|---|---|---|---|---|---|
| Both Sexes, All Races | 34,228 | 42,174 | 54,862 | 69,524 | 91,770 | 104,132 |
| **RACE** | | | | | | |
| White (alone, not Hispanic) | 36,540 | 45,523 | 56,187 | 69,786 | 92,193 | 111,679 |
| Black (alone) | 30,136 | 36,155 | 47,487 | 57,856 | 80,975 | 72,452 |
| Asian (alone) | 30,664 | 41,078 | 53,230 | 80,767 | 92,366 | 118,512 |
| Hispanic (all races) | 29,808 | 37,073 | 50,033 | 62,439 | 83,970 | 60,907* |
| **GENDER** | | | | | | |
| Male (all races) | 39,478 | 50,303 | 62,444 | 79,342 | 100,740 | 123,243 |
| Female (all races) | 29,002 | 37,240 | 46,757 | 61,075 | 76,235 | 84,822 |

Source: U.S. Census Bureau. (2010). Current Population Survey: Annual Social and Economic Supplement, Numbers in thousands, People 25 years old and over. Retrieved December 1, 2011 from Current Population Survey website. http://www.census.gov/hhes/www/cpstables/032010/perinc/new03_000.htm

*This dollar amount is a substitute. There were not enough Hispanic lawyers and doctors who worked full-time, year-round to calculate the median with any confidence (under 75,000 of them in the nation). This amount, $60,907, is the median income of all Hispanic lawyers and doctors who may or may not have worked full-time, year-round.

## Possible Explanations

How can this disturbing reality be explained? I offer four possible explanations: the desire for homogeneity, unequal weak ties, the motherhood penalty, and segregated job markets.

### Desire for Homogeneity

Hiring agents are not immune to the pervasive desire for homogeneity. Neither are the managers who control promotions. Just as with marriage, people tend to hire and promote others who are similar to themselves (Essed, 2002; Petersen & Dietz, 2006). Obviously, this reduces opportunities for those who do not resemble the people currently in charge, thus maintaining the pattern of relative privilege.

### Unequal Weak Ties

As discussed earlier, weak ties (i.e., acquaintance networks) appear to be the best source of information about job opportunities. This is especially true for college-educated individuals who are searching for higher-end employment. Opportunities for lower-end jobs are usually local and are more likely to be found through the strong ties of friends and family (Granovetter, 1983).

Weak ties between individuals of different racial categories tend to be relatively few and far between. This means that people of color are less likely than whites to hear about the best positions or, if they do, they may find out too late. This reduces the diversity of applicant pools, leaving hiring agents with limited choices even when they are eager to diversify staff.

Women are more likely than people of color to have sufficient weak ties for a job search. But the weak ties of women may be less helpful than those of men. Sociologist Gail McGuire (2002) surveyed more than a thousand employees at a financial services firm. She discovered that the men received a great deal of work-related help from their acquaintances. This included help in getting around bureaucratic hurdles, getting one's work recognized, meeting influential others, and getting promotions. Equal help was offered to both white and black men, but only when their organizational positions were equal, which was rare. Women were offered less help than men regardless of race. This was true even when comparing women and men who had equal positions.

Most workplaces can claim that their official, formal procedures are fair. Discrimination is far likelier to show up in everyday, informal interactions. This is important because such interactions have consequences for promotion outcomes (James, 2000; Powell & Butterfield, 1997). Often, the informal harm is done through exclusion. For example, not being invited to lunch can mean missing out on an informal planning session. Not being included in hallway conversations can mean not even coming to mind for important assignments. When informal exclusion results in missed opportunities, the economic consequences can be serious.

### The Motherhood Penalty

Women are still more likely than men to take time off from work, or to work only part-time, in order to care for their young children. This translates into lower incomes despite equivalent education in three ways:

- Direct loss of wages due to fewer hours worked.
- Loss of opportunities for promotions and career-building assignments.
- Automatic responses—unintended but damaging—from employers and managers based on beliefs about mothers.

Such automatic responses were documented through an experiment by Correll and Benard (2005). They gave hiring agents two applicant profiles that were equally strong for the position of marketing director. In an attached memo, one applicant was described as the mother of two children, while the other woman was believed to be childless. The hiring agents were twice as likely to report wanting to hire the childless applicant (84 percent vs. 47 percent). They also offered an average of $11,000 per year more to her. Further, the hiring agents indicated a greater willingness to tolerate absences from the "non-mother." Correll and Benard ran the experiment again, this time with the equally strong applications of a father and a "non-father" and the opposite trend was observed. The father was offered an average of $6,000 more and was granted more tolerance for absences. Employers appear to consider parenthood an asset for men, but a liability for women.

*Segregated Job Markets*

Women and men still tend to predominate in different kinds of jobs. On the whole, "her" typical jobs pay far less than "his" typical jobs. This is true even when required skills and training are taken into account. For example, in 2010, the median wage for a state-licensed daycare provider ("her" job) in the United States was $10.15 per hour. Meanwhile, a garbage collector ("his" job) earned a median wage of $16.50. For both jobs, a completed high school education is preferred, and on-the-job training is available. For the licensed daycare provider, additional training hours were required, such as first aid and child abuse prevention.

The same pattern is observable in higher-end jobs. In 2010, the average wage for a social worker specializing in hospital care ("her" job) was $63,510 per year. Meanwhile, the average wage for a mechanical engineer ("his" job) was $82,480. Both jobs require master's degrees and internships (Bureau of Labor Statistics, 2010).

Neither women nor racial minorities receive an equitable return on their investment in education. Their educations will still benefit them greatly, but not equally.

# Bureaucratic Organizations Have a Life of Their Own

Each social condition that I described above (homogeneity, job markets, etc.) tends to create harmful inequality, but mostly without the conscious intention of anyone involved. Remember that conformity also typically operates without awareness. This is because all social forces have their own power, independent of individual will.

The power of social groups to live above and beyond their members is especially evident in bureaucracies. A **bureaucracy** is defined by the following features (Weber, 1947). Each feature contributes to a bureaucracy's ability to control its members:

1. A set of statuses and roles is arranged in a *fixed hierarchy*.
2. All activity is governed by a strict set of *rules* and tracked by keeping formal *records*.
3. Each status and role is *specialized*, responsible for a small piece of the bureaucracy's overall task. This makes every worker an *expert* in his or her own area.
4. Relationships are intended to be *impersonal* with every individual entirely focused on the demands of his or her bureaucratic role.

This arrangement has both benefits and detriments.

## The Benefits of Bureaucracy

More than any other kind of group, a bureaucracy is designed to provide consistency, efficiency, and neutrality.

Devotion to rules and records maximizes *consistency*. Insisting on rules keeps individual efforts stable and predictable. Maintaining a formal record of what everyone is doing helps bureaucracies enforce those rules. Beyond that, the records provide information useful for tracking progress and analyzing the effectiveness of different strategies.

Specialization maximizes *efficiency*. Remember from our earlier discussion that even small groups benefit from splitting up the work. This is the fastest and easiest way to get a massive or complex task done. Saving time and effort also reduces the need for other resources, such as money, required to keep the bureaucracy running.

The prototypical example of maximized efficiency and consistency is an assembly line. In an assembly line, a product is moved, usually by machine, past a series of workers. Each worker adds a single piece or performs a single operation. Because the product parts are interchangeable, and the process of assembly has been worked out ahead of time, workers do not need to spend any time or effort on creating designs or solving problems.

Henry Ford is often given credit for inventing the assembly line, but the process is much older, used by a variety of militaries to produce weapons, starting with ancient China. It was also used in the

1800s by the U.S. meat industry for butchering (Aeragon, 2006). It would be more accurate to say that in 1913, Ford *perfected* the assembly line, at least enough to achieve a dramatic drop in automobile prices. This placed cars within reach of average consumers.

Efficiency is also served by bureaucracy's expectation that workers will remain impersonal. This minimizes daily distractions. However, staying impersonal offers a deeper benefit: *neutrality*. Transcending the personal keeps the workplace free from political or emotional concerns. This is especially important when the bureaucracy is one that serves the public. For example, judges in criminal courts used to hand out sentences according to their personal assessments. Unfortunately, that included personal biases. In the mid-1980s, the U.S. government established sentencing guidelines, a bureaucratic list of rules that limited the possibilities. In the years directly following, there was a significant reduction of racial and gender bias in sentencing (Anderson, Kling, & Stith, 1999; Barkan, 2006). As time wore on, however, there began to be complaints that the prosecutor now had too much influence on sentencing and that the biases had simply moved (Bowman, 2005). The federal guidelines were not able to achieve long-term equality, but they are still an example of a worthy attempt at bureaucratic impartiality.

## The Detriments of Bureaucracy

Ironically, each strength of bureaucracy is also a source of difficulty. Each feature seems designed to make human creativity and emotion, and ultimately humans themselves, entirely unnecessary. This arrangement has the power to last far into the future through "bureaucratic inertia" and "routinization."

Weber provided the definition of bureaucracy that we have been using for this discussion. He also hated and feared what he described. He complained that bureaucratic efficiency and consistency are bought at an unacceptable price: the *suffocation of human creativity*. Bureaucratic tasks are purposely spelled out so that creativity will not be necessary. Innovative thought is too slow and effortful. Besides, it might suggest changes in the rest of the bureaucracy that would cost too much.

When organizations resist beneficial change, this is called **bureaucratic inertia**. The main root of inertia is the complexity that comes with specialization. Rules are carefully designed to ensure that each specialty area makes its proper contribution to the whole. Therefore, making a change in one area usually demands adjustments in several others. A daunting amount of paperwork and meetings is required to shift so many bureaucratic pieces. Workers may resist such extra work if the required change does not make immediate sense for their area, even if it will benefit the overall organization. Their specialized concerns block their view of the "big picture" (Caiden, 1991). Political scientist William West explains one example. When a U.S. president wants to introduce an innovative change in Washington, his main obstacle is not usually Congress. Rather, it is the bureaucratic inertia of his own support staff that tends to frustrate him (West, 2005).

When creativity and change are limited, complained Weber, the human spirit suffers. Bureaucracy squeezes the individual even tighter through the *denial of human emotion*. Weber argued that, although people have always been subject to authority, they used to obey from their hearts. Feelings of devotion once inspired people to obey traditional leaders. Once in a while, a charismatic leader would arise, someone with new ideas who was considered exceptional. Then people would obey with enthusiastic hero worship. But now, lamented Weber, since the Industrial Revolution, authority has become rational, based on a set of logical rules. With rational authority, there is no need for feelings or personal attachments (Weber, 1946).

The main vehicle of rational authority is bureaucracy, and it is specifically designed to inhibit human emotion. Bureaucrats are expected to remain impersonal, concerned only with their own piece of the organizational task. Another way to say this is that everyone must be "professional." For example, when I enter a classroom—whether face-to-face or online—I must leave much of myself behind. The same is true for students. If any of us is especially sad, or angry, or even happy and celebrating, we must put that away and focus on our bureaucratic tasks. If I share a personal story about my life with students, the story had better have an educational purpose. Otherwise, I'm misusing everyone's time. I must not be too capricious about my grading either. I must follow the rules as exactly as possible. Yes, such bureaucratic neutrality is valuable, but also inhuman.

None of us dares to truly be ourselves. We must each play our predetermined roles and eventually be replaced by others who will do the same. In other words, we, personally, are entirely replaceable. This was Weber's final complaint: He was horrified by the *dispensability of human beings*.

Some of us might try to comfort Weber by pointing out that exciting charismatic leaders still show up from time to time. Perhaps they can free us from our bureaucratic non-existence. But Weber would answer that charismatic authority is inherently unstable. It only lasts as long as the leader is both popular and alive. After that, the new ideas and loyal followers may simply vanish. There is only one way for a charismatic leader to leave a lasting legacy: routinization. **Routinization** is the reduction of innovation into bureaucratic routine. Once the leader is gone, followers organize to keep his or her dream alive. In organizing, they are likely to adopt bureaucratic strategies: Tasks will be split, rules will be defined, and so on. From Weber's perspective, bureaucracy wins again, trapping us in its "iron cage."

In fact, Weber believed that rational systems like bureaucracies will always triumph. Worse, they will spread everywhere, replacing more human systems all over the world. A present day sociologist, George Ritzer, agrees. He points to McDonald's restaurant as a prime example (Ritzer, 2000).

McDonald's was not the first fast food restaurant chain. That honor goes to White Castle, established in 1921 (Wisconsin Historical Society, 2008). In 1948, the McDonald brothers, Richard and Maurice, were the first to retool their diner for assembly line production. As a result, they no longer needed to pay the wages of skilled chefs. At the same time, they switched to disposable utensils and packaging, which allowed them to fire their wait staff and dishwashers. With maximized speed and minimized prices, they became industry leaders (Costin, 2007).

Ray Kroc, a milkshake machine salesman, made a proposal to franchise the restaurant for a percentage of sales, and in 1955 the first franchise opened in Des Plaines, Illinois. In the 1960s, McDonald's began to franchise outside of the United States, and it now has restaurants in 119 countries (Parks, 2006).

McDonald's, besides leaping international boundaries, is also being replicated through imitation. Other industries such as toy manufacturing and banking are reorganizing to match its strategies and structure. Ritzer describes this process as **McDonaldization**. Given the financial success attached, conforming to this corporate trend is the rational choice. Yet, Ritzer warns that all of Weber's worst fears are coming true. In exchange for "big business" success, humans are giving up what should not be for sale: freedom, dignity, creativity, and close relationships (Ritzer, 2000).

## Humanity May be Underestimated

As for me, I think both Weber and Ritzer have underestimated the power of humanity to shine through rational rule systems. At least four conditions encourage an optimistic view:

1. The difference between informal and formal structure within a bureaucracy.
2. The partial humanization of big business through imitation of the *Japanese model*.
3. The development of alternatives to big business through a variety of "stay local" movements.
4. The ability of local populations across the world to choose their responses to global forces.

## Informal vs. Formal Structure

The informal reality of a bureaucracy is not likely to match the formal expectations. The official rule book is likely to describe only a fraction of the actual behavior in an office. Likewise, the organizational flowchart is supposed to show how authority and information move between positions and in what direction; yet, the actual flow may differ significantly. For example, employees may learn not to make requests of the manager since it is more effective to simply go to her secretary. This **informal organizational structure** of the way things really work is not written anywhere. No one has planned it out; it simply emerges as people interact.

According to Weber, people must stay impersonal in order to get their jobs done. But co-workers may easily become friends, especially if work-related frustrations are shared (Sias & Cahill, 1998). Indeed, office friendships influence the use of work-related resources, whether or not work-related information is passed on, and whether or not consensus is reached in group decisions (Lincoln & Miller, 1979; Rawlins, 1992). Boss-to-employee relations are also likely to involve strong feelings, although often hidden, rather than neutrality. Some workers have even reported that being able to trust a boss is more important to them than being able to trust a close friend (Cann, 2004).

The expected bureaucratic neutrality is often saved for customers and clients (Tschanh, Sylvie, & Dieter, 2005). Since neutrality is accomplished through strict obedience, the bureaucrat's contact with the public tends to be rigidly rule-focused, though individual humanity can still break through. This is illustrated by a story from my youth:

> Long ago, I lived in Los Angeles. In those days and in that city, getting your driver's license was an all-day ordeal. At the DMV, every step in the process involved a two-hour line (e.g., a two-hour line to take the test, another two-hour line to get the results, etc.). Well, I waited in one of these lines, finally arrived at the front, and discovered to my horror that I had been waiting in the wrong line. Now, if Weber were entirely right, the bureaucrat on the other side of the counter should have said simply, "Next window, please." The regulations would not allow anything else. But, as it happened, there was actually a human on the other side of the counter. Observing the moisture that was beginning in my eyes, she whispered, "I'm not supposed to do this, but I can help you. Here's the form you need...." I burst into full tears and sobbed, "You're my b-best fr-friend!"

Perhaps human emotion and variation are not so easily obliterated after all.

## Humanization of Big Business: The Japanese Model

American business has been humanized through imitating the *Japanese business model*. Despite a disappointing reversal in recent years, many benefits of the original change remain.

In the 1970s, the American business community began to admire the Japanese business model. The Japanese model does not contain any of the bureaucratic features that Weber found so dehumanizing. For example, in a typical American bureaucracy, employees are only welcome as long as they are considered useful by management. Likewise, employees freely abandon companies when they find better opportunities elsewhere. But in a Japanese business, there is a personal devotion between managers and employees; both are committed to a life-long relationship (Workman, 2008).

Many American companies have adopted their favorite pieces of the Japanese model. Especially popular has been the Japanese decision-making style. First, the decision-making is *collective*. Decisions are made in teams, so credit or blame is shared. This is in sharp contrast to the typical Western focus on personal performance and incentive plans. Second, decision-making is *bottom-up* instead of *top-down*. Work teams participate in key structural decisions such as how the work will be divided, how it will be completed, and how it will be rewarded. In a typical American bureaucracy, such decisions are designed and enforced by management (Egawa et al., 2007).

As long as the Japanese were envied competitors, the number of American companies eager to imitate them increased. Unfortunately, in the 1990s, Japan suffered an economic downturn. Many companies could no longer honor the life-long commitment between workers and management, so there were record layoffs (Japan Echo, 1998).

Since 2002, the direction of imitation reversed: At least 30 Japanese companies have now adopted some American business practices. Specifically, these companies have introduced performance-based pay. Previously, pay had been seniority based. They are also now willing to sell off company divisions that are not performing well. Before, they would have protected all employees no matter what.

Further, these companies now devote more energy to maintaining shareholders than to sustaining employees. Financially, this strategy has paid off, but humanity-wise, it is disappointing. For example, the distance between rich and poor has noticeably increased since these changes were made (The Economist., 2007).

How do I maintain an optimistic view in the face of such events? First, I find it encouraging that business communities, both Japanese and American, have demonstrated the capacity to make substantial changes. It means that Weber's "iron cage" has a door that can be opened. Second, Japanese-inspired changes in American business have survived. Compared with companies before the 1970s, current businesses are more accepting of employee control and innovation. (For examples, see Berg, Appelbaum, Bailey & Kalleberg, 2004; Gallup, 2006.)

## Alternatives to Big Business: "Stay Local" Movements

Remember that Weber's nightmare of inescapable bureaucracy has been updated in Ritzer's nightmare of global and eternal corporate control. In direct opposition to such a possibility, *stay local* movements provide alternatives for both workers and consumers. Such movements include:

- The *local business* movement.
- The *local farming* movement.
- The *buy local* movement.
- The *eat local* movement.

Although each of these movements developed independently, they share a common goal. All hope to encourage individuals at the community level to resist corporate harm. For example, when corporations control job markets, workers are at constant risk of unemployment because jobs can be auto-

In your own life, do you participate in any of the "stay local" movements?

mated or sent overseas. Further, when corporations control product markets, they also control prices and quality. While product prices can strike at consumer wallets, product quality can threaten consumer health. Finally, corporate damage can include resource depletion and pollution, even though many companies only contribute to these by transporting their goods long distances (Pollan, 2006).

One leading developer of local businesses, Judy Wicks (2006), explained the benefits of local control this way:

> Local business owners can provide more fulfilling jobs, healthier communities, and greater economic security in their region. Success can mean more than growing larger or increasing market-share. It can be measured by increasing happiness and well being, deepening relationships, and expanding creativity, knowledge, and consciousness.

Unfortunately, Wicks was compelled to acknowledge the corporate ability to overwhelm such efforts. Many local businesses fail because of big business competition. But it's almost worse to know that if they succeed, eventually, they are likely to be absorbed by the big players. For example, ice-cream maker Ben & Jerry's was once a main inspiration for the local movement, but it was recently bought by Unilever. Likewise, the juice maker Odwalla was bought by Coca-Cola (Wicks, 2006).

Despite these defeats, local movements hope to survive through forming alliances with each other. Additional allies have been found in related efforts such as the organic farming movement and the "slow food" movement which, of course, is specifically opposed to fast food (Wood, 2008).

## Local Choice: Globalization Meets "Glocalization"

**Globalization** refers to the international spread of cultural items, practices, and ideas that were once local, such as chopsticks, the Olympic Games, and the Internet. Could globalization eventually lead to the development of a single world culture? Some eagerly anticipate such a day, hoping that a unified culture would bring peace and prosperity to all. Per-

haps if this occurred we would pool our resources and enjoy the benefits of our collective wisdom.

Others dread the idea of one global culture. A homogenous world, by definition, would have lost its diversity. If the unified culture ends up being a globalized version of corporate America, we would be back to the same Weber/Ritzer scenario we keep discussing.

Many imagine that the West is bulldozing over the rest of a helpless world, but I don't think that gives sufficient credit to local populations. When pieces of a culture are globalized, the receiving populations do not always accept them. Instead, they are likely to take what they want of the global input, mix it with what they want from their local culture, and create something new. When globalized items, practices, and ideas are tailored to meet local needs, this is called **glocalization**.

My favorite example of creative glocalization is offered by the Mam, who are descendents of the ancient Mayans. The Mam were growing coffee on small plots of land in Mexico when the North American Free Trade Agreement was signed in 1994. Under NAFTA, participating governments are required to maximize trade of certain products across their borders. This was to take place no matter what the costs and meant discarding national laws that protected local businesses from corporate competition. The Mam feared that their little coffee industry would not survive. The Mexican government had been trying to "modernize" Mam coffee production for more than a decade. Despite the government's generous provision of pesticides and chemical fertilizers, the crops were meager (Castillo & Nigh, 1998). Mam coffee growers decided that the chemicals were part of the problem, and they returned to their indigenous farming practices. But the Mam had a new tool this time: direct access to potential buyers through the Internet. They soon discovered that the global community viewed their farming as "organic" and would pay higher-than-average prices for their coffee (Casillo & Nigh, 1998). The success of the new global business, Café Mam, is a triumph of glocalization.

Glocalization tends to be beneficial, even when it does not result in financial rewards. In Singapore, public housing serves 90 percent of the population and consists of high-rise apartment buildings. The buildings were designed by a Western firm, and each has an open parking garage as the first level. The people in Singapore never use the garage for parking, though. Instead, this space is known as a "void deck" and is used for weddings, funerals, club meetings, after-school parties, and other neighborhood gatherings (Khondker, 2004).

Ironically, when the term glocalization was introduced, it did *not* refer to this kind of local empowerment. The word originally meant that a corporation was tailoring a global product to local tastes in order to increase sales (Robertson, 1994). Actually, corporations still use the word this way. For example, McDonald's glocalizes. In India, Big Macs cannot be sold because beef is prohibited, so the Maharaja Mac is made with lamb or chicken. In Germany, McDonald's offers beer. In Hong Kong, instead of using buns, sandwich ingredients are held between two rice patties, and the list goes on (Adams, 2007).

Perhaps you will not be surprised to hear that George Ritzer is offended by the corporate version of glocalization. Ritzer wants to keep this term for describing local resilience (as I did above). He recommends calling what corporations do **grobalization**. The "gro" is short for "grow" since corporations only want to accommodate local needs in order to fuel their own expansion (Ritzer, 2003).

## Application: Whistle While You Work

At the beginning of this chapter, I asked why so many people are willing to give up so much of their humanity for a job. Our discussion of bureaucracies and corporations has provided some partial answers.

Now I would like to turn that question upside down: Which work conditions help individuals to *keep* their humanity? Specifically, what helps to keep people happy and healthy on the job? A list of obvious variables has been confirmed by research as having the expected benefits for job satisfaction and worker health. These include: sufficient pay (Terpstra & Honoree, 2004), sufficient resources to get the job done (Backman, 2000), recognition for achievements (Bialopotocki, 2006), and hope for advancement (Tian & Pu, 2008). There are some others that I will discuss in greater detail: autonomy and leadership, co-worker relationships, and the bottom line.

## Autonomy and Leadership

Workers appear to thrive best when they have considerable control over their own work through managing their own schedules and choosing between task options, as two examples. This is called **autonomy**. Job autonomy is strongly correlated with both happiness and health (Ala-Mursula, Vahtera, Pentti, & Kivimaki, 2004; Jamal, 2004; Pousette & Johansson, 2002).

Lower-paying jobs, such as food service and some factory work, tend to offer less autonomy than higher-paying jobs, such as college instruction and architectural design. This may be one of the reasons that social class is correlated with life expectancy (along with other variables such as nutrition, access to health care, etc.). Although life expectancy has risen for all social classes over the last three decades, the pattern of inequality remains. Currently, males in the professional class have a life expectancy of 80 years while males in the manual unskilled class have an expectancy of 73 years. Likewise, professional women are likely to live to be 85 while unskilled manual class women are likely to live 78 years (National Statistics, 2007).

Autonomy's direct opposite is **micromanagement**, which is the unrelenting managerial control of the smallest tasks. One study estimated that 80 percent of American workers have been subjected to micromanagement at least once. There appears to be a broad consensus that this strategy results in unhappiness and interferences with job completion (Chambers, 2004).

Workers are most likely to enjoy autonomy when their managers favor a **democratic leadership style**. This means involving workers in most decision-making. In contrast, an **authoritarian leadership style** is characterized by giving commands, and a **laissez-faire leadership style** is typified by leaving workers alone. It comes as no surprise that many studies demonstrate a connection between democratic leadership and high worker satisfaction. Such satisfaction includes feeling competent and valued, having lower stress, and feeling safe from abuse (Abbasi, Hollman, & Hayes, 2008; Hauge, Skogstad, & Einarsen, 2007; Kinjerski & Skrypnek,

2008).

It should be noted that effective leadership is actually more complex than I have suggested so far. Different leadership styles are called for in different situations. For example, in a crisis, authoritarian leadership is necessary to prevent confusion and reduce response time. In a non-crisis situation that is unfamiliar, it is best to proceed cautiously, gather information, and involve all players in democratic brainstorming. Further, when employees are new and inexperienced, an authoritarian style may be necessary. On the other hand, when employees are professional experts, it may make sense for a boss to stay out of the way and adopt a laissez-faire style. Finally, it may be necessary to use each style in sequence: authoritarian at the beginning of a project to get everyone moving, democratic as complexities arise, and laissez-faire once decisions have been made and employees are sent on their way to implement them (Clark, 1997).

## Co-worker Relationships Matter

Bosses and their leadership styles are important to employee happiness, but perhaps co-workers matter even more. Unfortunately, co-workers can easily reduce job satisfaction. One study found that co-worker conflict can create lasting stress, with an individual still reporting painful feelings long after the employment and relationship have ended (Hogh, Henriksson, & Burr, 2005). If co-workers disapprove of an individual's innovation, much of the person's creative joy is diminished, even when management rewards the effort (Janssen, 2003).

The good news is that co-workers are much more likely than not to be a source of happiness (Abualrub, 2006; Ducharme & Martin, 2000). The support of co-workers has even been credited with reducing blood pressure in the face of crisis (Quigley, 2003).

For employees, working in teams can significantly improve individual satisfaction. Studies disagree about whether work teams achieve more than individuals working alone. Some researchers claim that they have proven it (Hagman & Hayes, 1986; Laughlin, Hatch, Silver, & Boh, 2006; Moreland, Argote, & Krishnan, 1996; Valacich, Dennis, & Nunamaker, 1992). Others claim that they have disproved it (Allen & Hecht, 2004; Mullen, Johnson, &

Salas, 1991). But that only matters from a management perspective. Employees tend to enjoy group work whether or not the job gets done.

## The Bottom Line

Intangible sources of happiness and health, such as relationships with co-workers, matter. Their influence, however, can be overshadowed by the practical bottom line: Having a job is a necessary prerequisite to all the rest. For example, having a meaningful and engaging job usually seems important. A survey of more than 107,000 individuals in 49 countries confirmed that job satisfaction is greater when work is intrinsically interesting. But there was an important exception: Intrinsic interest did *not* increase happiness in countries where inequality was high and government assistance was low. In other words, under difficult circumstances, nothing but job security would satisfy (Huang & Van de Vliert, 2003).

# The Future?

Throughout this chapter we have discussed and documented the incredible power of groups. Yet, along the way, we have identified ways that individuals can be heard and contribute some influence. What does all of this suggest about the possible future? Predictions require some guessing and therefore depend on your perspective.

If Max Weber was right, "routinization" is an eternal force that will continue to limit our humanity. Remember that routinization transforms creative effort into bureaucratic rules. One example is emotional labor. **Emotional labor** (Hochschild, 1983) requires workers to manipulate their feelings in order to serve bureaucratic goals. For example, a waitress is required to give customers a "real" smile. To be convincing, the waitress must find a way to actually feel like smiling even if customers, co-workers or bosses happen to be rude.

A creative development in emotional labor was the *Fish!* philosophy. *Fish!* originated in a Seattle fish market as employees found ways of making their job fun. They would throw fish to each other to entertain the customers, speak in rhyme, anything to create surprise and excitement. Customers loved it, and the company made record sales. What made *Fish!* different from other emotional labor is that it was employee-created rather than management-driven. However, now that other companies are imitating the idea, this has become a management agenda, no different than any other bureaucratic demand. In other words, *Fish!* has been routinized. Weber would have predicted as much.

But maybe Weber only saw a small part of the near future. Maybe, in the long run, the post-Marxists will be proven right. From a post-Marxist perspective, any individual, group, or culture that succeeds in grabbing power will eventually lose it. Power is inherently unstable, they argue, because it always contains the seeds of its own destruction. They call this process "the dialectic," as Karl Marx did (Finlayson, 2003). For example, corporate culture seems unstoppable now, but it may self-destruct

given enough time. Possibly, corporate degradation of the environment will create a planet-wide collapse of industrial societies. Or maybe industrial societies will cease to function because corporate monopolies will raise prices and lower wages so much that consumers can no longer buy their products. Either way, humans would have to start over and find a new way of living together.

Or maybe it's Durkheim who understood the truth. He envisioned a future of rich connection between the peoples of the globe. Perhaps the resilience of local communities despite the odds is evidence of an optimistic future. Families tend to be resilient, too. Relationships may be transformed by divorce or death, but they remain significant to the individuals involved who manage to find ways to keep them. From this perspective, humans will always need groups and will always benefit from drawing together.

Source: John Walker

Have you ever had a job that involved emotional labor? If so, how did you feel about it?

# Summary

Groups have extraordinary power over individuals. The power of a group is above and beyond the individual wills of those involved. Group dynamics are often acted out without conscious awareness.

Members of a group have shared interaction and identity. Groups help individuals live healthier, longer and happier. In return, groups demand conformity from their members. Groups achieve conformity by using three main tools: internalized norms, identity control, and the power of division.

Conformity can be wonderful when it means healthy habits, academic success, and lawful society. But conformity is terrifying when it means obedience to a destructive agenda. Even stable, compassionate individuals often can end up participating in group violence. This can happen through deindividuation and dehumanization.

Despite the extreme power of groups, it is possible for individuals to resist. Social factors that help individuals stand up to groups include having an ally, self-confidence, high status, and a smaller group to face.

Diversity benefits both groups and individuals by offering new information, strategies and opportunities. Despite the benefits of diversity, both groups and individuals strongly prefer homogeneity (i.e., similarity between group members). This helps to explain why race and gender still make a difference in the United States, even though we say we value equality.

Bureaucracy is the result of formal organization. Its benefits include consistency, efficiency, and neutrality. But each of the strengths of bureaucracy is also a source of trouble. The downside includes the suffocation of human creativity, bureaucratic inertia, the denial of human emotion, and finally, the dispensability of humans themselves. Bureaucracy has a frightening durability, turning all innovations into routines.

Yet, just as individuals can stand up to groups (with some help), humanity can also stand up to global routinization (and its incarnation in big business). Encouraging social dynamics include: the freedom of informal interaction, the compassion of the Japanese business model, the empowerment of the stay local movements, the creativity of glocalization, and the resilience of workplace happiness.

Predictions about the future of groups depend on your theoretical position. Some predict that all current systems must eventually self-destruct, while others predict that destructive systems will rule forever. Those who favor Durkheim are the most optimistic. They remind us that groups benefit individuals. They do so in multiple ways that only groups can and always will provide.

## Review/Discussion Questions

1. What are the three main tools groups use to achieve the conformity of their members?
2. How can secondary groups transform into primary groups?
3. If you are ever in trouble, and a crowd of people is nearby, you may not receive help because of the *bystander effect*. What advice is given in the chapter for overcoming this phenomenon?
4. What are four of the features that define bureaucracy?
5. What is the difference between "glocalization" and "grobalization"?
6. Which groups have you been member of, and how did they influence you?
7. Would you rather work for a small independent startup business, or a large well-established bureaucratic one, and why?

## Key Terms

**Autonomy** is when individuals have considerable control over their own work.

**Authoritarian leadership styles** are characterized by a leader giving commands to subordinates.

**Bureaucracies** are organizations with statuses and roles arranged in a fixed hierarchy. Activity is governed by strict rules and tracked through the keeping of formal records. Each status and role is specialized so that each person is only responsible for one small aspect of the organization, making each worker an expert in his or her own area. Relationships are impersonal, with everyone's main concern being their own bureaucratic role.

**Bureaucratic inertia** is an organizational resistance to beneficial change.

**Bystander effect** is a term used to describe the tendency of individuals not to get involved in emergency situations if they are part of a crowd.

**Deindividuation** occurs when a person loses his or her individual identity and effectively disappears into a group.

**Dehumanization** involves depriving others of their humanity.

**Democratic leadership style** is a term for involving workers in the decision-making process.

**Diversity** is the existence of differences.

**Emotional labor** requires workers to manipulate their feelings in order to serve bureaucratic goals.

**Globalization** is the deepening, broadening and speeding up of worldwide interconnectedness in all aspects of life.

**Glocalization** describes when globalized items, practices, and ideas are tailored to meet local needs.

**Grobalization** is the desire of corporations to accommodate local needs in order to fuel their own expansion.

**Groupthink** occurs when individuals value a group enough to accept group decisions against their own better judgment.

**Homogeneity** is the existence of sameness.

**Idiosyncrasy credits** are permissions granted by a group that allow high-standing members to act in a nonconforming manner, thus allowing them to break group norms.

**Informal organizational structure** includes any group—not formally planned—that forms within an organization and develops through personal relationships and interactions among its members.

**In-groups** are those in which an individual is a valued member.

**Laissez-faire leadership style** involves leaving workers to function on their own.

**McDonaldization** refers to the global spread of bureaucratic efficiency and profitability at the expense of human creativity, dignity, freedom, and relation-ships.

**Micromanagement** is the unrelenting managerial control of even the smallest tasks.

**Norms** provide guidance on how to think, act and feel.

**Out-groups** are those in which an individual is not a member.

**Primary groups** are organized around togetherness and are assumed to be long-lasting.

**Reference groups** include any group that an individual admires enough to use as a standard for his or her identity.

**Routinization** is the reduction of innovation into bureaucratic routine.

**Secondary groups** are organized around a task and assumed to be short-term.

**Self-efficacy** is a person's confidence that he or she can accomplish what is desired and manage what is necessary.

**Social aggregates** include people who share a space and purpose but do not interact.

**Social categories** have members who share similar traits but do not interact or know one another.

**Social groups** involve two or more people who have a shared a sense of identity and shared interaction.

**Social networks** are webs of social ties among individuals and groups.

**Social rituals** are sets of behaviors that symbolize a relationship.

**Superordinate goals** involve people or groups working together to achieve a goal that is deemed important to everyone involved. The people tend to become friends and their attitudes, values, and goals will become similar, even if those involved originally disliked one another.

# Bibliography

Abbasi, S. M., Hollman, K. W., & Hayes, R. D. (2008). Bad bosses and how not to be one. Information Management Journal, 42 (1), 52-56.

Abualrub, R. F. (2006). Replication and examination of research data on job stress and coworker social support with internet and traditional samples. Journal of Nursing Scholarship, 38 (2), 200-204.

Adams, L. L. (2007). Globalization of Culture and the Arts. Sociology Compass, 1 (1), 127-142.

Aeragon (2006). Industrial politics and economics: The history of the assembly line. <http://www.aeragon.com/02/02-04.html> (2008).

Ala-Mursula, L., Vahtera, J., Pentti, J., & Kivimaki, M. (2004). Effects of employee worktime control on health: a prospective cohort study. Occupational and Environmental Medicine, 61, 254-261.

Allen, K., Blasovich, J., & Mendes, W. B. (2002). Cardiovascular reactivity in the presence of pets, friends, and spouses: The truth about cats and dogs. Psychosomatic Medicine, 64, 727-739.

Allen, N. J., & Hecht, T. D. (2004). The romance of teams: Toward an understanding of its psychological underpinnings and implications. Journal of Occupational and Organizational Psychology, 77, 439-461.

Anderson, J. M., Kling, J. R., & Stith, K. (1999). Measuring interjudge sentencing disparity: Before and after the federal sentencing guidelines. The Journal of Law and Economics, 42 (S1), 271-301.

Aronson, E., Wilson, T. D., & Akert, R. M. (2005). Social psychology (5th ed.). Upper Saddle River, NJ: Pearson Education.

Asch, S. (1955). Opinion and social pressure. Scientific American, 31-35.

Backman, A. (2000). Job satisfaction, retention, recruitment and skill mix for a sustainable health care system. Report to the Deputy Minister of Health for Saskatchewan. <http://209.85.173.104/search?q=cache:XcfAQs6GJ2sJ:www.health.gov. sk.ca/health-worcs+sufficient+resources%2Bjob+satisfaction&hl=en&ct=clnk&cd=30&gl=us> (2008).

Barkan, S. (2006). Criminology: a sociological understanding (3rd ed.). Upper Saddle River, NJ: Pearson Prentice Hall.

Baron, R. (2005). So right it's wrong: Groupthink and the ubiquitous nature of polarized group decision making. In M. P. Zanna (Ed.) Advances in experimental social psychology, (Vol. 37). San Diego, CA: Elsevier Academic Press.

Baumeister, R. F., & Bushman, B. J. (2008). Social Psychology and Human Nature. Belmont, CA: Thompson Wadsworth.

Berg, P., Appelbaum, E., Bailey, T., & Kalleberg, A. (2004). Contesting time: International comparisons of employee control of working time. Industrial and Labor Relations Review, 57 (3), 331-349.

Berger, J., Wagner, D. G., & Zelditch, M. (1985). Expectation states theory: Review and assessment. In J. Berger & M. Zelditch (Eds.). Status, rewards, and influence. San Francisco, CA: Jossey-Bass.

Bialopotocki, R. N. (2006). Recognition and praise relate to teachers' job satisfaction. Doctoral dissertation. University of Nebraska-Lincoln. <http://digitalcommons.unl.edu/dissertations/AAI3238255/> (2008).

Bonner, B. L., & Baumann, M. R. (2008). Informational intra-group influence: the effects of time pressure and group size. European Journal of Social Psychology, 38 (1), 46-66.

Bowman, F. O. (2005). The failure of the federal sentencing guidelines: A structural analysis. Columbia Law Review, 105, 1315-1350.

Brodbeck, F., Kerschreiter, R., Mojzisch, A., Frey, D., & Schulz-Hardt, S. (2002). The dissemination of critical, unshared information in decision-making groups: The effects of pre-discussion dissent. European Journal of Social Psychology, 32 (1), 35-56.

Bureau of Labor Statistics (2005). Occupational Outlook Handbook. <http://www.bls.gov/oco/ocos170.htm#earnings> (2005).

Bureau of Labor Statistics (2010). Occupational employment statistics: May 2010 national occupational employment and wage estimates. <http://www.bls.gov/oes/current/oes_nat.htm> (2011).

Burger, J. M. (2009). Replicating Milgram: Would people still obey today? American Psychologist, 64, 1-11.

Caiden, G. E. (1991). What really is public maladministration? Public Administration Review, 51 (6), 486-494.

Cann, A. (2004). Rated importance of personal qualities across four relationships. The Journal of Social Psychology, 144 (3), 322-335.

Castillo, R., & Nigh, R. (1998). Global processes and local identity among Mayan coffee growers in Chiapas, Mexico. American Anthropologist: New Series, 100 (1), 136-147.

Chambers, H. (2004). My Way or the Highway. San Francisco, CA: Berrett Koehler Publishers.

Chan, A., & Smith, K. (2001). Perceived marital quality and stability of intermarried couples. Sociological Imagination, 37, 230-256.

Choi, H. S., & Levine, J. M. (2004). Minority influence in work teams: the impact of newcomers. Journal of Experimental Social Psychology, 40, 273-280.

Costin, R. (2007, April 20). Fast food history. <http://referat.clopotel.ro/Fast_food_history-12767.html> (2008).

Conroy, S., & Emerson, T. (2004). Business ethics and religion: religiosity as a predictor of ethical awareness among students. Journal of Business Ethics, 50 (4), 383-396.

Correll, S. J., & Benard, S. (2005, August 15). Getting a job: Is there a motherhood penalty? Presented at the American Sociological Association's 100th annual meeting, Philadelphia, PA.

Correll, S. J., & Ridgeway, C. L. (2003). Expectation states theory. In J. Delamater (Ed.), Handbook of social psychology and social research (pp. 29-51). New York, NY: Kluwer Academic/Plenum.

Davis, M. H., Morris, M. M., & Kraus, L. A. (1998). Relationship-specific and global perceptions of social support: Associations with well-being and attachment. Journal of Personality and Social Psychology, 74, 468-481.

De Dreu, C., & West, M. (2001). Minority dissent and team innovation: The importance of participation in decision making. Journal of Applied Psychology, 86 (6), 1191-1201.

Ducharme, L. J., & Martin, J. K. (2000). Unrewarding work, coworker support, and job satisfaction. Work and Occupations, 27 (2), 223-243.

Egawa, S., Ito, A., Kokubo, Y., Ishiguro, D., Boozel, K., Osakada, M., & Ogawa, N. (2007). Who's really running the show? <http://www.winadvisorygroup.com/Who'sReallyRunningShow.html> (2007).

Essed, P. (2002). Cloning cultural homogeneity while talking diversity: Old wine in new bottles in Dutch organizations. Transforming Anthropology, 11 (1), 2-12.

Estrada, M., Brown, J., & Lee, F. (1995). Who gets the credit? Small Group Research, 26 (1), 56-76.

FBI (U.S. Dept. of Justice, Federal Investigation Bureau). (2010). Uniform crime reports: Hate crime statistics 2010. <http://www.fbi.gov/about-us/cjis/ucr/hate-crime/2010/narratives/hate-crime-2010-victims> (2011).

Finlayson, A. (Ed.). (2003). Contemporary political thought: A reader and guide. Edinburgh: Edinburgh University Press.

Fox News Network (2008, June 6). Video of gruesome hit-and-run released by Connecticut police. <http://www.foxnews.com/story/0,2933,363493,00.html> (2008).

Gallup, Inc. (2006, October 12). Gallup study: Engaged employees inspire company innovation. Gallup Management Journal. <http://gmj.gallup.com/content/24880/Gallup-Study-Engaged-Employees-Inspire-Company.aspx> (2008).

Garfinkle, H. (1967). Studies in ethnomethodology. Englewood Cliffs, NJ: Prentice-Hall.

Granovetter, M. (1983). The strength of weak ties: A network theory revisited. Sociological Theory, 1, 201-233.

Hagman, J. D., & Hayes, J. F. (1986). Cooperative learning: effects of task, reward, and group size in individual achievement. Report for the Army Research Institute for the Behavioral and Social Sciences, Alexandria, VA. <http://www.storming-media.us/82/8283/A828371.html> (2008).

Hamon, R. R., & Ingoldsby, B. B. (2003). Mate Selection Across Cultures. Thousand Oaks, CA: Sage.

Hauge, L. J., Skogstad, A., & Einarsen, S. (2007). Relationships between stressful work environments and bullying: Results of a large representative study. Work & Stress, 21 (3), 220-242.

Heaton, T. B., & Pratt, E. L. (1990). The effects of religious homogamy on marital satisfaction and stability. Journal of Family Issues, 11 (2), 191-207.

Hersh, S. M. (2004, May 10). Torture at Abu Ghraib. The New Yorker. <http://www.newyorker.com/archive/2004/05/10/040510fa_fact?currentPage=all> (2008).

Hochschild, A. (1983). The managed heart: The commercialization of human feeling. Berkeley, CA: The University of California Press.

Hogh, A., Henriksson, M. E., & Burr, H. (2005). A 5-year follow-up study of aggression at work and psychological health. International Journal of Behavioral Medicine, 12 (4), 256-265.

Hollander, E. P. (2004, December 6). Leadership perspectives: influence, inclusion, and idiosyncrasy credit. Speech delivered at the New York Academy of Sciences. <http://www.nyas.org/events/eventDetail.asp?eventID=2256&date=12/6/2004%207:15:00%20PM> (2008).

Hollander, E. P. (1958). Conformity, status, and idiosyncrasy credit. Psychological Review, 65, 117-127.

Huang, X., & Van de Vliert, E. (2003). Where intrinsic job satisfaction fails to work: National moderators of intrinsic motivation. Journal of Organizational Behavior, 24 (2), 159-179.

Idson, T. L. (1990). Establishment size, job satisfaction and the structure of work. Applied Economics, 22 (8), 1007-1018.

Jamal, M. (2004). Burnout, stress, and health of employees on non-standard work schedules: A study of Canadian workers. Stress & Health: Journal of the International Society for the Investigation of Stress, 20 (3), 113-119.

James, E. H. (2000). Race-related differences in promotions and support: Underlying effects of human and social capital. Organization Science, 11, 5, 493-508.

Janis, I. (1972). Victims of groupthink. Boston, MA: Houghton-Mifflin.

Janssen, O. (2003). Innovative behavior and job involvement at the price of conflict and less satisfactory relations with co-workers. Journal of Occupational and Organizational Psychology, 76 (3), 347-364.

Japan Echo (1998, July 31). Record unemployment: A cloud of anxiety looms over Japan's work force. Trends in Japan. <http://web-japan.org/trends98/honbun/ntj980730.html> (2008).

Kana'iaupuni, S., Donato, K., Thompson-Colon, T., & Stainback, M. (2005). Counting on kin: social networks, social support, and child health. Social Forces, 83 (3), 1137-1165.

Kemelgor, B. H. (2007). Job satisfaction as mediated by the value congruity of supervisors and their subordinates. Journal of Organizational Behavior, 3 (2), 147-160.

Kerr, N. L., & Bruun, S. E. (1983). Dispensability of member effort and group motivation losses: Free-rider effects. Journal of Personality and Social Psychology, 44, 78-94.

Khondker, H. H. (2004). Glocalization as globalization: Evolution of a sociological concept. Bangladesh e-Journal of Sociology, 1 (2), 1-8.

Kinjerski, V., & Skrypnek, B. J. (2008). Four paths to spirit at work: Journeys of personal meaning, fulfillment, well-being, and transcendence through work. Career Development Quarterly, 56 (4), 319-329.

Kiser, L., Bennet, L., Heston, J., & Paavola, M. (2005). Family ritual and routine: comparison of clinical and non-clinical families. Journal of Child & Family Studies, 14 (3), 357-372.

Kleinfeld, J. (2002). The small world problem. Society, 39 (2), 61-66.

Kuntzman, G. (2001, October 1). Thugs are people, too. Newsweek: American Beat. <http://www.msnbc.com/news/636423.asp> (2001).

Latane, B., & Darley, J. (1968). Group inhibition of bystander intervention in emergencies. Journal of Personality and Social Psychology, 10, 215-221.

Laughlin, P., Hatch, E., Silver, J., & Boh, L. (2006). Groups perform better than the best individuals on letters-to-numbers problems: Effects of group size. Journal of Personality and Social Psychology, 90 (4), 644-651.

Lincoln, J. R., & Miller, J. (1979). Work and friendship ties in organizations: A comparative analysis of relational networks. Administrative Science Quarterly, 24, 181-199.

Lortie-Lussier, M. (1987). Minority influence and idiosyncrasy credit: a new comparison of the Moscovici and Hollander theories of innovation. European Journal of Social Psychology, 17 (4), 431-446.

McFarland, D., & Pals, H. (2005). Motives and contexts of identity change: A case for network effects. Social Psychology Quarterly, 68 (4), 289-315.

McGuire, G. M. (2002). Gender, race, and the shadow structure. Gender & Society, 16 (3), 303-322.

Meir, E., Hadasi, C., & Noyfeld, M. (1997). Person-environment fit in small army units. Journal of Career Assessment, 5 (1), 21-29.

Milgram, S. (1967). The small-world problem. Psychology Today, 61-67.

Milgram, S. (1963). Behavioral study of obedience. Journal of Abnormal and Social Psychology, 67, 371–378.

Mills, C. W. (1956). The power elite. New York: Oxford University Press.

Moreland, R., Argote, L., & Krishnan, R. (1996). Socially shared cognition at work: Transactive memory and group performance. In J. Nye & A. Brower (Eds.), What's social about social cognition? Research on socially shared cognition in small groups (pp. 57-84). Thousand Oaks, CA: Sage.

Mouritzen, P. E. (2006). City size and citizens' satisfaction: two competing theories revisited. European Journal of Political Research, 17 (6), 661-688.

Mullen, B., Johnson, C., & Salas, E. (1991). Productivity loss in brainstorming groups: A meta-analysis. Basic and Applied Social Psychology, 12, 3-23.

Nath, P., Borkowski, J., Whitman, T., & Schellenbach, C. (1991). Understanding adolescent parenting: The dimensions and functions of social support. Family Relations, 40 (4), 411-420.

National Statistics (2007, October 24). Variations persist in life expectancy by social class. National Statistics: News Release. <http://www.statistics.gov.uk/pdfdir/le1007.pdf> (2008).

Ng, K. Y., & Dyne, L. V. (2001). Individualism-collectivism as a boundary condition for effectiveness of minority influence in decision making. Organizational Behavior and Human Decision Processes, 84 (2), 198-225.

Nemeth, C. J., & Kwan, J. L. (1987). Minority influence, divergent thinking, and detection of correct solutions. Journal of Applied Social Psychology, 17, 788-799.

Pachana, N. A., Ford, J. H., Andrew, B., & Dobson, A. J. (2005). Relations between companion animals and self-reported health in older women: Cause, effect, or artifact? International Journal of Behavioral Medicine, 12 (2), 103-110.

Parks, B. (2006, December 11). McDonald's and global marketing. <http://www.bizcovering.com/Marketing-and-Advertising/McDonalds-and-Global-Marketing.26899> (2008).

Perrone, K. M., & Sedlacek, W. E. (2000). A comparison of group cohesiveness and client satisfaction in homogenous and heterogenous groups. The Journal for Specialists in Group Work, 25 (3), 243-251.

Petersen, L., & Dietz, J. (2006). Prejudice and enforcement of workforce homogeneity as explanations for employment discrimination. Journal of Applied Social Psychology, 35 (1), 144-159.

Pollan, M. (2006). The omnivore's dilemma: A natural history of four meals. New York, NY: Penguin Press.

Pollard, J. A., & Hawkins, J. D. (1999). Risk and protection: Are both necessary to understand diverse behavioral outcomes in adolescence? Social Work Research, 23 (3), 145-158.

Pousette, A., & Johansson, H. (2002). Job characteristics as predictors of ill-health and sickness absenteeism in different occupational types: A multigroup structural equation modeling approach. Work & Stress, 16 (3), 229-250.

Powell, D., & Butterfield, A. (1997). Effect of race on promotions to top management in a federal department. Academy of Management Journal, 40, 1, 112-128.

Quigley, A. (2003, April 9). Social support at work protects the heart. Health Behavior News Service. <http://www.hbns.org/news/support04-09-03.cfm> (2008).

Rawlins, W. K. (1992). Friendship matters: Communication, dialectics, and the life course. New York, NY: Aldine de Gruyter.

Ritzer, G. (2003). Rethinking globalization: Glocalization/grobalization and something/nothing. Sociological Theory, 21 (3), 193-209.

Ritzer, G. (2000). The McDonaldization of society: An investigation into the changing character of contemporary social life. Thousand Oaks, CA: Pine Forge Press.

Robertson, R. (1994). Globalisation or glocalisation?, The Journal of International Communication 1(1), 33–52.

Rosenthal, R., & Jacobson, L. (1968). Pygmalion in the classroom: Teacher expectation and pupils' intellectual development. New York: Rinehart and Winston.

Ruef, M. (2002). Strong ties, weak ties, and islands: structural and cultural predictors of organizational innovation. Industrial and Corporate Change, 11 (3), 427-449.

Sanders, J. (2002). Ethnic boundaries and identity in plural societies. Annual Review of Sociology, 28, 327-357.

Sherif, M., Harvey, O. J., White, J., Hood, W., & Sherif, C. W. (1961). Intergroup conflict and cooperation: The robber's cave experiment. Norman, OK: Institute of Intergroup Relations, University of Oklahoma.

Sias, P. M., & Cahill, D. J. (1998). From coworkers to friends: The development of peer friendships in the workplace. Western Journal of Communication, 62 (3), 273-300.

State of the Union Address (2002, January 29). President delivers state of the union address. <http://www.whitehouse.gov/news/releases/2002/01/20020129-11.html> (2008).

Terpstra, D. E., & Honoree, A. L. (2004). Job satisfaction and pay satisfaction levels of university faculty by discipline type and by geographic region. Education. <http://findarticles.com/p/articles/mi_qa3673/is_200404/ai_n9345191> (2008).

The Economist (2007, November 29). Business in Japan: Special report: Going hybrid. <http://www.economist.com/specialreports/displayStory.cfm?story_id=10169956> (2008).

Tian, X., & Pu, Y. (2008). An artificial neural network approach to hotel employee satisfaction: The case of China. Social Behavior & Personality: An International Journal, 36 (4), 467-482.

Tschanh, F., Sylvie, R., & Dieter, Z. (2005). It's not only clients: Studying emotion work with clients and co-workers with an event-sampling approach. Journal of Occupational & Organizational Psychology, 78 (2), 195-220.

Vaillant, G. E. (2002). Adaptive mental mechanisms: Their role in positive psychology. American Psychologist, 55, 89-98.

Valacich, J. S., Dennis, A. R., & Nunamaker, J. F. Jr. (1992). Group size and anonymity effects on computer-mediated idea generation. Small Group Research, 23 (1), 49-73.

Walther, E., Bless, H., Fritz, S., Rackstraw, P., Wagner, D., & Werth, L. (2002). Conformity effects in memory as a function of group size, dissenters and uncertainty. Applied Cognitive Psychology, 16 (7), 793-810.

Weber, M. (1947). The theory of social and economic organization. (A. M. Henderson & T. Parsons, Trans.). Glencoe, IL: Free Press.

Weber, M. (1946). Types of authority. In H. H. Gerth & C. W. Mills (Eds.), Max Weber: Essays in sociology (pp. 224-229). New York, NY: Oxford University Press.

West, W. F. (2005). Neutral competence and political responsiveness: An uneasy relationship. Policy Studies Journal, 33 (2), 147-161.

Charthouse Learning (2008). What is Fish! <http://www.charthouse.com/content.aspx?nodeid=1066> (2008).

Wicks, J. (2006). Local living economies: The new movement for responsible business. <http://www.vtcommons.org/journal/2006/02/judy-wicks-local-living-economies-new-movement-responsible-business> (2006).

Wills, T. A., & Fegan, M. (2001). Social networks and social support. In A. Baum, T. A. Revenson, & J. E. Singer (Eds.), Handbook of health psychology (pp. 209-234). Mahwah, NJ: Erlbaum.

Wisconsin Historical Society (2008). Roadside Highlight: White Tower Hamburgers. Wisconsin History Explorer. <http://www.wisconsinhistory.org/archstories/restaurants/fast_food.asp> (2008).

Wood, C. (2008, June 19). Eat for the environment: Take charge, and start to live life in the slow lane. Pharmacy News, 34.

Workman, D. (2008, March 4). Japanese corporate culture: Japan's business model and project management approach. <http://globalization.suite101.com/article.cfm/japanese_corporate_culture> (2008).

Zapf, D., Seifert, C., Schmutte, B., Mertini, H., & Holz, M. (2001). Emotion work and job stressors and their effects on burnout. Psychology & Health, 16 (5), 527-546.

Zimbardo, P. G. (1972). Pathology of imprisonment. Society, 9 (6), 4-8.

CHAPTER SIX

# Deviance and Social Control

## Sally A. Stablein

---

**Chapter Objectives**
At the end of this chapter, students should be able to:

- Define and explain basic terms and concepts related to deviancy.
- Define the relationship between social norms and deviant behavior.
- Identify the major theories of deviance.
- Identify theoretical concepts related to the control and identification of deviancy.
- Analyze the historical course of deviancy from a global context.
- Differentiate between the cultural universals regarding deviance and culturally determined definitions of deviant behavior.
- Objectively analyze personal attitudes and beliefs regarding various deviancies.
- Categorize and explain recognized forms of social deviance.
- Describe society's changing solutions to the problems of deviance, analyze them, and propose alternatives.

---

This chapter defines deviance and deviant behavior, and explores deviance from several theoretical perspectives. Criminal behavior, crime and punishment also will be covered. An important point to take away from this chapter is that individuals convicted of wrong-doing don't always fit the common stereotype of a street criminal.

## What is Deviance?

When asked to describe deviant behavior, most people have a vision of what a deviant person looks or acts like. They may assume that a deviant is someone who breaks the law and goes to prison. But this is not always the case. In his classic 1965 study, sociologist Jerry L. Simmons asked a sampling of people to describe examples of deviance. The replies were many and varied. Respondents listed 252 kinds of people, including prostitutes, homosexuals, alcoholics, drug addicts, murderers, the mentally ill, Communists, atheists, liars, Democrats, Republicans, reckless drivers, retirees, career women, divorcees, Christians, suburbanites, movie stars, perpetual bridge players, prudes, pacifists, psychiatrists, priests, girls who wear makeup, smart-aleck students—and know-it-all professors.

The point is, deviance is not easy to define, and there is a lack of consensus as to what constitutes deviant behavior.

## How Do Sociologists Define Deviance?

Deviance is a behavior that violates the standards of conduct or expectations of a group or a society (Wickman, 1991). From a sociological perspective, **deviance** can be anything that violates a cultural norm and elicits a reaction.

This straightforward definition can be deceiving as it is difficult for an entire society to agree on what deviant behavior is, and it takes us to the heart of the sociological perspective on deviance, which sociologist Howard S. Becker (1966), described this way: "It's not the act itself, but rather the reactions to the act, that make something deviant."

Deviant behavior is not set in stone; rather, it is subject to social definition within a particular society at a particular time. This means the term is neutral, not a judgment about behavior. It is a relative concept, meaning different groups have different norms, and because of this, deviance varies by culture, gender, social class, race, ethnicity and historical context.

Consider tattoos. They vary greatly from culture to culture. History shows us that tattoos spread across many cultures, including the world's ancient cultures and historical eras. Christian Europe portrayed tattooing as deviant or pagan behavior. This belief was likely based on the Bible: "Ye shall not make any cuttings in your flesh for the dead, nor

print any marks upon you: I *am* the Lord" (Leviticus 19:28). Captain James Cook's voyages in Polynesia began a tradition of tattooing in the British navy, which likely spread from port to port. And, up until the late 20th century, tattoos flourished only among enlisted members of the military, criminals and circus performers. They were considered socially deviant or part of lower-class culture.

Now, however, tattoos are extremely popular, particularly in North America, Japan and Europe. What was once considered deviant by mainstream society has been relabeled as non-deviant in many cultures. This is referred to as **tertiary deviance**. People with tattoos consider them artwork that represents something permanent and unique. Many people articulate becoming tattooed at a point in their lives when they were undergoing personal growth or transformation, and their tattoos provide a feeling of empowerment. It is common among tattooed people to view their tattoos as *psychic armor,* fortifying their mind or spirit, reinforcing their image of themselves. This is a common historical theme drawn from so-called primitive cultures, as is the adoption of tribal designs as representations of spiritualism or amulets as protection in warrior cultures (Wiley, 1997; Designboom, 2008).

But tattoos are still considered deviant by many. Tattooing for women, in particular, can carry social stigmas above and beyond what men may experience. When a woman has a tattoo on her lower back, it is commonly referred to by the slang term "tramp stamp" (Ross & Lester, 2011). Yet, as the popularity of tattooing increases, its association with deviance may begin to fade, since it is becoming more of a cultural norm rather than a violation of what people expect to see in everyday life.

What is normal, though? Most societies define normal by what is standard within their culture. For example, in most of the United States, men may walk down the street without their shirts on, but women cannot do so because it goes against our cultural norms. Norms dictate social life. Without norms, there would be chaos. They also lay out the basic guidelines for how we should fulfill our roles and interact with others. Basically, norms bring about **social order**, and social order is necessary in all societies. Our lives of "normal" behavior are dependent on social arrangements, which is why deviance is so threatening. Deviance undermines predictability, the foundation of social life. Human groups develop a system of social control, as well, with formal and informal means of enforcing norms by using social control, which will be discussed later in this chapter.

## Sanctions

**Sanctions** promote conformity and discourage nonconformity. A sanction may be defined as any formal or informal reaction to an individual or group behavior that breaks a particular norm. A *positive sanction* rewards people for positive behavior, such as getting a good grade on a sociology exam or perhaps a raise from a job. *Negative sanctions* could be failing an exam or getting fired.

## Who or What is Deviant?

Sociologists believe that all people are deviants since everyone violates rules from time to time. In sociology, the term "deviance" refers to all violations of social rules, regardless of their seriousness, from committing a faux pas to exhibiting criminal behavior.

Speeding is breaking the law and may result in a speeding ticket, a negative sanction. But in some locations, speeding is considered the norm, and people may receive negative sanctions from other drivers who wonder why they are driving so slowly. As discussed previously, deviance is often in the eye of the beholder. Nothing is inherently deviant.

*Do your own experiment for fun*
Do something harmless that is against the social norms. Violate a folkway, such as wearing fingernail polish if you're a man, wearing a shirt inside out or giving a full-blown reply to the question, "How are you?"

How would this woman have been viewed in the 1950s?

Source: John Ramspott

## Explanations of Deviance: Sociobiology, Psychology and Sociology

### Sociobiology

Sociobiology focuses on genetic predispositions. A century ago, most people understood or, more correctly, misunderstood human behavior to be the result of biological instincts. Early interest in criminality focused on biological causes. In 1876, Cesare Lombroso, an Italian physician who worked in prisons, theorized that criminals exhibited such physical traits as low foreheads, prominent jaws and cheekbones, big ears, lots of body hair and unusually long arms. It was alleged that people with these characteristics were more likely to commit crimes. In the middle of the 20th century, William Sheldon also suggested that body structure might predict criminal behavior (Sheldon, Hartl, & McDermott, 1949). He cross-checked hundreds of young men for body type and criminal history and concluded that criminal behavior was most likely among boys with square, muscular, athletic builds. Sheldon Glueck and Eleanor Glueck (1950) confirmed Sheldon's conclusion but warned that a powerful build does not necessarily cause criminal behavior. Rather, parents tend to be somewhat distant from their powerfully built sons, who, in turn, show less sensitivity toward others when they grow up.

Today, genetic research seeks possible links between biology and crime. In 2003, a scientist at the University of Wisconsin reported the results of a 25-year study based on 400 boys. Researchers had collected DNA samples from each boy and noted any trouble they had with the law. The researchers concluded that genetic factors, especially defective genes that make too much of an enzyme, together with environmental factors, especially abuse early in life, were strong predictors of adult crime and violence. They noted that these two factors combined were better predictors than either one alone (Lemonick, 2003; Pinker, 2003).

## Psychology

Psychological explanations of deviant behavior focus on mental disorders, personality disorders and individual abnormalities. Some traits are certainly hereditary, but most psychologists believe personality is shaped by social experience. Classic research by Walter Reckless and Simon Dinitz (1967) illustrates the psychological approach. These two researchers asked several teachers to categorize 12-year-old male students as either likely or unlikely to get into trouble with the law. They then interviewed the boys and their mothers to assess how the boys felt about themselves (self-concept) and how they related to others. Analyzing the results, the researchers found that the "good boys" had a strong consciousness, what Freud would refer to as the "superego," and could handle frustration, and identify with cultural norms and values. The "bad boys" had a weaker consciousness, displayed little tolerance for frustration and felt out of place in conventional culture. The "good boys" went on to lead successful lives and had fewer run-ins with the law than the "bad boys."

As Dan Kindlon and Michael Thompson (2000) point out in their best-selling book, *Raising Cain*, there are no simple answers when it comes to the nature-versus-nurture debate. The authors point out

that multiple forces, from biology to community, influence every behavior. Both the biological and psychological views refer to deviance as a trait of the individual, but current research puts far greater emphasis on social influences than genetics and personality. As a matter of fact, the research is so strong that more and more criminology majors and people in the criminal justice field are taking sociology courses to try to understand why people behave the way they do.

## Sociology

Sociologists focus on outside factors, such as social background, peers and schools, which contribute to deviant behavior, and they believe that deviance is a learned behavior. There are reasons, sociologists say, why rules are broken or someone acts out. **Criminology** is a branch of sociology; criminologists study the causes of criminal behavior by looking at social structure.

Again, deviance varies according to cultural norms. For example, in the United States, drug use is considered deviant behavior. Vast amounts of time and money have been spent on the war on drugs, and there are serious consequences and negative sanctions for people who use and deal them. A large part of our recent prison population has been incarcerated for drug offenses rather than violent crimes such as rape, murder, and armed robbery. Eric Schlosser (2004) points out in his controversial book *Reefer Madness* that in some cases, people spend more time in jails and prisons for drug offenses than for violent crimes.

But in Amsterdam, drug laws are quite different. This Dutch capital boasts cafés that sell marijuana and hashish. Consumers enter, purchase a cup of coffee and a marijuana cigarette, then sit back and smoke, listen to music, and perhaps play some backgammon or chess, without fear of getting arrested (Pauker, 2006).

The United States, on the other hand, has arrested even people who use marijuana for medicinal reasons. The enforcement of state and federal laws regarding marijuana serves to guide its production and set the punishments for its users, suggesting the arbitrary nature of many cultural taboos. Americans not only imprison more people for marijuana but also smoke more marijuana than any other Western industrialized nation (Schlosser, 2004).

As you can see, laws are defined differently in different geographical locations. Some may suggest that the U.S. war against drugs is repressive and hypocritical, while others believe that Amsterdam's coffee shops are atrocious and lack moral character. Since those who devise our laws often define deviance, these relative definitions become part of our cultural norms.

Denver became the first city in the nation to make the private use of marijuana legal for adults age 21 and older. Will it become the norm for Colorado residents to see legal marijuana shops in metropolitan areas? Only time will tell.

# The Functionalist Perspective on Deviance

## Durkheim's Functionalist Theory

The key insight of the functional approach is that deviance is a necessary part of the structure of society. This point was made a century ago by French sociologist Emile Durkheim (1893), who suggested that there is nothing abnormal about deviant behavior and that it contributes to social order. He said that deviance performs four essential functions:

1. *Affirms cultural values and norms.* Without deviance, how do we know what is good or evil? There can be no good without evil and no justice without crime. Deviance is needed to define and support morality.
2. *Promotes social unity.* People typically react to serious deviance with shared outrage. A nation can react to deviant behavior and integrate, just as we saw after the attacks on September 11, 2001. In doing so, they reaffirm the moral ties that bind them.
3. *Clarifies moral boundaries.* By defining some individuals as deviant, people tend to draw a boundary between right and wrong. Punishing deviance affirms the groups' norms and clarifies

what is projected to be a member of said groups.

4. *Promotes social change.* Deviant people push a society's moral boundaries, suggesting alternatives and encouraging change. For example, rock-n-roll music was considered immoral in the 1950s but has since become a multibillion-dollar industry. In the 1950s, Elvis Presley was thought of as deviant for the way he moved his pelvis while performing. Today, he is considered tame compared with Marilyn Manson or Lady Gaga.

## Robert Merton's Strain Theory

Robert Merton used Durkheim's concept of **anomie**, a social condition in which norms and values are conflicting, weak or absent, to support his **strain theory**. According to Merton, while some deviance may be necessary for a society to function, too much deviance can result from specific social arrangements or flaws within the social structure. The kind of deviance that results depends on whether a society provides the means or opportunities to achieve **cultural goals**, such as financial success.

Merton (1968) suggests that some people feel more strain and frustration than others, due to their social location and unequal access to the institutional or conventional means to achieve cultural goals. Everyone in the United States, for example, is socialized with the idea of achieving the American Dream. But if people can't achieve that dream by legitimate means and mainstream norms, they may attempt to achieve it illegally. Social class and location within the social structure may determine what kind of illegitimate opportunities are available.

Merton (1968) presented five modes of adaptation to classify where individuals fit into the continuum of adopting cultural values.

Merton's first mode of adoption is **conformity**—using socially acceptable means to reach cultural goals. This category probably includes most of us. In industrialized societies, the majority of people will try to get an education and good jobs. If the economy is poor, and people cannot find higher-

**TABLE 6.1** Merton's Five Modes of Adaptation

| Mode of Adaptation | Cultural Goals | Institutional Means |
|---|---|---|
| Conformity | Accept | Accept |
| Innovation | Accept | Reject |
| Ritualism | Reject | Accept |
| Retreatism | Reject | Reject |
| Rebellion | Reject/Replace | Reject/Replace |

paying jobs, they often are willing to take less desirable positions. If students are denied access to Ivy League schools, they will likely go to less reputable schools. If people cannot take time off work during the day to attend school, they often will attend classes at night or online, or go to vocational schools. Overall, most people take the socially acceptable road to success.

*Innovation* occurs when a person accepts the cultural goals of society but rejects or lacks the socially legitimate means to achieve those goals. Drug dealers, for example, accept the idea of achieving wealth but reject the legitimate processes to achieving it. Thus, innovation is the mode of adaptation most associated with criminal behavior.

*Ritualism* involves following the rules. Ritualists are people who become discouraged and often give up on advancing in society; instead, they survive by following the regulations of their jobs. People using this mode of adaptation reject cultural goals but accept institutional means. They play by the rules of conventional conduct. An example of a ritualist may be a teacher who becomes disillusioned with teaching but, rather than change the situation, remains in the classroom where he or she continues to teach without enthusiasm. There are many examples of people who become burned out but stay in their jobs. This is considered deviant behavior because they have abandoned their dreams and goals.

*Retreatism* involves rejecting both cultural goals, such as success, and the institutionally legitimate means to achieve them. Retreatists withdraw from society, by way of alcohol or drugs, for example. Retreatists commonly stop trying to act as if they

share society's goals.

The final mode is *rebellion*. Like retreatists, rebels reject cultural goals and the socially legitimate means to achieve them. Unlike retreatists, however, rebels seek to replace existing goals and means with new ones. As an example, rebels may use political activism as a means to replace the goal of personal wealth with the goal of social justice. Revolutionaries are the most common type of rebels.

## Opportunity Theory

Sociologists Richard Cloward and Lloyd Ohlin (1966) theorized the existence of a criminal subculture that offered illegal opportunities and called it an **illegitimate opportunity structure**. To them, crime was not simply the result of limited legitimate (legal) opportunities, but also the result of readily accessible illegitimate (illegal) opportunities. Deviance or conformity arises from the relative opportunity structure that frames a person's life.

The 2007 film *American Gangster* is based on the life of Frank Lucas, who grew up facing the barriers of poverty and racial prejudice that lowered his odds of being successful in conventional terms. Not only was Lucas poor, but he also grew up in a time of violence against African Americans. He witnessed his 12-year-old cousin's murder at the hands of the Ku Klux Klan, apparently for simply looking at a white woman. Lucas led a life of petty crime, stealing to help feed his family, and one day he got in a fight with a former employer. He left the South for New York City. He began stealing to survive and eventually teamed up with notorious Harlem gangster Bumpy Johnson. Lucas started importing illegal drugs into the United States.

Lucas' actions are neither justifiable nor acceptable; however, by applying opportunity theory to his life, we can get a better picture as to why he made the choices he did. People do things for reasons, whether right or wrong, and sociologists are interested in understanding those reasons. In the film, Lucas (played by Denzel Washington) asks the rhetorical question, "Do you want to be a somebody or a nobody?" Lucas clearly wanted to be a "somebody," and he achieved that through illegitimate means. Lucas did not have access to **institutional means**, such as education and access to a well-paying job, so he achieved those cultural goals by using illegitimate means. Just imagine what Lucas could have accomplished or who he could have become with a business degree.

## Control Theory

**Control theory** proposes that a society's values, norms, and beliefs cause them not to deviate or break the law. People who have not been socialized will not have internalized the values and norms of society, and their actions won't be limited to those that are legal or legitimate.

Sociologist Walter Reckless (1973) developed **containment theory**, which is based on control theory and focuses on a strong self-image as a means of defending against negative peer pressure. This theory suggests that we have two control systems: inner containment (positive sense of self) and outer containment (supervision and discipline). Each of us is propelled toward deviance, but our inner and outer controls keep us from actually deviating. Our inner controls include morality, conscience, religious beliefs, and ideas of right and wrong. Inner controls also include fear of **punishment**, integrity and the desire to be a "good" person (Hirschi, 1969; Rogers, 1977; Baron, 2001). Our outer controls consist of people who cause us not to deviate, such as family, friends and police officers.

Control theory suggests that the stronger our bonds to society—for example, our commitment to legitimate opportunity, respect for authority and involvement in jobs, clubs, or sports—the more likely we are to conform to societal norms. On the other hand, people with weak social bonds are more likely to deviate from social norms. Bonds are based on attachments and commitments. People also may have a status in society that they don't want to jeopardize, such as a respected place in their families, communities, workplaces or schools.

Let's apply control theory to "Howard." Howard was recently released from prison and was told he could complete his parole in a halfway house in the city where he was arrested. Howard was dropped off by the Department of Corrections with $100 to his name. It was his responsibility to find a job and pay for his basic necessities, including his stay at the halfway house, but he was having a difficult time with this process. No one wanted to hire him because he was a convicted felon. Time was running out, and feelings of hopelessness were setting in. He soon met up with some old friends and decided to participate in some criminal activity.

If he doesn't get caught, he will have the money to meet his needs. But if he is caught, Howard will go back to prison. At this point, does Howard have a strong bond with society? What are his risks? What are society's risks?

You can see how someone in Howard's circumstances might take the risk and commit the crime versus someone in a college classroom, who has much more to lose if caught. Howard's criminal behavior is unwarranted, but it's clear why he makes this decision. Howard doesn't have a strong bond with society, so he is willing to take the risk.

# Conflict Theory

Conflict theory suggests that individuals or groups who have power over others can impose rules with which to construct social order. From a conflict perspective, all of the major institutions, laws and traditions of a society serve to support those in power. Laws are an instrument of oppression used to maintain power and privilege, which the ruling class, through the **criminal justice system**, use to punish the poor. Conflict theory links deviance to social inequality.

The group in power may be referred to as the **capital class** because it owns the capital (money) and does not need to sell its labor. Most prison inmates fit into the **marginal working class** category. This class consists of a group of people with modest skills and little job security and who are frequently unemployed. Often desperate, these people commit street crimes and/or have severe drug problems, and because their crime or behaviors threaten the social order, they end up being punished.

According to conflict theorists, the idea that the law operates impartially, treating people in a fair manner, is a myth promoted by the capital class. Conflict theorists see the law as an instrument of oppression designed to maintain the powerful in their privileged position. Conflict theorists suggest that the criminal justice system does not focus on the owners of corporations and the harm they do through pollution, unsafe products and poor working conditions because the system's purpose is to protect those in power. When the working classes rebel, social order is threatened, and they are imprisoned.

# Feminist Theory

Most theories about deviance take for granted that they apply to both sexes. Feminist theorists disagree. They argue that conventional theories of deviance describe men and are valid for men but not applicable to or valid for women. Feminist theorists also believe that the status of women as victims and offenders reflects the continuing subordination of women in a patriarchal society. Feminist theorists explain that in a patriarchal society, men and women have been socialized differently and, therefore, different deviant acts and behavior result. For example, more men are involved in violent criminal behavior in comparison to women, who tend to commit crimes that are less violent, such as forgery or embezzling from their places of employment.

# The Symbolic Interactionist Perspective

As we examine symbolic interactionism, it will become clearer why sociologists are not completely satisfied with theories of biology and personality. Symbolic interactionists emphasize our social environments and how our associations explain quite a lot about whether we will deviate or conform al norms.

## Differential Association Theory

Contrary to theories built around genetics, sociologists believe deviance is a learned behavior. Edwin Sutherland (1947) coined the term **differential association** to indicate that we learn to deviate or conform to society's norms based on the groups with whom we associate. This theory contradicts the view that deviance is biological or psychological. Humans are essentially social and need to feel a sense of belonging. Membership in groups, especially peer groups, is a primary way through which people meet this need.

Have your peer groups ever influenced you to engage in deviant behavior?

Eric Harris and Dylan Klebold, the two teens who committed the Columbine High School shootings in Colorado in 1999, most likely would not have committed the atrocities without one another. It could be said that differential association is one theory to apply to the boys' violent acts.

Families have a significant impact on the behavior of children. Providing a safe and caring environment typically falls to parents and other family members. At least until children begin school, the family has the important job of teaching them skills, values and beliefs. Research suggests that nothing is more likely to produce a happy, well-adjusted child than growing up in a loving family (Kindlon & Thompson, 2000).

Friends, neighborhoods and subcultures also influence and shape individuals. When children start school, they are exposed to groups that influence their behavior positively and negatively. Location will also have a significant impact on what opportunities are available.

## Labeling Theory

**Labeling theory** is a viewpoint developed by symbolic interactionists which holds that the labels people are given affect their own and others' perceptions of them. This theory focuses on how labels funnel people into or away from deviance. People who commit deviant acts often use **techniques of neutralization** to continue to think of themselves as law-abiding citizens.

Labeling theory does not focus on why some individuals resort to committing deviant acts. Instead, it attempts to explain why certain people are viewed as deviants, delinquents, bad kids, losers or criminals, while others exhibiting similar behaviors are not. Labeling theory emphasizes how a person labeled as deviant will then accept that label. Sociologist Howard Becker (1966) summed it up with this statement: "Deviant behavior is behavior that people so label."

How do certain behaviors come to be seen as a problem? Take smoking cigarettes. At one time, smoking was admired and considered attractive. On film, actors and actresses were seen smoking constantly, and cigarettes were considered eye-catching to the public. Today, however, most people view smoking as deviant behavior. What are your thoughts when you see a driver with a lit cigarette and a child in the car? This scene was frequent just 25 years ago. Many states have banned smoking in restaurants, while some towns have banned smoking in public, including at beaches and parks. As illustrated by these examples, views on behavior change over time and implementing specific laws regarding behavior contribute to society's change in perspective.

## Primary and Secondary Labels

Edwin Lemert (1951, 1993) observed that some violations of norms, such as skipping school or underage drinking, provoke slight reactions from others and have little effect on a person's self-concept. Lemert refers to this as **primary deviance**.

A person's perception may change, however, if someone else notices the deviance and points it out. For example, if people begin to describe a young man as an alcoholic or drug abuser and exclude him from their friendship group, he may become bitter, drink or use drugs more and eventually seek the company of others who approve of his behavior. The response to primary deviance sets in motion **secondary deviance**, by which a person repeatedly violates a norm and begins to take on a deviant identity. With secondary deviance, situations defined as real become real in their consequences (Merton, 1968).

Evaluate this example: The Saints and the Roughnecks were two groups of high school males who engaged in excessive drinking, reckless driving, petty theft, truancy and vandalism. None of the Saints was ever arrested, but the Roughnecks were continually in trouble and harassed by the police and townspeople. Why the difference in treatment? Sociologist William Chambliss (1973) conducted research in the boys' high school based solely on observation and concluded that social class played a significant role in the different treatment the boys received.

The Saints hid behind a façade of respectability and a higher social status based on their parents' income and the neighborhoods where they lived. They came from good families, were active in school organizations, received good grades and planned on attending college. People viewed their acts as a few isolated incidences of "sowing wild oats." The Roughnecks lived on the other side of town, came from a lower social class, drove around town in beat-up cars, were generally unsuccessful in school and were always viewed suspiciously regardless of their actions.

The Saints and the Roughnecks lived up to the labels the community gave them. The Saints grew up, went to college (all but one) and were successful. Two of the Roughnecks earned athletic scholarships and became coaches, but the rest did not do so well. Two dropped out of high school, later become involved in separate killings and went to prison. One became a local bookie. No one knows the whereabouts of the others.

How much of what the Roughnecks became had to do with the fact they were labeled "bad" and received negative treatment from their community?

Most people attempt to resist negative labels that others try to pin on them. Some are so successful at this that, even though they participate in deviant acts, they still consider themselves conformists.

People who commit deviant acts often use techniques of neutralization to continue to think of themselves as conformists. Sociologists Gresham

Sykes and David Matza (1964) studied boys who behaved deviantly and found that they used five techniques to neutralize society's norms (see table 6.3).

Matza and Sykes point out that it's not only delinquents who try to neutralize the norms of mainstream society; most people tend to justify their actions.

Erving Goffman (1963) says that secondary deviance marks the start of a deviant career. As people develop a stronger commitment to deviant behavior, they typically acquire a **stigma**, which is a powerfully negative label that greatly changes a person's self-concept and social identity. Perhaps this was the case for the Roughnecks.

Gays and lesbians face a negative stigma in parts of the United States and other Western societies as well. The view of same-sex orientation as deviant is condemned by many religious groups. The gay rights movement began in the late 1940s, when individual gays and lesbians discovered they were not alone. At present, we have made significant progress with respect to the treatment of gays and lesbians; eight states and Washington, D.C., as of mid-2012, had passed laws allowing same-sex couples to marry. But that means we have 42 states to go, and there are still laws that discriminate against gays, specifically, the Defense of Marriage Act.

Passed in 1996, this federal law states:

1. No state needs to treat a relationship between persons of the same sex as a marriage, even if this relationship is considered a marriage by another state.
2. The federal government may not treat same-sex relationships as marriage for any purpose, even if conducted in and recognized by one of the states.

This law exists because many people believe that legal gay marriage threatens the "natural order" of society.

Source: Sandra Bader

Do you think gay marriage will ever be legal in all 50 states?

# Crime and Types of Crime

## National Crime Rates

Sociologists and criminologists study crime patterns by examining crime rates. Contrary to popular belief, the crime rate in the United States has actually fallen in recent decades. Crime rates are not static, instead they rise and fall as chart 6.2 indicates. Since 1980, the national crime rates in the U.S. have trended downward (Federal Bureau of Investigation, 2011).

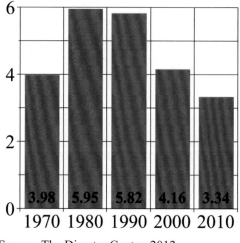

**CHART 6.2** U.S. Crime Rate Per 100 Inhabitants

| 1970 | 1980 | 1990 | 2000 | 2010 |
|------|------|------|------|------|
| 3.98 | 5.95 | 5.82 | 4.16 | 3.34 |

Source: The Disaster Center, 2012

**TABLE 6.3** Sykes and Matza Techniques of Neutralization

| Denial of Responsibility | I am not responsible for what happened because it was either an accident that couldn't be helped or I was the victim. |
|---|---|
| Denial of Injury | No one got hurt. What's the big deal? |
| Denial of a Victim | They had it coming! Did you see what she was wearing? They deserved what they got.got. |
| Condemnation of Condemners | Who are you to judge? Who are they to judge me? |
| Appeal to High Loyalties | I had to help my friends. Wouldn't you have done the same thing? |

The chart 6.2 shows the crime rate percentage (known and reported to the police) per 100 inhabitants.

Looking further into crime data reveals that the majority of crimes committed are property not violent crimes. In 2010, for example, there were a little over 10 million crimes reported to the police and of those 10 million roughly 1 million were considered violent crimes (murder, rape, robbery and assault) while the remaining were property (burglary and theft) (Federal Bureau of Investigation, 2012). It should also be pointed out that crime data always under represents reality this is because the data relies on individuals to report the crimes of which they are a victim. Some people fail to report crimes because they think the crime was too petty, or because they believe the police won't be able to do anything, or the perpetrator of the crime was a family member or close friend of theirs or for a number of other reasons.

But, despite a drop in crime rates, there has been an increase in prison inmates. The number of people in state and federal prisons continues to rise even with the drop in the crime rate. In per capita terms, in 1980 the incarceration rate, or the number of people in a state or federal prison, was 138 per 100,000; in 2010 it was 522 per 100,000—an increase of 378 percent over the 30 year period (Austin & Irwin, 2001; Bureau of Justice Statistics, 2011).

According to Bryon Stevenson, the executive director of the Equal Justice Initiative, in 1970 there were 350,000 people in our jails and prisons. Today, there are more than 2.2 million, with another 5 million on probation or parole (Stevenson, 2012). Stevenson believes that mass incarceration is a direct result of poverty and mental illness. In addition, laws passed in the 1990s led to more imprisonments and longer sentences (Federal Bureau of Investigation, 2005). Regardless of the decline, the public views crime as a major social problem. It remains to be seen whether this pattern will continue, and how we will deal with the mandatory minimums and drug offenses that are responsible for overpopulating our prisons.

## Hate Crimes

A **hate crime** is a criminal act motivated by bias against a race, ethnicity, religion, sexual orientation or disability. The term "hate crime" did not enter the nation's vocabulary until the 1980s, though crimes based on hatred and prejudice are a poignant fact in the nation's past and present.

The case of Matthew Shepard, who was tortured and killed in Laramie, Wyoming, in 1998 for

Source: Carles Pierre-Oliver

If your bike was stolen, would you report it to the police?

being gay, was a well-known and despicable hate crime. This particular case touched hearts across the nation. His murder brought national and international attention to the debate on hate crime legislation (Loffreda, 2000).

It is argued that the 1994 genocide in Rwanda had its roots in ethnic hatred. Belgium had colonized Rwanda and created social distinctions that gave one group power over another. By measuring one's nose and taking note of who had lighter skin two ethnic groups were created, the Hutus and the Tutsis. The Tutsis were given privilege at the beginning of colonization. But when the Belgians left, they left power to the Hutus, who had been oppressed for years. The Hutus took their revenge on the Tutsis by slaughtering 1 million people (Umutesi, 2006).

Was this genocide considered deviant behavior in Rwanda or did it become the cultural norm during this time period? What do you think?

## Juvenile Crime

Youth crimes committed by minors consist of, but are not limited to, theft, drug use, vandalism and, in some cases, extreme violence. **Juvenile delinquency** is participation in illegal activity by minors who fall under the statutory age limit, such as tobacco and alcohol violations, curfew and running away from home. Often, mental illness is part of the problem in youth crimes and in many cases is the more serious issue. But society closes its eyes to mental illness and punishes troubled juveniles instead, which typically doesn't work.

Many juveniles have had traumatic childhoods and may show signs of attachment disorder, which is always a red flag for possible violent behavior. Juveniles are works in progress. Their brains are not fully developed. If they get the proper help when they are young, they definitely have a better chance of staying out of the prison system (Shoemaker, 2009; Watkins, 2009).

## Organized Crime

When thinking of organized crime, people typically think of Al Capone, the mafia or gangsters.

**Organized crime** is a highly disciplined business organization whose profits come from illegal activity. Unfortunately, organized crime takes place all over the world. Earlier in this chapter, Frank Lucus was discussed. Frank Lucas was a former heroin dealer and organized crime boss who operated in Harlem during the 1960s and early 1970s.

## Gender and Crime

Often, when people think of a criminal, they envision a man. But women are committing a larger proportion of almost all crimes, from car theft to burglary, than they once did. There are 200,000 women in prison, another 94,400 on parole and 958,000 on probation. The number of incarcerated women has jumped 757 percent since 1977, nearly twice the growth rate of male incarceration (Talvi, 2007). On the other hand, women tend to serve shorter sentences than men, though this is likely due to differences in the majority of crimes committed by each of the genders (Mallicoat, 2012).

## Why is the Percentage of Female Offenders on the Rise?

A feminist approach suggests that in the past women did not have the same access to resources and opportunities as men and that it is difficult to commit crimes when you have to be home all day caring for the family. Adler suggests that it's difficult for a woman to embezzle when she has no access to a company's funds, or to get into a bar fight if she never goes to a bar (Adler, 1975). Yet as women have become more liberated and entered the workforce and the social community in greater numbers, they have had a better chance to commit crimes. It can therefore be understood that women are not less criminal than men; they simply have historically had fewer opportunities to commit crime.

## Women and Crime

In *Good Girls Gone Bad* (as cited in Ramsland, n.d.), journalist Susan Nadler talked with a variety of women in prison and found that they tended to fit into one of several categories:

- The majority of female convictions were for drug crimes.
- 90 percent of women in prison had substance abuse problems.
- Women offenders were more likely than their male counterparts to have been victims of abuse.
- Women who were victims of sexual abuse were 130 percent more likely to be arrested for a violent offense.
- Some women ended up in prison because they had retaliated against abuse as a way to protect themselves and their children. The majority of violent crimes committed by women fell into this category.
- Adolescent children of incarcerated mothers dropped out of high school at a rate three times that of their peers.
- Children with incarcerated mothers engaged in more delinquent behaviors such as lying, stealing and cheating
- It was estimated that children with an incarcerated mother were six times more likely than their peers to go to jail.
- Children with an incarcerated mother were more likely to be sexually promiscuous.
- Children with an incarcerated mother were more likely to experience a teenage pregnancy.

## Race and Crime

If we were to judge solely by arrest and conviction rates, we might conclude that the gender of crime is male and the race of the criminal is black (Pettit & Western, 2004). African Americans are arrested at a rate two, three or even five times greater than statistical probability.

Blacks represent just 12 percent of the U.S. population, yet their percentages in arrest statistics are extremely high. African American men are being imprisoned at an unsettling rate. Black males make up nearly 75 percent of the prison population. Out of 10.4 million black males in the United States, nearly 1.5 million are in prisons and jails, with another 3.5 million currently or formerly on probation or parole (Boothe, 2007). According to a New York Times article by Heather Mac Donald, the New York City Police Department, like many police departments across America, have oppressed some of the city's minority populations with racial tactics. Blacks and Latinos were nine times more likely to be stopped by an officer than whites in New York City in 2009 (Mac Donald, 2010).

Many consider Demico Boothe an expert on the criminal justice system as it relates to African Americans. He served 12 years in prison on a drug charge. He was released in 2003 and has been mentoring young minorities at local halfway houses and drug rehabilitation centers. In Boothe's book, *Why Are So Many Black Men In Prison*, he points out that a variety of laws are racist and implicitly target African Americans. For example, the "crack versus powder policy" adopted in 1986 states that cocaine and cocaine base, which is generally called crack, are the same drug chemically, but the two forms carry very different sentences. In 1988, Congress made crack the only drug that carries a five-year minimum penalty for possession. The penalty for possessing any other drug is only one year (Boothe, 2007). Boothe believes that this is one reason why so many African Americans are in prison.

Michelle Alexander, author of *The New Jim Crow*, emphasizes that our criminal justice system is set up in such a way that it allows legal discrimination against African Americans. She tells of a man, Jarvious Cotton, who doesn't have the legal right to vote in the United States because he is a convicted felon. Cotton's great-great grandfather couldn't vote because he was a slave, and the Ku Klux Klan beat his great-grandfather to death because he attempted to vote. His grandfather was intimidated by the Klan and consequently did not vote, and his father was barred from voting because of poll taxes and literacy tests (Alexander, 2010).

Cotton's family tree shows that even though we have come a long way in regards to discrimination, we clearly still have a long way to go.

## Social Class and Crime

One of the more interesting sociological findings in the study of deviance is that social classes have distinct styles of crime. Structural functionalists point out that street crime is typically committed by the lower classes.

**Street crime** includes robbery, drug dealing, burglary, prostitution and gambling. Industrialized societies have no trouble socializing the poor into wanting what everyone else has. Television and movies show images of middle-class residents enjoying the good life, reinforcing the idea that every American can afford society's goods and services.

The public school system, which is the most common route to success, habitually fails the poor, who are more likely to drop out than their more privileged counterparts (more on this in chapter 11).

## Political Crime

Liu Xiaobo received the Nobel Peace Prize in 2010, but he was not present to receive it because he is serving an 11-year prison sentence in China. China believes him to be guilty of breaking Chinese law for "inciting subversion" after drafting Charter 08, which called for multi-party democracy and respect for human rights. China considers this a political crime, but many others do not (Bristow 2010).

A **political crime** occurs when someone commits a criminal act to harm the state, the government or the political system in general. Political crimes vary from one place to another and can include tax evasion and espionage. What is important to remember about political crime is that often it is defined very differently depending on one's perspective. For example, many believe Gandhi committed political crimes by opposing British rule over India, but others view him as the leader of the nation's independence movement.

## White-Collar Crime

More privileged people also are tempted by crime but may have opportunities to commit more sophisticated forms of crime. You probably have heard about bookkeepers who embezzle from their employers, doctors who cheat Medicare and mortgage companies that knowingly grant bad home loans.

Sutherland (1947) coined the term **white-collar crime** to refer to crimes committed by people of high social status at their jobs.

White-collar crime is not a classic, clear-cut case of deviance. It has one foot in conventionality and one foot in deviance.

To benefit themselves or the companies that employ them, executives sometimes commit **corporate crimes**. In December 2001, Enron declared bankruptcy following the public disclosure of significant debt that had been hidden by fraudulent and labyrinthine accounting practices. Top executives were deeply tied to this scheme and personally received tens of millions of dollars from it. This gigantic fraud was pulled off with the help of Arthur Andersen, formerly one of the top five international accounting firms. As Enron's stock price collapsed, senior executives at the company sold hundreds of millions of dollars' worth of stock to unwary investors, even as employees were prevented from selling the stock they held in their 401(k) retirement plans (Desjardins, 2009).

More recently, we have witnessed the financial meltdowns that threatened not just the U.S. economy, but the global economy as well. In March 2008, the Bear Stearns investment firm failed, followed by brokerage firm Merrill Lynch and Washington Mutual bank. The Federal Reserve stepped in to take over mortgage finance agencies Fannie Mae and Freddie Mac as well as one of the world's largest insurance firms, AIG (American International Group). In October 2008, the Fed announced it would lend money directly to U.S. corporations, and Congress approved a $700 billion plan to assist the nation's financial systems, also known as the "bailout" (Crotty & Epstein, 2009).

While these corporations continued operating on Wall Street, many Americans went downhill financially, losing their homes, becoming unemployed, and struggling with a high debt rate. All the while, AIG executives were giving out $165 million in bonuses to their executives (Parrott, 2010).

The demise of these firms was largely related to the housing bubble in which loan money flowed freely from lenders to home buyers. After loans were approved, banks quickly packaged and sold them to investors as mortgage-backed securities. Many of these investors thought the mortgage-backed securities they were buying were high quality, but many were not, as home buyers no longer had to provide down payments or proof of income and assets and were thus approved for loans they could not afford. With the abandonment of the typical mortgage safeguards, loans started going bust as more and more on-the-edge borrowers could not keep up with their payments. More foreclosures began to occur, and home prices began to slide downward.

While formal criminal charges have not yet been filed against anyone at any of these firms for the financial crises, calls for prosecution persist (Berman, 2011; Wyatt, 2012). In 2010, Angelo Mozilo, the former CEO of Countrywide Financial, a mortgage company, agreed to pay a $67.5 million fine to the Securities and Exchange Commission (SEC) over securities fraud and insider trading charges. In settling with the SEC, Mozilo was able to avoid criminal charges (Morgenson, 2010).

The federal government, through its housing arm Federal Housing Finance Agency, has filed a lawsuit against 17 banks such as J.P. Morgan, which now owns Washington Mutual, and Bank of America, which now owns Countrywide Financial and Merrill Lynch, asking for billions in compensation for losses on mortgage-backed securities it purchased. They argue that the banks failed to do the due diligence required by law when packaging and selling mortgage-backed loans as securities and allowed unqualified home buyers to attain mortgages they could not afford. In all, the Federal Housing Finance Agency claims it lost $30 billion as a result of these deals, losses now mostly borne by taxpayers (Mak, 2011).

## Professional Crime

When someone uses special skills, experience, methods or instruments to commit a crime, it is called a **professional crime**. All professional crime is for personal gain, the most common type being fraud. In capitalist countries, professional crime outstrips other types of crime. Associations of professional criminals, known as syndicates, are growing and monopolizing various spheres of criminal business, such as drug traffic, kidnapping for ransom, extortion, stealing works of art,

smuggling and operating dens of vice. The activities of the syndicates can extend over entire countries or even groups of countries.

As we can see, people in higher social classes often lie, cheat, and steal just as people in lower classes do.

Those of us who are guilty of some of the above practices most likely justify these actions, continuing to think of ourselves as conformists.

- Have you ever taken office supplies from your place of employment?
- Have you ever been late to work, or left early, and not documented your hours correctly on your timesheet?
- Have you ever lied about your income on your taxes?
- Have you ever downloaded music and not paid for it?
- Have you ever been overpaid and just not mentioned it?

Functionalists conclude that street crime is the consequence of socializing everyone to equate success with owning material possessions, while denying many of those in the lower classes the means to achieve that success.

While it's clear that some people in lower classes commit crimes, it's still difficult to understand why more privileged people in higher social classes commit crimes. What is your take?

# Controlling Deviance and Social Control Mechanism

## Social Control

Every culture, subculture and group has distinctive norms dictating appropriate behavior. **Social order** is made possible by **social control**, which includes the various ways a social organization attempts to control the individual. Social control can be defined as all the pressures by which society and its component groups influence the behavior of individuals toward conformity with group norms (Rouck, 1978).

Social control and order are essential for societies to flourish. Though control and order are often positive factors that allow the continuation of the social organization, we should not always presume they are good. A society that oppresses its people should not be supported simply because control and order are necessary. Many changes take place because people refuse to be controlled by social patterns they regard as unjust. For example, women fought for the right to vote, as did African Americans. Laborers fought for fair working conditions and a 40-hour week.

Occupy Wall Street is a recent example of Americans uniting for change. This social movement started on September 17, 2011, in Zuccotti Park in New York City's Wall Street financial district. The protests were against high unemployment rates, greed, corruption and corporate influence on politics, specifically from the financial district. The slogan for this protest, "We are the 99 percent," refers to the growing wealth inequality in the U.S. between the wealthiest 1 percent and the rest of the population. The protest

Source: Christopher Smith

What is your opinion of the Occupy Wall Street movement?

in New York City sparked protests and movements around the world (Cook, 2011).

People like the Rev. Dr. Martin Luther King Jr. are seen as positive role models who made significant changes to the structure of our society. One also might ask about Angela Davis, the civil rights activist who was imprisoned for her views on communism during the civil rights movement. She was imprisoned in Marin County, California, when one of her guns was matched to the gun that killed a judge. Some people, however, believe that her real offense was belonging to the Communist Party and participating in the Black Panther movement. She was trying to get a message across and, instead, was penalized for it because she belonged to groups that were actively challenging the existing social order (Bukhari & Whitehorn, 2010).

## Social Control Methods Used to Control Deviance and Crime

### The Medicalization of Deviance as Social Control

Over the past 50 years, the growing influence of psychiatry and pharmaceuticals in the United States has led to the **medicalization of deviance**, which transformed moral and legal deviance into medical conditions. Labeling people with disorders that need to be treated by physicians has become quite widespread. But sociologists believe that confused or tortured minds are not necessarily something biological. Instead, these mental states may be directly related to particular life experiences.

Thomas Szasz (2008), a professor of psychiatry, argues that mental illness is simply a term for problem behaviors and is not a disease. Some forms of mental illness, such as depression, have organic causes like chemical imbalances in the brain, but others are responses to troubles with coping devices or specific circumstances. For example, many homeless people have been labeled or diagnosed as mentally ill. For sociologists, the question is: Were they mentally ill before they became homeless or did they become mentally ill after becoming homeless? If you lost your home and place of employment, and were then forced to live on the streets, could this make you mentally ill? Professor

Szasz suggests our social experiences, rather than mental illness, underlie bizarre behaviors.

## The Criminal Justice System as Social Control

The criminal justice system is a complex set of institutions that include the police, the courts and corrections.

The criminal justice system uses diverse methods to control deviance. For example, when crime soared in the 1980s, the "three strikes" laws were implemented with the goal of lowering crime. Three strikes laws are statutes enacted by state governments in the United States that require the state courts to impose a life sentence (usually with the possibility of parole) to people found guilty of a new offense who have been previously convicted of two or more other serious crimes (Walsh, 2007).

On the other hand, the people in power, as a conflict theorist would suggest, did not limit these laws to violent crimes, nor did they seem to realize that some minor crimes would become felonies. The functionalist perspective would assert that there were many unintended consequences to this type of law, such as overpopulated prisons and people doing time for petty theft. Imprisonment is an increasingly popular reaction to crime, but it does not seem to teach inmates to stay away from crime. The **recidivism rate** runs as high as 80 percent. Recidivism is measured by criminal acts that have resulted in the re-arrest, reconviction or return to prison with or without a new sentence during a three-year period following the prisoner's release (Spelman, 1994).

From 1994 to 2007, national recidivism rates hovered around 40 percent (Pew, 2011). This means that 4 out of 10 adult offenders returned to prison within 3 years of release. It is important to note that recidivism numbers vary by state. Between 2004 and 2007, Alaska, California, Illinois, Minnesota, Missouri and Utah had recidivism rates in excess of 50 percent, while Oregon, Virginia, West Virginia and Wyoming had recidivism rates under 30 percent (Pew, 2011).

While the criminal justice system serves a purpose in society, the conflict perspective would take the view that police, prosecutors and judges have dramatic influence on who gets punished and what types of deals are made. The limits of discretion vary from state to state. For example, some state judges have wide discretion in the types of sentence they impose. Other states have sought to limit a judge's discretion by passing mandatory sentencing laws that require a proscribed number of years for certain offenses (Gelsthorpe & Padfield, 2003).

Ninety percent of all criminal matters are resolved as a result of plea-bargaining. Young, poorly educated and scared defendants can easily

Source: Roland Lakis

If you were charged with a crime of which you were innocent and the prosecutor offered you three years of probation instead of going to trial and facing up to ten years in prison if found guilty, what would you do—take the probation or risk the prison time trying to prove your innocence?

be persuaded to plead guilty to crimes they did not commit, agreeing to receive lesser sentences than the ones they would receive if found guilty by a jury. They are often persuaded by public defenders to take the lesser of the two evils, even when they are innocent (Medwed, 2012).

Capital punishment is the most extreme action the state takes to control deviance and crime. There is much controversy regarding the death penalty, primarily based on moral and philosophical grounds. DNA testing has given opponents of the death penalty a strong argument: Innocent people have been executed.

What is your position on the death penalty? Should it be legal or should it be abolished? Why? Do you think it deters crime?

In 1986, Congress enacted minimum sentencing laws, which apply to 64,000 defendants a year and mandate specific sentences for specific crimes, allowing no room for discretion. The laws are designed to be tough on crime and eliminate bias in the courts (Vincent & Hoffer, 1994). The U.S. Census Bureau and the Department of Justice have each concluded that mandatory sentences have contributed greatly to prison overcrowding. More than 80 percent of the increase in the federal prison population from 1985 to 1995 was due to drug convictions based on mandatory minimums (U.S. Department of Justice, 2005).

The broader issues include how to protect people from deviant behaviors that are harmful to their welfare, tolerate those who are not and develop systems to ensure fair treatment for those who deviate from societal norms.

Deviant behavior often can be dealt with through socialization of youth by helping them internalize norms against harmful and illegal behavior. Informal methods such as the constructive influence of families, peer groups, schools and social pressure are the major crime fighters. They do not do a perfect job, though, and law enforcement has to deal with the failures. Formal methods in responding to crime include hiring more police, building more prisons and toughening penalties for crimes. A consequence to this approach is that punishment doesn't always equal change.

Perhaps we should take a more creative approach and study the ways other countries control deviance and rehabilitate their prison populations. Dr. Kiran Bedi changed the lives of thousands of desperate prisoners when she embarked on a mission to reform one of the world's largest prison systems. She transformed the inhumane conditions of India's Tihar Central Jail, which was a cesspool of drugs, gang wars, corruption and extortion by guards and powerful inmates. Today, thousands of inmates gather in clean, tree-shaded courtyards every morning for prayer and meditation. Volunteer groups are allowed into Tihar to provide counseling, meditation classes, legal aid, vocational training and entertainment.

In her book *It's Always Possible* Bedi discusses her approaches and how she achieved the changes (Bedi, 2002). Bedi used a hands-on approach by visiting and talking with inmates. She learned that inmates lived in horrible living conditions at the hands of the guards, and she also learned that the drug trade was alive and well inside the prison. One of the first things she did was to put in a complaint box. Inmates could make complaints or express concerns on paper. They would then place the paper in the box that was locked until Bedi opened it. She personally read these complaints every day and acted upon them. She addressed sanitation issues and implemented a nutrition program. Drug treatment programs and literacy programs opened the environment for positive behavior and created an atmosphere that encouraged prayer and meditation. These are just a few of the things Bedi did to change the lives of thousands of prisoners.

In the Philippines, Cebu Provincial Detention Center and Rehabilitation Center, a maximum-security prison, is best-known for the worldwide viral version of Michael Jackson's *Thriller* video. Byron F. Garcia, head of the prison, is credited for starting a program of choreographed exercise routines for the inmates. He initially wanted to start an hour-a-day exercise program but took it a step further after being inspired by the film *The Shawshank Redemption*, particularly by the scene in which Mozart's *Figaro* flooded the prison yard. The goal was to keep the body fit, which would keep the mind fit. Garcia believes that part of the rehabilitation process is combining the need for physical exercise with song and dance. (Ferran, 2007).

Cathy Lachman, a retired police officer who works with newly released felons in the Gateway program at Red Rocks Community College in the Denver, Colorado area, believes that many people with substance abuse issues who end up in prison are often very creative. She believes that dance, art, theater, or any positive creative outlet are beneficial not only to former inmates but to their environment as well. Much of the Gateway program focuses on finding meaning and purpose in life. Once the former offenders have found this purpose and meaning, they thrive and become passionate about what they can do and achieve.

Five major tenets make this program successful:

1. Every human being, no matter what his or her background, has a purpose and a meaning, and it is in the process of discovery that true change is possible.

2. People need people who believe in them and support them in their growth.
3. Individuals must be encouraged to take personal responsibility for their choices rather than using external threats of punishment as a motivator.
4. Through our giving, we shall receive.
5. Necessary for success is changing what we think about and how we think about it.

Recidivism for the Gateway program is less than 3 percent (Lachman, 2011).

Why do you think the Gateway program participants have had such low recidivism rates?

Source: Sally Stablein

# Summary

Definitions of deviance and deviant behavior depend on culture, social ties, race, ethnicity, gender, social class and historical context. Several explanations and theoretical perspectives help us explain deviance and deviant behavior. Biological, psychological and sociological theories offer much insight, though most theories suggest that social environment and one's position within the social structure play important roles in whether a person deviates from, or conforms to, societal norms.

The theories of structural functionalism, conflict and symbolic interactionism allow us to view deviant behaviors from different perspectives. Sociologists are interested in why people do the things they do, right or wrong, and these perspectives can provide some answers.

People of all social classes, ethnic groups and genders commit crimes.

Social control and social order are necessary, but not all forms of control and order are good. A society that oppresses its people should not be supported simply because control and order are necessary. Organizations that violate our values should not be supported. History reminds us that much change has taken place as a result of people refusing to be controlled by unjust social patterns.

The criminal justice system uses several methods to control deviance, depending on the crime, and may include mandatory sentencing minimums, prison terms and the death penalty. Despite the decrease in national crime rates, the number of prison inmates has increased. System administrators need to take a look at more creative approaches to reduce prison populations, and focus on additional systems that work.

Society should think about rehabilitation alternatives, as harsh punishment doesn't necessarily fix the problems of deviance. We can learn great things from the Gateway program, Kiran Bedi and other alternative ways of controlling deviance. Hopefully, this chapter has given you some insight on deviant behavior and awareness that individuals convicted of wrongdoing do not always fit the common stereotype of the "street criminal" or "deviant" person.

## Review/Discussion Questions

1. What are the central ideas of the conflict approach to deviance, and in what ways are economic and cultural conflict involved in the definition and control of deviance?
2. Are all deviants oppressed workers, or is deviance caused by other factors? How so?
3. Define and discuss the definition of deviance. Why is there often disagreement over what constitutes deviant behavior?
4. Discuss the death penalty. Are you for it or against it, and why?
5. It makes sense to apply the theories in this chapter to deviant behavior and street crime. Can we apply these same theories to people who commit white-collar crimes?
6. Do childhood experiences contribute to whether a person will deviate or conform? Why or why not?
7. Discuss whether the laws of society represent the interests of the public at large (public good) versus the interests of the power elites?
8. Identify and discuss major components of the U.S. criminal justice system.
9. Identify and discuss three different types of crimes.
10. What is Robert Merton's Strain Theory? Do you agree with it?
11. Have others ever labeled you? If so, did it change or alter your behavior in some way?
12. Give some examples of white-collar crime.
13. How is discretion used in the criminal justice system?
14. What happens to people when they have no meaning in their lives?

# Key Terms

**Anomie** is a social condition in which norms and values are conflicting, weak, or absent.

**Capital class** refers to the people who own the capital and do not have to sell their labor.

**Conformity** may involve going along with peers and/or following societal norms.

**Containment theory** is based on control theory and focuses on a strong self-image as a means of defending against negative peer pressure.

**Control theory** is the idea that there are two control systems, inner and outer, that work against our tendencies to deviate.

**Corporate crimes** are the illegal actions of people acting on behalf of the corporation.

**Criminal justice system** includes the police, courts and prisons that deal with criminal laws and their enforcement.

**Criminology** is the scientific study of the causes of criminal behavior in the individual and society.

**Cultural goals** are the legitimate objectives of members of society.

**Deviance** is a violation of rules or norms.

**Differential association** is a theory of deviance that believes people will deviate or conform depending on their associations.

**Hate crime** refers to criminal acts against a person or a person's property by an offender who is motivated by racial or other biases.

**Illegitimate opportunity structures** are relative opportunity structures outside laws and social norms that frame a person's life.

**Institutional means** include approved ways of reaching cultural goals.

**Juvenile delinquency** is participation in illegal activity by minors who fall under the statutory age limit (youth crime).

**Labeling theory** is the idea that the labels people are given affect their own and others' perceptions of them, and, therefore, channel behavior either into or away from conformity.

**Marginal working class** includes the most desperate members of society who have few skills and little job security. They often are unemployed.

**Medicalization of deviance** means to relate deviance to an underlying illness that needs to be treated by physicians.

**Organized crime** is a highly disciplined business organization whose profits come from illegal activity.

**Primary deviance** is the first occurrence of a violation of a norm, which the committing actor does not view as deviant. Thus, it would have little to no effect on a person's self-concept.

**Professional crime** is when someone uses special skills, experience, methods or instruments to commit a crime while considering the activity to be that person's basic occupation or as a main or additional source of income. The most common type is fraud, and all professional crime is for personal gain.

**Political crime** refers to crime or acts committed to harm the state, the state's government or the political system in general.

**Punishment** is an authoritative imposition of something negative or unpleasant on a person in response to behavior considered bad.

**Recidivism rates** represent the number of people rearrested for committing the same types of crimes.

**Sanctions** refer to rewards for normal behaviors and penalties for abnormal behaviors.

**Secondary deviance** is a response to primary deviance by which a person repeatedly violates a norm and begins to take on a deviant identity.

**Social control** involves techniques and strategies for maintaining order and preventing deviant behavior in a society.

**Social order** includes social arrangements upon which members depend.

**Stigmas** discredit a person's claim to a normal identity.

**Strain theory** was developed by Robert Merton to describe the strain felt by some members of society when they do not have access to the institutional means to achieve cultural goals.

**Street crimes** are crimes that occur in public places.

**Techniques of neutralization** are ways of thinking or rationalizing that help people deflect society's norms.

**Tertiary deviance** is normalizing behavior considered deviant by mainstream society, or relabeling behavior as non-deviant.

**White-collar crimes** are illegal acts committed by affluent individuals in the course of business activities.

# Bibliography

Adler, F, (1975). Sisters in Crime: The rise of the New Female Criminal. New York, NY: McGraw-Hill Book Company.

Alexander, M. (2010). The New Jim Crow: Mass Incarceration in the Age of Colorblindness.New York, The New Press.

Austin, J., & Irwin, J. (2001). It's About Time: America's Imprisonment Binge. Belmont, CA: Wadsworth/Thompson Learning.

Bedi, K. (2002). It's Always Possible: One Woman's Transformation of India's Prison System. Honesdale PA: Himalayan Institute Himalayan.

Baron, S. W. (2001, May). Street Youth: Labour Market Experiences and Crime. Canadian Review of Sociology and Anthropology, 38, (2), 24-31.

Becker, H. S. (1966). Outsiders: Studies in the Sociology of Deviance. New York: Free Press.

Berman, J. (2011). Financial Executives Likely Won't Face Criminal Charges For Role In Financial Crisis: Former Investigator. The Huffington Post. <http://www.huffingtonpost.com/2011/12/06/criminal-prosecution-financial-crimes_n_1131639.html> (2012).

Boothe, D. (2007). Why Are So Many Black Men in Prison? United States: Full Surface Publishing.

Bristow, M. (2010). Liu Xiaobo: 20 years of Activism. BBC News: Beijing < http://www.bbc.co.uk/news/world-asia-pacific-11492131> (2010).

Brooks, T. (2003). University of Maryland. < http://www.bsos.umd.edu/gvpt/lpbr/subpages/reviews/Gelsthorp.> (2012).

Bukhari, S., & Whitehorn, L. (2010). The War Before: the True Life Story of Becoming a Black Panther, Keeping the Faith in Prison & Fighting for those Left Behind. New York City: Feminist Press at the City University of New York.

Bureau of Justice Statistics (2011). Prisoners in 2010 (Revised). <http://bjs.ojp.usdoj.gov/index.cfm?ty=pbdetail&iid=2230> (2012).

Chambliss, W. J. (1973). The Saints and the Roughnecks. New York: Free Press.

Cloward, R. A., & Ohlin, L. (1966). Delinquency and Opportunity: A Theory of Delinquent Gangs. New York: Free Press.

Cook, C. D. (2011). Naomi Klein ``I've Never Seen Anything like the Occupy Wall Street Movement in my Life,'' Says the Author of The Shock Doctrine. Progressive. 75/76 (12/1), 54-55.

Crotty, J., & Epstein, G. (2009). Avoiding Another Meltdown. Challenge. 52 (1), 5-26.

Daly, K. (1989). Neither Conflict Nor Labeling Nor Paternalism Will Suffice: Intersections of Race, Ethnicity, Gender and Family in Criminal Court Decisions. Crime and Delinquency, 35, 136-168.

Defense of Marriage Act (2008). Doma Watch. <http://www.domawatch.org.> (2012).

Denver Legalizes Marijuana (2005). Cannabis Culture Magazine. < http://www.cannabisculture.com/articles/4570.html.> (2012).

Designboom (2008). A Brief History of Tattoos. <http://www.designboom.com/history/tattoo_history.html> (2012).

Desjardins, J. (2009). An Introduction to Business Ethics (3rded.). New York: McGraw Hill.

Donohue, J. (2005). Fighting Crime: An Economist's View. The Milken Institute Review, 7 (46) 46-58.

Drucker, E. (2011). A Plague of Prisons: The Epidemiology of Mass Incarceration In America. New York: The New Press.

Drug Policy Alliance (2008). Fighting Drug War Injustice. <http://www.drugpolicy.org/drugwar/mandatorymin.> (2012).

Durkheim, E. (1893). The Division of Labor in Society. New York: Free Press.

Federal Bureau of Investigation (2005). <http://www.fbi.gov/homepage.htm.> (2012).

Federal Bureau of Investigation (2005). Crime in the United States. <http://www.fbi.gov/ucr/05cius/.> (2012).

Federal Bureau of Investigation (2011.) Crime Statistics. <http://www.fbi.gov/stats-services/crimestats.> (2012).

Federal Bureau of Investigation (2012). Crime in the United States: 2010. <http://www.fbi.gov/about-us/cjis/ucr/crime-in-the-u.s/2010/crime-in-the-u.s.-2010> (2012).

Ferran, L. (2007, August 14). Boogie Behind Bars: Inmates Dance the Days Away. ABC News. <http://abcnews.go.com/icaught/story?id=3415920&page=1.> (2012).

Gaines, L. K., & Roger, L. M. (2004). Criminal Justice in Action: The Core. Belmont, CA:Wadsworth/ Thompson Learning.

Gelsthorpe, L., & Padfield, N (2003). Exercising Discretion: Decision Making in the Criminal Justice System and Beyond. Law & Politics Book Review. <http://www.bsos.umd.edu/gvpt/lpbr/subpages/reviews/Gelsthorpe-Padfield204.htm.> (2012).

Glassner, B. (1999). The Culture of Fear: Why Americans are Afraid of the Wrong Things. New York: Basic Books.

Glueck, S., & Glueck, E. (1950). Unraveling Juvenile Delinquency. New York: Common Wealth Fund.

Goffman, E. (1963). Stigma. Englewood Cliffs, NJ: Prentice Hall.

Herivel, T., & Wright, P. (2007). Prison Profiteers: Who Makes Money From Mass Incarceration.New York London: The New Press.

Herman, J. (1992). [Review of the book Skin and Ink: Artists and Collectors]. The Journal of American Folklore, 105 (415), 83-85.

Hirschi, T. (1969). Causes of Delinquency. Berkeley, CA: University of California Press.

Hubbard, G. R., & Mayer, C. J. (2009). The Mortgage Market Meltdown and House Prices. The B.E. Journal of Economic Analysis & Policy, 9 (3).

Kindlon, D., & Thompson, M. (2000). Raising Cain: Protecting the Emotional Life of Boys. New York: Ballantine Books.

Kozol, J. J. (1995). Amazing Grace: the lives of children and the conscience of a nation. New York: Harper Perennial.

Kushner, H. (2006). Man's Search For Meaning: Viktor E. Frankl. Boston: Beacon Press.

Lachman, C. (2011). Gateway program. A conversation with the author.

Langan, P., & Levin, D. (2002). Special Report: Recidivism of Prisoners Released in 1994.Bureau of Justice Statistics. <http://www.bjs.gov/content/pub/pdf/rpr94.pdf.> (2012).

Lemert, C. (1993). Social Theory: The Multicultural & Classic Readings. Boulder, CO: Westview Press.

Lemert, E. M. (1951). Social Pathology: a systematic approach to the theory of sociopathic behavior. New York: McGraw Hill.

Lemert, E. M. (1972). Human Deviance, Social Problems, & Social Control (2nd ed.). Englewood Cliffs, NJ: Prentice Hall.

Lemonick, M. D. (2003, January 20). The Search for a Murder Gene. Time, 100.

Loffreda, B. (2000). Losing Matt Shepard: Life and Politics in the Aftermath of Anti-Gay Murder. New York: Columbia University Press.

Lucas, F. (n.d.). In Wikipedia. <http://en.wikipedia.org/wiki/Frank_Lucas.> (2012).

Mac Donald, H. (2010, May 14). Distorting the Truth About Crime and Race. City Journal. <http://www.city-journal.org/2010/eon0514hm.html> (2012).

Mak, T. (2011). Fed Sues Banks Over Mortgage Fraud. <http://www.politico.com/news/stories/0911/62534.html> (2012).

Mallicoat, S. L. (2012). Women and Crime. Thousand Oaks, CA: Sage.

McCormack, J. (1999, February 22). The Sorry Side of Sears. Newsweek, 36-39.

Medwed, D. S. (2012). Prosecution Complex: America's Race to Convict and its Impact on the Innocent. New York: New York University Press.

Merton, R. K. (1968). Social Theory and Social Structure. New York: Free Press.

Merton, R. K. (2008). The Thomas Theorem and the Matthew Effect. Eugene Garfield, Ph.D. <http://garfield.library.upenn.edu/merton/thomastheorem.pdf.> (2012).

Morgenson, G. (2010) Angelo Mozilo of Countrywide Settles Fraud Case for $67.5 Million. The New York Times, 16 October 2010.

Office of Justice Programs (n.d.). <www.ojp.usdoj.gov.> (2012).

Parrott, J. (2010). New York City's Tale of Two Recessions. Challenge. 53 (3). 32-48.

Pauker, J. (2006). Get Lost: the cool guide to Amsterdam (10th ed.). Amsterdam: Get Lost Publishing.

Pettit, B., & Western, B. (2004). Mass Imprisonment and the Life Course: Race and Class Inequality in U.S. Incarceration. American Sociological Review, 69, 151-169.

Pew (2011). State of Recidivism: The Revolving Door of America's Prisons. <http://www.pewcenteronthestates.org/uploadedFiles/Pew_State_of_Recidivism.pdf> (2012).

Pinker, S. (2003, January 20). Are Your Genes to Blame? Time, 98-100.

Pinker, S. (1994). The Language Instinct. New York: Morrow.

Ramsland, K. (n.d.). Female Offenders. Bad Girls. TruTV. Retrieved from <http://www.trutv.com/library/crime/criminal_mind/ psychology/female_offenders/1.html> (2012).

Reckless, W. C., & Dinitz, S. (1967). Pioneering with Self Concept as Vulnerability Factor in Delinquency. Journal of Criminal Law, Criminology, and Police Science, 58 (4).

Reckless, W. C. (1973). The Crime Problem (5th ed.). New York: Appleton-Century-Crofts.

Rogers, J. W. (1977). Why are you not a Criminal? Englewood Cliffs, NJ: Prentice Hall.

Ross, S. D., & Lester, P. M. (2011). Images That Injure: Pictorial Stereotypes in the Media. Santa Barbara, CA: Praeger.

Rouck, J. (1978). The Concept of Social Control in American Sociology. Westport, CT: Greenwood Press.

Schlosser, E. (2004). Reefer Madness: Sex, Drugs, and Cheap Labor in the American Black Market. Boston: Houghton Mifflin Company.

Sheldon, W. H., Hartl, E. M., & McDermott, E. (1949). Varieties of Delinquent Youth. New York: Harper Brothers.

Shoemaker, D. J. (2009). Juvenile Crime. Lanham, MD: Rowman & Littlefield Publishers.

Simmons, J. L. (1965). Public Stereotypes of Deviants. Social Problems, 13, 223-224.

Spelman, W. (1994). Criminal Incapacitation. New York: Plenum Press.

Stevenson, B (2012). Why Are Millions of Americans Locked Up? Special to CNN <http://www.cnn.com/2012/03/11/opinion/ stevenson-justice-prison/index.html?hpt=hp_bn9> (2012).

Sutherland, E. H. (1947). Principles of Criminology (4th ed.). Philadelphia: Lippencott.

Sykes, G. M., & Matza, D. (2002). Techniques of Neutralization: A Theory of Delinquency. In E. J. Clarke (Ed.). Deviant Behavior: A Text-Reader in the Sociology of Deviance. (pp. 122-127). New York: Worth.

Szasz, T. (2008). The Myth of Mental Illness. YouTube. <http://www.youtube.com/watch?v=ea1yHguAWKQ.> (2012).

Talvi, S. (2007). Women Behind Bars: The Crisis of Women in the U.S. Prison System.Emeryville California: Seal Press.

The Disaster Center (2012).United States Crime Rates 1960 - 2010. <http://www.disastercenter.com/crime/uscrime.htm.> (2012).

U.S. Department of Justice (2005). <http://www.justice.gov/.> (2012).

Umutesi, M. B. (2006). Is Reconciliation Between Hutus and Tutus Possible? Journal of International Affairs. 60 (1), 157.

Vincent, B. S., & Hoffer, P. J. (1994). The Consequences of Mandatory Minimum Prison Terms: a Summary of Recent Findings. Washington D.C.: National Government Publication.

Walsh, J. E. (2007). Three Strike Laws. Westport, CT: Greenwood Press.

Watkins, C. (2009). Teens at Risk: Opposing Viewpoints. Detroit: Greenhaven Press.

Wickman, P. M. (1991). Deviance. Pp. 85-87 In Dushkin Publishing (Ed.), Encyclopedia Dictionary of Sociology (4th ed.) (pp.85-87). Guilford, CT: Dushkin Publishing.

Wiley, M. (1997). Filipino Martial Art Culture. Boston: Tuttle Publishing.

Wyatt, E. (2012). Obama Urges Tougher Laws on Financial Fraud. The New York Times. 24 January 2012.

Young, T. R. (n.d.). Teaching Criminology: Part VI. Critical Criminology Information and Resources.< http://critcrim.org/ redfeather/lectures/techcrm6.htm.> (2012).

The sign reads:

HOMELESS + DISABLED - with
NEUROPATHy in both Legs.
CAN you PLease help w/anything??
TO GET MEDiCiNE and FOOD etc.
This Lady
THANk's you        God BLess you

# CHAPTER SEVEN

# Social Stratification in the United States and the World

## Kwaku Obosu-Mensah

---

**Chapter Objectives**
At the end of this chapter, students should be able to:

- Understand the basis of stratification.
- Explain the main systems of stratification.
- Explain the class system in the modern world.
- Identify the consequences of stratification.
- Explain the types of poverty.
- Identify the poor in the United States.
- Explain the types of social mobility.
- Identify the factors that influence social mobility.
- Compare and contrast the three types of countries in the world.
- Understand the theories that explain global stratification.

---

 **ocial stratification,** the ranking of people within a society, is a very important issue because it determines the living standard of individuals. Stratification also determines how valuable resources are distributed in the society.

---

## Basis of Stratification

The Ashanti people of Ghana have a proverb that states, "The fingers are not equal." The literal meaning of this expression is that our fingers are not of the same length. Figuratively, this proverb means that human beings are not equal,

---

Chapter 7: Social Stratification in the United States and the World   179

implying that in every society some people have more privileges, power, prestige, and burdens than others. The saying acknowledges that stratification and, consequently, inequality are endemic to all human societies. It should be remembered that stratification explains differences in lifestyle, attitudes, and social behavior among people.

In a typical society, the basis of stratification may be put on a continuum from the most important to the least important factor that determines privileges. Such factors include class (economic position), prestige, status (such as age, profession, gender, and family), caste, and power (for example, party affiliation and noble lineage). The placement of profession is fluid because it can be considered class as well as status. Under class, the most important factor is income. Under status, the most important factor is the prestige or respect accorded to individual professions. According to the German sociologist Max Weber, status is recognition given to a person or group. This recognition could be based on an economic factor such as income or on the prestige or respect accorded to a profession (Kimmel & Aronson, 2009).

## Income and Wealth

In modern societies, the most important determinant of stratification is class, followed by the statuses accorded to different professions. Generally, the factors that determine stratification are achieved through an individual's own efforts. In the United States, a person's profession, which determines income and wealth (economic determinism), is the most important influence on his or her privileges. Thus, access to the necessities of life is determined by a person's income and wealth. People with high income or wealth are highly regarded in modern societies. If Bill Gates walked into your classroom, your reaction toward him would be different than your reaction toward a homeless person. Thus, you are treating these two individuals differently on the basis of their income or wealth. In modern societies, power gained through political affiliation may not be as important in determining a person's position as income.

A related question is, "Why is income so important in modern societies?" The simple answer is that people in such societies are materialistic. Materialism develops after people are able to satisfy their basic needs; they tend to spend more money on ostentatious goods and services. This is what sociologist and economist Thorstein Veblen termed conspicuous consumption—the public display and consumption of expensive items (Ashley & Orenstein, 2001). When wealthy people exhibit their affluence, others want to be like them. It is for this reason that a relatively poor family may be tempted to purchase a larger, more expensive home than they can afford, all in an attempt to appear better off than they actually are.

It is also true that without an adequate income, one may not be able to meet even his or her basic needs in a modern society. In modern societies, the accepted ideology is that hard work pays, so those who are poor must not be hard-working people. One way of showing that you are a hard-working person is to acquire material goods. Thus, since most people do not want to be stigmatized as lazy, they acquire material goods. The importance of income in modern societies cannot be overemphasized.

In traditional societies, the root of stratification is power, followed by status. Thus, income and wealth may not be the most important determinant of the stratification system. In such societies, stratification may be based on *ascriptive* factors—factors that individuals do not control. For example, no individual determines the family into which he or she is born.

Tradition may determine the stratification system. For example, by tradition the local or traditional chief may be the most powerful person in a society. Most important decisions may be made by the chief, as tradition has always dictated. In every Ghanaian town and village, for example, there is a local leader selected from the royal family to be chief. He is accorded the highest position in the stratification system. The chiefs are custodians of common lands, and all development projects in the town should be approved by the chief. In addition, disputes are settled by the chief. Although the power of chiefs in Ghana is waning in the face of modern challenges, they still wield enormous power over their subordinates.

## Prestige

In both modern and traditional societies, **prestige** given to an individual is next in importance in the stratification system. Prestige differs from wealth and power in that it is entirely subjective. A person may have wealth and power regardless of what others think of him or her, but in order for one to have prestige, one must be perceived by others as having it. In this sense, there exists a **status system** which ranks people based on their social prestige. One area that contributes to this ranking system is a person's profession. In a typical traditional society, a high percentage of the people are illiterate. These illiterates depend on the few literates to read and translate their letters and help them with situations requiring reading or writing. Teachers in such societies, by the singular fact that they are literate, are accorded high status, even though they may not earn high incomes. The same applies to priests who may not be rich but are accorded high status because of their profession. This can result in **status inconsistency** in which a person is given conflicting statuses; he may have the respect of the people and the prestige that comes with it, but lacks wealth or power.

## Power

In capitalistic societies, **power** is very important—it determines who gets the best of the society's resources. Indeed, the power structure of a society determines every aspect of life in the society. For example, power determines who gives instructions and who obeys instructions. Since power is so important, people in every capitalistic society try to gain power in order to exert influence and control. To achieve this goal, some people, through interactions and associations, form the power elite. In the United States, the governing elite, or **power elite**, draws its members from the following areas: (1) the highest political leaders, including the president and a handful of key cabinet members and close advisers; (2) major corporate owners and directors; and (3) high-ranking military officers (Mills Wright, 1958). A combination of these groups of people wields the most power and controls American society.

# Historical Systems of Stratification

Historically, there are five main systems of stratification. These are egalitarian, slave, feudal, caste, and class systems. In a typical society, two or more of these systems may exist at the same time. For example, during the time of slavery in the United States, the class system also existed.

## Egalitarianism

This type of structure has the least amount of inequality. Some examples are the hunting and gathering societies in which everyone worked together and then equally shared the proceeds of their combined labor. Some inequalities did exist, particularly in the area of status, with men viewed more highly than women or children, and the skilled and successful hunters the most prized. This type of society did not value the accumulation of wealth.

## Slavery

Under slavery, some people are owned by others. There are several ways of acquiring slaves. The most common methods are capturing and purchasing. Since nobody works to acquire or achieve the position of slavery, slavery is an *ascribed* status, meaning people are born or forced into slavery.

Slavery is the most extreme form of legalized social inequality because a slave owner always has control over slaves. In slavery, human beings are treated as property. Slave owners determine the schedule of their slaves' daily routines, as well as when to dispose of or sell their slaves and for how much. In most cases, the children of slaves become the property of the slave owner, just as the puppies your dog gave birth to become your property.

Technically, slavery has been abolished, but the practice still exists in various forms around the world. On the website of the U.S. State Department (2007), there is a letter dated June 12, 2007, written by Condoleezza Rice, then Secretary of State. In the letter, she notes that, "Trafficking in persons is a modern-day form of slavery, a new type of global slave trade. Perpetrators prey on the most weak among us, primarily women and children, for profit and gain. They lure victims into involuntary servitude and sexual slavery." The U.S. Central

Intelligence Agency estimates that 50,000 people each year are trafficked into, or transited through, the United States as sex slaves, domestics, garment workers, and agricultural slaves. Thus, slavery exists even in America. Most of the slaves in the United States are there for the purpose of labor and sexual exploitation. Though most of these slaves come from East Asia, Mexico, and Central America, quite a number of them are native-born Americans (Central Intelligence Agency, 2008).

In a remote area of Ghana, people practice a type of slavery called *trokosi*. It is a practice in which children, mostly girls, are sent to shrines to atone for the crimes of their relatives. Such supposed crimes might have been committed hundreds of years ago, but the family has to send a replacement when the girl entrusted to the shrine dies. Thus, the punishment for a past crime is perpetual. Let's examine an example. Let's say a hundred years ago, Mr. Kankan borrowed some money from Mr. Kosi but was not able to repay it at the agreed time. Mr. Kosi, the lender, would report Mr. Kankan, the borrower, to a priest in the community, who would pay Mr. Kosi. Mr. Kankan would now be indebted to the priest. If Mr. Kosi were not able to pay the loan at the agreed time, the priest would require him to send a girl from his family to serve him in his shrine. The priest would threaten that if Mr. Kosi did not comply, he (the priest) would use supernatural powers to kill all of Mr. Kosi's family members. Mr. Kosi's family is made to promise to replace the girl if she dies. The girls handed over to the priest would become his slaves because he could use them any way he wanted, even for sexual exploitation.

## Feudalism

Feudalism, also known as the *estate system*, was associated with societies during the Middle Ages. Feudalism was most common in England. By its very nature, feudalism gave rise to a hierarchy. Originally, the nobles were at the top and the commoners at the bottom. The commoners were mostly peasants, who demographically were the majority of the population. During this period, land was the most important commodity because almost everybody depended on it. The most powerful people in the society, the nobles, apportioned all the land to themselves. Thus, the nobles were a powerful land-holding class.

Under this system, the peasants swore homage to the nobles and, in return, the nobles promised to protect the peasants and to see that they received justice. There were minor variations of feudalism, but generally peasants were not paid, and instead were allotted small plots of land to grow food for themselves and their families. After working long hours for the noble, the peasant could cultivate his allotted plot of land to feed his family. Some people associate the estate system with enclosures. The term **enclosure** was used to describe, among other things, the process by which the most powerful and rich people fenced their land to the exclusion of all others. Before the period of enclosures, there was a sort of communal ownership of land. Consequently, Marxists see enclosures as a ploy used by the rich people who controlled state processes to appropriate public land for their private benefit. Thus, the "enclosure was a plain enough case of class robbery" (Thompson, 1991).

To prevent the parceling of land into small pieces, feudalism sanctioned *primogeniture*, by which all property of a deceased landowner was passed on intact to his eldest son. This type of inheritance was one of the factors that contributed to the demise of the feudal system. Younger sons of nobles who could not inherit their fathers' land eventually became priests, merchants, and artisans who challenged the positions of their elder brothers. For example, some of the merchants started cottage industries that attracted peasants from the fields, thus weakening the positions of the nobles. For the first time, some wealthy people—the priests, merchants, and artisans—were not dependent upon land.

## Castes

In a **caste system**, people inherit their caste from their parents. The caste system is maintained through inheritance and is generally justified and perpetuated through religion. As in slavery, the level of inequality in a caste system is very high. You are born into your caste and you cannot change it. That means the caste system is based on ascription.

## The Caste System in India

Historically, the caste system was most common in India, where it is still practiced in some form. Hindus believe that the caste you were born into was determined by a previous life. One's caste determines the type of job one can hold. Thus, there is occupational specialization on the basis of caste. In addition, the caste system determines power relations, residential patterns, and the types of food one can eat. One's caste determines one's life opportunities.

In India, people are born into four main castes (varnas). The highest caste, the one considered spiritually and socially superior and the one that enjoys the most privilege, is called the *Brahmin*. Members of this caste are considered pure. Traditionally, this is the priestly caste, with members of this category performing priestly duties. Since the caste system is based on religion, it is not surprising that the highest caste category is composed of those who supervise religion. In a traditional and highly religious society, people will accord the highest privileges to priests and priestly families. This supports the argument that status is the most important aspect of stratification in traditional societies.

The second highest caste is the *Kshatriya*. Generally, this caste is composed of the warriors and the political upper crust. During the period when people were consolidating their societies, different groups waged wars against each other. Therefore, soldiering was very important for the survival of every society. This may explain why warrior families are accorded such a high position in the caste system of India.

The third highest caste is the *Vaishnava*—the merchants, traders, and business people. Members of this category ensured that certain important goods were available in the society, hence their relatively average position in the caste system.

At the bottom of the system is the *Shudra*. This caste is composed of peasants, cleaners, and laborers. They do menial jobs, and their contribution to the society is not as valued as that of the other castes already mentioned.

A group called the *Dalit,* or *Untouchables*, is considered so low and unclean that it is not considered part of the caste stratification system. According to Smita Narula, "Dalits are not allowed to drink from the same wells, attend the same temples, wear shoes in the presence of an upper caste,

What are some of the main differences between the caste system in India and the class system in the United States?

or drink from the same cups in tea stalls" (Mayell, 2003). Traditionally, the Untouchables have been tasked with dirty jobs like washing blood from accident scenes. Most of them are condemned to begging for their survival. It could be said that they live to beg. In recent times, even though most are still sweepers and mowers, some Untouchables have attained executive posts as mayors, chairmen, and chancellors. In 1992, K.R. Narayanan, an Untouchable, became the vice president of India. He went on to become president in 1997. It should be noted, though, that in India, the position of president is largely ceremonial.

Since people are born into their castes, a person who belongs in one caste cannot move into another. In 1949, the Indian government abolished the caste system. However, as is the case in periphery countries, it is one thing to abolish an established cultural or religious practice, but it is another thing to enforce the abolition. Officially, the caste system has been stopped, but it is still practiced in some parts of the country, especially in rural India.

The caste system is not going away for two main reasons. First, those who are privileged by the system want to maintain their privileges. In many instances, through violence and the threat of violence, members of the upper castes have resisted the upward mobility of the lower castes. National Geographic News (2003) published an article *India's Untouchables Face Violence, Discrimination*, written by Hillary Mayell in which the author noted that:

> Human rights abuses against these people, known as Dalits, are legion. A random sampling of headlines in mainstream Indian newspapers tells their story: "Dalit boy beaten to death for plucking flowers"; "Dalit tortured by cops for three days"; "Dalit 'witch' paraded naked in Bihar"; "Dalit killed in lock-up at Kurnool"; "7 Dalits burnt alive in caste clash"; "5 Dalits lynched in Haryana"; "Dalit woman gang-raped, paraded naked"; "Police egged on mob to lynch Dalits." (p. 1)

The second factor that maintains the caste system is the religious belief of the people, including people of the lower castes and the Untouchables. Hindus believe in reincarnation and that an individual's position in the next life is dependent upon the way that person lives today. Thus, if you obey God and do what the Hindu doctrine expects of you, you may be born into a higher caste in your next life. On the other hand, if you do not obey the Hindu doctrine and you elevate yourself, you may be punished in your next life and relegated to a lower caste, or remain in your lower caste. This means that even people in lower castes may resist change.

# Class Systems

In a class system, people are categorized on the basis of their level of education, occupation, income, wealth, prestige and status. In such a system, rewards, positions, etc. are based on **meritocracy**. Thus, in a class system, a person's income, position, etc. are determined on the basis of their competency, education, credentials, talents, achievement and so on. A **social class** is made up of people similarly situated with roughly the same income, power, burden and prestige. The higher your class, the more privileges you enjoy in society. Under a **class system**, an individual's position is not fixed; instead, it is relatively open as one can ascend from a lower class to a higher one or descend in the opposite direction. Sociologists call this process social mobility. Through education and the acquisition of additional skills, individuals can make themselves more valuable and thus command more resources. In a capitalist society, there are five main classes: the upper class, the middle class, the working class, the lower class, and the underclass.

## The Class Structure in the United States

### The Upper Class

Whoever has the greatest influence on the government controls the economy. The upper class is politically the most influential class through direct participation in politics, selection of government leaders, the activities of lobby organizations, and organizations established to shape the development of government policy (Kerbo, 2009). At times, they determine how the people upon whom the president relies, like cabinet ministers and national security/policy advisers, are chosen. For example, President Jimmy Carter chose his running mate from the Trilateral Commission, which is an upper-class organization. Many of his cabinet members and special advisers were also members of the Trilateral Commission, which had been formed in 1973 by private citizens from the European Union, Japan, Canada, and the United States to encourage cooperation among the countries. Of the 90 top appointments made by President Reagan, 31 were members of the upper-class Council on Foreign Relations, a nonpartisan think tank, and 12 were members of the Trilateral Commission (Domhoff, 2006). Another 32 were members of the Committee on the Present Danger, an organization of upper-class members (Kerbo, 2009) focused on confronting terrorism. The trend of choosing members of the upper class for important political positions continues today.

The upper class can be divided into two categories, namely, the upper-upper class and the lower-upper class. There are interrelationships or overlaps between the upper-upper and the lower-upper subclasses.

## The Upper-Upper Class

The upper-upper class is made up of a group of families who are descendants of successful individuals from generations past. Some researchers call this the capitalist class or the super-rich. Their money is *old money*. Upper-upper class families are the wealthiest and the most influential families. They show a higher degree of class-consciousness and unity of action than any other class. Membership is mostly by birth and marriage. Examples of such families are the Rockefellers, the Carnegies, the Mellons, the Vanderbilts, and the Kennedys.

According to Rossides (1997), this class is very exclusive because 2 percent or less of the population belongs to it. Some researchers, such as Gilbert (2011), Kerbo (2009) and Marger (2005), believe that the upper-upper class comprises no more than 1 percent of the population. Members of this class associate in exclusive clubs and tend to marry within their class.

## The Lower-Upper Class

The lower-upper class, also known as the *nouveau riche*, comprises mostly very wealthy individuals and their families who made their fortunes relatively recently. This category comprises 2 to 3 percent of the population. Membership in this category is based on earnings rather than on inheritance. Bill Gates is one of the richest men in the United States and the world, but his family is not considered a part of the upper-upper class. This is because the wealth of the family was acquired very recently—it is *new money*. Billionaire Donald Trump is not listed in the Social Register of the upper-upper class—the wealthiest one-tenth of 1 percent of the American population. Donald Trump's response to the omission was that his heirs would be included in the Register. Like Bill Gates, Donald Trump does not belong to the upper-upper class because his money is new money. To this category, we can include top-rated sports personalities, movie stars, media personalities such as Oprah Winfrey, and some senior government officials and top executives of major corporations.

## The Middle Class

The middle class is also known as the white-collar class because its members don't generally engage in strenuous, repetitive, monotonous work; instead, their jobs typically involve dealing with people and data and require many years of educational training. In the occupational structure, most of the members of the middle class receive orders from the elite, and they in turn give orders to those in the working class. Examples of members of the middle class are physicians, professors, lawyers, office workers, insurance agents, and public school teachers. It is easier for people from lower-class backgrounds to join the middle class than it is for them to join the upper class.

Economic historians have pointed out the importance of a middle class for economic development. David Landes (1998) notes that the "ideal growth and development society" would have "a relatively large middle class" (pp. 217-18). According to Landes, England was the first country to industrialize because of "the great English middle class" (p. 221).

Besides construction, what other working-class professions can you name?

The notion that the middle class is the driving force behind the economic development of a society is supported by Adelman and Morris (1967) when they note that in the economic development of Western Europe, the middle classes were a driving force.

This is an indication that the general success of every economy is more dependent upon the middle class than it is upon the upper class. Collectively, the middle class earns and spends a lot of money. It is the backbone of the economy; when the size of the middle class increases, the economy booms. From a governmental point of view, the middle class is the money-maker; that is to say, it pays the bulk of the country's taxes. In addition, members of the middle class are more likely to demand infrastructure and services from the government—schools, highways, law enforcement—and tax reforms than any other class. Over the past decade, the middle class in the United States has shrunk in size and in its share of the nation's income (see Gilbert, 2011, and Marger, 2005).

Gilbert (2011), Thompson and Hickey (2005), and Beeghley (2004) agree that the middle class comprises between 46 and 50 percent of the population. Because the middle class consists of a wide range of professions, it is divided into two categories: the upper-middle class and lower-middle class.

### The Upper-Middle Class

The upper-middle class makes up about 15 to 19 percent of the population (Gilbert 2011, Thompson & Hickey 2005). This class is made up of highly paid professionals like doctors, lawyers, accountants, architects, and professors. Their positions are considered highly prestigious, and they are respected in society. Politically, they are active and very influential.

*The Lower-Middle Class*

The lower-middle class makes up 31 percent of the population (Gilbert 2011). Compared to the upper-middle class, members of the lower-middle class are paid less and include public school teachers, nurses, office workers, and technicians.

## The Working Class

The working class comprises about 35 percent of the population (Gilbert, 2011). Members of this class are also known as blue-collar workers. They perform primarily manual work—in a sense, using their muscles more than their brains. Examples of working-class professions are factory laborers, construction workers, and farm laborers. Compared to the upper and middle classes, members of the working class earn significantly lower incomes. The children of the working class often remain at that level; however, some are able to move to the middle class through higher education.

## The Lower Class

In a typical capitalist society like the United States, the lower class makes up of about 12 to 13 percent of the population (Gilbert, 2011, Beeghley, 2004). Many people in this class are employed part-time, seasonally or intermittently. When employed, they earn very little. Members of the lower class are politically weak. They may be struggling to put food on the table and not have enough time to engage in the political process. Historically, many of them haven't even voted. It is very difficult for these people to rise above the lower class because they don't have the money or time to attend college, with many working double shifts to make ends meet. The typical education level is high school or lower. Most of their children remain in the lower class because their parents lack the resources to push them up through the stratification system. Members of the lower class bear most of the burdens in society.

## The Underclass

The underclass is also known as the poorest of the poor, or the chronically poor. In a capitalist society, the underclass may comprise about 4 percent of the population. One of the differences between the underclass and the lower class is that while members of the lower class may be unemployed for a short time, underclass members are unemployed for a long time or perpetually. The underclass is outside the mainstream of the American occupational system. As noted by Gilbert (2011), members of the underclass have limited or erratic participation in the labor force and do not have wealth to fall back on. Thus, they are not essential to the efficient functioning of a capitalist economy. This class consists of people who dropped out of elementary school, those who engage in petty crime, as well as some elderly or disabled people. Members of the underclass possess few skills and are not able to secure jobs. Most of these people depend on the welfare system.

# Consequences of Stratification

## Income and Wealth Disparity

### Position

An individual's position in the stratification system determines his or her wealth and income. Stratification, therefore, denotes income and wealth disparity. In the United States, 24 percent of all income goes to the richest 1 percent, 50 percent of all income goes to the richest 20 percent of people, and only 3 percent of total income is earned by the bottom 20 percent. In 2006, the income of the top 1 percent increased by 14 percent, while that of the bottom 90 percent dropped by 0.6 percent (Saez & Piketty, 2006). Statistics from the U.S. Census Bureau (2011) indicate that in 2010, the income gap widened.

### Education

Income is influenced by education. On average, the higher your educational background, the higher your income. According to the Bureau of Labor Statistics (2011), in 2010 people with professional degrees earned an average of $77,280, those with doctoral degrees earned $74,400, those with master's degrees earned $61,056, those with bachelor's degrees earned $49,824, and those with associate's degrees earned $36,816. On the other hand, those with some college education (no degree) earned on the average $34,176, those with high school diplo-

**TABLE 7.1** Percentage of Total Household Wealth in the United States

| Population | 1992 | 1995 | 1998 | 2001 | 2004 | 2007 | 2010 |
|---|---|---|---|---|---|---|---|
| Top 1% | 37.2 | 38.5 | 38.1 | 33.4 | 34.3 | 34.6 | 37.1 |
| Top 20% | 83.8 | 83.9 | 83.4 | 84.4 | 84.7 | 85.0 | 87.7 |
| 2nd 20% | 11.5 | 11.4 | 11.9 | 11.3 | 11.3 | 10.9 | 10.0 |
| 3rd 20% | 4.4 | 4.5 | 4.5 | 3.9 | 3.8 | 4.0 | 3.2 |
| Bottom 40% | 0.4 | 0.2 | 0.2 | 0.3 | 0.2 | 0.2 | 0.3 |

Sources: Wolff, Edward N. (2010). "Recent Trends in Household Wealth in the United States: Rising Debt and the Middle-Class Squeeze," Working Paper No. 589. The Levy Economics Institute of Bard College

Montopoli, Brian (2011). "Left Behind in America: Who's to Blame for the Wealth Divide?" www.cbsnews.com

mas earned $30,048, and those without high school diplomas earned only $21,312.

## Government Tax Favoritism

In some ways, the rich cost the government a considerable amount of money. For example, according to the Associated Press, two-thirds of U.S. corporations did not pay federal income taxes, even though they made trillions of dollars in sales between 1998 and 2005 (Kerr, 2008). Some of these corporations are owned by the richest people in the country. Thus, the rich do not pay their fair share of tax.

## Wealth

In 2010, the richest 20 percent of families owned 87.7 percent of America's wealth, while the bottom 40 percent of the population owned less than 1 percent of the wealth. During the same year, the top 1

percent of families owned about 37.1 percent of the nation's wealth (Table 7.1).

It should be noted that wealth disparity is more pronounced than income disparity. For example, in 2010, while the richest 20 percent of the population controlled 87.7 percent of wealth in the country, they earned about 50 percent of all income. The bottom 60 percent of households possessed only 3.5 percent of the nation's wealth, while they earned 23.4 percent of the income (U.S. Census Bureau, 2011).

According to Wolff (2007), between 1983 and 2004, the largest gains in wealth and income in relative terms were made by the wealthiest households. The top 1 percent saw their average wealth rise by over 6 million dollars, or 78 percent; those in the top quintile experienced increases from 78 percent to 92 percent. Wealth increased by 57 percent for the fourth quintile, and 27 percent for the middle

**TABLE 7.2** Poverty Threshold

| Size of Family Unit | Weighted Average Thresholds |
|---|---|
| One Person | $11,139 |
| Two People | $14,218 |
| Three People | $17,374 |
| Four People | $22,314 |
| Five People | $26,439 |
| Six People | $29,897 |
| Seven People | $34,009 |
| Eight People | $37,934 |
| Nine People or More | $45,220 |

Source: U.S. Census Bureau, 2011: Poverty Threshold for 2010 by Size of Family and Number of Related Children Under 18 Years

**TABLE 7.3** Health Insurance Coverage in the United States

| Household Income | Percentage Uninsured | Number Uninsured |
|---|---|---|
| Less than $25,000 | 26.9% | 16.1 million |
| $25,000 to $49,999 | 21.8% | 15.4 million |
| $50,000 to $74,999 | 15.4% | 8.8 million |
| $75,000 or more | 8.0% | 9.4 million |

Source: U.S. Census Bureau, Current Population Survey, 2011 Annual Social and Economic Supplement

quintile. People in the bottom two quintiles lost 59 percent of their wealth. By 2004, the average wealth of the poorest 40 percent of the people had fallen to $2,200. In 2010, many Americans had negative wealth, meaning they were in debt. When this is factored in, the average wealth of the poorest 40 percent of the people has fallen below the 2004 figure of $2,200.

## Debt and Stocks

Important measurements of wealth include debt and stocks. All things being equal, the wealthier you are, the less debt you have. Additionally, upper-class people have more financial investments than members of other classes. For example, the richest 1 percent of households own about half of all outstanding stock shares, financial securities, trust equity, and business equity, along with 37 percent of non-home real estate. The top 20 percent of families account for 84 percent of the same assets. The remaining 80 percent of American families own only 16 percent of such **marketable assets**, or things that can be quickly converted into cash when cash is needed (Domhoff, 2006). According to Wolff (2010), 73 percent of all debts are the debt of the bottom 90 percent. On the other hand, the top 1 percent owes only 5 percent of the debt, and the next 9 percent owes 21 percent of all debt.

## Hunger

Testifying before the Subcommittee on Income Security and Family Support of the House Committee on Ways and Means on February 13, 2007, Robert Rector, a senior policy analyst of The Heritage Foundation, noted that 13 percent of poor families, and 2.6 percent of poor children, experience hunger at some point during the year. In most cases, their hunger is short-term. Eighty-nine percent of the poor report their families have "enough" food to eat, while only 2 percent say they "often" do not have enough to eat (Rector, 2007).

In 2010, Feeding America (the largest organization that feeds the poor) served 37 million Americans. Feeding America notes that 36 percent of its client households experienced food insecurity with hunger, meaning they were sometimes completely without a source of food (Feeding America, 2011).

## Health Insurance Coverage

In 2010, 16.3 percent or 49.7 million Americans were without health insurance. Poor people are less likely to have insurance coverage. For example, 26.9 percent of Americans who earned less than $25,000 did not have any insurance coverage in 2010 (U.S. Census Bureau, 2011). Comparatively, only 8 percent of those who earned $75,000 and above were not insured (Table 7.3).

## Income Gap

The income gap between the rich and the poor is increasing. The share of the total income going to the top 1 percent of Americans went from 8 percent in 1980 to 16 percent in 2004. Between 1970 and 2008, the income of the richest 10 percent increased by 38 percent while that of the bottom 90 percent decreased by 1 percent (Washington Post, 2011).

In 1978, corporate chief executive officers earned on the average 35 times as much as the average worker. In 1989, the gap increased to 71 times, and by 2000, the average CEO typically earned at least 300 times as much as the average worker (Mishel, 2006). Actually, figures provided by the U.S. Bureau of Labor Statistics indicate that in 1999, CEO pay surged to a record 419 times the average worker's wage.

**TABLE 7.4** Median Earnings by Race and Gender

| Race | Median Earnings | |
|---|---|---|
| | Men | Women |
| Asian | $52,154 | $42,232 |
| White | $49,643 | $37,456 |
| Native Hawaiian | $37,576 | $33,279 |
| African American | $37,392 | $32,299 |
| Native American | $35,780 | $30,196 |
| Hispanic | $30,798 | $27,035 |

Source: U.S. Census Bureau, 2010 American Community Survey, 2011

According to the U.S. Census Bureau (2010), in 2009 the income gap between the richest and poorest Americans grew to its largest margin ever. The top-earning 20 percent of Americans (those making more than $100,000 each year) received 49.4 percent of all income generated compared with the 3.4 percent made by the bottom 20 percent of earners. Poverty has driven many Americans to rely on food stamps. In 2009, the number of U.S. households receiving food stamps increased by 2 million to 11.7 million. This means 1 in 10 families was receiving government aid. This is the highest level on record.

## Poverty: What is it?

There are two main types of poverty: absolute poverty and relative poverty.

## Absolute Poverty

**Absolute poverty** may be termed complete poverty, occurring when people are desperately poor and may not even know where they will get their next meal. Absolute poverty connotes unemployment, homelessness, lack of health insurance, and, at times, going to bed hungry. The man or woman you see scavenging for food in other people's garbage is a typical example of a person who is absolutely poor. Nobody should be absolutely poor, but we find such people in all societies.

## Relative Poverty

A college class was once asked, "Is there anybody here who thinks he or she is poor?" The hand of a young lady shot up. She was asked to tell the class why she considered herself a poor person.

**TABLE 7.5** Top Ten Poverty Rates in the U.S.

| Rank | State | Poverty Rate (%) |
|---|---|---|
| 1. | Mississippi | 22.7 |
| 2. | Louisiana | 21.6 |
| 3. | District of Columbia | 19.9 |
| 4. | Georgia | 18.7 |
| 5. | New Mexico | 18.6 |
| 6. | Arizona | 18.6 |
| 7. | Texas | 18.4 |
| 8. | Kentucky | 17.7 |
| 9. | North Carolina | 17.4 |
| 10. | Alabama | 17.3 |

Source: U.S. Census Bureau. Current Population Survey. Annual Social and Economic Supplements, 2011

**TABLE 7.6** Americans Without Health Insurance Coverage by Race

|  | 2009 | | 2010 | |
|---|---|---|---|---|
|  | **Number** | **Percent** | **Number** | **Percent** |
| Whites | 22,715,000 | 11.5 | 23,093,000 | 11.7 |
| Asian Americans | 2,317,000 | 16.5 | 2,600,000 | 18.1 |
| African Americans | 7,838,000 | 20.3 | 8,132,000 | 20.8 |
| Hispanics | 15,450,000 | 31.6 | 15,340,000 | 30.7 |

Source: U.S. Census Bureau. Income, Poverty, and Health Insurance Coverage in the U.S., 2010

After struggling for a second, she said she drove an old car. She hesitated again and declared, "I know I am poor." The young lady, who was always neatly dressed, was asked to answer a few simple questions: "Have you ever gone to bed hungry? Do you own a house? Do you have a job?" She had never gone to bed hungry, she owned a vehicle, and she had a house and an income, yet she considered herself poor. Obviously, when she compared herself with other people in her milieu, others had more, so she thought she was poor. This type of "poverty" is called **relative poverty**, which is the feeling that you are poor when you compare yourself with other people. People in this category are often those who call for changes in society.

## Who Are the Poor?

The overall U.S. poverty rate increased from 14.3 percent in 2009 to 15.1 percent in 2010. For people aged 18 to 64, the poverty rate increased to 13.7 percent in 2010 from 12.9 percent in 2009. That means the number of people in poverty within that age group increased from 24.7 million in 2009 to 26.3 million in 2010.

Between 2009 and 2010, the poverty rate for children under age 18 increased to 22.0 percent from 20.7 percent. This translates into an increase from 15.5 million to 16.4 million children. These numbers indicate that the poverty rate for children was higher than the rates for adults. In all, children accounted for 35.5 percent of people in poverty but only 24.4 percent of the total population.

Poverty rates are different among races. The highest rate of poverty is found among Native Americans, followed by African Americans, then Hispanics (Table 7.8). This is due to a relative lack of education and marketable skills in these groups.

Educational achievement is the most important

**TABLE 7.7** Poverty Rate, Top Ten Poorest Cities

| Rank | City | Poverty Rate (%) |
|---|---|---|
| 1. | Detroit, MI | 36.4 |
| 2. | Cleveland, OH | 35.0 |
| 3. | Buffalo, NY | 28.8 |
| 4. | Milwaukee, WI | 27.0 |
| 5. | St. Louis, MO | 26.7 |
| 6. | Miami, FL | 26.5 |
| 7. | Memphis, TN | 26.2 |
| 8. | Cincinnati, OH | 25.7 |
| 9. | Philadelphia, PA | 25.0 |
| 10. | Newark, NJ | 23.9 |

Source: U.S. Census Bureau, 2006 American Community Survey, August 2007

factor in explaining the high earnings of Asians and whites. Since Asians and whites tend to have higher levels of education, they have learned skills that secure them high-paying jobs.

As expected, the rate of poverty is not the same in all states. As noted by Hill (2008), poverty is a major problem confronting the South, particularly Mississippi, where about one out of every five people lives in poverty. Among the top nine states with the highest poverty rates, eight are Southern states (Table 7.5). This means, comparatively, that an American is more likely to be poor if he or she lives in the South.

Southern states are poorer than Northern states due to less economic development and more limited access to higher education. In 2007, Mississippi ranked at the bottom in academic achievement (LeFevre, 2007). In Mississippi, industrialization, which is the engine of economic growth, did not come to many areas until the late 20th century. This was because the farmers were less than enthusiastic about new industry that would compete with them for unskilled black laborers. When mechanized agriculture was introduced to the South, many farm workers lost their jobs. Unfortunately, there were few industrial jobs to absorb these laid-off workers. This contributed enormously to poverty in the region, and, at the same time, many of the young and the educated left the South for the North.

Poverty rates differ by city, as well. Table 7.7 shows the top ten cities (250,000 or more in population) with the highest rates of poverty. The poorest cities have the highest concentration of minorities. Incidentally, most of the poorest cities are in the North and have high immigrant populations.

Compared with Northern states, Southern states are poorer. However, poverty is less concentrated in the South's large cities.

One common characteristic of poor cities is job loss. Detroit, for example, was once considered the automobile production headquarters of the United States and is still home to the nation's three biggest automobile companies: General Motors, Ford, and Chrysler. At the height of its industrial boom, Detroit boasted many factories. However, due to competition from foreign companies in the international market, some industries in the Detroit area have closed down. This has created unemployment and, hence, poverty.

Most of the poor are women. Pearce (1978) describes this as the feminization of poverty. Women are more likely to be unemployed and, if employed, a woman is more likely to have a part-time position. Another factor that has contributed to the feminization of poverty is an increase in female-headed households. More women are solely responsible for the financial upkeep of their households because of the higher number of deadbeat fathers. Many women are poor because their wages are lower than the wages of men. According to the U.S. Census Bureau (2011), in 2010, the median earnings of men were $46,376, and for women they were $36,142, or nearly 78 percent of what men earned. Traditional gender roles which socialize women to put family ahead of their education and careers have also contributed to the feminization of poverty.

## Disparity in Life Opportunities

Another consequence of stratification manifests itself in how long an individual lives. Various factors influence longevity, but poverty is certainly the

**TABLE 7.8** Poverty Rate by Race

| Poverty by Race | Poverty Rate | Number in Poverty |
|---|---|---|
| Native Americans | 28.4% | 1.0 million |
| African Americans | 27.4% | 10.6 million |
| Hispanics | 26.6% | 13.2 million |
| Asian Americans | 12.1% | 1.7 million |
| Whites (non-Hispanic) | 9.9% | 19.5 million |

Source: U.S. Census Bureau. Income, Poverty, and Health Insurance Coverage in the U.S., 2010

**TABLE 7.9** Life Expectancy by Income and Race

| Race | Income/Year ($) | Life Expectancy (years) |
|------|-----------------|--------------------------|
| Asian Americans | $21,566 | 84.9 |
| Whites in Appalachia | $16,390 | 75.0 |
| Blacks | $15,412 | 72.9 |
| Native Americans | $10,029 | 72.7 |

**TABLE 7.10** Correlation between Income and Life Expectancy

| Retirees | Low Income<br>Age at Death | High Income<br>Age at Death |
|----------|-----------------|------------------|
| White Males | 78.9 | 80.8 |
| Black Males | 76.8 | 79.5 |
| White Females | 82.1 | 84.7 |
| Black Females | 81.3 | 85.6 |

Source: Duggan, James E., Robert Gillingham, and John S. Greenlees (2007)

most important factor. More affluent people live longer than those who are less affluent because the former have easier access to health care, material goods, and better living and working conditions. Income influences what people eat and how they behave. For example, poor people are more likely to be obese, eat fatty foods, abuse alcohol and tobacco, and have high blood pressure and high cholesterol than rich people. A common finding is that **life expectancy** is higher for high-income people (Brown, 2002). Manchester and Topoleski (2008), note that there is a growing disparity in life expectancy between individuals with high and low incomes. Murray (2006) found that Asian American women can expect to live 13 years longer than low-income black women in the rural South.

The effect of income on longevity can be seen within race as well. For example, wealthy whites live longer than poor whites, and wealthy blacks live longer than poor blacks (Table 7.10).

The percentage of Americans reporting fair or poor health is considerably higher among people living below the poverty line than it is for those with incomes at least twice the poverty threshold. As noted by the Institute for Research on Poverty (2008), "Poor people are less healthy than those who are better off, whether the benchmark is mor-

tality, the prevalence of acute or chronic diseases, or mental health." In addition, the poor in the United States are exposed to more environmental health hazards.

## Disparity in Worker Satisfaction and Alienation

In general, high-level employees tend to be happier with their work than low-level employees. Workers at lower levels are also more likely to be alienated from their work. **Alienation** refers to the condition of powerlessness, estrangement or dissociation from the workplace and/or society. One reason low-level workers feel alienated and dissatisfied is that they always have to take instructions from others. In addition, most of the jobs of low-level employees are repetitive, offering workers little or no meaning in the work they do. Low-level workers are often not satisfied with their jobs because of their lower rate of pay.

# Social Mobility

On August 15, 2008, the media reported that Donald Trump was buying the Beverly Hills mansion of television personality Ed McMahon. Trump intended to rent the mansion to McMahon after buying the home to prevent it from going into

How do your goals today match up with the goals you had for yourself when you graduated from high school?

foreclosure, since McMahon could no longer afford to pay his $4.8 million mortgage. Obviously, McMahon was once wealthy. However, as of August 2008, he had moved to a lower social position. This is an example of **social mobility**, which describes the movement of one or more individuals from one social position to another. This move can be the result of **individual mobility** through hard work and perseverance at the individual level. Social mobility can also be the result of **structured mobility**, in which events happening in society allow groups of people to move up or down. An example of structured mobility is the reduction of manufacturing jobs in the United States. These jobs had allowed workers with little education and few skills to move upward into the middle class. With many plants shutting down their U.S. factories and moving their production overseas, these once middle-class workers are finding themselves reduced to the working or lower classes. Social mobility is more viable in open societies like capitalist societies than in closed societies like communist and traditional societies. This is because the rewards for hard work are higher in open societies than in closed societies.

## Types of Social Mobility

### Vertical Mobility

At the University of Ghana in Legon (Accra), there is an amazing story about one of the professors of sociology. This professor started work as a porter at the university. Through private studies, mostly using the university library, he passed the required preliminary courses and was admitted to the university for his bachelor's degree. Eventually, he obtained his doctorate from Oxford University in Britain and became a professor at the University of Ghana.

Another man became the branch manager of a bank in Ghana. He misappropriated some funds and was fired, and eventually became a subsistence farmer. Both his income and status diminished substantially. Thus, socially, he moved downward.

Both stories are examples of **vertical mobility**—moving up or down from one social position to another of a different rank and prestige.

## Horizontal Mobility

John was a high school teacher but decided to change professions. Consequently, he trained to become a registered nurse, where his income was similar to what he earned as a teacher. Nurses and high school teachers also attract similar levels of prestige. Thus, movement from teaching to nursing did not significantly change his income or prestige. This is an example of **horizontal mobility**, which is the movement from one social position to another of the same rank. If both professions attract the same prestige, why would an individual change professions? A person may change professions due to burn-out, which is often the result of exhaustion and decreased interest in one's work, possibly caused by stress.

## Intergenerational Mobility

The concept of **intergenerational mobility** is used to describe changes in the social positions of children in comparison to their parents. To make a fair comparison, it may be better for sons to compare their social positions with those of their fathers and daughters to compare themselves with their mothers. This is because the chances of succeeding are different for males and females. On a personal level, it will be helpful to compare yourself with your parent at specific ages. For example, if you are a 20-year-old male, you may compare your position with your father when he was 20 years old. Normally, children have access to more resources than their parents had when growing up, so they are expected to do better in their lives.

## Intragenerational Mobility

**Intragenerational mobility** involves changes in social positions within a person's adult life. In this case, you might compare yourself to yourself at different stages in your lifetime. Many people reach their peak social position at mid-life and continue to have a high social position, especially as far as income is concerned. They maintain this position until retirement, when the social position diminishes due to lower income at retirement, sickness, or other factors. These are normal or expected factors that explain why position may change over a person's lifetime. A factor expected to produce intragenerational mobility might be unemployment or a career change. A person occupying a highly respected position in the community may be fired, dramatically lowering his or her status in the community. On the other hand, an individual's status in the society may be enhanced by a job promotion.

**TABLE 7.11** Mean Earnings by Sex and Degree

| Race and Gender | Mean Earnings by Level of Highest Degree (Dollars) | | | | | | | |
|---|---|---|---|---|---|---|---|---|
| | No High School Diploma | High School Graduate | Some College | Associate Degree | Bachelor's Degree | Master's Degree | Doctorate | *Professional* |
| **White** | **20,457** | **31,429** | **33,119** | **40,632** | **57,762** | **73,771** | **104,533** | **127,942** |
| Male | 23,353 | 36,418 | 40,352 | 48,521 | 71,286 | 91,776 | 115,497 | 149,149 |
| Female | 15,187 | 24,615 | 25,537 | 33,996 | 43,309 | 58,036 | 85,682 | 89,526 |
| **Black** | **18,936** | **26,970** | **29,129** | **33,734** | **47,799** | **60,067** | **82,510** | **102,328** |
| Male | 21,828 | 30,723 | 33,969 | 41,142 | 55,655 | 68,890 | * | * |
| Female | 15,644 | 22,964 | 25,433 | 29,464 | 42,587 | 54,523 | * | * |
| **Hispanic** | **19,816** | **25,998** | **29,836** | **33,783** | **49,017** | **71,322** | **88,435** | **79,228** |
| Male | 21,588 | 28,908 | 35,089 | 38,768 | 58,570 | 80,737 | 89,956 | * |
| Female | 16,170 | 21,473 | 24,281 | 29,785 | 39,566 | 61,843 | * | * |

\* No data available because base figure is too small.

Source: U.S. Census Bureau. Statistical Abstract of the United States, 2012

# Factors That Influence Social Mobility

Social mobility is influenced by the occupational structure (parents' background) of a society, education, gender, race, and ethnicity. It should be noted that these factors work in conjunction with each other. For example, regardless of your gender or racial background, if you acquire a college education, you are likely to secure a higher-paying job than a high-school graduate. Similarly, regardless of your gender or racial background, your parents' background will affect your social mobility.

## Family Background

Family background is very important in determining an individual's social mobility. Thus, the parents' occupations influence the social mobility of their children. Professionals are more able and willing to spend the money necessary to ensure that their children acquire higher education and better jobs. Though children typically do better than their parents, they don't tend to move very far from their parents' social positions. Hence, if your parents are lower class, you are more likely to be lower class or, at best, lower-middle class.

## Education

Since higher education levels lead to more employment opportunities and higher incomes, people with higher levels of education attain higher social positions than those with lower educational backgrounds. Higher education may propel an individual into the middle class, while a high-school education might keep an individual in the working class. The educational background of parents also influences the social positions of their children. Research shows that children whose parents have a higher educational background tend to achieve higher educational levels.

Education is also the strongest single predictor of good health. It is known that individuals with high levels of education are less likely to engage in health-risk behaviors such as smoking and heavy drinking. Women with high levels of education are more likely to seek prenatal care and are less likely to smoke during pregnancy. This explains the low infant mortality rate among children of highly educated mothers.

## Gender

Compared with men, women have limited employment opportunities and their salaries are lower. Comparatively, women are more likely to be in lower-prestige occupations and less likely to achieve upward social mobility than men. In some cultures, females are discouraged and, at times, prevented, from pursuing higher education. Thus, gender is a factor in determining an individual's social mobility.

## Race and Ethnicity

Overall, most minorities have little or no wealth, little savings, and are more likely to lose their jobs. Thus, it is easier for a dominant group member to succeed than for a minority member. Many minority members, compared with dominant group members, are born into poverty. Consequently, they are not able to achieve a higher educational background and, therefore, are not able to move up in the stratification system.

# Global Stratification

The differences between countries can be measured using factors such as life expectancy, population growth rates, and literacy rates. The infant mortality rate—the number of deaths among children under 1 year of age per 1,000 live births—also illustrates the differences between countries. When making comparisons, countries are traditionally grouped into three categories: core, semi-periphery, and periphery countries.

## Core Countries

Core countries are also known as industrialized nations, first-world countries, high-income countries, developed countries, and the North. Most of these countries are located in the Northern Hemisphere. Examples include the United States, Japan, Canada, Britain, Norway, Germany and other countries in Western Europe. It should be remembered that Australia and New Zealand, which are in the Southern Hemisphere, are also core countries. Core countries are the richest countries in the world.

In what ways would your life be different if you had been born in a periphery country?

Most of the people in these countries are employed in the non-agricultural sector of the economy. For example, in the United States, only 1.9 percent of the population was involved in agriculture, forestry, fishing, or hunting in 2010 (U.S. Census, 2011). It is estimated that by 2016, the percentage of Americans engaged in agriculture will decline to 1.2 percent. On the average, primary products—consumed in their natural state—comprise less than 25 percent of the exports from core countries (Allen, 2006).

In core countries, the infant mortality rate is very low. The infant mortality rate in the United States is 7 deaths per 1,000 live births (UNDP, 2011). This rate is high compared with other core countries, but it is very low compared with non-core countries. People in core countries typically live longer than those in semi-periphery and periphery countries. For example, a baby born in the United States in 2011 will live an average of 79 years (UNDP, 2011). Many other core countries have life expectancy

rates higher than the United States.

Conditions such as life expectancy, infant mortality, literacy, and **purchasing power**, which is the number of goods and services that can be purchased with a unit of currency, are better in core countries than in semi-periphery and periphery countries (see Table 7.12)

## Semi-periphery Countries

Semi-periphery countries are known as newly industrializing countries or middle-income countries. Examples include Russia, China, India, South Korea, Malaysia, Brazil, Argentina, and most countries in Eastern Europe and the Middle East. In semi-periphery countries, the agricultural sector of the economy is shrinking in relation to other sectors of the economy. For example, at the start of the economic boom in 1963, the majority of South Koreans were farmers. Sixty-three percent of the population lived in rural areas. During the next

25 years, South Korea grew into an urban, newly industrialized country, and the agricultural work force shrunk to only 21 percent by 1989 (Savada & Shaw, 1990). Savada and Shaw also note that South Korean government officials expected urbanization and industrialization to further reduce the number of agricultural workers to well under 20 percent by 2000. By 2009, the share of agriculture in the national economy of South Korea had decreased to 3 percent (USDA, 2009).

The infant mortality rate in semi-periphery countries is generally between the low rate experienced in core countries and the high rate experienced in periphery countries. In China, the infant mortality rate is 22.1 deaths per 1,000 life births, and in India it is 34.6. Life expectancy in semi-periphery countries is also between that found in core and periphery countries. In Bulgaria, life expectancy is 73 years, in Brazil it is 74 years, and in Poland it is 76 years (WHO, 2011).

## Periphery Countries

Periphery countries are also known as the South, agricultural countries, Third World countries, low-income countries, and less-developed countries. They are the poorest countries in the world and are mostly in Africa, Asia, and Central and South America. Though the agricultural sector is declining as a reserve for surplus labor, most of the people in periphery countries are still employed in that sector of the economy. As noted by Díaz-Bonilla and Gulati (2004), "Although primary agricultural activities are declining over time as a share of the economy, they still represent about one-fourth of total economic activity and 60 percent of total employment in low-income developing countries." Commodities such as cocoa, coffee, and bananas make up 75 percent or more of the exports from periphery countries.

The infant mortality rate is highest in periphery countries. In Angola, the rate is 98 deaths per 1,000 live births (WHO, 2011). Life expectancy is also low in many periphery countries. In Zambia, for example, life expectancy is 49 years (UNDP, 2011).

## Theoretical Explanation of Global Stratification

An important question is, "Why are some coun-

tries rich and others poor?" To answer this question we need to look at some theories.

## Modernization Theory

Advocates of the **modernization theory** argue that societies started as traditional and simple societies and moved, or are moving, toward being modern (developed) societies. Thus, societies go through a number of stages of development. The more developed countries moved faster through the stages of development. Such countries have access to higher education, faith in science and technology, a free press, mass production and consumption of goods and services, political freedom, and other privileges. Conversely, less-developed countries fall behind in the stages of development. These countries lack political freedom, are superstitious, and lag behind in science and technology. They also do not provide their citizens with many privileges.

## Dependency Theory

**Dependency theory** advocates argue that some countries are poorer and less developed because they are dependent on more-developed countries. According to this school of thought, the more developed countries keep other countries poor through political and economic exploitation. The poor countries are compelled to sell their agricultural and mineral products cheaply, and to buy secondary products at exorbitant prices from the rich countries. The unequal trade relationships siphon wealth out of the poor countries and into the rich ones. As a result, the poor countries have a trade deficit, meaning they buy more than they sell. Since they make less money than what is needed to provide basic necessities for their citizens, the poor countries borrow a lot of money from the rich countries. These poor countries are indebted to the rich countries and are dependent upon their good will. In addition, the poor countries are dependent upon the rich ones for exports and investment capital. This unequal relationship resulted from colonialism in which some countries, notably European countries, ruled and exploited other countries.

An important version of the dependency theory is *World-Systems Analysis*, proposed by Immanuel Wallerstein. Wallerstein (1974) is responsible for

**TABLE 7.12** Life Conditions in Selected Core, Semi-periphery, and Periphery Countries

| Examples of: | Life expectancy (2011) | | | Infant mortality per 1,000 live births (2010) | Literacy rate percent (2009) | GNI per capita in puchasing power parity (PPP) in dollars (2011) |
|---|---|---|---|---|---|---|
| | Both Sexes | Male | Female | | | |
| **Core countries** | | | | | | |
| Japan | 83 | 80 | 86 | 2 | 99 | 32,295 |
| Australia | 82 | 80 | 84 | 4 | 99 | 34,431 |
| Switzerland | 82 | 80 | 84 | 4 | 99 | 39,924 |
| Canada | 81 | 79 | 83 | 5 | 99 | 35,166 |
| Norway | 81 | 79 | 83 | 3 | 99 | 47,557 |
| Sweden | 81 | 79 | 83 | 2 | 99 | 35,837 |
| Netherlands | 81 | 78 | 83 | 4 | 99 | 36,402 |
| Germany | 81 | 78 | 83 | 3 | 99 | 34,854 |
| Belgium | 80 | 77 | 81 | 4 | 99 | 33,357 |
| Finland | 80 | 77 | 83 | 2 | 99 | 32,438 |
| UK | 80 | 78 | 82 | 5 | 99 | 33,296 |
| USA | 79 | 76 | 81 | 7 | 99 | 43,017 |
| **Semi-periphery countries** | | | | | | |
| South Korea | 80 | 77 | 83 | 4 | 99 | 28,230 |
| Poland | 76 | 71 | 80 | 5 | 99 | 17,451 |
| Argentina | 76 | 72 | 79 | 12 | 98 | 14,527 |
| Turkey | 74 | 72 | 76 | 14 | 87 | 12,246 |
| China | 74 | 72 | 76 | 16 | 93 | 7,476 |
| Brazil | 74 | 72 | 76 | 17 | 90 | 10,162 |
| Serbia | 74 | 72 | 76 | 6 | 96 | 10,236 |
| Malaysia | 74 | 72 | 76 | 5 | 91 | 13,685 |
| Thailand | 74 | 72 | 76 | 11 | 94 | 7,694 |
| Bulgaria | 73 | 70 | 75 | 11 | 98 | 11,412 |
| Russia | 69 | 64 | 74 | 9 | 99 | 14,561 |
| India | 65 | 63 | 67 | 48 | 66 | 3,468 |
| **Periphery countries** | | | | | | |
| Bangladesh | 69 | 68 | 70 | 38 | 53 | 1,529 |
| Pakistan | 65 | 63 | 67 | 70 | 54 | 2,550 |
| Ghana | 64 | 62 | 66 | 50 | 65 | 1,584 |
| Haiti | 62 | 60 | 64 | 70 | 62 | 1,123 |
| Sudan | 62 | 60 | 64 | 66 | 60 | 1,894 |
| Ethiopia | 59 | 56 | 61 | 68 | 36 | 971 |
| Kenya | 57 | 55 | 60 | 55 | 73 | 1,492 |
| Nigeria | 52 | 50 | 54 | 88 | 72 | 2,069 |
| Angola | 52 | 51 | 53 | 98 | 67 | 4,874 |
| Mali | 51 | 50 | 52 | 99 | 26 | 1,123 |
| Chad | 50 | 48 | 52 | 99 | 32 | 1,105 |

Sources: World Health Organization (WHO) 2010 and 2011, and United Nations Development Programme (UNDP) 2011

grouping world countries into core, semi-periphery and periphery countries. The world system is dominated by core countries like Japan, the United States, and European countries. The most dominated countries are the periphery countries.

## Neo-colonialism

**Neo-colonialism** is the indirect continuation of colonialism by economic means. Some countries were poor under the rule of foreign European powers. This is because the colonial masters appropriated the products, including the minerals, of the colonized countries. For example, Ghana was colonized by the British for 136 years from 1821 to 1957 (Hatch, 1969). Though Ghana's first encounter with Europeans (the Portuguese) was in 1471, it was not until 1821 that the British colonized Ghana. During the period that Ghana was a colony of Britain, every important decision was made by the British in their own interests. Consequently, Ghana could not develop its interests as a nation.

Generally, colonialism around the world ended in the 1970s. An important question is, "If colonialism ended in the 1970s, why are former colonies still poor?" According to one school of thought, it is because of neo-colonialism. It is argued that through multinational corporations, the former colonial masters are still exploiting the former colonies. Most multinational corporations are headquartered in developed countries and have branches in developing countries. This means they repatriate wealth in the form of profits from poor countries to the rich countries. This keeps the former colonies poor.

# Sociological Theories of Stratification

## Structural Functionalist Perspective on Stratification

In order to clearly understand the position of *structural functionalism* on stratification, we have to examine how structural functionalists would answer the question, "Is social stratification necessary for society?"

The simple answer from structural functionalists would be, "Yes." According to structural functionalists, inequality is important for the survival of a society because it ensures that its most important needs are met. It also ensures that people who work harder than others are better rewarded. Every society has some necessary functions that must be performed in order for the society to survive, or to maintain social order. To qualify to perform these functions, people have to be able to invest resources like time and money. For example, the physician's role is very important in society, and it takes a lot of time and money to train to become one. Stratification motivates people to fill the most important positions in society; it encourages hard work, although many positions are only available to those who can afford the education. Thus, stratification is a structural arrangement by society to motivate or induce people to perform the duties that are important for a smoothly running society. These inducements take the form of high rewards for the important jobs in society. According to functionalists like Davis and Moore (1967), stratification is both universal and necessary in the society.

## Conflict Perspective on Stratification

Though *conflict theorists* admit that stratification is universal in human societies, they don't believe that it is necessary for a society to run smoothly. They believe that stratification is the root cause of tension and conflict in human societies. This is because stratification breeds inequality, and inequality leads to conflict.

Conflict theorists do not accept the functionalists' view that a person's position is dependent upon the importance of his or her contribution to a society. They challenge this theory on two main grounds.

First, what criterion is used to determine the importance of professions? For example, who is more important to a society, a farmer or a physician? Many people are quick to say that farmers are more important than physicians because the former produce the food we consume. If farmers are more important or critical to the survival of a society, then, going by the structural functionalist perspective, farmers should earn more than physicians. However, physicians earn more than farmers. Therefore, it is not true that the different professions

What are your thoughts on the sociological theories of stratification? Which perspective do you believe is the most accurate?

attract different salaries on the basis of their importance to society.

Second, how do we measure importance regarding different professions? Let's assume that it is true that the physician's role is more important than the role of the garbage collector. The average U.S. physician earns about $203,000 per year (Adams, 2006), while a garbage collector may earn about $30,000 per year (Employment Development Department, 2006). Thus, a physician's income is almost seven times as much as that of a garbage collector. Conflict theorists question whether a physician is indeed about seven times more important than a garbage collector. If not, then why are physicians rewarded seven times more than garbage collectors? This shows that it is not the importance of professions that determines how they are valued and rewarded.

Considering the above examples, it is obvious that the factors that determine a person's place on the stratification ladder are not straightforward. Conflict theorists assert that the most powerful people determine the stratification system ambiguously, placing some professions above others. Thus according to Mosca (1939), every society stratifies itself along lines of power, which is the main determinant of stratification.

According to the Marxist school of conflict theory, since stratification is not important, and since it is the source of conflict in society, it should be eliminated from society. One way of eliminating stratification in society is to pay people according to their needs, not according to their professions.

According to conflict theorists, one of the reasons that more has not been done to address the above issues in the United States is that Americans tend to have a poor level of **class consciousness**. Class consciousness refers to class members' shared awareness of their rank and status within a society, as well as their interests. Conflict theorists blame this low level of class awareness, in part, on false consciousness. **False consciousness** is a belief in ideas that are contrary to one's own best interests. An example would be an individual owning no investments and yet favoring a reduction of capital gains tax.

## Symbolic Interactionist Perspective on Stratification

*Symbolic interactionists* are interested in how stratification affects people's behavior. For example, they are interested in the importance of social class in shaping a person's lifestyle (Schaefer, 2008). After meeting their basic needs, people spend a lot of their resources on goods and services. Incidentally, not all people in society are able to meet their necessities. Those at the top of the social hierarchy have met their necessities and consequently spend part of their wealth on luxury yachts, fleets of vehicles, private jets, mansions, and other luxury items. On the other hand, those at the bottom of the social hierarchy spend a considerable amount of their wealth on food.

Stratification influences people's lifespans. In every society, the rich live longer than the poor because the former have access to better health care and more nutritious food. The definition of crime and the enforcement of criminal law may vary on the basis of the class system. While some actions by the rich may be ignored by police, the same actions, when taken by the poor, may result in arrest and prosecution. The definitions of crime and law enforcement biases tend to stigmatize the poor and minorities. Consequently, interactionists maintain that people are treated differently according to their position in the class system. Thus, stratification influences our lives, how others view us, and how we view ourselves.

## Feminist Perspective on Stratification

Most societies are patriarchal in the sense that they are male-dominated. Even in developed countries such as the United States, males dominate females. Even when a man and woman have the same qualifications and experience, men typically earn more than women (Eitzen & Baca-Zinn, 2003). Thus, according to functionalists, men are more important than women. In addition, the responsibilities and jobs men hold are more important than the jobs women hold. However, feminists do not agree with the views of functionalists. Feminists say that since men earn more than women even when they perform the same jobs, it is obvious that rewards such as wages are not determined by the importance of the jobs performed; rather, they are determined by a person's sex and gender expectations. Like conflict theorists, feminists assert that power relations determine the structure of stratification in society. The main goal of feminists is the practice of gender equality in society.

# Summary

Social stratification and, for that matter, inequality, are universal. The criteria used to stratify people may differ from society to society and may change from time to time. However, the consequences are the same—some people are more privileged than others. The consequences of stratification include differences in power, income, wealth, health care, and lifespan.

From the perspective of structural functionalists, stratification is positive for society because it encourages competition and motivates people to work hard. Thus, if you work hard you will secure a high-paying job and live comfortably. However, stratification is also the source of conflict in human societies. According to conflict theorists, since stratification breeds inequality, which is the main source of conflict, stratification is not good for a society. For symbolic interactionists, stratification gives some people the power to label others in a society. For example, the richest and most powerful people in a society define crime in a way that favors themselves and stigmatizes the poor and powerless. Interactionists maintain that people are treated differently according to their position in the class system. Feminists state that we live in a male-dominated society in which most important decisions are made by men, at times to the detriment of women.

## Review/Discussion Questions

1. What is the basis of stratification?
2. What is conspicuous consumption?
3. In your view, do you think stratification is positive or negative for society? List and explain some advantages and disadvantages of stratification.
4. Do you know anybody who is poor? Why do you consider that person poor?
5. List some families who belong to the American upper class. What are the criteria you used to determine the class of the families you listed?
6. What are the occupations of your father and mother? In which class category do you put your parents? Does your family background give you an edge over other students you know? Explain.
7. Who is to be blamed for the plight of the underclass? Is it the government's responsibility to assist the poorest people in society? Why or why not?
8. Who is more important to a society—a farmer or a physician? Explain your answer. Ask your friends the same question; do they have the same answer as you?
9. Your friend insists that there is too much income and wealth disparity in society, so there should be income redistribution to ensure that the gap between the rich and the poor is not too wide. Do you agree? Explain.
10. If you have never been to a Third World country, find someone from such a place and ask him or her to tell you about the conditions of life in that country. Based on the answers from this person, what do you suggest as solutions to Third World poverty?

## Key Terms

**Absolute poverty** describes people who are desperately poor and may not know where their next meal will come from.

**Alienation** refers to the condition of powerlessness, estrangement or dissociation from the workplace and or society.

**Caste systems** are based on stratification, classifying people at birth into social levels in which they remain.

**Class consciousness** is the shared awareness class members have of their status and rank within a society, as well as their interests.

**Class systems** are stratification systems in which an individual's position is not fixed but instead is relatively open, allowing the individual opportunities to move between levels.

**Conspicuous consumption** involves the public display and use of expensive items.

**Dependency theory** advocates argue that some countries are poorer and less developed because they are dependent on more developed countries.

**Economic determinism** is one of the theories attributed to Karl Marx to mean that social differentiation and class conflict resulted from economic factors.

**Enclosure** is the process by which the powerful and rich people fence (enclose) their land in order to exclude others.

**False consciousness** is a belief in ideas that are contrary to one's own best interests.

**Horizontal mobility** is the movement from one social position to another of the same rank and/or prestige.

**Individual mobility** is the result of hard work and perseverance by an individual.

**Intergenerational mobility** describes changes in the social positions of children in comparison to their parents.

**Intragenerational mobility** relates to changes in social position over the course of person's lifetime.

**Life expectancy** is the number of years that a person can expect to live within a given society, or as the number of further years of life a person can expect at a given age.

**Marketable assets** are things that can be quickly converted into cash when cash is needed.

**Materialism** occurs when people are able to satisfy their basic needs and have money left over to spend on goods and services.

**Meritocracy** is a system in which people are rewarded on the basis of their talents and achievements.

**Modernization theory** states that societies started as simple and traditional, then moved, or are moving toward, being modern (developed) societies.

**Neo-colonialism** is the indirect continuation of colonialism through economic means.

**Power** is the ability to achieve one's goals despiteopposition from others.

**Power elite** describes a small group of high-ranking leaders from government, corporations, and the military.

**Prestige** is the level of respect accorded to individuals and groups of people, especially on the basis of their occupation or profession.

**Purchasing power** is the number of goods and services that can be purchased with a unit of currency.

**Relative poverty** is the feeling or belief that you are poor when you compare yourself with other people.

**Social class** is made up of people in relatively similar situations with roughly the same power, income, and prestige.

**Social mobility** is the movement from one social position to another.

**Social stratification** is the systematic ranking of categories of people on a scale of social worth, which affects how valued resources are distributed in a society.

**Status** refers to a social position that is held by a person and characterized by rights and duties.

**Status inconsistency** occurs when people experience mismatch between their statuses, or when a person experiences mismatching statuses him or herself.

**Status systems** rank people based on their social prestige.

**Structured mobility** involves societal events that allow entire groups of people to move up or down the social structure together.

**Vertical mobility** is the movement from one social position to another of a different rank and/or prestige. This change can be in an upward or downward direction.

# Bibliography

Adams, D. (2006). Physician Income Not Rising as Fast as Other Professional Pay. American Medical News. <http: www.ama-assn.org/amednews/site/free/prsc0724.htm> (2008).

Adelman, I., & Morris, C. T. (1967). Society, Politics, and Economic Development: a Quantitative Approach. Baltimore, MD: Johns Hopkins Press.

Allen, J. L. (2007). Student Atlas of World Politics. New York: McGraw-Hill.

Ashley, D., & Orenstein, D. M. (2001). Sociological Theory: Classical Statements. Boston: Allyn and Bacon.

Beeghley, L. (2004). The Structure of Social Stratification in the United States. Boston, MA: Pearson/Allyn and Bacon

Brown, J. (2002). Differential Mortality and the Value of Individual Account Retirement Annuities. In M. Feldstein & J. Liebman (Eds.), The Distributional Aspects of Social Security and Social Security Reform (pp.401-440). Chicago: University of Chicago Press.

Bureau of Labor Statistics (2011). Current Population Survey.

Bureau of Labor Statistics (2007). Industry output and employment projections to 2016. November 2007 Monthly Labor Review. Washington, DC: U.S. Government Printing Office.

Butler, R. (2006). South Korea: Economy. <http://www.mongabay.com/reference/new_profiles/289.html> (2008).

Central Intelligence Agency (2008). The World Factbook. <https://www.cia.gov/library/publications/the-world-factbook/> (2008).

Davis, K., & Moore, W. (1966). Some Principles of Stratification. In R. Bendix (Eds.). Class, Status, and Power. New York: Free Press.

Díaz-Bonilla, E., & Gulati, A. (2004). 2002-2003 Annual Report Essay: Developing Countries and the WTO Negotiations. Washington, DC: International Food Policy Research Institute.

Domhoff, W. G. (2006). Who Rules America Now? Boston: McGraw-Hall.

Duggan, J. E., Gillingham, R., & Greenlees, J. S. (2007). Mortality and Lifetime Income Evidence from Social Security Records, Research Paper No. 2007-01. <www.ustreas.gov/official/economic-policy/papers> (2008).

Eitzen, S. D., & Baca-Zinn, M. (2003). Social Problems (9th ed.). Boston: Allyn and Bacon.

Employment Development Department (2006). California Occupational Guide #460. Sacramento: EDD.

Feeding America (2011). Hunger Study 2010. http://feedingamerica.org/hunger-in-america/hunger-studies/hunger-study-2010/key-findings.aspx

Gilbert, D. (2003). The American Class Structure in an Age of Growing Inequality (6th ed.). Belmont, CA: Wadsworth.

Gilbert, D. ( 2011). The American Class Structure in an Age of Growing Inequality. Los Angeles, CA: SAGE/Pine Forge

Hatch, J. (1969). The History of Britain in Africa. New York: Frederick A. Preager.

Hill, M. (2008). Solving the Poverty Problem in Mississippi. <http://www.mississippi.edu/urc/downloads/solvingpoverty_problem.pdf> (2008).

Infoplease (2007). Infant Mortality and Life Expectancy for Selected Countries. <http://www.infoplease.com/ipa> (2007).

Institute for Research on Poverty (2008). Health in the United States, Institute for Research on Poverty, University of Wisconsin-Madison. <http://www.irp.wisc.edu/research/health.htm#pubs> (2008).

Kerbo, H. R. (2009). Social Stratification and Inequality. Boston: McGraw-Hill.

Kerr, J. C. (2008). Most Companies in U.S. Avoid Federal Income Taxes. Associated Press. <http://news.yahoo.s/ap/20080812/ap_on_bi_ge/corporations_income_tax> (2008).

Kimmel, M., & Aronson, A. (2009). Sociology Now. Boston: Pearson/Allyn and Bacon.

Landes, D. (1998). The Wealth and Poverty of Nations. New York: Norton.

LeFevre, A. T. (2007). 2007 Report Card on American Education: A State-by-State Analysis. Washington, DC: American Legislative Exchange Council.

Manchester, J., & Topoleski, J. (2008). Growing Disparities in Life Expectancy. Washington, DC: Congressional Budget Office.

Marger, M. N. (2005). Social Inequality: Patterns and Processes. Boston: McGraw-Hill.

Mayell, H. (2003, June 2). India's Untouchables Face Violence, Discrimination. National Geographic News.

Mishel, L. (2006). CEO-to-worker Pay Imbalance Grows, Economic Snapshots: Economic Policy Institute. <http://www.epi.org> (2008).

Mills Wright, C. (1958). The Power Elite. New York: Oxford University Press.

Montopoli, B. (2011). "Left Behind in America: Who's to Blame for the Wealth Divide." <http://www.cbsnews.com> (2012).

Mosca, G. (1939). The Ruling Class. New York: McGraw-Hill.

Murray, C. J. L., Kulkarni, S., Michaud, C., Tomijima, N., Bulzacchelli, M. T., Iandiorio, T. J., & Ezzati, M. (2006). Eight Americas: investigating mortality disparities across races, counties, and race-counties in the United States. PLoS Medicine 3(9), e260.

Pearce, D. (1978). The feminization of poverty: Women, work and welfare. Urban and Social Change Review, 11, 28-36.

Rector, R. (2007). Statement of Robert Rector, Senior Policy Analyst, The Heritage Foundation. Committee on Ways and Means: Hearing Archives. http://waysandmeans.house.gov/hearings.asp?formmode=view&id=5454 (2008).

Rossides, D. W. (1997). Social Stratification: The Interplay of Class, Race, and Gender. Upper Saddle River, NJ: Prentice Hall.

Saez, E., & Picketty, T. (2008) Striking it Richer: The Evolution of Top Incomes in the United States. <http://elsa.berkeley.edu/~saez/saez-UStopincomes-2006prel.pdf> (2009).

Savada, A. M., & Shaw, W. (1990). South Korea: A Country Study. Washington: GPO/Library of Congress.

Schaefer, R. T. (2008). Sociology. New York: McGraw-Hill.

Thompson, E. P. (1991). The Making of the English Working Class. Harmondsworth: Penguin, New Edition.

Thompson, W., & Hickey, J. (2005). Society in Focus. Boston, MA: Pearson/Allyn and Bacon

United Nations Development Program (2010). Economic and social statistics on the countries and territories of the world. <http://data.un.org/Data.aspx?d=SOWC&f=inID%3A74> (2011).

United Nations Development Program (2011). Human Development Index and its Components. <http://hdr.undp.org/en/media/HDR_2011_EN_Table1.pdf> (2011).

United Nations Development Program (2011). International Human Development Indicators. <http://hdrstats.undp.org/en/indicators/100106.html> (2011).

United Nations Development Program (2008). Human Development Report: 2007/2008 Report. New York: UNDP.

USDA (2009). South Korea Agricultural Economy and Policy Report. <http://www.fas.usda.gov/country/Korea/South%20Korea%20Agricultural%20and%20Economy%20Policy%20Report.pdf> (2011).

U.S. Census Bureau (2006). American Community Survey. <http://www.factfinder.census.gov/servlet/DTTable?> (2008).

U.S. Census Bureau (2007). People and Families in Poverty by Selected Characteristics: 2006 and 2007. <http://factfinder.census.gov> (2008).

U.S. Census Bureau (2008). Current Population Survey, 2008, Annual Social and Economic Supplement. <http://factfinder.census.gov> (2008).

U.S. Census Bureau (2010). 2009 American Community Survey.

U.S. Census Bureau (2011). 2010 American Community Survey.

U.S. Census Bureau (2011). Current Population Survey. Annual Social and Economic Supplements, 2011

U.S. Census Bureau (2011). Income, Poverty, and Health Insurance Coverage in the United States 2010. <http://www.census.gov/prod/2011pubs/p60-239.pdf> (2012).

U.S. Census Bureau (2011). Poverty Threshold for 2010 by Size of Family and Number of Related Children Under 18 Years.

U.S. Census Bureau (2012). Statistical Abstract of the United States: 2012. <http://www.census.gov/population/www/socdemo/educ-attn.html> (2012).

U.S. Centers for Disease Control and Prevention (2008). Life expectancy at birth, National Center for Health Statistics, CDC. <http://www.cdc.gov> (2008).

U.S. Department of State (2007). Trafficking in Persons Report. <http://www.state.gov/g/tip/rls/tiprpt/2007/82798.htm> (2008).

Washington Post (2011). (Not) spreading the Wealth. <http://www.washingtonpost.com/wp-srv/special/business/income-inequality/> (2011).

Wallerstein, I. (1974). The Modern World System. New York: Academic Press.

World Health Organization (WHO) (2011). Life Expectancy and Mortality. <http://www.who.int/whosis/whostat/EN_WHS2011_Part2.pdf> (2012).

World Health Organization (WHO) (2011). Mortality and Burden of Disease Global Health Observatory Data Repository. <http://apps.who.int/ghodata/?theme=country> (2012).

Wolff, E. N. (2010). Recent Trends in Household Wealth in the United States: Rising Debt and the Middle-Class Squeeze, Working Paper No. 589. <http://www.levyinstitute.org/pubs/wp_589.pdf> (2011).

## CHAPTER EIGHT

# Race and Ethnicity

## Sergio Romero and Dara G. John

**Chapter Objectives**
At the end of this chapter, students should be able to:

- Understand the different forms of discrimination.
- Describe how structural functionalism, conflict and symbolic interaction theories view race.
- Give examples of ways in which life chances are different for minorities.
- Explain the history of slavery in the United States.
- Explain white privilege and its ramifications.
- Discuss some of the minority groups living in the United States.

A s one of the most diverse societies in the world, the United States influences the ways other nations treat minority groups. Race and ethnicity define our lifestyles, preferences, and identity. Think about who you are. Imagine yourself as a member of another racial group. What would you experience? How would you think differently? What do you think life is like for those who live it? Such an existence is nearly impossible to comprehend because the interactions you would have, the experiences you would know, and the thoughts you would be most concerned with would be shaped by a reality you had little control over. It is ironic that nearly everything you do, everyone you know, and every issue that matters to you is filtered by a reality above and beyond your choosing. Race and ethnicity remain two of the most defining features of people in our country, especially as determinants of social inequality.

## Social Construction of Race

If the goals of this chapter are accomplished, you will have been challenged to think about some of the concepts and beliefs that you hold, and what you understand to be "natural." In order for you to consider what is presented here, you will need to use your sociological imagination to analyze and understand how the idea of normal is, in fact, socially constructed. To say that something is a **social construction** is to realize that society and the ideas that influence and govern it are human products. Society and its many aspects are not to be taken for granted or accepted as given. Social constructs change alongside aspects of society because people and institutions change. History tells us a lot about the foundations of race and other social constructions.

## Slavery in History

As long as there has been recorded history, there have been reports of slavery. In ancient Greece, people were categorized by citizenship, language, or religious beliefs, but not by any physical characteristics. People became enslaved as a consequence of conquest, war, or debt. The word "slave" may have come from the word "slav," which referred to the prisoners from tribes captured by Germans and sold to Arabs in the medieval period.

When the British first settled in what later became the 13 colonies, neither they nor the Native Americans were categorized by race. Primary differentiation at that time was based on economic or social status or religious beliefs.

When enslaved Africans were first brought to the North American colonies in the early 1600s, they were traded for food. It is believed they were indentured servants, people who work for a specific period of time in exchange for their travel and living expenses. The first evidence of slavery is found in Virginia records as early as 1656, but the definition of a slave as a black person took longer to appear. As plantation-style capitalism developed, it came to rely heavily on enslaved Africans to work in the tobacco fields and to provide services for the plantation owners. The large amount of "free" labor was what made plantations so profitable. The slaves were racialized as a category of people who could be bought and sold without incrimination.

In 1705, the Virginia General Assembly facilitated this process with a declaration that would redefine life for African Americans for centuries:

All servants imported and brought into the Country...who were not Christians in their native Country...shall be accounted and be slaves. All Negro, mulatto and Indian slaves within this dominion...shall be held to be real estate. If any slave resist his master...correcting such slave, and shall happen to be killed in such correction...the master shall be free of all punishment...as if such accident never happened.

In his book, *On the Natural Varieties of Mankind*, published in 1776, German anthropologist Johann Blumenbach inadvertently created the foundations for racial definitions. Blumenbach believed in the equality of people and, as a professional physician and anthropologist, dispassionately provided a detailed discussion of the various appearances and physical types of humans around the globe.

Blumenbach placed the "white" skin color at the head of the list, not because of some presumed superiority, but simply because his descriptive list proceeds from lighter to darker shades of color. He described a skull found in the Caucasus Mountains as the "most beautiful form of the skull, from which...the others diverge." This description of the skull, coupled with the placement of the white skin color at the head of the list, inadvertently reflected a stratified ranking for which the white "Caucasian" racial category was its ideal.

Statements in the U.S. Declaration of Independence in 1776 about equality and "natural" human rights created a quandary for the leaders of the new country. How could a nation that declared individual liberty as preeminent nevertheless enslave a group of people to be bought and sold as property? Yet this recognition didn't prevent signatories of the U.S. Constitution from approving the counting of African slaves as three-fifths of a person for political representation to the U.S. House of Representatives. Ironically, it is Thomas Jefferson, the primary author of the Declaration of Independence who penned "life, liberty, and the pursuit of happiness," who also originated the scientific search for biological definitions of difference and inferiority.

In his *Notes on the State of Virginia*, Jefferson contemplated Blumenbach's hierarchy and suggested the innate inferiority of the black person: "I advance it therefore, as a suspicion only, that blacks … are inferior to the whites in the endowments of body and mind." He called on the scientific community to provide evidence that supported his thinking.

But race is not the biological distinction it has been believed to be. We share a biological heritage with no genetic difference. While it is likely that people of similar appearance will reproduce and create other people who share these characteristics, the idea that this is a natural desire or outcome is not accurate. Researchers who study the physical characteristics of humans find without challenge that people are far more alike both physically and emotionally than they are different. In fact, Joseph Chang, a professor of statistics at Yale University, and Steve Olson, a genetics researcher, show that if you go back in time about 30 generations, roughly 750 years ago, anyone whose children had children is likely to be one of your ancestors.

What we have then is a misinterpreted schema, supported by a desire to legitimize zealous "scientific" research, which has resulted in a set of falsely defined categories that have in very real ways determined the lives of millions of people. W.I. Thomas in his 1928 work, *The Child in America*, presented a social analysis that is accurate and appropriate here. He stated:

> If men define situations as real, they are real in their consequences (Thomas 1928, p.572).

We call this statement the Thomas Theorem. What this means in relation to race, and its manifestations in the form of racism, is the *idea* that races are real, biological distinctions. The owning, buying, selling, and even killing of members of a so-called race are legitimized by the idea of racial categorization and also by their institutionalization. The consequences of this phenomenon were real for many in the past, and the present inheritors live with them also.

# Understanding Race

The most recent U.S. Census was conducted in 2010. In the questionnaire sent to all households, two related questions asked everyone to self-select race and ethnicity. **Race** refers to a social definition that hierarchically ranks groups by physical features and cultural characteristics. The federal government keeps track of the nation's racial makeup for a number of reasons, including to: enforce civil rights laws (which also protect women, the disabled, and veterans); develop social service programs; implement equity decrees handed down by courts; and report racial disparities. The ongoing legacy of racial disparity necessitates these actions.

In our social understanding, race is more than a category on a questionnaire. Often, it shapes our attitudes and beliefs about other people, how we see ourselves, how we behave, and with whom we interact. We learn at a young age how to value people based on their skin color, the shapes of their eyes, or even the sizes and shapes of their noses. Unfortunately, these notions come with predefined behavioral expectations about how a person should act or think. This is called **stereotyping**—rigid mental images that cause us to expect a category of people to behave in a certain way, overgeneralized as true regardless of whether there are instances confirming the behavior. Stereotyping presumes that a certain trait is characteristic for all members of an identifiable group.

Stereotypes stem from **prejudice**, an attitude that one has about a person or a group. Prejudices may be favorable or negative but are not based on social reality. Rather, people often impute their feelings and attitudes from limited personal experiences. This can lead to the unfair treatment of people based on prejudices, also known as **discrimination**. Prejudicial attitudes and discriminatory practices are often based on **racism**, a set of beliefs and behaviors that is used to justify the unfair treatment of a racial group and its members for their alleged inferiority. Discrimination is present at every level of society.

The most common form of racism is **individual discrimination**, when one person treats another unfairly, and that treatment is attributed to the victim's membership in a **minority group**. The members of a minority group have significantly less power and, consequently, less access to and use of important resources in society than members of the majority group. These acts of discrimination can range from name calling to the denial of a job interview to racially motivated violence. For example, in 1998, two men in Texas dragged James Byrd to death behind a pickup truck because he was a black man. Another even less understood level of racism is **institutional discrimination**, which is more pervasive and damaging than individual discrimination. With institutional discrimination, the way in which society is organized is accepted as normal, and even necessary, while it confers disproportionate benefits to members of the **majority group**—the social group that holds and exercises the most power. Institutional racism is reflected in the advantages whites possess and successes they experience such as income, wealth, education, health care, and life expectancy. Unprejudiced whites may defend traditional institutional arrangements that protect these advantages because that's the way things have been done.

Mechanisms that maintain the status quo become apparent when crises erupt. When Hurricane Katrina was moving toward Louisiana in 2005, buses were sent to upscale neighborhoods to help the residents leave the area. Transportation was not sent to lower-income districts, where many people did not have cars or other means to leave. A majority of these residents were African Americans, and many died as a result of the lack of an organized response (Dyson, 2006).

The **Jim Crow laws** that existed in our country before the civil rights movement and the Civil Rights Act are examples of institutionalized, **legal discrimination**. Upheld by the laws, discrimination was a foregone conclusion. These laws, from the late 19th to the mid-20th centuries, allowed restaurants, businesses, and governments to deny services and employment or comparable wages to racial minorities. Additional requirements were written into many states' voting procedures that

If you saw a "white customers only" sign on a vending machine, how would you react?

made it extremely difficult, if not impossible, for minority groups to take part in the democratic process. There were even areas in the country where minority group members were not legally allowed to be in public, due to what were called *sunset laws*, after nightfall. Some forms of institutionalized racial **segregation**—the physical separation of individuals or groups from each other—were eliminated in civil rights legislation or court decisions such as the *Brown v. Board of Education* decision in 1954. With the enactment of civil rights laws, gradually all of the states repealed their bans on interracial marriage, although as late as 1999, Alabama still had this law on its books. In March 2000, Bob Jones University in South Carolina finally eliminated its ban on interracial dating.

## What is Ethnicity?

Another way in which social groups are distinguished is by **ethnicity**—a shared heritage defined by common characteristics such as language, religion, cultural practices, and nationality that differentiate it from other groups. The United States is one of the most ethnically diverse countries in the world. Many people thought of as white today would have been considered ethnic immigrants at one time. Books such as *How the Jews Became White Folk* (1998) or *How the Irish Became White* (1996) document this phenomenon. **Emigrants**, people moving from their home countries to live and establish lives in a new one, and the continued presence of Native Americans (despite the federal government's legacy of trying to exterminate them) are examples of the ethnic diversity in the United States.

Even though there is a widely accepted story of the nation as an immigrant country, as told from the perspective of the conquerors, there is continuing debate concerning the place of immigrants. Some think that once a person resides in another country, that person needs to shed his or her cultural traits and become like the members of the dominant group. This is called **assimilation**. Another way to view this issue is to see the United States as an **amalgamation**, a collection of various cultural groups that makes up society. In this manner, societal culture evolves in some ways while other aspects remain unchanged. What happens more often than not is immigrants **acculturate**; they incorporate facets of the dominant culture while retaining aspects of their ethnic origin. Over time, the host society reflects these interactions. For example, *Cinco de Mayo* is a Mexican holiday often celebrated by non-Mexicans in the United States.

One current debate focuses on language. Language is the means by which socialization occurs. It affects how we think and perceive the world. English, a unique blend of languages from multiple cultures, is the primary language in the United States. However, it is not the official language of the country. One of the historic reasons for this comes from the *Treaty of Guadalupe Hidalgo*, signed by the United States and Mexico in 1848, in which Mexico lost half of its territory after a two-year war. The treaty indicated the Spanish language would be respected alongside English to the extent that the new California constitution was written in the native tongue. New Mexico, Colorado, Nevada, Arizona, and California were some of the U.S. territories populated by Mexicans,

who spoke only Spanish. Even today, more than 50 percent of the population of New Mexico speaks Spanish as a first language, and that's not a recent development. Many people recognize U.S. city names that are Spanish—such as Los Angeles or El Paso—but are unaware that Nevada is Spanish for snowy and Colorado is Spanish for red.

According to the 2010 American Community Survey by the U.S. Census Bureau, Spanish is spoken by 12.8 percent of households, or roughly 37 million people who are at least 5 years of age and older. Among those who speak Spanish at home, more than half say they speak English "very well." While our country is improving in its ability to speak more than one language, something all industrialized countries already do, many groups oppose the provision of services and education in another language, Spanish or otherwise. They argue that if a person wants to live in the United States, he or she should learn the English language. They fear that Euro-American culture in the United States, and by extension American society, will be corrupted if another language becomes too common (U.S. Bureau of the Census, 2010b).

What are your views on current immigration laws?

Source: Laura Elizabeth Pohl.Bread for the World

Anxieties over language are connected to the ongoing issue of undocumented immigration. In April 2010, Arizona passed Senate Bill 1070, a law permitting police officers to stop anyone suspected of being an illegal immigrant and request documentation to prove his or her legal status. If a person fails to do so, he or she will be arrested and possibly deported. There was a large outcry against this law as it allows discrimination against legal residents and citizens who share physical characteristics of suspected undocumented immigrants, an act known as **racial profiling**.

# A Glimpse into Minority Group Differences

The experiences and characteristics of minorities differ along racial and ethnic lines. Their stories are comparable yet distinct, as are the terms used to identify them. Social identity labels are generally imposed by society. When immigrants from Italy began settling in the United States, they were bewildered at being called Italians or, much later, Italian Americans (when they weren't being bombarded by racial epithets). In Italy, their identity was regionally specific: Sicilians, Romans, Venetians, etc.

Every racial or ethnic minority group also has differences within it. Ethnic similarity does not translate into ethnic solidarity. As you will see, the terms that identify groups don't necessarily correspond to the varied identities, experiences, and histories within these heterogeneous groups. The members of these groups even differ on what to call themselves. The point is that as much as these pan-ethnic identity labels denote diversity in our society, there is as much diversity within each group.

## Native Americans

The stereotype of indigenous Americans as head-dress-wearing, horseback-riding, buffalo-chasing hunters is so ingrained that it leaves little room to imagine their actual diversity (Strickland, 1997). Before Christopher Columbus called the people who greeted his landing party *Indians*, this population was, as it still is, vast and varied in culture. Each tribe has a distinct and rich heritage and tradition. American Indians are, in fact, the first group in America to be racially tagged and subjugated to extreme and harsh treatment based on that identity.

Albert Memmi, an author and scholar whose work focused on the social effects of colonization, wrote that it is necessary for colonized people to be dehumanized by their oppressors and their history rewritten so that conquest may be complete (1965). In Columbus' diary, he made the following observation:

> It appears to me that the people [of the New World] are ingenious and would be good servants…These people are very unskilled in arms…With fifty men they could all be subjected to do all that one wishes.

The 2010 Census tells us that there are approximately 5.2 million people, or 1.7 percent of the population, who identify with an American Indian and/or Alaska Native tribe. There are more than 800 tribes, and nearly 70 percent are federally recognized. Seventy-eight percent of Native Americans live outside reservations or rancherias. According to the Census, the cities with the largest populations of Native Americans, in order, are New York City, Los Angeles, Phoenix, Oklahoma City, Anchorage, Tulsa, Albuquerque, Chicago, Houston, and San Antonio (U.S. Bureau of the Census, 2010a).

There are 566 federally recognized reservations and lands held in trust in 33 states. This is only about 2 percent of the land in the country. European settlers and then the federal government confiscated nearly all the land that originally was inhabited by indigenous people through force, deception, and legal trickery. Much of this land was turned over for homestead lots and private business development in the 19th century. Tribes were pushed onto reservations, often on lands they didn't originally live on. Native American reservations are highly regulated by the federal government and are controlled more than any other group of people in the country except the military. Tribal leaders are consulted regarding the affairs of reservations, but many decisions are still made at the federal government level, especially the one that defines who is an *Indian* (Wilkins, 2004).

Native Americans have the highest levels of poverty of any racial-ethnic group in the country.

Why do you think American Indian casinos benefit so few Indians?

Centuries-long discrimination prevented wealth accumulation. Reservations often are highly undeveloped and lack adequate resources for education and employment. Unemployment on and near reservations averages 49 percent. Thus, many are dependent on federal and state social welfare programs. Approximately 47 percent of all Native Americans, on or off reservations, live at or below the poverty level (Bureau of Indian Affairs, 2005; U.S. Bureau of the Census, 2010a).

The introduction of casino gambling on reservations has resulted in a higher standard of living for some Native Americans. Some casinos have seen enormous success, such as the Soaring Eagle Casino and Resort in Mount Pleasant, Michigan. Proceeds from the casino are shared with tribal members. For example, these returns have been used to build a support system for members of the Saginaw Chippewa Tribe, including a tribal police force and court system, a Montessori school and tribal college, and a social services bureau. However, gaming chiefly benefits the management companies that run these operations and a small percentage of Native Americans who live where gambling profits are high. These gains do not bring the Native Americans' overall standard of living to the American median (Barlett & Steele 2002; Sahagun, 2004).

## African Americans

People of African descent have been present in the Americas since the earliest years of European colonization. However, African "emigration" was forced through kidnapping and bondage, not by choice. The struggle for social, educational and economic equality for African Americans has framed the history of our country since its beginning.

In 2010, 42 million people, or 13.6 percent, identified as African Americans in the United States. They make up the second-largest minority population; Latinos make up the largest. The South continues to be the region with the highest proportion of African Americans (20 percent). The 10 states with the largest black populations in 2010 – New York, Florida, Texas, Georgia, California, North Carolina, Illinois, Maryland, Virginia, and Michigan – represented 58 percent of the country's total black population. Louisiana is no longer in the top 10 as a result of the Hurricane Katrina disaster in 2005. Of the 10 largest U.S. cities with a population of 100,000 or more, Detroit, Michigan, has the largest proportion of blacks (84 percent) followed by Jackson, Mississippi, with 80 percent (Office of Minority Health, 2010).

Education is a resource that affects quality of life, and blacks are less likely than whites to obtain an education. By 2010, 82 percent of African Americans, compared with 90 percent of whites, had attained at least a high school diploma. In terms of higher education, the disparity is much greater: Approximately 35 percent of African Americans had earned college degrees compared with 62 percent of whites. The lack of educational attainment combined with discrimination leads to high unemployment. For example, black males without criminal records are less likely to receive a callback from an employment application than are whites with criminal records. As a result, African American unemployment is generally twice as high as the national rate in any given year (Pager, 2003; Office of Minority Health, 2010).

According to a 2010 Census Bureau report, the average black family median income was $32,068, or 58.7 percent, in comparison to $54,620 for non-Hispanic white families. Approximately 27.4 percent of blacks were at or below the poverty level compared with 9.9 percent of non-Hispanic whites. The unemployment of black males and females is double that of their white counterparts (U.S. Bureau of the Census 2010b; Office of Minority Health 2010).

Income is one resource that affects quality of life; wealth is another, affecting the long-term quality of life for multiple generations. Wealth is the accumulated sum of assets minus the sum of debt (Pew Research Center, 2010).The median wealth of African American households is 20 times *less* than that of whites. Between 2005 and 2009, inflation-adjusted black wealth fell 53 percent in comparison to 16 percent for white households. Moreover, 35 percent of black households had zero or negative wealth (i.e., debt) compared with 15 percent for whites.

In 2010, 20.8 percent of African Americans, compared with 11.7 percent of non-Hispanic whites, did not have health insurance. Of those who were covered, 44 percent of African Americans depended on employer-sponsored health insurance, compared with 62 percent for non-Hispanic whites. When it came to publicly funded health insurance, 28 percent of African Americans, compared with 11 percent of non-Hispanic whites, relied on it (Office of Minority Health, 2010).

Racism is a fundamental cause of health disparities. A combination of resource deprivation and physiological and mental reactions to racism negatively affects racial minorities. Stress responses to racism are demonstrated to be related to hypertension, heart disease, mental health, and other negative states of health.

In a report on the state of national health, the death rate from 11 of the leading causes of death is 21 percent higher for African Americans than the national average. Blacks have significantly higher rates of death from heart disease (24 percent), diabetes (52 percent), HIV (89 percent), and homicide (82.5 percent) compared with whites. African Americans are 11.4 percent more likely to experience hypertension without getting it treated and 40.7 percent more likely to visit the emergency

room compared with whites. Consequently, the life expectancy of African Americans is five years less than whites (National Center for Health Statistics, 2011).

## Latinos

Latinos in the United States are a heterogeneous population of minority and immigrant groups. According the 2010 Census, they number 50.4 million people, or 16.3 percent of the U.S. population, making them the largest racial-ethnic minority. The vast majority are of Mexican extraction (63 percent) followed by Puerto Ricans (9.1 percent), Cubans (3.5 percent), Salvadorans (3.2 percent), Dominicans (2.8 percent), and other Central and South Americans (U.S. Bureau of the Census, 2010b).

Latinos are expected to number 132.7 million, or 30.2 percent, by 2050 when 53.7 percent of the national population will have racial-ethnic minority backgrounds. According to this projection, Latinos will continue to be the largest racial-ethnic group in the nation (U.S. Bureau of the Census, 2009).

According to the 2010 Census, 61 percent of Latinos age 25 and older had at least a high school diploma, and 12.6 percent possessed a bachelor's degree or higher; 1.1 million Latinos 25 years and older have advanced degrees (e.g., master's, professional, doctoral). In 2008, 12 percent of full-time college students were Latino. Despite these numbers, Latinos had the highest high school dropout rate in 2010 at 17.6 percent. "Some 41 percent of Hispanics ages 20 and older in the United States do not have a regular high school diploma, versus 23 percent of comparably aged blacks and 14 percent of whites" (Fry, 2010; U.S. Bureau of the Census, 2010b).

According to the Census Bureau, 26.3 percent of Latinos, compared with 14.9 percent of whites, work in service-level occupations, while 18.6 percent of Latinos work in managerial or professional occupations compared with 39.6 percent of whites. Consequently, wage incomes are significantly less. Among full-time year-round workers, the median income for Latino families was $37,359, compared with $54,620 for non-Latino whites. This means Latino households earn 68 cents for every dollar non-Latino white families earn. The Census Bureau reports that 26.6 percent of Latinos live at or below the poverty level; it's the population with the largest in-group poverty (U.S. Bureau of the Census, 2010b).

The median wealth of Latino households is 18 times *less* than whites. The typical Latino household has $6,325 compared with $113,149 for non-Latino whites. Between 2005 and 2009, inflation-adjusted Latino wealth fell 66 percent in comparison to just 16 percent for white households. Moreover, 31 percent of Latino households had zero or negative wealth (i.e., debt) compared with 15 percent for whites (Pew Research Center, 2011).

Latinos have the highest uninsured rates of any racial-ethnic group. In 2010, 30.7 percent did not have health insurance coverage. Health disparities are a complex phenomenon, but the combination of discrimination in employment, low-wage work, lower levels of education, and lack of health insurance coverage contributes to it. For example, 14.2 percent of Puerto Ricans—higher than whites and African Americans—have asthma compared with 7.8 percent of the general population. Latinos have an HIV infection rate that is 205 percent higher than that of whites. Latinos have the second highest rate of diabetes at 10.7 percent, 26.2 percent higher than the national average (Center for Disease Control, 2011; Office of Minority Health, 2010).

While Latinos have high indices in some areas of health disparities, they nevertheless have a higher than average life expectancy of 77.7 years. They have a lower mortality rate from chronic diseases than whites. They are less likely to smoke and drink alcohol excessively than whites. These differences are owed in large part to the fact that 41 percent of Latinos are foreign-born immigrants who bring healthy lifestyles with them. However, as Latino immigrants acculturate to U.S. society, they adopt the unhealthy diet and behavioral patterns of mainstream culture such as incorporating more processed foods into their diet, increasing the use of alcohol and cigarettes and decreasing fiber consumption (National Center for Health Statistics, 2011; Pew Hispanic Center, 2010; U.S. Bureau of the Census, 2010).

## Arab Americans

Prior to the World Trade Center attacks on Sept. 11, 2001, the U.S. Arab population received little attention from the rest of the country. It is a heterogeneous population from about 22 countries in Africa and Asia. Worldwide, the majority adhere to Islam and—as with Christians—there are many sects that emphasize certain aspects of their teachings while de-emphasizing others. However, Arab Muslims make up about one-fourth of all Muslims in the world. An unfortunate consequence of the 9/11 attacks was the conflation of Arab Americans and Muslims. Racism begets a rigid belief system that homogenizes a targeted group. In the case of Arab Americans, the racism net grouped them with Muslim extremists and non-Arabs and non-Muslims such as Sikhs (Southern Poverty Law Center, 2011; Pew Forum on Religion and Public Life, 2009).

Arab Americans live in all 50 states. At least 1.7 million Americans are of Arab descent, with 94 percent concentrated in the Los Angeles, Detroit, New York/New Jersey, Chicago, and Washington, D.C., metropolitan areas.[1] Some 89 percent of Arab Americans age 25 or older have at least a high school diploma. Forty-five percent have a bachelor's degree or higher, compared with 28 percent of all Americans. Furthermore, 18 percent have a post-graduate degree, which is nearly twice the U.S. average of 10 percent (Arab American Institute

---

1 The Census Bureau asks only for ancestry on the American Community Survey (ACS). The ACS is distributed to 250,000 households on a monthly basis. A household participates every six months for up to one year and a half. The ancestry question is open-ended, meaning the respondent self-identifies. The Arab American Institute and demographers estimate an undercount by a factor of three for several reasons, including: distinguishing the ancestry question apart from the race and ethnicity questions; "the effect of the sample methodology on small, unevenly distributed ethnic groups; high levels of out-marriage among the third and fourth generations; distrust/misunderstanding of government surveys among more recent immigrants, resulting in non-response by some; and the exclusion of certain subgroups from Arabic-speaking countries, such as the Somali and Sudanese, from the Arab category. It is estimated that the actual population, adjusting for underreporting, is around 5.1 million" (Arab American Institute, 2012).

Foundation, 2012).

Of working Arab Americans, 73 percent are employed in professional, managerial, technical, sales, or administrative fields. Fourteen percent are employed in service jobs compared with the 17 percent national average. Most Arab Americans work in the private sector (88 percent), though 12 percent are government employees (Arab American Institute Foundation, 2010).

The median income for Arab American households in 2008 was $56,331 compared with $51,369 for all households in the United States. Mean individual income is 27 percent higher than the national average; 13.7 percent of Arab Americans live below the poverty line, though the figure increases to more than 28 percent for single mothers (Arab American Institute Foundation, 2010).

Roughly two-thirds of Arab Americans are Christian. About 25 percent of Muslims worldwide are Arabs. Religious practices that direct personal behavior—including the five-times-daily prayers, month long fast at Ramadan, beards for men and the wearing of the *hijab* (head cover) for women—make Muslims more visible than most religious minorities and thus more vulnerable to bigotry. As the narrator for the documentary *Reel Bad Arabs* (2006) says, "Arabs are the most maligned group in the history of Hollywood…. [W]e've unlearned many of our prejudices against blacks, Native Americans, Jews, other groups. Why can't we unlearn our prejudices against Arabs and Muslims?" (Media Education Foundation, 2006; Samhan, 2001).

## Asian Americans

Asian Americans are a heterogeneous group that includes long-standing minority and immigrant groups from China, India, Japan, Korea, Vietnam, the Philippines, and other nations in Asia. The ethnic groups are diverse in language and culture. A majority (59 percent) were born outside the United States. The 2010 Census identified 14.6 million people, or 4.8 percent, who claimed complete or partial Asian heritage. Since 2000, the presence of Asian Americans grew by 43.3 percent. California has the largest population (4.8 million), and Hawaii

is the state where Asians make up the highest proportion (38.6 percent) of the population (U.S. Bureau of the Census, 2012a & b).

A common stereotype about Asian Americans is that they are a model minority group that has "made it," unlike other non-whites. This is a case of racialized deception. Students of Asian descent who do well in education, like any other group, correlate with the income and education level of their parents. For example, "most of the nation's Hmong and Cambodian adults have never finished high school" (Lewin, 2008).

The increases of Asian Americans in higher education parallel those of African Americans and Latinos. Contrary to stereotype, most Asian American students receive bachelor's degrees in business, management, social sciences, or humanities, not in the science, technology, engineering, or math fields. The Census Bureau reports that 49 percent of Asian Americans age 25 and over have a bachelor's degree or higher (M.A., PhD, M.D. or J.D.). Yet, 14 percent of Asian American adults do not have a high school diploma or equivalent. More than 2.3 million are uninsured for health care, and 12.4 percent live at or below the poverty line. Nevertheless, the median income of Asian American households is 18.2 percent higher than it is for whites (U.S. Bureau of the Census, 2010b).

However, the image of a model minority group does not protect Asian Americans from either prejudice or violence. Hate crimes are not uncommon, and these increased following 9/11. A 2002 report by the National Asian Pacific American Legal Consortium documented these crimes. "A Pakistani American family in Heber City, Utah, had their motel business set on fire…. The family stated that they had been receiving telephone threats from an anonymous person for about a year, warning them that they did not belong and to get out" (National Asian Pacific American Legal Consortium, 2002).

Many people today equate Asian products with the lowest quality. "Made in China" is perceived as an indication of poor quality and cheap labor. This attitude continues today, even in the face of high-quality production economic policies by Congress over the decades that encouraged overseas production.

## Whither Race *and* Ethnicity?

In 1903, the great sociologist W. E. B. DuBois foretold, "The problem of the twentieth century is the problem of the color-line." Enlightened perspectives on racism emerged as the last century unfolded. One of the insights that came to light was how race and ethnicity are intertwined. The basis for understanding the fluidity of racial categorization—who is racially superior, who is racially inferior—is premised on the stratification of ethnicity. For example, though Caribbean immigrants of African descent have distinct dialects and cultural practices, they are racially tagged as African Americans in the United States. They endure much of the prejudicial stereotyping and discriminatory acts meted against African Americans. Thus, they constitute a **racial-ethnic group**, a socially subordinate group that is culturally distinct.

Race or ethnicity, like other social structures such as gender, sexual orientation, disability, and social class, are ranked socially in terms of value, known as **social stratification**. In traditional American culture, implicit value is ascribed to whites and American culture at the top while others are tolerated, marginalized, ignored, or demeaned. Whites and American culture are considered the ideal with which others are compared. The combination of racism and **ethnocentrism**, the belief that one's culture is superior and other **ethnic groups** or nations are inferior, reinforces stratification of people in society.

Race and ethnicity coexist alongside other social structures. We tend to discuss them separately as though they are not interrelated. In reality, they are interdependent. For example, the persistence of racism often coexists with social structures such as gender and social class. We can perceive these dependencies as relational circles that overlap each other. Each circle represents a social structure, and the overlapping areas are where combined forms of inequality are reinforced. The mutual dependencies expand and contract, but they are ever-present.

The understanding of race relations changes as the racial and ethnic composition of social organizations, from small units like families to large units like a society, also changes. Consequently, society creates and transforms racial categories over time. Sociologists Michael Omi and Howard Winant call this phenomenon **racial formation** (1994). The composition of racial categories is altered over time. Groups previously defined by their ethnicity are racialized. For example, Native American Indians are a diverse group of ethnicities. Many of the tribes speak languages unrelated to each other, practice different cultural traditions, and engage in unique forms of religious worship. Yet they are racialized by society as though they are one group with the same cultural background and traditions.

## Sociology and the Study of Race and Ethnicity

Sociology—the systematic study of social behavior and organization—is an ideal platform from which to consider the issues connected to race and ethnicity. Indeed, the study of race and race relations has long been a focus of the discipline. The three major classical theories of sociology—structural functionalism, conflict theory, and symbolic interactionism—can be used to describe how race and society intersect.

### Structural Functionalism

The structural functionalist theory of society focuses on a social system of interdependent parts that maintains order. All elements of society have functions that serve to help that society maintain consistency and stability in its structure. All parts of society have a purpose, even those that may be seen as undesirable. How can we understand the persistence of race, which has had such negative effects on society, in a functionally, positive way?

We first recognize that the resources that exist in our society do, in fact, benefit the dominant group—whites. The legacy of Euro-American history on Western industrialization and development has maintained the existence of racism. Racism functions in many ways, including:

1. Racist ideologies of superiority that justify maintaining a society that favors the idealized, majority group.
2. Discouraging, if not limiting, many in subordinate groups from collectively challenging the status of the majority group for fear of reprisal.
3. Racialized institutions that reinforce the sense of identity; that is, who is part of the "in-group" or "out-group."
4. A sense of entitlement and gains from privilege that deter members of the majority group from altering the status quo that reproduces inequality.

Dysfunctions in society also exist because of racism. These dysfunctions affect not only the subordinate group, but also the dominant one. Adjustments are made in order to restore stability, not necessarily for redress. Ways in which racism is dysfunctional for society include:

1. The talents and skills of the members of the subordinate group are underutilized, causing a loss to society. Those that are used in society are exploited.
2. Discrimination compounds the effects of social problems.
3. Racial prejudice affects international relations and intercultural communication.
4. Social discord and disagreement are created, interfering with issues that require resolution.

Structural functionalism does not attempt to define a moral ground or determine which attitudes are good or bad. Functionalism simply describes what exists in a society. It is up to members of the society to determine their ethical foundations.

## Conflict Theory

Much of Karl Marx's work, which later developed into what is known as conflict theory, was about inequity in life. He saw serious abuse of workers during the expansion of capitalism known as industrialization. He argued capitalism would implode and would cease to exist after a worker revolt. As this theory was expanded by others, social class and racial inequality were examined in a combined manner as primary issues of research.

The focus of conflict theory is that social change comes about from the conflict generated in a capitalistic society that divides and conquers. The constant struggle for power and the ensuing conflict over resources make this theory a device for examining and understanding race relations. Conflict theorists explain that there are limited resources in society and various groups compete constantly to gain power over these resources. Within a racialized lens, conflict theorists ask: Who benefits?

This perspective of society works quite well to explain the ongoing tension between whites and racial minority groups. Whites in positions of power reinforce racial inequalities by favoring other whites for resources while exploiting and discriminating against non-whites. Assimilation is not perceived as a desirable condition or readily available option for non-whites because of the persistence of racism. Non-whites are asked to sacrifice their heritage for the cultural practices of society. In the 1980s and 1990s, many states passed English-only laws to reinforce the cultural dominance of English out of fear American society was culturally and socially deteriorating with the presence of foreign speaking immigrants.

## Symbolic Interaction Theory Functionalism

Symbolic interaction outlines a framework to understand the ways in which individuals understand, interpret, and create social reality with symbols consisting of images, spoken language, expressions, body language, and appearances. Norms, rules, and expectations influence the use of symbols to communicate a shared understanding. In symbolic interaction, racism contains symbols that reproduce racial inequality. People who feel otherwise also point out how these symbols distort our perceptions of racialized people. For example, studies show that the entertainment media's emphasis on comedic performances by African

Americans influences how audience members stereotype these performers and African Americans as a whole. The media are a source for many of the studies that employ symbolic interaction theory (Ford, 1997).

Interactionism also studies how people learn to become members of their culture and to share the beliefs and attitudes of that culture, dominant or not. From this perspective, one can see that existing prejudices and stereotypes can be perpetuated simply by socializing the next generation into that belief structure. Socialization is continuous throughout one's lifetime. The reality that results significantly affects the lives of all. The perspective individuals hold reflects how they interpret symbols, including those related to racial inequality. The effects of racialized socialization vary depending on one's racial, gender, and class identities. Structural functionalist and conflict theories focus on society, while symbolic interactionism examines aspects of it at the micro, individual level.

# Life Chances for Minorities

In every aspect of life, such as education, income, and health care, disparities between the life circumstances of whites and non-whites are noticeable when we examine the statistics. As shown earlier, the **life chances**—the ability to experience the opportunities and corresponding resources held by a society—experienced by racial minorities illustrate racial inequality.

There is no universal health care in the United States, so people must either buy their own insurance or work for an employer that provides coverage as a benefit. Many people cannot afford individual health insurance, and many companies offer insurance policies with high deductibles that price out employees. The federal government enacted health care reform in 2010, but many of the programs do not take full effect for several years while the costs of health care continue to rise.

Minority and immigrant populations are most affected by the increase in health insurance costs. Non-whites comprise 57.5 percent of the uninsured, even though these groups are only 36.3 percent

of the U.S. population. People who are not white are more likely to be locked in low-wage jobs that do not provide health insurance benefits. In some cases, health insurance is offered, but the deductible is very high or the low wages prevent the workers from paying the premiums. Often, non-whites work in part-time or temporary jobs and are three to four times as likely to be unemployed as white Americans. The U.S. Census Bureau reported in 2010 that 8.9 percent of whites, 20.8 percent of blacks, 30.7 percent of Latinos, 33 percent of Native Americans, 18.1 percent of Asians, and 16.3 percent of Pacific Islanders had no health insurance (U.S. Bureau of the Census, 2010b).

A mistaken common belief is that everyone has access to a good education and can secure a solid career if he or she chooses. According to the U.S. Census Bureau, of those students who dropped out of high school in 2009, 9.1 percent were white, 20.8 percent were Latino, and 11.6 percent were African American. Only Asian Americans show a vastly lower drop-out rate at 2.2 percent. The disparities in educational attainment repeat themselves at the post-secondary level as well. In 2010, 71.5 percent of bachelor's degrees were earned by whites, followed by 9.8 percent African Americans, 8.1 percent by Latinos, 7 percent by Asian Americans or Pacific Islanders, and 0.8 percent by Native Americans (U.S. Bureau of the Census, 2012; U.S. Bureau of the Census, 2010b).

Reasons for not finishing high school or not attaining a postsecondary degree are multi-faceted. The interplay of structural, political, economic, and cultural factors above and beyond individual capacity is involved. Also, minority students often face an adversarial environment in school. Their culture is devalued in the curriculum and students with names that are not conventional in society (e.g., not Mary, John, Bill, etc.) are the object of ridicule on the playground. The burden of success is hoisted on the individual, with teachers not realizing the external impediments that limit, if not destroy, social mobility.

Educational attainment correlates with work and income. Careers and positions that require more education, and pay higher salaries, are typically filled by whites. In 2010, only 7.7 percent of executive and managerial professionals were African American and only 8.2 percent were Latino. This does not match with the workforce ratio of 10.8 percent African American and 14.3 percent Latino. In other words, blacks and Latinos are more likely to work in low-end, service-oriented jobs where career advancement and income gains are non-existent (U.S. Bureau of the Census 2010b).

Housing is also a major area in which there is systemic discrimination. One academic offers her story as an example. Patricia Williams, a law professor at Columbia University in New York City, decided to buy a house in the mid-1990s. She researched available options and chose a home in her price range in a good neighborhood. She had an excellent credit history. This, combined with her prestigious position, allowed her to obtain a mortgage with a phone call.

When the mortgage forms arrived in the mail, she noticed that the bank had identified her race as white. She corrected this error, checked the African American box, and returned the signed forms to the bank. Immediately the bank wanted more money and increased her lending rates. The professor threatened to sue and the bank backed down, telling the professor that it was concerned with falling property values in that neighborhood.

This puzzled her. She had done her research and found no issues in the neighborhood. Then she realized that her *blackness* was the reason values might fall (Williams, 1997).

Source: White House

Do you know people who think racism is dead in the United States because we have a black president?

## The Consequences of Race

The concept of racism has existed in our society long enough for many to understand that it is unacceptable to publicly ridicule, utter racial epithets at, or physically harm racial minorities. These practices didn't end because upstanding, moral people decided to change their belief systems. It took the sacrifices, and sometimes lives, of many people of color and their allies to challenge the social systems at the micro- and macro-levels that maintained racial inequalities. Much of what was understood as racist from the past is no longer pervasive. High-profile racial minorities exist in many areas of society. U.S. President Barack Obama is a bi-racial African American.

However, do these developments mean that racism has ceased to exist? Are we living a color-blind era in the United States? If we relied on public opinion polls to inform our understanding of reality, we might conclude things are quite satisfactory. In a 2008 Gallup poll, 60 percent of whites believed racial minorities have equal job opportunities, 65 percent thought racial discrimination against African Americans is a minor problem or none at all, and 81 percent had great or a fair amount of confidence that the police treat blacks and whites equally. Similarly, studies of white college students indicate they believe that the socioeconomic playing field has been leveled for all races, especially African Americans (Gallagher, 2004).

## We Have Moved On: The Quandary of Color Blindness

There is a genuine feeling that society has moved beyond the significance of skin color. Every January when the birthday of Martin Luther King Jr. is recognized, excerpts from his famous 1963 "I Have a Dream" speech are played. The line "I have a dream that my four little children will one day live in a nation where they will not be judged by the color of their skin but by the content of their character" is extolled by the media and in U.S. classrooms.

There is a general consensus that overt white supremacy is a thing of the past. Civil rights laws making it illegal to deny housing, employment, and public accommodations give many a feeling a new era exists. Moreover, many also perceive a disconnect of the present to the past, when blatant racism was the norm. There is a strong feeling that people in the modern era are not accountable for what took place in the past because they weren't there. When blatant racism does arise, such as in 2012 when a boys high school basketball team from a white Pittsburgh suburb racially taunted its rivals, who were mostly black, or when a black man in Jasper, Texas, was dragged to death in 1998, it is roundly condemned. The public notoriety of many non-whites, including President Obama, underscores a belief we live in a morally superior period of U.S. history.

Yet, virulent, explicit expressions of racism persist. For example:

• The former secretary of education turned talk-show host Bill Bennett said in 2005, "if you wanted to reduce crime, you could—if that were your sole purpose—you could abort every black baby in this country, and your crime rate would go down." Bennett quickly added that such an idea would be "an impossible, ridiculous and morally reprehensible thing to do." But, he said, "Your crime rate would go down." (According to FBI crime records, the most common average street criminal is a young white male between the ages of 18 and 24.)

• Boston radio talk-show host Jay Severin said of Mexicans on his show in 2009: "It's millions of leeches from a primitive country come here to leech off you and, with it, they are ruining the schools, the hospitals, and a lot of life in America." Responding to a caller in 2004 about developing relationships with Muslims, he said: "You think we should befriend them. I think we should kill them."

• The website *Media Matters* posted a list of racial comments by on-air personalities in 2009, including:

Jesse Lee Paterson: "I think we all agree that Barack Obama was elected by, mostly by black racists and white guilty people."

Michael Savage: Obama is the "biggest liar in the history of the presidency, and he's getting away with it … because he's a man of color."

Bill O'Reilly: "Should white Americans be concerned about Judge [Sonia] Sotomayor?"

Jim Quinn to "race-baiting" African-American "ingrates": "get on your knees" and "kiss the American dirt" because slavery brought them to the United States.

On the January 15 edition of his nationally syndicated radio show in a monologue about Martin Luther King Jr. Day, Michael Savage called "civil rights" a "con" and asserted, "It's a racket that is used to exploit primarily heterosexual, Christian, white males' birthright and steal from them what is their birthright and give it to people who didn't qualify for it." Savage then said, "Take a guess out of whose hide all of these rights are coming? ... [T]here is only one group that is targeted, and that group is white, heterosexual males."

These statements were made in an era that many believed was long gone. How are powerfully situated individuals motivated, and secure enough, to make such unambiguous, racially charged statements?

One way to grasp how this happens is to understand **scapegoating**. This concept refers to the singling out of a group or individual for unmerited blame. The legacy of scapegoating immigrants, or the poor, is longstanding in U.S. history (Acuña, 2010). When economic crises occur and large swaths of **majority group** members lose their financial footing, opportunists exploit this condition, thereby reinforcing the inequality that is at the heart of social problems. It is easier to blame a minority group for social problems rather than recognize the structural flaws that tolerate the persistence of these problems. It is always easier to blame the victim than it is to challenge structural problems from the way a society is organized.

Racism is one of those features in society that transforms itself. The absence of overt instances of racism is muted in subtle, yet pervasive, forms of it. One of the more clever forms is racially coded imagery. Let's look at some instances of this.

- In a 2005 CNN report during the aftermath of Hurricane Katrina in New Orleans, two contrasting images were displayed: One was of two white men in a boat, filled with supplies who, according to the reporter, were "scavenging for survival materials." The other image was of some black men leaving a store with various supplies in their arms. The same reporter called these men "looters."
- In 2011, Newt Gingrich, a candidate for the Republican Party's presidential nomination said: "It would be great if inner city schools and poor neighborhood schools actually hired the children to do things. ... What if they cleaned out the bathrooms, and what if they mopped the floors?" (References to "inner city" or "urban" are widely agreed to be euphemisms for African Americans.)

The subtle forms of institutionalized racism contain an assortment of practices that preserves advantages and power for whites. In nearly every quality of life index that is valued in our society—education, employment, income, health care, life expectancy, home ownership, and wealth—whites come out ahead. In nearly every index that is feared—criminal conviction, sentencing, mortality, unemployment, debt, health ailments and afflictions—racial minorities suffer disproportionately. The resource inequalities reflected in these quality of life indices are meted out institutionally but experienced personally.

## Racial Inheritance

The nation's culture, and the country itself, was structured at its inception by whites for whites. Native Americans and people of African descent were not considered fully human and treated accordingly. Over the centuries, various systems were organized to ensure racial advantages that reflect the Euroamerican experience. This is called **white privilege**. In general, privilege refers to unearned power (Johnson, 2005). It is inherited and confers benefits not of an individual's choosing but as a consequence of birth.

One of the earliest descriptions of white privilege was offered by Peggy McIntosh (1989), an American feminist and anti-racist activist. She identified it as an "invisible knapsack" that whites carry with them of "special provisions, maps, passports, codebooks, visas, clothes, tools, and blank checks" encoded in laws, resources, images, language, traditions, and assumptions of life. McIntosh (1992) listed up to 46 examples including:

- To be taught that people of your race had created a civilized democracy.
- To see yourself widely (and for the most part positively) represented in the media.
- To not be followed when shopping.
- To not be viewed as representing or speaking for your racial group.
- To find greeting cards, dolls, and toys depicting people who look like you.
- To not have to protect your children from racism.
- To not be considered a "credit to your race" when you excel.

# Ten Things Everyone Should Know About Race

1. *Race is a modern invention.* Ancient societies, like the Greeks, did not divide people according to physical differences, but according to religion, status, class or even language. The English word "race" turns up for the first time in a 1508 poem by William Dunbar referring to a line of kings.

2. *Race has no genetic basis.* Not one characteristic, trait or even gene distinguishes all the members of one so-called race from all the members of another so-called race.

3. *Human subspecies don't exist.* Unlike many animals, modern humans simply haven't been around long enough, nor have populations been isolated enough, to evolve into separate subspecies or races. On average, only one of every thousand of the nucleotides that make up our DNA differ one human from another. We are one of the most genetically similar of all species.

4. *Skin color is only skin deep.* The genes for skin color have nothing to do with genes for hair form, eye shape, blood type, musical talent, athletic ability or forms of intelligence. Knowing someone's skin color doesn't necessarily tell you anything else about him or her.

5. *Most variation is with, not between, "races."* Of the small amount of total human variation, 85 percent exists within any local population. About 94 percent can be found within any continent. That means, for example, that two random Koreans may be as genetically different as a Korean and an Italian.

6. *Slavery predates race.* Throughout much of human history, societies have enslaved others. But it was often as a result of conquest or debt, not because of physical characteristics or a belief in natural inferiority. Because of a unique set of historical circumstances, North America had the first slave system where all slaves shared a common appearance and ancestry.

7. *Race and freedom were born together.* The United States was founded on the principle that "All men are created equal," but the country's early economy was based largely on slavery. The new idea of race helped explain why some people could be denied the rights and freedoms that others took for granted.

8. *Race justified social inequalities as natural.* The "common sense" belief in white superiority justified anti-democratic action and policies like slavery, the extermination of American Indians, the exclusion of Asian immigrants, the taking of Mexican lands, and the institutionalization of racial practices within American government, laws, and society.

9. *Race isn't biological, but racism is still real.* Race is a powerful social idea that gives people different access to opportunities and resources. The government and social institutions of the United States have created advantages that disproportionately channel wealth, power, and resources to white people. This affects everyone, whether we are aware of it or not.

10. *Colorblindness will not end racism.* Pretending race doesn't exist is not the same as creating equality.

Source: Independent Television Service www.itvs.org

One could add the cultural space to laud your success as the result of individual effort free from the stigma of government intervention. Consequently, whites feel "more at home in the world" and "escape [the] penalties or dangers that others suffer" (1992, p. 72). As Tim Wise, in his book *White Like Me* (2010), states:

> To be white not only means that one will typically inherit certain advantages from the past but also means that one will continue to reap the benefits of ongoing racial privilege…" (xi)

A common reaction to this way of understanding privilege is to look at the various social programs and affirmative action laws that attempt to help minorities and women gain access to resources otherwise out of reach. It is a common misconception that these laws create such favoritism for minority groups that white males are now the underprivileged group. Radio talk-show host Michael Savage, in 2007, used his powerful media status to claim: "[White males] are the new witches being hunted by the illiberal left using the guise of civil rights and fairness to women and what not."

Tim Wise provides a thought-provoking response to grievances of the type quoted above. He creates a scenario in which he has possession of a pill. This pill will render a white person black; he or she will be black to police officers, who stop people on the street, as well as to store owners, to loan officers, and to college admissions counselors. If it is true, he argues, that black people now have all of the privilege and opportunity of white people, people will not only accept the pill, people will demand the pill.

In reality, there is a substance that can turn skin black, yet there is no demand for it. There isn't any increase in its production or distribution. Why? Because we know that African Americans are not treated equally; therefore, no one who is not black would want to become so. It's understood, at least implicitly, that white privilege is an advantage. Does this mean that every white person is better off than non-whites?

## Intersectionality of Race

The significance of race—a social structure that profoundly affects everyone—does not stand alone. Racial issues are generally understood as an independent force. The competitive value system in society often leads many to rank them in a form resembling **oppression olympics**. For example, race and gender compete against each other to be the single most important expression of domination. Oppression olympics can lock us into a competition for attention, resources, and ideational supremacy. But race depends on other social structures like gender, ethnicity, sexual orientation, age, and social class for its persistence.

Race, gender, and social class are the most well-known social structures of oppression. Patricia Hill Collins (2012) describes these as a matrix of domination. Race is, along with the other social structures, stratified in an interlocking structure of domination and subordination. Thus, one's advantage in a particular environment or period of history is contingent on the disadvantage of others. Consequently, the institutional, symbolic, and individual dimensions of oppression render disadvantages and privileges. They affect an individual's life chances.

The interaction of race with other social structures occurs simultaneously, though not to the same degree. Therefore, not every white person is successful and not every racial minority dies prematurely. There are more whites who are poor and on welfare than any other racial group; race as well as social class are determinants of these outcomes. Latina college graduates earn less than white males with a high school diploma; race and gender explain these differences.

What is our point with these illustrations? We are attempting to help you understand that even though social progress has been made since the civil rights era, there is still a great deal of work left to change the system. Only about five percent of the population was involved in the civil rights movement, yet it profoundly changed the course of this country. Social movements draw from each other as well as create alliances for the future.

# Making a Difference

For many centuries, society has adhered to a notion that everyone can be unambiguously defined as a member of a race. Anyone who had any non-white ancestry was essentially not white—a uniquely American principle of blood quantum. As recently as 1983, a Louisiana court ruled that a woman who was the great-great-great-great-granddaughter of a slave, but whose other ancestors were white, was nonetheless an African American (Sharfstein, 2007; Marger, 2000).

One of the primary issues in debate today is affirmative action. **Affirmative action** is defined as a policy or program that seeks to redress past discrimination by increasing opportunities for underrepresented groups. The federal government has passed various forms of affirmative action legislation, but the laws that were passed in response to the civil rights movement in 1963 are those that initiated our current debate.

Some of the arguments against affirmative action are:

- Affirmative action is reverse discrimination. The white males who lose opportunities have done nothing personally to merit not being hired, promoted or admitted.
- It is demeaning to minorities and women. Saying that they need extra consideration is the same as saying that they are incapable. People who receive affirmative action benefits never escape a cloud of suspicion about their abilities.
- Affirmative action can result in hiring marginally less qualified people.
- Finally, affirmative action helps only people who are qualified for hiring or admission, those who don't really need the help, while doing little or nothing to help the poor and uneducated.

Advocates of continuing affirmative action say the following:

- Reverse discrimination, if it occurs at all, is very rare. Within the court system, only 3 percent of the affirmative action cases were reverse discrimination, and only 6 percent of that 3 percent were upheld.
- Research clearly indicates that discrimination in areas like housing and education is still widely practiced and experienced. The claim that affirmative action is no longer needed is mistaken in its platform that these practices no longer occur.
- Much evidence shows that affirmative action works. Following affirmative action guidelines has resulted in the education and hiring of many women and minorities as compared to those who do not follow these guidelines. When the law schools at the University of California and the University of Texas stopped using affirmative action, the percentage of minorities enrolling dropped sharply.

Since race is a social category rather than a biological concept, racial labels are not immutable. The dynamics of race are in constant flow and adaptation. Today in the United States, there is increasing support at the federal level for multiracial identification, as evidenced by the Census 2000 and 2010 forms. Not only are there multiple race categories to select from, but a person may also check more than one category. In addition, there is space to write in a racial or ethnic category. Over 9 million self-identified a multi-racial background in Census 2010, with black and white being the most prevalent combination. Golfer Tiger Woods and U.S. President Barack Obama identify with multiple racial groups, and this has helped elevate awareness of the racial heterogeneity of our society (U.S. Bureau of the Census, 2010a).

The civil rights movement has helped the United States move closer to equality in many ways, but there is a great deal that still needs to change. As with most social change, cultural lag is in full effect. While changes need to occur at every level, it is important to understand that responsibility for change does not rest solely in the hands of our officials. Each of us can and should work actively to correct discrimination.

The Southern Poverty Law Center (2010)

publishes a series of education packages on how to avoid acting in discriminatory ways. Below is a list of those things we can each do to work toward equality.

# Ten Ways to Fight Hate: A Community Response Guide

All over the country people are fighting hate—standing up to hate—mongers and promoting tolerance, acceptance and inclusion. The Southern Poverty Law Center (2010) published a community response guide to fight hate. This guide sets out 10 principles for fighting hate along with a collection of inspiring stories of people who acted, often alone at first, to push hate out of their communities. Their efforts usually made smaller headlines than the acts of the haters, but they made a difference. The steps outlined in this guide have been tested in scores of communities across the U.S. by a wide range of human rights, religious and civic organizations. One person, acting from conscience and love, can neutralize bigotry. A group of people can create a moral barrier to hate.

Ten Ways to Fight Hate:

1. *ACT.* Do something. In the face of hatred, apathy will be interpreted as acceptance—by the haters, the public, and worse, the victim. Decency must be exercised; if it isn't, hate invariably persists.
2. *UNITE.* Call a friend or co-worker. Organize a group of allies from churches, schools, clubs and other civic sources. Create a diverse coalition. Include children, police and the media. Gather ideas from everyone, and get everyone involved.
3. *SUPPORT THE VICTIMS.* Hate-crime victims are especially vulnerable, fearful and alone. Let them know you care. Surround them with people they feel comfortable with. If you're a victim, report every incident and ask for help.
4. *DO YOUR HOMEWORK.* Determine if a hate group is involved, and research its symbols and agenda. Seek advice from anti-hate organizations. Accurate information can then be spread to the community.
5. *CREATE AN ALTERNATIVE.* Do NOT attend a hate rally. Find another outlet for anger and frustration and people's desire to do something. Hold a unity rally or parade. Find a new hook, like a "hate-free zone."
6. *SPEAK UP.* You too, have First Amendment Rights. Hate must be exposed and denounced. Buy an ad. Help news organizations achieve balance and depth. Do not debate hate-mongers in conflict-driven talk shows.
7. *LOBBY LEADERS.* Persuade politicians, business and community leaders to take a stand against hate. Early action creates a positive reputation for the community, while unanswered hate will eventually be bad for business.
8. *LOOK LONG RANGE.* Create a "bias response" team. Hold annual events, such as a parade or culture fair, to celebrate your community's diversity and harmony. Build something the community needs. Create a website.
9. *TEACH TOLERANCE.* Bias is learned early, usually at home. But children from different cultures can be influenced by school programs and curricula. Sponsor an "I have a dream" contest. Target youths who may be tempted by skinheads or other hate groups.
10. *DIG DEEPER.* Look into issues that divide us; economic inequality, immigration, homosexuality. Work against discrimination in housing, employment, and education. Look inside yourself for prejudices and stereotypes.

We often tell students in discussions about affirmative action that the equality pendulum swings both ways. What we want is for it to come to an even center, but for centuries it has been held tightly by the dominant establishment for whites. In order for it to come to that center, it must swing in the other direction. It is only through that momentum that we can reach the balanced medium.

Can you name some other ways to fight hate?

Source: Robert Thivierge

# Summary

In addition to the details of the lives of many who share our membership as citizens and residents of the United States, we have also offered new and challenging ways to think to understand and know people, without the definition of a racial category. We have also asked that you understand, if you possess racial privilege, the symbolic, individual, and institutional advantages that exist for you, a life that has the solidity of many generations of support.

If you need to rebuild a house to suit a new way of life, you first examine what the existing house looks like, what you want to keep, and what doesn't work – those things you want to change to improve it. So it is with culture and ideology. We have things to change to sustain a new, and improved, way of life.

Tim Wise has spent his adult life working to help us understand that. He concludes in his book, *White Like Me* (2005):

> I have no idea when, or if, racism will be eradicated. I have no idea whether anything I say, do, or write will make the least bit of difference in the world. But I say it, do it, and write it anyway, because as uncertain as the outcome of our resistance may be, the outcome of our silence and inaction is anything but. We know exactly what will happen if we don't do the work: *nothing*. And given that choice, between certainty and promise, in which territory one finds the measure of our resolve and humanity, I will opt for hope (p. 154).

Our hope is that, through reading this chapter, we encourage your optimism. "While a piece of the oppressor may be planted deep within each of us, we each have the choice of accepting that piece or challenging it as part of the 'true focus of revolutionary change'" (Hill Collins, 2012).

## Review/Discussion Questions

1. What are the dimensions of racial inequality?
2. What is racial privilege and how is it premised on racial inequality?
3. How does institutional discrimination occur?
4. In what ways do the life chances for members of minority groups differ from those of whites?
5. What forms of white privilege can you identify both historically and presently?
6. What examples of acculturation can you identify?
7. How is the history of slavery connected with present-day racial inequality?
8. What are your thoughts on affirmative action?
9. How are affirmative action and racial privilege similar and dissimilar?

## Key Terms

**Acculturate** is to incorporate aspects of the dominant culture while retaining aspects of a group's ethnic origin.

**Affirmative action** is a policy or program that seeks to redress past discrimination by increasing opportunities for underrepresented groups.

**Amalgamation** happens when various cultures combine to create a new culture.

**Assimilation** occurs when a person from a minority cultural group adopts the cultural characteristics of the dominant group while discarding their ethnic traits.

**Discrimination** is differential treatment of people based on superficial characteristics such as skin color or accent.

**Emigrants** are people who leave their home countries and establish citizenship in a new country.

**Ethnic groups** are people with shared cultural heritages that others regard as distinct.

**Ethnicity** is a shared heritage defined by common characteristics such as language, religion, cultural practices, and nationality that differentiate it from other groups.

**Ethnocentrism** is the belief that one's culture is superior and other ethnic groups or nations are inferior. All other cultures and societies are judged according to the standards of the society or culture that one belongs to.

**Individual discrimination** occurs when one person treats another unfairly, and that treatment is based on the person's social status.

**Institutional discrimination** results from society operating in ways that allow certain groups to receive better treatment and opportunities than other groups.

**Jim Crow laws** allowed restaurants and business owners to legally deny services to members of minority groups.

**Legal discrimination** is unequal treatment that is upheld by laws.

**Life chances** are the ability to experience the opportunities and corresponding resources held by a society.

**Majority group** is the social group that holds and exercises superior power and resources that derive from this power. Population numbers do not equate to this power.

**Minority group** is a subordinate group whose members have significantly less power and access and use of important resources in society than members of a majority group.

**Oppression olympics** is a competition for attention, resources, and ideational supremacy between aggrieved groups or individuals.

**Prejudice** is an attitude about a person or a group that is not based on social reality.

**Race** is understood as a group of people defined by obvious physical characteristics such as skin color.

**Racial-ethnic group** refers to a socially subordinate group that is culturally distinct.

**Racial formation** is how society creates and transforms racial categories over time.

**Racial profiling** is a discriminatory law-enforcement tactic aimed at targeting racial minorities.

**Racism** is a set of beliefs used to justify the unfair treatment of a racial group and its members.

**Scapegoating** is the singling out of a group or individual for unmerited blame.

**Segregation** is the physical separation of individuals or groups from each other.

**Social construction** refers to the belief that the ideas that influence and govern social organizations are human inventions.

**Social stratification** is the systematic ranking of categories of people on a scale of social worth, which affects how valued resources are distributed in a society.

**Stereotyping** refers to pre-defined, rigid mental images about how a person or group should act or think, held to be true regardless of whether there is evidence and data disproving these images. They may be positive or negative.

**White privilege** is a cultural superiority given to people who have "white" skin and is not based on their skills, talents, or merit.

# Bibliography

Acuña, R. F. (2011). Occupied American: A History of Chicanos, 7th Edition. New Jersey: Prentice Hall.

Arab American Institute Foundation (2010). Quick Facts about Arab Americans. Washington D.C. <www.aaiusa.org> (2011).

Arab American Institute Foundation (2012). <http://www.aaiusa.org/pages/about-foundation/> (2012).

Barlett, D. L., & Steele J. B. (2002). Indian Casinos: Wheel of Misfortune—Who Gets the Money? Time, December 16.

Becker, E. (1999). Chronology on the History of Slavery. Washington, DC: The Office of Architectural History and Preservation, Smithsonian.

Bolander, D. O. (1969). Instant Quotation Dictionary. Mundelein, Ill: Career Institute

Brodkin, K. (1998). How Jews Became White Folks and What that Says About Race in America. Piscataway, NJ: Rutgers University Press.

Brown, R. E., Roberta, W., & Teleki, S. (2000). Disparities in Health Insurance and Access to Care for Residents across U.S. Cities. UCLA Center for Health Policy Research.

Blumenbach, J. F. (2005). On the Natural Varieties of Mankind. Elibron Classics, Boston, MA: Adamant Media Corporation.

Bureau of Indian Affairs (2005). American Indian Population and Labor Force Report. Washington DC: United States Department of Interior.

Chang, J. T. (1999). Recent common ancestors of all present-day individuals. Advances in Applied Probability. 31 (4), 1002-1026.

CNN (2000). Bob Jones University Ends Ban on Interracial Dating. <www.cnn.com> (2011).

DuBois, W. E. B. (1994). The Souls of Black Folk. Dover Publications, Mineola, N.Y.

Dyson, M. E. (2006). Come Hell or High Water: Hurricane Katrina and the Color of Disaster. New York: Basic Civitas Books.

Encyclopedia of Everyday Law (2010). Affirmative Action. <www.enotes.com> (2011).

Ford, T. E. (1997). Effects of Stereotypical Television Portrayals of African-Americans on Person Perception. Social Psychology Quarterly, 60: 266-278.

Fry, R. (2010). Hispanics, High School Drop Outs, and the GED. Pew Hispanic Center, May 13.

Gallagher, C. A. (2004). Color-Blind Privilege: The Social and Political Functions of Erasing the Color Line in Post-Race America. In Rethinking the Color Line, 2nd Edition, edited by Charles A. Gallagher, 575-588. New York: McGraw Hill.

Hill Collins, P. (2012). Toward a New Vision: Race, Class, and Gender as Categories of Analysis and Connection. In Race and Ethnicity in Society: The Changing Landscape, edited by Elizabeth Higginbotham and Margaret L. Anderson, 216-222. Belmont, CA: Wadsworth.

Ignatiev, N. (1996). How the Irish Became White. New York: Routledge Books.

Independent Television Service (2003). Ten Things Everyone Should Know about Race. San Francisco, CA.

Johnson, A. G. (2005). Power, Privilege, and Difference, 2nd Edition. New York: McGraw Hill.

Lewin, T. (2008). "Report Takes Aim at 'Model Minority' Stereotype of Asian American Students." New York Times, June 10.

Loury, G. C. (2002). The Anatomy of Racial Inequality. Boston: Harvard University Press.

Marger, M. N. (2000). Race and Ethnic Relations: American and Global Perspectives. Belmont, CA: Wadsworth.

McIntosh, P. (1992). White Privilege and Male Privilege: A Persona Account of Coming to See Correspondences through Work in Women's Studies. In Race, Class, and Gender: An Anthology, edited by Margaret Anderson and Patricia Hill Collins, 70-81. Belmont, CA: Wadsworth.

McIntosh, P. (1989). White Privilege: Unpacking the Invisible Knapsack. Peace and Freedom, July/August: 10-12.

Media Education Foundation (2006). Reel Bad Arabs: How Hollywood Vilifies a People. New York: Director, Sut Jhally.

Media Matters (2007). On MLK Day, Savage called Civil Rights a "racket" Designed to Steal "white males' Birthright. <www.mediamatters.org> (2011).

Media Matters (2009). Most outrageous comments of 2009. <www.mediamatters.org> (2011).

Memmi, A. (1965). The Colonizer and the Colonized. Boston: Beacon Press.

National Asian American Pacific Legal Consortium (2002). 2002 Audit of Violence Against Asian Pacific Americans. Washington, D.C.

National Center for Education Statistics (2007). Status and Trends in the Education of Racial and Ethnic Minorities. Washington, DC: U.S. Government Printing Office.

National Center for Health Statistics (2011). Health, United States, 2010: With a Special Feature on Death and Dying. Hyattsville, MD: U.S. Department of Health and Human Services.

Office of Minority Health, U.S. Department of Health and Human Services (2010). African American Profile. Washington, DC: U.S. Government Printing Office.

Omi, M., & Winant, H. (1994). Racial Formation in the United States, 2nd Edition. New York: Routledge.

Outwin, C. P. M. (1996). Securing the Leg Irons: Restriction of Legal Rights for Slaves in Virginia and Maryland, 1625-1791. Archiving Early America, <www.earlyamerica.com> (2012).

Owens, G. (2000). Alabama voters decide fate of miscegenation ban. <www.stateline.org> (2012).

Pager, D. (2003). The Mark of a Criminal Record. American Journal of Sociology, 108: 937-975.

Pew Forum on Religion and Public Life (2009). Mapping the Global Muslim Population: A Report on the Size and Distribution of the World's Muslim Population. Washington, DC: Pew Research Center.

Pew Research Center (2011). Wealth Gaps Rise to Record Highs between Whites, Blacks, and Hispanics. Washington, D.C.

Sahagun, L. (2004). Communities to Get Help from Tribes for Services, Equipment. LA Times, March 30.

Samhan, H. H. (2001). Who are Arab Americans? Washington DC: Arab American Institute.

Sharfstein, D. J. (2007). Crossing the Color Line: Racial Migration and the One-drop Rule, 1600-1860. University of Minnesota Press.

Southern Poverty Law Center (2011). 9/11 Anniversary Sparks Hate Crimes Against Muslims. Intelligence Report, Winter.

Southern Poverty Law Center (2010). Ten Ways to Fight Hate: A Community Response Guide. Montgomery, AL.

Strickland, R. (1997). Tonto's Revenge: Reflections on American Indian Culture and Policy. Albuquerque, NM: University of New Mexico Press.

Temple-Ralston, D. (2002). A Death in Texas. New York: Henry Holt and Company.

Thomas, W. I. (1928). The Methodology of Behavior Study. In The Child in America: Behavior Problems and Programs. New York: Alfred A Knopf.

U.S. Bureau of the Census (2012). Statistical Abstract of the United States, 2012, Table 271. Washington, DC: U.S. Government Printing Office.

U.S. Bureau of the Census (2010a). 2010 Census, Summary Files 1 and 2. Washington, DC: U.S. Government Printing Office.

U.S. Bureau of the Census (2010b). 2010 American Community Survey, 1-Year Estimates. Washington, DC: U.S. Government Printing Office.

U.S. Bureau of the Census (2009). United States Population Projections: 2000 to 2050. Washington, DC: U.S. Government Printing Office.

Wilkins, D. E. (2004). A Tour of Indian Peoples and Indian Lands. In Rethinking the Color Line, 2nd Edition, edited by Charles A. Gallagher, 66-86. New York: McGraw Hill.

Williams, P. J. (1997). Of Race and Risk. The Nation. December 29, 1997,10.

Wise, T. (2005). White Like Me. New York, NY: Soft Skull Press.

CHAPTER NINE

# Inequality and Stratification by Sexual Orientation, Gender and Age

## Liza L. Kuecker

**Chapter Objectives**

At the end of this chapter, students should be able to:

- Distinguish between the concepts of sex and gender.
- Identify variations in sexual orientation and the discrimination that often surrounds it.
- Explain how we become gendered individuals.
- Describe how gender is structured into social institutions, and provide examples.
- Describe how gender stratification has changed throughout history.
- Discuss the status of men and women in the United States in three major institutions: education, the economy and the political system.
- Describe how gender is analyzed by sociologists operating from the major sociological perspectives.
- Describe the effects of an ageist ideology on an elderly population.
- Describe how the status of the elderly is analyzed by sociologists operating from the major sociological perspectives.

an you identify any society in the world where men and women participate as equals in every aspect of social life? Where all age groups are equally valued and treated with respect? Where a person's sexual orientation does not become a social issue? Where the idea of difference just means different and not inferior?

If you are struggling to answer any of these questions, you are not alone. The reality is that every society stratifies its members, assigns a status value to each group, and distributes valued resources accordingly. The result is a system of structured inequalities. Sociologists use the concept of **social stratification** to refer to the way groups are ranked on a scale of perceived social worth and how that ranking affects access to resources such as property, prestige and power.

Gender, age and sexual orientation serve as a basis for stratification. In this chapter, we will focus on the inequalities associated with each. We will also learn how sociologists operating from the functionalist, conflict and symbolic interactionist perspectives analyze gender and age inequality. We will end with a brief discussion of intersectionality, a framework that highlights the importance of understanding the interconnections of gender, age and sexual orientation, and how they affect our experiences in society.

## Boy or Girl?

When a child is born, everyone wants to know: Is it a boy or a girl? The answer to the question is one that typically sends the child down a socialization path that presumes that biological sex is interwoven with gender. Gender identity emerges, and gender expectations will be socially learned through interaction with family and peers, and often reinforced by images in mass media. Then, as children reach puberty, it is also presumed they will develop an attraction to the opposite sex. It sounds pretty straightforward, doesn't it? Actually, the relationships between sex, gender and sexual orientation are quite complex. Let's begin by making distinctions among the three concepts and exploring how sex, sexual orientation and gender can serve as the basis for social inequality.

## Sex: The Biological Dimension

**Sex** refers to the biological and anatomical differences between females and males. What differentiates them is their role in reproduction. At birth, infants have **primary sex characteristics**—the genitalia involved in the reproductive process. As children reach puberty, an increase in hormone production results in the development of **secondary sex characteristics**. Males develop greater height, more muscular build, and enlarged genitalia and grow body/facial hair. Females develop larger breasts and wider hips, and begin menstruation (Benokraitis, 2012).

The assignment of biological sex is not always clear-cut. Some babies are born **intersexed**, or without genitalia that is clearly male or female. Originally, the term hermaphrodite was used to describe these babies (Weitz, 2010). About 2 percent of babies are born intersexed (Blackless et. al, 2000). Since they were not sure how to proceed with the socialization process, physicians in the 1940s in the United States began recommending that intersexed children be surgically changed to become male or female. Surgery, combined with lifelong hormonal injections, became standard medical practice. While the practice has increasingly come under attack (you can follow the debate by visiting The Intersex Society of North America website), the verdict is still out on whether sex assignment helps or harms children (Navarro, 2004). What is clear is the rationale for the procedure: Biological sex must be known in order to proceed with "appropriate" gender socialization.

*Transsexuality* presents another sex variation. A transsexual has a gender identity that is opposite of the physical sex organs of his or her body, and awareness of these differences may emerge early in life. Some transsexuals take hormone treatments or have sex change operations, decisions that are often made after extensive counseling. According to Vitello (2006), thousands of transsexuals who have undergone sex change surgery report satisfaction with the outcome and no regrets.

A clear form of sex inequality, rooted in biology but also incorporating gender expectations, is a worldwide cultural preference for male children. This has led to a phenomenon known as the "missing girls," where female fetuses are aborted or baby girls killed or neglected to death. It has been estimated that there are more than 100 million "missing girls." This has led to skewed sex ratios in several countries. For example, in China in the 1980s, there were on average 108 boys to 100 girls; in 2010, it was 124 boys to 100 girls. In this case, the skewed sex ratio is the outcome of three social forces coming together: the consequences of China's one-child policy introduced in 1979 in a culture with an enduring preference for sons; a modern desire for small families; and technology that can identify the sex of the fetus. Girls also are missing in India and other South Asian countries (Xue, 2010). Thus, we can see how biological sex is linked to gender expectations. Being born male results in a gender socialization process by which boys and men learn they have higher value, carry on the family line, inherit property and perform the tasks of a dutiful son in caring for elderly parents.

Are most of the differences we see in the behaviors of men and women rooted in biology? Sociologists maintain that the majority of differences we see are an outcome of gender socialization and are thus socially constructed.

## Sexual Orientation

**Sexual orientation** refers to a person's direction of sexual and emotional interest. Attraction may be toward members of the opposite sex (heterosexuality), the same sex (homosexuality), or both sexes (bisexuality). Sexual orientation results from a complex interplay of biological and social factors. Most societies reinforce heterosexuality as the norm, based on their cultural and/or religious systems. **Heterosexism** is the belief that heterosexuality is superior and more natural because it is linked to reproduction. **Homophobia** is the fear and hatred of homosexuality. Homophobia can take many forms: anti-gay comments, harassment, bullying or violence against gays or lesbians. The degree of acceptance of homosexuality varies from one society to the next. For example, in Egypt and other African countries where homosexuality is illegal, gays can be stoned, imprisoned or killed (Murdock, 2005; Wax, 2005). In India, where homosexual acts are illegal, gays and lesbians

could lose their jobs and possibly be sentenced to long prison terms (Wax, 2008). Greater acceptance appears to be the norm in Northern and Western Europe. Some countries, such as the Netherlands, Belgium, Spain, Canada, Norway, Sweden, Portugal and Iceland, have legalized same-sex marriage.

In the United States, attitudes toward and beliefs about homosexuality are changing, mostly in a more inclusive direction. For example, in 1973, the American Psychiatric Association removed homosexuality from its *Diagnostic* and *Statistical Manual*, no longer identifying it as a "mental disease " (Weitz, 2011). In a 2009 Gallup poll, 49 percent of those polled believed that homosexuality was "morally acceptable" as compared to 47 percent that considered it "morally unacceptable." The same poll found that 89 percent believed that homosexuals should have equal rights in terms of job opportunities (Saad, 2009). A poll conducted by the Pew Research Center in fall 2011 found the American public almost evenly divided on the issue of gay marriage, with 46 percent favoring it and 44 percent opposing it (Pew Research Center for People and the Press, 2011). As of 2012, same sex marriage has been legalized in seven states and the District of Columbia. The American Academy of Pediatrics now supports co-parent or second-

Have you ever witnessed instances of homophobia?

Source: David Shankbone

parent adoption by same-sex couples (Seccombe, 2012). The U.S. military officially rescinded its "Don't Ask, Don't Tell" policy in September 2011, joining 29 nations that allow gays and lesbians to serve openly in their militaries. Pre-repeal training occurred across the armed forces, and other military policies were also examined to ensure "sexual orientation neutrality." Surveys of military personnel and their families conducted before the repeal indicated that the majority had no issues with the repeal, but that does not guarantee everyone will accept the change (Miles, 2012). While there is no evidence that the repeal has harmed unit cohesion, as predicted by opponents, prejudice and discrimination likely persists.

Becoming a victim of a hate crime continues to be a major issue for gay, lesbian, bisexual and transgendered people. In 2010, law enforcement agencies reported 1,470 hate crimes based on sexual orientation (U.S. Department of Justice, 2010). Gay, lesbian, bisexual and transgendered youth also remain at high risk for being bullied, threatened or injured at school, and are more likely to report feeling unsafe at school than their heterosexual peers (GLSEN—the Gay, Lesbian, and Straight Education Network, 2010). Lesbian, gay and bisexual youth also have higher rates of suicide attempts than their straight peers (Hatzenbuehler, 2011). Consider the tragic circumstances that led to the suicide of Rutgers University student Tyler Clementi in September 2010. Tyler's roommate and a female friend secretly videotaped him having sex with a man, and the video was streamed online. The next day, Tyler threw himself off the George Washington Bridge. His body was later pulled from the Hudson River. The two perpetrators were charged with invasion of privacy; gay and lesbian students on campus as well as gay activists in the community wanted the pair to be charged with a hate crime, arguing that the incident was motivated by anti-gay sentiment. As the case was making its way through court, the charges were dropped for the young woman in exchange for her testimony against Tyler's roommate (Foderaro, 2010; Pilkington, 2010). The case is still pending.

# Gender: The Social Dimension

**Gender** refers to the socially and culturally constructed differences between males and females. Evidence supports the notion that gender is more than an expression of biology; gender expectations vary by culture, and also change over time in a particular society. In the Western world, gender has been presented as a binary: We are either masculine or feminine. Other cultures recognize at least three genders, if not more. Multiple genders have long been recognized in more than 150 Native American tribes (Jacobs, Thomas & Long, 1997). Originally called *berdache*, two spirits has become the preferred term to describe males who take on women's ways, or females who take on men's ways. The two most important aspects of two spirits are the gendered occupational roles they assume and the spiritual power they are thought to possess. Sexual orientation is not a defining characteristic, as two spirits may be heterosexual, homosexual or hold sexual attraction for other two-spirits members. Based on studies of two spirits, the evidence supports the idea that they are so significantly different from the men and women in their societies that they can be considered another gender (Roscoe, 1991). The *hijras* of India, described as neither men nor women, are another example of third gender (Nanda, 1999).

How do we become gendered? We learn gender expectations early in life. **Agents of socialization**, such as parents, extended family members, teachers and peers, guide this process. We also observe images of gender daily in mass media and witness gender performances in our social environments. One of the most interesting aspects of learning gender is that we are socialized to expect difference (Renzetti & Curran, 2003). In most cultures, men and women look different (by hairstyle and dress), act differently (mannerisms expressed, language used) and hold different positions. It has also been suggested that men and women think differently, but this might be better addressed through psychology than sociology.

To see an example of how we learn gender and difference, try going back to your early childhood.

While the first toys that you played with were probably selected for you by your parents and probably reflected their gender expectations, you later let your toy preferences be known. Were your favorite toys in any way gender-typed? Recent research indicates that toys are still gender-specific and that "girl toys" are the most obvious in transmitting gender expectations in terms of beauty, nurturance and emphasis of future domestic roles (Diekman, 2004; Cheney & London, 2006; Williams, 2006). Investigate this for yourself. Visit any local toy store or browse through toy catalogs online. What do you see?

Gender socialization continues throughout life. In elementary school, our peers often act as "gender police" to reinforce gender norms. You are likely to hear the comment, "Boys (or girls) don't do that." Teachers reinforce gender expectations as well, but less overtly. We are probably most aware of gender expectations when we violate them and others respond negatively, or when we see someone behaving in a way that doesn't meet our gender expectations. Throughout our lives, we will be reminded that gender matters.

Gender also is built into our social institutions. Gender is used to establish the division of labor, allocate valued resources and distribute power. All cultures have associated certain activities with women and others with men. Anthropologist George Murdock (1937) in his analysis of data collected on 324 societies found that in all of them, the work was gendered. While he noted that there were many commonalities in gender assignment of tasks across cultures, he discovered that activities that might be considered "women's work" in one society were considered "men's work" in another. One category of work that varied was taking care of cattle. In many horticultural societies, including the Masaii of Africa, women tend to cattle but do not own them. He also found that while there was no specific task assigned universally to either gender, the care of children and other domestic tasks were typically assigned to women, and waging war to men. While a gendered division of labor does not necessarily produce gender inequality, research indicates almost universally greater prestige given to "men's work,"

Source: Derek Kaczmarczyk

In your household are tasks divided up based on gender?

regardless of the task (Lerner, 1986; Linton, 1936; Rosaldo, 1974).

When one gender's activities are seen as more valued in society, and that gender is rewarded with a disproportional share of resources and opportunities, a gender stratification system has been established. **Gender stratification** refers to unequal access to property, power and prestige. It is supported by **sexism**—the belief that one sex and, by extension, one gender, is superior to another. Throughout the history of human societies (with perhaps the notable exception of hunting and gathering societies), men have been accorded more status, thus resulting in their ability to control property, experience high prestige and exercise power.

**Patriarchy** is the term used when men control the cultural, political and economic institutions in a society. We should note that the degree of patriarchy varies by society. Let's see what history can tell us. A gendered division of labor is found in all societies. But does a gendered division of labor always result in gender inequality? The answer appears to be no.

## Hunting and Gathering Societies

The earliest known division of labor between women and men was found in hunting and gathering societies, where women's primary responsibilities were the birthing and care of children. Other tasks assigned to women were based on their compatibility with child care. In most discussions of hunting and gathering societies, the basic distinction is that man was hunter and woman was gatherer. In some societies, women trapped or killed small game as they went out gathering.

What seemed to distinguish men's and women's hunting was the size of the animal, the weapon and the killing technique used.

Men in some hunting and gathering groups also participated in gathering and the care of children. Since both men and women contributed to the immediate survival of the group, there was greater equality. In fact, in some hunting and gathering groups, it has been estimated that women contributed between 60 and 80 percent of the subsistence. Less equality can be found in societies that were more dependent on men's large-game hunting.

Men who enjoyed success as hunters were accorded more prestige as they were able to distribute meat beyond immediate family use. But, since there was seldom surplus, and most hunting and gathering groups were nomadic and did not accumulate many possessions, there was limited opportunity to establish status differences between men and women (Nolan & Lenski, 2010).

## Agrarian Societies

The patriarchal system reached its peak in agrarian societies (3000 BC-1800 AD), with men controlling virtually all aspects of women's lives. Technology transformed crop cultivation and increased crop yield. Innovations also removed or limited women's participation. With the advent of the plow, use of draft animals, fertilization and the development of more sophisticated methods of irrigation, farming became men's work. Men took control of the fields and the crops that were produced, often for trade instead of immediate use. Largely removed from farming because of incompatibility with child-rearing, women became economically dependent on men, and their tasks centered on raising children and performing domestic chores.

A clear-cut distinction arose between men's work and their participation in political, legal, religious and civic life, and women's domestic roles. Culturally, men's work was given greater status, and women's work took on lesser value. The sexist ideology that emerged espoused superiority of men and inferiority of women, and was reinforced in the legal, moral and religious traditions associated with agrarian states. This included the beliefs about men and women found in the theologies of Confucianism, Hinduism, Judaism and Christianity (Scupin, 2012). As women became relegated to the private sphere, they were not allowed to own property, were often denied educational opportunities and were excluded from political participation (Martin & Voorhies, 1975).

Cultural practices developed that enforced men's control of women. For example, in China, the tradition of binding women's feet emerged around 1,000 AD. The practice is said to have originated after an emperor expressed admiration for a dancer's small feet. Foot binding involved binding a young girl's feet so they would not grow. The ideal foot size was said to be no more than 3 inches for upper class women, and 4 to 5 inches for other women. The result was decreased mobility, as you can probably imagine, and for some women, the inability to walk at all. The practice was less prevalent in South China, where women's role in rice production was still viewed as necessary. It has been estimated that 50 to 80 percent of Chinese women had bound feet in the 19th century (Scupin, 2012; Chang, 1991).

Other cultural practices focused on controlling women's sexual behavior. An important consideration for men was the assurance of the legitimacy of their heirs, so women were expected to be chaste before marriage and monogamous during marriage.

One notable practice was *purdah*, a system of secluding women and enforcing a rigid standard of female modesty. *Purdah* has been practiced in the Near East, North Africa and South Asia, involves the separation of men and women in daily life, and demands the deference of women to men. To leave the home, women may need the permission of their husbands or another male relative and must be accompanied by a male relative or servant in their travels. When venturing out in public, women's bodies must be well-covered, and clothing may include a *hijab* or *burqa*. Consequences can be severe for a woman suspected of sexual deviance, whether premarital sex or marital infidelity. In some Islamic countries, women who have been accused of sexual misconduct have been executed in what are referred to as "honor killings" (Scupin, 2012).

Although female circumcision has come under fire globally, it continues to be widely practiced in many African countries, Malaysia and Indonesia (World Health Organization, 2008). Also known as genital mutilation, it includes several different procedures, ranging from removal of the clitoris to the most severe practice, known as pharaonic infibulation, which involves stitching the cut labia to cover the vagina (Walker & Parmar, 1993; Fluehr-Lobban, 2003). The procedure varies by country, as does the age at which it is performed. Most commonly, the girls are between the ages of 4 and 8. The procedure is done without anesthesia and can result in death from blood loss or infection. Chronic infections throughout life is a likely outcome for those who survive the procedure. The intended purpose is to reduce female sexual desire, and make it more likely that a girl will remain a virgin until married and remain faithful to her husband, as sexual intercourse will always involve pain. Another concern is the complications that may arise during childbirth, placing both mother and baby at risk.

A growing social movement to ban female genital mutilation has developed, with the World Health Organization framing it as not only a human rights issue but also a health issue (World Health Organization 2008). Fifteen African countries have banned the practice, but enforcement of the law is weak (Corbett, 2008). Many women in countries where female genital mutilation is prevalent continue to support it for cultural reasons. Mothers in these countries want their daughters to marry well, and it is believed that an uncircumcised woman is impure, not respectable and, therefore, not marriageable (Flueher-Lobban, 2008).

As noted above, *purdah* and female circumcision are still maintained in some parts of the world. But consider this question: Is it appropriate for us to condemn such cultural practices in other societies?

# Gender Stratification in Contemporary Societies: A Global Perspective

In 2006, the World Economic Forum introduced the Global Gender Gap Index to assess gender equality in countries around the world. The index examines the gap between men and women in four areas:

- Economic participation and opportunity.
- Educational attainment.
- Health and survival.
- Political empowerment.

The final composite score for each country is presented as a percentage, which represents the degree of gender gap closure in the four areas. A score of 100 percent would indicate complete gender equality. Data on 135 countries were examined. Table 9.1 contains the Global Gender Gap 2011 Rankings for the Top 20 Countries.

Other key findings are that over the past six years, 85 percent of the countries have improved their gender equality ratio; the four top Nordic countries have consistently scored highest on gender equality over six years; and the gap remains widest in the Middle East and North Africa. As a general trend, the gaps in health and education are closing more rapidly than the gaps in economic and political participation (Hausmann, Tyson, Bekhouch & Zahidi, 2011).

Measuring gender equality by this method has earned one major criticism: No measure compares men's and women's participation in family work, including the care of children and domestic labor. Excluding such participation reinforces the idea that unpaid labor in the home is not really "work."

**TABLE 9.1** Global Gender Gap 2011

| Country | Gender Gap |
|---|---|
| 1. Iceland | 85.3% |
| 2. Norway | 84.0% |
| 3. Finland | 83.8% |
| 4. Sweden | 80.4% |
| 5. Ireland | 78.3% |
| 6. New Zealand | 78.1% |
| 7. Denmark | 77.8% |
| 8. Philippines | 76.9% |
| 9. Lesotho | 76.3% |
| 10. Switzerland | 76.3% |
| 11. Germany | 75.9% |
| 12. Spain | 75.8% |
| 13. Belgium | 75.3% |
| 14. South Africa | 74.8% |
| 15. Netherlands | 74.7% |
| 16. United Kingdom | 74.6% |
| 17. United States | 74.1% |
| 18. Canada | 74.1% |
| 19. Latvia | 74.0% |
| 20. Cuba | 73.9% |

## Gender Stratification in the United States: A Current Status Report

As we discovered in the previous section, the United States is ranked 17th in the degree of gender gap closure on the measurements identified. Let's take a closer look at how the United States fared in three areas: educational attainment; occupation and income; and political office-holding.

### Education

The United States scored a 1 (no gender disparity) in the educational attainment measure of the Global Gender Gap Index. This places the country alongside most of Northern and Western Europe in providing equal educational opportunities. This may not be surprising as most Americans equate completion of educational degrees with more and better employment opportunities. However we

might define a "better job," most of us recognize that completion of a postsecondary degree is likely a requirement. The data support this; Americans have become more educated over the past 40 years. The number of Americans attending college and obtaining degrees has dramatically risen since 1970. In 1970, 8.5 million attended institutions of higher education; by 2009, more than 20 million did (U.S. Department of Education, National Center for Education Statistics, 2011). The percentage of Americans attaining at least a bachelor's degree has risen from 11 to 30 percent over the same time period. The pattern holds true for women and men, and for all racial and ethnic categories (Pollard, 2011). And we can confirm this for ourselves through personal experience. Take a minute to think about why you are in college. Do you think your intended degree will lead to better employment opportunities than you currently have?

Historically, men comprised the majority of college students in all degree programs. This should not be surprising because men were expected to be the breadwinners. It is interesting to note that men's college attendance rose dramatically in the 1950s with the introduction of the G.I. Bill. At that time, men made up 70 percent of college enrollment. When we examine the gender composition of college students over the past 40 years, we see a dramatic shift in enrollment and degree completion patterns. In 1970, men comprised 58 percent of college students and women 42 percent. By 2010, women made up 57 percent of college students and men 42 percent. Women also became more likely to graduate from college than men. By 2010, women earned 57 percent of all bachelor's degrees and 60 percent of all master's degrees. They have also made significant progress in the completion of professional degrees, and earned nearly 50 percent of all law and medical degrees (Statistical Abstracts of the United States, 2011).

But gender differences can still be found in the selection of college majors. In the United States, men are more likely to major in engineering (84 percent), mathematics and computer science (69 percent), law and public policy (59 percent), and physical science (58 percent). By comparison, women are more likely to major in nursing and allied health sciences (85 percent), education (77 percent), psychology and social work (74 percent) and the arts (61 percent). One notable change in gender composition has occurred among business majors, where men and women pursue the degree in roughly comparable numbers. It can be argued that gender socialization channels women and men into different educational tracks. As a result, it may lead to very different wage and benefit structures for them. For example, in 2011, the median annual salary for engineers was $75,000; it was $70,000 for computer scientists. Compare those with the median annual salary in education, psychology or social work of $42,000 (Center in Education and the Workforce, 2011). It is possible that the wage differences among various fields are a contributing factor in the persistence of the gender pay gap, which we will discuss in the next section.

## Occupation and Income

In the early stages of industrialization and the rise of the factory system in the 19th century, it was common to find men, women and children working for wages. Most industrialized societies eventually enacted laws that either banned or restricted female and child labor. Industrial work became men's domain, and their wages were considered a family wage. This continued the pattern of women's economic dependence on men that had emerged during agrarian times. However, young, poor, immigrant and minority women have always been part of the paid labor force, more so than any other groups of women, although the rates of women's participation in the labor force remained low well into the 20th century. Until 1900, less than 20 percent of all women 14 and older were in the paid labor force at any one time (Kessler-Harris, 1981). Their participation steadily increased after that and rose dramatically after World War II. By 2011, 61 percent of women 16 and older were in the paid labor force, and they comprised 47 percent of all workers (Bureau of Labor Force Statistics, 2011).

Despite nearly equal rates of labor force participation, a gender pay gap persists between men and women. The **gender pay gap** refers to the differences in men's and women's average earnings, when controlling for full-time employment. In 1970, the pay gap was 59 percent, meaning that for every $1 earned by a man, a woman earned 59 cents. By 2011, the gap had narrowed to 77 percent. The gap has been closing over the past 30 years as women's levels of education and labor force participation have increased. Additionally, men's wages have been slow to rise and in some cases have stalled or declined. It appears, however, that the gap will not disappear any time soon (AAUW, 2011).

Numerous factors contribute to the persistence of the gender pay gap. Some of the most significant ones are:

- Women and men are not in the same occupations. **Sex segregation** refers to the concentration of men and women in different jobs. Women are still concentrated in low-pay, low-prestige jobs with few benefits and opportunities for advancement, such as secretaries, daycare providers, elementary and secondary schoolteachers, food service workers, entry-level retail sales, nurses and maids/housekeepers. By comparison, men are more likely to be dispersed across occupational categories but predominate in the better-paid blue collar trades, such plumbing, construction, mining and electrical work, and the professions, including engineering, dentistry, and architecture (Statistical Abstract of the United States, 2012). The higher the income and prestige accorded an occupation, the more likely it is filled by men. We also find that both men and women are disadvantaged when employed in an occupation that is considered a female one (England, 1992).

- Even when men and women are in the same occupation, women earn less. While this looks like a violation of the Equal Pay Act, upon closer examination, we can see that men and women enter different specialties within an occupation. For example, in medicine, men are more likely to specialize in higher-paid specialties such as surgery and cardiology. Women are more likely to become generalists (primary care) and internists, thus earning less.

- Educational attainment does not have the same economic benefit across the sexes. According to a recent American Association of University Women study, women earn only 80 percent of what their male counterparts make a year after college graduation. Ten years later, they were earning only 69 percent of what men earned. While researchers have been able to identify numerous factors that explain the gap, such as choice of major, occupation entered, family status and geographical location, a 5 percent difference in the first year was still unexplained (AAUW, 2011). Is it possible that men are better at negotiating wages?

- The cost of being female has many employment implications. A major factor to consider is how employers perceive men and women as prospective employees. A gender stereotype that stubbornly persists is that women have a lower level of commitment to labor force participation than men do and that their primary responsibilities as family caregivers may interfere with their job duties. It is true that women frequently leave the labor market to care for children and aging family members, and re-enter when these responsibilities lessen. Women also are more likely to consider part-time employment or seek jobs that allow work flexibility so they can better juggle the demands of work with family care. Unfortunately, women also pay a price for this in what Ann Crittendon has referred to as the "mommy penalty" (Crittendon, 2001). Another problem many women face is the **glass ceiling**, when they are blocked from upward mobility in their chosen field. Part of the problem may be that women typically do not have mentors to help them in their career advancement. Perhaps the most dramatic example of the glass ceiling is in Fortune 500 companies, where only 12 women serve as chief executive officers (VanderMey, 2011).

There are several strategies to consider when it comes to closing the gender pay gap. The first is encouraging girls to pursue an educational path that will open the doors to better paid, male

Source: Dan Thompson

What are some reasons the job of elementary school teacher appeals to women?

dominated occupations. School districts across the United States have implemented STEM programs, which promote opportunities for girls in science, technology, engineering and mathematics.

A second strategy requires that we do nothing since men's wages do not look to improve in the foreseeable future. A third and more radical strategy is to value women's work more highly and compensate them accordingly. Implementing this strategy, however, might prove the most difficult, as it would require a drastic change in gender ideology.

## Holding Political Office

American women have made significant progress in politics over the past four decades, especially at state and local levels. Since 1970, the number of women serving in state legislatures has more than quintupled. In 2011, 24 percent of all state legislators were women, compared with 6 percent in 1970 (CAWP, 2011). Additionally, thousands of women now serve as mayors and successfully run for city or county councils and local school boards. While these gains are impressive, women continue to be poorly represented in national elective office, where the biggest political decisions are made from enacting federal laws to establishing national policies and priorities. In the 112th Congress, women held 17 percent of 535 seats: 17 of 100 Senate seats, and 73 of 435 seats in the House of Representatives. Three women also served as delegates from Guam, the Virgin Islands and Washington, D.C. (CAWP, 2011).

Low representation in national elective office may be partly attributed to the position requirements. Congressional seats are full-time jobs, with hours that can be long and unpredictable. In addition, extensive travel is often necessary, so the positions are routinely held by men who have made politics a career. We previously noted that women frequently consider family responsibilities in making job decisions, so they may be more likely than men to find the demanding and highly public nature of national office incompatible with family life. Another part of the explanation is linked to gender socialization. To what extent are girls socialized to consider politics as a career choice?

Women's political achievements at the national level include some recent milestones:

- In 1992, Carol Moseley Braun (Democrat-Illinois) became the first African American elected to the U.S. Senate.

- In 2002, Nancy Pelosi (Democrat-California), a mother of five, became the first woman to become minority leader in the House of Representatives. In 2007, she became speaker of the House then later reassumed the minority leader position.

- In 1984, Geraldine Ferraro became the first woman chosen to be the Democratic vice-presidential candidate. In 2008, Sarah Palin was chosen as the Republican vice-presidential running mate of John McCain.

- In 2008, Hillary Clinton came close to becoming the Democratic presidential nominee.

- Women have been appointed to Cabinet positions, including secretary of state. Women have served in this position in the three most recent administrations: Madeline Albright under Bill Clinton, Condoleezza Rice under George W. Bush, and Hillary Clinton under Barack Obama.

# Theoretical Perspectives on Gender and Gender Stratification

## Functionalist Perspective

Sociologists with a functionalist perspective view society as a system, structured so that all the social components are interrelated. When all components work together, social stability and integration are achieved. Functionalists argue that sex, and by extension gender, is a fundamental principle of social organization. They point out that the division of labor by sex is universal and, therefore, must contribute to the operation of society. Based on biological determinism, functionalists claim that the sexual division of labor reflects task assignments for men and women for which they are "best suited." Once the division of labor into "male tasks" and "female tasks" is established, socialization transmits expectations from one generation to the next.

An example of a functionalist perspective on gender comes from Talcott Parsons and Robert Bales' (1955) analysis of the family in industrial society. They argued that the nuclear family was most functional when men and women held distinct yet complementary roles. Men were assigned the breadwinner role, in which they were responsible for bringing economic resources into the family. They also served as the family's link to the larger society. Women were assigned the roles of taking care of children and meeting the emotional needs of family members. Women's true calling, as depicted in popular culture at the time, was management of hearth and home.

This perspective was popular during the 1950s as post-World War II America moved into the baby boom era. While men and women may have seen themselves as equal partners, in the larger social picture the person who brought more resources into the family certainly had more power. And more value became attached to roles outside the home.

## Conflict Perspective

Sociologists who adopt a conflict perspective view society as being organized into groups that compete with one another for control of valued resources, such as property, power and prestige. The outcome of the various groups struggling over valued resources results in the creation of structural inequalities. One of the earliest theoretical analyses of gender inequality was offered by Frederick Engels in *The Origin of the Family, Private Property and the State* (1884). Engels asserted that men and women held relatively equal status in early societies until the rise of advanced agriculture as a major mode of production. Prior to that, men and women shared the work of production, and what was produced was primarily for immediate consumption.

With the adoption of improved technology, especially the plow and irrigation, men took over production, and surplus was generated. Since men generated surplus, they took ownership. Women, thus, became dependent on men for financial support. As men's economic power rose, so did their control of politics, religion and civic life. To ensure that private property would be passed on to legitimate heirs, women's sexuality needed to be controlled, and monogamy, at least for women, was vigorously enforced. While the evidence that Engels used to support his analysis was questionable, he did lay out a plausible explanation for the rise of patriarchy.

The conflict perspective contained the seeds of feminist perspectives. In addition to providing a framework for analyzing gender inequality, feminist perspectives also attempt to identify what needs to change to make women equal partners with men in all spheres of social life. **Feminism**, in its most basic form, is a perspective that advocates for equality between women and men. While there are many forms of feminist thought, liberal feminism is most recognizable in practice in the United States. Liberal feminists emphasize the importance of individual rights and equal opportunity as the basis for social reform. They advocate for the removal of barriers that impede women's ability to make choices regarding their participation in social institutions. The liberal feminist framework has been used to support many of the legal changes that have occurred to bring about greater equality.

Consider the three following examples:

- Passage of the 19th Amendment in 1920, guaranteeing woman the right to vote.
- The Equal Pay Act, passed in 1963, which prohibits paying women less than men for doing the same job (although this has proved difficult to enforce).
- Passage of the 1964 Civil Rights Act, which outlawed discrimination in unions, public schools and the workplace on the basis of race, creed and color.

Legislating equality does not necessary bring the end to discrimination against women. We can change the law, but we cannot always force a change in behaviors.

## Symbolic Interactionism

Symbolic interactionists focus on how people interact with one another using a shared symbol system. They are most interested in the meaning attached to social life. One way symbolic interactionists analyze gender is by using the concept of "doing gender," which interprets gender as an act performed in ongoing social interactions (West & Fenstermaker, 1995). For example, what does "acting like a man" look like? What does "acting like a woman" look like? Consider your own behaviors for a day. Can you catch yourself, and others, performing gender?

Sociologists who adopt the "doing gender" framework argue that it is through our daily construction of gender that the existing social order is reproduced.

---

# Age and Age Stratification

Every society categorizes and ranks its population by age. Age categories are socially constructed and assigned a **status value**, and valued resources are thus unequally distributed. Structured age inequality is reinforced by an ageist ideology. **Ageism** is prejudice and discrimination directed against people based on age. Any age category can experience ageism, but consequences certainly differ. Consider the following scenarios:

Scenario One: Your 7-year-old daughter asks to borrow the car to take her friends for a spin. Surprised by her request, you say no. When she asks why, you explain that she is too young but add that someday she will be allowed to drive.

Scenario Two: Your 86-year-old father was recently in a fender bender that was his fault. Your siblings think he might be getting too old to drive, and they want you to talk to Dad about it. What will you say to him? To an older person, the loss of driving privileges represents a loss of freedom and independence.

The scenarios demonstrate the difference between the consequences of being told you are too young vs. being told you are too old. When we are young, we look forward to growing older as we acquire new opportunities. Then, when we reach a certain age, we begin to dread aging. This is what happens in a society that values youth over age. "Old" has become a devalued social category. Images of aging as depicted in mass media certainly do not help. For example, how often do you see "anti-aging" products marketed on television, on billboards or in magazines?

Stereotypes play an important role in perpetuating an ageist ideology. These stereotypes are based on the assumption that with advancing age comes significant physical and psychological decline. The stereotypes can then be used to justify the exclusion of older people from full participation in society.

Some prevalent myths are identified below, as well as the reality supported by research.

*Myth 1*: *Older people are less productive.* Ideas that feed into this myth include: Older workers work slower; they are less creative; they do not adjust well to workplace changes; and they have a hard time adopting new technology. *The reality*: Compared with younger workers, workers over age 55 are more likely to demonstrate better job attitudes, higher job loyalty and lower rates of absenteeism. They can and do learn how to use new technologies, though for some it does take longer. As with any other worker, motivation to work, be productive and learn is the key (Hillier & Barrow 2012; Merman et. al 2008). With research supporting the idea that older workers are among the best workers in the economy, why would they face discrimination in the labor force? They often experience pressure to retire or leave their jobs and, in fact, may be forced out. This may not be because of their abilities but because older workers are generally better paid. Also, many employers may be concerned about the benefit packages that are part of a worker's compensation. The decision to replace older workers with younger ones is likely to be more about a company's bottom line than individual ability.

*Myth 2*: *With age comes physical decline*; mobility may become so limited that full participation in social life is problematic. *The reality*: Most elders in the United States rate their physical health as good to excellent (National

---

What kinds of physical activities do you often see the elderly engaged in?

Center for Health Statistics, 2000). While physical limitations are more common in the 75+ age category, elders often benefit from the use of assistive technologies that let them remain socially active and independent (Hooyman & Kiyak, 2008).

*Myth 3: With age comes significant mental decline*, including problems with memory, diminished capacity to learn and loss of problem-solving skills. *The reality*: While the development of certain diseases such as Alzheimer's certainly concerns many as they age, research shows that memory and learning ability do not decline appreciably until after age 80 (Novak, 2012). Short-term memory is usually affected before long-term memory, and the speed with which one recalls information may slow. But what is most important to recognize is that for most elders who remain socially engaged and mentally stimulated, clarity of thought, expression of creativity and retention of critical problem-solving skills continue well into later life (Cohen, 2005).

*Myth 4: Older people are asexual.* Are you familiar with the stereotype of the "dirty old man"? Interestingly enough, there is no comparable concept for older women. *The reality*: Elders actively reject the stereotype of asexuality. Sexuality is an important part of the human experience. Given good health and a willing partner, sexual intimacy, if it is important at midlife, will continue to be so in later life (Hillier & Barrow, 2012).

The list of stereotypes could go on and on. More

negative stereotypes regarding aging exist than positive ones. What has happened to the notions that with age comes wisdom and that elders should be treated with respect?

The persistence of negative stereotypes of older people, particularly in the United States, reinforces negative consequences, including:

- Perpetuating ageism, often resulting in discriminatory practices in social institutions directed toward older people.
- Creating a fear of aging.
- Stifling the potential of elders. A self-fulfilling prophecy can emerge when an older person is constantly told, "You shouldn't do this."
- Maintaining a social system segregated by age.
- Drawing attention away from the healthy, active and socially engaged elders.

What can be done to remove stereotypes? It has been suggested that more education about the realities of aging and the creation of more opportunities for intergenerational activities would go a long way to dismantling stereotypes (Novak, 2012).

# Theoretical Perspectives on Aging and Age Stratification

## Functionalist Perspective

Structural functionalists conceptualize society as a system of interrelated components, all contributing to social stability and order. To promote stability, one organizing principle found in all societies is **age grading**.

Attached to each socially constructed age category are expectations for behaviors, including what social roles will be available. We learn and are expected to conform to the norms that are associated with age grades. For example, small children are expected to learn language and develop basic skills that allow them to fit into society. Although most social expectations are relatively clear, with increasing longevity the social expectations attached to later life have not been clearly established.

It is within this context that the first sociological theories about aging emerged. One of the earliest theorists was Talcott Parsons. In his essay "Toward a Healthy Maturity" (1960), he argued that in the United States, we needed to create roles for older people so they would remain engaged in society and meaningfully contribute to social institutions. He further suggested that these roles take into account the individual's *advanced age.*

Parsons' work influenced the development of *disengagement theory* (Cumming & Henry, 1961), the idea that as we age we are no longer able to perform our social roles competently. As a result, it becomes dysfunctional for both the individual and society to expect that the aging individual can remain in certain social roles, especially the work role. Therefore, it is in the best interest of older people and society that a mutual disengagement occurs. Younger people will benefit by gaining access to the social roles previously held by older people. And, according to Cumming and Henry, older people can then invest their waning energy in preparing for their final disengagement—death. How depressing! Critics quickly pointed out that older people do not disengage from all social roles; they selectively do so, and it is in the best interest of society that the individual's decision to disengage is made by choice.

It was soon recognized that older people disengage from some roles but not others. This recognition led to the development of another functionalist theory, *activity theory.* Based on a different set of assumptions, the main idea is that older people, especially those in good health, can and should be encouraged to remain active and productive in their communities. Everyone will benefit. If it becomes too difficult for older people to continue in some roles, such as work, other roles should be sought out.

The message is that older people need to keep busy, productive and contributing to society.

A final functionalist theory to consider is **age stratification** (Riley, Foner & Riley, 1999). More of a framework than a theory, the key ideas are that each age cohort will experience its elder years differently, based on historical and social contexts.

For example, it is now being suggested that baby boomers (those born between 1946 and 1964) will have a major impact on redefining later life in America.

## Conflict Perspective

The conflict perspective conceptualizes society as groups competing over valued resources. The question of which groups benefit from the way society is structured is an important consideration in analyzing age stratification. When we examine the age stratification system in the United States, does it appear that any age category controls a disproportionate share of societal resources? For example, given the current economy, in which jobs are disappearing, unemployment is high, and drastic cuts have been made to federal social programs, there is a growing concern over how resources are distributed by age. In such a tight economy, there is a perception (or misperception) that those over the age of 65 control a disproportionate share of economic (jobs, Social Security, Medicare, pensions, savings) and political (elected officials and lobby groups such as the AARP) resources. The stereotype of the "greedy geezer" has arrived; older people have too much power, and they are doing too well at the expense of other age categories, especially young adults and children. Referred to as the **new ageism**, elders are resented for their age-based entitlement programs and political clout (Novak, 2012; Palmore, 2004). The stereotype obscures the diversity in our elderly population; elderly women, minority elders and the oldest of the old (85+) remain at high risk of poverty (Hillier & Barrow, 2011). The whole question of which age categories control a disproportionate share of resources raises another interesting question: Is an intergenerational conflict over resources in America's future?

## Symbolic Interactionist Perspective

Symbolic interactionists focus on the social meaning attached to social life. In the construction of our social world through the process of symbolic interaction, we create categories and attach meaning to them (Blumer, 1969). As with sex and gender, age is a social construction, with social meaning in terms of attitudes, values and behaviors.

The symbolic meaning of old age is rooted in culture; therefore, how it is valued and experienced varies across cultures. Furthermore, its meaning can shift over time. For example, in colonial America, elders were treated with deference and respect. Advancing age was accorded prestige; in fact, people would often lie about their age to present themselves as older than they actually were. Powdered wigs were all the rage, and men's clothing was designed to enhance the look of age.

But the status of elders started to shift during the 1800s. America was a young nation, with a Constitution emphasizing equality in all matters political, economic and social. The availability of land in the western United States gave younger people greater independence because they didn't have to wait to inherit property. Perhaps most important was the change in values as the "cult of youth" emerged, which still influences American society (Fischer, 1978). A more contemporary example is how the status of elders is changing in China. Historically, that country was well-known for its elder respect; elders were considered a source of wisdom. But in modern China, that respect has been diminished as several factors have come together: With longer life expectancy, there are more elders to support. Young people's success in the market economy has weakened the bonds between parents and children. And the success of the one-child policy has led to fewer adult children who can care for their aging parents (Chen, 2005).

# The Intersectionality Approach

So far, we have examined the effects of stratification by sex, gender, sexual orientation and age. However, we occupy multiple statuses, and they are interconnected. For example, your chapter author is a white, middle class, heterosexual, middle aged woman. Take a minute to list some of the social statuses that you occupy. Who are you, according to your sex, gender, race, social class, sexual orientation and age? Can you identify the possible advantages/disadvantages you might experience that are associated with each status?

The **intersectionality approach** was originally developed by black feminist scholars as they analyzed the status of black women, taking into consideration how their lives were affected by race, class and gender (Pacific Sociological Association, 2012).

The intersectionality approach provides a framework that allows us to examine the interconnections among socially constructed categories (including sex, gender, sexual orientation and age), and how they combine in complex ways that result in different constellations of privileges and penalties. **Privileges** are advantages and opportunities, often unearned, attached to a social status. **Penalties** are disadvantages or constraints on opportunities or choices attached to a **social status**.

Sociologist Patricia Hill Collins has been a key figure in the development of this approach. In her book, *Black Feminist Thought: Knowledge, Consciousness and the Politics of Empowerment* (2000), she argues that each of us derives varying degrees of privilege and penalty from the multiple systems of structured inequalities that frame our lives.

The value of the intersectionality approach is that it "provides a conceptual space needed for each individual to see that she or he is born a member of multiple dominant groups and multiple subordinate groups" (Collins, 2000: 230). While Collins' analysis focuses on the influence of race, gender and class on black women's lives in the United States, we can see the potential for using the intersectionality approach in other social statuses.

A somewhat related approach helps us make sense of the effects that holding multiple statuses have on age inequality. Emerging from a life course perspective on aging, **cumulative disadvantage theory** holds that disadvantages experienced while we are younger accumulate and lead to greater inequality in later life (Kail, Quadagno & Keene, 2009). As a result, inequality among people age 65 and older in the United States is the highest of all age groups (O'Rand, 2006). Older women have twice the poverty rate of older men, and older African American women have twice the poverty rate of older white women (Novak, 2012).

# Summary

In this chapter, we have examined social stratification by sex, gender, sexual orientation and age. We have discovered how each dimension of structured inequality has been supported by an ideology that argues the superiority of men over women (sexism), the young over the old (ageism) and heterosexuality over other forms of sexual expression (heterosexism).

We also have learned how sociologists operating from functionalist, conflict and symbolic interactionist perspectives have analyzed gender and age inequality. We have identified how the degree of patriarchy differs by type of society, with the greatest gender equality found in early hunting-and-gathering societies and the greatest inequality found in agrarian societies.

We looked at the current status of gender inequality, making some global comparisons. We then shifted our focus to an analysis of the myths and realities of aging, and how the myths perpetuate age inequality.

The chapter concluded with a brief explanation of the intersectionality approach, which provides sociologists with a framework to analyze the interconnectedness of social statuses, including sex, sexual orientation, gender and age. Adopting an intersectionality framework can help us better understand how the various social statuses we all hold result in a different constellation of privileges and penalties.

Now that you have read the chapter, I ask you to return to the questions posed in the introduction. Give each question serious thought and engage your sociological imagination: How close is the United State to achieving equality by sex, sexual orientation, gender and age?

## Review/Discussion Questions

1. How would you explain the difference between sex and gender?
2. How would your life change if you woke up tomorrow and found yourself to be a member of "the opposite sex" or gender?
3. Reflect back on your gender socialization. How obvious was the process in your life?
4. What factors are important in explaining the gender pay gap in the United States?
5. If more women held high political office in the United States, would any national priorities change?
6. How often do you hear ageist comments or observe ageist behaviors?
7. What kinds of intergenerational activities may prove helpful in breaking down age-group boundaries in the United States? Could these activities contribute to more positive views of aging?
8. What do you think is the future of gay and lesbian rights in the United States?

## Key Terms

**Age grading** is the creation of age categories in a society and the attachment of certain rights, expectations and duties to each.

**Age stratification** is a structural system of inequality in which different age groups are ranked in a hierarchy based on status value.

**Ageism** is prejudice and discrimination directed against people based on age.

**Agents of socialization** are people or groups that affect our self-concept, attitudes, behaviors or other orientations toward life.

**Cumulative disadvantage theory** states that disadvantages experienced in youth accumulate and lead to greater inequality in later life.

**Feminism** is a broad perspective that advocates for equality between men and women.

**Gender** is the socially and culturally constructed differences between males and females that are found in the meanings, beliefs and practices associated with masculinity and femininity.

**Gender pay gap** refers to the differences between men's and women's earnings, controlling for full-time employment.

**Gender stratification** is men's and women's unequal access to property, power and prestige.

**Glass ceiling** describes what happens when women are blocked from upward mobility in their chosen field.

**Heterosexism** is the belief that heterosexuality is superior to homosexuality, as it is "more natural" since it is tied to reproduction.

**Homophobia** is the fear and hatred of homosexuality.

**Intersectionality approach** is a conceptual framework that allows for the examination of interconnections among socially constructed statuses, which can include sex, gender, sexual orientation, and age.

**Intersexed** describes babies born with genitalia that are neither clearly male nor female.

**New ageism** in which elders are resented for their age-based entitlement programs and political clout.

**Patriarchy** is a structural system of inequality in which men control the major social institutions, including the family, the economy, politics and religion.

**Penalty** is a disadvantage or constraint attached to a social status.

**Primary sex characteristics** are the genitalia involved in the reproductive process.

**Privilege** is an advantage or opportunity, often unearned, attached to a social status.

**Secondary sex characteristics** are the changes that occur at puberty as a result of hormonal production.

**Sex** refers to the biological and anatomical differences between females and males.

**Sex segregation** refers to the concentration of men and women in different occupations.

**Sexism** is the belief that one sex and, by extension, one gender is superior to another.

**Sexual orientation** is the direction of sexual and emotional interest.

**Social status** is a socially created structural category or position in society. Each status carries with it certain rights, expectations and duties.

**Social stratification** is the systematic ranking of categories of people on a scale of social worth, which affects how valued resources are distributed in a society.

**Status value** is the social value assigned to social statuses whereby some statuses are treated as more valuable or worthy than others.

# Bibliography

American Association of University Women (2011). The Simple Truth about the Gender Pay Gap.

Atchley, R., & Barusch, A. (2003). Social Forces and Aging, 10e. Belmont CA: Wadsworth, Cengage Learning.

Associated Press (2011). Military's Ban on Gays Ends Tuesday. Billings Gazette, September 18, 2011; A3.

Benokraitis, N. ( 2012). Marriages and Families: Changes, Choices and Constraints, 7e. Boston MA: Pearson Learning.

Blackless, M., Charoavastra, A., Derryck, A., Fausto-Sterling, A., Lauzanne, K., & Lee, E. (2000). How Sexually Dimorphic Are We? Review and Synthesis. American Journal of Human Biology. 12: 151-166.

Blumer, H. (1969). Symbolic Interactionism. Englewood Cliffs, NJ: Prentice Hall.

Chang, J. (1992). Wild Swans: Three Daughters of China. New York, NY: Doubleday.

Center for American Women and Politics (2011). Women in Elective Office, 2011. <www.cawp.edu> (2012).

Center for Education in the Workforce (2011). What's It Worth: The Economic Value of College Majors-Interactive Summary Tables. Washington, D.C.: Georgetown University. <http://cew.georgetown.edu/219725.html> (2011).

Chen, K. (2005). China's Growth Places Strains on Family's Ties. Wall Street Journal, April 13, 2005.

Cherney, I. D., & London, K. (2006). Gender-Linked Differences in the Toys, Television Shows, Computer Games and Outdoor Activities of 5- to 13- Year Old Children. Sex Roles: A Journal of Research 54 (9-10). May: 717-726.

Cohen, G. D. (2005). The Mature Mind: the Positive Power of the Aging Brain. New York: Basic Books.

Collins, P. H. (2000). Black Feminist Thought: Knowledge, Consciousness and the Politics of Empowerment. New York, NY: Routledge.

Corbett, S. (2008). A Cutting Tradition. New York Times, January 20, 2008.

Cumming, E., & Henry, W. E. (1961). Growing Old: The Process of Disengagement. New York: Basic Books.

Diekmann, A. B., & Murnen, S. K. ( 2004). Learning to be Little Women and Little Men: The Inequitable Gender Equality of Nonsexist Children's Literature. Sex Roles: A Journal of Research, March 2004.

Engels, F. (1972). The Origin of the Family, Private Property, and the State. New York: Pathfinder Press. (Original publication date of 1884).

England, P. (1991). Comparable Worth: Theories and Evidence. New York, NY: Aldine de Gruyter.

Fischer, D. H. (1978). Growing Old in America, Expanded Edition. New York: Oxford University Press.

Foderaro, L. W. (2010). Private Moment Made Public, Then A Fatal Jump. New York Times, September 29, 2010. <http://www. nytimes.com/2010/09/30/nyregion/30suicide.html> (2011).

Fluehr-Lobban, C. (2003). Ethics and the Profession of Anthropology: Dialogue in Ethically Conscious Practice. Walnut Creek, CA: AltaMira Press.

GLESEN (the Gay, Lesbian and Straight Education Network) (2010). The 2009 National School Climate Survey Executive Summary. <http://www.glsen.org> (2011).

Hatzenbuehler, M. L. (2011). The Social Environment and Suicide Attempts in Lesbian, Gay, and Bisexual Youth. Pediatrics, 127(5): 896-903.

Hausmann, R., Tyson, L. D., Bekhouch, Y., & Zahidi, S. (2011). Global Gender Gap Report, 2011. World Economic Forum Publication. <http://www.reports.weforum.org/global-gender-gap-2011> (2011).

Hillier, S. M., & Barrow, G. M. ( 2011). Aging, the Individual and Society, 9e. Belmont, CA: Wadsworth, Cengage Learning.

Hooyman, N. R., & Kiyak, H. A. (2008). Social Gerontology: A Multidisciplinary Perspective, 8e. Boston, MA: Pearson, Allyn &

Bacon.

Howard, J. A., & Hollander, J. ( 2000). Gendered Situations, Gendered Lives. Lanham MD: Altamira Press.

Institute for Women's Policy Research (2011). IWPR Fact Sheet: The Gender Gap by Education. Washington, D.C.: IWPR <http://www.iwpr.org/pdf/C350.pdf> (2011).

Jacob, S. E., Thomas, W., & Long, S. (1997). Two-Spirit People: Native American Gender Identity, Sexuality and Spirituality. Urbana, IL: University of Illinois Press.

Kail, B. L., Quadagno, J., & Keene, J. R.( 2009). The Political Economy of Aging. In Bengston, V. M. Silverstein, M.M. Putney, and D. Gans (Eds.) Handbook of Theories of Aging. New York, NY: Springer.

Kessler-Harris, A. (1981). Women Have Always Worked: A Historical Overview. Old Westbury, NY: Feminist Press.

Lerner, G. (1986). The Creation of Patriarchy. New York: Oxford Press.

Linton, R. (1937). The Study of Man. New York, NY: Appleton, Century and Crofts.

Lorber, J. (2005). Night to His Day: The Social Construction of Gender. The Spirit of Sociology: A Reader by R. Matson. New York: Penguin Press.

Lorber, J. (1994). Paradoxes of Gender. New Haven, CT: Yale University Press.

Martin, K., & Voorhies, B. (1975). The Female of the Species. New York, NY: Columbia University Press.

Mermin, G. B. T., Johnson, R. W., & Tooder, E. J. ( 2008). Will Employers Want Aging Boomers? The Urban Institute, December. <www.urban.org> (2011).

Miles, D. (2011). Officials Expect Smooth Don't Ask, Don't Tell Repeal. <http://www.defense.gov/utility/print.aspx?print=http://www.defense.gov/news/newsart> (2011).

Murdock, G. P. (1937). Comparative Data on the Division of Labor by Sex. Social Forces, 15, 4: 51-553.

Nanda, S. (1999). Neither Man nor Woman: The Hijras of India, 2e. Belmont, CA: Wadsworth.

Navarro, M. (2004). When Gender Isn't a Given. New York Times, September 19, 2004.

Nolan, P., & Lenski, G. (2010). Human Societies: An Introduction to Macrosociology, 10e.Boulder, CO: Paradigm Publishers.

Novak, M. (2012). Issues in Aging, 3e. Boston, MA: Pearson.

O'Rand, A. M. (1996). The Precious and the Precocious: Understanding Cumulative Advantage and Cumulative Disadvantage over the Life Course. The Gerontologist 36: 230-238.

Pacific Sociological Association (2011). Theme: Intersectionalities and Inequalities: Knowledge and Power for the 21st Century. <http://www.pacificsoc.org/2006/08/2012-annual-meeting.html> (2011).

Palmore, E. B. (2004). Ageism Survey: First Findings. The Gerontologist, 4 (5): 431-437.

Parsons, T. (1960). Toward a Healthy Maturity. Journal of Health and Social Behavior. 1:163-187

Parsons, T., & Bales, R. F. (1955). Family, Socialization and Interaction Process. Glencoe, IL: Free Press.

Pew Research Center for People and the Press (2011). The Generation Gap and the 2012 Election. <http://www.people-press.org/2011/11/03/section-8-domestic-and-foreign-policy-views/> (2011).

Pilkington, E. (2010). Tyler Clementi, student outed as gay on internet, jumps to his death. The guardian, September 30,2010. <http://www.guardian.co.uk/wordl/2010/Sep/30/tyler-clementi-gay-suicide> (2011).

Pollard, K. (2011). The Gender Gap in College Enrollment and Graduation. Population Reference Bureau, 2011.<http://www.prb. org/Articles/2011/gender-gap-in-education.aspx?p=1> (2011).

Renzetti, C. M., & Curran, D. J. (2003). Women, Men and Society, 5e. Boston, MA: Allyn & Bacon.

Rosaldo, M. Z., & Lamphere, L. (1974). Women, Culture and Society. Palo Alto, CA: Stanford University Press.

Roscoe, W. (1991). The Zuni Man-Woman. Albuquerque, NM: University of New Mexico Press.

Saad, L. (2008). By Age 24, Marriage Wins Out. Gallup Poll. <http://www.gallup.com/poll/10609/Romance-Break-Nationalwide-Weekend.aspx> (2012).

Saad, L. (2009). Republicans Move to the Right on Several Moral Issues. Gallup Poll. <http://www.gallup.com/poll/118546/ republicans-veer-right-seveal-moral-issues.aspx> (2011).

Scupin, R. (2012). Cultural Anthropology: A Global Perspective, 8e. Boston, MA: Pearson.

Seccombe, K. (2012). Exploring Marriages and Families. Boston, MA: Allyn & Bacon.

Statistical Abstract of the United States (2012). Table 616. Employed Civilians by Occupation, Sex, Race, and Hispanic Origin, 2010. Washington, D.C.: United States Census Bureau.

United States Department of Education, National Center for Education Statistics (2011). Digest of Education Statistics, 2010 (NCES 2011-015): Table 199.

United States Department of Justice (2011). Uniform Crime Report: Hate Crime Statistics 2010.

VanderMay, A. (2011). Fortune 500 Women CEOs. CNN Money, May 5, 2011.

Vitello, P. (2006). The Trouble When Jane Becomes Dick. New York Times, August 20: H1, H6.

Walker, A., & Parmar, P. (1993). Warrior Marks: Female Genital Mutilation and the Sexual Blinding of Women. New York, NY: Harcourt Brace & Company.

Wax, E. (2008). For Gays in Indian, Fear Rules. Washington Post, October 24, 2008. A1.

Wax, E. (2005). Namibia Chips Away at African Taboos on Homosexuality. Washington Post, October 24, 2004.

Weitz, R. (2010). The Sociology of Health, Illness and Health Care: A Critical Approach, 5e. Boston, MA: Wadsworth, Cengage Learning.

Williams, C. L. (2006). Inside Toyland: Working, Shopping and Social Inequality. Berkeley, CA: University of California Press.

World Health Organization (2008). Eliminating Female Genital Multilation: An Interagency Statement. United Nations Publication.

Xue, X. (2010). Gendercide: The Worldwide War on Baby Girls. The Economist (8672): Pp.72-74.

# CHAPTER TEN

# Families

## Cheryl Boudreaux

---

**Chapter Objectives**

At the end of this chapter, students should be able to:

- Understand that there are different family forms.
- Recognize the diversity of the American family.
- Explain the three sociological theories that can be used as lenses to understand families.
- Think critically about the modern family as a living, changing, growing, social institution.
- Define the family life cycle perspective.
- Understand marriage as a social institution that is important to the formation and maintenance of the family.
- Be aware of alternatives to marriage.
- Recognize the different parenting styles.
- Understand that there are social problems common to all families.
- Explain the view that the family can be a force for social change.

---

The group of people we are born into is our family. Our first and most intimate social contact is with the family. As we grow older, however, we may find ourselves in living situations that reflect the changing nature of American households and families. According to the 2010 census count, there were 39.2 million households (33.6 percent of the 116.7 million households in the United States) designated as **"nonfamily households,"** a census designation for people living together who are not related to the head of household by birth, marriage or adoption. If you live with roommates or an unmarried partner, for example, you count as a nonfamily household (Suchan et al., 2007).

Sociologists understand the family as a basic social institution or building block of society. The family is a *universal social institution*, meaning that it is a patterned way of solving problems and needs that exists in all societies. The family is our most important social institution. We are socialized in and come to understand who we are and our place in society as part of a family. When we are sick and dying, it is the responsibility of the family to take care of us. When we are dead, it is the family's responsibility to dispose of the body.

## Which of the Examples Listed Below Are Families?

- A mother and her child, living with the mother's partner whom the child also calls "mommy."
- An unmarried man and woman.
- A grandfather and his two grandchildren.
- A married couple with no children.
- Two men who were married in Canada.
- A single woman and her child.
- A group of young adults who bought a house together and share the bills.
- A woman with her mother and children.

Defining the family is not a simple task. The U.S. Census Bureau must have a legal definition of family to use when conducting its counts of the population in the United States. These counts are completed once a decade, and the information is used to distribute scarce resources to families as well as to inform the public about the state of the American family. The U.S. Census definition of **family** is "a group of two or more people who reside together and who are related by birth, marriage, or adoption" (Suchan et al., 2007).

While individuals may live with others in a household not related by birth, marriage or adoption, for legal purposes they are not considered a family even if they treat each other as family and think of each other as family. The Census Bureau distinguishes between a family and a household. According to the Census Bureau, a **household** "includes all the people who occupy a housing unit as their usual place of residence" (U.S. Census Bureau, 2003). You can therefore live together in a household but not be considered a family. By using this distinction, the federal government defines *kinship*,

or relatives, not just in the present, but for past and future generations. Definitions of family and kinship present obvious problems for the sociologist or anthropologist studying the family not only in America, where individuals may experience and define their families in ways different from the official census definition, but in other parts of the world as well.

The distinction between families and households raises a number of issues for groups that feel discriminated against when they are left out of programs and services targeted at helping families in need. These groups include gay and lesbian couples living in states that do not grant them the right to marry, cohabiting heterosexual and homosexual couples, and children living with adults not related by blood, marriage or adoption. In 2010, the Census Bureau reported that cohabiting heterosexual households represented 5.4 percent of all households. Families come in many forms, and different societies recognize different forms as legitimate family.

### Family Forms

Although the family is nearly universal, present in all societies throughout history, it exists in many forms. It can exist as a **matrilineal descent** system, tracing descent through the mother's line, a **patrilineal descent** system, tracing the descent through the father's line, or a **bilateral descent** system, tracing the line of descent through both the mother's and the father's families. In the United States, the family line of descent is patrilineal, illustrated by the fact that in most cases the child is given the father's last name at birth.

Families can be **consanguine families**, meaning they are formed and recognized through blood ties, or they can be **conjugal families**, meaning they are formed and recognized through the mating of a couple. When the family is formed through consanguine ties, it is usually an **extended family**, including aunts, uncles, grandparents, and other blood ties. This is an important distinction from the conjugal family, which is usually a **nuclear family**, composed of two adults and their children, if they have any. While the extended family is inherited, the nuclear family is usually formed through marriage. An analysis of the American Community Survey

2008 shows that 16.1 percent of all households were **multigenerational family** households, consisting of more than two generations living together as a family.

**Patriarchy** means "rule of the father" and is usually associated with **patrilocal residence**, which is the man's family residence. In a patriarchal family, the father is head of the household. **Matriarchy** means "rule of the mother" and is usually associated with matrilocal residence. In a matriarchal family, the mother is the head of the household. In a **matrilocal residence**, married couples live with the woman's family. There are families that have matrilineal descent systems and matrilocal residence patterns that are patriarchal. In these cases, the person considered the father might not be the biological father, but rather the mother's brother or some other man in her family of origin. In America, which is primarily patriarchal and patrilineal, young couples are more **neolocal**, meaning that they leave their parents' residence and find one of their own. Young married couples living on their own in a sense have two families. The one they grew up in, their **family of orientation** made up of their parents and siblings, and their **family of procreation** made up of the spouse and the couple's children.

## An Inclusive Definition of the Family

Variations found in different parts of the world can make it difficult to study the family. In order to do a systematic study of the family, we need to have a definition that allows us to recognize family in whatever form we find it. In the United States, the family is legally defined as a household related by blood, marriage, or adoption, a definition that has been challenged because it is not inclusive of all households that consider themselves family. Researchers need a more inclusive definition of family that does not rely on blood ties, marriage, or adoption alone. Anthropologist George Murdock (1949), studying families in more than 250 different societies, developed a functional definition of the family as a social group characterized by a common residence, reproduction or economic cooperation. Using his definition, we can observe who performs certain functions, and there we would find the family, no matter which society we are studying.

## Theory and Research: Strategies for Understanding the Family

There are many theories or perspectives for understanding the family. The different views and perspectives are used somewhat like the lens of a camera. When we change the lens, we have a different focus that allows us to perceive different parts of the picture. Each theory provides a different view of what family life means at the micro or macro level. Three of those lenses are structural functionalist, conflict and symbolic interactionist perspectives.

### Structural Functionalist Perspective

Structural functionalists look for persistent patterns in society and view them as serving a positive role or function in the maintenance of the society as a whole. The family is one such pattern that serves certain functions in nearly all societies throughout history. From the functionalist perspective, if a function is being met in other ways, a particular pattern is no longer needed to serve its function, and that pattern will cease to exist. This leads some to conclude that the family is in danger of ceasing to exist, since professionals are paid to perform many of its most basic functions, such as child care, housekeeping and education. The functionalist perspective defines the family in terms of the vital functions it serves to the individual and the society. The family functions as an institution through which to reproduce and maintain the society. It does this through the reproduction and socialization of children, the passing on of rules and social status and the provision of economic and emotional support (Eshleman, 2003; Ogburn, 1938; Murdock, 1949).

*Major functions of the family include*: reproduction of children, nurturing and socialization of children, emotional and economic support of its members, and sexual rules and regulations.

*Reproduction* and the *nurturing* and *socialization of children* are universal functions necessary for the reproduction of the family and perpetuation of the society. It is the family's responsibility to help children become good citizens in the society to which they are born.

The family is responsible for the passing on of *ascribed* or *inherited status*, including race, ethnicity, social class, and religion.

As an *economic unit,* the family must cooperate to provide food, clothing and shelter for its members. The family also functions to prescribe the division of labor within the family, making sure that all of the necessary tasks, such as making money, housecleaning, cooking, and laundry, get accomplished. Labor, as well as authority, in the family is divided by age and sex.

*Sexual rules and regulations*, or taboos, are present in every society, although not every society has the same incest taboos. The family makes the distinction between kin and non-kin, teaching us which individuals are off-limits for marriage and sexual relationships. In some societies it might be permissible, and even encouraged, to marry cousins, while in others it is completely taboo. A society's definition of family specifies who are considered close relatives, and therefore off-limits.

## Conflict Perspective

Conflict perspective as it relates to families sug-

gests that family forms develop as a result of the particular mode of production, or economic system, of a society. The United States has a capitalist society in which investors, workers and consumers are important. A family in a capitalist society produces good workers trained to consume, and investors with capital ready to invest in order to produce more. Nuclear families produce more consumption and, ideally, more savings for investment.

From a conflict perspective, it is the power relationships between different groups in society, including families, that are important. Power in society is divided by class, race, gender, and age.

Building on the conflict perspective, the feminist perspective turns our attention to gender and the inequality between men and women. An important institution in society, the family maintains and perpetuates the inequalities between men and women. The United States, along with most cultures in the world, is a **patriarchal society** where men are dominant and social institutions are set up to sustain a system of male rule. The feminist and conflict perspectives

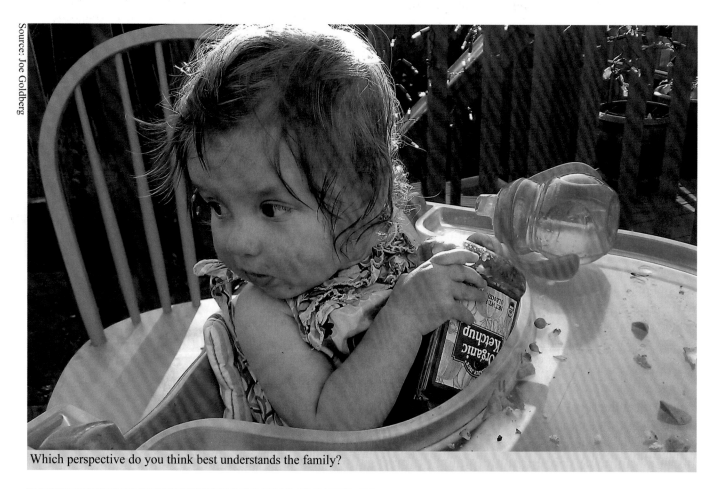

Source: Joe Goldberg

Which perspective do you think best understands the family?

look at the division of labor both within the family and within the larger society. Within the household, women do a full extra month of work a year more than men. Arlie Hochschild (1989) calls this extra unpaid labor of women the *second shift*, representing a "leisure gap" between men and women, and illustrating the gendered unequal division of unpaid labor in the family.

## Symbolic Interactionist Perspective

Symbolic interactionism focuses on the signs and symbols that are used to construct reality. The structural functionalist perspective and conflict feminist perspectives are both macro-level perspectives that sociologists use to get a broader view. In these perspectives, the focus is on the family as an institution in the larger society. The lens is wider and we take into account the harmony or disharmony of the institutions in society.

The symbolic interactionist perspective is a micro-level perspective that focuses closely, paying attention to symbols and their meaning created in social interaction with others. These symbols include language, gestures, body language, role making, and role taking in everyday interactions among the individual, the family and the society. In this perspective, the formation of individual identity is important, as well as the role of the individual in the social construction of reality. The dramaturgical perspective described by Max Weber (1864-1920), George Herbert Mead (1863-1931), and Erving Goffman (1922-1982), reflects aspects of symbolic interactionism. The dramaturgical perspective examines the context of human behavior, rather than the cause, because a person's actions are dependent on time, place, and audience. Through the lens of Goffman's dramaturgical perspective, one can see the family as a staging place for the theater of life, its members learning to play various roles, roles associated with identity, gender and social relationships. The audience would be composed of all the members of society that we interact with. Learning and playing our roles well would be essential to society (Goffman, 1959).

## Introducing a Family Life Cycle or Development Perspective

A family life cycle looks at the roles, problems and issues of families over the course of a lifetime. It relies on an expectation that there are major life events or stages that families typically go through. Major life events include dating, marrying, becoming parents, having children leave home (the empty nest syndrome), taking care of elderly parents and losing a partner. By looking at a family in a particular stage of this life cycle, we can spot common problems and issues. This perspective is criticized because not all families or individuals go through the same life events in the same order. For example, a single mother might not yet have faced the issue of marriage.

## Dating and Mate Selection

Almost everyone expects to, and does, marry at some point in his or her life. Marriage is such a strong social expectation that those who do not marry are more likely to have their motivations questioned than those who do. In many societies, and in most of human history, parents or matchmakers **arrange marriage**. In the United States, and increasingly the rest of the modern world, individuals are expected to make a *love match*, which puts the pressure on the individual to find his or her marriage partner. That choice, however, feels more individual than it really is.

Turning our attention to the patterns of mate selection, we can see that we are guided by social rules to fall in love with, and marry, the appropriate person. In the United States, most people fall in love with, and marry, someone similar to themselves. Through socialization and nurturing, we have, in a sense, been programmed to fall in love with those within our group. This practice is known as **homogamy**. We tend to fall in love with and marry someone like us in race, class, education, religion, age, and *propinquity* or geographic region. Marrying someone within one's social and economic group is known as **endogamy**. Homogamy is the opposite of **heterogamy**, which is the practice of choosing someone different than one's self. Those who select mates that come from different regions, or from

Source: Mel Rowling

How long do you think a couple should date before getting married?

other social and economic categories, can be said to practice **exogamy**.

## Marriage: The Social Institution

Marriage is seen as an essential right all over the world. According to the Universal Declaration of Human Rights adopted by the United Nations (1948):

> Men and women of full age, without any limitation due to race, nationality or religion, have the right to marry and to form a family. They are entitled to equal rights as to marriage, during marriage and at its dissolution. Marriage shall be entered into only with the free and full consent of the intending spouses. The family is the natural and fundamental group unit of society and is entitled to protection by society and the State (Article 16).

Marriage is an important part of the formation and maintenance of the family as a basic social institution. The form of marriage tends to fit with the particular society where you find it. Forms of marriage include **polygyny**—when a husband is allowed to have more than one wife and historically the most common form of marriage; **polyandry**—allowing a woman to have more than one husband at a time; **polygamy**—having more than one mate; **monogamy**—allowing for only one mate at a time or **serial monogamy**—cycles of divorce and remarriage in which the person becomes less capable each time of making a permanent commitment. Many sociologists claim that the modern marriage arrangement has become one of serial monogamy as evidenced by the high divorce rate and the individual pursuit of satisfaction and personal growth over self-sacrifice for the good of the family (Cherlin, 1978; Furstenberg, 1980; Giddens, 1992).

The *marriage premise* is one of *sexual exclusivity*, which is to have only one sexual partner, and *permanence*, the expectation that the relationship will last a lifetime. The premise supports long-lasting happy relationships, allowing for trust and the growth of intimacy. In modern society, more and more people are marrying and hoping for the ideals of sexual exclusivity and permanence, while being less able to believe in them. The divorce rate and the rate of affairs began to increase in the 1970s and has remained high since then, leading some theorists to suggest that marriage may be in decline and, thus, less important as a social institution than it once was. Although we continue to marry, and married individuals report being happy more often than single individuals, we are less and less likely to stay together or to remain sexually faithful to our partners (Campbell & Wright, 2010; Giddens, 1993; Gove, Style & Hughes, 1990; Lee & Roebuck, 2004).

## Parenting

*Fertility* rates are not consistent over time, fluctuating within the social economic and historical context. They are lower than they were in the 1950s, but higher than they were in the 1970s, and currently hover around two children per woman in the United States. Perhaps this low fertility rate is due to the fact that more women are delaying having children in order to complete their education and start careers. Children are expensive, time-consuming and can strain a couple's relationship. For working women, children also represent an *opportunity cost*, the value of the next-best alternative that will be forgone as a result of choosing to have a child.

Do you believe in the marriage premise?

Even so, the average person in the United States still wants to have two children (Carroll, 2007; Saad, 2011).

Children are no longer the assets that they were in preindustrial society when they could work and contribute to the family. Children are, however, seen as an important part of creating a family and living the American Dream. Having children means sharing a special kind of love and creating an environment similar to our *family of orientation*, the one we grew up in, passing on those customs that we inherited from our families. Children today are an emotional asset rather than an economic one. Increasingly, men and women are making the decision to remain child-free.

Social programs and public policy have an effect on the fertility rate, depending on whether the society is *pro-natal*, encouraging and supporting the reproduction, nurturing and socialization of children, or *anti-natal*, putting up road blocks which make it more difficult for people who choose to parent. The pervasive assumption that everyone will have children and the need to explain a decision not to have children is pro-natal. Social programs, tax breaks, and child care that aid working parents in doing the work of parenting are all pro-natal. Isolating women who have children, denying parental leave from work, and cutting programs and services to families with children are anti-natal. A society can have features of both.

## Three Parenting Styles

Theory and research suggest that parenting styles can have a dramatic effect on a child's grades, behavior, tendency toward substance abuse, and chances of success in life. Children have a greater chance of success if their parents are consistent, monitor their children's activity and discipline to train, rather than to punish. Three basic parenting styles discussed are authoritarian, permissive and authoritative (Baumrind, 1991; Clark, 1983; Dornbusch, et al., 1987; Steinberg, et al., 1989).

Source: Matthew Hoelscher

Which parenting style do you like best?

## Authoritarian Parenting Style

For the authoritarian parent, the child is like a lump of clay to be molded and shaped into a good citizen; a child's success or failure is seen as a reflection of the parent's ability to control that child's behavior. The parent controls the child's behavior with little emotion or explanation. The child is told to "do it because I say so" or face punishment. This parenting style is described as "demanding and directive, but not responsive" (Baumrind, 1991, p. 62).

## Permissive Parenting Style

The permissive, or non-directional, parent's goal is to manipulate the child into thinking that he should behave a certain way because he wants to, because it is good for him. This parent does a lot of talking, answering the "why" questions with "because it is the right thing to do" and explaining for as long as it takes. This parent leans heavily on the child's ability to make decisions for him/herself. These parents are more "responsive than they are demanding" (Baumrind, 1991, p. 63).

## Authoritative Parenting Style

Most experts agree that the authoritative parenting style facilitates success in children. It involves fewer rules, with strict adherence to those rules. This style is thought to give the child more autonomy. Parents using this style are "both demanding and responsive," wanting their children to follow the rules and be able to assert themselves and their own ideas as well. "Children from authoritative homes have consistently been found to be more instrumentally competent—agentic, communal, and cognitively competent—than other children" (Baumrind, 1991, p. 63).

# Empty Nest and Sandwich Generation

*Empty nest* is a term used to describe the reorientation that takes place after 18 years of parenting. This reorientation happens when parents have spent 18 or more years raising their children, who then go off to college and start their lives as adults. As parents of adults, they then have to find a new focus and find out who they are without their children. If married, they need to reintroduce themselves to each other as individuals and as part of a couple. This can be a difficult but necessary transition.

With new technology and improvements in medicine, people are living longer, giving rise to the *Sandwich Generation* where young couples spend their time raising children and taking care of aging parents. Often, these couples do not get the luxury of the empty nest because they are sandwiched between the younger and older generations.

There is also emerging evidence that more and more adult children return home after college, so that we now have more *intergenerational households*. This number is expected to grow in the future as people wait later and later to marry (Messineo, 2005).

# The Single Life

According to the U.S. Census, since 1950 there has been a continual decline in married-couple households. In 1950, one-person households represented 9.5 percent of the households counted, while in 2010, one-person households represented 27 percent of the population (Census, 2010).

In the age of *Sex and the City*, a popular cable television show and movie about four single girls and their exploits in New York, being single no longer bears the stigma that it once did. Today's non-married couples are seeking satisfaction from other life experiences. They are "reworking those norms and inventing alternatives. Some strategies included having 'emotional monogamy' but not sexual monogamy; refusing to cohabit; maintaining long-distance-partner relationships; and focusing on strong ties with friends" (Budgeon, 2008, p. 319). They don't need to be married to be happy and respected by their peers (Giddens, 1992).

Some people choose to be single. Other people remain single because they never find a partner with whom they can trust their future selves. Others are single because their partner left or died. Those people who choose a single lifestyle are happier than those who look back and realize that they have lived a single lifestyle, not by choice. Most happy singles have satisfying careers and good social networks.

# Cohabitation

*Cohabitation*, or "living together," might be more of an emerging lifestyle than a substitute for marriage. According to Brown (2008), cohabiters are most likely to have the lowest socioeconomic status, which suggests that they may not feel their economic status is sufficient to justify marriage. Cohabiters do raise children and do not feel the need to marry because of pregnancy as in previous generations. We may see a developing trend of intergenerational cohabitation, since 40 percent of children are expected to spend some time in a cohabitating household. Just as living single has become an acceptable life choice, cohabitation is a lifestyle that has steadily increased since the 1970s. Cohabitation does not necessarily lead to marriage, especially among blacks and Hispanics (Brown, 2008; Bumpass, 2000).

*Same sex or gay and lesbian couples* form households and live together in most counties within the United States. Almost one-quarter of the gay male households and one-third of the lesbian households are raising children. These are committed relationships that are more similar to married heterosexual relationships than they are to cohabiting heterosexuals. The children of gay and lesbian parents do not have different outcomes than children raised by heterosexual parents, and they are not more likely to be homosexual themselves. Overall, "children raised in same-sex environments show no differences in cognitive abilities, behavior, general emotional development, or such specific areas of emotional development as self-esteem, depression, or anxiety" (Meezan, 2005, p. 103). Further, one study showed that preschool children raised by lesbians were less aggressive, bossy, and domineering than children with heterosexual mothers (Meezan, 2005).

# Domestic Partners

Some cities, counties and states in the United

States offer a legal status known as **domestic partnership** for two unrelated, unmarried adults who share the same household. They may be gay or heterosexual couples who are not married but want legal recognition of their relationship. There is no consistent set of benefits for domestic partnership; its rights and responsibilities will depend on the state in which it exists. Domestic partnerships can be valuable for sharing employee benefits, designating rights to medical visitations, health care directives and child custody agreements. Domestic partnerships do not solve all the problems of those who do not want to or cannot marry. Most states do not offer domestic partnerships, and even in states where they are legally recognized the status does not confer on a couple any of the more than 1,000 rights and privileges that come with legal marriage. The federal government does not recognize domestic partnerships even when the state does.

## The Socially Diverse American Family

America is a pluralistic, culturally diverse nation. All American families share in the larger American culture. Americans of all ethnicities are more like each other than they are like individuals from other cultures. The continually negotiated, changing American dream includes the romance of a white wedding, two kids, a house, a middle-class job, and two or more cars.

American culture includes the more static features of patriarchy, heterosexism, white privilege, and individualism. America is also a culture made up of subcultures. While we share the larger culture, which includes much of our lifestyles, eating habits, education, and national identity, we also each inhabit subcultural identities that are important and meaningful to us.

Many people think of race as the source of our diversity; however, there is no objective biological fact of race, and cultural diversity is not based on a biological fact of race. The socially agreed upon perception of race is just as important, though. Racial discrimination and prejudice do exist. Early studies of the black family, for example, contrasted black and white families and expected to, and did, find differences, which were seen as pathological compared with the white middle class family (Glazer, 1963). Black children were seen as coming from a culturally disadvantaged background. This influenced social policy and programs aimed at helping black children transcend their culturally impoverished backgrounds. In reality, both black and white children in poverty experience similar kinds of problems, issues, and coping mechanisms.

Belief in race and racial differences influences our families and our social policies. Although so far there is no scientific evidence for the existence of race as a biological fact, race is a very important concept for social scientists looking to explain family experience and social status in the United States. Social scientists tend to focus on class and ethnicity, which is based on cultural tradition, experience, and identity, when looking at diversity. Families within the same class are more alike than those of the same race.

The majority of families in America are non-Hispanic white, or European-American. According to the U.S. Census in 2010, the non-Hispanic white population represented 72.4 percent of the population, and if white Hispanics are included, the white population represented 76.2 percent of the population. The black, or African American, population represented 12.6 percent of the population. In 2010, other large and growing racial groups in America included Asian, 4.8 percent; American–Indian and Alaska native, 0.9 percent; and Hawaiian and other Pacific Islander, .02 percent of the population. The Hispanic population in America was seen as a language ethnicity rather than a race, and so could self-classify as any race. The perception of race in America affects a family's experiences and opportunities and its subcultural participation. America is still segregated in terms of neighborhoods, religions, churches, and schools, not because of laws, but because of choices, economic opportunities or lack thereof, preferences, privileges, and prejudices.

Most of us associate class with income, and there is a relationship between the two; however, sociologists attribute much broader meaning to class. *Social class* represents opportunity, income, education, values, beliefs, preferences, and even family size. Whether a child is born into a working-class family or a middle-class family will greatly influence every aspect of that child's life. Parenting styles may also be related to class. The schools, churches and social programs available to any child will be different according to his or her social class.

# Divorce

The divorce rate in the United States reached an all-time high in 1979 and then began to level off, so that now about 40 to 50 percent of new marriages are likely to end in divorce (National Center for Health Statistics, 1983; National Vital Statistics Reports, 2010). Arlene Skolnick (1997) discusses the contradictory views of "Middletown" Americans on the question of divorce. We believe in marriage as a forever proposition, so we oppose divorce. However, we also believe that no one should have to stay in a loveless or abusive marriage, so our pragmatic side recognizes the necessity of divorce. Louisiana, Arizona, and Arkansas have enacted *covenant marriage*, which is a marriage contract that is much more difficult to dissolve than the regular marriage contract. This kind of contract is very similar to marriage before the advent of no-fault divorce; at that time, couples had to have concrete evidence to prove adultery or physical abuse before a divorce would be granted. Since most people today agree that there are situations where divorce is the preferred outcome of a marriage gone wrong, covenant marriages do not seem to be the solution to the high divorce rate. Rather, we might do better to direct our energy at some of the problems that cause people to have troubled marriages. Some of these problems are related to poverty, inequality, poor conflict resolution skills, and unrealistic expectations. Many of these problems can be helped with education. As the Middletown families in Skolnick's study suggest, divorce is a remedy. If we find other remedies to these problems, divorce will cease to be functional and rates will decrease.

# Remarriage

Many Americans remarry or cohabit after a divorce, forming stepfamilies. Individuals with children are less likely to remarry, and remarriages are more likely to end in divorce. Goldscheider and Sassler (2006) found that "being a co-resident father dramatically increases forming a union with a woman with children. Women's co-residential children reduce women's odds of forming unions with men who do not have children and increase them for unions with men who do" (p. 275). Overall, women have a more difficult time and are less likely than men to remarry when they have children.

# Social Problems, Change and Justice

The baby boom generation has begun to retire, and it is the largest cohort to retire since the Social Security Administration was established in 1935. This group is expected to live longer because of technology, improved health care, and a better standard of living than any other group to grow old in American history. We worry that this group will put an unprecedented strain on family resources. Social policy regarding retirement has already begun to change, as people are expected to work longer and longer before retirement. Indeed, there is worry that retirement will no longer be an option for many Americans.

With all of the support, joy and love associated with the family, it is important to remember that it can also be a source of great pain for its members. According to the Bureau of Justice Statistics (BJS) the overall rates of intimate-partner violence have decreased steadily between 1976 and 2005. **Intimate partners** are defined by the BJS as spouses, ex-spouses, boyfriends and girlfriends. Gender matters when looking at intimate-partner violence. In 2005, intimate partners killed about 3 percent of male murder victims and about a third of female murder victims.

In addition to intimate-partner violence, the family is host to many other social problems, including child abuse, neglect, divorce, extramarital affairs, single parenthood, poverty, and the feminization of poverty, making the family a good place to direct our attention for social change.

The family can be a force for change through nurturing and socialization. With the support of positive social policy, families can lower the incidence of violence, rape, incest, alcoholism, homophobia, racism, and sexism in society.

Problems faced by today's families lead many experts to believe that the family is becoming an institution in decline. Other experts argue that the family is not in decline; rather, the modern family is described as changing to meet the demands of modern society. The concept of the family is changing. The family has existed throughout human history,

and it is an essential part of the human journey. The family as a social institution has ensured that young adults find appropriate mates, children are nurtured and properly socialized, the elderly are cared for, and the dead are buried, while important customs and traditions are passed from one generation to the other. The family is not a static institution; it can be made better. The institution of family has continually changed as other elements of social reality have changed. The family in an advanced capitalist society is very different than the family in hunter/ gatherer, agricultural or preindustrial societies. In the future, we may not recognize its form, but it will continue to exist as an important institution that serves basic functions in support of society.

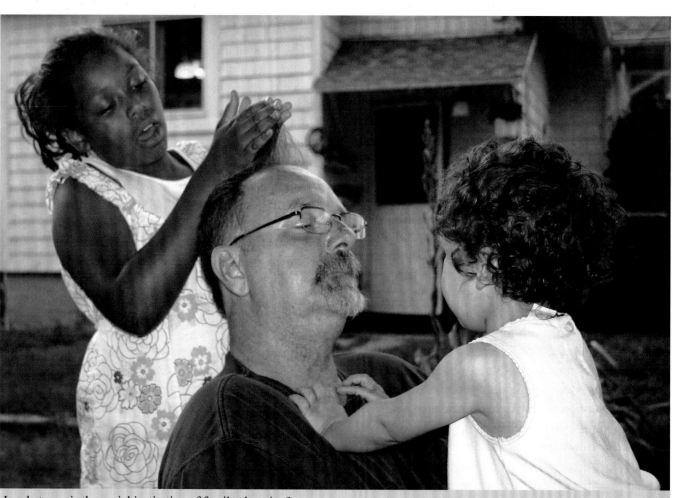

In what way is the social institution of family changing?

# Summary

This chapter has provided a brief overview of the study of the family, along with some of the problems and concerns involved in this research. It is meant to whet your appetite so that you will want to learn more. The family is a universal social institution legally defined for purposes of the U.S. Census as a "group of two or more people who reside together and who are related by birth, marriage, or adoption" (Suchan et al., 2007). Families come in many forms, though, and this definition makes it difficult to study families that are not included. Social scientists use a theoretical understanding of the family, allowing us to recognize and include families that do not fit our expectations, and to study families in many societies and subcultures. The structural functionalist definition, for example, allows us to define family in terms of the functions that it serves to perpetuate and maintain the society. Family functions include economic and emotional support, and the reproduction and socialization of children. Additionally, conflict and feminist perspectives introduce power relations and gender into the analysis; the symbolic interactionist perspective allows us to focus more closely and look at the production of symbols and meanings for our actions. Symbolic interactionism allows sociologists to explore how socialization takes place and how identities are formed.

The family has undergone tremendous change in the last 40 years and is expected to continue to change. The society as a whole has also changed, growing through several large and important movements, including civil rights, women's liberation and gay rights. As a result of these historical changes, birth control is more effective and more readily available; jobs are more accessible to women and more women have careers; privacy has become a protected right; and, in some states, marriage and domestic partnerships are an option for gay and lesbian couples. Advances in technology have helped more people to have children and a new generation to live longer.

The family is also the source of many social problems, illustrating that in many ways the family is not functioning well in modern society. Examining social problems such as the high number of divorces, affairs and single-parent families, the intergenerational transmission of divorce, the extra burden of taking care of the growing elderly population and the rate of violence and abuse in the family, it is easy to see why some experts argue that the institution of family is in decline.

Families are increasingly more diverse. Two categories used to deliver social programs and services based on the census count are race, a social reality rather than a biological one, and ethnicity. In recent years, the census has had to add categories for unmarried partners and for people who define themselves as more than one race. There are more people cohabiting than ever before, and more people are choosing to remain single or to not have children.

Another change in family is represented by the substantial percentage of gay and lesbian families that include children by birth and or adoption. Families are being blended through divorce and remarriage. With all of this change, we can still look to the family to serve the basic functions for the individual and society. Most people continue to describe getting married and having at least two children as a major part of their American Dream. In this chapter, we have taken a view that the family will continue to undergo tremendous change and growth, and it will continue to exist as an important institution that serves basic functions in support of society.

## Review/Discussion Questions

1. What does patriarchy mean?
2. Which of the three parenting styles do you think works best? Explain.
3. Why do you think more people are choosing to cohabit rather than get married?
4. Should the government allow individuals to marry more than one person? Why or why not?
5. If one of your friends started dating someone 30 years older than him or her, what would you think? What kind of advice would you try to offer your friend, if any?

## Key Terms

**Arranged marriage** means that parents or match-makers decide who is going to marry whom.

**Bilateral descent** traces the line of descent through both the mother's and the father's family.

**Conjugal families** are formed and recognized through the mating of a couple.

**Consanguine families** are formed and recognized through blood ties (birth).

**Domestic partnership** is a legal status offered by some cities, counties and states in the United States for two unrelated, unmarried adults that share the same household.

**Endogamy** involves marrying someone from within one's social and economic group.

**Exogamy** involves marrying someone from a different region, or other social and economic categories.

**Extended family** includes two parents and their children, as well as other blood relatives such as aunts, uncles, and grandparents.

**Family**, for purposes of the U.S. Census, is a group of two or more people who reside together and who are related by birth, marriage, or adoption.

**Family of orientation** is the family a person grows up in, including parents and siblings.

**Family of procreation** is a family made up of a person, that person's spouse and their children.

**Heterogamy** means choosing to marry someone who is different from one's self.

**Homogamy** involves people falling in love with, and marrying, someone similar to themselves.

**Household** includes all the people who occupy a housing unit as their usual place of residence.

**Intimate partners** are defined by the Bureau of Justice Statistics as spouses, ex-spouses, boyfriends, and girlfriends.

**Matriarchy** means that the mothers rule and are in charge of the family.

**Matrilineal descent** traces the descent through the mother's line.

**Matrilocal residence** means that when couples marry, they live with the wife's family.

**Monogamy** allows a person only one mate.

**Multigenerational family** households consist of more than two generations living together as a family.

**Neolocal** means that young couples leave their mother and father's residence and find one of their own.

**Nonfamily household** is a census term used to describe people living together who are not related to the head of household by birth, marriage or adoption.

**Nuclear families** are composed of two adults and their children, if they have any.

**Patriarchal society** is one in which men are dominant and social institutions are set up to sustain a system of male rule.

**Patriarchy** is a structural system of inequality in which men control the major social institutions, including the family, the economy, politics and religion.

**Patrilineal descent** traces the descent through the father's line.

**Patrilocal residence** means that a married couple lives with the father's family.

**Polyandry** allows a woman to have more than one husband at a time.

**Polygamy** allows marriage of one person to two or more others of the opposite sex.

**Polygyny** allows a man to have more than one wife at a time.

**Serial monogamy** involves cycles of divorce and remarriage allowing people to marry multiple partners, but only one at a time.

# Bibliography

Baumrind, D. (1991). The influence of parenting style on adolescent competence and substance use. Journal of Early Adolescence, 11, 56-95.

Budgeon, S. (2008). Couple Culture and the Production of Singleness. Sexualities, 11, 301-326.

Brown, S. L. (2008). Generational Differences in Cohabitation and Marriage in the US. Population research and policy review (0167-5923), 27 (5), 531.

Bumpass, L. L., & Lu, H. (2000). Trends in cohabitation and implications for children's family contexts in the United States. Population Studies, 54, 29–41.

Bureau of Justice Statistics (BJS) (2007). Intimate Partner Violence in the United States. <http://bjs.ojp.usdoj.gov/content/pub/pdf/ipvus.pdf> (2012).

Caetano, R. (2008). Intimate Partner Violence Victim and Perpetrator Characteristics Among Couples in the United States. Journal of Family Violence (0885-7482), 23 (6), 507.

Campbell, K., & Wright, D. (2010). Marriage Today: Exploring the Incongruence Between Americans' Beliefs and Practices. Journal of Comparative Family Studies (June 1, 2010): 329-345.

Cherlin, A. (1978). Remarriage as an Incomplete Institution. American Journal of Sociology, 84 (3), 634-650.

Clark, R. (1983). Family life and school achievement: Why poor black children succeed or fail. Chicago: University of Chicago Press.

Dornbusch, S. M., Ritter, P. L., Leiderman, P. H., Roberts, D. F., & Fraleigh, M. J. (1987). The relation of parenting style to adolescent performance. Child Development, 58, 1244-1257.

Eshleman, J. R. (2003). The Family (10th ed.). Boston: Allyn & Bacon.

Furstenberg, F. Jr. (1980). Reflections on Remarriage: Introduction to Journal of Family Issues Special Issue on Remarriage. Journal of Family Issues, 1 (4), 443-453.

Giddens, A. (1992). The Transformation of Intimacy: Sexuality, Love & Eroticism in Modern Societies. Stanford, CA: Stanford University Press.

Giddens, A. (1993). The Transformation of Intimacy: Sexuality, Love, and Eroticism in Modern Societies. Stanford University Press.

Glazer, N., & Moynahan, D. P. (1963). Beyond the Melting Pot. Cambridge, MA: M.I.T. Press and Harvard University Press.

Goffman, E. (1959). The Presentation of Self in Everyday Life. Carden City New York: Doubleday Anchor Books. Doubleday & Company, Inc.

Goldscheider, F., & Sassler, S. (2006). Creating Step-families: Integrating Children into the Study of Union Formation. Journal of Marriage and Family (0022-2445), 68 (2), 275.

Gove, W., Style, C., & Hughes, M. (1990).The effect of Marriage on the Well-Being of Adults: A Theoretical Analysis. Journal of Family Issues, 11, 4–35.

Hochschild, A. R. (1989). The Second Shift: Working Parents and the Revolution at Home. New York: Viking.

Kurdek, L. (2008). Change in relationship quality for partners from lesbian, gay male, and heterosexual couples. Journal of Family Psychology, 22 (5), 701-11.

Kurdek, L. (2007). The Allocation of Household Labor by Partners in Gay and Lesbian Couples. Journal of Family Issues, 28 (1), 132-148.

Lee, G. R., & Roebuck, J. (2004). Change and consistency in the Relation of Marital Happiness, Conference Papers: American Sociological Association; 2004 Annual Meeting, San Francisco, p1-21, 21p, 2 Charts.

Meezan, W., & Rauch, J. (2005). Gay Marriage, Same-Sex Parenting, and America's Children. The Future of Children (1054-8289), 15 (2), 97.

Messineo, M. (2005). Influence of Expectations for Parental Support on Intergenerational Coresidence Behavior. Journal of Intergenerational Relationships, 3 (3), 47-64.

Murdock, G. P. (1949). Social Structures. New York: MacMillan.

National Center for Health Statistics: Advance report, final divorce statistics (1983). Monthly Vital Statistics Report. Vol. 32-No, 3, Supp, DHHS Pub. No. (PHS) 83–1 120. Public Health Service, Hyattsville, Md., June 1983.

National Vital Statistics Reports (2010). Births, Marriages, divorce, and Deaths: Provisional Data for 2009. National Vital Statistics Reports, Volume 58, Number 25.

Ogburn, W. F. (1938). The Changing Family. Family, 19, 139-143.

Rennison, C. M. (2003, February). Intimate Partner Violence, 1993-2001. Bureau of Justice Statistics Crime Data Brief. <http://www.ojp.usdoj.gov/bjs/pub/pdf/ipv01.pdf> (2008).

Skolnick, A. (1997). Family values: the sequel. The American Prospect, 32, 86-94.

Smock, P. J. (2000). Cohabitation in the United States: An appraisal of research themes, findings, and implications. Annual Review of Sociology, 26, 1–20.

Smock, P. J., Manning, W. D., & Porter, M. (2005). Everything's there except money: How money shapes decisions to marry among cohabitors. Journal of Marriage and Family, 67, 680–696.

Steinberg, L., Elmen, J. D., & Mounts, N. S. (1989). Authoritative parenting, psychosocial maturity, and academic success among adolescents. Child Development, 60, 1424-1436.

Suchan, T. A., Perry, M. J., Fitzsimmons, J. D., Juhn, A. E., Tait, A. M., & Brewer, C. A. (2007). Census Atlas of the United States, Series CENSR-29. Washington, DC: GPO/U.S. Census Bureau.

United Nations (1948). The Universal Declaration of Human Rights. <http://www.un.org/Overview/rights.html> (2008).

U.S. Census Bureau (2008). American Community Survey <http://www.census.gov> (2010).

U.S. Census Bureau (2003). 2000 Census of Population and Housing, Summary Social, Economic, and Housing Characteristics, Selected Appendixes, PHC-2-A. Washington, DC: GPO.

U.S. Census Bureau (2010). American Community Survey <http://www.census.gov> (2012).

# CHAPTER ELEVEN

# Education and Religion

## Josh Packard

---

**Chapter Objectives**

At the end of this chapter, students should be able to:

- Identify how the institutions of religion and education serve to socialize members into a society.
- Identify how social class affects education and religion.
- Describe how education and religion contribute to a stable society.
- Recognize the key challenges faced by educational and religious institutions in the United States.
- List the major world religions.
- Connect important sociological theories to the institutions of religion and education.
- Explain why some believers use violence in the name of religion.

---

ducation and religion are two of the primary institutions used for socializing members of any society in a process called **acculturation**. What is acculturation? Think about the differences between a typical Sunday morning church service and an average college classroom. Aside from the topics being discussed, an outside observer could make the case that they constitute the same kind of experience. People arrive at a scheduled time and participate in activities directed by a person who is in charge of the group by virtue of his or her training and credentials. At some point, when the leader talks, people sit quietly and listen carefully (or at least pretend to do so) in order to gain knowledge or understanding that will help them later.

---

A sociologist can easily see how a general set of norms about the correct way to conduct oneself in public is being transmitted, along with the religious beliefs or class content. People are being socialized to listen to authority figures, to arrive on time, pay attention and be respectful of others. As you might imagine, these same traits and values are important in other spheres of American life as well (e.g. participatory democracy). One could argue that many of the things that religious services and classrooms have in common make up the foundation of what it means to be American. Indeed, one of the primary ways new groups of people are **assimilated** into U.S. culture is through participation in these key institutions.

In this chapter, we will take a close look at exactly how this socialization takes place. We will also examine how socialization experiences are determined by social class and how the symbolic elements of religious and educational institutions add structure to people's lives.

# Education

We devote a tremendous amount of time, money and other resources to education in the United States. Each year, roughly $650 billion is spent on public, K-12 education alone, which amounts to about $10,400 per student per year. College expenditures total another $200 billion annually. Over the course of their lives, college graduates will have spent one-fifth of their time in school. Across the nation, full-time teachers number 3.6 million, making this profession the U.S.'s third-largest employment sector (National Center for Educational Statistics, 2010).

Clearly, there is a strong commitment to education—or rather, to schooling in the United States. What is the difference between these two terms? **Education** refers to the social institution that provides formal training for people to gain knowledge and skills, as well as learn values and norms. **Schooling** refers to education in a classroom setting. Some societies strongly emphasize education in a very broad sense. In America, we use schools to do the vast majority of this work.

This has broad implications for how our society is structured because, unlike some other countries, the United States takes a very decentralized approach to schooling, with no comprehensive, national curriculum or standards. Instead, educational standards are left up to the individual states. Adding to the complexity of this system is the practice of **credentialism**, which involves a reliance on conferred degrees and diplomas as universal markers of educational achievement, even though educational standards vary greatly. This diversity of educational approaches allows us to look at the various roles that schooling plays in our society.

## Three Perspectives on Education

### Functionalist

Sociologists have long understood that education plays a major role in creating and maintaining societies. Whether education occurs institutionally or more informally, it is crucial that people have a way of systematically passing on knowledge and developing intellectual capacity. A smart, well-informed citizenry results in a more productive society that can solve problems and create new industries and sources of wealth. Everyone benefits from a system that maximizes people's talents and abilities. This is the functionalist perspective of education.

Functionalists take the position that the **manifest function**—things that are destined to occur—of education is to place the brightest, most talented people into the most difficult jobs. High-achieving students are rewarded with better grades and promoted to ever higher levels of education. To entice smart, talented people to devote their late teens and twenties to pursue higher education, we offer incentives (e.g., better pay, prestigious jobs) to those who pursue advanced degrees. For example, becoming a physician requires enormous amounts of time and money for medical school and training. Consequently, doctors are among the most prestigious and best-paid professions in our society. This is exactly what comprehensive public education is intended to do: provide opportunities so high-achieving students can put their talents to good use.

Universal public education also results in a citizenry that learns the same values and lessons, ultimately creating a cohesive society that shares civic pride and duty to country. This is, however, somewhat undermined by a lack of national standards and the ability of some, such as the rich, to opt out of the public system and into private schools. But lessons learned in school still provide one of the biggest sources of national identity in the United States. Often, these efforts at national socialization take explicit forms, such as reciting the Pledge of Allegiance or taking government and history classes that focus on U.S. civics and political structures.

Attendant with this kind of educational system are **latent functions**, or unintended consequences. Schools are typically where some of our earliest lessons about gender roles and class boundaries are learned. Sometimes through the activation of stereotypes, students discover which behaviors are appropriate or expected of them by both their peers and authority figures. These latent functions structure social life as much as the manifest functions of education.

## Conflict Theory

For conflict theorists, school is less about trying to find the most qualified, talented people and more about replicating class standing and privilege. In most parts of the country, schools are financed through property taxes, resulting in inequities between school districts that may be right next to each another. Wealthy districts with a high percentage of homeowners can funnel more money toward buildings and teacher salaries than poorer ones. When coupled with the significant racial segregation and inequality still present in the U.S., the result is a school system that can look very different for wealthy, white students than poor, non-white students.

Of course, this is not the only way to fund public schools. Critics of the district approach point out that taxes could simply be distributed equally on a per-student basis. Conflict theory, however, suggests that we choose not to fund schools this way because the wealthy and powerful control a system that

Source: Steven Hoover

Aside from the Pledge of Allegiance, what other forms of national socialization occur in schools?

Do you think funding public schools through property taxes is fair?

works well for them.

Conflict theorists also point to the **hidden curriculum**—which includes the non-instructional items learned in school that reward upper-class students for the habits and norms they bring into the classroom—as evidence that the school system, while it might be educating students, is certainly working to replicate class privilege. For example, students who come to the classroom with significant amounts of **cultural capital**—those who speak and write well with standard English, who have been raised to sit through a long story or to listen patiently to instructions from adults—will have an advantage in an environment where not everyone possesses those skills. Teachers tend to confer status on students who already possess these traits and punish those who don't display appropriate behavior.

The result, say conflict theorists, is that wealthier students are viewed, and begin to view themselves, as superior. They are more eagerly engaged in school and leadership positions from a young age, while students from lower social classes learn how to avoid drawing attention to themselves, to show up on time and to not question authority, among other things.

## Symbolic Interactionist

The interactionist perspective focuses on interactions between students and teachers. In particular, symbolic interactionists are concerned with what happens when a teacher forms an impression of a student as a "good" or a "bad" student. These impressions tend to result in different behaviors, expectations and, ultimately, outcomes. The core idea is that impressions become self-fulfilling prophecies. As a teacher labels a student "good," for example, the student receives increased attention, reaches higher expectations and internalizes a general feeling of superiority and competency. The result is often an increase in outcomes, whether in test scores or grades, that serves to confirm both the student's belief in her or his own abilities and the teacher's initial assessment.

This dynamic was illustrated in the now-classic experiment by Rosenthal and Jacobsen (1968) in which they described the Pygmalion effect. In the experiment, Rosenthal and Jacobsen informed teachers that some of their students were poised to see a significant increase in their IQ scores based on a series of tests they had run at the beginning of the year. When they were retested at the end of the year, sure enough, the identified students saw their scores improve significantly.

Rosenthal and Jacobsen, however, had not actually sorted the students. Instead, the students were simply chosen at random. The study confirmed the notion of the self-fulfilling prophecy. As, over the course of the school year, teachers treated students as if they were special, the students internalized this, and they proceeded to, indeed, become special.

In its most explicit form, this differential treatment leads to **tracking**, or ability grouping. This occurs when students are divided and sometimes physically separated from one another in order to receive separate instruction in a particular subject or comprehensively. Gifted and talented, advanced placement and honors classes are modern versions of educational tracking, but educators have been attempting to provide challenging instruction for bright students for a long time. The problem is that it is extremely difficult to move up into this track once you have been slated for a lower-achieving track. As time goes on, the content and instructional differences between the two groups continue.

Tracking is one of the most formal ways that labels get attached to a student. A major part of the **adolescent subculture** is the self-esteem that emerges from such labels, whether they come from formal sources or from peers. Geeks, jocks, preppies and others are all designations that come with a particular self-image. A good self-image and corresponding high self-esteem that comes from positive peer relations determine to a large extent how adolescents view their own abilities. Those with confidence tend to perform better in school.

The interactionist interpretation of schooling finds natural allies with the conflict understanding as educators' biases frequently form the basis for their initial perception. Students from socioeconomic groups with the appropriate cultural capital have a leg up on other students when it comes to making favorable first impressions (Bourdieu, 1996; Stanton-Salazar & Dornbusch, 1995). Gender and race biases also play into these dynamics. Such stereotypes not only help formulate these perceptions but are strengthened by the ultimate outcomes as well.

### Which Perspective is Correct?

Does formal education act as a mechanism of class reproduction, or does it help people reach their full potential? Does it enable social mobility and bring citizens together or draw boundaries around social class and give a leg up to those who already possess power and privilege? As with most things in sociology, the answer is "all of the above."

This understanding of education is confirmed in the very foundations of formal schooling in the United States. As one of the first countries to set a goal of providing **universal education** for its citizens, America engaged in a significant social experiment in its public education system, which took off in the second part of the 1800s. By the 1920s, every state had mandatory education laws on the books, and only 100 years after the movement began, most American adults had graduated from high school (Graham, 1974; Stark, 2007). Today, education dominates a significant portion of our lives.

From the beginning, however, people were conflicted about the nature of public education. On one hand, they understood that a well-informed citizenry was necessary for a functioning democracy, and businesses increasingly needed qualified workers for new, highly specialized industries. Along with these manifest functions of education, the rapid industrialization of 19th-century America, as early

proponents of universal education understood, often resulted in both parents working outside the home, leaving children unsupervised. Thus, one latent function of early education was to control the children of the working class, provide some structure and middle-class values, and reduce street crime and violence (Kaestle, 1972).

It was clear from the outset that those who could afford to do so were receiving vastly superior educational experiences. In 2003, for example, The New York Times famously profiled the so-called "Baby Ivies," where the wealthy send their sons and daughters to prepare them for entry into top colleges and universities.

But these are not prep schools or even high schools. They are preschools for 2- to 5-year-old children. They come complete with on-site child psychologists and test prep for admission to the best private kindergartens. The Times article refers to research done by the National Institute for Early Education Research, which shows that children who attend top preschools do end up earning significantly more over the course of their lifetimes. It is unclear, however, whether these children earn more because they are actually smarter or because they simply know the "right" people. What do you think conflict theorists would argue? (The New York Times, 2003).

Diplomas from elite private schools and universities signal to others a myriad of things regarding a person's social class and cultural background and status. To be sure, schools like Harvard and Yale require dedication, hard work and intelligence for admission and graduation, but it is just as true that wealthy families are in a much better position to provide their children with the kind of preparation necessary for entrance into those schools.

## Educational System Today

The contemporary American educational system faces unique challenges. Though universal schooling helped vault the United States to become a world leader during the 20th century, we are no longer educationally dominant. Other countries now outpace us both in terms of hours spent in school and test scores in key areas such as math, science and reading. American students rank 23rd in science and 36th in math test scores worldwide (Baldi et al., 2007).

The United States ranks in the top five in overall educational and per-pupil spending. But the distribution of that money is far from universal, and per-student spending is outstripped by other budgetary priorities. For example, states spend approximately three times as much to incarcerate a prisoner as they do to educate a student (Goodman, 2004).

In addition to disproportionate funding, the American school year and day are becoming comparatively shorter than those of other countries. While American students typically receive about 180 days per year of instruction, countries such as Japan, South Korea and Israel have well over 200 instructional days of education. Recent research by Karl Alexander, made popular in the book *Outliers* by Malcolm Gladwell, suggests that during the summer, children whose families possess few resources to continue their education actually regress significantly during their time away from school (Gladwell, 2008). Meanwhile, children in other countries get more instruction and also have fewer opportunities to forget the things they have learned.

Many of these outcomes can be understood by exploring the specific challenges that the United States faces in terms of public education. Unlike many of the other countries that perform better, the U.S. has an extremely diverse population, with students from many backgrounds. It also lacks a consistent educational approach. The sections below explore some of the unique challenges faced in American public education.

## Diversity in Education

One of the greatest challenges to universal education in the U.S. is racial diversity. In a country highly segregated by geography and neighborhood, it is rarely the case that K-12 schools reflect the diversity of the population at large. When this segregation is coupled with the historic advantages and privilege held by white families, the result is a two-tiered system, with wealthy, suburban, largely white school districts spending vastly more per student on public education when compared to their overwhelmingly non-white peers in the urban core.

In 1954, the United States Supreme Court ruled that school districts could not legally sustain separate facilities for white and non-white students, claiming that "separate educational facilities are inherently unequal." In the years following this decision and other court rulings prohibiting **de jure**, or legal, segregation, a system of **de facto**, or segregation in practice, arose. White families with means fled to suburbs, and better schools, in a phenomenon known as **white flight**. The result is that, 55 years after *Brown v. Board of Education*, many of America's schools are more segregated than they were before the ruling (Orfield, 2009).

Because most states hold that students must attend schools in the district where they reside, and because our communities are highly racially homogenous—meaning largely made up of one race—the result is that the average white student attends a school that is nearly 80 percent white while non-white students attend schools that are almost completely nonwhite (New York Times 2003). There are obvious implications here not only for racial equality in the United States but also for our ability to guarantee everyone an equal chance at success.

## Spotlight on Research

The national debate surrounding **affirmative action** policies in higher education has prompted numerous examinations of the effects of diversity. These studies overwhelmingly concluded that a diverse campus leads to increased educational and social outcomes for all students (Appel et al., 1996). This research has been at the heart of two Supreme Court decisions regarding university affirmative action policies. First, in *Regents of the University of California v. Bakke* (1978), the high court identified diversity in higher education as a compelling national interest. Later, Justice Sandra Day O'Conner cited the social science research directly in her majority opinion upholding the University of Michigan Law School's affirmative action plan.

Current research on diversity in higher education has demonstrated the benefits that accrue from diverse campuses: increased retention and overall satisfaction (Astin, 1993); gains in cultural awareness (Chang, 2002); intellectual motivation and engagement (Gurin et al., 2002); ability to solve problems and evaluate arguments (Pascarella et al., 2001);

self-confidence (Hu & Kuh, 2003); and the ability to integrate multiple perspectives (Marin, 2000). There is a simple assumption that undergirds these findings: A diverse student body yields a broader collection of thoughts and opinions. Exposure to this wider range of perspectives leads to intellectual advancement.

Researchers have repeatedly asserted that the interactions that lead to this exposure cannot be assumed but rather must be actively attended to. While sheer numbers can be counted on to increase the likelihood that informal interactions between racial groups can happen, research suggests that key learning outcomes are more likely to result from intentional curricular efforts to expose students to different backgrounds and opinions.

In an attempt to uncover the processes responsible for producing the links between campus diversity and student learning, Pitt and Packard (forthcoming) analyzed student contributions to course discussions. They found that students of different races actually make different contributions to class discussions. That is, they talk about different things and in different ways. Their examination confirms that even in the classroom, diversity is an important resource that results in a better-informed and educated student body.

## Dropout Rates

Dropout rates in the United States have generally decreased from 15 percent in the 1970s to less than 10 percent today (Planty et al., 2008). This total, however, obscures some important trends. For example, student background significantly affects the likelihood of dropping out. Foreign-born students and racial minorities are far more likely to drop out of school (Statistical Abstract, 2005). Additionally, the shift to high-stakes standardized testing for school assessment has proven to increase dropout rates when these results are tied to school funding, an unintended consequence of the school accountability movement exemplified by the passage of the Bush administration's 2001 No Child Left Behind education bill (Orfield & Wald, 2001). The Obama administration's recent Race to the Top initiative also places a strong emphasis on standardized tests.

While teenage pregnancy and juvenile delin-quency remain predictors of dropout rates, working at a job more than 20 hours a week is also an important factor (Rumberger & Lim, 2008). These same dynamics are true in higher education as well. The most common reasons students discontinue postsecondary education are financial. The need to work more and longer hours was given as the primary reason students drop out of college (Ashburn, 2009).

## Home Schooling

The number of home-schooled children in the United States has risen dramatically in the past decade. There are currently around 1.5 million home-schooled children, up from 850,000 in 1999 (National Center for Education Statistics, 2011). Despite this 75 percent increase, the population of home-schooled children is strikingly homogenous. The vast majority are white (77 percent), from two-parent households (89 percent), with middle-class household earnings. Although parents cite a variety of reasons, one driving force behind the home-school movement is a desire to provide specific religious or moral instruction (Princiotta & Bielick, 2006).

While there is nothing inherently problematic about home schooling, that does not mean there is no effect on the overall society. As families withdraw their children from public schools, they withdraw their resources as well. While they cannot opt out of taxes (unless they move out of the school district), families do withdraw their involvement and participation in the community of education. The homogeneity of home-schooled students means that school districts are losing families that typically make up the bulk of their involved parents—that is, people with knowledge, time and motivation to improve their child's educational experience. In the United States, the courts have tended to rule in favor of the right to home school as long as parents can demonstrate they are providing a quality educational experience (Mehta, 2008). In other countries, such as Germany, the courts generally uphold the notion of a public good, and rule that everyone should participate in public education because it makes for a more cohesive and functional society (Spiegler, 2003).

## Community Colleges

Community colleges are increasingly the option of choice for many students in America. More than one-third of current postsecondary students are in a two-year, or community, college. At their best, community colleges offer a route through higher education for nontraditional and/or disadvantaged populations, opening up more opportunities for people who have been traditionally kept out of higher education. Flexible learning options, including online, evening and weekend classes, increase the likelihood of diverse student bodies at community colleges.

This flexibility reflects changes in the larger society. The shift in the United States from a manufacturing to a service-based economy has meant a demand for more specialized and skilled labor for high-end, good-paying jobs as well as an increase in shift labor and nontraditional work weeks for lower-paying jobs. Community colleges, with their multitude of options, have exploded as a way for people to move into more stable, higher-paying careers. Recognizing the increasingly important role such colleges play in this regard, President Obama recently held the first White House Summit on Community Colleges, calling them the "unsung heroes" of higher education (Schlesinger, 2010).

## For-Profit Higher Education

The largest university in the United States is the University of Phoenix. It is a for-profit university with more than 400,000 students in hundreds of campuses around the world (Wilson, 2010). Phoenix, like other for-profit universities, focuses its attention on non-traditional students, many of whom are balancing a full-time job and family life with college. The flexible schedules, convenient locations and ability to earn degrees online appeal to many people. But such convenience comes at a cost.

Traditionally, education has been separate from the profit motive. Educators have reasoned that the incentive to make money would potentially compromise the quality and purity of the intellectual product. Professors at for-profit colleges are not protected by tenure and have little academic freedom. Additionally, the drive to enroll students has led many for-profit universities to come under

fire from federal and state governments. In August 2010, the Governmental Accounting Office found that for-profit universities often engage in deceptive recruiting practices in order to increase enrollment (GAO, 2010).

The vast majority of the funding for these universities (more than 90 percent, in many cases) comes in the form of financial aid that the federal government pays to students, such as the G.I. Bill, Pell Grants or subsidized loans. But often these loans are never repaid. The ability of the for-profit education sector to place its graduates in jobs upon matriculation has been seriously questioned (Perez, 2011).

With Americans now owing more in student loans than in credit card debt, the value of for-profit education has come under increased scrutiny (Kantrowitz, 2010). The fear is that these degrees will leave students heavily in debt and with training and credentials that will not get them the jobs they need to pay off their loans, leaving taxpayers to foot the bill. Some critics are even calling student loans the next "bubble" in our economy as students take out increasing amounts of loans that they cannot repay (Pope, 2011).

Despite such concerns, for-profit institutions continue to earn profits and have been a steady growth industry. For-profit colleges and universities now enroll more than 12 percent of all students in the United States, and revenues have tripled in the past decade (Nocera, 2011). Additionally, there is some evidence that when measured simply in terms of a college degree, for-profit institutions are cheaper for the taxpayer than traditional universities with vast facilities, expansive campuses, dining halls, labs and research faculty.

# Religion

Sociology, as a discipline, can trace its roots back to a concern with the role of religion in society. The major upheavals in Europe during the 1700s and 1800s left an entirely new social order. The scientific, French and industrial revolutions coming directly on the heels of the Reformation dramatically altered the power and scope of the Catholic Church. Where once the Church had controlled nearly all social institutions throughout much of Europe, the revolutions significantly eroded the authority of the papacy and the institution of religion. Increasingly, religion was undergoing a process of **secularization**, where religious authority declined and was relegated to its own sphere in the social world rather than dominating all aspects—a process that continues today (Chaves, 1994).

While this came as a welcome change for some, it left a burning question in the minds of many philosophers and social critics. If the Church did not keep social order, then what would? How would society function and survive without a dominant social institution?

The answer they found—that something happens when people get together in groups that causes them to develop regulatory habits, practices and institutions—launched the study of society. In many ways, our understanding of religion in the modern world is still shaped by these early inquiries into the importance of religion.

## Three Perspectives on Religion

### Functionalism

Perhaps no body of thought places more importance on the role of religion in creating a cohesive society than functionalism. Religion does a number of things that functionalists recognize as being essential for a stable social structure. Emile Durkheim famously observed that regardless of whatever else might occur at a religious worship service, what is certainly happening is that people are worshiping themselves.

Of course, he did not mean that people literally worship other people but that people collectively affirm what they value and believe in—and what they do not. Durkheim called this the sacred-profane division (Durkheim, 1912 [1995]). The **sacred** are those things that are set apart from everyday life and regarded as extraordinary. Religious texts, places, objects and rituals can all be regarded as sacred as long as people collectively regard them as special and deserving of importance. Objects and practices that are **profane**, on the other hand, are not necessarily bad or evil, they just are not sacred. They are the mundane, everyday things.

Sacred practices and beliefs generally result in cooperation and self-sacrifice, and reaffirm the importance of social stability. Functionalists point to the importance of things such as family, marriage, personal restraint and charity, which are found in every major religion, to show that the primary result of religion in society is to facilitate social interaction and reduce chaos.

For example, nearly every religion emphasizes helping the poor and refraining from self-indulgence. Being able to provide security for the poorest citizens and cooperation among everyone is a core component of any functioning society. Whether compelled by religion or some other force, societies need a way to help the impoverished, and people need a motivation other than their own desires.

### Conflict

Conflict theorists, following up on the ideas of Karl Marx, take a decidedly different approach to religion. They understand social class and power as the primary organizing schemas of modern life. Religion is generally regarded as an ideology—a set of ideas that legitimates or supports the status quo. Marx famously wrote that religion "is the sigh of the oppressed creature…It is the opium of the people" (Marx, 1977 [2000]:72). Essentially, Marx argued that religion, as a social system, is controlled by people in power in order to maintain their power. To take an example from the dominant religion of his day, Christianity, one could look at the Beatitudes. The Beatitudes are a list of blessings Jesus bestows on a crowd in the books of Matthew and Luke in the New Testament. They contain such statements as "Blessed are the poor: for yours is the kingdom of God" (Luke 6:20) and "Blessed are the meek: for they shall inherit the earth" (Matthew 5:5). These are read by conflict theorists as simply a way to keep the poor and oppressed focused on the afterlife and not on the injustices they face in this world.

Modern conflict approaches to religion have kept this focus on social class and extended their analysis to focus on racial segregation and gender inequality as well. Conflict theorists draw a straight line from the fact that men have historically held most positions of power in major religions, and

In Judaism, bar mitzvahs represent a coming of age ritual. What other religions have similar rituals?

many interpretations and teachings give women secondary status to men. Similarly, Sunday mornings, often said to be the most segregated time of the week in the United States, highlight the racial divide that still exists in the United States even as we collectively want to believe in equality. Church segregation is not officially mandated, of course, but reflects the socioeconomic disparity in our neighborhoods and is enforced in a much more informal way.

## Interactionism

Symbolic interactionism focuses on the way religion adds meaning to a person's day-to-day life by focusing on rituals and symbols. These rituals and ceremonies help people navigate and make sense of not only day-to-day living but also major events or transitions. For example, most religions have a symbolic ceremony to mark going from childhood to adulthood. Many Christians have the ceremony of Confirmation, Jews observe bar and bat mitzvahs, and Muslim children limit their fasting during the month of Ramadan but

are expected to fully participate upon reaching adulthood.

More than simply celebrations of adulthood, these rituals and ceremonies provide structure and confer both responsibility and expectations on the members, clearly signaling that the person is no longer a child but should be treated as an adult. Although in modern times we rarely treat the newly confirmed or bar mitzvahed as adults at age 13, it is clearly still seen as a transition from childhood into adolescence.

## Organization of Religion

The way people organize their religious activity takes many forms. One is what sociologists refer to as **animism**, the belief that all forms of life contain elements of the supernatural. This belief system is associated with the hunter-gatherer tribes of Africa and North America.

In contrast, the form of religion that currently dominates the world is **theism**. This is the belief that god(s) reside separately from humans and other living things even though they may occasionally inhabit their bodies.

Sociologists tend to classify religious activities into organizations that range from groups that have high engagement with the rest of society to those that are minimally engaged. **Churches** exhibit the highest degree of engagement with other social institutions. The values and practices of these large and long-established religions often mirror those of society in general. Examples include mainstream Protestant denominations (e.g., Methodists, Lutherans, Presbyterians), the Roman Catholic Church and Reformed Judaism.

Leadership in churches is tied less to charisma than to a training and credentialing process that results in a very stable organization, even when it experiences turnover. When a pastor leaves or retires, a new one is "called" from among a select pool of candidates with the correct credentials.

The message espoused in churches is rarely controversial or even critical of the status quo. In part, this is so it can appeal to as many people as possible—and because these religious organizations benefit from existing social arrangements. In the United States, for example, some church leaders enjoy tax breaks, privileged social status, even political access, leaving them less inclined to advocate for social upheaval.

The result is an organization that requires relatively little from its members. Most churches don't make major demands on a congregant's resources. There may be requests for money, time and talents, but typically there is no enforcement mechanism. The term sociologists give to people who take the benefits offered by the church while making few contributions in exchange is **free riders**. Large churches can tolerate free riders because usually there are enough other people who pitch in to keep the organization running.

One of the biggest challenges facing churches, however, is the inevitable disillusionment some people experience in large organizations that tolerate high numbers of free riders. Frequently, groups will assert that a church has become too worldly and accommodating of those who are not upholding the foundational tenets of the faith.

When these people break away to form their own, independent groups, these are called sects. A **sect** is typically small, and the barriers to joining the group usually involve significant amounts of time, money and/or religious adherence. Although most sects are short-lived, some cycle into full-blown churches. Still others such as the Amish, Quakers and Hasidic Judaism, persist long-term.

**Cults**, or New Religious Movements, are typically centered on a charismatic leader. The distinguishing feature of a cult is that it offers a new understanding of the world and the afterlife. Early Christianity could easily be considered an NRM. Jesus was a charismatic figure who offered a concept of heaven that was different than the major understandings of the time, and he encouraged his followers to have relatively little engagement with the secular world. Over time, of course, Christianity moved steadily into the realm of a church, but most NRMs remain small and relatively unheard from. Typically, when a charismatic founder leaves or dies, the movement dissolves. Although cults sometimes make headlines, they rarely effect large-scale social change even though their belief systems may often be highly critical of the status quo.

## Evangelicals, Fundamentalists and Extremists

While most Christians share similar beliefs, other religious adherents have much in common as well. The term **evangelical** typically refers to any group of conservative Christians that focuses explicitly on spreading religious beliefs and converting people. We typically understand evangelicals to be Protestants who believe in proselytizing—that is, actively converting others—to get people to believe the idea that Jesus Christ is the one true source to eternal salvation. Evangelicals also have a fundamental belief in the inerrancy of the Bible.

But fundamentalism is not found only among conservative Christians. We see evidence of religious **fundamentalism** in each of the three types of religious organizations discussed above, though probably most prominently in religious sects. The very nature of the sect as a breakaway from what is perceived as a "corrupt" or wayward church lends itself to a literal interpretation of a religious text. While Christian fundamentalists share an understanding of the Bible similar to that of evangelicals, they do not necessarily have the same drive to spread the teachings of the message or to convert others.

Religious **extremists** can be found in most major world religion. Extremists take the same literal interpretation of a religious text as fundamentalists and combine elements of conversion found among evangelicals. Religious extremists, however, take their beliefs a step further. Rather than simply believing that theirs is the one true religion, they take the stance that other religions must be done away with through conversion or violence. Religious extremism is often rooted in turbulent political and social conditions.

## Religions of the World

Throughout the world, the vast majority of people are religious. While the principles guiding the organization and development of the major world religions are strikingly consistent, the intricacies of the various belief systems are as varied as their believers. Humans have found a variety of ways to express religious belief. Some religions emphasize a set of practices; others focus on having the right beliefs. Some make exclusive claims of truth; others are open to a variety of paths. Many of these distinctions can be understood by focusing on the differences between Western and Eastern religions.

## Western Religions

### Abrahamic

The religions that dominate in the global West—Judaism, Christianity and Islam—appear to most people as separate and distinct belief systems. And while this is true today, it is also true that these major world religions share a common background, development and god. These religions are often referred to as the Abrahamic religions because they all trace their roots to a singular event that occurred in the Middle East more than 4,000 ago. It was then that an ancient tribe came to believe its god was not particular to its people but rather was the one and only god for the whole world. Abraham,

a member of the tribe, is recognized as the first to establish a **monotheistic** belief system, known as Judaism after the land of Judea where the tribe settled. Christianity developed out of this tradition 2,000 years later as many people came to believe that mainstream Judaism was not keeping the laws of its god. Islam was developed by people who were dissatisfied with Christianity some 500-600 years after the followers of Jesus established Christianity (Armstrong, 1994).

### Judaism

Judaism is the oldest of the modern, major world religions, but its adherents make up less than 1 percent of the world population. Judaism developed the earliest monotheistic belief system in the Western world, around 2,000 BCE (Armstrong, 1994). Jews are distinctive because their religion includes no unifying creed other than a belief in one god. This does not mean, of course, that they have no common bonds. Rituals and commandments make up the bulk of Jewish practice. The Talmud, for example, includes more than 600 commandments for Jews to follow daily. Their main holy book is the Torah, which includes the bulk of what Christians refer to as the Old Testament.

Like all major religions, Judaism includes liberal interpretations of the religion, called Reformed Judaism. Hasidic and Orthodox Jews, on the other hand, interpret the Torah and Talmud much more literally, taking a fundamental approach to their religious teachings. Jews around the world have been persecuted throughout their long history. This persecution throughout the Middle East and Europe makes up a strong component of Jewish identity worldwide. Although these persecutions occurred regularly throughout the history of Jewish people, the Holocaust in Germany during World War II, where Hitler's regime exterminated 6 million Jews, stands as the dominant symbol of Jewish oppression and a modern act of genocide.

### Christianity

Christianity is the world's largest religion, with approximately one-third of the world claiming adherence to some form of it. Of course, there is much to choose from, as the various denominations within Christianity number into the tens of thousands with over 200 in the United States alone (Barret, 2001). Christianity developed as an offshoot of Judaism; the schism surrounds the divinity of Jesus Christ. Christians believe in Jesus as the immaculately conceived son of the one god and the one true messiah. The teachings of the New Testament announce Jesus as the one true path to Heaven and that Jesus came to Earth and was killed to redeem the sins of humanity. This was necessary because people had stopped following the ways and teachings of God. The New and Old Testaments make up the Christian Bible.

Christians believe that eventually Jesus will return to this world from Heaven, and there will be an ultimate day of judgment for everyone. Unlike Jews, who believe there are multiple paths to the afterlife or heaven, Christians believe that only those who affirm a belief in Jesus Christ as the son of God and redeemer of humanity will be judged favorably.

There have been two major schisms within Christianity. The first, known as the Great Schism, took place in the 11th century and led to the development of the Roman Catholic Church in the West and what is now known as the Orthodox Church in the East. These groups make up the two largest branches within Christianity.

The second major schism occurred in 1517, when Martin Luther nailed a list of 95 complaints against the Roman Catholic Church onto the door of a church in Germany. This act began the Reformation and led to the development of Protestant Christianity, which is now composed of thousands of denominations (Nichols, 2007).

### Islam

The most recent of the major world religions is Islam. Developed about 1,400 years ago, Islam centers on the teachings in the Koran as revealed through the prophet Mohammed. These new teachings were deemed necessary because people had failed to live up to the standards God revealed through Judaism and Christianity. Islam literally means "submission (to God)" and now counts nearly one-fifth of the world as believers (Emerson et al., 2011).

The basic beliefs and duties of Islam are laid out in the five pillars of the Islamic faith that Muslims are expected to observe. *Shahadah* is the profession that there is only one god and that Mohammed

What other religious pilgrimages can you name?

Source: Fadi El Binni

was God's messenger. *Salat* is Islamic prayer, which occurs five times daily: before dawn, in the afternoon, when the sun is fading, at sunset and in the evening. In all cases, the supplicant should be facing the holy city of Mecca in Saudi Arabia. *Sawm* refers to ritual fasting that primarily occurs during the holy month of Ramadan. *Zakat* obliges Muslims to give alms, or charity, to the poor, and the *Hajj* is the pilgrimage to Mecca that able-bodied Muslims are obligated to make at least once in their lifetimes (Kurtz, 2007).

The major divisions within Islam occur between the Sunni and the Shi'ite denominations. The vast majority of the world's Muslims are Sunni, while the Shi'ite comprise a minority in most areas. The division traces its roots back to the prophet Mohammed's rightful successor. While the Sunnis believe that the rightful successor to Mohammed was his father-in-law, Abu Bakr, Shi'ite Muslims believe that Mohammed's son-in-law, Ali, was the rightful successor. Sunni-Shi'ite relations have at times been violent and at other times harmonious.

### Similarities

Christianity and Islam, which developed originally as sects, have many of the common characteristics of sects. Rather than relying on birth and socialization for increasing membership, both had to have a strong evangelistic focus, especially in their early days. In other words, they wanted people to convert to their belief systems.

Though both are now well-established, they often retain this evangelizing focus. Additionally, unlike Judaism, they both boast an exclusive claim to universal truth. For example, Christians believe that a belief in Jesus is the one true way to reach the afterlife. Muslims believe that religious adherence to Islam is necessary to enter the highest orders of heaven.

Additionally, both religions are **messianic**—that is, they believe God will come to Earth in some form in order to redeem humanity. Christians believe this has already happened in the form of Jesus Christ, who will return to Earth. Muslims likewise assert the importance of a messiah but are divided over who that will be and whether the messiah has already been here.

## Eastern Religions

Eastern religions also share many similarities as well as several elements that believers in the Western world may find very strange. In general, these religions are polytheistic or at least recognize multiple versions or spirits of the same god (not unlike the Christian concept of the trinity: the Father, Son and Holy Spirit). Additionally, these religions are not mutually exclusive. That is, a person could be both Buddhist and Sikh. There is typically no heaven or hell or any concept of afterlife at all. Reincarnation in the search for enlightenment replaces judgment and condemnation.

These religions comprise about one-fifth of the world's population, with Hindus being the largest group (15 percent of the world population) (Emerson et al., 2011).

### Hinduism

The oldest and largest of the Eastern religions, Hinduism stretches back to around 1,500 BCE. The third-largest religion in the world, Hinduism developed out of thousands of indigenous religions in what is now India and has no identifiable founder. Although Hinduism is **polytheistic**, consisting of many gods, most believers follow Brahman, Vishnu, or Shiva. These are the creator, preserver and destroyer of life, respectively. The teachings in the Vedas and Upanishads give the basic tenets of the faith, but many other sacred texts exist (Kurtz, 2007).

Hindus have a strong belief in reincarnation. Enlightenment, or Nirvana, which ends the cycles of reincarnation, is achieved only after many lifetimes. All living things contain Brahma, or God, and enlightenment is reached when a person is in harmony with God.

Central to the cycle of reincarnation is the notion of karma, which holds that good deeds and thoughts and bad deeds and thoughts come back to the individual in the form of cosmic rewards and punishments in this life or in a future one.

Although the caste system is strongly associated with Hinduism, it is by no means particular to the religion or necessary for it. Four basic castes

# Religion and Consumption

A few years ago, a friend invited me to attend his church. "I know you're interested in religion," he said "so why don't you come and check out my church. We're a little different than most places." Intrigued, I took him up on his offer. That Sunday night, I set out with directions in hand to meet him for the weekly worship service but was surprised when I ended up in a residential neighborhood cul-de-sac. Confused, I called my friend to explain that I was lost. "No, you're not," he told me. "I can see you out the window. Just come on in." I looked around and realized that the "church" was in a house. He was right—this was going to be different.

I walked up the steps and into a gathering of about 20 adults and children just getting ready to share a pot-luck dinner. The evening was more like a gathering of friends than a typical worship service. People talked and laughed and helped each other with dishes and kids. After the meal, everyone gathered in the living room for a worship service. There was communion, a sermon, an offering, prayers and music—all typical elements of Christian worship.

What I didn't find out until later was that the people in charge of coming up with the service change on a weekly basis. Sometimes, the worship elements are decided on the spot, based on someone's needs or desires.

When I asked my friend why he belonged to this church, he explained it to me this way: "So many other churches I have been to were all about creating programs and resources for the members to use—bigger buildings, more staff, more events. We don't do that here. We meet at people's houses because we're small. We don't need to pay for a building or a pastor. We would rather use our resources to help others."

My friend was drawn to this church because of his dissatisfaction with mainstream religion. Social scientists are increasingly referring to these people, who drop out of mainstream organized religion, as the **dechurched** (as opposed to the unchurched, who have never been part of organized religion on a regular basis). The dissatisfaction expressed by the dechurched frequently revolves less around theological issues and more around the ways church resources are consumed. *Time Magazine* profiled the movement in 2006, noting that the appeal of flexible resources was a major draw for participants. While buildings typically consume around 75 percent of a congregation's resources, house churches spend only 10 percent of offerings on non-service-related activities (Healy, 2006).

Another friend of mine, Dr. George Sanders, a sociologist at Oakland University in Michigan, recently found himself in a local **megachurch**, marveling at the spectacle that had been created by this modern-day cathedral. Stadium seating, state-of-the-art audio-visual systems, satellites and TV cameras to carry the message to congregations around the country and people at home were all part of the weekly experience. The sermon was even made available on DVD or podcast before the service was finished.

Throughout the week, innumerable programs and services were available for the local congregation to take part in—computer skills classes, child-care facilities, workout facilities, a coffee shop and bookstore, even a dry cleaner—all on the grounds of the church "campus."

The modern megachurch movement is one of the fastest-growing religious movements in the United States (Thumma, Travis & Bird, 2005).

As sociologists interested in religion, our task is to uncover exactly why these two religious expressions, so different from each other, would show up at exactly the same time. The key lies in recognizing that whenever one form of expression comes to dominate a field (in this case, the large, consumer-driven church dominating the field of religion), we will inevitably see alternative movements arising to meet the needs of those who oppose the movement (in this case, the smaller, more relational house church). Sociologists pay attention to both of these things as we seek to understand how societies work.

Source: Sunciti Sundaram

Do you believe, like the Hindus, that the concept of karma is real?

is gained by following the path of the Buddha to end desire and suffering. This path is known as the Eight-Fold Path and consists of:

1. *Right view:* accepting the Four Noble Truths.
2. *Right intention:* the commitment to neither act nor think cruelly, instead focusing on compassion.
3. *Right speech:* choosing words carefully so as to do little harm and not lie.
4. *Right action:* refraining from harming others and endeavoring to treat people kindly and respectfully.
5. *Right living:* obtaining a living in an honest and peaceful way.
6. *Right effort:* acting from pure states of mind rather than being motivated by jealousy or anger.
7. *Right mindfulness:* seeing the world objectively and clearly.
8. *Right concentration:* through mediation focusing clearly with little effort (Kurtz, 2007).

Although Buddhism is still found primarily in Asia, it has spread throughout the world. The religion's major focus is on the individual, and worship can happen at home, individually, or at a temple with others. This makes it appealing to many in the West, where individuality in other aspects of life is emphasized. Thus, elements of Buddhism, such as meditation and yoga (which originally developed with Hinduism), are practiced by a variety of people in the U.S.

traditionally make up the social classes in India. At the bottom are the untouchables who reside outside traditional Hindu society, although this category was officially banned in the middle of the 20th century. Caste position is determined by birth, not deeds, and cannot be changed. Religious scholars generally regard the caste system as a political vestige and not necessarily tied to the religion (Kurtz, 2007).

## Buddhism

Just as Christianity broke off from Judaism (and Islam from Christianity), Buddhism arose as a reaction to corruption within Hinduism. Its founder, Siddhartha Gautama, was a Hindu in line to become a king. His father tried to shield him from the outside world to ensure his son fulfilled his destiny, but Siddhartha left the temple, saw visions of human suffering and eventually renounced material goods in a quest for true enlightenment.

For Buddhists, enlightenment means the absence of desire. Siddhartha, the first to achieve true enlightenment, or Nirvana, is known as the Buddha. While he is not directly worshiped, his life is seen as a model for others to follow and emulate (Kurtz, 2007).

Buddhism is strikingly diverse in practice but can be loosely centered on the Four Noble Truths, which were among the earliest teachings of the Buddha. They assert that 1) The modern world produces suffering; 2) Suffering arises from desire; 3) When desire ends, suffering ends; and 4) Enlightenment

## Sikhism

Sikhism, the world's fifth-largest religion and one of the fastest-growing, was founded in the 1500s in Pakistan and stresses equality among believers. Guru Nanak founded the religion, which is monotheistic. Its core teachings were revealed to him and the nine gurus who followed him. The 10th and final guru, Guru Gobind Singh, declared he would be the last human guru, and from then on the Sikh scripture, Guru Granth Sahib, was known as guru (Sikhs.org).

Sikhism places little emphasis on religious rituals. Instead, the focus is on doing good deeds.

Do you think you could live like a Buddhist monk for an entire year?

Overall, a high degree of importance is placed on the individual's relationship with God. Sikhs believe everyone is equal in the eyes of God and has direct access to God. Furthermore, Sikhism holds that God is without form or gender. Thus, Sikhs have no idols or representations of God, opting instead to worship only God in the abstract form.

Sikhs can worship at any time and place, but the religion teaches that life lived in a community is the most important. Communal worship, then, is important to Sikhs and takes place at Gurdwaras, where anyone of any faith is welcome. The most prominent Gurdwara is the Harmandir Sahib in Punjab, India, which has been the site of many battles over the years.

The monotheistic stance and equality of all believers regardless of social class sets Sikhism in stark contrast to the dominant religion in India, Hinduism. Sikhism not only eschews the caste system, which was so closely associated with Hinduism when Sikhism was founded, but also accords far more rights to women than Hinduism.

## Religion in America

### Beliefs and Adherence

Measuring religious adherence and practice, what researchers call **religiosity**, has long posed problems for researchers. Part of this is due to the lack of consistency between what people profess and what they do. For example, although 60 percent of Americans claim that religion is "very important" in their lives, only 24 percent of citizens attend religious services weekly (Pew, 2002). Regardless of how religious commitment and adherence are measured, however, the United States ranks as one of the most religious countries in the world, especially among Westerners. In fact, twice as many Americans think religion plays an important role in their lives as Canadians, Britons and Italians.

Not only do the vast majority of Americans say that they belong to a church (65 percent, according to a Gallup Poll in 2005), nearly 90 percent profess a belief in God, with 63 percent saying they have "no doubt that God exists" (Gallup, 2005). These numbers have not changed much over recent decades, either, regardless of the fact that many high-profile pastors bemoan what they see as the secularization of America.

Secularization occurs when religion becomes less influential over other social institutions. In Europe during the Middle Ages, for example, the Catholic Church controlled nearly all aspects of political, social and economic life, in addition to dominating the religious sphere. Now, however, while the influence of the Catholic Church has not disappeared entirely, institutions such as government, education and the economy operate independently. In America, these spheres have always been somewhat separated, and there is no evidence that the United States is becoming dramatically more secularized. In fact, for Protestant churches, attendance has actually increased over the last 50 years (Hout & Greely, 1987; National Opinion Poll, 2000).

## Civil Religion

The United States has a strong element of what sociologists refer to as **civil religion**. Robert Bellah (1967) was the first to describe this system, in which Americans are united by certain common beliefs, some of which are explicitly religious, that bring together a diverse people under a common umbrella. Civic rituals, ceremonies and symbols form the basis for bonds between groups that otherwise might have little in common. Scholars point to events such as presidential inaugurations as examples of common rituals that bring people across the country together. These events, along with symbols of America such as the flag, can let civic life take on the dynamics of a religious experience.

## Pluralism and Diversity

The United States protects diversity within religion through laws and regulations that prohibit the favoring of any one religion or belief system by the government. The First Amendment to the Constitution ensures that Americans have both freedom of religion and freedom from religion. In effect, this sets up a religious marketplace where various religions, denominations and churches compete for members (Iannaccone, 1997; Stark & Bainbridge, 1996). This marketplace reflects the diverse ethnic and racial makeup of the country, as well as the distinct emphasis on individuality and personal fulfillment found here.

Unlike elsewhere in the world, no religion is supported either ideologically or financially by the state. This means that without weekly attendees and participation, most churches here would cease to exist. The result is a religious landscape characterized by a high degree of **religious pluralism**, with a wide variety of practices and beliefs. There is a startling array of churches in the United States as congregations have broken off from existing groups or sprung up to meet the needs of people in the community. Many pastors act like religious entrepreneurs and specialize in "church planting," where they establish a church, get it up and running, and then move on to the next community.

The racial and ethnic diversity in the United States contributes to a unique religious landscape characterized by both a high degree of religiosity and a wide variety of choices.

## Religion and Violence

Religion has often been the subject of global interest because of the role religious extremists play in acts of terrorism. Most Americans associate religious violence and terrorism with the hijackers from the 9/11 attacks or with the ongoing turmoil in the Middle East, but religious terrorism has a long history and spans every major belief system. In the Western world alone, such acts include race riots in the Southern United States, Catholic/Protestant violence in Northern Ireland, the Inquisition in Europe and Latin America, and the Crusades, among many other examples. In the United States and Canada, for example, Christian terrorists have been responsible for the vast majority of abortion clinic violence, including more than 40 clinic bombings, eight murders and hundreds of death threats (NAF, 2010).

Mark Jurgensmeyer, who wrote *Terror in the Mind of God,* (2003), points out that the motivations behind religious terrorists are varied and that many acts serve symbolic as well as strategic purposes. These ideologies are frequently supported by turbulent political and economic circumstances. Many scholars understand acts of religious terrorism to be only tangentially connected with religion. Instead, they say, these acts are more about achieving political goals and protesting unequal conditions (Pape, 2005). Religion is simply the justification people use to explain their actions, because the reality of an increasingly globalized world, where some countries and people prosper, while others do not, is complex and difficult to understand. Religion offers a compelling framework for the explanation of these murky global dynamics.

# Summary

Education and religion are important areas of study for sociologists. They not only help structure the world through their socialization efforts but also reflect back the inequalities present in any society. Both institutions remain as important as ever. An educated citizenry is increasingly vital for countries to remain competitive in a global marketplace. Anything that bars or prohibits some members of society from getting an education is to the detriment of the society as a whole. Similarly, we see that as the world becomes more connected, religion plays an increasingly important role in many people's lives as they seek structure and understanding in a complex and seemingly chaotic world. Religion provides not only comfort but also a framework around which to interpret world events.

## Review/Discussion Questions

1. What are the key differences between Western and Eastern religions?
2. What are the similarities between Judaism, Christianity and Islam?
3. Explain the hidden curriculum and give an example.
4. How do labels and self-image factor into an individual's education?
5. How religious is the United States?
6. Why are churches able to be tolerant of "free riders"?
7. How might one explain the popularity of Sikhism in India?
8. How do social class and race affect education in the United States?

## Key Terms

**Acculturation** is the passing along of norms, practices and values from generation to generation.

**Adolescent subculture** is made up of attitudes and values that are specific to youth, especially in contrast to adults.

**Affirmative action** is a policy or program that seeks to redress past discrimination by increasing opportunities for underrepresented groups.

**Animism** is the belief that all forms of life contain elements of the supernatural.

**Assimilation** occurs when a person from a minority cultural group adopts the cultural characteristics of the dominant group while discarding their ethnic traits.

**Church** is a kind of religious organization with high engagement with mainstream society.

**Civil religion** is a collection of beliefs and rituals that exists outside of institutional religion and unites people in a celebration of society.

**Credentialism** is the practice of relying on conferred degrees and diplomas as universal markers of educational achievement.

**Cult** is a kind of religious organization, typically centered on a charismatic leader, which offers a new interpretation of the afterlife.

**Cultural capital** is Pierre Bourdieu's term for the cultural elements—tastes—that distinguish people of different classes.

**De facto** means "in practice."

**De jure** means "by law."

**Dechurched** refers to people who have left institutional religion because of dissatisfaction with its structure, organization, politics or attitudes.

**Education** is the social institution that encompasses all aspects of formal training in which people gain knowledge and skills as well as learn values and norms.

**Evangelical** are religious adherents with a strong focus on spreading their religion to other people.

**Extremists** are religious adherents who believe that their religion is the one true religion and others must be done away with.

**Free rider** is a person who attends religious services and takes advantage of congregational resources without contributing time or money.

**Fundamentalism** are religious adherents who take a literal interpretation of a religious text or teaching.

**Hidden curriculum** involves the mechanisms through which schooling rewards upper-class habits and values through non-instructional items taught in schools.

**Latent functions** are unintended consequences or results.

**Manifest functions** are intended consequences or results.

**Megachurch** is a congregation with at least 2,000 weekly attendees.

**Messianic** are religions that believe in the coming of a divine figure for the redemption of humanity.

**Monotheism** is the belief in and worship of only one god.

**Polytheism** is the belief in and worship of multiple gods.

**Profane** are mundane, everyday things.

**Religiosity** is the measure of religious belief in a population.

**Religious pluralism** is the coexistence of a wide variety of religious beliefs in a single society.

**Sacred** are those things that are set apart from everyday life and regarded as extraordinary.

**Schooling** is when education occurs in a formal, classroom setting.

**Sect** is a religious organization that breaks off from a mainstream church and is less integrated with the surrounding culture.

**Secularization** is the decline of religious authority and separation of society into various institutional components.

**Theism** is the belief that god(s) reside separately from humans and other living things.

**Tracking** is the separation of students into different ability groups to receive different levels of instruction.

**Universal education** is the granting of free education to all citizens in a country.

**White flight** is the systematic movement of upper-middle-class families out of the inner-city cores and into the suburbs.

# Bibliography

Appel, M., Cartwright, D., Smith, D., & Wolf, L. (1996). The Impact of Diversity on Students: A Preliminary Review of the Research Literature. Association of American Colleges and Universities, Washington, DC.

Armstrong, K. (1994). A History of God: The 4,000 Year Quest of Judaism, Christianity, and Islam. New York, NY: Random House.

Ashburn, E. (2009). Why Do Students Drop Out? Because They Must Work at Jobs Too. <http://chronicle.com/article/Why-Do-Students-Drop-Out-/49417/> (2011).

Astin, A. (1993). What Matters in College: Four Critical Years Revisited. San Francisco, CA: Jossey-Bass.

Aud, S., Hussar, W., Kena, G., Bianco, K., Frohlich, L., Kemp, J., & Tahan, K. (2011). The Condition of Education 2011 (NCES 2011-033). Washington, D.C., National Center for Education Statistics, Institute of Education Sciences, U.S. Department of Education.

Baldi, S., Jin, Y., Skemer, M., Green P. J., & Gerget, D. (2007). Highlights from PISA 2006: Performance of U.S. 15 Year Old Students in Science and Mathematics Literacy in an International Context. Washington, D.C.: U.S. Department of Education.

Bellah, R. (1967). Civil Religion in America. Daedalus. 96(1): 1–21.

Bourdieu, P. (1996). The State Nobility. Translated by Lauretta C. Clough. Foreword by Loic J. D. Wacquant. Stanford, Calif.: Stanford University Press.

Chang, M. (2002). The Impact of an Undergraduate Diversity Course Requirement on Students' Racial Views and Attitudes. The Journal of General Education 51:21-42.

Chaves, M. (1994). Secularization as Declining Religious Authority. Social Forces. 72(3):749- 774.

Durkheim, E. (1995, [1912]). Elementary Forms of Religious Life. New York, NY: Free Press.

Emerson, M., Mirola, W., & Monahan, S. (2011). Religion Matters: What Sociology Teaches Us About Religion in Our World. Boston, MA.: Allyn and Bacon.

GAO (2010). For-Profit Colleges: Undercover Testing Finds Colleges Encouraged Fraud and Engaged in Deceptive and Questionable Marketing Practices. Testimony Before the Committee on Health, Education, Labor, and Pensions, U.S. Senate.

Gladwell, M. (2008). Outliers: The Story of Success. New York, NY: Little, Brown and Co.

Goldman, V. (2003). The Baby Ivies. The New York Times. Jan. 12, 2003.

Goodman, D. (2004). Class Dismissed. Mother Jones. 29, May/June, 41-47.

Graham, P. (1974). Community and Class in American Education: 1865-1918. New York, NY: Wiley.

Gurin, P., Dey, E., Hurtado, S., & Gurin, G. (2002). Diversity and Higher Education: Theory and Impact on Educational Outcomes. Harvard Educational Review 72.

Healy, R. (2006). Why Home Churches are Filling Up. Time, February 27th.

Hout, M., & Greeley, A. (1987). The Center Doesn't Hold: Church Attendance in the United States, 1940-1984. American Sociological Review. 52: 325-345.

Hu, S., & Kuh, G. (2003). Diversity Experiences and College Student Learning and Personal Development. Journal of College Student Development 44:320-334.

Iannaccone, L. (1997). Rational Choice: Framework for the Scientific Study of Religion. Rational Choice Theory and Religion: Summary and Assessment, edited by Lawrence Young. New York: Routledge.

Jurgensmeyer, M. (2003). Terror in the Mind of God: The Global Rise in Religious Violence. 3rd Edition. Berkeley, CA.: University of California Press.

Kaestle, C. (1972). Social Reform and the Urban School. History of Education Quarterly. 12(2): 211-228.

Kantrowitz, M. (2010). Total College Debt Now Exceeds Total Credit Card Debt. Fastweb. <http://www.fastweb.com/financial-aid/articles/2589-total-college-debt-now-exceeds- total-credit-card-debt> (2011).

Kurtz, L. (2007). Gods in the Global Village: The World's Religions in Sociological Perspective. London: Pine Forge.

Marin, P. (2000). The Educational Possibility of Multi-Racial/Multi-Ethnic College Classrooms. American Council on Education and American Association of University Professors, Washington, DC.

Marx, K. (1977, [2000]). Towards a Critique of Hegel's Philosophy of Right: Introduction. In Karl Marx: Selected Writings. Edited by David McLellan. Oxford: Oxford University Press.

Mehta, S. (2008). Parents may Home-School Children Without Teaching Credential, California Court Says. Los Angeles Times. <http://articles.latimes.com/2008/aug/09/local/me- homeschool9> (2011).

NAF (2010). Incidents of Violence and Disruption Against Abortion Providers in the U.S. and Canada. National Abortion Federation. <http://www.prochoice.org/pubs_research/publications/downloads/about_abortion/vi olence_stats.pdf.> (2011).

National Center for Education Statistics (2010). Digest of Educational Statistics. <http://nces.ed.gov/programs/digest/d10/.> (2011).

National Opinion Research Center (NORC) (2000). General Social Survey: Cumulative Codebook. Chicago, IL: University of Chicago Press.

The New York Times (2003). Fighting School Resegregation. (January 27). <http://www.nytimes.com/2003/01/27/opinion/fighting-school-resegregation.html.> (2011).

Nichols, S. (2007). The Reformation. Wheaton, IL: Crossway Books.

Nocera, J. (2011). Why We Need For-Profit Colleges. The New York Times Magazine. <http://www.nytimes.com/2011/09/18/magazine/why-we-need-for-profit- colleges.html?pagewanted=all.> (2011).

Orfield, G., & Wald, J. (2001). High Stakes Tests Attached to High School Graduation Lead to Increased Drop-Out Rates, Particularly for Poor and Minority Students. In Motion. April 29. Pp. 1-2.

Orfield, G. (2009). Reviving the Goal of an Integrated Society: A 21st Century Challenge. Los Angeles, CA.: UCLA Civil Rights Project.

Pape, R. (2005). Dying to Win: The Strategic Logic of Suicide Terrorism. New York, NY: Random House.

Pascarella, E., Palmer, B., Moye, M., & Pierson, C. ( 2001). Do Diversity Experiences Influence the Development of Critical Thinking? Journal of College Student Development. 42:257- 271.

Perez, E. (2011). Low Job Placement Rates Put For-Profit Colleges at Risk. California Watch. <http://californiawatch.org/dailyreport/low-job-placement-rates-put-profits-risk-13649.> (2011).

Pew (2002). Among Wealthy Nations ...U.S. Stands Along in its Embrace of Religion. The Pew Global Attitudes Project. Washington, DC: The Pew Research Center.

Pitt, R., & Packard, J. (forthcoming). Activating Diversity: Examining the Impact of Student Race on Contributions to Course Discussions. The Sociological Quarterly.

Planty, M. W., Hussar, T., Snyder, S., Provasnik, G., Kena, R., Dinkes, A., Ramani, K., & Kemp. J. (2008). The Condition of Education 2008 (NCES 2008-031). Washington, D.C.: National Center for Education Statistics, Institute of Education Sciences, U.S. Department of Education.

Pope, J. (2011). Student Loans: The Next Bubble? The Huffington Post. <http://www.huffingtonpost.com/2011/11/06/student-loans-the-next- bu_n_1078730.html.> (2011).

Princiotta, D., & Bielick, S. (2006). Homeschooling in the United States: 2003 (NCES 2006- 042). Washington, D.C., National Center for Education Statistics, Institute of Education Sciences, U.S. Department of Education.

Regents of the University of California v. Bakke, 438 U.S. 265 (1978).

Rosenthal, R., & Jacobson, L. (1968). Pygmalion in the classroom. New York: Holt, Rinehart & Winston.

Rumberger, R., & Lim, S. A. (2008). Why Students Drop Out of School: A Review of 25 Years of Research. California Dropout Research Project. UC Santa Barbara: Gevirtz Graduate School of Education.

Schlesinger, J. (2010). Obama: Community Colleges are the 'Unsung Heroes.' ABCNEWS. Political Punch Blog. <http://abcnews.go.com/blogs/politics/2010/10/obama-community- colleges-are-the-unsung-heroes/.> (2011).

Sikhs.org. <http://www.sikhs.org/.> (2011).

Spiegler, T. (2003). Home Education in Germany: An Overview of the Contemporary Situation. Evaluation and Research in Education. 17(2-3):179-190.

Stanton-Salazar, R., & Dornbusch, S., (1995). Social Capital and the Reproduction of Inequality: Information Networks among Mexican-Origin High School Students. Sociology of Education. 68:2.

Stark, R. (2007). Sociology. 10th ed. Belmont, Calif.: Thomson.

Stark, R., & Bainbridge, W. S. (1996). A Theory of Religion. New Brunswick, N.J.: Rutgers University Press.

Statistical Abstract of the United States (2005). Washington, D.C.: U.S. Bureau of the Census.

Thumma, S., Travis, D., & Bird, W. (2005). Megachurches Today. Hartford, Conn.: Hartford Institute for Religion Research.

Wilson, R. (2010). For-Profit Colleges Change Higher Education's Landscape. Chronicle of Higher Education. February 7, 2010. <http://chronicle.com/article/For-Profit-Colleges- Change/64012/.> (2011).

# CHAPTER TWELVE

# Politics and the Economy

## Steven D. Williams

**Chapter Objectives**
At the end of this chapter, students should be able to:

- Understand the difference between power and authority.
- Distinguish between Max Weber's three forms of authority.
- Distinguish between the concepts of politics, government, and the state.
- Understand the distinction between civic and ethnic nationalism.
- Define the different forms of government.
- Understand the pluralist and elite models of political power.
- Define the concept of the military-industrial complex.
- Distinguish between use value and exchange value.
- Name the three sectors of the economy.
- Distinguish between the economic systems of capitalism and socialism.
- Understand the concept of economic globalization.
- Distinguish between the methods of Fordism and post-Fordism.
- Articulate the significance of the modern corporation.
- List the various categories of occupation.
- List the various forms of unemployment.

In the 1975 science-fiction film *Rollerball*, economics and politics have melded. In this future world, war is obsolete, but so is the concept of the nation-state. Nationalism has given way to corporate loyalty. Individuality is looked on with suspicion, and the corporation is the dominant model of social organization. Violence and crime have been virtually eliminated, and the populace is generally content in its materialistic utopia. The people are allowed only one spectacle of violence, the sport of rollerball (a hybrid of roller derby and hockey). Rollerball is designed to reflect the ideology that individual effort is futile while a smooth-functioning group like a team or a corporation is efficient and powerful.

For most of us, a life of material abundance free of crime and war may sound very appealing. But the vision of society presented in *Rollerball* is actually meant to be a dystopia—a society of unimaginative, uninspired sheep. The film's protagonist is a rebellious individual who questions the social order and champions the idea of individual accomplishment—a very American perspective. But of course, this is only science fiction, and corporations would never gain that much power in our society—or would they?

## Power and Authority

In many sociology textbooks, the institutions of politics and the economy are combined in the same chapter. Although one could certainly make a case for combining any of the five traditional sociological institutions (as Josh Packard does regarding education and religion in chapter 11), it is the combination of economics and politics that seems most inevitable. The election of politicians all the way up to the president often hinges on the perception of who can run the economy best, and our political leaders often receive either credit or blame for presiding over strong or weak economic conditions.

But ultimately, as Max Weber, a German sociologist and political economist at the turn of the 20th century, asserted, politics is about **power**, the ability to accomplish goals despite the resistance of others (Weber, 1947). Systems of government based solely on the naked wielding of power, however, are inherently fragile and usually seen as illegitimate. Power, then, must be made acceptable to those who are subjected to it. Imagine driving home from campus and being forced to the side of the road by another car. The driver gets out of his vehicle, opens your car door before you can lock it, and forces you to hand over all your cash. Now imagine that on that same stretch of road you are pulled over by a police officer for speeding. The officer writes you a ticket for the same amount of money you were previously

bullied out of. Both individuals exercised power over you, but the former situation seems much more disturbing and unjust. This is because most of us would agree the bully had no right to take your money. This, Weber argued, is the distinction between power and **authority**, which is defined as power that is perceived as legitimate. Weber proposed three general means by which power is translated into authority: traditional, charismatic, and rational-legal.

**Traditional authority** is power that has been legitimated through a history of long–standing rituals and customs, often containing an appeal to the sacred or supernatural. Traditional authority is commonly found in small-scale hunting-gathering, pastoral, or horticultural societies, but it can build up a social and historical inertia such that it is seldom challenged. Thus, large-scale agricultural or industrial societies have operated with traditional authority into the modern era. Ruling dynasties based on heredity from ancient Egyptian pharaohs to the British House of Windsor are prime examples. Traditional authority can be exceptionally stable for the individual leader and even for the group, but there is a built-in danger in terms of continuity. If a sitting monarch dies unexpectedly before a clear successor has been established, the ensuing power struggle could escalate to civil war.

**Charismatic authority** depends on the extraordinary characteristics of individuals and their ability to inspire others. The charismatic leader may also make an appeal to the supernatural and even claim a degree of divinity. In extreme cases, as in the leadership of religious cults, followers may be persuaded to engage in activities that outside observers would consider bizarre or destructive. In most cases, the charismatic leader is a gifted orator who presents a compelling or even utopian vision, and followers become convinced that only he or she can lead them. For the leader, charismatic authority is particularly tenuous and dangerous. The charismatic leader may be in a position to take credit for almost every success an organization or society enjoys, but he or she must also take the blame for events or conditions over which he or she has no control. For the social group itself, charismatic authority can be potentially disastrous if the leader becomes convinced of his or her own divinity or genius to the point of irrationality.

**Rational-legal authority** refers to power that is legitimated through formal, standardized legal procedures. Such authority is clearly and precisely prescribed in its responsibilities, duties, and limitations, often in the form of a constitution or similar charter. Ideally, rational-legal authority ensures that any person wielding it cannot step outside its boundaries to become despotic. This form of authority is most closely associated with such governmental forms as constitutional monarchies and democracies. The past 200 years have seen a significant increase in the prevalence of rational-legal authority. Max Weber understood this as part of the general trend of **rationalization** he observed in modern, particularly Western, societies. One advantage of rational-legal authority is that power moves away from the individual *per se* and toward the formalized system. If either a charismatic or traditional leader makes decisions destructive to the group, it may be difficult or impossible to remove the individual. With rational-legal authority, mechanisms to do that are built into the system (impeachment, elections, etc.). If a charismatic or traditional leader dies suddenly, the group or society may be thrown into chaos. With rational-legal authority, a clear line of succession is spelled out. Weber also knew, however, that rationalization usually entails *bureaucratization,* and although theoretically more efficient, such authority can also be slow and cumbersome.

It is important to realize that all three forms of authority are ideal types (in the sense described by Weber) and that in reality, two or all three may be combined. All American presidents, for example, rely on rational-legal authority, but some may utilize a degree of charismatic leadership, and a few (e.g., the Kennedy and Bush families) may draw on familial history to exercise traditional authority as well.

## Politics, Government and the State

**Politics** is the institution through which power, and, one hopes, authority, is exercised, particularly at the macro level. People may speak of "office politics" or the politics of gender, and these ideas are certainly of interest to sociologists. But generally, we refer here to the use of institutionalized norms and laws to organize societies according to the will of particular groups or individuals. When groups or individuals legally exercise political power, they are usually part of a formal organization called **government**. A functioning government requires both motivated individuals and the appropriate apparatus of governance, that is, the **state**. To illustrate the distinctions between the terms, consider the transition of power immediately following an election in, say, the United Kingdom. The newly elected members of Parliament constitute a group that shares a generally similar political perspective and may have already informally divided responsibilities in anticipated Cabinet positions. As a matter of tradition, the sovereign (Queen Elizabeth II) invites these individuals to form a government. They then take over the apparatus that is waiting for them—the state. Regardless of which party is in power, the state remains. But the state cannot operate to its potential without a government. And the institutionalized norms, laws, and traditions that govern the entire process is politics.

The state is the apparatus of governance, but Max Weber also defined the state as the entity claiming a monopoly on the legal use of violence within its borders (Weber, 1994). This may seem a strange definition at first glance. In the United States, how does this mesh with, for example, the mythology of the "Wild West," the ideology of the rugged individual, or the constitutionally protected right of citizens to bear arms? In theory, we do not tolerate vigilantes; in practice, many might admire them under certain circumstances. To clarify, the posse is legal, but the lynch mob is not. The difference between them is clear: The former is sanctioned by a recognized legal authority while the latter is not. If someone breaks into your home with the intent to rob you or do you physical harm, you may choose to defend yourself in a violent manner. If you do so, you must be able to demonstrate to the legal authorities that you were only defending yourself; otherwise, you may be arrested, tried, imprisoned, and possibly even executed. The "violence" of the state, in other words, is manifested in the police, courts, and prison system. What we are left with in terms of legal violence not administered by the state are the simulations of violence found in television and movies, as well as the tightly controlled and regulated pseudo-violence of spectacles such as boxing and wrestling.

## The Nation-State

Humans, being the inherently social creatures they are, have always organized themselves into groups. From small, kinship-based bands to continent-spanning empires, people have been held together by a variety of social, political, and economic forces. The relatively recent rise of the **nation-state** organizes virtually the entire planet into territorial and political units. At present, there are approximately 200 such internationally recognized entities (CIA World Factbook, 2012). Each of these units possesses its own distinct symbols of identity, most notably its flag. Most also issue their own currency (though the European Union has recently bucked this trend) and passports; have their own national anthem; and adopt such symbols as national animals and mottos.

Part of the function of macro-level politics is to foster and perpetuate a sense of belonging and loyalty to the nation-state. Governments adopt many strategies in this regard depending, in part, on the cultural makeup of the population. In a culturally homogenous state such as South Korea or Japan, for instance, political leaders may refer to shared norms and beliefs in areas like language, ethnicity, or religion with the confidence that most of the population will feel a shared resonance and sense of peoplehood along those dimensions. In multicultural nation-states like the United States or Australia, a sense of shared identity is more abstract and potentially less stable. Lacking an authoritarian central government, the ethnically diverse nation-state of Yugoslavia fell into civil war and "ethnic cleansing" in the 1990s. In the United States, a diverse population is held together by a relentless **civic nationalism** that socializes its members into identifying not with any particular ethnic or religious tradition but with the concept of the nation-state itself and the values it represents. Thus, each successive American government must utilize at least part of its political power to uphold and entrench nationalism.

## Forms of Government

In developing his theory of historical materialism in the 19th century, Karl Marx modified the **dialectic** principle of philosopher Georg Wilhelm Friedrich Hegel to posit an ultimate "end point" to history—the communist revolution. Marx's theory implies that in a classless society, there would no longer be a need for an ideology that produces **false consciousness** and inevitable class conflict, and the dialectical process of history would reach its conclusion (Marx & Engels, 1970). Despite the fact that none of the communist societies that were formed in the 20th century followed Marx's model, the collapse of Soviet communism in 1989-91 seemed to some a reversal of Marx's prediction. In 1992, Francis Fukuyama wrote of the failure of both communism and authoritarianism (fascism) as indications that liberal democracy had finally revealed itself as the self-evident form of human government. Thus, the **"end of history"** came with the end of the Cold War, and all that remains is to perfect and spread the basic form of Western, capitalist, democratic society (Fukuyama, 1992) This assertion, however, ignores the fact that many other forms of government still exist.

## Authoritarianism

**Authoritarian governments** concentrate power in the hands of a small group, usually with a military dictator as the absolute ruler. They often come about as the result of a military *coup d'etat*, a swift, usually violent takeover of the government and may initially enjoy popular support, especially among the poorer social classes. The apparatus of the state is often used in a brutal fashion to suppress or eliminate rival political parties, and the mass of the population is keenly aware that the police or military may be used against them. But if the authoritarian leaders are satisfied that their own goals (wealth, power, prestige) are adequately met, there may be little attempt to interfere with the daily operation of civil society. Authoritarian regimes often have no coherent political ideology to impose on their people other than obedience.

## Totalitarianism

**Totalitarian** systems of government resemble authoritarian regimes in their concentration of absolute power, but they typically attempt to control virtually all aspects of public and even private life. Totalitarian governments frequently attempt to manufacture the effects of charismatic authority or a cult of personality through propaganda. As in authoritarian regimes, the apparatus of state violence can and often is used against the population. In totalitarian systems of government, however, rulers use modern technologies of surveillance to monitor and control civil society. Other social institutions—the economy, religion, the mass media, and, particularly, education—are controlled by the state in the service of consolidating power. Impressive but sometimes horrific large-scale changes can be made with alarming speed and efficiency, such as the elimination of entire "subversive" elements (e.g. the educated, or those of a particular ethnicity or religion). Totalitarian governments may foster the exaggerated image of a benevolent ruler, but it is the overall efficiency of the system rather than the person that renders totalitarian states so powerful and difficult to overthrow. The image of the totalitarian state is particularly frightening to many Americans, fostering, among other things, their distrust in "big government" and the use of such adjectives as "**Orwellian**" to describe what they consider its manifestations.

## Monarchies

As ideal types, monarchies come in two general forms: absolute and constitutional. In an **absolute monarchy**, a king or queen rules by hereditary right until death or abdication. In the 17th and early 18th centuries, Louis XIV of France epitomized many of the qualities of an absolute monarch, famously stating "I am the state." Such monarchs may personally take charge of any aspect of government at any time and have traditionally claimed a "divine right" of rule. In reality, few have been able to rule effectively without making concessions to such social forces as the church or the aristocratic class. Absolute monarchies are relatively rare in the 21st century; Saudi Arabia and Swaziland are two of the few remaining examples. Absolute monarchies operate almost exclusively with traditional authority, while constitutional monarchies utilize both traditional and rational-legal authority. In a **constitutional monarchy**, the power of the monarch is limited by the legal guidelines of a formal constitution or charter. Thus, in most constitutional monarchies, the king or queen serves only as a symbolic figurehead while the real power resides in a **parliament** or similar legislative body. The United Kingdom and Sweden are contemporary examples of such a system. Technically, many members of the British Commonwealth remain constitutional monarchies, and the queen's representative, the governor-general, has the legal right to strike down legislation passed in Canada or Australia, for example. In reality, however, this right is virtually never exercised, and for all intents and purposes, most constitutional monarchies operate as democracies.

## Democracies

Again, as an ideal type, a **democracy** refers to direct rule by the people themselves. In practice, however, such a system would be unworkably slow and awkward since every policy and decision would require a public referendum. The operation of government would become slow and ineffective. It should be noted, though, that the evolution of communications technology, particularly the widespread use of the Internet, could render participatory democracy much more feasible, provided that Internet access is available to all voters and reasonable security measures instituted. For now, a system of representative democracy has evolved, whereby individuals from various political parties are elected for specific terms and are expected to represent the interests of their constituents, their party, and the political unit as a whole (city, state, country). If the elected representative does not perform to the satisfaction of his or her constituents, he or she is likely to be voted out in the next election. If legal or ethical

Have you ever been involved in helping a candidate get elected?

guidelines are violated, mechanisms of removal or correction, such as impeachment, exist. Thus, democracies operate primarily with rational-legal authority.

## Other Political Systems

Given the dwindling of absolute monarchies, the defeat of authoritarian fascism in World War II, and the collapse of most totalitarian communist regimes in the late 20th century, can we now embrace Francis Fukuyama's "triumphalist" declaration that liberal democracy is the final form of human government? It is impossible to be certain, but we might take note of at least two challenges to this prediction. In the United States and other multicultural Western societies such as Canada, Australia, and the United Kingdom, civic nationalism may seem self-evidently normative. Citizens grow up socialized into patriotism to the "imagined community" of a nation-state, with its positive social values, internal tolerance and righteous history stressed. Regardless of their ethnic, religious or linguistic origins, Americans are expected to place their highest loyalty in their country, and the crime

of treason is viewed with such revulsion that it approaches the level of a social taboo. But much of the world embraces not civic but an **ethnic nationalism**, deriving identity not from nation-state loyalty but cultural or ethnic homogeneity (Marger, 2009). Thus, it is quite common for citizens in other parts of the world to place religious devotion above that of country. The possibility exists, then, of governments combining these loyalties into a **theocracy**, where spiritual and secular leaders are one and the same, and state policy is determined by religious dogma. In democracies that embrace free-market capitalism, the potential exists for informal **plutocracies** to form. The concentration of wealth in a relatively small part of the population means that political influence may also concentrate there, and state policies that favor the rich may become entrenched. In effect, a democracy may end up becoming a system that protects a small ruling class. So, while democracies have significantly increased in almost all parts of the world, their continued dominance is not inevitable.

# The Political Spectrum

In most democracies (and constitutional monarchies), a number of political parties vie for power by appealing to citizens with coherent stances on particular issues as well as a general philosophy or political ideology. Usually, this is expressed in terms of "left" or "right," that is, relative points on the **political spectrum**. The political spectrum is a socially constructed and historically relative continuum with a center that supposedly represents a moderate position. In the United States, the left corresponds to a generally liberal political and social ideology and is represented by the Democratic Party. The right, then, corresponds to a conservative ideology and is represented by the Republican Party. Although other political parties have existed and continue to exist in American politics, these two major parties effectively monopolize political choice in the United States. Under parliamentary systems (internationally more common than the American model), a greater variety of parties, with sometimes more particular or more extreme positions, proliferates. The leader of whichever party elects the greatest number of representatives automatically becomes the prime minister. If the ruling party holds a majority of the seats in parliament, and the members of the government all vote along party lines, it is rare that proposed legislation does not become law. But in a multi-party system it is possible to win the greatest number of seats without winning a majority. In the case of a **minority government**, the ruling party's position is more tenuous, requiring it to make concessions to other parties or face the possibility of consistently blocked legislation. Multi-party parliamentary democracies also allow for relatively obscure political parties to hold at least a few seats in parliament and thus have some voice in governmental debate.

Generally speaking, liberal and conservative political ideologies take predictable stances on certain social issues. In the United States, conservatives are more likely to oppose abortion; be in favor of the death penalty; support the Second Amendment right to bear arms; and oppose government-supported social programs. Liberals are more likely to support abortion; oppose the death penalty; favor some degree of gun control; and see value in the role of government programs. As an overall ideology, conservatives claim to support individual freedom; the traditional model of the family; the value of religion (specifically Christianity); law and order; and an economic environment that allows capitalism to flourish with minimal government "interference." Liberals, by contrast, will place more emphasis on overall social justice; tolerance for alternatives to traditional institutions (including support for the rights of the gay community); the value of science and separation of church and state; and an economic environment that regulates the "excesses" of capitalism in order to protect the working classes and the poor.

# Sociological Perspectives on Politics in Democracies

## The Functionalist Perspective

The two major macro-level sociological paradigms, functionalist and conflict, are usually applied to politics as pluralist or elite models. The two perspectives see political power as either dispersed or concentrated. Those who adhere to the **pluralist model** believe that political power should be shared equally among a diverse assortment of groups: individual voters, political parties, small businesses, large corporations, labor unions and a plethora of special interest groups (Dahl, 1961). Although many might complain about the influence of **special interest groups**, pluralist model theorists point out that these groups may be formed for virtually any cause so that, for example, a group promoting the protection of the environment will have a voice equal to that of a group promoting its exploitation. Since so many groups and social forces are at work, many will have competing interests so that no one group can gain too much power, and politics becomes "the art of compromise."

## The Conflict Perspective

In the **elite model**, power is seen as unbalanced in favor of particular social groups, as theorized by sociologists C. Wright Mills and G. William Domhoff. Although not necessarily adherents to historical materialism or Marxism *per se*, elite model theorists recognize, as Marx did, that a ruling class may exist even in democracies and that political power may concentrate in the hands of a minority at the expense of the majority. For Marx, this class—the bourgeoisie—consisted of those who owned and controlled the means of industrial production. Rich factory owners may not have held all the seats in British parliament, but laws were usually made for their benefit. In the modern American context, Mills saw the power elite consisting of the corporate rich working with the executive branch of government and top military leaders. Members of Congress, the Supreme Court, political interest groups, and media figures hold a secondary position. Finally, he characterized the great majority of the population as not only powerless but unorganized and largely apathetic (Mills, 1956).

G. William Domhoff's elite model differs from Mills' in the coherence of the ruling elite. Where Mills saw a relatively unified set of goals pursued by corporate, political, and military leaders, Domhoff notes there are often significant disagreements within such factions. Domhoff's model also expands the definition to include powerful interest groups and labor unions (Domhoff, 2002). Elite model theorists have also noted that the elite are primarily white and male.

## The Symbolic Interactionist Perspective

As a generally apolitical and micro-level sociological perspective, symbolic interactionism might not seem particularly useful in the macro-realm of politics. But symbolic interactionism can provide fascinating insights into individual and group behavior in the political arena. The study of communication patterns from body language to voice inflections can tell us much about what makes a politician successful. In 1960, for example, the first televised presidential debate in American history took place between Richard Nixon and John F. Kennedy. It is generally agreed that, controlling for the variable of party identification, those who listened to the debate on the radio believed Nixon won, while those who watched it on television believed Kennedy won (Schroeder, 2000; Hellweg, Pfau & Brydon, 1992). The manner in which politicians speak when campaigning; the strategic use of repetition and rhetorical questions; the rhythm of discourse; and the tactical pauses for audience applause are all examples of symbolic interaction. Similarly, the behavior of individuals at political speeches and rallies or the means by which people account for their political beliefs can often be understood through the principles of symbolic interactionism.

## American Political Participation

One might expect that in a country like the United States, which spends so much time and energy celebrating the idea of democracy, citizens' political participation would be exceptionally high. This is not the case. U.S. voting rates are noticeably lower than in many other democracies. In national elections, American voting rates usually range from 50 to 60 percent (Center for the Study of the American Electorate, 2012; U.S. Census Bureau, 2012), while in countries as diverse as Germany, Israel, Japan, Australia and Brazil, voter turnout is routinely above 80 percent (Pintor & Gratschew, 2002). In the United States, sociologists have found a positive correlation between voting and such variables as gender, age and education. That is, the older one is and the more years of formal education one has, the more likely one is to vote. Women, on average, are also somewhat more likely to vote than men (U.S. Census Bureau, 2012). But what accounts for the relatively low rate of American political participation? Can it be that in many other democracies a higher proportion of the population does not take its right to vote quite so much for granted? Certainly there are those still alive in Germany or Italy who remember fascism, and many nation-states have a much shorter history of political

Why do you think voter participation is so low in the U.S.?

Source: Paul Garland

freedom than that of the United States. Or, perhaps, an increasing proportion of the American citizenry has become disillusioned with the political process. If so, we might trace much of the cause to a primary source: money.

According to the U. S. Constitution (Article II, Section 1) only two basic qualifications are necessary to become president: one must be a natural-born citizen and be at least 35 years old. In practical terms, however, there have been many more. Only recently, for example, has it seemed feasible that a woman might be president, and it was not until the election of Barack Obama in 2008 that a non-white man held the office. And although the presidents' degree of religious commitment has varied, there have been no non-Christian presidents and only one (John F. Kennedy) who was Roman Catholic. The overriding qualifications to successfully run for high political office are beyond demographic; they are financial. It requires a great deal of money to run a campaign, and few individuals have the private fortune necessary. Thus, candidates must raise funds both from private citizens and large organizations. Many of these organizations will expect certain concessions in return for their financial or public support. And although an elected member of Congress is under no legal obligation to do so, he or she may find future fundraising more difficult if such concessions are not made.

More specifically, we may note the influence of **political action committees** and **527 organizations**. The former is any group that spends more than $1,000 in an effort to affect the outcome of an election or the passing of legislation. Political Action Committees are one of the ways through which organizations such as corporations or labor unions financially influence the political process. A corporation or union may legally draw not from its profits or treasury but only from the contributions of individual members. PACs are limited in the amount they can directly contribute (e.g., at the federal level, only $5,000 per candidate per election is allowed) but unlimited in the amounts they may spend if not coordinated directly with a candidate (Federal Election Commission, 2007). Thus, many PACs actually spend millions to affect elections "independently." Similarly, so-called "super PACs" may also raise and spend unlimited amounts of money but cannot donate any money directly. The organizers of a PAC or super PAC may have as much or more access to a candidate's political strategy as any public organization, but as long they do not directly consult with a candidate, they may spend as much as they like on supportive advertising, pamphlets, signs, attack ads or any other legal campaign strategy.

A 527 organization (named after Section 527 of the Internal Revenue Code) is created to influence the outcome of an election, particularly at the federal level, and primarily through advertising. As with a PAC, a 527 organization cannot legally coordinate with a candidate, but unlike a PAC, it cannot directly advocate the election of a particular candidate. It may, however, construct its message such that its influence is just as effective. In the 2004 presidential election, for example, the 527 organization Swift Boat Veterans for Truth could not ask anyone directly to vote for George W. Bush or to not vote for John Kerry, but it could create advertisements that questioned Kerry's military record and thus increase the chances of Bush's re-election. These organizations do not have spending limits, and anyone may contribute (Federal Election Commission, 2012; Open Secrets, 2012).

# Politics and War

The Prussian military theorist Carl von Clausewitz famously stated, "War is the continuation of politics by other means" (von Clausewitz, 1976). One might hope that human social groups could interact without large-scale conflict, but history has not confirmed this idea. One reason behind feudalism's growth in the European Middle Ages was the need for defense against invasion from other kingdoms. Eventually, standing armies were instituted, and nobles no longer took up this responsibility. In the age of the nation-state, militaries became further responsible for the patriotic socialization of citizens. The military of any nation-state is its most obvious symbol of direct power. It is thus an entity with the inherent potential to impose its will on its own citizenry. This has indeed occurred, from the Roman Empire to contemporary military dictatorships.

So, is the military its own separate institution? Traditionally, it is thought of as being under the control of the institution of politics. In the United States, the legislative branch of government declares and appropriates funding for war. In the executive branch, the president serves as commander-in-chief. But even though the U.S. Congress has not officially declared war since 1942, there has been no shortage of military conflict over the past 70 years. A critical aspect of politics, then, is the maintenance and control of the military, and the decision of when to wage war.

On Jan.17, 1961, President Dwight D. Eisenhower gave his farewell address to the nation as he prepared to hand the office over to President-elect John F. Kennedy. On that day, Eisenhower, a Republican and a former Army general and NATO Supreme Commander, brought a new phrase to the consciousness of the American public: the **military-industrial complex**:

> Now this conjunction of an immense military establishment and a large arms industry is new in the American experience. The total influence—economic, political, even spiritual—is felt in every city, every statehouse, every office of the federal government. We recognize the imperative need for this development. Yet, we must not fail to comprehend its grave implications. Our toil, resources, and livelihood are all involved. So is the very structure of our society. ...In the councils of government, we must guard against the acquisition of unwarranted influence, whether sought or unsought, by the military-industrial complex. The potential for the disastrous rise of misplaced power exists and will persist (National Archives, 2012).

Recall that C. Wright Mills considered America's ruling elite to be composed of a corporate, political, and military coalition. Individuals of high rank and influence in these three areas may see a shared interest in a heightened state of preparation for war or even in war itself. The military, more specifically the Department of Defense, has a vested interest in procuring more resources and increasing its budget. Corporations, such as defense contractors like Lockheed Martin and Northrop Grumman, have an obvious interest in winning DoD contracts to increase their profits. The president of the United States may believe that significant political capital could be gained by appearing "strong" against communism or terrorism. Many presidencies have, in fact, been defined through war.

This is not to suggest that all individuals involved in this "**iron triangle of power**" are motivated by nefarious impulses. Defense contractors provide thousands of jobs and develop many important technological innovations. The Department of Defense is filled with many dedicated and selfless individuals who believe deeply in defense rather than aggression. And one hopes that the executive branch of government does respond to real threats but does not lead the nation into war for personal political gain. Yet it is possible for this coalition to develop a certain momentum to the point where the abstract idea that war is "good for business" can overshadow its human cost. U.S. military expenditures are nearly equal to the rest of the world's nation-states' combined. It is also worth noting that the United States is the world's largest arms supplier (SIPRI, 2011).

An argument may be made that much of

American society and a substantial portion of American civic nationalism are organized around the principle of war. The United States was born out of war. As a part of **political socialization**, American schoolchildren are taught the names of military heroes, from Nathan Hale to Audie Murphy. American mass media, particularly film and television, have dramatized and often glorified war for decades. The images of Uncle Sam and the flag raising on Iwo Jima are instantly recognizable, as are slogans, from "Remember the Alamo" to "Remember the Maine." If we take American history beginning in 1776, we can note at least 11 major wars: the Revolutionary War (1776-83), War of 1812 (1812-15), Mexican-American War (1846-48), Civil War (1861-65), Spanish-American War (1898), World War I (1917-18), World War II (1942-45), Korean War (1950-53), Vietnam War (1964-72), Persian Gulf War (1990-91) and the Afghanistan/Iraq wars (2001/03-2011/12). Thus, in its 236-year history, the nation has experienced a major war on average every 21.4 years. This does not include such relatively minor conflicts as our involvement in Guatemala (1954), Grenada (1983), Somalia (1992-93) or the former Yugoslavia (1991-95).

If we look past official military conflicts to include wider historical patterns, an even more pronounced emphasis on war becomes evident. Much of the 19th century, approximately 1817 to 1898, included consistent military campaigns against the Native American population. Both the Korean and Vietnam wars were manifestations of the wider Cold War from 1946 to 1989. If we include these dates (and do not double count other concurrent wars), the United States has been at war for 158 of 236 years, or almost exactly two-thirds of its history. This is not to suggest that we are a nation of war-mongers, but simply that war is an entrenched aspect of a national consciousness. U.S. political leaders have exploited this "war" imagery to organize and inspire domestic policy as well. In 1964, President Lyndon Johnson started a "war on poverty." In 1971, President Richard Nixon's administration proposed a "war on drugs." More recently, conservative media commentators have warned against an apparent "war on Christmas" as part of the overall culture wars. Clearly, the word is understood, or at least believed, to be a primary means by which Americans are motivated.

## The Economy

The **economy** is the social institution responsible for the production, distribution, and consumption of goods and services. This is a traditional and deceptively simple definition, as the national and global economic systems of the 21st century are remarkably complex. Through most of human history, "the market" was understood as an actual, physical place. A public square at the center of town, perhaps; an exciting hub of activity where people met to exchange goods, hear news and socially interact. And while many in our contemporary consumer society still congregate for social interaction in places like shopping malls, "the market" now means something much larger, more abstract and, for most of the population, quite mystifying. Economics itself is a complex social science, and even the most learned individuals cannot always predict the vagaries of inflation, unemployment, interest rates, stock market fluctuations or consumer behavior.

## Value and Price

To further illustrate this complexity, let us consider what seems a simple problem: How is the price of a product determined? For most of human history, the value of something had at least some relationship to how useful it was. The simplest examples would be growing one's own food or making one's own clothing; these things are valuable because they help us survive. The usefulness of a product, however, is increasingly less powerful in determining how much it is sold for. Consider clothing: One pair of jeans is as useful as another in terms of keeping you warm (or avoiding arrest for indecent exposure), but the price of jeans can vary from one dollar at a yard sale to hundreds at an upscale boutique.

Classical economic theorists such as Adam Smith and David Ricardo introduced certain principles that might help us understand the way value is determined for a product. Smith's "law" of supply and demand dictates that as the supply of a product increases, its demand decreases, and its price will fall until a point of equilibrium is reached (Smith, 1991). Ricardo's labor theory of value tells us that the value of a product should be related to the amount of labor it took to produce it (Ricardo, 2004). This principle was seized upon by Karl Marx in his 1867 book *Capital* when he analyzed the exploitation of labor under capitalism. Marx believed that human labor was the primary determinant of value; in fact, he believed it was the only thing that really created value (Marx, 1976). But how can we be sure just how much labor has gone into the products we purchase? Is a mass-produced assembly-line item worth less than one made by hand? And if labor really is the prime determinant of value (and therefore price), how can we explain such phenomena as the pet rock (a novelty item briefly popular in the 1970s) or the selling of virtual gifts on social networking sites? When a late-night infomercial tells us that we can receive an item as a free bonus that is actually a "$20 value," how can we confirm this?

Clearly, "value" has become a rather nebulous concept. **Use value** has largely given way to **exchange value**; that is, the amount that a commodity will exchange for in the market according to a variety of changing factors (Marx, 1976). Exchange value can be difficult to predict, particularly in the largely service-based economies of contemporary nation-states. How much value, for example, does a professor create through his or her teaching, research, and service activities, and how could this be quantified?

The matter is further complicated by the manner in which we encounter the ultimate exchange value commodity: money itself. In any society not reliant on simple **barter**, a recognized system of currency exchange exists, which greatly expands the reach and stability of trade. Many mediums have existed, but by far the most common has been coinage produced from silver and gold. Both have

recognizable use value: gold in particular is highly malleable, conductive, and resistant to corrosion. One could always determine the inherent value of a gold or silver coin regardless of where and when it was produced by establishing its weight and purity. With the introduction of paper money (bank notes), currency became more abstract and symbolic. A $1 bill has precisely the same use value as a $100 bill (which is to say, very little), but the difference in exchange value between the two is equally precise. At one time, a bank note could theoretically be exchanged for a set amount of gold held in reserve by the government.

But movement off this form of **gold standard** introduces another layer of abstraction: Now, the bank note's exchange value is determined by—among other things—the number of other bank notes in circulation, which is limited or expanded by a central banking agency like the Federal Reserve. It is the responsibility of this agency to ensure there is neither too much nor too little currency so as to moderate inflation and the interest rates that other banks will charge on loans.

Further abstraction is introduced by the continued waning of physical bank notes themselves. Cash has increasingly given way to credit and debit cards, and especially the instantaneous electronic transfer of funds over computer networks and the Internet. So money, which was once felt as weight in human hands, is now most often encountered as simply numbers on screens. To return to our original problem: How, again, is the price of a product determined? It is determined not simply by its usefulness, its supply, or the labor time involved in its production, but by a number of socially constructed forces.

## Economic Sectors

The economy can be broken down into three fundamental sectors: primary, secondary and tertiary. The **primary sector** provides value through the exploitation of natural resources. This includes mining, fishing, hunting and trapping, forestry and agriculture. A nation-state rich in natural resources like the United States can therefore ensure that its citizens are fed and housed at a basic level. Smaller countries or those with limited resources are in a more vulnerable position, particularly if the national economy depends on only one or two particular resources. Of course, if that resource happens to be gold or oil, its exchange with other countries can provide abundance for either the ruling elite or the general citizenry. Still, a danger exists when factors beyond national control affect the value of the resource. A drought that wipes out the primary agricultural crop; an international reduction in demand; or the introduction of new resources rendering the old less valuable can devastate a national economy.

It is therefore desirable to develop a **secondary sector** of the economy. In this sector, natural resources are made into finished products that sell for more than their raw components. Trees become paper, cod become packaged fish sticks, and crude oil becomes refined petroleum. More complex manufacturing develops with technological innovation, and eventually highly specialized products from a variety of materials are created, from Chevrolets to computer chips. In the 20th century, the United States became a leading industrial nation, contributing greatly to its economic and military power.

But the **tertiary sector** of the economy has recently grown in importance, particularly among so-called developed nations. In fact, the term "developed" itself indicates an advanced industrialization. The term "high-income countries" is also used to acknowledge that the tertiary sector of the economy has at least partially eclipsed the secondary (World Bank, 2012). In the tertiary sector, people use their expertise to provide services rather than tangible products. A thriving service sector requires a literate and educated populace in its more prestigious and information-oriented occupations such as those in health care, legal services, education and finance. But the service sector also includes low-paying, lower-status jobs in retail sales, waste disposal and telemarketing. It is possible for small nation-states with few natural resources and little industry to survive in the service sector. Banking in the Cayman Islands and tourism in Aruba are pertinent examples.

In its first century of independence, the United States had a primary-sector economy. Raw materials such as cotton and animal pelts were shipped to Europe for processing in the more advanced secondary economies that had developed there. By the mid-19th century, the northern states were moving into the secondary sector, though the plantation system of the South remained economically critical. The advanced industrial capacity of the North became a significant contributing factor to its victory in the Civil War. In the post-World War II era and especially since the 1970s, however, the American economy has moved decidedly into the tertiary sector.

In most high-income countries, most of the population, often more than 70 percent, is employed in the tertiary sector (International Labor Organization, 2012). This is not to suggest that the other sectors are no longer important; part of the reason for this shift is simply the greater efficiency that is now applied to the secondary and, particularly, the primary sectors. Large-scale mechanized agriculture in the United States, for example, means that a great deal of food can now be produced by a relatively small workforce.

# Economic Systems

## Capitalism

**Capitalism**, sometimes referred to as free enterprise, is a relatively recent and extremely powerful economic system that developed in Western Europe following the demise of feudalism. It was quickly adopted in 19th century America and now has spread to (or been imposed on) most of the world. As an ideal, capitalism contains the following components:

1. Private ownership of the means of production.
2. The pursuit of individual profit.
3. Free-market competition.
4. Lack of government intervention.
5. Wage labor.
6. Reinvestment and expansion.

The idea of private ownership in the pursuit of personal profit free of government control might appear to be a chaotic system. But the profit motive is a powerful force, and if providing a good or service can create profit, it is almost certain that someone will undertake it to do so. Free-market competition means that, theoretically at least, all citizens have an equal chance to succeed if they provide a better good or service at a lower price. Competition spurs the process forward, keeping prices lower and quality higher. The "free market" can only do this effectively if no outside force, particularly government, interferes with the operation of private enterprises. Classical economist Adam Smith believed that if left to itself, the "laws" of the market would benefit society as a whole, as if an "invisible hand" were guiding the system (Smith, 2007). Of course, such competition means that some will be more successful than others. Unfortunately, inequality under capitalism is inevitable.

A critical aspect of capitalism is reinvestment. If business people spent all their profits on, say, vacations or cars, or shut down their businesses the moment they had made a certain amount of money, the system would indeed not work. But as Max Weber theorized in *The Protestant Ethic and the Spirit of Capitalism*, the strategy of reinvesting a substantial portion of profit into expanding a business became the catalyst that allowed capitalism to be the global force it is today.

Sociologists consider the rise of capitalism to be one of the most significant developments in human history. Its establishment was intertwined with such shifts as the industrial revolution, the rise of democracy, scientific rationalization and the reorganization of Western class structure. It is this enormous nexus of change, spearheaded by the energy of capitalism, that made sociology itself a necessary new science.

## Socialism

As an economic system, **socialism** takes a different approach. Here, limited private enterprise may exist, but the entire economy is centrally planned and administered. The government sets wages and prices in an attempt to find an equitable balance. The means of production are publicly owned, and the motivation is not personal profit but a fair and equal distribution of goods and wealth. In this way, gaps between rich and poor can be closed, and every citizen is assured that his or her basic needs of food, housing, employment and health care will be met. It is important to distinguish between socialism as an economic system and communism as a political system. Under communism as it existed in the 20th century, the economy was centrally planned in a socialist model, but a nation-state may have a largely socialist economy without being communist. For countries afflicted with poverty and social inequality, there is appeal in the socialist model. Logistically, however, complete socialism can be difficult to achieve, and its failures can be disastrous. In the Soviet Union of the early 1930s, for example, the rapid reorganization of agriculture was poorly implemented. Combined with the authoritarian excesses of the Stalinist regime, the result was widespread famine and a death toll in the millions, particularly in Ukraine. In some countries, however, a more limited degree of socialism has been quite successful. In the Scandinavian countries of northern Europe, citizens routinely pay a higher proportion of their income in government taxes than in the United States, but they also enjoy extensive and efficient social programs, such as universal health care, without having their political freedom or economic creativity curtailed.

## Mixed Economies

Our descriptions of capitalism as *laissez-faire* free enterprise and socialism as a completely centrally planned economy are of course ideals. In reality, most economies are a mixture of these systems. China has capitalistically expanded its "special economic zones," and even the United States employs a degree of socialism. Technically, whenever a government collects taxes from its citizens and uses that revenue to provide a free or subsidized public service, it is a limited form of socialism. Thus, as taxpayers, we all contribute to the existence of public schools, libraries, national parks, the interstate highway system and more. Moreover, there are certain essential services that might be better administered by a central government than left to private enterprise. It may not be in a country's best interests, for example, to leave its national defense in the hands of private mercenaries. And it is generally accepted that government intervention is sometimes needed in order to protect capitalism. Laws prohibiting monopolies, for example, ensure that free-market competition exists.

# Globalization

Economic **globalization** refers to the increasing interconnectedness of economic activity around the world. It takes the form of reductions in trade barriers such as tariffs, duties and import quotas. The 1994 North American Free Trade Agreement (NAFTA), for example, further entwined the economies of Canada, the United States and Mexico. From the standpoint of Americans, globalization is most often encountered in the form of lower prices for goods imported from other countries, especially China and Mexico. Since wages are significantly lower in such places, goods have always been theoretically cheaper but were kept artificially high by the imposition of tariffs. Another result of NAFTA has been the movement of industry from the United States to areas where operating costs are lower. This has most often taken the form of U.S.-based companies moving their manufacturing facilities to northern Mexico in order to take advantage of lower labor costs and less-stringent environmental regulations. Thus, American manufacturing jobs have decreased, a phenomenon sometimes referred to as outsourcing or offshoring. While these effects may be criticized as harmful to workers, they should not be surprising given the primacy of the profit motive in capitalism.

Marxian theorist Rosa Luxemburg believed capitalism was inherently aggressive on an international scale and must "always and everywhere fight a battle of annihilation against every form of natural economy it encounters" (Luxemburg, 1951). She points to historical examples such as British and French colonial policy in India and Algeria, respectively, as well as the transformation of small family farms in late 19th century America. According to Luxemburg,

capitalism has historically destroyed self-sufficient productive units, such as small farms and cottage industries, in order to introduce wage labor and reduce the influence of use value. Those who take a dim view of this process highlight the exploitation of less-developed countries and refer to it as **economic imperialism**.

# Sociological Perspectives on the Economy

## The Functionalist Perspective

From the functionalist perspective, the economy is an essential institution of stability that provides for the material needs of society's members. Ideally, it efficiently produces and distributes goods and services for all to consume at or above the level of basic needs. If some members of society enjoy a greater accumulation of goods or access to services, it is simply the inevitable effect of differences in the

Source: Robert Scoble

What are some of the benefits and drawbacks associated with globalization?

abilities and efforts of individuals. Functionalists believe that the economy is part of an overall **meritocracy**, that is, a system whereby everyone gets what he or she merits. In a meritocracy, the wealthy are so because of their superior intelligence and effort, while the poor deserve their lot due to their lack of these qualities.

## The Conflict Perspective

For the conflict theorist, the economy, particularly capitalism, is the primary institution through which inequality and oppression are perpetuated. Conflict theorists believe the exploitation of working-class labor and concentration of wealth in the hands of a societal elite are inherent in the system. Thus, although some members of society are indeed more intelligent or motivated than others, these qualities do not always correlate with economic success. So, while the functionalist may see the idea of the meritocracy as useful in motivating individuals, the conflict theorist is more likely to see it as an ideological construct that disguises structural inequality as individual failure.

## The Symbolic Interactionist Perspective

Symbolic interactionists are less interested in how the institution of the economy as a whole functions and more concerned with how individuals interact with it and with others under certain economic conditions. Individuals in a circumstance of poverty, for example, may distance themselves from a definition of "poor," or they may embrace it, or they may redefine it according to their own criteria. To a 20-year-old university student, it may be perfectly acceptable to publicly discuss one's (relative) poverty and creative strategies for dealing with it. But as a 40-year-old parent, one may be less motivated to admit one's diet of ramen soup. Still others may employ creative justifications to distance themselves from a societal image of poverty, citing such circumstances as unexpected medical bills or other factors beyond their control. The style of dress individuals adopt (to hide or display their economic position) or their attitudes regarding governmental programs like food stamps are all of interest to the symbolic interactionist.

## The Consumer Society

At the dawn of the 20th century, sociologist Thorstein Veblen published *The Theory of the Leisure Class*, in which he criticized wealthy individuals (particularly the emerging upper-middle class) who engaged in "**conspicuous consumption**" rather than productive work (Veblen, 1899). His work was, perhaps, prophetic in that he anticipated the importance that consumerism would have in 20th century America. Western society has been described as a "consumer society." That is, it's a society that has become more materialistic, defines itself by spending habits, and measures economic health by the amount of goods consumed rather than produced. To understand this shift, it is instructive to trace certain developments, particularly a shift from Fordism to post-Fordism. First used by Italian sociologist Antonio Gramsci, the term **Fordism** refers to the assembly-line manner of production exemplified by Henry Ford in the automotive industry. By using standardized machinery to construct more standardized machinery and needing only specialized but unskilled labor, Ford was able to produce the Model T automobile at a price low enough for the "great multitude," including most of his own employees, to afford. Fordism is an economy of scale that cheaply produces a large number of the same products. Ford famously stated that customers could order the Model T in "any color as long as it is black" (Ford, 2009). Fordism assumes the pre-existence of a need that may be most efficiently met through mass production. The system was successfully applied to industry in general and helped increase the wealth and power of the United States through the first half of the 20th century. In fact, it may be argued that the United States became too good at Fordism, producing, or at least gaining the potential to produce, more goods than were necessary. Eventually, the problem facing many companies was no longer how to produce enough goods in order to meet needs, but how to create needs to consume all the goods produced. Although assembly-line production remains effective, over the past several decades, the economy of scale has given way to an economy of flexibility or **post-Fordism**.

Here, the assumption is that consumers desire products that reflect their individuality and that consumer behavior is as much (or more) emotional as rational (Amin, 1994). As of early 2012, the Ford Motor Co. offered 18 models of cars, trucks, vans and SUVs. The Ford Mustang alone is available in 11 versions. Each version is available in eight exterior and 11 interior colors. One can then choose between a manual or an automatic transmission and five optional upgrades. So, while all 1922 Model T's were exactly the same, there are potentially 9,680 variations on the 2012 Mustang (Ford, 2012).

One of the most pronounced effects of post-Fordism is the proliferation of advertising. If goods can now be produced in virtually unlimited amounts, it is consumer desire that must be stimulated, and this is best undertaken through skillful, even manipulative advertising. Indeed, advertising has become a major U.S. industry. **Planned obsolescence** and disposability are also crucial. Goods become obsolete not necessarily because they no longer function, but because they are perceived to be out of style. Disposable paper and plastic versions of goods that were once permanent are now commonplace. Consumption and production are, of course, both necessary; neither makes sense without the other. But living a life of **consumerism** may have unintended negative consequences. While it provides a source of instant gratification, it also promotes the perception that non-material needs (affection, friendship, self-respect) can be met through material means.

How goods are produced and where they go when we are finished with them are virtually invisible. Most consumers do not see or contemplate processes like strip mining, deforestation or **sweatshop** labor, nor do we need to see sewage disposal or landfill sites. What we do see is a compelling world of exciting advertising and attractive packaging. Measuring consumer spending as an indicator of economic vitality makes sense to a point, but it does not necessarily correlate with the health and happiness of a population. The social emphasis on consumption is often undertaken at the expense of personal financial stability as consumers are encouraged to purchase goods on credit and take on debt.

---

# The Rise of Corporation

Consider for a moment the largest, most impressive buildings humans have ever created. From the Great Pyramids of Egypt to the Palace of Versailles in France, these structures are tangible representations of wealth, power and prestige. Most were built to enhance the glory of rulers or gods. For centuries, the skylines of Europe were dominated by cathedrals. Now consider the skylines of contemporary cities and their tallest structures: the Sears (Willis) Tower in Chicago; the Transamerica Pyramid in San Francisco; the CN Tower in Toronto; the Petronas Towers in Kuala Lumpur. Today, in almost every major city on the planet, the skyline is dominated by structures that are designed for corporations, run by corporations, or named by corporations.

The institution of politics is not the only place where power resides. At the end of the 19th century, when Emile Durkheim published his influential work *Suicide*, he considered the problem of societal anomie to be caused not only by rapid social change but by insufficient social regulation. In such a context, he believed, human appetites would run unchecked and people would not know what they could reasonably expect out of life. As Durkheim saw the problem: "Religion has lost most of its power. And government, instead of regulating economic life, has become its tool and servant" (Durkheim, 1951). The institutions of religion and government, in other words, were now subservient to that of economics. Large economic organizations, particularly corporations, can exercise enormous power, often in ways less visible to citizens. **Multinational corporations** can mobilize resources equal to or greater than the governments of most nation-states.

The **corporation** as a general concept has existed in America since the colonial period, but the modern corporation became a significant social, political and economic force only in the last century. A business corporation, as opposed to a partnership or association, is a rather peculiar thing in that it is given by government the same status as a person. A corporation, for example, may sue a person or be sued in turn. It can be held legally responsible for criminal offenses. In conjunction with an 1886 Supreme Court case regarding railroad taxation, Chief Justice Morrison Waite officially enshrined an opinion that corporations enjoyed the protection of the 14th amendment to the U.S. Constitution (Horwitz, 1985).

Ratified in 1868, the amendment defined citizenship at least in part to ensure the voting rights of African Americans. It also, however, formed the basis for the concept of **corporate personhood**. In 1976, a Supreme Court decision (*Buckley v. Valeo*) regarding limits on campaign contributions ruled that money in this context is a form of speech and thus protected under the First Amendment (Oyez, 2012a). In January 2010, the Supreme Court in a 5-4 decision ruled in the case of *Citizens United v. The Federal Election Commission* that "no distinction can be drawn between the First Amendment rights of individuals and corporations in the electoral context" (Oyez, 2012b). Thus, the free speech of persons/corporations is constitutionally protected and money recognized as a form of free speech. The ruling may be interpreted as creating the right for large corporations to affect the political process to an even greater extent. Modern corporations often undertake impressive and socially important projects, using their financial resources to provide many crucial goods and services. It does, however, potentially create a situation in which corporate political speech becomes increasingly influential. As Justice John Paul Stevens noted in his dissenting opinion, "While American democracy is imperfect, few outside the majority of this Court would have thought its flaws included a dearth of corporate money in politics" (Oyez, 2012b).

On occasion, a corporation may become so successful that it eliminates its competition. Ironically, in the case of some **monopolies**, one of the crucial aspects of functioning capitalism—free-market competition—can produce as an end-point the lack of such competition. At this point, the incentive to improve through innovation and cost reduction is limited, and government intervention may be needed to break up the monopoly, as in the case of AT&T in 1984. Though monopolies tend to be short-lived, **oligopolies** and **shared monopolies** often endure. These terms refer to a situation in which a relatively small number of corporations control a disproportionately large percentage of a market or industry. A shared monopoly refers to four or fewer companies controlling more than half of the market for a particular good or service. **Conglomerates** exist when several corporations operating in different areas of business are owned by one parent company. **Interlocking directorships** occur when members of the board of directors of one corporation also sit on the boards of others. Thus, the potential exists under capitalism for both real and corporate "persons" to acquire tremendous wealth and power. Both entities may choose to utilize these resources for socially constructive purposes, but even benevolent motives cannot be realized unless a profit is made.

Some corporations become so large, so interconnected, providing such vitally important goods or services and employing so many people that their failure would have a significant effect on the economy. A pure *laissez-faire* approach to capitalism would insist that the success or failure of any business should be left to the unregulated operation of the market and that any business that fails deserves to fail. There have been several instances, however, when the potential bankruptcy of a corporation has been averted through government intervention because such a business is considered "too big to fail." Loan guarantees to the Chrysler Corporation in 1979 and the more recent Troubled Asset Relief Program to aid financial institutions such as AIG and Citigroup, and the auto industry bailout, are pertinent examples.

# Work and Occupations in the United States

For centuries, particularly in feudal-era Europe, the nobility or aristocracy was understood to exist above the daily concerns of the common people. Though they may have had a legal responsibility to protect the peasants on their estates, generally speaking, they did not work; they owned. The earlier meaning of the term "gentleman" in fact referred to this reality. But in the prelude to the French Revolution of 1789, Henri de Saint-Simon, a French nobleman, denounced his own class as contributing nothing substantial to French society. He declared instead that "all men must work" (Collins & Makowsky, 1993). In the two centuries since the revolution, the social class of the nobility has faded into virtual extinction. And while inherited wealth certainly exists in contemporary society, it is now generally accepted that all men, and increasingly women, must work.

Not only must all members of society work, but the majority are expected to engage in the form of work known as wage labor. At a certain age, we are expected to leave the financial care of our parents and earn our own way. Thus, we enter into a contract with an employer, agreeing to perform certain tasks for specified periods of time, receiving a specified amount of money. One's occupation is likely to be the activity that takes the greatest amount of one's time and energy and may even be the aspect of one's life that provides the greatest source of self-definition.

As Emile Durkheim noted, one defining characteristic of a complex society is a high **division of labor**. Occupations have become increasingly specialized, and new types are constantly appearing. Some occupations are classified as **professions**, which usually require advanced training and/ or education. Professions rely on specialized knowledge and usually confer relatively high status and remuneration. Professionals such as doctors, lawyers, professors and scientists are likely to also enjoy a higher degree of autonomy in their work. As sociologist Frank Parkin has noted, professionals also are able to protect themselves from outside scrutiny through technical jargon and closed systems of self-regulation and evaluation (Parkin, 1979).

Traditionally, most occupations are divided into **white collar** and **blue collar work**. The terms referred to the types of dress expected in the workplace, with the white shirt and tie serving as a service sector stereotype. While the proportion of blue collar jobs has diminished, it should be remembered that not all occupations in the service sector carry high salaries or extensive benefits. Occasionally, the term **pink collar work** has been used to refer to service sector jobs, traditionally performed by women, carrying low-to-moderate levels of payment and status (e.g. waitress, flight attendant, and receptionist). Although the proportions of, for example, male nurses and female doctors have both increased, many service occupations are still performed by women. Clearly, some jobs are more desirable and carry greater rewards than others. Sociologists Kingsley Davis and Wilbert Moore believed such inequality is justified. They reasoned that if society does not reward the occupations that require high levels of skill or training, there will be a shortage of people to fill them. Similarly, one may take an occupation that is of less importance and requires less skill or training, but one should not then expect a high level of reward (Davis & Moore, 1945). The logic seems reasonable at first glance, but a careful examination of the rewards associated with certain professions puts the hypothesis in doubt. Professional athletes, for example, are some of the most skilled people on the planet, but is the social importance of their occupation enough to justify multimillion-dollar salaries when compared to such occupations as social workers or daycare workers? The labor market of a capitalist economy is a system of competition that almost all of us must negotiate. In all probability, one of the main reasons you as a student are reading these words is to perform well on your next exam, earn a university degree and thus elevate your position when searching for your occupation.

## Unemployment

**Unemployment** refers to the inability of individuals to secure jobs despite their efforts to do so. Sociologists and economists generally refer to three types: structural, cyclical and seasonal. **Structural unemployment** can occur when there is a lack of congruence between jobs needing to be filled and the skills or situations of potential workers. A sudden change in dominant technology, for example, can cause significant structural unemployment until corrected by shifts in education or training. A milkman in the 1970s or a switchboard operator in the 1980s probably found his or her job obsolete and needed retraining.

**Cyclical unemployment** ebbs and flows with the contraction or expansion of the economy. In times of recession, many workers may lose their jobs through **layoffs** as businesses reduce their operating costs.

**Seasonal unemployment** occurs due to shifts in demand in industries such as retail, tourism or agriculture.

The overall **unemployment rate** is the percentage of individuals in the labor force who are available for work and have actively looked for work in the previous four weeks but do not have a job (Bureau of Labor Statistics, 2012a). In the past 60 years, the overall American unemployment rate has varied from a low of 2.5 percent in June 1953 to a high of 10.8 percent in December 1982 (Bureau of Labor Statistics, 2012a). Given the official definition, unemployment is usually higher than the published rates since many individuals may become discouraged and stop actively looking for work, and those people are not counted in unemployment statistics.

## Labor Unions

**Labor unions** are collective organizations of employees designed to protect workers' rights and maximize their benefits. Because they can organize workers to act as a unit, unions enhance their bargaining position with ownership or management and may threaten to strike if their demands are not met. Unions in the United States began forming in the mid-19th century and are generally credited with bringing about such conditions as the five-day and 40-hour workweek, enhanced workplace safety standards, unemployment benefits, pension plans, health benefits and sick leave. In recent decades, proportional union membership in the United States has decreased, as has the frequency of work stoppages. As of 2010, the proportion of the American workforce belonging to a labor union was between 11 and 12 percent (Bureau of Labor Statistics, 2012b; OECD, 2012). This is relatively low compared with the rates in similar countries such as Australia at 18 percent, Canada at 27.5 percent, Italy at 35.1 percent, and Sweden at 68.4 percent (OECD, 2012). While labor unions have historically served a crucial function in protecting the rights of workers, they also are often large, bureaucratized organizations that can lose touch with the concerns of their rank-and-file membership.

Source: Fibonacci Blue

Why do you think labor union membership in the U.S. has been declining?

# Summary

Politics and the economy are crucial social institutions that have become increasingly intertwined. They are both so large and complex that they may seem beyond our comprehension. They also appear to contain opposing or even contradictory forces. Politics is the institution through which power is overtly exercised. It is possible, however, for democratic governments to be disproportionately controlled by a relatively small elite. The United States is perhaps the world's most successful democracy but has one of the lowest rates of political participation by its citizens.

The economy organizes the production, distribution and consumption of goods and services. The United States was once a primary economy, relying on the export of natural resources. In the 19th and especially 20th centuries, it became a global leader in the secondary economic sector of manufacturing. Like other high-income nation-states, it is now very much a tertiary economy based on the service and information industries. Yet many people are concerned that the U.S. economy and society have become focused on consumption over production. The two major economic systems of capitalism and socialism are distinct in their ideal types, yet most modern economies are a mixture of the two. Capitalism puts more emphasis on private ownership, competition and personal profit. Socialism emphasizes public ownership, cooperation and the equitable distribution of resources. Capitalism is increasingly dominant, and the world is becoming more economically interdependent through globalization. From the standpoint of the individual, capitalism is a system of occupations, requiring varying degrees of education and training, that must be successfully negotiated so that unemployment can be avoided.

To return to the example of the film *Rollerball*, by the end the protagonist, "Jonathan E," has resisted attempts by the international coalition of corporations to force his retirement. But as the wielders of economic and political power, they are able to change the rules of the sport to ensure he will be either crippled or killed in the championship match. It being a movie, he not only survives but is the last man standing after this brutal display of state-sanctioned violence.

As Jonathan scores the winning goal and skates around the ring to the sound of the spectators chanting his name, the frame freezes on his image and the credits roll to the strains of the corporate anthem. So, did our hero's survival actually mean anything? Are we meant to believe that his momentary triumph will ignite a social revolution of individualism and creativity? Or will corporate culture and the executive ruling class continue as before, providing the populace with "bread and circuses?"

Is such a society possible in our future? For the viewers of a 1975 science-fiction movie, the fictional inhabitants of the film's 2018 world, and for us, the questions remain open.

## Review/Discussion Questions

1. Do you agree that liberal democracy is the final form of human government?
2. Which model of political power, pluralist or elite, do you think best describes American politics?
3. Do you think American society could become (or has already become) a plutocracy?
4. Why do you think the voting rate is lower in the United States compared to most other democracies?
5. Do you agree American society is organized around the concept of war?
6. Should the United States try to increase the secondary sector of the economy and provide more "made in America" products?
7. Is globalization/free trade a positive or negative influence in the world?
8. Should corporations be considered persons?
9. Should more or less of the American workforce be unionized?
10. Is American freedom threatened by "big government," "big business," neither, or both?

## Key Terms

**527 organizations** are organizations designed to influence the outcome of elections through technically indirect mass media advertising.

**Absolute monarchy** is hereditary rule until death or abdication with the authority to personally control any aspect of governance.

**Authoritarian government** is a government that suppresses political opposition through violence or the threat of violence.

**Authority** is power that is perceived as legitimate by those over whom it is exercised.

**Barter** is the direct exchange of goods or services in the absence of currency.

**Blue collar work** is an occupation in the secondary sector of the economy, particularly manufacturing.

**Capitalism** is an economic system stressing private ownership in the pursuit of personal profit.

**Charismatic authority** is power that is legitimated by the extraordinary characteristics of an individual.

**Civic nationalism** is nationalism based on loyalty to the nation-state.

**Conglomerate** is one large holding company that owns several corporations operating in different goods and/or services markets.

**Conspicuous consumption** involves the public display and use of expensive items.

**Constitutional monarchy** is hereditary rule that is legally limited by a constitution or charter such that the monarch becomes a symbolic figure.

**Consumerism** is the social preoccupation with consumption as a defining aspect of life.

**Corporate personhood** is the legally defined status of a corporation that endows it with similar but not identical rights and responsibilities as a person.

**Corporation** is a legally created business entity that has an existence independent of its members.

*Coup d'etat* is a swift, usually violent takeover of a government.

**Cyclical unemployment** is unemployment caused by fluctuations in the economy.

**Democracy** is a political system based on direct rule by the people themselves.

**Dialectic** is a view of change or progress based on the interaction of opposing forces.

**Division of labor** is the degree to which the total percentage of labor in a society or organization is subdivided into particular tasks.

**Economic imperialism** is the forceful implementation of capitalism for the purpose of exploiting less-developed nations.

**Economy** is the social institution that organizes the production, distribution and consumption of goods and services.

**Elite model** is a model of politics stressing the concentration of power in the hands of a small minority.

**End of history** is a doctrine proposing that Western liberal democracy has been accepted as the final form of human government.

**Ethnic nationalism** is nationalism based on loyalty to a shared cultural or ethnic identity.

**Exchange value** is the value of a commodity based on its anticipated price in relation to other commodities in the marketplace.

**False consciousness** is a belief in ideas that are contrary to one's own best interests.

**Fordism** is an economy of scale using efficient, low-cost assembly-line production methods.

**Globalization** is the deepening, broadening and speeding up of worldwide interconnectedness in all aspects of life.

**Gold standard** is a system whereby currency is stabilized by its actual or symbolic relationship to a specified amount of gold.

**Government** is the formal organization that exercises power through the state.

**Interlocking directorships** is when members of the board of directors of one corporation also sit on the boards of others.

**Iron triangle of power** is the closed system of mutual benefit between Congress, military contractors and the Department of Defense; the specific manifestation of the military-industrial complex.

**Labor unions** are organizations of workers that collectively bargain with ownership or management for improvements in wages, benefits or working conditions.

*Laissez-faire* is the doctrine of complete marketplace freedom.

**Meritocracy** is a system in which people are rewarded on the basis of their talents and achievements.

**Military-industrial complex** is the informal coalition between government, the military and the arms industry.

**Minority government** is a democratic government in which the ruling party wins the greatest number but less than 50 percent of the total seats in parliament.

**Monopoly** is the control of a particular goods or services market by one company.

**Multinational corporation** is a corporation that operates in more than one country.

**Nation-state** is a modern territorial and political entity recognized by other nation-states, with precise borders and unique symbolic representations.

**Oligopoly** is the control of the majority of a particular goods or services market by a small number of companies.

**Orwellian** is a term used to invoke fears of a totalitarian or "big brother" government. Inspired by the George Orwell novel *1984*.

**Parliament** is a democratic legislative body composed of representatives elected from specified districts within a territory.

**Pink collar work** is a low to moderate-status occupation traditionally held by women.

**Planned obsolescence** is the built-in obsolescence of goods due to changing style or disposability.

**Pluralist model** is a model of politics stressing the relatively even distribution of power between many societal groups.

**Plutocracy** is formal or informal political rule by the wealthy.

**Political action committees** are organizations designed to influence the outcome of an election or the passing of legislation through use of financial donations to candidates or political parties.

**Political socialization** is the process through which one acquires political beliefs from societal agents of socialization (family, peers, education and mass media).

**Political spectrum** is a socially constructed and historically shifting continuum of political ideology generally divided between left/liberal and right/conservative.

**Politics** is the social institution that organizes macro-level power in society.

**Post-Fordism** is an economy of flexibility responding to individual tastes and using advertising to create the perception of new needs.

**Power** is the ability to achieve one's goals despite opposition from others.

**Primary sector** is the sector of the economy based on the direct exploitation of natural resources.

**Profession** is a high-status occupation requiring specialized knowledge.

**Rational-legal authority** is power that is legitimated through formalized, standardized regulations and procedures.

**Rationalization** is the process by which society becomes increasingly dominated by regulation, standardization and bureaucratization.

**Seasonal unemployment** is unemployment caused by predictable shifts in demand for a good or service through an annual cycle.

**Secondary sector** is the sector of the economy based on the transformation of natural resources into finished products.

**Shared monopoly** is the control of at least 50 percent of a particular goods or services market by four or fewer companies.

**Socialism** is an economic system stressing public ownership in pursuit of the equal distribution of goods and wealth.

**Special interest group** is a group formed for the purpose of lobbying government in order to pass or block legislation.

**State** is the apparatus of governance that exists independent of government but which cannot function effectively without government.

**Structural unemployment** is joblessness due to a mismatch between available work and the skills or situations of potential employees.

**Sweatshop** is a place of labor where workers are paid very low wages and operate in substandard conditions often for long hours.

**Tertiary sector** is the sector of the economy based on the provision of services rather than tangible goods.

**Theocracy** is a political system with no separation between church and state such that spiritual and secular leaders are one and the same.

**Totalitarian government** is government that suppresses political opposition and attempts to control all aspects of civil society.

**Traditional authority** is power that is legitimated by long-standing custom.

**Unemployment** is the inability to find work despite actively seeking it.

**Unemployment rate** is the percentage of the potential labor force that is not employed despite actively seeking work in the previous four weeks.

**Use value** is the value of an item based on its inherent usefulness.

**White collar work** is an occupation in the service sector of the economy, particularly office work.

# Bibliography

Amin, A., ed. (1994). Post-Fordism. Oxford: Blackwell Publishers.

Bureau of Labor Statistics (2012a). Overview of BLS Statistics on Unemployment. <www.bls.gov> (2012).

Bureau of Labor Statistics (2012b). Union Members Summary. <www.bls.gov> (2012).

Center for the Study of the American Electorate (2012). Study: African-Americans, Fear and Youth Propel Highest Turnout Since 1960. <www.american.edu> (2012).

C.I.A. World Factbook (2012). People and Society. <www.cia.gov> (2012).

Collins, R., & Makowsky, M. (1993). The Profits of Paris: Saint-Simon and Comte, In The Discovery of Society. Fifth Edition. New York: McGraw Hill.

Dahl, R. A. (1961). Who Governs? Democracy and Power in an American City. New Haven: Yale University Press.

Davis, K., & Moore, W. (1945). Some Principles of Stratification. American Sociological Review, 10, 242-49.

Domhoff, W. G. (2002). Who Rules America? Fourth edition. Boston: McGraw Hill.

Domhoff, W. G. (2012). Power in America. <www2.ucsc.edu> (2012).

Durkheim, E. (1951). Suicide: A Study in Sociology. Translated by John A. Spaulding and George Simpson. New York: The Free Press.

Federal Election Commission (2007). Federal Election Campaign Guide: Corporations and Labor Organizations. <www.fec.gov> (2012).

Federal Election Commission (2012). What is a 527 organization? <www.fec.gov> (2012).

Fukuyama, F. (1992). The End of History and the Last Man. New York: Avon Books.

Ford, H. (2009). My Life and Work - An Autobiography of Henry Ford. New York: Classic House Books.

Ford Motor Company (2012). All Legend. Zero Compromise. <www.ford.com> (2012).

Gramsci, A. (1971). Selections from the Prison Notebooks. Edited by Quintin Hoare and Geoffrey Nowell-Smith. New York: International Publishers.

Hellweg, S. A., Pfau, M., & Brydon, S. R. (1992). Televised Presidential Debates: Advocacy in Contemporary America. New York: Praeger.

Horwitz, M. J. (1985). Santa Clara Revisited: The Development of Corporate Theory. West Virginia Law Review, 88, 173-224.

International Labor Organization (2012). Main statistics (annual): 2B Total employment, by economic activity. <www.ilo.org> (2012).

Jordan, T. L. (2002). The U.S. Constitution and Fascinating Facts About It. Naperville, IL: Oak Hill Publishing Company.

Luxemburg, R. (1951). The Accumulation of Capital. London: Routledge & Kegan Paul.

Marger, M. N. (2009). Race and Ethnic Relations: American and Global Perspectives. Eighth Edition. Belmont, CA: Wadsworth.

Marx, K., & Engels, F. (1970). The German Ideology. New York: International Publishers.

Marx, K. (1976). Capital, volume 1. London: Pelican Books.

Mills, W. C. (1956). The Power Elite. New York: Oxford University Press.

Open Secrets (2012). Types of Advocacy Groups: 527 Group. <www.opensecrets.org> (2012).

Organization for Economic Co-operation and Development (2012). Trade Union Density. <www.oecd.org> (2012).

Oyez: U.S. Supreme Court Media. (2012a). *Buckley v. Valeo.* <www.oyez.org> (2012).

Oyez: U.S. Supreme Court Media. (2012b). *Citizens United v. Federal Election Commission.* <www.oyez.org> (2012).

Parkin, F. (1979). Marxism and Class Theory. New York: Columbia University Press.

Pintor, R. L., & Gratschew, M. et al. (2002) Voter Turnout Since 1945: A Global Report. Stockholm: International Institute for Democracy and Electoral Assistance.

National Archives (2012). Public Papers of the Presidents. <www.archives.gov> (2012).

Ricardo, D. (2004). The Principles of Political Economy and Taxation. Mineola, NY: Dover Publications, Inc.

Schroeder, A. (2000). Presidential Debates: Forty Years of High-Risk TV. New York: Columbia University Press.

Smith, A. (1991). Wealth of Nations. Amherst, NY: Prometheus Books.

Smith, A. (2007). The Theory of Moral Sentiments. New York: Cosimo.

Stockholm International Peace Research Institute (2011). SIPRI Military Expenditure Database. <www.sipri.org> (2012).

U.S. Census Bureau (2012). Voting and Registration in the Election of November 2008. <www.census.gov> (2012).

Veblen, T. (1899). The Theory of the Leisure Class. New York: Viking Press.

von Clausewitz, C. (1976). On War. Edited and translated by Michael Howard and Peter Paret. Princeton, NJ: Princeton University Press.

Weber, M. (1947). The Theory of Social and Political Organization. Translated by A. M. Henderson and Talcott Parsons. New York: Oxford University Press.

Weber, M. (1994). "The Profession and Vocation of Politics." Weber: Political Writings. Edited by Peter Lassman and Ronald Speirs. Cambridge: Cambridge University Press.

Weber, M. (2002). The Protestant Ethic and the Spirit of Capitalism. Translated by Stephen Kalberg. Los Angeles: Blackwell Publishing.

World Bank (2012). How we Classify Countries. <www.worldbank.org> (2012).

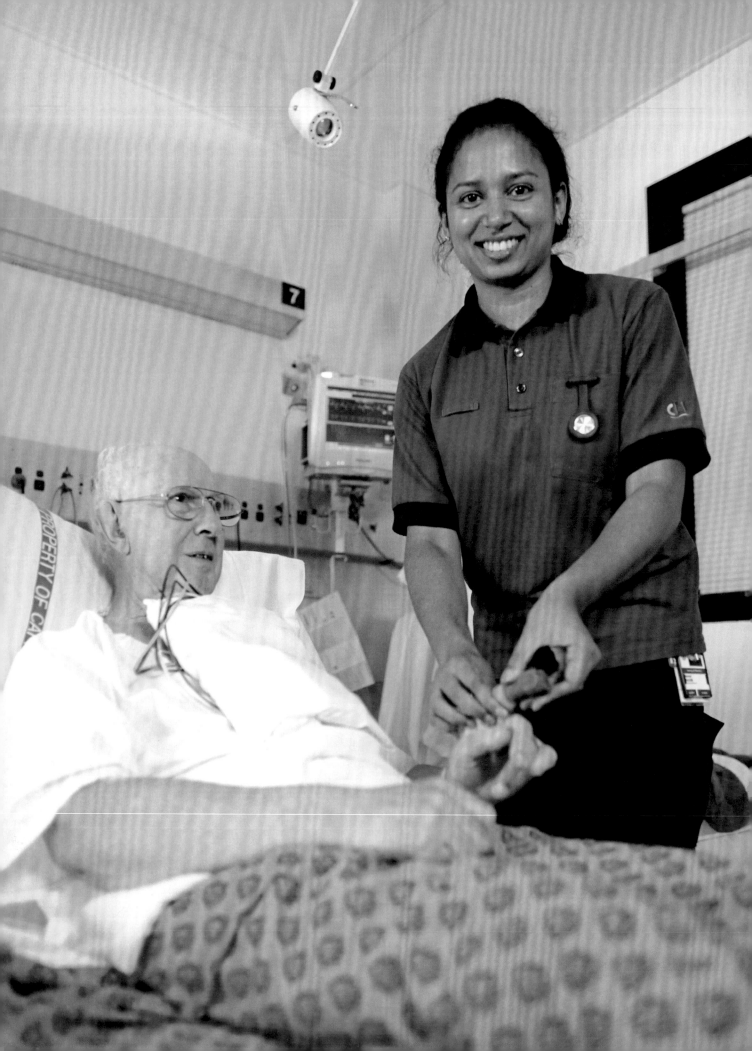

# CHAPTER THIRTEEN

# Health and Population

## Bruce D. LeBlanc

**Chapter Objectives**
At the end of this chapter, students should be able to:

- Describe three perspectives on health.
- Compare health care system models, including the dominant model in the United States.
- Describe various types of health care providers.
- Compare and contrast how each major sociological theoretical perspective views health care.
- Articulate the terms and concepts associated with population dynamics.
- Describe the population trends of over and under population.
- Describe the classical and contemporary theoretical approaches to viewing population dynamics.
- Compare and contrast how each of the major sociological theoretical perspectives views population dynamics.

ur own health is something we might not think much about until we aren't feeling well. Health care, on the other hand, is a topic we may think about often because it has been in the news regularly for more than a decade. The discussion is centered on one question: Who is financially responsible for a person's health care needs? Some people believe that health care is solely the financial responsibility of the individual; others believe that it is solely the responsibility of government. Then there is an entire spectrum of beliefs in between.

In the United States, the health care system was originally based on personal responsibility, and each individual paid for his or her own care in what is known as a *direct pay* model. The system has since been modified to include payments from the government to health care providers on behalf of the elderly, disabled, and impoverished—a form of *socialized medicine*—and payments from private insurance companies, which have created a *third-party payer* model. In the case of government payments to care providers, the taxpayers take on the responsibility of paying for the health care of certain groups of people. Third-party payments are covered by the premiums paid by individuals or by individuals and their employers.

With payment, comes control. When individuals pay for their own health care, they can choose who they can afford to see without limitations. They may choose to see a medical doctor who has met standards set by the government or professional associations, or they may choose people who offer complementary or alternative care, such as herbal remedies, homeopathy, massage therapy, yoga and meditation. Individuals are expected not only to shoulder the responsibility of paying their health care providers, but also to take care of themselves. If they have habits that may contribute to poor health, any resulting costs of that behavior are theirs.

When the taxpayers pay for the health care of others, control over how that money is spent is given to government agencies that determine who is covered by various programs and which health care providers are authorized to receive payments for treatment. Providers also may decide whether or accept patients whose care is paid for by the government because providers are reimbursed for care at a rate lower than what that provider would normally charge. The government can also determine whether a person has taken sufficient care of himself to receive treatment, and there is discussion regarding whether those who abuse substances ranging from tobacco and alcohol to food should be eligible for coverage under government-paid programs.

Under the third-party payment model, insurance companies have control over reimbursement payments and are able to set their own standards about which types of treatment are covered as well as different levels of reimbursement for different providers based on their participation in the company's networks. Individuals may choose where to seek treatment, or whether to pursue an unhealthy lifestyle, with the understanding that they may be responsible for paying for all or part of their care as a result.

The next section of this chapter provides a brief overview of four perspectives that can be used to view health care. As you read these descriptions, consider who bears the responsibility for health and health care, and how each perspective's views are represented in the public debate on these topics. Next is an overview of the foundations of sociological thought and how they relate to health, followed by a more detailed comparison of the models of health care. Health care as seen from the three main theoretical perspectives of sociology—structural functionalism, conflict theory, and symbolic interactionism—will then be discussed and applied to the issues of population and carbon footprinting.

## Perspectives on Health

There are many perspectives from which to view health and the systems and institutions of health care. This chapter begins with a brief exploration of four such perspectives: existentialist, medical, sociological, and sociocultural.

The **existentialist perspective** focuses on individual responsibility for health care issues. Such a perspective was advanced by LeBlanc (2000) in his health responsibility model. This model advocates individuals taking personal responsibility for not only knowing about their health status, but also for taking steps to correct both individual choices and social influences that have an impact on their health. An example of existentialist thinking is the soul life karmic perspective. According to this perspective, individuals through their soul life progressions experience certain life events, including health-related issues, as means of enlightening their souls.

The **medical perspective** views issues of health within a medical framework that attempts to examine pathogens that result in disease and illness. The medical perspective is clearly seen in the genome project through which researchers are identifying genetic factors and predispositions for diseases. Another example of the medical model is the identification of specific pathogens, such as HIV, and how those pathogens affect the health of individuals. Certainly the medical perspective is aware of, and incorporates, dimensions of the sociological perspective, but the core focus of the perspective remains the identification and treatment of pathogens and diseases.

The **sociological perspective** uses research and concepts at both a macro and a micro level to identify health care issues in a society. From a macro-sociological perspective, sociologists examine the functions of the health care system within a particular society, determining if they are functional or dysfunctional. At this level, they might also examine the tensions between groups such as professional and ideological organizations (e.g., anti-abortion or pro-choice camps). Conflicts over scarce resources in the health care system, like access to primary care physicians and medical facilities, are also studied. The micro-sociological level looks at various types of credentialism illustrated by the use of letters to designate one's professional status within the field of health care, such as CNP (certified nurse practitioner), RN (registered nurse), LPN/LVN (licensed professional or licensed vocational nurse), and CNA (certified nursing assistant).

The sociocultural perspective views health care issues as the responsibility of not only an individual, but also his or her family members and sometimes even the community. The sociocultural perspective is different from the sociological perspective because it doesn't consider the responsibility for health-related problems at a micro level. Two examples of the sociocultural perspective include the Navajo and the Chinese. Within both of these cultures, illness is seen as a "disease," or imbalance, in the human system, which includes not only the biological system, but also the social system—family and community. Consequently, restoring a person to health involves restoring the balance within both of the systems.

# Social and Sociological Foundations and Dynamics of Health Care

Sociologists examine health-related issues through the use of categories associated with socio-economic status, including gender, race, and class.

According to Quimby and Friedman (Blankenship, 1989), it must be recognized that power and influence are unequally distributed across the social continuum, especially for women, racial minorities, and the poor. These inequalities are evident in the ability of social institutions and activist groups to effectively address the public health issues of each of these sociocultural minorities. As a result, individuals who belong to these groups can face special challenges in maintaining their health.

One example of the unequal distribution of resources occurred when HIV infections first were being documented. Initial educational endeavors conducted by the government and nonprofit organizations mostly were directed at the male homosexual community. The lack of similar proactive HIV education programs in the African American community led to the current wave of infections in that population.

The unequal educational system is another example. The inequalities between affluent suburban communities and inner-city minority communities have often resulted in minority students achieving a lower educational status than their suburban counterparts. Given the positive correlation between a higher level of education and good physical and mental health, the consequences to less-educated inner-city students become evident—potentially poorer health. Essentially, higher education can provide access to work with greater economic rewards, thus improving a person's well-being (Reynolds & Ross, 1998).

# Demographic Factors

Sociologists are interested in demographic factors such as gender, age, race, and geographical location as they attempt to understand the nature of health and health care institutions. We will briefly explore gender and how it relates to health. When sociologists consider chromosomal and physiological data, it appears that females are the stronger sex. Females can exist with only a single X chromosome, a condition referred to as Turner's syndrome; no male of the human species has been found to exist with only one Y chromosome. Additionally, females are protected by the *double X-factor*, where a dominant X chromosome blocks the expression of any recessive trait found on the second X chromosome. In comparison, the male Y chromosome is incapable of blocking the expression of a recessive trait found on the inherited X chromosome. Furthermore, from a physiological perspective, female brains have greater connectivity between the two hemispheres of the brain, which promotes quicker physiological recoveries from strokes and similar conditions. On the other hand, research on specific health conditions shows that males may be the stronger of the sexes. Women experience migraine headaches far more frequently than men as a result of sex hormones experienced post-puberty. Additionally, women experience arthritis at higher rates than men; men are potentially protected by genetics and testosterone. Eating disorders are also 10 times more prevalent in women, even though the risks for eating disorders are believed to be similar for both males and females. Women are more likely to experience anxiety disorders, while bipolar disorders are experienced equally for both sexes (Maloof, 2008).

# The Social Nature of the Sick Role

When we are sick, we tend to see our illness as an individual experience. Most of us, though, live and function within the social worlds of family and work. As a result of these involvements, our illness generally assumes a broader social impact. Not only do we assume the sociological status of being ill, we also take on roles associated with that status. These dynamics are referred to as the **sick role**, which involves a variety of social norms that specify the responsibilities, expectations, and rights of someone who is ill. Henderson (1935) and Parsons (1951) generally assign four characteristics to the sick role. An individual who is ill first acquires the freedom to not perform certain personal, familial, and work responsibilities. Secondly, because the individual has manifested the illness, s/he is not blamed for being ill. Although there is no blame, a third expectation requires the person to visit an appropriate medical professional. Finally, after having sought medical treatment, the individual is expected to comply with

the treatment plan in an attempt to restore his/her health (Abercrombie, Hill & Turner, 1984).

# Health Care Systems: Comparative Models

As we explore the social frameworks for providing health care to a nation's citizens, we will draw upon three prominent models: socialized medicine, socialist medicine, and decentralized national health care.

## Socialized Medicine

In the **socialized medicine** model, the government exercises some, but not total, control of the health care system. Cockerham (1995) identified five characteristics associated with socialized medicine. The first characteristic allows for the financing and organizing of health care services based on capitalistic economic factors that allow for supply and demand, as well as free-market competition. There is payment by government agencies to health care providers. Ownership of health care facilities can be either private or public, providing for limited, though often expensive, private caretakers for individuals. Finally, there is guaranteed access to medical care regardless of one's financial ability to pay.

Countries that have socialized systems include Canada, Great Britain and Sweden. In Great Britain, a primary care physician also acts as a gatekeeper, determining who should be referred to specialists. Canada ensures primary care physician coverage, as well as hospital care, but limits coverage for prescription drugs for those under 65. Dental care in Canada is not covered because it is seen as the responsibility of each individual. The Swedish system provides the greatest range of benefits, including payment for travel expenses and economic losses related to health care treatments.

## Socialist Medicine

**Socialist medicine** is a system of health care that is under the complete control of the government, or state. Hospitals and other medical facilities are owned by the government, and all health care workers are employed by the government. Medical treatment is seen as a benefit provided by a government to its citizens. Cockerham (1995) identified five key characteristics of a socialist health care system: (1) provisions for private health care are banned, (2) equal access to medical care is guaranteed for all citizens, (3) all health care facilities are government owned and operated, (4) health care providers are employees of the government, and (5) the health care system is financed through an economy based on socialist, and often communist, principles, wherein direct control and organization of the system fall under the auspices of the state.

Socialist forms of health care have traditionally been found in communist states such as Russia and Cuba. Russia is no longer communist, but its socialist medical system persists. Bribes are common to obtain better care, but the government spent $6.4 billion in 2008 on new facilities, equipment and raises for doctors (Los Angeles Times, 2008). In Cuba, not only is routine health care provided by the government, but so is treatment for some of the most challenging diseases, including AIDS. Although HIV-infected individuals and those who have developed AIDS often receive their care in isolated facilities, they are provided comprehensive treatment for this disease.

## Decentralized National Health Care

The third organizational model is **decentralized national health care**, in which government functions primarily as a regulator of the system. Regulation typically involves the government acting as a mediator between the providers of care and those organizations that pay for health care services within the system. Cockerham (1995) also identified five characteristics associated with this model: (1) the government may own some health care facilities, (2) equal access to care is guaranteed by the government, (3) payments made to providers are regulated, (4) individuals have access to some private care at their own expense, and (5) in capitalist economies, the government often indirectly controls the organization and financing of health care services.

Countries with decentralized national health care systems include Germany, the Netherlands, and Japan. Health care plans in Germany are managed by governmental bodies, and each citizen is required to belong to a plan. In the Netherlands, the fees that pay for health care are obtained through compulsory contributions from employees and employers, as well as from state subsidies. A second system exists where individuals earning higher wages can purchase private insurance with employer subsidies that equal the amount of the public contribution, supplemented by the individual's own money. Finally, in Japan the government establishes fee schedules for physicians and hospitals, but within a system that allows citizens to choose their own physicians.

# United States Model of Health Care

As with many other aspects of the social structure in the United States, the health care system offers diverse functional models that draw upon the experiences of other countries, including the three models discussed previously. For people not covered by a private insurance plan or a government program, their health care falls under an independent **direct pay model**. Under the direct pay model, each individual is legally responsible for paying all of his or her own health care costs. Many people who work are covered by employer-subsidized insurance plans, thus creating a third-party payer model.

At times in our lives, we may receive health care that incorporates features from other models. For example, both Los Angeles and Ventura counties in California have general hospitals where citizens are entitled to receive care. Although this health care is not provided free of charge, the counties will absorb the costs if the individual is indigent. Essentially, these costs are covered by the taxes paid by local residents, as they are in socialist medical systems. Medicare, which provides health coverage for those with qualifying disabilities or those 65 years and older, and Medicaid, health coverage for low income families and individuals, are also examples of socialized medicine. The government makes direct payments to health care providers on behalf of those people who qualify for coverage under Medicare and Medicaid. The U.S. health care model is a combination of several models. Fundamentally, though, it remains a direct pay system.

## Health Care Controversies in the United States

In the United States, there are a number of controversies surrounding health care. Because the economy is based on a capitalist system, profit motives are enmeshed within the direct pay and third-party models of health care. Even nonprofit entities have to pay competitive salaries to their employees, raising their operating costs. It is the for-profit sector of health care that receives the most attention from legislative bodies at both the state and national level. This sector is also responsible for conducting much of the research to formulate new medications and developing most new technologies for the diagnosis and treatment of disease.

Unlike more socialist and socialized models of health care systems, which negotiate prices to be paid for various health care advances, individuals in the United States pay fair market value (allowing for a profit) for medications and technology. It is often argued that the third-party system in the United States is more of a socialized or socialist health care system because it subsidizes other people's care through insurance premiums, co-payments, and other health care costs. The capitalistic for-profit nature of the U.S. health care system allows for the development of advanced technologies and new medications. Thus, it appears to be a double-edged sword. By paying significant health care costs, U.S. citizens have access to the most advanced health care in the world, but this access is not guaranteed because of the lack of universal health care.

The role to be played by public health departments is another controversial topic in health care. In 1920, Charles Edward Amory Winslow, a public health professor at Yale, defined public health as:

> The science and art of preventing disease, prolonging life, and promoting physical health and efficiency to organize community efforts for the sanitation of the environment, the control of community infections, the education of the individual and principles of personal hygiene, the organization of medical and nursing service for the early diagnosis, prevention and treatment of disease, and

the development of the social machinery which will insure to every individual of health (Starr, 1982).

Religious organizations raised objections, often along moral grounds, regarding any state endeavor that concerned public health. Medical professionals also raised objections, particularly when public health departments tried to involve themselves in the "organization of medical and nursing service." This aspect of health care related directly to the practice of medicine, and they wanted to keep it under their purview. The antipathy toward public health services is reflected in a comment by Dr. George Shardy, who noted that "poor people do not suffer from want of skilled medical attendants…on the contrary, they obtain vastly more than they have the right to expect…vast sums of money are wasted yearly on worthless and undeserving persons" (Starr, 1982).

Dr. Shardy's comment was related to public health dispensaries and appeared to be motivated by the fact that the dispensaries often were used as training facilities for medical interns. Physicians decreased the number of medical schools in the United States, thus eliminating the need for internships at public health dispensaries, which also reduced the interns' contact with the public health system. Because it is physicians who control the training of medical students, through the legislative authority given to the American Medical Association, we can see an organized effort on the part of doctors to limit access to free or reduced-cost health care services provided by public health organizations. Such endeavors raise serious questions about the motives of both physicians and the American Medical Association, particularly regarding their economic and profit motives. We continue to see the marginalization of public health care programs to services that they are "allowed" to provide within the health care system in the United States. The services typically provided by such departments include family planning, infant and child nutrition, and environmental and community health issues, including the diagnosis and treatment of sexually transmitted infections or diseases. These services generally do not generate high revenues.

# Health Care Providers

There are a variety of individuals who provide health care services in the United States yet it is physicians who reign supreme among health care providers, regulating the practice of medicine through their legislative and legal establishments. There are three broad classifications of providers: primary care providers, secondary care providers, and alternative health care providers.

**Primary care providers** are physicians who can practice medicine in all of its branches. Historically, this category has been composed of doctors of medicine (MDs). Doctors of osteopathic medicine (DOs) are another group of professionals that can function as primary care providers in the United States. These primary care providers are trained in much the same way as medical doctors, but they also learn holistic techniques that include physical adjustments to the body (similar to those made by chiropractors). A doctor of chiropractic (DC) can practice as a primary care provider if he or she takes additional training and refers patients as medically necessary to other primary care providers. While most states allow both MDs and DOs to practice in all medical branches, few states allow DCs to do the same. Illinois does allow chiropractic physicians this authority, provided that they complete additional courses as prescribed by the state's Department of Professional Occupations. An emergent primary health care provider, allowed in a limited number of states, is a doctor of naturopathic medicine (ND). Naturopathic doctors often use herbs as part of their treatment protocols. Like DCs, NDs must also make appropriate referrals when a medical condition is beyond the scope of their training and practice. Depending upon where they live, individuals may have any one of these four types of doctors as their primary health care provider.

**Secondary care providers** include professionals who extend the services of doctors. Doctors have the greatest degree of authority for providing health care within the United States. Those professionals who also provide health care services, but are not physicians, are referred to as secondary care providers. This categorization is not a reflection of their professional training but is rather a reflection of their secondary functionality in the delivery of health care.

When the health care system experienced a decline in the number of physicians, two classifications of professionals were added to help meet demand—physician assistants and nurse practitioners. These **physician extenders** can provide basic physical diagnoses and care. In most states, physician assistants are licensed to practice under the supervision of a physician, while nurse practitioners function fairly independently. This varies from state to state, however, depending on licensing laws.

While the impetus for the development of physician extenders was to meet the needs of the underserved, primarily those in rural areas of the United States, this health care model failed to make working in such areas a requisite for licensure. As a result, many physician assistants and nurse practitioners relocated to urban areas where they could receive higher wages.

Because of a shortage of nurses, there was a need to develop **clinical nurse extenders** (LeBlanc, 2006). These individuals provide limited nursing care to a level consistent with their training and licensing. Historically, nurses were trained in three-year diploma programs, often affiliated with particular hospitals. As the nursing shortage emerged, two-year degree programs were introduced to the community college system. When the demand for nurses was still not being met, one-year training programs for licensed vocational nurses (LVNs) and licensed practical nurses (LPNs) were developed. When there was a demand for still more nurses, combined with a need to reduce costs, a third category emerged—nursing assistants. This category evolved into a certified nursing assistant (CNA) health care professional. As pressure has mounted to provide nursing care, particularly in rural areas, the scope of practice for nurse extenders has been expanded. For instance, LPNs are generally not allowed to dispense medications, administer IV treatments, or act as charge nurses, but they can, with additional training, now assume these responsibilities in some states. Not only has the scope of practice expanded for LVNs and LPNS, it has also expanded for CNAs. In some states, CNAs can now dispense medications if they complete additional training.

Within the health care field there are also a variety of professionals with specialized occupational training who provide limited health care services. These professionals include physical therapists, respiratory therapists, speech pathologists, dietitians, health care educators, medical social workers, and even chaplains. These professionals supplement primary and secondary care providers, allowing them to focus on the diagnosis and treatment of illness and disease.

**Alternative health care professionals** do not practice health care within mainstream, Western modalities of health care. Such practitioners have existed in non-Western societies for centuries. Many early healers, including shamans in tribal cultures, used natural plants and herbs to treat human diseases. The Chinese have used not only herbs, but also needles (acupuncture) and the manipulation of the body's soft tissues.

A more contemporary alternative practitioner is a doctor of Oriental medicine (OMDs). Doctors of Oriental medicine generally have to complete 3,000 hours of formal training, guided by Eastern philosophical principles regarding "disease" and medical treatments that promote physiological integration through a holistic approach. Herbs are often a part of their clinical practice, as are nutritional counseling and massage. Acupuncturists are a related group of alternative practitioners, specifically trained in the Chinese practice of using needles to release energy—or chi—blockages. Many states require that an acupuncturist obtain a master's degree before seeking licensure. Though they may be licensed, some states do not allow them to practice independently of primary health care providers. For instance, to see an acupuncturist in Illinois, a patient must have a referral from a primary health care provider.

A massage therapist is another type of alternative health care provider. Most massage therapists complete a 500-hour training program that includes more anatomy and physiology information than is required of students in licensed vocational and practical nursing programs. Generally, the scope of practice for a massage therapist is the reduction of muscular tension in the human body. Finally, there is a range of alternative health care providers who may not be required to have much training to practice their professions. Examples include aromatherapists who use natural scented oils to work with human imbalances and hypnotherapists who may have as few as 100 hours of training.

# Theoretical Perspectives on Health Care

## Structural Functionalism

As a macro-sociological perspective, structural functionalism is more concerned with the larger social and societal dimensions of health care, focusing on the functions served by the system and its institutions.

For a society to function, it needs a healthy work force. Maintaining the health of the individual serves to stabilize the general health and well-being of the population, and it is the health of the population, particularly the work force, that allows a society to maintain itself economically. Thus, a manifest function of the health care system is to keep the citizenry healthy so it can be a productive work force serving to stabilize society.

A second manifest function of the health care system is to avoid increasing the burden placed upon the broader society to care for the health of the population. It has been proposed that one way to accomplish this is to provide, or mandate, health care coverage for all citizens. Providing universal health care has been discussed in the United States since the first Clinton administration, but only recently has major health reform been enacted. The Patient Protection and Affordable Care Act of 2010 requires most Americans to have health insurance. Massachusetts provides us with an example of how mandated universal health care coverage can be effective at dispersing the social and economic burdens that the uninsured and underinsured place upon society. Citizens of Massachusetts must have health insurance coverage or face economic penalties. If they do not have access to insurance through their employment, they must purchase insurance within a state-sponsored plan. Thus, Massachusetts is attempting to meet this second manifest function (Massachusetts Trial Court Libraries, 2008).

## Social Conflict

Like structural functionalism, social conflict is a macro-level theoretical perspective. It deals with the larger dimensions of society and, in particular, the tensions that exist between groups within that society. Although the classic social conflict perspective articulated by Marx involved tensions between the social classes, groups can also be in conflict over scarce resources other than money, such as a significant value within society including health care. Remember, also, that groups struggle to obtain and/or control scarce resources. Consequently, struggles for power often enter the social institutions of a society.

The health care system has many groups in conflict with one another. In the United States, we have to look no further than the power struggle over who can practice medicine, to what degree, and in what settings, to see that social conflict exists in the health care system. Historically, medical doctors have been able to practice in all branches of medicine in the United States. When more holistic practitioners, like doctors of osteopathic medicine, entered the practice of medicine, MDs fought their acceptance, both legislatively and professionally, arguing that their training does not adequately prepare them for the practice of medicine. While legislative efforts eventually failed, the MDs succeeded professionally by limiting where DOs can practice medicine. For instance, osteopathic physicians are not permitted to practice medicine in hospitals, thus limiting their work with patients in such settings. Further, when doctors of chiropractic medicine sought professional recognition, medical doctors attempted to prevent that change. It is believed that the economic motivation, with money being the scarce resource, is central to the conflict paradigm. The exercise of power by the MDs, demonstrated by their attempts to limit the acceptance of other doctors, is the mechanism by which they maintain that scarce resource for themselves.

Two examples further illustrate the conflict dynamics within the health care system. The first example occurred in Illinois, where doctors were successful at establishing a legislative requirement that individuals must have been referred by a medical doctor, doctor of osteopathic medicine, or chiropractor before seeing an acupuncturist (Illinois Compiled Statutes, 2008). It should be noted that a number of states allow acupuncturists and doctors of Oriental medicine to practice completely independent of mandated referrals. Such states recognize a specific scope of practice within the field of medicine for these practitioners. The second example involves an attempt by physicians to limit access to natural remedies, specifically herbs. Physicians attempted to define herbs as drugs because of their medicinal qualities. If classified as drugs, herbs would have fallen within the scope of practicing medicine, as only licensed physicians can prescribe drugs or medications. Individuals would then have had to acquire a prescription before purchasing herbs. Fortunately for these individuals, the efforts failed (Theil, 2003). One has to question the motives behind the actions of physicians, particularly since they have very little, if any, medical training in herbology, unlike naturopathic physicians and master herbologists, both recognized medical practitioners in other countries. Such physicians may argue that classifying herbs as drugs would lead to better regulation of substances that could have adverse effects if used improperly. Conflict theorists would say that there is an economic motivation on the part of physicians to limit and control access to a variety of health care professionals and medial interventions.

## Symbolic Interactionism

As a microsociological perspective, symbolic interactionism focuses on how symbols are defined and used, both contextually and socially. Equally important for symbolic interactionists are how social interactions are created and maintained and how they change society. When applying symbolic interactionism to the health care system, one needs look no further than the variety of requisite initials associated with the professional status of health care providers to see the use of symbols. The symbolic representation of something is central to this perspective; therefore, it is important to recall what each of these symbols means (see Table 13.1).

Each set of letters represents the symbolic nature of a profession, which is often a socially recognized credential that defines the legal parameters for practicing that profession.

From the symbolic interactionist perspective, how individuals create, maintain, and change the social world at a micro level is significant. We can see this

**TABLE 13.1** Professional Medical Designations

| Physicians | |
| --- | --- |
| DC | Doctor of Chiropractic Medicine |
| DO | Doctor of Osteopathic Medicine |
| MD | Doctor of Medicine |
| ND | Doctor of Naturopathic Medicine |
| OMD | Doctor of Oriental Medicine |
| **Nurses** | |
| CNA | Certified Nursing Assistant |
| CNP | Certified Nurse Practitioner |
| LPN | Licensed Practical Nurse |
| LVN | Licensed Vocational Nurse |
| RN | Registered Nurse |
| **Alternative Health Care Providers** | |
| CMT | Certified Massage Therapist |
| DPM | Doctor of Podiatric Medicine |
| LMT | Licensed Massage Therapist |
| NCMT | Nationally Certified Massage Therapist |
| NP | Naprapathic Practitioner |

within the practice of massage therapy. Historically, massage was taught through a mentoring process, and a person would be referred to as a massage therapist upon completion of the program. As society evolved, it demanded a more formal educational process for individuals studying massage; consequently, schools developed where, upon successful completion of a training program, individuals would receive a certificate recognizing their status as a certified massage therapist (CMT). Though professionally trained, these individuals often practiced without local or state licensure. The field then evolved to require licensing at a local or state level, resulting in the use of the initials LMT to represent a licensed massage therapist. A final evolution within the field

of massage therapy resulted in a number of states requiring not only licensure but also national certification. To become a nationally certified massage therapist (NCMT), individuals are required to pass an examination. The changes in this one field illustrate the importance of symbols in society and how they can change over time.

# Population Issues and Dynamics

Having covered health care issues from a sociological perspective, including some issues related to population dynamics, it is time to more directly examine population from a sociological perspective. This examination of population issues and dynamics begins by reviewing some foundational terms and concepts used by sociologists. After that review, sociological population theories will be briefly highlighted. These will be followed by factors that influence population growth, as well as a discussion of limited population trends seen both globally and in the United States. The final section of this chapter will examine how each of the three dominant sociological theories views population issues and dynamics.

Within the discipline of sociology, **demography** is generally defined as the study of growth and decline in the human population caused by migration, fertility, and mortality, as well as sex ratios and age cohorts (Scott & Marshall, 2005). Like many other areas in the field of sociology, there is complexity and interrelatedness in the population characteristics and concepts related to demography. Sociologists who investigate population characteristics are referred to as **demographers**, and they focus on population projections and the social consequences of those projections.

As noted in the definition, key concepts that would interest a demographer are birth and fertility rates, death (mortality) rates, life expectancies, human migration, sex ratios, and marriage rates. We will briefly discuss these terms, as defined by Scott and Marshall (2005), and provide tables comparing these statistics for countries in several regions.

Birthrates are used to compare the fertility rates of different populations. There are two common ways to calculate birthrates; the *crude birthrate* and the *general fertility rate*. The **crude birthrate** is defined as the number of live births in a year per 1,000 people (using midyear estimates). The **general fertility rate** is defined as the birthrate per 1,000 women of childbearing age. The fertility rate is calculated as the number of live births in a year, divided by the female population aged 15 to 44 years, times 1,000, and may also be referred to as the *total fertility rate*. As shown in Table 13.2, the crude birthrate in Mexico (19.13) is almost twice that of Canada (10.28), with the rate in the United States (13.83) falling about halfway between the two. Mexico (2.29) also has the highest fertility rate compared with the United States (2.06) and Canada (1.58) (Central Intelligence Agency, 2011). The terms *birthrate* and *fertility rate* are often used interchangeably, so it is important to note when the crude birthrate is being used to avoid confusion.

Death (mortality) rates are another demographic variable that interests sociological demographers. Just as with birthrates, death rates are generally defined in two ways. The **crude death rate** is the number of deaths in a year per 1,000 population in the defined geographical area. Another way of measuring death rates is the computation of a standard mortality ratio (SMR) for each sex, the sexes combined, or specific social groupings. The **standard mortality ratio** is defined as the actual or observed number of deaths of a group, divided by the expected number of deaths, and then multiplied by 100. Another key death rate examined by demographers is the **infant mortality rate**, which is defined as the number of deaths within the first year of life, divided by the number of live births in the same year, times 1,000. Mexico has the lowest crude death rate (4.86), but the highest infant mortality rate (17.29). The United States has the highest crude death rate (8.38), and Canada has the lowest infant mortality rate (4.92).

Life expectancy is often used by demographers as an indicator of the standard of living within a society, in particular as it relates to the health, social, and economic standards of living. **Life expectancy** is defined as the number of years that a person can expect to live within a given society. It can also be calculated as the number of additional years of life a person can expect for a given age. Demographers often delve beyond general life expectancy to examine differences between the genders within the same societies. Among the countries shown in Table 13.2. Canada has the highest life expectancy rate (81.38) and Mexico has the lowest (76.47). In all three of these countries, women can expect to live longer than men, on average. The largest gap between the average life expectancy for women and that for men

TABLE 13.2 Demographic Statistics for North and Central America

| 2011 Demographic Statistics | Canada | Mexico | United States |
|---|---|---|---|
| Crude Birthrate (per 1,000 population) | 10.28 | 19.13 | 13.83 |
| Total Fertility Rate (per woman) | 1.58 | 2.29 | 2.06 |
| Crude Death Rate (per 1,000 population) | 7.78 | 4.86 | 8.38 |
| Infant Mortality Rate (per 1,000 live births) | 4.92 | 17.29 | 6.06 |
| Life Expectancy - All (at birth) | 81.38 | 76.47 | 78.31 |
| Life Expectancy - Male (at birth) | 78.81 | 73.65 | 75.92 |
| Life Expectancy - Female (at birth) | 84.1 | 79.43 | 80.93 |
| Sex Ratio (at birth, males/females) | 1.05 | 1.05 | 1.04 |
| Sex Ratio (under 15 years, males/females) | 1.03 | 1.04 | 1.04 |
| Sex Ratio (15 - 64 years, males/females) | 1.02 | .94 | 1.00 |
| Sex Ratio (65 and over, males/females) | .78 | .82 | .75 |
| Sex Ratio (total population, males/females) | .98 | .96 | .97 |
| Net Migration Rate (per 1,000 population) | 5.65 | -3.24 | 4.18 |

Source: The 2011 World Factbook, CIA.

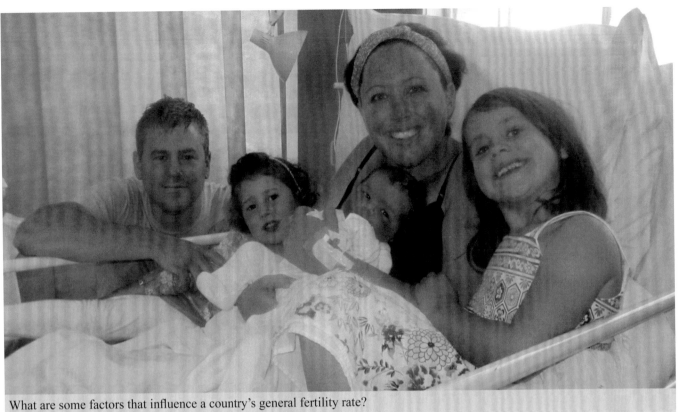

What are some factors that influence a country's general fertility rate?

is in Mexico, where the difference is 5.78 years.

In addition to looking at general life expectancies, demographers also examine **sex ratios**, which are calculated as the number of males per 1,000 females in the population. The sex ratios for Canada, Mexico, and the United States are fairly even up to 15 years of age, then the ratio for ages 15 through 64 in Mexico drops (0.94) compared with the United States (1.00) and Canada (1.02). That trend reverses in the 65 and older age range, with Mexico having the highest ratio (0.82), compared with Canada (0.78) and the United States (0.75).

The sex ratio of a country is an important social indicator because it affects the **marriage rate**, which is the number of marriages per 1,000 people in a given year. The participation of women in the labor force, and the expected or actual roles for males and females, may also be affected by sex ratios (Guilmoto, 2012). On the other hand, social policies, such as female infanticide, can have a large impact on sex ratios, affecting future trends like the availability of partners and fertility rates in a society. Too few women can relegate a significant portion of men to a single lifestyle.

**Human migration** is another factor that affects the population demographics of countries. Human migration is the permanent movement of individuals or groups across symbolic or political boundaries into new areas and communities (Scott & Marshall, 2005). The definition of human migration recognizes that there may be movement between areas within a society or a country, like the migration from rural areas to more urban areas, which has been happening within the United States over the past century. The definition also recognizes migration patterns from one nation to another, such as the movement of people from Mexico and countries in Central and South America to the United States, through both legal and illegal migration patterns. In 2011, Mexico had a negative net migration rate (-3.24), which indicates net emigration, while the rates for Canada (5.65) and the United States (4.18) were both positive, indicating net immigration.

Human migration patterns can be used to stabilize population demographics, or they can challenge sociocultural and economic stability. An example of migration stabilization, including illegal migration, is seen in the agricultural sector of the United

States. Many farmers could not economically produce and harvest their crops without the use of a migrant labor force that may include people who have entered the country illegally. One social consequence is the availability of affordable agricultural commodities, especially produce, for U.S. consumers. Yet, the use of this labor force can have destabilizing effects on other sectors of the economy, such as the demands placed on the health care and education systems by the illegal immigrant work force. It is estimated that five to six percent of California's K-12 student population is in the United States illegally (Miller, 1997). The presence of these students also stresses the economic resources of school districts due to the need to provide bilingual education.

# Population Trends

In this section, we will examine three population trends—overpopulation, underpopulation, and resource utilization, including carbon footprinting. Each of these population issues can affect not only a particular country, but also the international community, in very different but significant ways. These issues will be examined from both a regional and a global perspective.

## Overpopulation

**Overpopulation** is defined as the population of an environment by a particular species that exceeds that environment's carrying capacity. The effects of overpopulation can include depletion of resources, environmental deterioration, and a prevalence of famine and disease. With its over-dependence on internal resource production, Rwanda is experiencing overpopulation. It does not draw on the carrying capacity of other nations by importing significant resources. Consequently, Rwanda exceeds the carrying capacity of its own geographical and economic resources. Additionally, the rate at which the population is growing exceeds the country's ability to provide for its people, particularly when it comes to agricultural goods. This has resulted in an internal migration and a higher concentration of young men in urban areas. In turn, the level of violence committed by this group of dislocated men has increased

as they struggle to survive. Finally, deaths caused by HIV/AIDS have affected the employment sector and the development of human capital through teacher deaths and the production of agricultural resources through farmer deaths (Butler, 2004). In 2009, it was estimated that 2.9 percent of adults in Rwanda were living with HIV/AIDS, compared with 17.8 percent in South Africa and 0.6 percent in the United States (CIA, 2011).

India is also experiencing overpopulation while facing agricultural challenges. India has an amount of arable land only second in size to that of the United States. Yet India has to import wheat so that it can feed its more than one billion residents. Matters are further complicated by the demands of feeding the poor while at the same time providing the emergent affluent class in India more variety in food availability. Consequently, farmers are shifting crop production to maximize their return on investment. This has resulted in government incentives to farmers to produce the commodity staples of rice and wheat. Furthermore, climate changes related to water are forcing India to reexamine its food production system.

## Underpopulation

In contrast to overpopulation, **underpopulation** is defined as having a less than sustainable population density. One way of determining if a country is underpopulated is to learn whether it produces births equal to the necessary *replacement rate*, a figure presently established as about 2.1 children for each woman in a developed country. The replacement rate is the number of children each woman needs to have to maintain current population levels. If a country's fertility rate—the total number of children the average woman is likely to have—is below the replacement rate, underpopulation is a possibility. In 2011, the fertility rate was 1.96 in France, 1.91 in the United Kingdom, and 1.41 in Germany, as shown in Table 13.3. As a result of these low fertility rates, it is estimated that by the year 2030, Europe will have about 20 million fewer workers than it needs in order to have a strong economy. It is also estimated that within two generations in France and Germany, there is a potential for a Muslim majority, due to the high fertility rate of Muslim immigrants

**TABLE 13.3** Demographic Statistics for Europe

| 2011 Demographic Statistics | France | Germany | United Kingdom |
|---|---|---|---|
| Crude Birthrate (per 1,000 population) | 12.29 | 8.3 | 12.29 |
| Total Fertility Rate (per woman) | 1.96 | 1.41 | 1.91 |
| Crude Death Rate (per 1,000 population) | 8.76 | 10.92 | 9.33 |
| Infant Mortality Rate (per 1,000 live births) | 3.29 | 3.84 | 4.62 |
| Life Expectancy - All (at birth) | 81.19 | 80.07 | 80.05 |
| Life Expectancy - Male (at birth) | 78.02 | 77.82 | 77.95 |
| Life Expectancy - Female (at birth) | 84.54 | 82.44 | 82.25 |
| Sex Ratio (at birth, males/females) | 1.05 | 1.05 | 1.05 |
| Sex Ratio (under 15 years, males/females) | 1.05 | 1.05 | 1.05 |
| Sex Ratio (15 - 64 years, males/females) | 1.00 | 1.04 | 1.03 |
| Sex Ratio (65 and over, males/females) | 0.72 | 0.72 | 0.76 |
| Sex Ratio (total population, males/females) | 0.96 | 0.97 | 0.98 |
| NET Migration Rate (per 1,000 population) | 1.46 | 0.54 | 2.6 |

Source: The 2011 World Factbook, CIA.

(6.0). Additionally, it is estimated that Russia will lose one third of its population, primarily through the use of abortion as a method of birth control, by the year 2050 (Smith, 2008). Furthermore, it is estimated that 15 countries have fertility rates below 1.3, and six countries have rates between 1.3 and 1.4 (Abortion TV, 2006). As of 2011, it was estimated that 84 countries and territories had fertility rates below the replacement level, representing approximately 2.7 billion people, or roughly 44 percent of the world's population (Eberstadt, 2001; CIA, 2011).

A decrease in life expectancy is an additional area where population declines are of concern. As shown in Table 13.4, Russia's life expectancy was 66.29 in 2011, with the life expectancy for women (73.17) more than 13 years longer than that for men (59.8) (CIA, 2011).

There are several means of countering underpopulation. One way is through the regulation of abortion. In countries where abortion is illegal, such as Ireland and Portugal, there exist some of the highest fertility rates within any European nation (CIA, 2011). Another way of addressing underpopulation is through immigration. As a result of declining fertility rates, it is estimated that Europe would need to quadruple its number of immigrants to prevent a decline in the working-age population. To achieve

this, the net migration rates for the countries included in Table 13.3 would have to increase substantially from their 2011 levels of 1.46 for France, 0.54 for Germany, and 2.6 for the United Kingdom. For Japan, it is estimated that nearly 600,000 immigrants are necessary to keep the working population from shrinking and having a negative impact on the country's economy (Eberstadt, 2001). Immigration is also a factor in the stabilization of total fertility rates within the United States. In the United States, the fertility rates for Hispanics (2.9) and blacks (2.1) were at or above the replacement level needed to maintain the current population (2.1) in 2008. The rates for Asians (2.0) and whites (1.84) were below the replacement rate (Khan, 2010). Thus, it can continue to be said that the population of the United States is being stabilized mostly by the fertility rates of the Hispanic and black communities (Currie, 2007).

Finally, China presents us with a population paradox. Some researchers believe that because China has the highest population in the world, with approximately 1.2 billion people, it is overpopulated, particularly in certain regions such as urban centers. Other researchers believe that China faces a population shortage, particularly as it deals with an aging population. In 1979, China introduced a one-child-per-family policy to help it control its exponential

**TABLE 13.4** Demographic Statistics for Asia

| 2011 Demographic Statistics | China | India | Japan | Russia |
|---|---|---|---|---|
| Crude Birthrate (per 1,000 population) | 12.29 | 20.97 | 7.31 | 11.05 |
| Total Fertility Rate (per woman) | 1.54 | 2.62 | 1.21 | 1.42 |
| Crude Death Rate (per 1,000 population) | 7.03 | 7.48 | 10.09 | 16.04 |
| Infant Mortality Rate (per 1,000 live births) | 16.06 | 45.57 | 2.78 | 10.08 |
| Life Expectancy - All (at birth) | 74.68 | 66.8 | 82.25 | 66.29 |
| Life Expectancy - Male (at birth) | 72.68 | 65.77 | 78.96 | 59.8 |
| Life Expectancy - Female (at birth) | 76.94 | 67.95 | 83.72 | 73.17 |
| Sex Ratio (at birth, males/females) | 1.13 | 1.12 | 1.05 | 1.06 |
| Sex Ratio (under 15 years, males/females) | 1.17 | 1.13 | 1.06 | 1.06 |
| Sex Ratio (15 - 64 years, males/females) | 1.06 | 0.91 | 1.02 | 0.92 |
| Sex Ratio (65 and over, males/females) | 0.93 | 0.91 | 0.74 | 0.44 |
| Sex Ratio (total population, males/females) | 1.06 | 1.08 | 0.95 | 0.86 |
| NET Migration Rate (per 1,000 population) | -0.33 | -0.05 | 0 | 0.29 |

Source: The 2011 World Factbook, CIA.

population growth. As shown in Table 13.4, China's fertility rate (1.54) was significantly below the 2.1 replacement rate but higher than the rates for Russia (1.42) and Japan (1.21) in 2011 (CIA, 2011).

The one-child policy benefited China economically by raising the standards of living for its citizens, including the introduction of birth insurance and worker's compensation benefits (Cook, 1999). However, China still faces two emergent population concerns. It was speculated that by the year 2010, China's capital, Beijing, would face a water shortage because its population was expected to exceed 17 million, which is at least three million more than the carrying capacity of the city's water system (China.org.cn, 2009). In 2010, Steven Mufson of *The Washington Post* quoted Ma Jun, director of the Beijing-based Institute of Public and Environmental Affairs, as saying, "China is facing prominent challenges: water shortages and pollution." Mufson commented, "The source of the water predicament is China's own economic success" (Mufson, 2010). Additionally, by 2050, China will face a shrinking working-age population that will be expected to take care of the elderly, both physically and economically. Matters are further complicated by the entry of females into the labor force, as well as the decreasing number of young Chinese females, who are traditionally expected to take care of the elderly,

especially in the home (Kaneda, 2006).

Next we will focus on resource utilization and carbon footprinting as a means of examining a person's impact on not only the social but also the physical world. The U.S. Energy Information Association (2011) reports on the 2009 oil consumption rates for the top consuming countries. While the United States is ranked third in terms of total population size with just under 5 percent of the world's population (U.S. Census Bureau, 2012), it consumes a vast amount of oil compared to other countries. The EIA reports that the United States consumed an average of 18.8 million gallons of oil per day. The average daily gallons of oil, in millions of gallons, consumed by China is 7.8, Japan 4.4, India 3.1, Russia 2.9, Germany 2.5, Canada 2.2, Mexico 2.1, Saudi Arabia 2.1, Iran 1.7, Spain 1.5 and Indonesia 1.3. Clearly the use of oil within the United States is not only disproportional based on mere "raw" usage; when the percentage of the world's population is considered, the disparity is further magnified.

In North America, we consumed 60 barrels of oil per capita. This compares with 9 barrels of oil for Latin America, 29 barrels of oil for Europe, 3 barrels of oil for Africa, and 7 barrels of oil for Asia (Population Connection, 2007). Access to and utilization of land are also significant for North America. Regarding access to arable—crop-producing—land, each individual in North America has an equivalent of 1.7 acres, compared with 0.8 acres in Latin America, 1.0 acres in Europe, 0.6 acres in Africa, and 0.4 acres in Asia.

The populations of different regions have different effects on the natural resources of the world. Concerns have been raised about the impact of unequal utilization of natural resources on the environment. Out of this concern, an interest in measuring the carbon footprint of societies and individuals developed. A **carbon footprint** is "the impact our activities have on the environment, and, in particular, climate change. This relates to the amount of greenhouse gases produced in our day-to-day lives through burning fossil fuels for electricity, heating, and transportation" (Carbon Footprint Ltd., 2008).

The chart below illustrates the unequal carbon footprints of different regions of the world, as measured by population versus the amount of carbon emissions.

From these statistics we see that North America—the United States in particular—consumes a disproportionate amount of the world's natural resources. One final comparison will be noted: Developing countries in the world hold approximately 79 percent of the world's population and emit approximately 41.4 percent of the world's

carbon dioxide. This compares with the approximately 12 percent of the world's population that reside in developed countries and produce a similar amount of carbon dioxide emissions. It is this disproportionate production of carbon dioxide that has raised international concerns about the impact on the environment, specifically global warming, by the world community (United Nations Development Programme, 2008).

Our final trend affecting population is related to HIV/AIDS infection rates. It is estimated that 5.4 percent of the adult population in Uganda is infected with HIV, and in urban centers the rate is much higher (10.1 percent). Although rates of infection appear to have stabilized, the impact on the population of Uganda has been the death of approximately one million people and a significantly reduced life expectancy. The labor force has been depleted, which affects agricultural productivity, and the health care and educational sectors of the economy have been weakened. Furthermore, the epidemic has resulted in more than one million orphans, and a disproportionate number of women are affected, representing 59 percent of all those infected (Avert, 2008). South Africa has a very high prevalence of HIV/AIDS (21.5 percent) (CIA, 2008). It is estimated that of those people under age 24, 23 percent

**TABLE 13.5** Unequal Carbon Footprints

|  | Population | Carbon Emissions |
|---|---|---|
| **Canada** | 0.5% | 2.2% |
| **Central and Eastern Europe** | 6.4% | 11.0% |
| **East Asia and the Pacific** | 30.2% | 23.0% |
| **Latin America and the Caribbean** | 8.5% | 4.9% |
| **South Africa** | 0.7% | 1.5% |
| **South Asia** | 24.0% | 7.0% |
| **United States** | 4.0% | 21.1% |
| **Other Areas** | 25.70% | 29.30% |

Source: United Nations Development Programme, 2008.

are HIV positive. This high rate of infection, combined with a younger age of infection, was projected to result in two million orphans by 2010 (Malebo, 2002). While such a large number of orphans were projected, China's Ministry of Health estimates that there were only 100,000 AIDS orphans in China, while UNICEF's office in China estimates that a range of 150,000 to 250,000 will be added to that number in China within the next five years (Chelala, 2010). The HIV/AIDS epidemic shows how a health-related issue can affect death rates and life expectancy for an entire population.

# Theories Related to Population Dynamics

As we begin to examine theories related to population dynamics, it is important to recall the distinction between a theory and the theoretical perspectives used within the discipline of sociology. A theory attempts to explain a particular social behavior, and the next section will be an exploration of the theories that explain population dynamics. These explanations will draw on two classic theoretical perspectives, drawing on the works of Malthus and Marx, that attempt to explain population dynamics, as well as a more contemporary perspective based on the works of Nam. In contrast, the theoretical perspectives presented near the end of this chapter provide the overarching framework for sociological study.

## Classic Approaches

Most sociologists credit Thomas R. Malthus for presenting the first significant theory about population and population changes. The foundations of Malthus' position were that "(1) the rapid growth of population would outstrip the resources needed to provide for it; and (2) this growth was due to the excess of births over deaths" (Nam, 1994, p. 33). Malthus recognized the necessity of resources, most notably food, as well as the reality of the birthing process, thus including the sexual drives found and expressed within the human condition. As a result of these two population dynamics, Malthus believed that population numbers would increase geometrically, while food and sustenance production would increase only arithmetically. Additionally, he believed that humans would be limited by sustenance issues. Furthermore, he believed that a set of preventative checks would address these issues. For example, preventative checks might include unsafe occupations, difficult labor circumstances, extreme poverty and diseases, military conflict, and famine—all of which result in deaths. Malthus believed that excesses were also part of population balance, particularly moral excesses. He proposed a number of checks and balances to address some of these issues, beginning with restraining excesses through willful acts or by avoiding behaviors that may predispose a person to the miseries noted. Thus, moral restraint becomes a positive preventative check in dealing with these issues (Nam, 1994).

In response to the writings of Malthus, Karl Marx and Friedrich Engels became his antagonists. Rather than directly challenging Malthus' dynamics of population growth and population sustenance, Marx and Engels, being true to their fundamental class position, believed that population pressures really resided within the social dimensions of one's "means of employment." Consequently, population growth dynamics are continually relevant because each stage of development will have a "law" related to population dynamics. In capitalist societies, there is often a surplus population of laborers that exceeds the needs of production demands. Regarding the surplus population, Marx and Engels maintained that Malthus failed to recognize potential progress within the sciences that could address related sustenance issues and, thus, meet the needs of a population. Additionally, the ideas of Marx, although modified, are seen within democratic socialism, which makes provisions for the less fortunate within a society based on their social class standing.

The Chinese sociologist Zheng noted that a society can exercise plans to control overpopulation dynamics, in particular population reduction, "in line with the needs of the developing social productive forces" (Nam, 1994, p. 72). We can clearly see the influences of Marx and Engels within these positions articulated for Chinese society.

## A Contemporary Approach

While the writings of Malthus, Marx and Engels provide the classic theoretical foundations, it was Charles B. Nam (1994) who articulated theoretical positions of population dynamics at the macro, micro, and medial sociological levels, thus reflecting the three dominant perspectives of analysis within the discipline of sociology. Nam provided four macro perspectives that allow us to understand population dynamics at the aggregate or societal level. These perspectives include an ecological, a sociocultural, and a modernization approach, and a final approach that is institutional in nature.

The ecological perspective is based on the position that organisms adapt biologically to their environments, in this case referring to human beings adapting to their geographical areas. This approach uses a framework of technology, natural environment, and social organization. In contrast, the sociocultural position recognizes both the social and cultural dimensions of the human system as shaping demographic processes. The nature of values within a society and how these values influence where people live is of particular interest, as is how reproductive patterns are influenced by these residential choices. The third macro approach, modernization, recognizes divisions of labor within social

institutions and how traditions are modernized and transformed. Thus, it is through the process of modernization that adaptations to living conditions are incorporated in societies and communities. The final macro approach stresses the connection between population changes and the institutional forms and mechanisms that are created within this environment. One example would be the changes within the economic system that allow for improvements within health care institutions, resulting in extending life expectancy.

In contrast to these macro positions, Nam (1994) articulated a micro-level position focusing on the decision-making processes within any small group situation that includes individuals and couples. At the micro level, it is the questions regarding population dynamics that must be answered by an individual or a couple that are most relevant. Such questions might involve the number of children desired and the types of family planning to be utilized. The sociological, psychological, economic and cultural factors that may influence these decision-making processes might also be included.

Nam concluded his examination by noting two medial approaches for understanding population changes and dynamics. His first medial approach, the normative perspective, recognizes that there are changes in societal norms at either the micro

**TABLE 13.6** Demographic Statistics for Africa

| 2011 Demographic Statistics | Rwanda | South Africa | Sudan | Uganda |
|---|---|---|---|---|
| Crude Birthrate (per 1,000 population) | 36.74 | 19.46 | 36.12 | 47.49 |
| Total Fertility Rate (per woman) | 4.9 | 2.3 | 4.89 | 6.69 |
| Crude Death Rate (per 1,000 population) | 9.88 | 17.09 | 11 | 11.71 |
| Infant Mortality Rate (per 1,000 live births) | 64.04 | 43.2 | 68.07 | 62.47 |
| Life Expectancy - All (at birth) | 58.02 | 49.33 | 55.48 | 53.24 |
| Life Expectancy - Male (at birth) | 56.57 | 50.24 | 54.18 | 52.17 |
| Life Expectancy - Female (at birth) | 59.52 | 48.39 | 56.71 | 54.33 |
| Sex Ratio (at birth, males/females) | 1.03 | 1.02 | 1.05 | 1.03 |
| Sex Ratio (under 15 years, males/females) | 1.01 | 1.00 | 1.04 | 1.01 |
| Sex Ratio (15 - 64 years, males/females) | .99 | 1.02 | 1.01 | 1.01 |
| Sex Ratio (65 and over, males/females) | 0.67 | 0.68 | 1.05 | 0.7 |
| Sex Ratio (total population, males/females) | 0.99 | 0.99 | 1.03 | 1.01 |
| NET Migration Rate (per 1,000 population) | 1.06 | -6.89 | -0.29 | -0.02 |

Source: The 2011 World Factbook, CIA.

or macro level that might emerge in response to these dynamics. Changes in the norms then have an impact on the social world at the micro or macro level. Nam's second medial approach involves socialization processes, which relates to the normative perspective. As norms emerge, individuals and societies must be socialized into the emergent normative framework. Consequently, socialization is a mechanism for disseminating the new normative processes within a society.

The classic and modern theories used to understand population changes demonstrate that there are a variety of ways from which to frame these issues. Just as with the sociological theoretical perspectives and paradigms that dominate the discipline, we're cautioned not to rely on one theoretical explanation to offer a conclusive explanation for population changes and dynamics. Thus, we must conclude that these theories and theoretical frameworks should be utilized as a way of deepening our understanding of the relevant issues.

# Theoretical Perspectives: Differing Views of Population Issues

As we examine each sociological topic, it is important to recall our foundational discussions of the three dominant sociological perspectives or paradigms within the discipline of sociology. Remembering that each perspective is a way of viewing the social world and not necessarily the "correct" way of viewing the social world, we now examine how each of these three theoretical perspectives views population dynamics, beginning with structural functionalism.

## Structural Functionalism

Structural functionalism asserts that within societies there is a great deal of social stability and harmony, which promote a state of homeostasis. However, it is recognized that manifest functions can sometimes be dysfunctional if they promote social instability or disharmony. In addition, there are latent, or unintended, functions that can also be either functional or dysfunctional for a society. China's one-child-per-family policy will be used

to analyze structural functionalism. China formalized its one-child policy as a means of controlling the country's population growth. Therefore, this policy had manifest functions of controlling the population, limiting the effects of population dynamics, preventing a population explosion, and protecting the sociocultural and economic resources of the country. From this perspective, it can be argued that the one-child policy was functional for China because it resulted in the direct control of population growth. While functional in this capacity, it can also be argued that the one-child policy is, at the least, potentially dysfunctional because it can create an imbalance of male-to-female birth ratios, with substantially more males born than what is normally seen in societies. Scholars believe that this imbalance may have resulted from sex-selective abortions, female infanticide, or the nonregistration of female births (Rosenberg, 2008). In response, China outlawed the practice of sex-selecting abortions. Another direct response from the Chinese government has been to allow families to have two children if the first child is a girl, modifying its one-child-only policy while not officially abandoning it (Research Directorate, 2007). A latent function of China's policy, which may prove dysfunctional, is its effect on divorced individuals. Technically, divorced and remarried individuals are not allowed to have a child if their spouse has a child. This policy has been modified in Shanghai, and divorced individuals are no longer required to wait for years before having a child (Watts, 2004). These examples illustrate the nature of manifest and latent functions and dysfunctions of the one-child-per-family policy in China.

## Social Conflict

Before exploring the specific conflict tensions within the anti-abortion and pro-choice positions, let's first establish that abortion, to a certain degree, is a scarce resource. While the U.S. Supreme Court decision in *Roe v. Wade* established a legal right for women to have abortions, both the states and federal government have enacted measures to limit the use of this right. At the federal level, the Hyde Amendment, passed by Congress in 1976, ".... excludes abortion from the comprehensive health care services provided to low-income people by the federal government through Medicaid." Additionally, soon after the passage of the 2010 health care bill by Congress, President Obama signed an executive order "....designed to ensure that no federal money can be used for elective abortions under the nation's new health care law" (Werner, 2010). This is now occurring in a context where most Americans will be required to have health insurance but will be denied access to a legal medical procedure through those mandated plans of coverage.

Facts and initiatives at state levels further substantiate that abortion is a scarce resource. The Guttmacher Institute (2010) notes that as of 2005 there were no abortion providers in 87 percent of counties in the United States, with one-third of all women living in these counties. In Mississippi, the geographic scarcity is even more pronounced,

where 99 percent of counties in that state have no doctors or facilities providing abortions, with 91 percent of women in that state living in those counties. Additionally, although the state had two providers of abortions services in 2005, a 2010 online search found that Mississippi by then had only one clinic providing abortion services to the women of that state.

Additional state initiatives to limit abortions include: Nebraska's 2010 law that sought to establish fetal pain as the point at which abortion rights are limited, Tennessee's restriction on abortion coverage in any health exchange programs in the state and 22 states' legislation to increase required counseling and/or waiting periods for abortions (Young, 2010). It now seems appropriate to explore the conflict perspective by examining the positions of the anti-abortion and pro-choice movements. Although

Source: Andre Kiwitz

Do you support the Chinese government's one-child per family policy? Why or why not?

the classic social conflict perspective articulated by Marx involved tensions between the social classes, modern conflict theory seeks to identify relevant social tensions between various groups in society. Groups struggle to obtain, and eventually maintain, power once they control a particular scarce resource in a society. Struggles for power, therefore, often enter the political and social institutions of a society. As it relates to population dynamics, there is no more salient example of social conflict than in the tensions expressed by the anti-abortion and pro-choice communities. The groups associated with each of these positions determine their meaning within the social conflict paradigm.

In its mission statement, the National Right to Life organization defines its ultimate goal as "to restore legal protection to innocent human life." Although concerned with this central issue, it includes within its mission statement the "related matters of medical ethics which relate to the right to life issues of euthanasia and infanticide." The social organization, founded in 1973 as a nonsectarian and nonpartisan organization, believes that it has been influential within legislative reforms, particularly at the national level. At that level, it has contributed to the ban on non-therapeutic experimentation on unborn and newborn babies, as well as the establishment of a federal conscience clause that allows medical personnel the right to refuse to participate in abortion procedures. The organization also reported being successful at advancing various amendments to appropriation bills limiting the use of federal funds for abortions and related research, both in the United States and overseas. The National Right to Life organization has also helped to pass laws in 11 states that require a woman seeking an abortion to view an ultrasound of her unborn fetus.

In contrast to this position, Planned Parenthood "is committed to protecting and defending women's access to the full range of reproductive health care—including access to abortion. Decisions about childbearing are to be made by women, their families, and their doctors—not politicians." Planned Parenthood says choice is central to maintaining reproductive rights and maintains that it will work within the states, at the federal level, and around the

world to "protect every woman's right to make her own decisions about childbearing." Planned Parenthood states that those who are anti-abortion "extremists" push for restrictions on basic health care and "harass women seeking preventative family planning services." Such individuals and organizations are also accused of supporting abstinence-only programs that deny medically accurate information about preventing unintended pregnancies or sexually transmitted infections. Planned Parenthood also maintains that anti-abortion groups distort information regarding birth control safety, condom effectiveness, and the side effects of abortion. Planned Parenthood goes on to mention that it fights "anti-choice extremism," by advocating common-sense policies at all levels. Finally, it highlights that the legislative lobbyists at Planned Parenthood attempt to protect everyone from what it calls intrusive laws through use of the court system.

While *Roe v. Wade* established the constitutionality of abortion within the United States, it is clear from the foregoing presentations of both the National Right to Life organization and Planned Parenthood that conflict and tensions still exist over the use of abortion and other population control procedures. The scarce resource involved in this ongoing struggle is often identified as abortion, and the conflict is fueled by the question, "When does life begin?" However, the positions of both organizations, as well as their interventions within the sociopolitical arena, show that the scarce resource is really the power to choose what happens once fertilization occurs and who will have it—government or women?

## Symbolic Interactionism

The symbols that are used when discussing various sociological and societal concepts are a foundation of the symbolic interactionism perspective. Just as important is how interactions at a micro social perspective create, maintain, and also change the social world.

We only need to return to the first part of this chapter to begin to understand the various symbols associated with population dynamics. Recall that we defined a number of key concepts and terms related to the study of the population, beginning with the use of the term demography or demographics as the area of study regarding population. The use of each definitional term is merely a symbolic representation of a meaning that can be used by demographers (and you as a student of sociology) to understand the issues and dynamics of population studies. Yet, the nature of symbols goes beyond their operational definitions and can often reflect sociocultural and political tensions with a society.

Though abortion is legal in the United States, considerable symbolic tensions remain regarding its utilization. The symbolic camps in the United States are commonly referred to as either pro-life or pro-choice. It is clear that each of these terms communicates a great deal symbolically, using meanings that are significant for individuals and social movements. Not only are these words symbolic socially, they are value-laden within the political arena, particularly in the United States. The symbolic value of these words is clearly seen when political candidates are asked to state their positions as either pro-life or pro-choice.

Returning to the earlier discussion of China's one-child-per-family policy, we can see a clear illustration of the creation, maintenance, and change of a social policy dealing with the attempt to control a population. While the policy in China was developed at a macro sociological level, it was the dynamics at the micro sociological level that appear to have motivated changes in the country's official childbearing policy. For example, the creation of the policy was the apparent result of individuals in China choosing to give birth to children at a rate that was exponentially increasing China's population. Because of these individual choices, China had to address the situation, resulting in its one-child policy. After establishing its policy, China also needed to maintain it and did so through the imposition of fines for violators. Social circumstances like divorces, remarriages and the deaths of children resulting from the 2008 earthquake led China to change its policy in response to the child-rearing challenges faced by individuals and families who lost children through death or divorce.

# Summary

This chapter presents two distinct, yet related, sociological concepts—the health care system and population dynamics. Students of sociology must remember that the foundation of any society is its inhabitants and the population issues that exist, or emerge, within that social context. There is an inherent drive for every society to perpetuate itself, not only for intrinsic psychological reasons, but as a means of perpetuating a cultural way of life. The perpetuation of life is affected by birth and death rates, immigration and emigration patterns, and social policies. The existence of overpopulation or underpopulation can place stresses on not only the economy but also the social institutions of a society. These population tensions are often addressed by a variety of social institutions.

One institution tasked with addressing population issues is the health care system. The central task, or function, of the health care institution is to maintain a healthy population for the well-being of society. A healthy population allows for the development of a strong economic sector within a society, and a strong economy promotes the maintenance of the social contract for inter-generational support and care. This well-being and care are the motivating factors for some form of comprehensive or universal health care as seen in socialized, and often democratic, societies. In the United States, the health care system can become a significant factor within the economic sector because of the increasing costs associated with providing technologically advanced health care to all of its citizens, and the inability of citizens to pay these costs.

We can see a complexity regarding the health care institution and population dynamics and the various theories that attempt to explain these issues. Just as with the rest of the discipline of sociology, these issues have multiple orientations and dimensions. Within the health care institution, this is seen in the diversity of systems utilized to meet the needs of various societies. A further demarcation of sociological diversity is presented through the exposition of the three classic theoretical perspectives of the discipline and how each views either population dynamics or the health care institution.

Students should leave this chapter with a solid foundational knowledge of the sociological dynamics in societies regarding population issues and health care institutions. Within this disciplinary foundation, you should be able to articulate the diverse ways in which both of these social dimensions of life can be viewed within the discipline of sociology. Grasping this complexity will ground you well as an emergent sociologist.

## Review/Discussion Questions

1. What is the sick role?
2. How does the U.S. model of health care differ from the socialized-medicine model?
3. Which health care model do you prefer and why?
4. What is demography?
5. What factors contribute to underpopulation?
6. A hundred years from now, do you think the life expectancy in the United States will be higher or lower than it is today?

## Key Terms

**Alternative health care professionals** are individuals providing care outside the mainstream or western modalities of health care.

**Carbon footprint** is the impact a person's activities have on the environment in general and climate change in particular.

**Clinical nurse extenders** are individuals who are trained and licensed to provide a limited level of nursing care.

**Crude birthrate** is the number of live births in a year per 1,000 people during a given time period in a defined geographical area.

**Crude death rate** is the total number of deaths per 1,000 people during a given time period in a defined geographical area.

**Decentralized national health care** is a system in which the government functions primarily as a regulator.

**Demographers** are sociologists who investigate population characteristics.

**Demography** is the study of the characteristics of human populations, including the increases and decreases caused by migration, fertility and mortality.

**Direct pay model** is a system wherein individuals are legally responsible for paying all of their own health care costs.

**Existentialist perspective** asserts that individuals are responsible for their own health care issues.

**General fertility rates** measure the number of live births divided by the female population aged 15 to 44 years (childbearing years), times 1,000.

**Human migration** is the permanent movement of individuals or groups across symbolic or political boundaries into new residential areas and communities.

**Infant mortality rate** is the number of deaths within the first year of life, divided by the number of live births in the same year, times 1,000.

**Life expectancy** is the number of years that a person can expect to live within a given society, or as the number of further years of life a person can expect at a given age.

**Marriage rate** is the number of marriages per 1,000 people in a given time period.

**Medical perspective** focuses on the medical framework that attempts to examine pathogens that result in disease and illness.

**Overpopulation** is the population by a particular species in excess of the environment's carrying capacity.

**Physician extenders** are secondary health care providers who can provide basic physical diagnosis and care.

**Primary care providers** are physicians who can practice medicine in "all of its branches."

**Secondary care providers** include professionals who extend the services of doctors.

**Sex ratios** are the number of males per 1,000 females in the population of the society.

**Sick roles** involve a variety of social norms specifying the responsibilities, expectations, and rights of someone who is ill.

**Socialized medicine** is composed of health care systems over which the government exercises some, but not total, control.

**Socialist medicine** involves a system of health care that is under the complete control of the government.

**Sociocultural perspective** views health issues as the responsibility not only of each individual, but also of their family members and sometimes even their community.

**Standard mortality ratio** is a measure indicating the actual or observed number of deaths in the group of interest, divided by the expected number of deaths, then multiplied by 100.

**Underpopulation** is the lack of normal or desirable population density for economic viability.

# Bibliography

Abortion TV (2006, September 7). European Countries Have Underpopulation Problem Because of Abortion. <http://www.abortiontv.com/Lies%20&%20Myths/underpopulation.htm> (2008).

Abercrombie, N., Hill, S., & Turner, B. S. (1994). The Penguin Dictionary of Sociology (3rd ed.). New York: Penguin Books.

American Civil Liberties Union (2004). Public Funding for Abortion. July, 21. <www.aclu.org/reproductive-freedom/public-funding-abortion> (2010).

Avert (2008). HIV and AIDS in Uganda. <www.avert.org/aidsuganda.htm> (2008).

Blankenship, K. (1998, Summer). A race, class, and gender analysis of thriving. Journal of Social Issues, 54 (2), 393-403.

Butler, C. D. (2004). Human Carrying Capacity and Human Health. Public Library of Science, 1 (3), e55. (doi:10.1371/Journal.pmed.0010055)

Carbon Footprint, Ltd. (2008). What is a Carbon Footprint? <www.carbonfootprint.com/carbonfootprint.html> (2008).

Central Intelligence Agency (2008). The 2008 World Factbook. <https://www.cia.gov/library/publications/the-world-factbook/index.html> (2008).

Central Intelligence Agency (2011). The 2011 World Factbook. <.https://www.cia.gov/library/publications/the-world-factbook/index.html> (2012).

Chelala, C. (2010). "AIDS Orphans in China." The Epoch Times, Sunday, April 11, 2010.

China.org.cn (2009). Beijing may get Yangtze water in 2014. <http://www.china.org.cn/china/news/2009-01/14/content_17104224.htm> (2009).

Cockerham, W. (1995). Medical Sociology (6th ed.). Englewood Cliffs, NJ: Prentice Hall.

ConsumerAffairs.com (2007, August 6). Study Finds 24% of Americans Underinsured. <http://www.consumeraffairs.com/news04/2007/08/cu_insurance.html> (2008).

Cook, J. (1999, December 5). Population Control and Consequences in China. <http://maps.unomaha.edu/peterson/funda/sidebar/chinapop.html> (2008).

Currie, D. (2007, September 28). Population Wars, Why Europe's demography is more complicated than you think. The Weekly Standard.

Democratic Policy Committee (2005). <http://democrats.senate.gov/dpc/dpc-printable.cfm?doc_name=fs-109-1-85-9k> (2008).

Eberstadt, N. (2001, May 18). Underpopulation, Not Overpopulation, the Real Global Problem. The Washington Post.

Gilland, B. (2008). What is Overpopulation? <http://www.globalpolitician.com/print.asp?id=4818> (2008).

Grinnell College (2008). <www.grinnell.edu> (2008).

Guilmoto, C. Z. (2012). Skewed Sex Ratios at Birth and Future Marriage Squeeze in China and India, 2005-2100. Demography, 49 (1), 77-100.

Guttmacher Institute (2010). <www.guttmacher.org/pubs/sfaa/mississippi.html> (2010).

Henderson, L. J. (1935). Physician and patient as a social system. New England Journal of Medicine, 212, 819-823.

Illinois Compiled Statutes (2008). <http://www.ilga.gov/legislation/ilcs/ilcs.asp> (2008).

Kaneda, T. (2006). China's Concern Over Population Aging and Health. <http://www.prb.org/articles/2006/chinasconcernoverpopulationagingandhealth.aspx?.=1> (2008).

Khan, R. (2010). Which American Racial Group has the Lowest Fertility? Discover Magazine. <http://blogs.discovermagazine.com/gnxp/2010/09/which-american-racial-group-has-the-lowest-fertility/> (2011).

LeBlanc, B. (2000). Health Responsibility Model: Promoting Responsible Health from the Human Factor Perspective. Review of Human Factor Studies, 5, (1-2), 43-58.

LeBlanc, B. (2006). Health. Everyday Sociology (5th ed.). Elmhurst, IL: Starpoint Press.

Los Angeles Times (2008, March 16). Russia's outdated healthcare mired in corruption. <http://articles.latimes.com/2008/mar/16/world/fg-russia16plr> (2008).

Malebo, W. (2002). Country Statement on Population Matters, Policies, and Interventions, Reproductive Rights and Health, with Special Reference to HIV/AIDS. Conference on Population and Development Programme of Action, Yaounde, Cameroon.

Maloof, R. (2008). Men: The Stronger Sex? <http://health.msn.com/print.aspx?cp-documentid=100204784&page=0> (2008).

Massachusetts Trial Court Libraries (2008, October 15). Mass Law About Health Insurance. <http://www.lawlib.state.ma.us/healthinsurance.html> (2008).

Miller, B. (1997, October). Educating the "other" children-education of illegal immigrants may be necessary. American Demographics, pp. 49–54.

Mufson, S. (2010). "As economy booms, China faces major water shortage." The Washington Post, March 16, 2010.

Nam, C. (1994). Understanding Population Change. Itasca, IL: FE Peacock Publishers.

National Right to Life (2008). <http://www.nrlc.org> (2008).

Parsons, T. (1951). The Social System. New York: Free Press.

Planned Parenthood Federation of America (2008). <www.plannedparenthood.org> (2008).

Population Connection (2007). Teaching Population: Hands-on Activities [CD-ROM]. <http://www.populationeducation.org/index.php?option=com_content&task=view&id=174&Itemid=10> (2008).

Research Directorate, Immigration and Refugee Board of Canada, Ottawa (2007, June 26). Responses to Information Requests: China: Treatment of "illegal," or "black," children born outside the one-child family planning policy; whether unregistered children are denied access to education, health care and other social services (2003-2007). <http://www.irb-cisr.gc.ca/en/research/rir/?action=record.viewrec&gotorec=451354> (2008).

Reynolds, J., & Ross, C. (1998, May). Social stratification and health: education's benefit beyond economic status and social origins. Social Problems, 45 (2), 221-247.

Rosenberg, M. (2008, June 18). China's One Child Policy. About.com: Geography. <http://geography.about.com/od/populationgeography/a/onechild.htm?p=1> (2008).

Scott, J., & Marshall, G. (Ed.). (2005). Oxford Dictionary of Sociology. New York, NY: Oxford University Press.

Smith, D. E. (2008, March 1). The World's Underpopulation. <http://illinoisreview.typepad.com/illinoisreview/2008/03/under-population.html> (2008).

Starr, P. (1982). The Social Transformation of American Medicine. New York: Basic Books.

Theil, R. (2003, August 9). Compromises and Betrayals: How the So-Called California Naturopathic Physicians are Digging a Hole to Bury the Natural Health Movement. <http://naturalsolutionsradio.com/articles/article.html?id=6639&filter=topic> (2009).

Thompson, B. (2000). Ecotracs, Salt Lake City, Utah. <www.ssc.wisc.edu/~jraymo/links/soc674/674_3.pdf> (2009).

United Nations Development Programme (2008). Human Development Reports. <http://hdr.undp.org/external/flash/shares> (2008).

U.S. Census Bureau (2012). <http://www.census.gov/population/popclockworld.html> (2012).

Watts, J. (2004, April 14). Shanghai eases China's one-child rule. The Guardian.

Werner, E. (2010). Obama signs order blocking abortion funding. The Boston Globe, March 26, 2010. <www.boston.com/news/nation/washington/articles/2010/03/25/> (2010).

Xinhua News Agency (2006, December 12). Overpopulated Beijing Facing Water Crisis. <http://www.china.org.cn/english/environment/192116.htm> (2008).

Young, A. (2010). States seek new ways to restrict abortions. USA Today. <www.usatoday.com/cleanprint/?1272820815989> (2010).

# CHAPTER FOURTEEN

# Urban and Environmental Sociology

## John Joe Schlichtman and Chris Biga

**Chapter Objectives**

At the end of this chapter, students should be able to:

- Describe the changes that occurred in American cities over the previous two centuries.
- Consider whether natural processes, larger forces or powerful decision-makers changed the city and how these perspectives agree or conflict.
- Identify key thinkers in urban sociology and explain their unique contributions.
- Be familiar with the three functions that the physical environment provides for humans.
- Think critically about the three functions of the physical environment and how they can be overused or placed in conflict with each other.
- Describe the three primary causes of anthropogenic environmental degradation.
- Describe the different theories explaining anthropogenic environmental degradation.
- Define the basic types of environmental problems facing human civilization.

eople have considerable ability to shape our environment. In this chapter, we begin by examining how urban settlements of several million people were rapidly carved into the plains, prairies, deserts and mountains of the United States. Then we will turn to the natural environment, our interaction with it and our management of its resources.

# The City

Just about a decade ago, the world reached an important milestone: The majority of its inhabitants lived in cities. The sociological study of cities is not only fascinating but important and relevant. If you look at the table of contents of this book, you will notice that this section is the only one that focuses on a *place*. Why? Because the social processes that unfold in cities are unique, prompting sociologists to deem them worthy of separate study. Some of these processes are so distinct that we consider them explicitly *urban* processes. Some concepts we will discuss in this section are considered by many **urbanists**, or people who study cities, to be distinctly urban phenomena. Other processes are not considered distinctly urban but take on a very distinct form in cities.

We are going to examine American cities chronologically in this chapter. We also are going to examine the major scholars who discussed cities in the periods they were conducting their work. We will examine the 19th century, the early 20th century and the 1950s to the present.

As we do, we will pay attention to the immense changes in transportation, production and communications technologies that enabled the urban transformation we discuss. When I say "enabled," I mean that we will consider transportation, production and communication technologies not as the cause of change, but as human-made factors that made the change possible. I encourage the reader to keep this in mind: It is ultimately *people* who change cities in response to different factors.

## American Cities in the 19th Century

At the dawn of the 19th century, less than 4 percent of the nation resided in communities of 8,000 people or more. But human-made transportation networks, such as rail, road and canal systems, were beginning to expand, and they intersected with waterways at the riverfronts, coasts and lakefronts of the nation's largest populations. The land located at these new intersections would become quite valuable, and powerful business leaders and politicians fought to ensure that these points were located on land that they owned or were in their districts.

Cities began to have more regular and dependable access to the resources of other places. They were becoming increasingly interconnected in a network of exchange. In other words, they had the opportunity to specialize in the production of some goods while importing other goods that were produced elsewhere.

Cities were growing as a result of **agglomeration**, the location of complementary functions near one another. What does this mean in practice? Quite simply, a factory is located near a railway; a company that supplies the factory is located nearby; workers are located near these employers; and the bar these workers patronize is located near them.

Meanwhile, changes in food preservation technology allowed people to settle farther from the farm. Changes in steam-powered production technology enabled factories to be more productive. The young nation's financial technology was also evolving, so as more cities began to be built, there were increasing opportunities to fund that development.

In the second half of the 19th century, cities started changing much more rapidly. Factories were innovating their production technologies, powered by coal. Agglomeration was intensifying. The raw materials going into factories and the finished products coming out were often large and bulky. Therefore, an increasing number of suppliers, clients, warehouses and distributors started locating in proximity to the factories. Workers, who often lived a few blocks from factories, were streaming into cities as our nation moved from an agricultural economy to an industrial one. Many of them were immigrants who, shortly after their arrival, were having children. Cities were burgeoning with people.

Unskilled work was plentiful. To be clear, many jobs were horrible, and those who obtained them might risk life and limb. But the draw of work was powerful, and there was plenty to be found. After all, our nation was being built, and cities were increasingly at the center of this growth. One representative urban project during this period was the Brooklyn Bridge, which took the lives of 27 laborers.

Powerful political and business leaders utilized innovations in financial, transportation, food preservation and communication technologies to connect the nation. In 1863, the National Bank Act established a framework for a national banking system. Railways, which had expanded during the previous period, reached a major milestone in 1879 as the nation completed the first transcontinental tracks. The 1880s saw the development of the first refrigerated railroad freight car.

In 1883, New York and Boston were linked by telephone, a very important step in connecting the nation's cities with communication infrastructure.

These changes were happening in Europe as well, in cities centuries older than the young agglomerations in the United States. It is not surprising, then, that European thinkers such as Friedrich Engels were the first to grapple with this new reality. Engels' (1952) first book was *The Condition of the Working Class in England in 1844*. German-born Engels wrote it while staying in Manchester, an emerging cotton manufacturing center, for a few years during the intense growth of the Industrial Revolution. One of Engels' key arguments was that the Industrial Revolution was making workers worse off. He chronicled the "filth, ruin, and uninhabitableness, the defiance of all considerations of cleanliness, ventilation, and health" in workers' neighborhoods.

In trying to describe the impact of these economic changes on social life in Germany, Ferdinand Tönnies (1955) contrasted the **gemeinschaft** of rural communities to the **gesellschaft** of urban communities. In gemeinschaft, people are connected and organized through kinship and long-held traditions. On the other hand, gesellschaft implies that people are connected only to accomplish their own interests. Tönnies envisioned what some researchers call strong ties—long-lasting, rich, family-like relations—being replaced with weak ties—impersonal, passing interactions motivated by self-interest.

Frenchman Emile Durkheim entered this conversation with two similar ideas that also attempted to capture the difference between rural and urban life. **Mechanical solidarity** is akin to Tönnies' gemeinschaft. It is a connection based on shared values. **Organic solidarity**, like Tönnies' gesellschaft, implies interpersonal ties that are based upon the interdependence of people who rely on one another for their different economic specializations. The increasing gesellschaft of urban life meant a change in the nature of community, just as Tönnies had suggested.

Tönnies' countryman Georg Simmel's (1971) thinking was also motivated by these huge economic and social changes, but the sociologist's observations dealt more with psychology. Simmel suggested that, due to the sheer number of people living in each other's faces, urban residents are overwhelmed by stimuli—screaming people, smelly streets, noisy traffic, theft, violence, etc. To survive, they must detach from their surroundings. Simmel called this detachment the **blasé attitude**. A week in current-day New York, Paris or London makes Simmel's concept come alive. If New Yorkers responded as they might wish to every stimulus they encountered on the street, they might never accomplish anything!

Interestingly, while contemporary sociologists were observing what some might consider negative changes in community, urban neighborhoods of the late 19th and early 20th century United States are often looked back on as having very strong communities when compared with neighborhoods today. Whereas people who do not like their neighbors due to differences in culture or class generally now have the ability to leave, at the turn of the 20th century, most urbanites were constrained to live—more or less, for better or worse—on top of one another. These communities, filling with the massive wave of European immigrants in the late 19th century, were supplying factory labor. As each ethnic group came to this nation, where racial groups were traditionally categorized as either "black" or "white," most were considered (at least eventually) to be on the white side of the color line, creating a black minority and white majority. These groups, in close proximity to one another in the city, would go on to build the urban industrial unions in the next period. Racial injustice, long a critical issue simmering under the foundations of American cities, would boil over during the next century.

## American Cities in the Early 20th Century

During the first half of the 20th century, massive innovations in communication, transportation and production technologies revolutionized cities. Communication advances intensified, and 1914 saw the construction of the nation's first transcontinental phone line. Ford built its first conveyor assembly line in 1914. This was a milestone in both transportation technology and production technology. First, of course, it made automobile travel more common and ushered in the era of using trucks for goods transport. In fact, during the 1910s, the U.S. railway system reached its peak length. After this point, goods would increasingly be transported on highways rather than railways.

More important, Ford's production innovation also marked a new age of industrial **automation**, using machinery rather than human laborers to control a process. This would increase productivity and—in time—decrease the need for workers. It also began a huge change in the tide of the potential power of workers vis-à-vis owners. Well-known leader of the automobile-workers' union Walter Reuther once mentioned that an automobile executive, sounding "slightly gleeful," asked him, "How are you going to collect union dues from all these machines?"

Signs of urban growing pains were becoming evident. The industries around which cities had developed were now discontent with their old arrangements. As production technology forged ahead, and mass production took hold, some stated that the urban layout in cities that had industrialized in the 19th century was not optimal for the new production processes.

As manufacturers adopted production-line technology, they wanted their factories to look more like a "line": a long single-story building. As we have learned, however, cities had become dense with industrial agglomeration. There was not much room to expand around existing factories, nor was there much vacant land on which to build new ones. Moreover, trucks could not get in and out to make deliveries on the small city streets that had been built for horses and cars. It turns out that the way cities had been developed for early factories—with dense agglomeration—made them less than optimal for new mass-production facilities. Many urban leaders stated that change of some sort was necessary, but it was not exactly clear what form that change would take.

The seemingly "natural" changes that cities experienced in the late 1800s and early 1900s begged for analysis. The best-known American sociologists to respond to this need were based at the University of Chicago and became known as the "Chicago School." This school of thought was associated with urban thinkers Ernest Burgess, Robert Park and Louis Wirth.

Burgess was interested in the ways in which cities expand and, in that vein, proposed what he called a **concentric-zone model**. The model included five different circles ranging from an inner circle—including the downtown or "central business district"—to an outer circle of suburbs that grew along transportation routes. While Burgess felt he had found a model for how cities naturally grow, many urbanists today feel that the model did not describe a city's natural growth as much as it captured a historically and culturally specific snapshot of the American city in Burgess' era.

This idea that there is something natural about urban growth came to be connected with the Chicago School. Park (1952) was a proponent, for example, of the *ecological approach*, an idea that emphasized the natural growth and organization of cities. This term borrows from the physical science idea of ecology, which studies how living things relate to each other and the environment around them. Living things, despite their biological diversity, reach a natural equilibrium with each other and a natural balance with their environment. The ecological approach assumed that urban society, wherever it is, tends toward this same type of balance.

Like Simmel and Durkheim before him, Wirth (1995) was far more interested in the social aspects of city life. Wirth was interested in the ways that **urbanism** was a distinct "way of life," different from life in other types of communities. For Wirth, the size, density and diversity of urban populations fostered this unique way of life. The city was a place where people's connections with one another weakened, and the importance of family bonds decreased. Neighborhoods were places of isolated individuals living in anonymity. There is potentially very little significant human interaction throughout the day for city dwellers, whose interactions—in today's terms—might be limited to saying "excuse me" to a person on the street, "thank you" to the cashier at McDonald's and "sorry" to the homeless person asking for money.

But Wirth also addressed another important idea: that urbanism affects the wider society around it. If you fast-forward to the present for a moment, you could likely think of slang terms, fashions and music that originated in cities but came to be assimilated into American society as a whole. Hip-hop music, fashions and slang, more limited to urban neighborhoods 30 years ago, have long since diffused to suburban and rural areas.

Studying the communities of the mid-20th century, other contemporary observers noticed something very different from the isolation that those before them had found. Herbert Gans (1962) noted that urban residents can create smaller communities within the city, such as the one he found in his study of Boston's West End. For them, the neighborhood was an "urban village." Such neighborhoods had strong **social capital**, connections among people that cause a social cohesion. It seemed as if everyone knew each other and understood one another. Residents in such communities were in very similar life situations. In this particular neighborhood, Gans discovered, people hung out on stoops, played games in the streets, leaned out of windows and felt free to discipline other people's children. The West End in Boston was mostly Italian when Gans wrote about it. But much of what he discussed applied to black neighborhoods of the same era.

From the early 1900s to about 1970, 6 million black Americans moved out of the American South. The peak of this migration was during the period under discussion. These migrants, taking part in what is termed **The Great Migration**, were pushed by severe racial violence and the scarcity of jobs,

How strong is the social capital in your community?

Source: Kelly Schott

for which they were fighting with white workers. They were drawn by the manufacturing jobs and seemingly less violent racial context in other regions of the country. They also were recruited by manufacturing firms that wanted them to function as "strikebreakers" when white workers went on strike for better work conditions. The underlying assumption by these manufacturers, of course, was that black and white laborers would not cooperate.

Black neighborhoods such as Houston's Third Ward, Chicago's Bronzeville, New York's Harlem and other "black metropolises" around the country were full of social capital. Bankers, janitors, lawyers, beauty-shop owners and politicians all lived next-door to one another. This was partly due to the desire of black residents, many of whom had recently arrived from the South, to live in close proximity to one another just as the Italians did in Gans' West End. But as St. Clair Drake and Horace Cayton (1962) argued in their masterful critique of social ecology, there was more than just personal preference or some "natural" process at work. These black neighborhoods were **ghettos**, neighborhoods where certain racial, ethnic or religious groups are in some way forced to live. Black ghettos were created and maintained by the larger society through a web of policies that made urban segregation a national issue, not merely a Southern issue.

One such policy was **racial zoning**, which restricted residences in certain city blocks by their race. When racial zoning became illegal in 1917, homeowners took it upon themselves to "protect" their own homes. They created **racial restrictive covenants**, which were legally binding provisions on the deed of a property specifying which groups could and could not own that property. The Federal Housing Administration initially encouraged this practice, which was made illegal in 1948. The covenants were worded with language such as, "No person or persons of Asiatic, African or Negro blood, lineage, or extraction shall be permitted to occupy a portion of said property."

**Redlining** was another policy used by the federal government. It instructed banks to avoid lending within certain less "secure" neighborhoods. A racially mixed neighborhood was, in this thinking, a less secure neighborhood. Realtor "codes of ethics," ironically, were another mechanism for reinforcing the boundaries of black neighborhoods. Realtors were required to abide by certain "ethical" standards, and one of these standards often was to avoid introducing members of a race that would be detrimental to property values. It was believed that black residents hurt the value of neighborhoods.

Some real estate agents, however, took advantage of certain fears of both white and black homeowners. **Blockbusting** was a practice of local real estate agents in which they would buy a house from a white owner for one price and sell it to a black owner for a higher price. The practice was premised on the idea that the real estate agent could get the white owner to sell for a low price in the fear that a black neighborhood would soon surround him. The real estate agent could then get the black homebuyer to pay a premium with the idea that few people wanted to sell to black households.

## American Cities in the Late 20th and Early 21st Century

As with every period that we have discussed thus far, our final period from 1950 to the present has been defined by even more intense technological changes. Production is now powered by computer chips. The machines producing goods now have some level of actual intelligence. They are able not only to make the same precise motions over and over without error but also to monitor and adjust their own movement, efficiency and performance. This innovation makes the unskilled human labor that had operated the factory machinery in the past even more expendable and, in some cases, actually increases the skill required of the few people who do operate it. Manufacturers have worked to give these technologies greater control over the production process and allow for less expensive, more efficient production.

Transportation technology transformed the nation during this period, as cars became the primary mode of transportation for most Americans. Many cities built modern airports during the 1950s and 1960s, with air travel becoming increasingly more common during this modern era. Once reserved for business travelers and the wealthy, air travel is now accessible for the masses.

Communication technology seemed to be reinvented every few years during this period, with the creation of the fax machine in 1975, the cellular phone in 1983 and the Internet in the 1990s. It was a new day in communications. From 1990 to 2010, cellular subscribers increased from around 12 million to over 4.5 billion. During this time, "Internet" became a household term, and "browsing" became a daily—if not hourly—habit for many Americans.

The developed world was in a race to connect and was becoming interconnected as never before. Of course, it had been connected for many centuries, but this type of interconnectedness was different. It was deepening, broadening and speeding up.

First, places that had been connected before were becoming more interconnected. While a person could get a message from New York to London in 1800, that capability has deepened. Today, you can choose the method that you want to use. Second, tasks that had never been "global" were becoming so. As I write this in a café, there are people playing chess on their iPad with an opponent across the world. The scope of interconnectedness has broadened to include even a casual board game! Finally, this interconnectedness is speeding up. That is to say that the changes leading to this interconnectedness are occurring at a faster and faster rate. David Held and Anthony McGrew (2000) call this deepening, broadening and speeding up of worldwide interconnectedness **globalization**.

Many scholars during this era followed in the path of Drake and Cayton in linking the radical urban changes cities were witnessing not to natural processes as the Chicago School suggested but to decisions made by powerful people. Henri Lefebvre, who lived through every decade of the 20th century, was a critical urban thinker who thought about the astounding changes that occurred in cities in light of Karl Marx's theories. The political economy approach that developed from his view takes into account, as one would guess, politics and economics. This approach applies Marxist analysis of the conflict over scarce resources to the urban context. David Harvey (1973, 1982, 1985) and Manuel Castells (1977, 1983) both analyzed the city as a **built environment**, the totality of human-made physical structures that provides the environment for human activity.

The built environment, Harvey explained, is constantly experiencing waves of restructuring due to firms' constant consideration of the profitability of new locations over current ones.

Capitalists, who in Marx's view are those who control society's means of production, shape the built environment to maximize profits. As places became more interconnected during this period, the ability of businesses to relocate to places that were more profitable increased. We term this state in the global economy in which profit-seeking enterprises are able to move where it is most profitable **capital mobility**. According to David Gordon (1982), manufacturers did not leave the city in the previous period simply in pursuit of more-efficient factories and cheaper land, as many suggested, but also to *escape* strong urban unions that demanded better working conditions. Suburbanization to Gordon, then, had much more to do with the interests of

capitalists than the consumer tastes of American homeowners.

If you think about it, the ability of a firm to locate anywhere in the world is a very recent development. One of the first types of businesses to act on this capital mobility was manufacturing firms. In the previous period, manufacturing leaders realized that the old urban layout was not the most efficient fit for factories built for the latest mass production. Over time, rapidly advancing production, communication and transportation technology enabled these firms to relocate. Many did, resulting in the removal or reduction of manufacturing activity in urban regions in what was the first stage of **deindustrialization**.

As these changes became apparent, economist Robert Reich (1992) created a useful typology of jobs to help classify their level of capital mobility. *Routine production* jobs require repetitive physical or mental tasks. These jobs, such as those in manufacturing, demand few social skills and little education. *In-person services* require physically or mentally repetitive tasks, but also require contact with customers. Positions such as cashier, administrative assistant or call center worker require some people skills but do not require high amounts of education. *Symbolic-analytic service* jobs, such as attorneys, financial analysts, accountants and marketing strategists, involve creative problem solving and complex strategy. These are the high-education, high-skills service jobs of the current economy. They are better known among urbanists by what sociologist Saskia Sassen (1991) terms them: **advanced producer services**. The first two types of jobs, which do not involve much skill, are most prone to elimination or relocation and therefore to lower wages.

The most vulnerable jobs are in manufacturing: This was the first industry to move out of American cities to places where production was potentially cheaper. For a typical manufacturer, the first move out of the city may have been to the suburbs; then perhaps to a rural area in the same state; then to the **Sunbelt** states; then eventually out of the country altogether.

The Sunbelt is a loosely defined area of the Southern and Western United States that generally has cheaper land, cheaper wages (often because workers are not unionized) and lower taxes (sometimes because these states offer high tax breaks). Sunbelt states saw a huge increase in population during this period as the Northeastern and Midwestern cities that people were leaving became known as the **Rustbelt**.

In-person services may not be as vulnerable to capital mobility as manufacturing because they require some customer contact. But "customer contact" is, as we know, relative. Have you ever called your neighborhood bank branch and had to talk to a computerized customer service representative? Have you ever skipped the cashier line at the grocery store and checked out at the self-checkout computer? These services are not so "in-person" anymore.

While they certainly could not imagine the scope, many American urban leaders saw these changes coming. In the 1950s, they began discussing what the city would look like without factories. These thinkers envisioned it as a place that no longer made tangible items but rather focused on the exchange of ideas and *services*, both non-tangible products. Rather than factories, for instance, the city would be filled with the corporate headquarters that run the companies that own the factories.

The policies that cities utilized to orchestrate what they viewed as the necessary transformation of the city were called **urban renewal**. Urban renewal was funded by the Housing Act of 1949, legislation originally intended to demolish inferior housing and replace it with more humane housing. The act called for the removal of "blighted" housing and provided federal funds for two-thirds of the cost of preparing the land it stood on for another use. Increasingly, however, the new use was not housing at all. Instead, city leaders often used urban renewal funds to create amenities that they saw as being important for the service-centered city after manufacturing, or the *postindustrial city.*

About half of Boston's West End, the area Gans studied, was demolished in urban renewal. This story was repeated around the nation. Cities used urban renewal's federal funding and invoked their authority of **eminent domain**, the power

of the government to seize private land for the public good. City leaders, who viewed these neighborhoods as slums, felt they had to go. In retrospect, it appears that the ideas of "slum" and "blight" were less attached to the quality of housing and more attached to the perceived "quality" of the residents in the housing.

After all, the neighborhoods being cleared could not be completely bereft of value. Cities wanted to acquire land that would be attractive for a new development once a neighborhood was demolished. Some scholars termed this balance of finding a neighborhood that is not so bad but bad enough to be classified as "blighted" as "the blight that's right." Close to 400,000 units of housing were destroyed by urban renewal, but because housing was often replaced with non-residential structures, such as parking garages, there was not nearly enough housing built in its place. And the housing built was often not only in a different community than the housing destroyed but also cost more to rent or own.

Urban renewal illustrated a simple but important idea highlighted by John Logan and Harvey Molotch (1987), the idea that the city is a *"growth machine"* utilized by powerful actors for their benefit. Included in the growth machine are **speculators**, people who buy land hoping it will increase in value. **Real estate developers**, other growth machine actors, build on the land to make it more profitable. Politicians benefit not only from the increased taxes that development brings but also from the attention-grabbing headlines that come with it. For this reason, Logan and Molotch rightly included the media as part of this growth coalition because they are able to build consensus for urban development projects.

The growth machine members, Logan and Molotch argued, assess the **exchange value** of land: how much it is or could be worth monetarily. Residents, on the other hand, appreciate the **use value** of property, the value they experience in using the spaces for resident-centered housing, community meeting places or houses of worship. Use value and exchange value, the thinking goes, are in conflict. Such conflict was very apparent during urban renewal.

Jane Jacobs (1961) played a major role in the fight against urban renewal. Jacobs is known as a public intellectual because she, a self-trained urbanist with a high school education, linked the conversations of urbanists to the typical resident and the conversations of the typical resident to urbanists. She argued that the types of neighborhoods destroyed by urban renewal were precisely the objective, not the problem. Such city blocks, with people sitting out in front of their house, watching their children play in the street and hanging out of windows observing the action, are safe, healthy neighborhoods.

When a city block features many kinds of uses with mostly "respectable" people coming and going, this combined bustle of community serves as the "eyes on the street," making sure order is maintained. Jacobs and others like her contributed to the end of this period of American urban renewal, which wound down by about 1974. Much of the American public had turned on the wholesale destruction of neighborhoods, with some activists pointing to the ethnic and racial discrimination that were a part of this process. As black novelist James Baldwin stated, urban renewal amounted to "Negro removal."

There was certainly truth to this statement: White middle-class urban leaders utilized urban renewal to remove areas they considered blight. As stated earlier, "blight" often had little to do with housing and much to do with the people in the housing. Some of the properties leveled during this time, with their oak, marble and wrought-iron detail, would have cost millions of dollars in today's economy (and those that were saved do): They were structurally and architecturally valuable.

As industry was leaving and urban leaders were orchestrating the reinvention of the city, the Federal Highway Act of 1956 was passed by Congress. The act, which was drafted to develop highways between cities, created more than 40,000 miles of highway. Due to pressure by urban leaders who wanted assistance connecting their own regions, 20 percent of the highway system was actually within metropolitan areas. The highway system was about

90 percent federally funded, with the rest coming from states. The funding for thousands of miles of highways within metropolitan areas provided a means for cities to connect their downtown with their outlying areas, but it also gave leaders another method by which they could eliminate undesired neighborhoods.

This high-speed connection of the city with its periphery paved the way for the development of the American suburb. Federal policies that encouraged suburban development helped reshape the city. One such policy was the **mortgage interest deduction**, which allowed homeowners to deduct the money they paid in mortgage interest and property tax from their income when they calculated their federal income taxes. This bonus for owning a home, which still exists, was available only on new construction in its early years, making most city dwellers ineligible.

All of these massive changes and important policies together resulted in an opportunity and— some might say—an invitation to leave the city. People responded. The urban exodus that resulted was profound. Manufacturing plants moved to the suburbs, where land was plentiful and new, cutting-edge factories could be built. The middle class moved to the suburbs in droves. Stores, restaurants and other establishments followed the middle class out of the city to a new, comfortable and convenient retail phenomenon: the suburban shopping mall.

When considering this economic restructuring, urban sociologists are careful not to make the error of suggesting that cities are slaves to technological changes. For instance, just because the federal government could build an expansive highway system, just because the technology was available for automobile companies to build more cars than ever, and just because factories needed open land to develop on does not mean it was inevitable or natural that the middle class and factories would abandon the city. The United States as a society made specific choices enabled by human-made technologies, and other societies made slightly different choices. The erroneous belief that technology is outside of social influence and actually structures social, economic and political

How will rising gas prices affect home values in the suburbs?

life is called **technological determinism**.

Nevertheless, urban economic restructuring, though a result of cumulative human action, is often experienced as a force acting upon cities and their residents. To give one example, if you were starting a plastic toy company today, you might feel like you have to locate your production in a place with cheaper land and labor costs in order to compete. But in the end, you have a choice not to. This is illustrated by the emerging trend of some U.S.-based companies bringing their manufacturing back to the United States. Perhaps if some of these firms had thought more creatively they would not have needed to move their production in the first place.

The urban renewal and highway building era is widely acknowledged as one of the most important eras of American urban development. These two policies have been called the "twin wrecking balls." They laid a foundation of inequality upon which future development would sit. Civil unrest in the 1960s in the black neighborhoods of Los Angeles' Watts neighborhood, Chicago's Division Street and

the city of Newark led President Lyndon B. Johnson to establish the National Advisory Commission on Civil Disorders (1968), on which urban sociologist Herbert Gans consulted. The commission was charged with determining what happened in each of the riots, why the riots happened and how future riots could be prevented. The commission found white society was deeply implicated in the ghetto. "White institutions created it, white institutions maintain it, and white society condones it."

In 1972, a Department of Housing and Urban Development official acknowledged that urban renewal policies fostered injustice. "It has been said by our critics that we are unresponsive to the relocation needs of…residents," he began (as quoted in Frieden and Sagalyn, 1989). "It has been said, for example, that 'urban renewal' is nothing more than 'Negro removal.'…We have been accused of violating the law and of contravening our own administrative regulations. And today, we have been called 'legal lawbreakers.'…It is time to be honest with one another and admit that there is some validity to these allegations."

Yet the leaders behind urban renewal were accurate about some things. Just as many city leaders imagined in the mid-century, individual cities would have to go through some process of change to prepare for the postindustrial economy. Once a center of manufacturing, downtowns were now populated with corporate headquarters and advertising, brokerage, consulting, financial, legal and accounting firms. While manufacturers complained about the density of the city, service firms benefited from this close proximity, which allowed face-to-face meetings about important business. Corporate headquarters that housed engineers, financial analysts, accountants, lawyers and other professionals benefitted from having them all under one roof. The city was experiencing a new agglomeration, one not built around the complementary functions of the industrial economy but built around the complementary functions of the post industrial economy.

As city leaders were reimagining the new postindustrial city, they understood it to be a "landscape of experience" whose success would increasingly rely on tourism and leisure. Cities worked to attract the leisure spending of suburbanites from a few miles away; producer service workers tempted to grab a bite in the city after work; conventioneers from far and near; and tourists arriving by car for a day trip or by plane for an extended urban vacation. Cities needed new economic activity, and one way they would encourage it was by being "alive after five." This required a new infrastructure of grand waterfronts, pedestrian-friendly areas, convention centers, museums, theaters, restaurants, retail centers, nightclubs, hotels, sports arenas and theaters. Many cities, even those that really did not have enough funding to do so, created landscapes with these components.

In some cases, this led to what Dennis Judd and Susan Fainstein (1999) termed the **tourist bubble**, a specialized area of a downtown that presents a coherent, easy-to-understand and safe version of the city in order to lure visitors who might otherwise be skittish of cities. The tourist bubble can lead

to what some urbanists see as two separate cities: the neighborhoods where the struggling residents live and the glistening tourist bubble that features a "Disneyfied" version of the city. **Disneyfication** can be described as the process of stripping a place of its authentic character and repackaging it in a sanitized and diluted format with the intention of making it more pleasant and easily consumable. Critics of this Disneyfied tourism infrastructure such as Christine Boyer (1992) bring attention to the **festival marketplace**, a type of urban mall featuring boutiques, restaurants and street entertainers, built in historic or historic-looking buildings. Usually absent of the large "anchor" stores that suburban malls feature, these malls are intended to offer an "urban" feel in a safe environment intended to make them attractive to suburbanites and tourists.

These Disneyfied landscapes, however, are not only for tourists. Some suggest that gentrifiers also contributed to the Disneyfication of the city, an oversimplified but important characterization. What is **gentrification**? Neil Brenner and Jason Patch (2007) define it as "the reinvestment of real estate capital into declining, inner-city neighborhoods to create a new residential infrastructure for middle- and high-income inhabitants." Gentrification implies, at its core, the displacement of lower-income residents as increasing demand by higher-income residents causes increased rents, increased home values and increased property taxes.

The transformation brought by gentrification also affects a neighborhood's politics and social life. The new residents often have more social power and, therefore, tend to nudge the neighborhood's future development in a very different direction. People who rented an apartment in the neighborhood before gentrification can no longer afford the rent. Old residents who own their home have a decision to make: cash in on their high-value home and leave or try to stay in the changing neighborhood.

Some residents who want to stay simply cannot due to the increasing property taxes. Their taxes grow to be higher than their mortgage payment as the home they purchased for $50,000 is now worth $500,000. One critical housing issue related to gentrification is whether city neighborhoods will be left that are affordable for low-income residents.

Japonica Brown-Saracino (2009) found that some gentrifiers move to neighborhoods precisely to live with people of a different racial, ethnic, religious or class group than themselves. Others, however, move to a neighborhood banking on the fact that it will change. They see, as geographer Neil Smith (1996) suggested, the land as an "urban frontier" populated by natives that are a hindrance to progress. These types of gentrifiers are quite uncomfortable living near their non-gentrified neighbors, making what may look like a racially, ethnically, religiously or economically "integrated" community anything but socially integrated in residents' daily lives. If you live in the city, you might hear people say something like, "It's a tough neighborhood, but it is gentrifying." For some urbanists critical of gentrification, this is "code" for, "This neighborhood is filled with people who make us uncomfortable, but if you get in now while it is still cheap, that will change soon enough—and you'll make a ton of money when your home rises in value."

The success of the old industrial city had been measured by how many tangible goods it produced. It was not quite as important how good-looking it was as this production occurred. The city was similar to a farm worker who works hard in the field: With leathery skin and soiled hands, he bears the marks of hard work. The city's marks of hard work were hulking buildings, polluted water, smoggy air and sooty streets. In the new postindustrial economy, the city was no longer valued for the goods it made. Instead, it was valued for the experience it fostered.

The new glass and steel buildings made up what Sharon Zukin (1991) calls a **landscape of power**, an impressive global landscape free of the **urban vernacular**, the complex grittiness of the local culture. The field worker, in other words, had become a fashion model.

Of course, not every city was able to make this transition. Although the process was tumultuous in all cities, larger ones that already had expansive, diverse service economies, such as Chicago and New York, made the difficult transition more smoothly than places like Detroit or Newark. Cities that developed later, such as the Sunbelt cities of Atlanta and Houston, were able to build new postindustrial downtowns as well as factories in outlying areas that were conducive to the latest production technology.

The old neighborhoods of the industrial economy and the residents who live in them have suffered tremendously as cities make this change. William Julius Wilson (1996) reported that work "disappeared" from these neighborhoods, leaving residents frustrated, isolated and without the skills to compete in the new post industrial economy. Their neighborhoods experienced **liminality**. This term, popularized by Turner (1970), describes a disoriented state characterized by ambiguity in which an old order has left, with no apparent new order to replace it; it is "neither here nor there." The film *Roger and Me* (1990) portrayed an excellent example of urban liminality in Flint, Michigan, the "motor city," which went from an American industrial success story to one of the dreariest cities in the United States. One worker said, "I feel bad for the people that have kids right now. What are they going to grow up to be? What are they looking forward to? Out there (pointing out to the city), it's nothing; they have a bleak future."

Part of Zukin's urban vernacular are the urban homeless. Homeless people are "out of place," according to Talmadge Wright (1997). First, they do not "fit" in the new postindustrial city; they don't fit into the image tourists or business people want the city to have. They also are "out of places" to live. Snow and Anderson (1993) and Wright showed how the urban homeless are pushed onto "marginal" land that people with money to spend (e.g. tourists, corporate leaders, developers) do not care about from "prime" land that people with money to spend do care about. This is problematic when gentrification decreases the amount of marginal land.

One way cities keep homeless people out of prime areas is through **illegal lodging citations**, which are tickets issued by police to homeless individuals for taking up lodging (usually sleeping) in a public place. So there are a decreasing number of places for low-income people to live off of the street, and there are a decreasing number of places for people to sit or sleep once they are homeless on the street. Marginal areas of cities used to be filled with residential options for low-income people such as single-room occupancy or **SRO hotels**. These were often little more than tiny 6-foot-by-8-foot cubicles that could be rented by the night. With gentrification, SROs are nearing extinction. With such options gone, it has been up to local government and nonprofits to pick up the slack with other kinds of shelter. Common Ground in New York City and other nonprofits are working to bring back these small units, but the new incarnation is often accompanied with services such as mental health and substance abuse treatment.

As the globalization that emerged around the 1950s began to become more important in economic, social and political realms, cities that were more interconnected became what Saskia Sassen (1991) termed the "command and control" centers for the world.

Sassen and others pointed to these cities' common characteristics: They are economic centers with global corporate headquarters, banking and finance functions, and major stock and commodities exchanges. They are political centers that are homes for international organizations, such as the United Nations, that influence world events. They are cultural centers with the world's leading media corporations, and they are on the cutting edge in the performing arts, the visual arts, popular music, sporting events and fashion. These world cities, or **global cities**, such as London, New York and Tokyo, sit atop a hierarchy of interconnected cities. There is much argument among urbanists as to what the rest of this "urban hierarchy" should look like, or whether what Jennifer Robinson (2004) calls "ordinary cities" should even be forced into these types of hierarchical classifications.

All cities are settlements that carve out huge swaths in the natural environment. A key topic of discussion today is the idea of sustainability.

Sustainability connotes endurance: What makes an entity endure? For instance, urbanists ask what makes for a sustainable neighborhood: One that allows residents to prosper? Others ask how a city might avoid growing too large for its own good. To be more specific, what if a city outgrows its water supply? Should it pipe in water from another city? This term "sustainable" can be used in a social sense, an economic sense or an environmental sense.

# The Environment

Most Americans view the natural environment as distinctly different from the human experience. This dichotomy can foster a belief that the relationship between human civilization and the physical environment is contentious, with humans objectifying and dominating the nonhuman world. *Anthropocentrism* is an interpretation of reality exclusively in terms of human values and experience, where humans are dominant over the nonhuman. Anthropocentrism "depicts nature as atomistic, passive, lifeless and wholly devoid of purpose" (Brown, 1992). Humans assigned the purpose of serving their needs and wants to the unrefined, raw environment. While this worldview has led to great economic wealth, technological advancements and material comforts, it has also contributed to toxic waste, air pollution, loss of biodiversity, the extinction of countless species of flora and fauna and global warming.

Hurricane Katrina came ashore just east of New Orleans, Louisiana, on August 29, 2005, as a Category 3 hurricane. In its wake, nearly 2,000 people lost their lives across the Gulf Coast, and 80 percent of New Orleans was submerged, flooded by a breached and battered levee system.

Hurricane Katrina was the most costly hurricane in U.S. history, causing more than $80 billion in damage. Events such as Katrina remind us that humans are not exempt from the ecological laws that govern our planet, though our Western, anthropocentric worldview suggests that they are.

In this chapter we will broadly discuss how humans are one member of our global ecosystem; how the physical environment serves three functions for human civilization; how human activities lead to environmental degradation; and how this degradation affects human civilization. We will also discuss briefly several environmental problems, including air, water and soil pollution, and provide an in-depth discussion of global climate change.

## Three Functions of the Environment

Earth serves three major functions for all living creatures that inhabit it. It is a *supply depot, waste repository,* and *living space* (Dunlap, 1994; Dunlap & Catton, 2002). When these functions break down due to overuse or competition, environmental problems emerge. But, when Earth can ensure these functions for humans, and the functions complement each other, sustainability is maintained. **Sustainability** is the "ability of Earth's various systems, including human cultural systems and economies, to survive and adapt to changing environmental conditions indefinitely" (Miller, 2007).

### Supply Depot

Earth serves as our largest shopping mall, providing all living creatures with everything necessary for survival. The air we breathe, the water we drink and the food we eat; the raw materials like petroleum and metals needed to assemble an iPod; and even the erythorbic acid, gum arabic and calcium disodium EDTA in a bottle of Mountain Dew, are materials that come directly from Earth or are derived from its resources.

There are two kinds of resources in this shopping mall: renewable and non-renewable. **Renewable resources**, like grains, trees for paper and wood, and cotton for clothes, can be regenerated. The key factor in determining whether a resource is renewable is its rate of regeneration. If the need/want for a resource outpaces Earth's ability to regenerate it, the resource is no longer considered renewable. **Non-renewable resources**, like fossil fuels (gasoline, coal and natural gas) and rare minerals (gold, platinum and uranium) cannot be regenerated in a timely manner, or at all, and may be permanently depleted (Holechek, Cole, Fisher, & Valdez, 2000).

While there can be shortages of renewable resources, such as when a freeze in Florida reduces the supply of oranges to consumers, non-renewable resources experience *scarcities*. Diminished oil reserves cannot be restored, and, therefore, are considered scarce (Dunlap & Catton, 2002).

### Waste Repository

Earth serves as a huge treatment plant, absorbing or storing all of the waste materials from all living creatures. Earth absorbs or recycles the bodily waste of every human being, animal and plant; the carbon dioxide and nitrogen dioxide waste from the combustion engines in our vehicles; the sulfur dioxide released from coal plants; the toxic metals like lead and cadmium released into rivers and streams from factories; and the plastic, paper and organic matter that we place in our garbage cans that find their way to city landfills and incinerators.

When waste is created faster than Earth can recycle or absorb it, pollution results. In an environment unaltered by industrialized human activity, the waste created by flora, fauna and humans can serve as a supply depot for other organisms. Alternatively, the waste created by modern civilizations is not always a resource for other organisms (Miller, 2007).

In 1900, there were approximately 4,200 passenger cars in the U.S., whereas now there are more than 600 million motor vehicles in use in the world (Stasenko, 2001). Air pollution, consisting of a high concentration of particulate matter from automobiles and other sources, has spurred many cities to adopt a system of air quality advisories and warnings similar to severe weather warnings. In 1900, Earth's atmosphere and biotic life could absorb and recycle the waste products of these early vehicles ($CO_2$ is absorbed by plant life and soils). While Earth will absorb today's carbon emissions, doing so will change the structure of our atmosphere. We will discuss this more later when we discuss global climate change.

### Living Space

Our planet provides shelter and refuge for all of the living creatures that dwell there. The dorm room you live in, the classroom your sociology class meets in, the Grand Canyon you may visit while on vacation and the house you may visit for a college party all take up space. As populations increase, crowding can occur. Just as our resources can be overused, so can our living spaces.

### Conflict Between Functions

Environmental problems occur when one of

What were your thoughts when you first saw the images from Katrina?

*Source: Mark Moran*

Earth's functions is stretched beyond its capabilities, or when functions collide, keeping each from operating properly. Often, the use of the environment for one function will interfere when it is used for another.

For example, the human health and ecological disaster at Love Canal illustrates what happens when functions of the environment conflict.

The community of Love Canal, a neighborhood of Niagara Falls, New York, is the site of one of the more notorious environmental tragedies in U.S. history (Blum, 2008; Fowlkes & Miller, 1983). At the turn of the century, William T. Love had a half-mile trench excavated as part of a project to connect the upper and lower Niagara River. But the project failed. The empty, partially dug canal was turned into a dumpsite for 22,000 tons of municipal and industrial waste by Hooker Chemical and Plastic Corporation. In 1953, the canal was capped and sold to the city of Niagara Falls for a single dollar to be the future home of an elementary school and hundreds of homes (Beck, 1979; Blum, 2008).

Love Canal turned into a human health and ecological disaster as 421 toxic chemicals from the landfill site leeched into people's basements and yards, contaminating the water, land and air around them (University of Buffalo University Archives, 2008). The overlapping functions of waste repository and living space led to high rates of miscarriages, birth defects, respiratory ailments and cancers (Environmental Protection Agency, 2007). This site could not safely function as both a waste repository and a living space for the community of Love Canal. In the end, the school closed, and more than 900 families were moved from the site at a cost of $100 million.

# Causes of Environmental Degradation

How does a society get to the point of overusing available resources, outpacing waste repository processes and damaging its own living spaces? We will examine these questions by discussing the three main functions served by Earth along with environmental degradation utilizing the IPAT model. The metaphor of the Tragedy of the Commons will also be outlined. And, finally, we will cover the sociological theory known as the Treadmill of Production.

## IPAT Model

Scientists have outlined the most important driving forces of human civilization that impact (I) the functions of the environment: population (P), social affluence (A) and technology (T) (Commoner, 1972; Dietz & Rosa, 1994; Duncan, 1961; Ehrlich & Holdren, 1971). The IPAT model has been called "the ecological complex" and describes the relationship between human civilization and the physical environment (Duncan, 1961).

### Impact

Environmental degradation can be observed on many levels, from the environmental impact of individual behaviors (electricity/natural gas usage, gasoline consumption, air travel hours, recycling habits, etc.) to the global impact of nation-states (greenhouse gas emissions, deforestation, loss of biodiversity, etc.). Later in this chapter, we will discuss several environmental problems, but first we will introduce the concept of an ecological footprint.

Environmental degradation can be broadly measured by the ecological footprint concept first proposed by Mathis Wackernagel and William Rees

(1996). A city, region or nation's ecological footprint is a measure of the land necessary to support the utilization of the three functions of the environment—resource depot, waste repository and living space—for a specified geographic region (Wackernagel & Rees, 1996; York, Rosa, & Dietz, 2003). In our globalized economy, a region's **ecological footprint** is an important measure of environmental degradation because resources are imported and wastes are often exported. For example, a Barbie doll is not just a plastic doll. Oil that is extracted and refined into ethylene in Saudi Arabia is turned into polyvinyl chloride (PVC) plastic pellets in Taiwan. The pellets are then shipped to factories in China, Indonesia and Malaysia where they are formed into 11.5-inch dolls by machines that were made in the United States. Barbie's hair is made in Japan; her clothes are made from Chinese cotton (Cha, 2008). One cannot measure one's complete environmental impact by looking only within one's own yard.

As an example, how much landmass does the United States need in order to sustain the American population at the current standard of living? An ecological footprint of "one" represents a sustainable region; an ecological footprint greater than one denotes an unsustainable region. In 2001, human civilization needed 1.2 "planet Earths" to sustain current resource consumption, waste production and living space, and it is projected to need 1.6 planet Earths in 2015 (Dietz, Rosa, & York, 2007). In comparison, the United States alone was using 1.5 times the landmass needed to sustain our land-rich country in 1999 (Wackernagel et al., 1999). This research suggests that human civilization is coming to an age of increased ecological degradation as we outpace Earth's ability to sustain our standard of living.

You may be wondering about the size of your own ecological footprint. On average, a U.S. citizen's ecological footprint is 30 times greater than that of an average citizen in India (Miller, 2007).

## Population

Danica May Camacho was born in the Philippians on October 30, 2011. She is only one of the 2 million children born in the Philippians every year. But Danica (which means "morning star") is spe-

cial. She has the symbolic distinction of being the 7 billionth person on the planet (Coleman, 2011). Consider that it took from the dawn of human existence, approximately 195,000 years ago, until the Common Era (1 C.E.) to amass 200 million people on the planet, but it took only another 1,800 years to reach 1 billion people (Census, 2008a). Since the Industrial Revolution, human population growth has exploded, reaching 2 billion in the 1930s, 3 billion in 1960, 4 billion by the mid-1970s, 5 billion in the late 1980s and 6 billion in 1999 (Harper, 2008; Kemp, 2004), and it is projected to increase to 9 billion by 2040 (Census, 2008b).

Humans use resources. The more people there are, the more resources are used. Two hundred years ago, demographer Thomas Malthus was one of the first scientists to shed light on the issue of population growth in relation to resource consumption, specifically of the food supply. Malthus was concerned that geometric population growth would outpace the growth of food production through technological advancements (Kemp, 2004). Population growth can also strain other resources, such as energy, water and housing. Population concerns are especially severe in urban areas where the local ecosystems cannot absorb the waste of human activity, causing pollution of the air, water and soil (Harper, 2008). Looking at our global measure of environmental impact, population size is directly related to ecological footprint (York, Rosa, & Dietz, 2003). The human population explosion did not happen in a vacuum; it occurred after the introduction of industrialization, a period of colossal increases in affluence and technology, including utilization of energy stores like wood, coal and oil.

## Affluence

In sociological literature, affluence refers to an individual's or group's level of social and economic abundance. Affluence is related to a person's access to resources, whether physical or social. More-affluent individuals and countries utilize more resources than less-affluent individuals and countries. In research utilizing the IPAT model, affluence is often measured by a country's gross domestic product (GDP) per capita (Chertow, 2001).

Although GDP per capita is a good measure of

affluence, it is difficult to visualize. Photojournalist Peter Menzel (1995) provided a stunning visualization of affluence through photos of statistically average families from across the world with all their worldly possessions. Utilizing data from the United Nations and the World Bank, Menzel determined what was average based on family size, annual income, occupation, religion and type of location (such as rural, urban or suburban).

Thorstein Veblen (1899) described how affluence leads to greater consumption of resources, but, more important, to *conspicuous consumption*. Conspicuous consumption is the demonstration of affluence through lavish consumption. Think of the suburban motto of "keeping up with the Joneses." People who have more control over resources show their power and status by out-consuming their neighbors, purchasing larger homes, expensive vehicles, stylish clothing and extravagant toys.

Conspicuous consumption leads to conspicuous waste. *Conspicuous waste* comes with affluence, allowing individuals to be more careless with their resources. Replacing possessions that are broken or worn, instead of reusing or repairing them, simply because one has the ability to do so, is conspicuous waste. Look at how fashion changes with the seasons. American teenagers participate in conspicuous waste by replacing perfectly usable clothing with the latest fashions to demonstrate their social status (Bell, 1998).

## Technology

Technology is the useful application of knowledge to a situation. Through the use of technology, societies can accomplish tasks that might otherwise be impossible, inefficient or difficult to accomplish. The invention of the wheel, plow, automobile and airplane; the domestication of animals and the planting of crops; the development of medicines, Velcro, personal computers, cell phones and the Internet are all applications of knowledge to accomplish tasks that would otherwise be exceedingly difficult or impossible.

Technology often makes life easier. The Internet, for example, has made writing college papers remarkably easier. Imagine how long it would take you to write a sociology paper if you had to go to the library and use a card catalog to find a book or journal article, rather than doing a search online. And imagine how boring life would be if you could surf through only four television channels.

While technology can make life easier, it can also generate unintended consequences that damage the environment and human societies. Technologies allow society to consume more, leading to diminished resources. Technologies also can create waste matter that has detrimental environmental effects. Even though fertilizers have allowed farmers to produce vast quantities of food, the nitrogen-rich chemicals they contain find their way into streams, rivers and oceans. Despite the fact that nitrogen is good for crop growth, it is not good for aquatic life. Nitrogen encourages the growth of plant life such as algae in water. This increase in plant life can also reduce the levels of oxygen in the water, making it difficult or impossible for animal life to exist. The nitrogen run-off from crop farming in the Midwest has led to the Gulf of Mexico dead zone, a 6,000- to 7,000-square-mile area where fish cannot live (Bruckner, 2008).

This does not mean that all technologies create environmental problems. Remember that technology is the application of knowledge, so it also is true that technology can be used to ease or eliminate environmental degradation. Front-loading washing machines and non-phosphorous laundry detergents are technological innovations that reduce the consumption of water as a resource as well as reduce the stress on environmental sinks (areas used to absorb wastes) to recycle phosphorous. Solar energy and wind turbines are sustainable energy technologies that we will be discussing later in this chapter. Because technology is the use of knowledge, it is up to the developers and users of this knowledge to understand the pros and cons involved, and to at least be cognizant of the negative consequences such technologies can have on society and the environment.

Population, affluence and technology are those components of human civilization that have the most significant impact on the physical environment. But they do not explain how societies become unmanageably populated, unsustainable societies

At what point would you consider a car's price excessive?

of wealth, or technologically savvy yet ecologically destructive. The following two sections will discuss how social processes lead to environmental degradation from the perspective of "the Tragedy of the Commons" and the "Treadmill of Production."

## Tragedy of the Commons

Garrett Hardin's (1968) influential *Tragedy of the Commons* thesis suggests that, in a finite world, the short-term interests of individuals and groups can come into conflict with long-term group and global interests. Using a community of herdsman as a metaphor, Hardin illustrates how a community can unconsciously degrade its local environment. Imagine herdsman sharing a community pasture (commons). Initially, each herdsmen has an equal number of cattle in the pasture; the ratio of cattle to land is sustainable. This means that the cattle do not deplete the resources of the pasture or permanently damage the living space with waste.

In a competitive economy, each herdsman attempts to reap the most profit. In our example, if a single herder wants to maximize her profits, she will add more cattle to her flock. As a consequence, the added cattle will use more of the pasture's resources (food), sinks (waste storage/absorption) and living space (land). If the other herdsmen are anything like the first herdsman, they will also want to maximize

profit and add cattle to the community pasture. The addition of one herder's cattle sets off a competitive battle over the shared finite resource. The new additions will apply more strain on the pasture's environmental functions, resulting in the loss of grazing foliage, increased waste matter and a more crowded living space. The competitive behaviors of the herdsmen become unsustainable given the finite resources of the community pasture, creating a *tragedy of the commons*.

## Treadmill of Production

Extrapolating the *Tragedy of the Commons* to our global village, with Earth as one large community pasture, one can begin to see how uncontrolled growth of society can outpace the environment's ability to maintain a healthy planet. Placing Hardin's *Tragedy of the Commons* thesis in the context of our global economy, and adding a dose of *neo-Marxist theory*, one can begin to outline the theory of the *Treadmill of Production*. According to Allan Schnaiberg and Kenneth Gould (1994), the *Treadmill of Production* is the motivating force of ecological degradation driven by modern economics, especially following World War II. The modern economic market, spurred by industrialization and an abundance of wealth, requires economic expansion. In other words, corporations seek profits; without profits, corporations fail. To maintain profits, corporations increase production. Increased production leads to competition between corporations (remember the competing herdsmen in the tragedy of the commons?), which leads to more production. The competition for wealth through the production and sale of goods places the community on a treadmill.

In an attempt to increase profits, two means of minimizing costs are addressed: reducing operating costs and externalizing production costs. One way to reduce operating costs is to invest in technologies that will replace expensive labor. While investing in technological infrastructure, such as factory equipment and computer technology, is initially expensive, these costs are offset by increases in production. Companies can reduce operating costs by substituting machines for part of their human work force, because the costs related to labor—salaries and benefits—typically increase over time.

The transition from labor-intensive production to technology-intensive production degrades the environment on two fronts (Gould, Pellow, & Schnaiberg, 2004). First, technologies increase production due to the increased time efficiency. Increases in production require more resource inputs, thus leading to the overutilization of environmental resources. Second, these technologies, while efficient in time of production, are often inefficient in energy and/or chemical use. The use of these technologies leads to overutilization of environmental resources; in addition, these technologies pollute more, leading to the congestion of waste sinks. The *Treadmill of Production* recognizes that investment in capital leads to increased demands for natural resources.

The second method used to decrease operating costs is to externalize them, predominately the costs related to waste disposal. Disposing of the waste resulting from the production of goods can be a costly endeavor, thereby reducing profits. Corporations may, therefore, attempt to externalize the costs of waste removal. Externalizing costs occurs when a company transfers some of its moral responsibilities to the community, either directly or as degradation to the environment.

Before environmental laws, such as the Clean Air Act of 1970 and the Clean Water Act of 1972,

corporations could dispose of waste in ways that were harmful to both the environment and human health, keeping the costs of disposal to a minimum. Laws that govern the level of pollutants that can be released into the environment serve to internalize some of the costs of production, placing them upon the company rather than the community. The *Treadmill of Production* perspective provides an excellent blueprint to understand how a society can get to a point of overusing available resources, outpacing waste repository processes and damaging its own living space.

# Environmental Problems

In the following section, we will discuss some of the larger environmental problems that human civilization is facing. Specifically, we will discuss pollution and global climate change. When you read about these environmental effects, think of how population, affluence and technology are leading to overutilization of, or competition for, resources, waste sinks and living space.

## Pollution

As the 2008 Summer Olympic Games began in Beijing, China, athletes, spectators and government officials worried about the effects that China's notoriously dismal air quality would have on the event. The Chinese government restricted car traffic in the city, banning the use of 2 million cars, and shut down heavily polluting factories, turning Beijing into the world's largest air quality experiment in an attempt to clean the air for the Olympic Games (Tran, 2008). Pollution is defined as the "destruction or damage of the natural environment by by-products of human activities" (McGraw-Hill, 2003). Sources of pollution include vibration, heat and noise that contaminate the air, water and land.

Air pollution is the presence of particulates and chemicals in the atmosphere that have negative effects on ecological and/or social systems. More than a billion people live in communities, predominately in developing countries, where the air is unhealthy to breathe (Miller, 2007). Air pollution is so pervasive in Southeast Asia that an enormous brown cloud over the area can be seen from space, and it is intensifying the melting of the Himalayan glaciers that serve as drinking water for the people of China and India (Environment News Service, 2007).

Most air pollution is the product of industrialization and the burning of fossil fuels. Although the atmosphere operates as an environmental sink, diluting contaminants by diffusion and wind or settling particulates to Earth by gravity or precipitation, present human activity is outpacing the ability of ecosystems to dilute pollution in many areas, leading to contaminated resources. Air-quality issues are more prevalent in industrialized urban areas where population and factory density are higher, especially in communities that rely on the burning of coal as an energy source. Not only is air pollution unsightly, but as many as 30,000 Americans die prematurely each year from air pollution, while another 125,000 get cancer from breathing air pollution from automobiles (Miller, 2007).

Pastor and his colleagues (Pastor, Sadd, & Morello-Frosch, 2004) found that Latino and other communities of color in California are more likely to live in proximity to manufacturing facilities that emit toxic air pollution. Not only are there trade-offs between the functions of the environment, but there are also social structures that may lead to inequitable distributions of environmental problems. **Environmental injustice** occurs when a social group based on race, ethnicity, gender, age or some other characteristic is burdened with an environmental hazard (Pellow, 2000).

Until now, we have focused on outdoor air pollution, but indoor air pollution is another major concern. In fact, indoor pollution is a greater risk than outdoor pollution. Not only does it have higher concentrations of harmful chemicals like carbon oxide, nitrogen oxides and sulfur dioxide, Americans spend 70 to 98 percent of their time indoors, leading to approximately 6,000 premature cancer deaths each year (Miller, 2007).

Water pollution is the presence of particulates, chemicals or temperature changes that have negative effects on the ecology of watersheds or the use of water sources by societies. Water is abundant—comprising 71 percent of Earth's surface. It is also

renewable because the global water system continually recycles itself. However, access to and pollution of water are two of the most contested environmental problems facing human societies today. Only 3 percent of the world's water supply is freshwater (drinkable), and close to 70 percent of that is locked in the icecaps and glaciers, leaving only 1 percent available for human consumption, of which the vast majority is groundwater (Geological Survey, 2008).

The most pressing global water concern is contaminated drinking water. Infectious bacteria, viruses and parasites from human and animal waste contaminate much of the drinking water in developing countries. Approximately 17 percent of the world's population lacks access to a safe drinking water source. Contaminated drinking water causes the premature deaths of more than 2 million people a year, most of whom are children. There are many types of water systems that can become polluted. We will discuss the pollution of two of these systems: freshwater streams and lakes, and groundwater.

Most surface water pollution is the result of agricultural, industrial and mining activities. Agricultural practices pollute freshwater streams and lakes with eroded sediment, fertilizer and pesticide runoff, and waste and bacteria from livestock. Industrial factories use streams and lakes as a waste sink for dumping inorganic and organic chemicals, and mining is responsible for polluting water systems with toxic chemicals and eroded sediments (Miller, 2007).

Because water is constantly moving, especially in rivers and streams, the natural processes of dilution and biodegradation recycle any environmental wastes placed in water systems. Remembering the lessons that we learned from the *Tragedy of the Commons*, this recovery system becomes ineffective if overloaded. In the United States, nine out of 10 aquifers are contaminated with volatile organic chemicals generated by people, and 50 percent of Americans get their drinking water from these aquifers (Miller, 2007). For example, in an attempt to reduce air pollution, the chemical MTBE was added to gasoline so that it would burn cleaner in automobile engines. Unfortunately, this carcinogenic chemical is very soluble in water and has been found to leak from more than a quarter-million underground storage tanks at gas stations, contaminating groundwater that serves as drinking water.

Access to fresh water is not just a problem for developing countries. While almost every American has access to healthy drinking water, our affluent society has strained the availability of water in many communities. Because the population of Atlanta doubled between 1980 and 2007, for instance, water demands have skyrocketed. This higher demand, coupled with a recent drought, led Georgia legislators to haggle with government officials in Alabama and Florida over access to the Chattahoochee watershed, which provides water for millions of people in the three states (CNN, 2007).

Soil pollution is the alteration of the natural soil environment. In 2003, every woman, man and child in the United States generated 1.3 tons (2,600

pounds) of garbage. This was an almost threefold increase in average waste production since 1960 (Royte, 2005). This waste included 25 billion Styrofoam cups, 22 billion plastic bottles, 186 billion pieces of junk mail and 25 million metric tons of edible food, plus countless other discarded materials (Miller, 2007).

Two types of pollution that contaminate soil are solid waste and hazardous waste. Solid waste includes all discarded material that is neither liquid nor gas. These materials are often stored in landfills (54 percent), incinerated (11 percent) or recycled (35 percent) (EPA, 2011). Some solid waste comes from individual consumer habits (municipal waste), but most of it (98.5 percent) comes from factories, mining operations, agriculture and businesses that produce these consumer products and services (industrial waste). In a landmark study on environmental inequality, Robert Bullard (1983) found that

Source: David Barrie

The air quality in Beijing is notoriously poor. In the U.S., which city do you consider as having the worst air pollution?

African American communities were disproportionately located in the vicinity of solid waste facilities in comparison to Caucasian communities in Houston, Texas.

The second type of soil pollution comes from hazardous waste, which includes all toxic, biological, infectious and radioactive waste that not only is discarded but threatens both human health and the ecosystems in which it is disposed. Household chemicals, batteries, pesticides, toxic chemicals and ash wastes from incinerators are all examples of hazardous waste (Miller, 2007). The largest producer of hazardous waste is the U.S. military, followed by the chemical industry. The Environmental Protection Agency identified approximately 450,000 hazardous waste sites. Twenty-five percent of Americans live near one of these hazardous waste sites.

## Global Warming

Daily temperatures can swing dramatically. The greatest temperature change recorded in a 24-hour period happened in Loma, Montana, on January 15, 1972, when the temperature rose from -54 degrees Fahrenheit to 49 degrees Fahrenheit, an increase of 103 degrees. For sustainable life to exist on Earth, though, the average global temperature cannot fluctuate dramatically. The average temperature of Earth's surface is 60 degrees Fahrenheit.

The sun's radiant heat warms our planet. While most of the sun's solar radiation (sunlight) is absorbed by Earth's surface (land and water), much of it is reflected back into space by Earth's surface and atmosphere. Earth's atmosphere—the layer of gases that surrounds the planet—acts as a blanket, keeping much of the sun's radiation from escaping, thereby warming the planet's surface and atmosphere and making it welcoming for life. This is called the *greenhouse effect*. Water vapor, carbon dioxide, methane, nitrous oxide and ozone are some of these heat-trapping gases. Water vapor and carbon dioxide make up approximately 90 percent of the insulating capacity of our atmospheric blanket and are the most important of the *greenhouse gases*.

**Global warming**, also called *global climate change*, is a gradual increase in Earth's average temperature (both ground and atmospheric). Earth's climate has continually fluctuated over the course of its planetary history (4.5 billion years), leading to cycles of ice ages and warm periods. For much of this time, Earth's climate was not conducive to human inhabitance outside our ancestral home of Africa (Fagan, 2004). Presently, Earth is going through a 20,000-year natural warming period (Dobson, 2002), which fostered human migration from Africa throughout every continent except Antarctica. The natural warming and cooling processes of our planetary climate should not be confused with anthropogenic global climate change.

Anthropogenic climate change is the relatively quick change in Earth's average temperature due to human activities. The rate of global warming has increased drastically in the past 200 years. In the past 100 years, Earth's average surface temperature has increased by 1.4 degrees Fahrenheit. The change in temperature from 1950 to 2000 was the largest increase in average surface temperature in 1,300 years, and the polar regions have not seen average temperatures this high in 125,000 years (Intergovernmental Panel on Climate Change, 2007b).

To a large extent, the type and concentration of gases in Earth's atmosphere determine the average temperature of the planet. Greenhouse gases are the specific gases that have the most warming effect on Earth's atmosphere. Just as having too many blankets on your bed can cause you to be too warm, an overabundance of greenhouse gases can over-insulate Earth's surface, influencing global warming and affecting human civilization. Water vapor, carbon dioxide, tropospheric ozone, methane, CFCs and nitrogen oxide are the most important insulating greenhouse gases (Harper, 2008).

Despite the fact that humans have had very little effect on the amount of water vapor in Earth's atmosphere, humans have had a major influence on the amount of carbon dioxide ($CO_2$) in the atmosphere (Harper, 2008). The relatively rapid warming of the past 200 years has been traced to anthropogenic sources, primarily the burning of fossil fuels (EPA, 2008; IPCC, 2007b). The burning of fossil fuels accounts for 75 percent of humankind's emissions of $CO_2$.

Earth's capacity to serve as a waste repository,

absorbing and recycling *greenhouse gases* produced since the Industrial Revolution, is having an impact on the planet's ability to function as a resource depot and a living space. Specifically, global warming will have negative effects on food supplies and coastal living spaces (Harper, 2008).

It is projected that global climate change will have a significant effect on the production of food grains. Even though many countries and regions, such as temperate regions in the mid to high latitudes, will be able to adapt to the changing climate with different crop rotations, many other countries and regions will not, such as those in tropical or dry regions in the low latitudes. Research indicates that maize production in southern Africa will decrease by 30 percent, and maize, rice and millet production in South Asia will decrease by 10 percent by 2030 (Lobell et al., 2008).

Global warming will have an effect on sea levels due to the melting of Arctic and Antarctic ice sheets and glaciers. Because cities often were settled on trade routes, 50 percent of the world population lives on coastal lands. The Intergovernmental Panel on Climate Change (2007a) predicts significant flooding in coastal areas, especially in delta regions, like New Orleans and the Netherlands, and island regions.

Inland communities are not immune to global warming; communities near river systems will also be affected. Early spring thaws will increase the probability of river system flooding worldwide. Global warming also will have an effect on human health. As the average global temperature increases, death and disease due to malnutrition, heat exhaustion, ozone exposure and vector-borne infectious diseases like Lyme disease, plague, encephalitis and yellow fever also will increase.

# Summary

It should be clear, even from this brief introduction, that cities and their surrounding regions are complex social creations, sometimes full of surprises and contradictions. It is possible to argue that sociology in the 21st century is, by definition, *urban* sociology, in that most of the world's population resides in cities and their surrounding regions. This is especially true for developed nations.

This chapter outlined how the environment provides everything for human existence, from the air we breathe to the shelters that keep us warm in the winter and cool in the summer, as highlighted in the three functions of the environment. These functions—supply depot, waste repository and living space—have come into competition with one another throughout human history, leading to shortages in resources and polluted neighborhoods. This derogated environment can be traced to three main attributes: population, affluence and technology, as discussed using the IPAT model. In this chapter, we proposed that the major causes of environmental degradation could be explained by the *Tragedy of the Commons* and the theory of the *Treadmill of Production*. This degradation can be better understood as a result of our discussion of air, water and soil pollution, as well as in our discussion of global climate change.

## Review/Discussion Questions

1. How has the way cities are judged changed over time?
2. Which thinker's perspective struck you as a class conflict perspective? Structural functionalist? Symbolic interactionist?
3. What is the debate regarding technological determinism?
4. How have communication, transportation and production technologies affected the city?
5. How have the decisions of powerful people and policies affected the lives of urban residents?
6. How has the urban economy changed over time?
7. What is urban economic restructuring, and what has been its effect?
8. Name some renewable resources.
9. List some causes of environmental degradation.
10. What are you doing, if anything, to reduce your carbon footprint?

## Key Terms

**Advanced producer services** are the highly skilled service jobs of the current economy.

**Agglomeration** is the location of complementary functions near one another.

**Automation** is the use of machinery to control a manufacturing process rather than human laborers.

**Blasé attitude** is an urban resident's detachment from his or her environment in response to an overabundance of stimuli.

**Blockbusting** was a practice of local real estate agents in which they would buy a house from a white owner for one price and sell it to a black owner for a higher price.

**Built environment** is the totality of human-made physical structures that provides the environment for human activity.

**Capital mobility** is the state in the global economy in which profit-seeking enterprises are able to locate where it is most profitable.

**Concentric-zone model** is a model of urban growth that includes five circles ranging from an inner circle, including the downtown or "central business district," to an outer circle of suburbs.

**Deindustrialization** is the removal or reduction of manufacturing activity in urban regions across the country.

**Disneyfication** is the process of stripping a place of its authentic character and repackaging it in a sanitized and diluted format with the intention of making it more pleasant and easily consumable.

**Ecological footprint** is a measure of how much land is necessary to support the utilization of the three functions of the environment (resource depot, waste repository and living space) for a specified geographic region.

**Eminent domain** is the power of the government to seize private land for the public good.

**Environmental injustice** occurs when a social group (race, ethnicity, gender, age, etc.) is burdened with an environmental hazard.

**Exchange value** is the value of a commodity based on its anticipated price in relation to other commodities in the marketplace.

**Festival marketplace** is a type of urban mall featuring boutiques, restaurants and street entertainers, built in historic or historic-looking buildings.

**Gemeinschaft** is the connection and organization of community through kinship and long-held traditions.

**Gentrification** is the reinvestment of real estate capital into declining, inner-city neighborhoods to create a new residential infrastructure for middle- and high-income inhabitants.

**Gesellschaft** implies that people are connected only to accomplish their own interests.

**Ghettos** are neighborhoods in which certain racial, ethnic or religious groups are in some way forced to live.

**Global cities** are the command and control centers of the world's economic, political and cultural activities.

**Global warming** is a gradual increase in Earth's average temperature.

**Globalization** is the deepening, broadening and speeding up of worldwide interconnectedness in all aspects of life.

**Illegal lodging citations** are tickets issued by police to homeless individuals for taking up lodging (usually sleeping) in a public place.

**Landscape of power** is an impressive global landscape that is relatively free of the urban vernacular.

**Liminality** is a disoriented state characterized by ambiguity in which an old order has gone with no apparent new order to replace it.

**Mechanical solidarity** is a form of social cohesion in which people do similar work and share the same values and beliefs.

**Mortgage interest deduction** is a federal policy allowing homeowners to deduct the money they paid in mortgage interest and property tax from their income when they calculate their federal income taxes.

**Nonrenewable resources** are resources that cannot be regenerated in a timely manner or that are permanently depleted.

**Organic solidarity** is a form of social cohesion in which people work in a wide variety of specialized occupations and thus gain their social consensus from their need to rely on one another for goods and services.

**Racial restrictive covenants** were legally binding provisions on the deed of a property specifying which groups could and could not own that property.

**Racial zoning** is the restriction of residents to certain city blocks based upon their race.

**Real estate developers** build on land to make it more profitable.

**Redlining** was a policy that instructed banks to avoid lending within certain less "secure" neighborhoods (around which a red line would be drawn on a map).

**Renewable resources** are those resources that can be regenerated, like food and trees.

**Rustbelt** is a loosely defined area of Northeastern and Midwestern states that factories and many residents have departed.

**Social capital** refers to the connections among people that cause social cohesion.

**Speculators** are people who buy land hoping that it will increase in value as they hold on to it.

**SRO hotel** or single-room occupancy hotel, is a house, apartment building or residential hotel where low-income tenants live in small, single units sharing a common bathroom and where rent can typically be paid in short-term increments.

**Sunbelt** is a loosely defined area of the Southern and Western United States that generally has cheaper land, cheaper wages and lower taxes.

**Sustainability** is the ability of Earth's various systems, including human cultural systems and economies, to survive and adapt to changing environmental conditions indefinitely.

**Technological determinism** is the erroneous belief that technology is outside of social influence and that it actually structures social, economic and political life.

**The Great Migration** was the movement of 6 million black Americans out of the American South in the 20th century.

**Tourist bubble** is a specialized area of a downtown that presents a coherent, easy-to-understand and safe version of the city in order to lure visitors who might otherwise be skittish of cities.

**Urban renewal** refers to the efforts of urban leaders in the 1950s through the 1970s, using federal housing funds, to create amenities that they saw as being important for the post-industrial city.

**Urban vernacular** refers to the visual manifestations of the complex grittiness of the local culture.

**Urbanism** is a distinct way of life that emerges in cities.

**Urbanist** is a person who studies cities.

**Use value** is the value of an item based on its inherent usefulness.

# Bibliography

Beck, E. C. (1979). The Love Canal Tragedy. EPA Journal.

Bell, M. (1998). An invitation to environmental sociology. Thousand Oaks, CA: Pine Forge Press.

Blum, E. D. (2008). Love Canal Revisited: Race, Class, and Gender in Environmental Activism. Lawrence, KS: University Press of Kansas.

Brown, C. S. (1995). Anthropocentrism and Ecocentrism: The Quest for a New World View. Midwest Quarterly, 36 (2), 191-202.

Brown-Saracino, J. (2009). A neighborhood that never changes : gentrification, social preservation, and the search for authenticity. University of Chicago Press, Chicago.

Bruckner, M. (2008). The Gulf of Mexico Dead Zone. Microbial Life Educational Resources. <http://serc.carleton.edu/micro-belife/topics/deadzone/> (2008).

Boyer, M. (1992). Cities for sale: Merchandising history at South Street Seaport. In M. Sorkin (ed.), Variations on a theme park: the new American city and the end of public space, Hill and Wang, New York, xv, 252.

Bullard, R. D. (1983). Solid Waste Sites and the Houston Black Community. Sociological Inquiry, 53, 273-288.

Castells, M. (1977). The urban question : a Marxist approach. MIT Press, Cambridge, Mass.

Castells, M. (1983). The city and the grassroots : a cross-cultural theory of urban social movements. E. Arnold; University of California Press, London Berkeley.

Cha, M. (2008). The Creation of Barbie. <http://www.lclark.edu/~soan221/97/Barbie5.html> (2008).

Chertow, M. R. (2001). The IPAT Equation and Its Variants: Changing Views of Technology and Environmental Impact. Journal of Industrial Ecology, 4, 13-29.

CNN (2007). Feds OK drought deal letting Georgia keep more water. <http://www.cnn.com/2007/US/11/16/southern.drought/index.html> (2008).

Coleman, J. (2011). "World's 'seven billionth baby' is born." The Gardian. <http://www.guardian.co.uk/world/2011/oct/31/seven-billionth-baby-born-philippines?intcmp=122> (2012).

Commoner, B. (1972). The Environmental Cost of Economic Growth. In R. G. Ridker (Ed.), Population Resources and the Environment (pp. 339-363). Washington, DC: Government Printing Office.

Dietz, T. & Rosa, E. A. (1994). Rethinking the Environmental Impacts of Pollution, Affluence, and Technology. Human Ecology Review, 1, 277-300.

Dietz, T., Rosa, E. A., & York, R. (2007). Driving the Human Ecological Footprint. Frontiers in Ecology and the Environment, 5, 13-18.

Dobson, D. M. (2002). From Ice Cores to Tree Rings. In S. L. Spray, & K. L. McGlothlin (Eds.), Global Climate Change, Exploring Environmental Challenges: A Multidisciplinary Approach (pp. 3-30). New York: Rowman & Littlefield Publishers, Inc.

Drake, S. C., & Cayton, H. R. (1962). Black metropolis; a study of Negro life in a northern city. Harper & Row, New York,.

Duncan, O. D. (1961). From Social System to Ecosystem. Sociological Inquiry, 31, 140-149.

Dunlap, R. E. (1994). The Nature and Causes of Environmental Problems: A Socio-Ecological Perspective. In K. S. Association (Ed.), Environment and Development (pp. 45-84). Seoul, Korea: Seoul Press.

Dunlap, R. E. & Catton, W. R. Jr. (2002). Which Function(s) of the Environment Do We Study? A comparison of environmental and natural resource sociology. Society and Natural Resources, 15, 239-249.

Durkheim, E., & Halls,W. D. (1984). The division of labor in society. Free Press, New York.

Ehrlich, P. R., & Holdren, J. P. (1971). Impact of Population Growth. Science, 171, 1212-1217.

Engels, F. (1952). The condition of the working-class in England in 1844 : with a preface written in 1892. Allen and Unwin, Ltd., London.

Environment News Service (2007). Asian Brown Clouds Intensify Global Warming. <http://www.ens-newswire.com/ens/aug2007/2007-08-01-02.asp> (2008).

Environmental Protection Agency (2008). Climate Change: Basic Information. <http://www.epa.gov/climatechange/basicinfo.html> (2008).

Environmental Protection Agency (2007). Continuing the Promise of Earth Day. <http://www.epa.gov/superfund/20years/ch1pg2.htm> (2008).

Environmental Protection Agency (2011). Municipal Solid Waste Generation, Recycling, and Disposal in the United States: Facts and Figures for 2010. EPA-530-F-11-005. <www.epa.gov/wastes> (2012)

Fagan, B. (2004). The Long Summer: How climate changed civilization. New York: Basic Books.

Fowlkes, M. R., & Miller, P. Y. (1983). Love Canal: The social construction of disaster. Washington, DC: Federal Emergency Management Agency.

Frieden, B. J., & Sagalyn L. B. (1989). Downtown, Inc. : how America rebuilds cities. MIT Press, Cambridge, Mass.

Gans, H. J. (1962). The urban villagers : group and class in the life of Italian-Americans. Free Press of Glencoe, [New York].

Gordon, D. M., Edwards, R., & Reich, M. (1982). Segmented work, divided workers : the historical transformation of labor in the

United States. Cambridge University Press, Cambridge [Cambridgeshire]; New York.

Gould, K. A., Pellow, D. N., & Schnaiberg, A. (2004). Interrogating the Treadmill of Production: Everything You Wanted to Know about the Treadmill but Were Afraid to Ask. Organization Environment, 17, 296-316.

Hardin, G. (1968). The Tragedy of the Commons. Science, 162, 1243-1248.

Harper, C. L. (2008). Environment and Society: Human Perspectives on Environmental Change. Upper Saddle River, NJ: Pearson Education, Inc.

Harris, C., & Ullman, E. (1945). The Nature of Cities. The Annals of the American Academy of Political and Social Science, 242 (1), 7-17.

Harrison, B., & Bluestone, B. (1990). The Great U-Turn: Corporate Restructuring and the Polarizing of America. New York: Basic Books.

Harvey, D. (1973). Social justice and the city. Johns Hopkins University Press, [Baltimore].

Harvey, D. (1982). The limits to capital. University of Chicago Press; B. Blackwell, Chicago Oxford [Oxfordshire].

Harvey, D. (1985). The urbanization of capital : studies in the history and theory of capitalist urbanization. John Hopkins University Press, Baltimore, Md.

Held, D., & McGrew, A. G. (2000). The global transformations reader : an introduction to the globalization debate. Polity Press in association with Blackwell, Malden, MA.

Holechek, J. L., Cole, R. A., Fisher, J. T., & Valdez, R. (2000). Natural Resources: ecology, economics, and policy. Upper Saddle River, NJ: Prentice-Hall.

Intergovernmental Panel on Climate Change (2007a). Climate Change 2007: Impacts, Adaptation and Vulnerability. Contribution of Working Group II to the Fourth Assessment Report of the Intergovernmental Panel on Climate Change, Cambridge, UK: Cambridge University Press.

Intergovernmental Panel on Climate Change (2007b). Climate Change 2007: The Physical Science Basis. Contribution of Working Group I to the Fourth Assessment Report of the Intergovernmental Panel on Climate Change, Cambridge, UK: Cambridge University Press.

Jacobs, J. (1961). The death and life of great American cities. Random House, New York.

Judd, D. R., & Fainstein, S. S. (1999). The tourist city. Yale University Press, New Haven.

Kemp, D. D. (2004). Exploring Environmental Issues: An Integrated Approach. London, UK: Routledge.

Lobell, D. B., Burke, M. B., Tebaldi, C., Mastrandrea, M. D., Falcon, W. P., & Naylor, R. L. (2008). Prioritizing Climate Change Adaptation Needs for Food Security in 2030. Science, 319, 607-610.

Logan, J. R., & Molotch, H. L. (1987). Urban fortunes : the political economy of place. University of California Press, Berkeley, CA.

McGraw-Hill (2003). McGraw-Hill Dictionary of Environmental Science. New York: McGraw-Hill.

Menzel, P. & Mann, C. C. (1995). Material World: A Global Family Portrait. San Francisco, CA: Sierra Club Books.

Miller, G. T. (2007). Living in the Environment: Principles, Connections, and Solutions. Belmont, CA: Thomson Higher Learning.

Moore, M., Smith, R. B., Boone, P., Bryant, A., Beaver, C., Stanzler, W., Beman, J., Warner Bros., Dog Eat Dog Films and Warner Home Video (1990). Roger & me. Warner Home Video, Burbank, CA.

Park, R. E. (1952). Human communities. Free Press, New York.

Park, R. E., Wirth, L., McKenzie, R. D., & Burgess, E. W. (1925). The city. The University of Chicago press, Chicago, Ill.

Pastor, M., Sadd, J. L., & Morello-Frosch, R. (2004). Waiting to Inhale: The Demographics of Toxic Air Release Facilities in 21st-Century California. Social Science Quarterly, 85, 420-440.

Patch, J., & Brenner, N. (2007). Gentrification. In G. Ritzer (ed.), Encyclopedia of Sociology, Blackwell, London.

Pellow, D. N. (2000). Environmental Inequality Formation: Toward a Theory of Environmental Injustice. The American Behavioral Scientist, 43, 581-601.

Reich, R. B. (1992). The work of nations : preparing ourselves for 21st century capitalism. Vintage Books, New York.

Robinson, J. (2004). Ordinary cities : between modernity and development. Routledge, London.

Royte, E. (2005). Garbage Land: On the secret trail of trash. New York: Little, Brown and Company.

Sassen, S. (1991). The global city : New York, London, Tokyo. Princeton University Press, Princeton, N.J.

Schnaiberg, A., & Gould, K. A. (1994). Environment and Society: The Enduring Conflict. New York: St. Martin's.

Simmel, G. (1971). On individuality and social forms; selected writings. University of Chicago Press, Chicago,.

Smith, N. (1996). The New Urban Frontier: Gentrification and the Revanchist City. Routledge, London ; New York.

Snow, D. A., & Anderson, L. (1993). Down on their luck : a study of homeless street people. University of California Press, Berkeley.

Stasenko, M. (2001). Number of Cars. The Physics Factbook. <http://hypertextbook.com/facts/2001/MarinaStasenko.shtml> (2008).

Tönnies, F. (1955). Community and association (Gemeinschaft und Gesellschaft). Routledge & Paul, London,.

Tran, T. (2008). Pollution curbs turn Beijing into urban laboratory. <http://hosted.ap.org/dynamic/stories/O/OLY_OLYMPICS_LABORATORY?SITE=NYMID&SECTION=HOME&TEMPLATE=DEFAULT> (2008).

Turner, V. W. (1970). The forest of symbols : aspects of Ndembu ritual. Cornell University Press, Ithaca [N.Y.], London.

U. S. Census Bureau (2008a). Historical Estimates of World Population. <http://www.census.gov/ipc/www/worldhis.html> (2008).

U. S. Census Bureau (2008b). World Population Information. International Data Base. <http://www.census.gov/ipc/www/idb/worldpopinfo.html> (2008).

U. S. Geological Survey (2008). Where is the Earth's Water's Located? Water Science. <http://ga.water.usgs.gov/edu/earthwherewater.html> (2008).

United States National Advisory Commission on Civil Disorders (1988). The Kerner report : the 1968 report of the National Advisory Commission on Civil Disorders. Pantheon Books, New York.

University of Buffalo University Archives (2008). Love Canal Collections. University Archives. <http://ublib.buffalo.edu/libraries/specialcollections/lovecanal/about.html#info> (2008).

Veblen, T. (1899, 1994). The Theory of the Leisure Class. London, UK: Constable.

Wackernagel, M., & Rees, W. (1996). Our Ecological Footprint: Reducing Human Impact on the Earth. Gabriola Island, BC: New Society Publishers.

Wackernagel, M., Onisto, L., Bello, P., Linares, A. C., López Falfán, I. S., Méndez García, J., Suárez Guerrero, A. I., & Suárez Guerrero, M. G. (1999). National natural capital accounting with the ecological footprint concept. Ecological Economics, 29, 375-390.

Wilson, W. J. (1996). When work disappears : the world of the new urban poor. Knopf, New York.

Wirth, L. (1995). Urbanism as a way of life. In P. Kasinitz (ed.), Metropolis : center and symbol of our times, Macmillan, Hound-mills, Basingstoke, Hampshire, 58-84.

Wirth, L., Furez, M., & Burchard, E. L. (1938). Local community fact book. The University of Chicago Press;, Chicago.

Wright, T. (1997). Out of place : homeless mobilizations, subcities, and contested landscapes. State University of New York Press, Albany.

York, R., Rosa, E., & Dietz, T. (2003). Footprints on the Earth: The Environmental Consequences of Modernity. American Sociological Review, 68, 279-300.

Zukin, S. (1982). Loft living : culture and capital in urban change. Johns Hopkins University Press, Baltimore.

Zukin, S. (1991). Landscapes of power : from Detroit to Disney World. University of California Press, Berkeley.

CHAPTER FIFTEEN

# Collective Behavior, Social Movements and Social Change

## Brian G. Moss

**Chapter Objectives**
At the end of this chapter, students should be able to:

- Describe how social movements and collective behavior differ.
- List the six factors required to produce social change.
- List the various forms of collective behavior.
- List and describe some of the methods used to disperse propaganda.
- List and describe the four main types of social movements.
- Describe three theories that attempt to explain the causes of social movements.
- Explain how convergence and divergence theories differ.
- Explain how functionalist, conflict and symbolic interactionist theories view social change.

The process by which social change occurs is extremely complex and composed of social, political and cultural elements. Social change can be caused by one event or be the result of a series of interrelated events. It can appear organized at some times and chaotic at others. Sociologists make a distinction between *social movements*, which tend to be more organized and purposeful, and **collective behavior**, which tends to be more random and spontaneous.

Two examples of social movements in the United States include the fight for civil rights and the advocacy for environmental responsibility. Both of these movements were systematically planned, with clearly defined goals, and included participation from private citizens, corporations, religious organizations and

Chapter 15: Collective Behavior, Social Movements and Social Change    387 politicians. Conversely, collective behavior often lacks structure.

For example, in late 2010, Egypt underwent a series of protests that spread across northern Africa and the Middle East which are often referred to as the "Arab Spring" or "Arab Awakening"(Khalidi, 2011). At first, the protests seemed relatively isolated and were purportedly caused by decades of economic and political oppression. But, over the course of 18 days, the spontaneous collective behavior quickly turned into a large-scale social movement that demanded the resignation of President Hosni Mubarak. Organizers harnessed the connectivity of social media, leading to well-organized demonstrations, marches and rallies throughout Egypt. On February 11, 2011, Mubarak resigned and transferred power to military commanders (Kirkpatrick, 2011).

As we study social change, we will see that it can occur quickly or more gradually. Generally, most change is so subtle we are unaware it is occurring. This chapter will highlight sociological concepts and theories that relate to the process of social change and how it dramatically transforms societies.

# Forms of Collective Behavior

## Panic

A **panic** is a flight to safety in response to the fear of immediate danger. In most instances, the fear is real—the building is on fire, for example, and failing to flee could result in serious injury or death. When groups of people panic together, they often act irrationally and selfishly, each person trying to save himself from the perceived danger.

An example of a panic occurred at the Hillsborough soccer stadium in Sheffield, England, on April 15, 1989. A group of 5,000 fans waited outside the stadium to be let in for a soccer match. Police worried that the crowd might cause a stampede, so they opened a small gate. The fans filled the gate and began to be crushed by others pushing from behind. The trapped fans panicked and began shoving each other trying to escape, while some tried to climb over the fencing. As a result, 96 people died and 766 were injured (Scraton, 1999).

## Mass Hysteria

**Mass hysteria** is similar to a panic except that there is no real danger, and the participants do not check to see whether the source of the fear is real or not.

In November 1994, a hospital received a call that a fire had broken out in a women's dormitory at United Arab Emirates University and some victims were on their way to the hospital. Once at the hospital, the students displayed a number of behaviors such as heavy breathing, shaking, dizziness, wailing, screaming and fainting. Physical examinations were conducted only to discover that the women were fine. So what had happened? A student had been burning incense in her room when the other women smelled the smoke and concluded the dorms were on fire, triggering mass hysteria (Amin, Hamdi & Eapen, 1997).

Mass hysteria includes situations in which one person exhibits very real symptoms and, upon seeing the symptoms, others in the group believe that they, too, are ill and begin displaying similar symptoms, even though they are not sick.

## Crowds: Types of Crowd Behaviors

**Crowds** are groups of people doing something together for a short period of time (Schnapp & Tiews, 2006). There are five types of crowds:

1. The *casual crowd* is the most loosely structured. Coined by Herbert Blumer, the term is used to describe groups of people who share only a minimum level of emotional or physical interaction (Blumer & Shibutani, 1970). People enter and leave the crowd easily, often without even talking to one another. This type of crowd would include a group of people listening to a street musician. People enter the crowd to see what is going on, stay if they like the music, and casually move on when they are finished listening.

2. A *conventional crowd* has a little more structure, and the behavior of the crowd is largely predictable. Examples of conventional crowds include the audience at a play or people riding a bus together. People in such crowds rarely

interact with each other and, when they do, the interaction is often minimal, with people tending to follow conventional norms (Le Bon, 2009).

3. An *expressive crowd* forms with the intent of giving its members the opportunity for personal expression. Examples include fans at a sporting event who may cheer and yell in support of their team, or people attending Mardi Gras in New Orleans, who shout and throw beads at one another. On the surface these crowds may appear to be out of control, but in reality there are roles and norms guiding their behavior. People in these crowds know the line between acceptable and unacceptable behavior, and most don't cross it; those who do are often removed (Le Bon, 2009).

4. *Solidaristic crowds* form in order to give their members a sense of unity and belonging (Le Bon, 2009). One example was the Million Man March organized by Nation of Islam leader Louis Farrakhan on October 16, 1995, in Washington, D.C. The march was designed to bring black men together and strengthen their sense

of solidarity. Many new organizations emerged in response to the march, including MALE (Maturing Africans Learning from Each other), which encourages men to work together to solve issues (Cooper, Groce & Thomas, 2003). Solidaristic crowds may appear spontaneous, but they are well-planned, and the activities are choreographed in advance.

5. *Reactionary crowds* form in response to some event or situation (Drury, 2002). Reactionary crowds are usually angry and hostile and can easily become violent. The two most common forms of reactionary crowds are mobs and riots (Drury, 2002). **Mobs** channel their anger onto a single target. They often have leaders and some degree of structure. After the goals of the mob are met, the crowd usually disperses. Examples include the Ku Klux Klan lynchings and fire bombings in the South, and the members of Islamic Jihad who target Jews (Drury, 2002; Borgeson & Valeri, 2007).

A **riot** is a violent crowd that moves from target to target over the course of hours or days. Riot-

How many casual crowds were you a part of today?

Source: Stu Spivack

ers often focus their anger on groups they dislike and engage in activities such as violence, looting and destruction of property. A riot occurred on the Cronulla Beach in Sydney, Australia, in December 2005. The week before the riot, three lifeguards had been taunting four men of Lebanese descent with comments such as "Lebs can't swim" (Poynting, 2006). The men retaliated by brutally beating two of the lifeguards. The media covered the story extensively, and a local radio show host called for a rally to take place as a show of force. When the weekend arrived, 5,000 participants descended on the beach. The crowd, many wearing T-shirts saying "100 Percent Aussie Pride" and "The Ethnic Cleansing Unit" then moved across the beach shouting racist slogans and attacking anyone they thought was of Middle Eastern descent (Poynting, 2006).

## Common Traits of Crowds

No matter the type of crowd, most share similar traits. The first is *uncertainty*—no one is exactly sure of the outcome, nor do they all have the same expectations regarding behavior. The second is a *sense of urgency*—there is often the sense that something must be done right away and that by simply standing around, time is being wasted. The third is *communication*—the ideas, as well as the mood and attitude shared by the group help force conformity among its members. The fourth is *suggestibility*—members of a crowd tend to be more open to suggestion and less likely to be critical of ideas suggested by others. The fifth is *permissiveness*—members of crowds often feel free of conventional norms and act and say things differently than they would on their own (McPhail, 1991).

# Theories of Crowd Behavior

## Social Contagion Theory

According to Gustave Le Bon's **social contagion theory**, crowds are in agreement in both thought and action, and in this sense, they share the same collective mind (Le Bon, 1960). According to Le Bon, the collective mind represents the mind of a barbarian: It is emotional and irrational. Le Bon argues that each of us deep down is a barbarian but that we hide our true thoughts and feelings in order

to fit into the social norms and values of society. All of that hiding is revealed among individuals in a crowd because they become emboldened by its numbers; acting as a group takes away their personal responsibility, releasing them to become more like their real selves (Le Bon, 1960).

Le Bon argued that people give up their individuality and willingly become part of the collective mind due to social contagion. **Social contagion** is the spread of certain emotions or actions from one member of the crowd to another (Le Bon, 1960). An example is laughter in a movie theater spreading from one audience member to many (Le Bon, 1960).

Recently, however, evidence provided by sociologists discredits Le Bon's idea of the collective mind. First, it ignores and downplays the differences among the individuals who make up the crowd (Abrams & Hogg, 1990). Second, it applies individual attributes, such as a mind or conscience, to a group when groups cannot possess these personal attributes.

## Convergence Theory

According to **convergence theory**, people in crowds share the same attitudes, views and beliefs, and it is these similarities that brought these individuals together in the first place (Turner & Killian, 1993). A gay rights rally is one example. People who support rights for gays are likely to be motivated, based on their beliefs, to attend the rally to show their support for the cause. Others may be attracted to the rally to protest gay rights, but they, too, would be motivated to attend based on their views and beliefs.

## Emergent Norm Theory

From the viewpoint of the **emergent norm theory**, crowds tend to approach unanimity because one set of behavioral norms is accepted by the entire crowd (Turner & Killian, 1993). Members of the crowd who refuse to adopt the emergent norms would receive social pressure from other crowd members to do so.

For example, a crowd protesting police brutality might begin throwing rocks at officers. Those who refuse to throw the rocks might still support the group and the emergent norm through their passive presence. Members of the group who urge others to stop throwing the rocks might likely be heckled or pushed aside (Turner & Killian, 1993). From outside the crowd, it could appear as if all were in agreement. That might not be the case, however, since those in attendance may remain only because they are afraid to leave.

# Crowds: Dispersed

## Fashions, Fads and Crazes

**Fashions** involve a large number of people adhering to a particular innovation. Fashions usually occur with clothes and style of dress, such as "pegging," or excessively taking in, jeans in the late 1980s and early 1990s. But fashions tend to burn out over a short period of time. They also are likely to be subject to traditional norms.

Fashion subcultures are outside the realm of popular fashion. In a fashion subculture, a trend might be popular only among a small percentage of the population. Goth fashion is an example of a fashion subculture. It is based in part on the dichotomy of light and dark, with the understanding that neither would exist without the other. Goths use white and black makeup to depict death and typically wear black clothing (Langman, 2008).

**Fads** are a temporary infatuation with a particular practice or innovation. Examples include the Pet Rocks and mood rings of the 1970s, Garbage Pail Kids and jelly shoes in the 1980s, and Beanie Babies and slap bracelets in the 1990s. Recent fads include Apple iPods and Texas Hold'em poker (Crazy Fads, 2008).

**Crazes** are fads that can bring serious consequences for those involved. Many crazes are financial in nature. One example, the dot-com stocks of the late 1990s, rapidly soared in value as everyone rushed in to buy, and then quickly deflated as everyone tried to sell before the dot-com companies went out of business. The value of many dot-com stocks, such as Metro One Telecom and Digital Island, went from more than a hundred dollars a share to only a few dollars (Lewis, 2008).

Source: Luz Alvarez

In your opinion, what fashion trends are popular right now?

## Rumors and Gossip

A **rumor** is an unverified story that spreads from person to person through sources such as the Internet or by word of mouth (Pratkanis & Aronson, 1992). As the story is retold, bits are left out or embellished so that even if it was originally based on facts, the resulting version may be entirely inaccurate. People often turn to rumors when trying to find out what is happening in situations where not a lot is known.

**Gossip** involves talk about the personal and private lives of others (Pratkanis & Aronson, 1992). The tabloid industry is almost entirely devoted to making money off the gossip surrounding celebrities.

## Public Opinion

In sociology, the **public** refers to a group that shares the same common interest, positions or thoughts (Pratkanis & Aronson, 1992). Examples of public groups include the Republican and Democratic political parties, the National Rifle Association, and the American Association of Retired Persons. The attitudes and beliefs held by the public are known as **public opinion** (Lewis, 2001).

## Propaganda

Public opinion is not concrete and can change over time. **Propaganda** refers to those methods designed to influence people's opinions (Lewis, 2001). Politicians and advertisers know public opinion can change, and they use various propaganda methods aimed at influencing it to be more favorable to them. Five of the more popular methods are:

1. *Ad nauseam:* Repeating a message over and over again. Examples include television ads for a product that are run repeatedly. In the political arena, this includes the placement of a candidate's advertisement in so many places that the average person encounters it wherever he or she goes.
2. *Bandwagon:* The idea that everyone is doing it, so you should, too. This method appeals to people's desire to be on the winning side and not get left behind. One example is advertisements telling the public that a popular band is coming to town: The message conveyed is that everyone is going to go and have a great time, and you do not want to miss out on the fun.
3. *Glittering generalities*: Applying emotionally appealing words to a product or cause without presenting any factual proof to support the claim. An advertisement might say that a particular restaurant has the "Best Burgers in America," for example, without offering proof.
4. *Transfer*: Associating one thing with something else that is already widely revered or desirable. For example, adding an American flag to a television commercial for an automobile might suggest that the vehicle is solid and strong like the idea of America, or that you would be performing some sort of patriotic duty if you bought the car.
5. *Testimonial*: Using the reputation of a person pitching the product as an endorsement. This method has celebrities claim a particular product or service is so good that they use it themselves.

## Media Influence

The media have the power to influence public opinion because newsroom leaders choose which issues and stories reporters are going to cover.

There are four ways in which the media influence public opinion. First, they *authenticate* information by showing images and discussing them, which make them seem more real. A person would have a difficult time trying to convince others that an earthquake had not hit China if everyone saw aftermath videos on television or YouTube.

Second, media *validate* private opinions and viewpoints. People's views might be strengthened if a commentator they respect offers similar views.

Third, media *legitimize* ideas, even unconventional ones. Ideas that at first glance appear crazy might seem more reasonable over time if a person routinely sees or hears them in the media.

Fourth, the media *concretize* unrestrained and poorly defined ideas. The media do this by providing labels such as "global warming" or "the housing bust" over larger issues, making them appear to be connected (McCombs, 2004).

# Social Movements

**Social movements** are collective efforts designed to bring about social change. They are usually conducted using non-institutionalized methods (Melbourne & Wilson, 1973). An example of a social movement that developed over time is the women's suffrage movement in the United States, which had its first meeting in Seneca Falls, New York, in 1848. Women signed the *Declaration of Sentiments and Resolutions*, which laid out the rights they wanted, including the right to vote. It was not until 1920, when the 19th Amendment to the Constitution was ratified, however, that women won this right (Barber, 2008). Social movements have a purpose and an agenda, so they generally involve more structure than other forms of collective behavior.

Social movements also tend to have more staying power, as illustrated by women's suffrage. While a riot or mob might be in action for a couple of hours, a social movement could last for decades (Melbourne & Wilson, 1973).

What forms of media have the greatest influence over you?

## Four Types of Social Movements

1. *Revolutionary movements*: They seek to overthrow a government and start a new and completely different one. In order to accomplish their goals, revolutionary movements usually take violent and illegal action (Stewart, Smith & Denton, 1994). Generally, it is considered an act of treason for a citizen to declare war on the federal government. But in the 1950s' Cuban Revolution, Fidel Castro overthrew President Fulgencio Batista, appointed himself leader of the country and installed a new socialist government (Montaner, 2007).

2. *Reform movements*: Such movements desire only limited change to the status quo. They believe the overall social structure is good enough and does not need to be completely torn down. But they still want minor changes to make the system better (Stewart, Smith & Denton, 1994).

3. For example, the push by U.S. workers in the 1930s for a national minimum wage was a reform movement. Business owners and other capitalists fiercely fought the idea of a minimum wage, arguing that workers should be able to contract their labor at any price they saw fit and that it was not the business of government to determine what workers could charge for their labor (Smith, 2008). It is interesting to note that some of the arguments made by business interests against minimum wage laws were similar to those made against the implementation of child labor laws (Fischer, 1995).

4. *Resistance movements*: These seek to maintain the status quo and to prevent any social change from occurring (Stewart, Smith & Denton, 1994). One example is the Know Nothings, so called because when asked about their movement, members would reply, "I know nothing."

The Know Nothings, along with the Ku Klux Klan and the Knights of Luther, opposed the advancement of Catholics in society. They saw them as a threat to democracy, believing they were mindless followers of the Pope, who they said had deviated from the Bible since they worshiped statues of the Virgin Mary. In an effort to stop Catholics from gaining power, these groups discriminated against them in employment by putting up signs such as "No Irish Need Apply." They also burned parishes, attacked convents, killed Catholics and vehemently opposed the first Catholic to run for U.S. president, Al Smith. (Davidson & Williams, 1997).

5. *Expressive movements*: This mind-set wants to change individuals, not society. Many religious organizations that aggressively try to recruit new members to their faith, such as Jehovah's Witnesses and Hare Krishna, are examples of expressive movements (Burns, 1990).

## Three Possible Causes of Social Movements

**Frustration theory**, developed by Eric Hoeffer (1966), claims that those who get involved in social movements are frustrated or disturbed. They join social movements as a way to divert attention away from themselves and their personal problems, putting their thoughts and energies instead into their "cause." By being part of a cause, they are able to view themselves positively as people trying to help not only themselves but others as well.

One problem with this theory is that it focuses blame on participants in the movement instead of on society and its deficiencies. People are often drawn to social movements because of racial and or sexual discrimination. It was societal problems that prompted them to get involved, not their own personal problems (Morris & Mueller, 1992).

**Breakdown-frustration theory** contends that social breakdowns lead to social movements when frustration mounts among the masses (Morris & Mueller, 1992). An example might be lack of food, as deprivation and hunger can lead to rebellion (Oberschall, 1995). Imagine the social unrest that

would develop if none of the supermarkets had food, and people were going hungry and could not feed their children.

**Resource mobilization theory** argues that social movements are initiated only when the necessary resources and mobilization tools are available. According to this theory, movements do not come into being simply because of frustration. Instead, they exist because core organizers garner the required support, money and media access.

This theory is often criticized for ignoring the role frustration plays in social movements. If the cause being advocated had lots of money and resources, then it would likely rely heavily on the methods laid out by the resource mobilization theory. If the movement, however, is made up of poor people with few resources, it is more likely to be formed through frustration (Morris & Mueller, 1992).

## Consequences of Social Movements

Although various causes of social movements were presented earlier in the chapter, we need to also understand the effects of these actions. More specifically, if a social movement's aim is to change society, what consequences will this have for a society and its members?

To help answer this question, we will examine the work of Dieter Rucht (1992), who provides a model for analyzing the consequences of social movements. His framework maintains that social movements possess both intended and unintended influences to those inside and outside the group. Table 1 applies Rucht's concepts to the prohibition movement.

During the early 1900s, the Prohibition Party made a concerted effort to make the sale of alcohol illegal in the United States. After years of planning, the movement successfully worked to pass the 18th Amendment to the Constitution, which outlawed the production, sale, transportation and import or export of alcohol.

With this action, the movement achieved its intended, external purpose. At the same time, however, there was an unintended, external consequence. Throughout the country, alcohol continued to be consumed primarily through a black

**TABLE 15.1** Applying Rucht's Consequences of Social Movements Model to the Prohibition Movement

|  | Internal | External |
|---|---|---|
| **Intended** | Shared Beliefs & Group Cohesion | 18th Amendment: Prohibition |
| **Unintended** | Disagreement of Purpose | Black Market & Organized Crime |

market. Prohibition also created an opportunity for organized crime to profit from bootlegging and speakeasies (illegal barrooms). The movement had intended to form an internal group of like-minded individuals to work on the shared belief that prohibition was necessary. The unintended, internal consequence was that two factions within the party began to disagree about the focus of the movement. Some members wanted to broaden the agenda to include other conservative social issues. But a second faction desired to keep a narrow focus on outlawing alcohol.

Rucht's model makes us realize that social movements have consequences beyond any outcome stated by the group. In fact, change spurred by social movements and collective behavior has implications for both the macro structure and the micro interactions of society.

## Changes in the Macro Structure

Various concepts and theories have been introduced that sociologists use to evaluate the impact of social change. We can now think about change occurring at two distinct levels of sociological analysis: Macro structure and micro interactions.

The 19th century sociologist Ferdinand Tönnies (2001) provides another perspective about changes in social structure and the consequences this has for people. Tönnies was interested in the how societies changed over time. His approach to understanding this process is referred to as the **Gemeinschaft-Gesellschaft transition**.

Tönnies made a distinction between Gemeinschaft and Gesellschaft social systems. Gemeinschaft communities consist of more intimate relationships, shared beliefs and stronger attachments. These type of communities differ from Gesellschaft societies, which are dominated by impersonal relationships and where individual accomplishments and self-interest are valued.

Tönnies believed that with social change, communities generally moved from Gemeinschaft to Gesellschaft. To Tönnies, the transition between these two classifications is a product of human action altering the social structure of the social system. For instance, the industrial revolution dramatically transformed some areas of the world from being primarily agricultural to being primarily industrial. This revolutionary form of modernization altered the components of the social structure. With industrialization came institutional changes, as well as new social roles, social statuses and group dynamics. The overall nature of interconnectedness changed as a consequence of the technological advances of the time period.

## Changes in Micro Interactions

As the large-scale social features of a society change, so do the interactions between its members. Changes in micro interactions often rapidly spread through societies and are a consequence of institutional transformations. Since the mid-1980s, electronic devices in the United States have become more integrated into our society. These technological advances have altered how many individuals interact. Mass availability of electronic communication devices has replaced face-to-face interactions. In a relatively short period of time, access to social media such as Twitter, MySpace and Facebook, the Internet, cell phones, email and text messaging have had profound implications for social interactions.

## A Global Approach to Social Change

Societies change around the globe. They change, in part, due to **modernization** and the development of new technologies. When a society moves from being agricultural to industrial, sociologists would say that the move represents modernization.

Modernization can serve to weaken traditions within a culture, though this is not always the case (Stahler-Sholk, Kuecker & Vanden, 2008). For example, researchers studied 496 television commercials aired on three networks in China during the summer of 2000. They examined the dominant values found in each commercial's theme and discovered that both traditional and modern values were present in most of the commercials, suggesting that tradition still plays a strong role in modern China (Zhang & Harwood, 2001).

Modernization is having the greatest effect on those societies that are the least modern. In parts of Africa and South America, many people have no access to phones. With the advent of cell phone technology, telephone and Internet access is often available (Racanelli, 2008). **Convergence theory** states that modernizations will bring Western and non-Western countries together as they become more and more technologically equal. It is believed that when this happens, countries not previously exposed to Western technology and ideas will abandon their old ways for more Western lifestyles (Sasaki, 2008).

The opposite view is offered by **divergence theory**, which argues that with modernization comes a growing divide between Western and non-Western societies as people in the non-Western societies reject Western values. Examples of this can be seen throughout Muslim societies in the Middle East. Middle Easterners may adopt Western technologies, but they still maintain their own traditions (Hunter & Malik, 2005).

## Social Factors Influencing Social Change

Collective behavior usually does not happen on its own. Triggers include life-threatening danger, potential economic loss and some forms of social injustice. The particular behavior depends on how the people involved view the problem. If they believe it is a relatively straightforward issue, they may engage in the least organized forms of collective behavior: a panic or riot. If, on the other hand, the problem is viewed as more multifaceted with difficult-to-achieve solutions, the people involved may choose to engage in a social movement.

According to Neil Smelser's *value-added approach* (1962), six factors are required to produce collective behavior:

1.  *Structural conduciveness.* The people involved

When it comes to the Middle East, which theory, convergence or divergence, do you think is the most likely outcome?

must be able to communicate their problems with each other. Face-to-face communication is possible for people living next to each other in a neighborhood or can occur using a phone or the Internet. Once the problems have been voiced, the people involved need to be able to take action.

2. *Social strain.* An injustice or conflict needs to be present in combination with an unwillingness or inability of the side holding the power to correct the situation or make amends.

3. *Generalized belief.* The people involved must have a shared understanding about the cause or causes of the conflict.

4. *Precipitating factors.* An event or spark intensifies the conflict, which pushes people into action.

5. *Mobilization for action.* The people organize, and leaders emerge and direct the people.

6. *Failure of formal social controls.* In most situations, agents of social control, such as the police or the National Guard, are able to prevent any collective action from occurring. This is why instances of collective behavior, such as riots, occur so infrequently. For collective action to occur, police and other social control agents must fail in their attempts to stop the people.

# Sociological Theories on Social Change

## Functionalist Perspective on Social Change

Those adhering to the functionalist perspective believe that social change is a gradual process. Below are three theories that attempt to explain how this happens:

### Evolutionary Theory

**Evolutionary theory** states that societies evolve over time from simple to more complex forms. One early supporter of this theory was Herbert Spencer, who believed that societies evolve on the basis of natural selection; good aspects of a society flourish, while bad aspects die off. He believed that society

is an organized entity that possesses organic properties. Over time, the evolutionary process allows societies to build on their strengths and discard their weaknesses.

Consequently, Spencer believed that social reformers or even policymakers can have a negative impact on the evolutionary trajectory of a social system and that societies should be allowed to unfold naturally.

One criticism of this theory is that societal evolution does not necessarily equal an improvement. Pastoral societies had their strengths and weaknesses, as do modern industrial societies (Goodwin & Scimecca, 2005).

### Cyclical Theory

Unlike evolutionary theory, **cyclical theory** argues that societies move back and forth in a continuous series of cycles. The following three theories all stem from the cyclical theory.

#### Spengler's Theory of Majestic Cycles

The majestic cycles theory was developed by German historian Oswald Spengler. His idea was that cultures are like living organisms: They are born, grow up, mature, grow old and then die. When cultures die, they are simply replaced by new ones, as once great societies like the Greeks and Egyptians have been replaced. When he wrote this theory, he was convinced that Western civilization was in a stage of old age and close to dying off (Spengler & Atkinson, 1926).

#### Toynbee's Theory of Challenge and Response

Arnold Toynbee agreed that civilizations rise and fall, but he argued that they did so not based on a life cycle, as suggested by Spengler, but based on the humans within the civilization and their environment. He saw change within a civilization as prompted mainly by two sources: that of the *challenge* and that of the *response* to the challenge. The challenges could come from nature, such as a hurricane, tornado or flood, or they could come from other humans, such as during war. How the civilizations changed depended on their responses and whether those responses were successful in overcoming their challenges (Toynbee & Fowler, 1950).

## Sorokin's Principle of Immanent Change

Pitirim Sorokin believed that societies bounced back and forth between two cultural extremes, which he referred to as ideational and sensate (Sorkin, 1941).

**Ideational culture** focuses on religion and spiritualism and believes they are essential ingredients to understanding knowledge. This view encourages people to be spiritually active. **Sensate culture** sees science and empirical evidence as the true source of knowledge. This view encourages people to engage in lifestyles that focus on being practical, materialistic and hedonistic. Sorokin believed that external forces, such as war, may speed up social change, but according to the **principle of immanent change**, all social change is the result of forces operating within the society. When change does occur, society simply rejects the side it currently supports and switches to the other side. Thus, societies go from being ideational to sensate, and eventually back to ideational (Sorkin, 1985).

## Equilibrium Theory

**Equilibrium theory** was developed by Talcott Parsons, who viewed society as made up of many interdependent parts, each contributing to society as a whole. Parsons believed that the natural condition of a social system is a state of equilibrium, in which all parts of society are in balance.

Parsons believed that a social system can change in two ways: Change can be generated by an outside social system, or it can come as a result of strain and pressure from within. Since each part of society is dependent on the others, even a minor change to one of the parts can cause the system to become unbalanced, creating a state of disequilibrium (Talcott, 1977). If social change does occur, then the social system needs to adjust to accommodate those changes.

For Parsons, social change did not involve a complete overhaul, in which the old system would be tossed out and replaced with a new one. Instead, social change would result from a process of gradual change, in which new elements are added to old elements in a moving equilibrium with the goal of becoming balanced again (Talcott, 1977).

## Conflict Perspective on Social Change

According to Karl Marx, all societies are in constant conflict, and it is that conflict that leads to revolutionary change. Marx viewed conflict as an even greater force in capitalist societies, which are divided into two groups: those with money, who own the factories and businesses; and those who sell their labor to those organizations.

It is this division which creates the conflict because the two groups have different goals in mind. Business owners want to pay the workers as little as necessary in order to keep their profit high. Workers, on the other hand, want to maximize their pay and earn as much for their labor as possible. Marx believed this exploitation of labor would eventually lead to a worker revolt in which the workers would take control of the factories and businesses where they worked.

Marx's predictions have not yet come to pass for a number of reasons, including the existence of a large middle class made up of many white-collar workers; the proliferation of laws requiring better and safer working conditions passed by governments in capitalist societies; and the relative affluence of workers in such societies, who have more today than the workers of the past. This makes them feel as though they have a stake in the system (Marx, 1964).

In 1965, only 10 percent of Americans owned shares of stock; in 1980, it was 20 percent; and, as of 2000, that number was at 50 percent (Norquist, 2000). It is important to note that this increase in stock ownership is not necessarily by choice. For example, 401(k) plans invest mostly in stocks and are increasingly common as private-sector pensions have largely disappeared.

## Symbolic Interactionist Perspective on Social Change

Symbolic interactionists focus on how social interactions change within a society. People interpret the world around them in order to determine how to interact with others. Part of this interpretation involves people's interpretation of themselves and how they want others to view them. This, in turn, influences how they interact with others.

Do you agree with Arnold Toynbee that natural disasters can prompt civilizations to change?

Source: Frank Pierson

As social change occurs, people must redefine their world and their self-perceptions. People living in traditional societies often have a more concrete sense of who they are, since they were born with their social status already determined. If their parents were farmers, then they, too, will become farmers; from before they can remember, to the day they die, their status as farmers remains the same.

In modern societies, this is not the case. People assume many statuses over a lifetime. For instance, after spending three years working as a high school science teacher, a person might go to school to become a dentist. This status change, from teacher to dentist, might cause the person to feel some anxiety and nervousness as he or she tries to fit into this new status without fully knowing what is expected.

People in traditional societies tend to place a high value on relationships, a sense of belonging and their role within their group. People in modern societies, on the other hand, tend to place a high value on individualism and privacy and may be less trusting of others.

# Summary

This chapter began by discussing collective behavior and the six factors that need to be present for collective behavior to occur. The various forms of collective behavior include panics, mass hysteria, crowds, fashions, fads, crazes, rumors, public opinion and social movements. The four main types of social movements were described, along with three possible reasons for their existence. Globally, change is occurring due in part to modernization, which different theories suggest will either push Western and non-Western societies together or pull them apart. The functional perspective on social change views change as occurring slowly over time. The conflict perspective on social change argues that societies are in constant conflict, with those who control the resources against those who do not. Symbolic interactionists focus on how people interpret and view the world around them and how that affects their interactions with others. Social movements have both intended and unintended consequences for individuals and social systems.

## Review/Discussion Questions

1. What are the five types of crowds?
2. What are some of the propaganda methods used to influence people's opinions?
3. What are three possible causes of social movements?
4. Which forms of collective behavior have you personally been involved in?
5. What might trigger you to join a riot?
6. What are some things in your life that were once considered fashionable but no longer are?
7. What are the consequences of social movements?

## Key Terms

**Breakdown-frustration theory** contends that social breakdowns lead to social movements when frustrations mount among many people at the same time.

**Collective behavior** is behavior that tends to be unorganized, unpredictable and spontaneous, with little structure or stability.

**Convergence theory**, as it relates to crowds, means that people in crowds share the same attitudes, views and beliefs, and it was their similarities that brought these individuals together in the first place. As the theory relates to social change, it means that modernization will bring Western and non-Western countries together as they become more technologically equal.

**Crazes** are fads that can bring with them serious consequences for those involved.

**Crowds** are groups of people doing something together for a short period of time.

**Cyclical theory** argues that societies move back and forth in a continuous series of cycles.

**Divergence theory** contends that with modernization comes a greater and growing divide between Western and non-Western societies.

**Emergent norm theory** asserts that crowds tend to approach unanimity because one set of behavioral norms is accepted by the entire crowd.

**Equilibrium theory** views society as made up of many interdependent parts, which all serve a function and are in balance with one another. Change in one part leads to change in other parts.

**Evolutionary theory** claims that societies evolve gradually over time from simple to more complex forms.

**Fads** are temporary infatuations with a particular practice or innovation.

**Fashions** are brief followings for a particular innovation by a large number of people.

**Frustration theory** claims that those people who get involved in social movements are themselves frustrated or disturbed.

**Gemeinschaft-Gesellschaft transition** describes the structural shift within a society from one that tends to be more cohesive to one more inclined to be impersonal or rational.

**Gossip** involves talk about the personal and private lives of others.

**Ideational culture** focuses on religions and spiritualism, believing that these are essential ingredients to understanding knowledge. This view encourages people to be spiritually active.

**Mass hysteria** is similar to panic, except that in panic the danger is real, while in mass hysteria the danger is absent, and participants engage in the frenzied behavior without checking to see if the source of their fear is real or not.

**Mobs** are groups of people who are angry and channel their anger onto a single target.

**Modernization** is the transformation of a society from agricultural to industrial.

**Panic** is a flight to safety in response to the fear of immediate danger.

**Principle of immanent change** states that all social change results from social forces operating within the society.

**Propaganda** refers to the methods used to influence public opinion.

**Public** refers to a group that shares the same common interest, positions or thoughts.

**Public opinion** is composed of the attitudes and beliefs held by the public.

**Resource mobilization theory** contends that social movements are initiated only when the organizers have the necessary resources. Without these tools, the movement cannot exist.

**Riots** are violent crowds that move from target to target over the course of several hours or days.

**Rumors** are unverified stories that spread from one person to another through a variety of sources, such as word of mouth or the Internet.

**Sensate culture** sees science and empirical evidence as the source of knowledge. This view encourages people to engage in lifestyles that focus on being practical, materialistic and hedonistic.

**Social contagion** is the spread of certain emotions or actions from one member of a crowd to others.

**Social contagion theory** claims that crowds are in agreement in both thought and action; in this sense, they share the same collective mind.

**Social movements** are collective efforts designed to bring about some social change.

# Bibliography

Abrams, D., & Hogg, M. A. (1990). Social Identifications: A Social Psychology of Intergroup Relations and Group Processes. New York: Routledge.

Amin, Y., Hamdi, E., & Eapen, V. (1997). Mass hysteria in an Arab culture. International Journal of Social Psychiatry, 43, 303-306.

Barber, E. (1998). One hundred years toward suffrage: An overview. Votes for Women: Selections from the National American Woman Suffrage Association Collection, 1848-1921. <http://memory.loc.gov/ammem/naw/nawstime.html> (2008).

Blumer, H., & Shibutani, T. (1970). Human Nature and Collective Behavior; Papers in Honor of Herbert Blumer. Englewood-Cliffs, N.J.: Prentice-Hall.

Borgeson, K., & Valeri, R. (2007). The enemy of my enemy is my friend. American Behavioral Scientist, 51, 182-195.

Burns, S. (1990). Social movements of the 1960s: Searching for Democracy. Boston: Twayne Publishers.

Cooper, R., Groce, J., & Thomas, N. (2003). Changing direction: Rites of passage programs for African American older men. Journal of African American Studies, 7 (3), 3-14.

Crazy Fads <http://www.crazyfads.com> (2008).

Davidson, J., & Williams, A. (1997). Megatrends in 20th-century American Catholicism. Social Compass, 44, 507-527.

DiMaggio, P., Hargittai, E., Neuman, R., & Robinson, J. P. (2001). Social implications of the internet. Annual Review of Sociology, 27, 307-336.

Drury, J. (2002). 'When the mobs are looking for witches to burn, nobody's safe': Talking about the reactionary crowd. Discourse & Society, 13, 41-73.

Fischer, L. (1995). American constitutional law (Vol. 1). New York: McGraw-Hill.

Gettleman, J. (2008, December 25). Coup in Guinea largely welcomed. International Herald Tribune.

Goodwin, G. A., & Scimecca, J. A. (2005). Classical Sociological Theory: Rediscovering the Promise of Sociology. Florence, KY: Wadsworth Publishing.

Harwood, J., & Zhang, Y. (2006). Modernization and tradition in an age of globalization: Current values in Chinese television commercials. Journal of Communication, 54, 156-172.

Hunter, S., & Malik, H. (2005). Modernization, democracy, and Islam. Westport, CT: Praeger Publishers.

Khalidi, R. (2011). The Arab Spring. The Nation. March 21st.

Kirkpatrick, D. D. (2011). Egypt Erupts in Jubilation as Mubarak Steps Down. The New York Times. February 11th.

Langman, L. (2008). Punk, porn, and resistance: carnivalization and the body in popular culture. Current Sociology, 56, 657-677.

Le Bon, G. (1960). The Crowd; a Study of the Popular-mind. New York: Viking Press.

Le Bon, G. (2009). Psychology of Crowds. Southampton, UK. Sparkling Books Ltd.

Lewis, J. (2001). Constructing Public Opinion: How Political Elites Do What They Like and Why We Seem to go Along With It. New York: Columbia University Press.

Lewis, M. (Ed.). (2008). Panic: The story of modern financial insanity. New York: Norton.

Marx, K. (1964). Selected Writings in Sociology and Social Philosophy. New York: McGraw-Hill.

McCombs, M. (2004). Setting the Agenda: The Mass Media and Public Opinion. Hants, UK: Polity.

McPhail, C. (1991). The Myth of the Madding Crowd. Piscataway, NJ: Transaction Publishers.

Melbourne, J., & Wilson, O. (1973). Introduction to Social Movements. New York: Basic Books.

Montaner, C. A. (2007). Fidel Castro and the Cuban Revolution: Age, Position, Character, Destiny, Personality, and Ambition. Piscataway, NJ: Transaction Publishers.

Morris, A. D., & Mueller, C. M. (1992). Frontiers in Social Movement Theory. New Haven, CT: Yale University Press.

Norquist, G. (2000). Elections 2000: The leave us alone vs. the takings coalition. <http://www.haciendapub.com/norquist.html> (2008).

Oberschall, A. (1995). Social movements: Ideologies, interests, and identities. New Brunswick: Transaction.

Poynting, S. (2006). What caused the Cronulla riot? Race & Class, 48 (1), 85-92.

Pratkanis, A., & Aronson, E. (1992). Age of Propaganda : The Everyday Use and Abuse of Persuasion. New York: W.H. Freeman.

Racanelli, V. (2008, December 29). Ringing up gains around the globe. Barron's.

Rucht, D. (1992). Studying the Effects of Social Movements: Conceptualization and Problems. Presented at ECPR Joint Session.

Sasaki, M. S. (2008). New Frontiers in Comparative Sociology. Leiden, South Holland: Brill Academic Pub.

Schnapp, J. T., & Tiews, M. (2006). Crowds. Palo Alto, CA: Stanford University Press.

Scraton, P. (1999). Policing with Contempt: The Degrading of Truth and Denial of Justice in the Aftermath of the Hillsborough Disaster. Journal of Law and Society, 26 (3), 273-297.

Smelser, N. J. (1962). Theory of Collective Behavior. New York: Free Press.

Smelser, N. J. (1963). Theory of Collective Behavior. New York: Free Press of Glencoe.

Smith, C. (2008). U.S. Minimum Wage History. Court's World. <http://oregonstate.edu/instruct/anth484/minwage.html> (2008).

Sorkin, P. A. (1941). The Crisis of our Age: the Social and Cultural Outlook. New York: Dutton.

Sorkin, P. A. (1985). Social and Cultural Dynamics: A Study of Change in Major Systems of Art, Truth, Ethics, Law, and Social Relationships. Piscataway, NJ: Transaction Publishers.

Spengler, O., & Atkinson, C. F. (1926). The Decline of the West. New York: A.A. Knopf.

Stahler-Sholk, R., Kuecker, G. D., & Vanden, H. E. (2008). Latin American Social Movements in the Twenty-First Century: Resistance, Power, and Democracy. Lanham, MD: Rowman and Littlefield.

Stewart, C., Smith, C., & Denton, D. E. (1994). Persuasion and Social Movements. Prospect Heights, IL: Waveland Press Inc.

Talcott, P. (1977). Social Systems and the Evolution of Action Theory. New York: Free Press.

Tönnies, F. (2001 [1887]). Community and Civil Society. New York, NY: Cambridge University Press.

Toynbee, A., & Fowler, A. V. (1950). War and Civilization. New York: Oxford University Press.

Turner, R. H., & Killian, L. M. (1993). Collective Behavior. Englewood Cliffs, NJ: Prentice-Hall.

Zhang, Y. B., & Harwood, J. (2004). Modernization and Tradition in an Age of Globalization: Cultural Values in Chinese Television Commercials. Journal of Communication, 54 (1), 156.

# Glossary

**527 organizations** are organizations designed to influence the outcome of elections through technically indirect mass media advertising.

**Absolute monarchy** is hereditary rule until death or abdication with the authority to personally control any aspect of governance.

**Absolute poverty** describes people who are desperately poor and may not know where their next meal will come from.

**Acculturate** is to incorporate aspects of the dominant culture while retaining aspects of a group's ethnic origin.

**Acculturation** is the passing along of norms, practices and values from generation to generation.

**Achieved status** refers to a social position that a person earns through effort and choice.

**Adolescent subculture** is made up of attitudes and values that are specific to youth, especially in contrast to adults.

**Adult socialization** is the process by which adults learn new statuses and roles.

**Advanced producer services** are the highly skilled service jobs of the current economy.

**Affirmative action** is a policy or program that seeks to redress past discrimination by increasing opportunities for underrepresented groups.

**Age grading** is the creation of age categories in a society and the attachment of certain rights, expectations and duties to each.

**Age stratification** is a structural system of inequality in which different age groups are ranked in a hierarchy based on status value.

**Ageism** is prejudice and discrimination directed against people based on age.

**Agents of socialization** are people or groups that affect our self-concept, attitudes, behaviors or other orientations toward life.

**Agglomeration** is the location of complementary functions near one another.

**Agrarian societies** are based on the technology of animal-drawn plows that support large-scale cultivation to acquire food supplies.

**Alienation** refers to the condition of powerlessness, estrangement or dissociation from the workplace and or society.

**Alternative health care professionals** are individuals providing care outside the mainstream or western modalities of health care.

**Amalgamation** happens when various cultures combine to create a new culture.

**Animism** is the belief that all forms of life contain elements of the supernatural.

**Anomie** is a social condition in which norms and values are conflicting, weak, or absent.

**Anticipatory socialization** involves learning the skills and values needed for future roles.

**Aptitude** is the capacity to develop physical or social skills.

**Arranged marriage** means that parents or matchmakers decide who is going to marry whom.

**Ascribed status** refers to a social position that a person receives at birth or assumes involuntarily later in life.

**Assimilation** occurs when a person from a minority cultural group adopts the cultural characteristics of the dominant group while discarding their ethnic traits.

**Authoritarian government** is a government that suppresses political opposition through violence or the threat of violence.

**Authoritarian leadership styles** are characterized by a leader giving commands to subordinates.

**Authority** is power that is perceived as legitimate by those over whom it is exercised.

**Automation** is the use of machinery to control a manufacturing process rather than human laborers.

**Autonomy** is when individuals have considerable control over their own work.

**Back stage** is the place where there is no audience, and a person does not play a role for the benefit of others.

**Barter** is the direct exchange of goods or services in the absence of currency.

**Beliefs** are specific ideas that people think are true.

**Bilateral descent** traces the line of descent through both the mother's and the father's family.

**Blasé attitude** is an urban resident's detachment from his or her environment in response to an overabundance of stimuli.

**Blockbusting** was a practice of local real estate agents in which they would buy a house from a white owner for one price and sell it to a black owner for a higher price.

**Blue collar work** is an occupation in the secondary sector of the economy, particularly manufacturing.

**Breakdown-frustration theory** contends that social breakdowns lead to social movements when frustrations mount among many people at the same time.

**Built environment** is the totality of human-made physical structures that provides the environment for human activity.

**Bureaucracies** are organizations with statuses and roles arranged in a fixed hierarchy. Activity is governed by strict rules and tracked through the keeping of formal records. Each status and role is specialized so that each person is only responsible for one small aspect of the organization, making each worker an expert in his or her own area. Relationships are impersonal, with everyone's main concern being their own bureaucratic role.

**Bureaucratic inertia** is an organizational resistance to beneficial change.

**Bystander effect** is a term used to describe the tendency of individuals not to get involved in emergency situations if they are part of a crowd.

**Capital class** refers to the people who own the capital and do not have to sell their labor.

**Capital mobility** is the state in the global economy in which profit-seeking enterprises are able to locate where it is most profitable.

**Capitalism** is an economic system stressing private ownership in the pursuit of personal profit.

**Carbon footprint** is the impact a person's activities have on the environment in general and climate change in particular.

**Caste systems** are based on stratification, classifying people at birth into social levels in which they remain.

**Charismatic authority** is power that is legitimated by the extraordinary characteristics of an individual.

**Church** is a kind of religious organization with high engagement with mainstream society.

**Civic nationalism** is nationalism based on loyalty to the nation-state.

**Civil religion** is a collection of beliefs and rituals that exists outside of institutional religion and unites people in a celebration of society.

**Class conflict** occurs between the capitalist class and the working class as they struggle for control over scarce resources, such as money.

**Class consciousness** is the shared awareness class members have of their status and rank within a society, as well as their interests.

**Class systems** are stratification systems in which an individual's position is not fixed but instead is relatively open, allowing the individual opportunities to move between levels.

**Clinical nurse extenders** are individuals who are trained and licensed to provide a limited level of nursing care.

**Coercion** is characteristic of oppositional interactions, and it occurs when one person or group forces its will upon another.

**Collective behavior** is behavior that tends to be unorganized, unpredictable and spontaneous, with little structure or stability.

**Competition** means that two or more people follow mutually accepted rules to achieve the same goal before the other person or people.

**Concentric-zone model** is a model of urban growth that includes five circles ranging from an inner circle, including the downtown or "central business district," to an outer circle of suburbs.

**Conflict** occurs when people who dislike or hate each other interact.

**Conformity** may involve going along with peers and/or following societal norms.

**Conglomerate** is one large holding company that owns several corporations operating in different goods and/or services markets.

**Conjugal families** are formed and recognized through the mating of a couple.

**Consanguine families** are formed and recognized through blood ties (birth).

**Conspicuous consumption** involves the public display and use of expensive items.

**Constitutional monarchy** is hereditary rule that is legally limited by a constitution or charter such that the monarch becomes a symbolic figure.

**Consumerism** is the social preoccupation with consumption as a defining aspect of life.

**Containment theory** is based on control theory and focuses on a strong self-image as a means of defending against negative peer pressure.

**Control groups** are those in which participants are not exposed to the variables.

**Control theory** is the idea that there are two control systems, inner and outer, that work against our tendencies to deviate.

**Conventional morality** is Kohlberg's term for people incorporating society's rules and laws into their own value systems and behaving accordingly.

**Convergence theory**, as it relates to crowds, means that people in crowds share the same attitudes, views and beliefs, and it was their similarities that brought these individuals together in the first place. As the theory relates to social change, it means that modernization will bring Western and non-Western countries together as they become more technologically equal.

**Cooperation** involves two or more people working together as friends or supporters to achieve a common goal.

**Corporate crimes** are the illegal actions of people acting on behalf of the corporation.

**Corporate personhood** is the legally defined status of a corporation that endows it with similar but not identical rights and responsibilities as a person.

**Corporation** is a legally created business entity that has an existence independent of its members.

**Correlation** exists when two (or more) variables change together.

**Counterculture** describes a cultural group whose values and norms are opposed to those of the dominant culture.

*Coup d'etat* is a swift, usually violent takeover of a government.

**Crazes** are fads that can bring with them serious consequences for those involved.

**Credentialism** is the practice of relying on conferred degrees and diplomas as universal markers of educational achievement.

**Criminal justice system** includes the police, courts and prisons that deal with criminal laws and their enforcement.

**Criminology** is the scientific study of the causes of criminal behavior in the individual and society.

**Crowds** are groups of people doing something together for a short period of time.

**Crude birthrate** is the number of live births in a year per 1,000 people during a given time period in a defined geographical area.

**Crude death rate** is the total number of deaths per 1,000 people during a given time period in a defined geographical area.

**Cult** is a kind of religious organization, typically centered on a charismatic leader, which offers a new interpretation of the afterlife.

**Cultural capital** is Pierre Bourdieu's term for the cultural elements—tastes—that distinguish people of different classes.

**Cultural diversity** refers to a variety of cultural differences within a society and across societies.

**Cultural goals** are the legitimate objectives of members of society.

**Cultural imperialism** refers to the widespread infusion of a society's culture into that of other societies.

**Cultural lag** is a discrepancy between material culture and nonmaterial culture that disrupts an individual's way of life.

**Cultural relativism** refers to the judging of another culture by its own standards.

**Cultural transmission** refers to a process through which one generation passes culture to the next.

**Cultural universals** refer to the culture traits that people share across cultures.

**Culture** refers to a way of life of a particular society or social group.

**Culture shock** refers to the disorientation that people feel when they experience an unfamiliar culture.

**Cumulative disadvantage theory** states that disadvantages experienced in youth accumulate and lead to greater inequality in later life.

**Cyclical theory** argues that societies move back and forth in a continuous series of cycles.

**Cyclical unemployment** is unemployment caused by fluctuations in the economy.

**De facto** means "in practice."

**De jure** means "by law."

**Decentralized national health care** is a system in which the government functions primarily as a regulator.

**Dechurched** refers to people who have left institutional religion because of dissatisfaction with its structure, organization, politics or attitudes.

**Dehumanization** involves depriving others of their humanity.

**Deindividuation** occurs when a person loses his or her individual identity and effectively disappears into a group.

**Deindustrialization** is the removal or reduction of manufacturing activity in urban regions across the country.

**Democracy** is a political system based on direct rule by the people themselves.

**Democratic leadership style** is a term for involving workers in the decision-making process.

**Demographers** are sociologists who investigate population characteristics.

**Demography** is the study of the characteristics of human populations, including the increases and decreases caused by migration, fertility and mortality.

**Dependency theory** advocates argue that some countries are poorer and less developed because they are dependent on more developed countries.

**Detached observation** involves a researcher observing behavior from a distance without actually getting involved with the participants.

**Developmental socialization** is the process by which people learn to be more competent in their currently assumed roles.

**Deviance** is a violation of rules or norms.

**Dialectic** is a view of change or progress based on the interaction of opposing forces.

**Differential association** is a theory of deviance that believes people will deviate or conform depending on their associations.

**Diffusion** is the spread of cultural traits from one group or society to another.

**Direct pay model** is a system wherein individuals are legally responsible for paying all of their own health care costs.

**Discovery** is the process of knowing and recognizing something previously in existence.

**Discrimination** is differential treatment of people based on superficial characteristics such as skin color or accent.

**Disneyfication** is the process of stripping a place of its authentic character and repackaging it in a sanitized and diluted format with the intention of making it more pleasant and easily consumable.

**Divergence theory** contends that with modernization comes a greater and growing divide between Western and non-Western societies.

**Diversity** is the existence of differences.

**Division of labor** is the degree to which the total percentage of labor in a society or organization is subdivided into particular tasks.

**Domestic partnership** is a legal status offered by some cities, counties and states in the United States for two unrelated, unmarried adults that share the same household.

**Dramaturgical analysis** is the perspective of social interaction that compares everyday life to a theatrical performance.

**Ecological footprint** is a measure of how much land is necessary to support the utilization of the three functions of the environment (resource depot, waste repository and living space) for a specified geographic region.

**Economic determinism** is one of the theories attributed to Karl Marx to mean that social differentiation and class conflict resulted from economic factors.

**Economic imperialism** is the forceful implementation of capitalism for the purpose of exploiting less-developed nations.

**Economy** is the social institution that organizes the production, distribution and consumption of goods and services.

**Education** is the social institution that encompasses all aspects of formal training in which people gain knowledge and skills as well as learn values and norms.

**Ego** is Freud's term for the part of the personality that deals with the real world on the basis of reason and helps to integrate the demands of both the id and the superego.

**Elite model** is a model of politics stressing the concentration of power in the hands of a small minority.

**Emergent norm theory** asserts that crowds tend to approach unanimity because one set of behavioral norms is accepted by the entire crowd.

**Emigrants** are people who leave their home countries and establish citizenship in a new country.

**Eminent domain** is the power of the government to seize private land for the public good.

**Emotional labor** requires workers to manipulate their feelings in order to serve bureaucratic goals.

**Enclosure** is the process by which the powerful and rich people fence (enclose) their land in order to exclude others.

**End of history** is a doctrine proposing that Western liberal democracy has been accepted as the final form of human government.

**Endogamy** involves marrying someone from within one's social and economic group.

**Environmental injustice** occurs when a social group (race, ethnicity, gender, age, etc.) is burdened with an environmental hazard.

**Equilibrium theory** views society as made up of many interdependent parts, which all serve a function and are in balance with one another. Change in one part leads to change in other parts.

**Ethnic groups** are people with shared cultural heritages that others regard as distinct.

**Ethnic nationalism** is nationalism based on loyalty to a shared cultural or ethnic identity.

**Ethnicity** is a shared heritage defined by common characteristics such as language, religion, cultural practices, and nationality that differentiate it from other groups.

**Ethnocentrism** is the belief that one's culture is superior and other ethnic groups or nations are inferior. All other cultures and societies are judged according to the standards of the society or culture that one belongs to.

**Evangelical** are religious adherents with a strong focus on spreading their religion to other people.

**Evolutionary theory** claims that societies evolve gradually over time from simple to more complex forms.

**Exchange** means that two or more individuals offer something in order to obtain a reward in return.

**Exchange value** is the value of a commodity based on its anticipated price in relation to other commodities in the marketplace.

**Existentialist perspective** asserts that individuals are responsible for their own health care issues.

**Exogamy** involves marrying someone from a different region, or other social and economic categories.

**Experimental groups** are those exposed to the independent variables, such as participation in a program or use of a medication.

**Experiments** are controlled environments in which variables can be closely managed.

**Extended family** includes two parents and their children, as well as other blood relatives such as aunts, uncles, and grandparents.

**Extremists** are religious adherents who believe that their religion is the one true religion and others must be done away with.

**Face-saving behavior** refers to techniques that people use to salvage their performance when they encounter a potential or actual loss of face.

**Face work** describes making an effort to give our best possible performance to avoid "losing face."

**Fads** are temporary infatuations

with a particular practice or innovation.

**False consciousness** is a belief in ideas that are contrary to one's own best interests.

**Family**, for purposes of the U.S. Census, is a group of two or more people who reside together and who are related by birth, marriage, or adoption.

**Family of orientation** is the family a person grows up in, including parents and siblings.

**Family of procreation** is a family made up of a person, that person's spouse and their children.

**Fashions** are brief followings for a particular innovation by a large number of people.

**Feminism** is a broad perspective that advocates for equality between men and women.

**Festival marketplace** is a type of urban mall featuring boutiques, restaurants and street entertainers, built in historic or historic-looking buildings.

**Folkways** refer to everyday customs that may be violated without formal sanctions within a society.

**Fordism** is an economy of scale using efficient, low-cost assembly-line production methods.

**Free rider** is a person who attends religious services and takes advantage of congregational resources without contributing time or money.

**Front stage** is the place where a person plays a specific role in front of an audience.

**Frustration theory** claims that those people who get involved in social movements are themselves frustrated or disturbed.

**Fundamentalism** are religious adherents who take a literal interpretation of a religious text or teaching.

**Gemeinschaft** is the connection and organization of community through kinship and long-held traditions.

**Gemeinschaft-Gesellschaft transition** describes the structural shift within a society from one that tends to be more cohesive to one more inclined to be impersonal or rational.

**Gender** is the socially and culturally constructed differences between males and females that are found in the meanings, beliefs and practices associated with masculinity and femininity.

**Gender pay gap** refers to the differences between men's and women's earnings, controlling for fulltime employment.

**Gender role** refers to how we should act as males or females.

**Gender stratification** is men's and women's unequal access to property, power and prestige.

**Gender typing** refers to the acquisition of behavior that is considered appropriate for one's gender.

**Genderlects** are the linguistic styles that reflect the different worlds of women and men.

**General fertility rates** measure the number of live births divided by the female population aged 15 to 44 years (childbearing years), times 1,000.

**Generalized others** are people who are not necessarily close to a child but still help influence the child's internalization of societal values.

**Gentrification** is the reinvestment of real estate capital into declining, inner-city neighborhoods to create a new residential infrastructure for middle-and high-income inhabitants.

**Gesellschaft** implies that people are connected only to accomplish their own interests.

**Ghettos** are neighborhoods in which certain racial, ethnic or religious groups are in some way forced to live.

**Glass ceiling** describes what happens when women are blocked from upward mobility in their chosen field.

**Global cities** are the command and control centers of the world's economic, political and cultural activities.

**Global perspective** concerns the impact our society has on other nations, and also the impact of other nations upon our society.

**Global warming** is a gradual increase in Earth's average temperature.

**Globalization** is the deepening, broadening and speeding up of worldwide interconnectedness in all aspects of life.

**Glocalization** describes when

globalized items, practices, and ideas are tailored to meet local needs.

**Gold standard** is a system whereby currency is stabilized by its actual or symbolic relationship to a specified amount of gold.

**Gossip** involves talk about the personal and private lives of others.

**Government** is the formal organization that exercises power through the state.

**Grobalization** is the desire of corporations to accommodate local needs in order to fuel their own expansion.

**Groups** are collections of people characterized by more than two people, frequent interaction, a sense of belonging and interdependence.

**Groupthink** occurs when individuals value a group enough to accept group decisions against their own better judgment.

**Hate crime** refers to criminal acts against a person or a person's property by an offender who is motivated by racial or other biases.

**Hawthorne effect** describes a phenomenon in which people modify their behavior because they know they are being monitored.

**Heterogamy** means choosing to marry someone who is different from one's self.

**Heterosexism** is the belief that heterosexuality is superior to homosexuality, as it is "more natural" since it is tied to reproduction.

**Hidden curriculum** involves the mechanisms through which schooling rewards upper-class habits and values through non-instructional items taught in schools.

**High culture** refers to cultural patterns that appeal to the upper class or elite of a society.

**Homogamy** involves people falling in love with, and marrying, someone similar to themselves.

**Homogeneity** is the existence of sameness.

**Homophobia** is the fear and hatred of homosexuality.

**Horizontal mobility** is the movement from one social position to another of the same rank and/or prestige.

**Horticultural societies** use hand tools to raise crops in order to acquire food.

**Household** includes all the people who occupy a housing unit as their usual place of residence.

**Human migration** is the permanent movement of individuals or groups across symbolic or political boundaries into new residential areas and communities.

**Hunting and gathering societies** use simple subsistence technology to hunt animals and gather vegetation.

**Hypotheses** are tentative statements about how different variables are expected to relate to each other.

**Id** is Freud's term for the part of the personality that is totally unconscious and consists of biological drives.

**Ideal culture** refers to the rules of expected behavior that people should follow.

**Ideational culture** focuses on religions and spiritualism, believing that these are essential ingredients to understanding knowledge. This view encourages people to be spiritually active.

**Idiosyncrasy credits** are permissions granted by a group that allow high-standing members to act in a nonconforming manner, thus allowing them to break group norms.

**Illegal lodging citations** are tickets issued by police to homeless individuals for taking up lodging (usually sleeping) in a public place.

**Illegitimate opportunity structures** are relative opportunity structures outside laws and social norms that frame a person's life.

**Impression management** refers to our efforts to present favorable images to the people around us.

**Inclusive communication** refers to an exchange where all parties are entitled to respect and the opportunity to express themselves.

**Individual discrimination** occurs when one person treats another unfairly, and that treatment is based on the person's social status.

**Individual mobility** is the result of hard work and perseverance by an individual.

**Industrial societies** are based on technology that mechanizes production to provide goods and services.

**Infant mortality rate** is the number of deaths within the first year of life, divided by the number of live births in the same year, times 1,000.

**Informal organizational structure** includes any group—not formally planned—that forms within an organization and develops through personal relationships and interactions among its members.

**In-groups** are those in which an individual is a valued member.

**Institutional discrimination** results from society operating in ways that allow certain groups to receive better treatment and opportunities than other groups.

**Institutional means** include approved ways of reaching cultural goals.

**Intelligence** is the capacity for mental or intellectual achievement.

**Intergenerational mobility** describes changes in the social positions of children in comparison to their parents.

**Interlocking directorships** is when members of the board of directors of one corporation also sit on the boards of others.

**Intersectionality approach** is a conceptual framework that allows for the examination of interconnections among socially constructed statuses, which can include sex, gender, sexual orientation, and age.

**Intersexed** describes babies born with genitalia that are neither clearly male nor female.

**Intimate partners** are defined by

the Bureau of Justice Statistics as spouses, ex-spouses, boyfriends, and girlfriends.

**Intragenerational mobility** relates to changes in social position over the course of person's lifetime.

**Invention** is the process of reshaping existing cultural traits into new forms.

**Iron triangle of power** is the closed system of mutual benefit between Congress, military contractors and the Department of Defense; the specific manifestation of the military-industrial complex.

**Jim Crow laws** allowed restaurants and business owners to legally deny services to members of minority groups.

**Juvenile delinquency** is participation in illegal activity by minors who fall under the statutory age limit (youth crime).

**Labeling theory** is the idea that the labels people are given affect their own and others' perceptions of them, and, therefore, channel behavior either into or away from conformity.

**Labor unions** are organizations of workers that collectively bargain with ownership or management for improvements in wages, benefits or working conditions.

*Laissez-faire* is the doctrine of complete marketplace freedom.

**Laissez-faire leadership style** involves leaving workers to function on their own.

**Landscape of power** is an impressive global landscape that is relatively free of the urban

vernacular.

**Language** refers to an organized system of symbols that people use to think and to communicate with each other.

**Latent functions** are unintended consequences or results.

**Laws** refer to formal norms that are enacted by governments and enforced by formal sanctions.

**Legal discrimination** is unequal treatment that is upheld by laws.

**Life chances** are the ability to experience the opportunities and corresponding resources held by a society.

**Life expectancy** is the number of years that a person can expect to live within a given society, or as the number of further years of life a person can expect at a given age.

**Liminality** is a disoriented state characterized by ambiguity in which an old order has gone with no apparent new order to replace it.

**Looking-glass self** is Cooley's theory that we are influenced by our perception of what others think of us and develop our self-image on that basis.

**Majority group** is the social group that holds and exercises superior power and resources that derive from this power. Population numbers do not equate to this power.

**Manifest functions** are intended consequences or results.

**Marginal working class** includes the most desperate members of society who have few skills and little job security. They often are unemployed.

**Marketable assets** are things that can be quickly converted into cash when cash is needed.

**Marriage rate** is the number of marriages per 1,000 people in a given time period.

**Mass hysteria** is similar to panic, except that in panic the danger is real, while in mass hysteria the danger is absent, and participants engage in the frenzied behavior without checking to see if the source of their fear is real or not.

**Master status** is a status that determines a person's overall social position and identity.

**Material culture** refers to physical or tangible creations that members of a society make and use.

**Materialism** occurs when people are able to satisfy their basic needs and have money left over to spend on goods and services.

**Matriarchy** means that the mothers rule and are in charge of the family.

**Matrilineal descent** traces the descent through the mother's line.

**Matrilocal residence** means that when couples marry, they live with the wife's family.

**McDonaldization** refers to the global spread of bureaucratic efficiency and profitability at the expense of human creativity, dignity, freedom, and relationships.

**Measurement** is the systematic process of assigning values or labels to concepts for research purposes.

**Mechanical solidarity** is a form of social cohesion in which people do similar work and share the same values and beliefs.

**Medical perspective** focuses on the medical framework that attempts to examine pathogens that result in disease and illness.

**Medicalization of deviance** means to relate deviance to an underlying illness that needs to be treated by physicians.

**Megachurch** is a congregation with at least 2,000 weekly attendees.

**Meritocracy** is a system in which people are rewarded on the basis of their talents and achievements.

**Messianic** are religions that believe in the coming of a divine figure for the redemption of humanity.

**Micromanagement** is the unrelenting managerial control of even the smallest tasks.

**Military-industrial complex** is the informal coalition between government, the military and the arms industry.

**Minority government** is a democratic government in which the ruling party wins the greatest number but less than 50 percent of the total seats in parliament.

**Minority group** is a subordinate group whose members have significantly less power and access and use of important resources in society than members of a majority group.

**Mobs** are groups of people who are angry and channel their anger onto a single target.

**Modernization** is the transformation of a society from agricultural to industrial.

**Modernization theory** states that societies started as simple and traditional, then moved, or are moving toward, being modern (developed) societies.

**Monogamy** allows a person only one mate.

**Monopoly** is the control of a particular goods or services market by one company.

**Monotheism** is the belief in and worship of only one god.

**Mores** refer to strongly held, formally enforced norms with moral overtones.

**Mortgage interest deduction** is a federal policy allowing homeowners to deduct the money they paid in mortgage interest and property tax from their income when they calculate their federal income taxes.

**Multiculturalism** refers to the coexistence and equal standing of diverse cultures within a society.

**Multigenerational family** households consist of more than two generations living together as a family.

**Multinational corporation** is a corporation that operates in more than one country.

**Nation-state** is a modern territorial and political entity recognized by other nation-states, with precise borders and unique symbolic representations.

**Neo-colonialism** is the indirect

continuation of colonialism through economic means.

**Neolocal** means that young couples leave their mother and father's residence and find one of their own.

**New ageism** in which elders are resented for their age-based entitlement programs and political clout.

**Nonfamily household** is a census term used to describe people living together who are not related to the head of household by birth, marriage or adoption.

**Nonmaterial culture** refers to abstract or intangible things that influence our behavior.

**Nonrenewable resources** are resources that cannot be regenerated in a timely manner or that are permanently depleted.

**Nonverbal interaction** is the exchange of information among people without the use of speech.

**Norms** provide guidance on how to think, act, and feel.

**Nuclear families** are composed of two adults and their children, if they have any.

**Oligopoly** is the control of the majority of a particular goods or services market by a small number of companies.

**Oppression olympics** is a competition for attention, resources, and ideational supremacy between aggrieved groups or individuals.

**Organic solidarity** is a form of social cohesion in which people work in a wide variety of specialized occupations and thus gain their social consensus from their need to rely on one another for goods and services.

**Organized crime** is a highly disciplined business organization whose profits come from illegal activity.

**Orwellian** is a term used to invoke fears of a totalitarian or "big brother" government. Inspired by the George Orwell novel *1984*.

**Out-groups** are those in which an individual is not a member.

**Overpopulation** is the population by a particular species in excess of the environment's carrying capacity.

**Panic** is a flight to safety in response to the fear of immediate danger.

**Parliament** is a democratic legislative body composed of representatives elected from specified districts within a territory.

**Participant observation** allows a researcher to observe a group's behavior from within the group itself.

**Pastoral societies** use technology that supports the domestication of animals in order to acquire food.

**Patriarchal society** is one in which men are dominant and social institutions are set up to sustain a system of male rule.

**Patriarchy** is a structural system of inequality in which men control the major social institutions, including the family, the economy, politics and religion.

**Patrilineal descent** traces the descent through the father's line.

**Patrilocal residence** means that a married couple lives with the father's family.

**Peer group** includes a person's same-aged friends who have similar interests and social positions.

**Penalty** is a disadvantage or constraint attached to a social status.

**Personal space** is the area surrounding a person.

**Personality** refers to a person's patterns of thoughts, feelings, and self-concepts that make him or her distinctive from others.

**Physician extenders** are secondary health care providers who can provide basic physical diagnosis and care.

**Pink collar work** is a low to moderate-status occupation traditionally held by women.

**Planned obsolescence** is the built-in obsolescence of goods due to changing style or disposability.

**Pluralist model** is a model of politics stressing the relatively even distribution of power between many societal groups.

**Plutocracy** is formal or informal political rule by the wealthy.

**Politeness theory** is the idea that communicators change and adapt their messages to protect and save the "face" of their listeners.

**Political action committees** are organizations designed to influence the outcome of an election or the passing of legislation through use of financial donations to candidates or political parties.

**Political crime** refers to crime or acts committed to harm the state, the state's government or the political system in general.

**Political socialization** is the process through which one acquires political beliefs from societal agents of socialization (family, peers, education and mass media).

**Political spectrum** is a socially constructed and historically shifting continuum of political ideology generally divided between left/liberal and right/conservative.

**Politics** is the social institution that organizes macro-level power in society.

**Polyandry** allows a woman to have more than one husband at a time.

**Polygamy** allows marriage of one person to two or more others of the opposite sex.

**Polygyny** allows a man to have more than one wife at a time.

**Polytheism** is the belief in and worship of multiple gods.

**Popular culture** refers to widespread cultural patterns that appeal primarily to the middle and working classes.

**Populations** are entire groups of people to be studied.

**Post-conventional morality** is the highest level of morality available, according to Kohlberg. At this level, people use broad ethical principles to guide their behavior, such as showing respect for human dignity,

equality, and, of late, respect for one's environment—even for the rights of animals and other living creatures.

**Post-Fordism** is an economy of flexibility responding to individual tastes and using advertising to create the perception of new needs.

**Post-industrial (postmodern) societies** are based on computer technology that produces information and supports service industries.

**Power** is the ability to achieve one's goals despite opposition from others.

**Power elite** describes a small group of high-ranking leaders from government, corporations, and the military.

**Pre-conventional morality** is Kohlberg's term for abiding by the law chiefly to avoid punishment or to gain some benefit.

**Prejudice** is an attitude about a person or a group that is not based on social reality.

**Prestige** is the level of respect accorded to individuals and groups of people, especially on the basis of their occupation or profession.

**Primary care providers** are physicians who can practice medicine in "all of its branches."

**Primary deviance** is the first occurrence of a violation of a norm, which the committing actor does not view as deviant. Thus, it would have little to no effect on a person's self-concept.

**Primary groups** are organized around togetherness and are

assumed to be long-lasting.

**Primary sector** is the sector of the economy based on the direct exploitation of natural resources.

**Primary sex characteristics** are the genitalia involved in the reproductive process.

**Primary socialization** is the period during which children learn language and the basic behavioral patterns that form the foundation for later learning.

**Principle of immanent change** states that all social change results from social forces operating within the society.

**Privilege** is an advantage or opportunity, often unearned, attached to a social status.

**Profane** are mundane, everyday things.

**Profession** is a high-status occupation requiring specialized knowledge.

**Professional crime** is when someone uses special skills, experience, methods or instruments to commit a crime while considering the activity to be that person's basic occupation or as a main or additional source of income. The most common type is fraud, and all professional crime is for personal gain.

**Propaganda** refers to the methods used to influence public opinion.

**Public** refers to a group that shares the same common interest, positions or thoughts.

**Public opinion** is composed of the

attitudes and beliefs held by the public.

**Punishment** is an authoritative imposition of something negative or unpleasant on a person in response to behavior considered bad.

**Purchasing power** is the number of goods and services that can be purchased with a unit of currency.

**Qualitative data** measures intangibles such as people's feelings and can include focus group results, interviews, and observations.

**Quantitative data** is data that can be measured in numbers.

**Race** is understood as a group of people defined by obvious physical characteristics such as skin color.

**Racial-ethnic group** refers to a socially subordinate group that is culturally distinct.

**Racial formation** is how society creates and transforms racial categories over time.

**Racial profiling** is a discriminatory law-enforcement tactic aimed at targeting racial minorities.

**Racial restrictive covenants** were legally binding provisions on the deed of a property specifying which groups could and could not own that property.

**Racial zoning** is the restriction of residents to certain city blocks based upon their race.

**Racism** is a set of beliefs used to justify the unfair treatment of a racial group and its members.

**Random samples** are those in which each person who is part of the population has an equal opportunity to be selected for participation in a study.

**Rational-legal authority** is power that is legitimated through formalized, standardized regulations and procedures.

**Rationalization** is the process by which society becomes increasingly dominated by regulation, standardization and bureaucratization.

**Real culture** refers to the values that people actually have.

**Real estate developers** build on land to make it more profitable.

**Recidivism rates** represent the number of people rearrested for committing the same types of crimes.

**Redlining** was a policy that instructed banks to avoid lending within certain less "secure" neighborhoods (around which a red line would be drawn on a map).

**Reference groups** include any group that an individual admires enough to use as a standard for his or her identity.

**Relative poverty** is the feeling or belief that you are poor when you compare yourself with other people.

**Reliability** refers to consistency, or receiving the same results every time the same study is conducted.

**Religiosity** is the measure of religious belief in a population.

**Religious pluralism** is the coexistence of a wide variety of religious beliefs in a single society.

**Renewable resources** are those resources that can be regenerated, like food and trees.

**Resocialization** is the process by which people must leave behind their old selves and develop new ones.

**Resource mobilization theory** contends that social movements are initiated only when the organizers have the necessary resources. Without these tools, the movement cannot exist.

**Riots** are violent crowds that move from target to target over the course of several hours or days.

**Role conflict** refers to conflicting demands connected to two or more statuses.

**Role exit** is the process by which people disengage from a role.

**Role expectation** relates to the expectations required of a role.

**Role performance** relates to the delivery of role expectation.

**Role set** refers to a number of roles attached to a single status.

**Role strain** refers to conflicting demands connected to a single status.

**Roles** are socially defined expectations associated with a given status.

**Routinization** is the reduction of innovation into bureaucratic routine.

**Rumors** are unverified stories that spread from one person to another through a variety of sources, such as word of mouth or the Internet.

**Rustbelt** is a loosely defined area of Northeastern and Midwestern states that factories and many residents have departed.

**Sacred** are those things that are set apart from everyday life and regarded as extraordinary.

**Samples** are smaller groups of individuals selected from larger populations.

**Sanctions** refer to rewards for normal behaviors and penalties for abnormal behaviors.

**Scapegoating** is the singling out of a group or individual for unmerited blame.

**Schooling** is when education occurs in a formal, classroom setting.

**Seasonal unemployment** is unemployment caused by predictable shifts in demand for a good or service through an annual cycle.

**Secondary care providers** include professionals who extend the services of doctors.

**Secondary deviance** is a response to primary deviance by which a person repeatedly violates a norm and begins to take on a deviant identity.

**Secondary groups** are organized around a task and assumed to be short-term.

**Secondary sector** is the sector of the economy based on the transformation of natural resources into finished products.

**Secondary sex characteristics** are the changes that occur at puberty as a result of hormonal production.

**Secondary socialization** takes place later in childhood and into maturity. In this phase, other agents of socialization take over some of the responsibility from family.

**Sect** is a religious organization that breaks off from a mainstream church and is less integrated with the surrounding culture.

**Secularization** is the decline of religious authority and separation of society into various institutional components.

**Segregation** is the physical separation of individuals or groups from each other.

**Self-efficacy** is a person's confidence that he or she can accomplish what is desired and manage what is necessary.

**Sensate culture** sees science and empirical evidence as the source of knowledge. This view encourages people to engage in lifestyles that focus on being practical, materialistic and hedonistic.

**Serial monogamy** involves cycles of divorce and remarriage allowing people to marry multiple partners, but only one at a time.

**Sex** refers to the biological and anatomical differences between females and males.

**Sex ratios** are the number of males per 1,000 females in the population of the society.

**Sex segregation** refers to the concentration of men and women in different occupations.

**Sexism** is the belief that one sex and, by extension, one gender is superior to another.

**Sexual orientation** is the direction of sexual and emotional interest.

**Shared monopoly** is the control of at least 50 percent of a particular goods or services market by four or fewer companies.

**Sick roles** involve a variety of social norms specifying the responsibilities, expectations, and rights of someone who is ill.

**Significant others** are those people who are the closest to and have the strongest influence on a child, and whose approval and affection the child desires most.

**Social aggregates** include people who share a space and purpose but do not interact.

**Social capital** refers to the connections among people that cause social cohesion.

**Social categories** have members who share similar traits but do not interact or know one another.

**Social class** is made up of people in relatively similar situations with roughly the same power, income, and prestige.

**Social conflict perspective** views society as a compound filled with inequalities in regard to the allocation of resources.

**Social consensus** occurs when nearly all members of a society want to achieve the same goals and work cooperatively to achieve them.

**Social construction** refers to the belief that the ideas that influence and govern social organizations are human inventions.

**Social contagion** is the spread of certain emotions or actions from one member of a crowd to others.

**Social contagion theory** claims that crowds are in agreement in both thought and action; in this sense, they share the same collective mind.

**Social control** involves techniques and strategies for maintaining order and preventing deviant behavior in a society.

**Social groups** involve two or more people who have a shared a sense of identity and shared interaction.

**Social institutions** are established ways that society organizes to meet basic needs.

**Social interaction** involves reciprocal communication between two or more people through symbols, words, and body language.

**Social mobility** is the movement from one social position to another.

**Social movements** are collective efforts designed to bring about some social change.

**Social networks** are webs of social ties among individuals and groups.

**Social order** includes social arrangements upon which members depend.

**Social rituals** are sets of behaviors that symbolize a relationship.

**Social status** is a socially created structural category or position in society. Each status carries with it certain rights, expectations and duties.

**Social stratification** is the systematic ranking of categories of people on a scale of social worth, which affects how valued resources are distributed in a society.

**Social structure** refers to the social relationships that exist within society.

**Socialism** is an economic system stressing public ownership in pursuit of the equal distribution of goods and wealth.

**Socialist medicine** involves a system of health care that is under the complete control of the government.

**Socialization** is the process whereby we internalize our culture's values, beliefs, and norms. Through this experience, we become functioning members of our society.

**Socialized medicine** is composed of health care systems over which the government exercises some, but not total, control.

**Societies** are diverse groups of people who share distinctive cultures in defined geographic locations.

**Sociocultural perspective** views health issues as the responsibility not only of each individual, but also of their family members and sometimes even their community.

**Sociological imagination** is the process of achieving a better understanding of our own experiences. We do this by discovering our place within society, including our experiences with social institutions and the historical period in which we live.

**Sociological paradigms** provide frameworks that allow us to study society and analyze data and research using sociological tools, methods, and theories.

**Sociological perspective** involves being able to see the general in the particular.

**Sociology** is the scientific study of human society and social interaction.

**Special interest group** is a group formed for the purpose of lobbying government in order to pass or block legislation.

**Speculators** are people who buy land hoping that it will increase in value as they hold on to it.

**Spurious correlation** occurs when two variables change together, not because of a causal relationship between the two, but because of a third variable. This result reminds us that correlation does not imply causation.

**SRO hotel** or single-room occupancy hotel, is a house, apartment building or residential hotel where low-income tenants live in small, single units sharing a common bathroom and where rent can typically be paid in short-term increments.

**Standard mortality ratio** is a measure indicating the actual or observed number of deaths in the group of interest, divided by the expected number of deaths, then multiplied by 100.

**State** is the apparatus of governance that exists independent of government but which cannot function effectively without government.

**Status** refers to a social position that is held by a person and characterized by rights and duties.

**Status inconsistency** occurs when people experience mismatch between their statuses, or when a person experiences mismatching statuses him or herself.

**Status set** refers to all the statuses that a person occupies at a given time.

**Status systems** rank people based on their social prestige.

**Status value** is the social value assigned to social statuses whereby some statuses are treated as more valuable or worthy than others.

**Stereotyping** refers to pre-defined, rigid mental images about how a person or group should act or think, held to be true regardless of whether there is evidence and data disproving these images. They may be positive or negative.

**Stigmas** discredit a person's claim to a normal identity.

**Strain theory** was developed by Robert Merton to describe the strain felt by some members of society when they do not have access to the institutional means to achieve cultural goals.

**Stratified sampling** makes sure that the people randomly selected to be in the sample match the proportions of the population being studied.

**Street crimes** are crimes that occur in public places.

**Structural functionalism** views society as an intricate structure, with many levels or parts all working together in collaboration for stability.

**Structural unemployment** is joblessness due to a mismatch between available work and the skills or situations of potential employees.

**Structured mobility** involves societal events that allow entire groups of people to move up or down the social structure together.

**Subculture** refers to distinctive lifestyles and values shared by a category of people within a larger society.

**Subordinates** are individuals or groups with less power than another individual or group in a coercive interaction.

**Sunbelt** is a loosely defined area of the Southern and Western United States that generally has cheaper land, cheaper wages and lower taxes.

**Superego** is Freud's term for the part of the personality that acts as the executive branch because it uses reason and deals with whether something is right or wrong.

**Superordinate goals** involve people or groups working together to achieve a goal that is deemed important to everyone involved. The people tend to become friends and their attitudes, values, and goals will become similar, even if those involved originally disliked one another.

**Superordinates** are individuals or groups with more social power than another individual or group in a coercive interaction.

**Sustainability** is the ability of Earth's various systems, including human cultural systems and economies, to survive and adapt to changing environmental conditions indefinitely.

**Sweatshop** is a place of labor where workers are paid very low wages and operate in substandard conditions often for long hours.

**Symbol** refers to anything that represents an idea.

**Symbolic interactionism** contends that society exists due to the everyday interactions of people.

**Taboos** refer to strongly held mores, the violation of which is considered to be extremely offensive.

**Techniques of neutralization** are ways of thinking or rationalizing that help people deflect society's norms.

**Technological determinism** is the erroneous belief that technology is outside of social influence and that it actually structures social, economic and political life.

**Tertiary deviance** is normalizing behavior considered deviant by mainstream society, or relabeling behavior as non-deviant.

**Tertiary sector** is the sector of the economy based on the provision of services rather than tangible goods.

**The Great Migration** was the movement of 6 million black Americans out of the American

South in the 20th century.

**Theism** is the belief that god(s) reside separately from humans and other living things.

**Theocracy** is a political system with no separation between church and state such that spiritual and secular leaders are one and the same.

**Theories** are integrated sets of propositions that are intended to explain specific phenomena and to show relationships between variables in order to gain understanding.

**Total institutions** are places where people are cut off from the larger society and forced to follow a strict set of rules.

**Totalitarian government** is government that suppresses political opposition and attempts to control all aspects of civil society.

**Tourist bubble** is a specialized area of a downtown that presents a coherent, easy-to-understand and safe version of the city in order to lure visitors who might otherwise be skittish of cities.

**Tracking** is the separation of students into different ability groups to receive different levels of instruction.

**Traditional authority** is power that is legitimated by long-standing custom.

**Underpopulation** is the lack of normal or desirable population density for economic viability.

**Unemployment** is the inability to find work despite actively seeking it.

**Unemployment rate** is the percentage of the potential labor force that is not employed despite actively seeking work in the previous four weeks.

**Universal education** is the granting of free education to all citizens in a country.

**Urban renewal** refers to the efforts of urban leaders in the 1950s through the 1970s, using federal housing funds, to create amenities that they saw as being important for the post-industrial city.

**Urban vernacular** refers to the visual manifestations of the complex grittiness of the local culture.

**Urbanism** is a distinct way of life that emerges in cities.

**Urbanist** is a person who studies cities.

**Use value** is the value of an item based on its inherent usefulness.

**Validity** means that indicators used in research, like rating scales, accurately measure the concepts they are intended to measure.

**Value contradictions** refer to values that conflict with each other, either within a culture or across cultures.

**Values** refer to collective ideas about what is right or wrong, good or bad, desirable or undesirable in a particular culture.

**Variables** are attributes that may change their values under observation. Variables can be assigned numerical scores or category labels.

**Vertical mobility** is the movement from one social position to another of a different rank and/or prestige. This change can be in an upward or downward direction.

**White collar work** is an occupation in the service sector of the economy, particularly office work.

**White flight** is the systematic movement of upper-middle-class families out of the inner-city cores and into the suburbs.

**White privilege** is a cultural superiority given to people who have "white" skin and is not based on their skills, talents, or merit.

**White-collar crimes** are illegal acts committed by affluent individuals in the course of business activities.

**Work spillover** refers to the effect that work has on individuals and families, absorbing their time and energy and impinging on their psychological states.

# Photo Credits

Chapter 1 p. 12 "Sidewalk" source David Bueso

Chapter 2 p. 34 "Hispanic festival" source Cliff

Chapter 3 p. 64 "Boy in the mirror" source Alan Turkus

Chapter 4 p. 88 "Celebrities" source Ryan Coleman

Chapter 5 p. 118 "Soccer" source Ronnie MacDonald

Chapter 6 p. 152 "Broken window" source Quinn Dombrowski

Chapter 7 p. 178 "Homeless woman" source Jeremy Brooks

Chapter 8 p. 208 "Marathon" source Alejandro Arce Herrero

Chapter 9 p. 234 "Couple" source Quinn Anya

Chapter 10 p. 256 "Family" source Howi Lee

Chapter 11 p. 274 "Learning" source MDgov

Chapter 12 p. 298 "President Bill Clinton" source World Economic Forum

Chapter 13 p. 326 "Nurse and patient" source DIAC

Chapter 14 p. 354 "New York City" source Karen Blaha

Chapter 15 p. 386 "Protest" source Al Jazeera English

# Name Index

# Subject Index

primogeniture 182
principle of immanent change 398
private schools 277, 279
privilege 250
profane 283
profession 317
professional crime 167
Prohibition 394-395
proletariat 21
pro-natal 263
propaganda 392
proscriptive norms 49
puberty 67
public 391
public opinion 391-392
public schools 246, 277-278, 281,
    312
punishment 159
purchasing power 197

Q

Quakers 285
qualitative data 24
quantitative data 24

R

race 211
Race to the Top 281
racial formation 219
racial profiling 214
racial restrictive covenants 360
racial zoning 360
racial-ethnic group 219
racism 211
Raising Cain 156
random samples 24
rationalization 301
rational-legal authority 301
reactionary crowds 389
real culture 48
real estate developers 362
recidivism rates 169
reciprocal inclusivity 54
redlining 360
Reefer Madness 156
Reel Bad Arabs 218
reference groups 121-122
reform movements 393
Regents of the University of
    California v. Bakke 280
relative poverty 190-191
reliability 26

religiosity 291-292
religious pluralism 292
renewable resources 368
Republican Party 224, 305
resistance movements 393
resocialization 80-81
resource mobilization theory 394
revolutionary movements 393
riots 389
Roe v. Wade 345, 347
Roger and Me 366
role conflict 93
role exit 93
role expectation 92
role performance 92
role set 92
role strain 93
roles 92
Rollerball 299-300, 319
Roman Catholic Church 285, 287
routinization 113, 135, 140
rumors 391
rustbelt 362
Rutgers University 238

S

sacred 283
Saginaw Chippewa Tribe 215
same-sex marriage 237
samples 24
sanctions 50, 155
Sandwich Generation 264-265
scapegoating 224
schools 276
seasonal unemployment 318
secondary care providers 333-334
secondary deviance 161-162
secondary groups 122-123
secondary sector 311
secondary sex characteristics 236
secondary socialization 78
sect 285
secularization 283
Securities and Exchange Commission
    167
segregation 212, 277, 280, 283
self-actualization 73-74
self-efficacy 128
semi-periphery countries 197-199
sensate culture 398
serial monogamy 262
service sector 43-44, 311, 317

sex 76, 236
Sex and the City 265
sex ratios 338
sex segregation 243
sexism 239
sexual orientation 237
shared monopoly 316
sick roles 330
significant others 70
Sikhism 290-291
skinheads 53, 228
Skype 57
slavery 39, 181-182, 210, 225
social aggregates 120
social capital 359
social categories 120
social class 165, 184
social conflict perspective 19
social consensus 19
social construction 210,
social contagion theory 390
social control mechanisms 50
social control 50, 155, 167-169, 397
social groups 120
social inequality 38, 39, 41-42, 58,
    159, 181, 209, 236, 312
social institutions 35, 37, 39, 40, 42,
    89, 94, 239, 283
social interaction 21, 89, 94, 96, 105,
    111, 261, 398
social learning theory 76
social mobility 193-194, 279
social movements 387, 392-395
social networks 130
social order 155
social rituals 125
social status 250
social stratification 179, 219
social structure 89
socialism 312
socialist medicine 330
socialization 65
socialized medicine 327, 330-331
sociobiology 67, 155
sociocultural evolution 36
sociocultural perspective 329
sociological imagination 14
sociological paradigms 14
sociological perspective 14, 329
sociology 14
solidaristic crowds 389
Southern Poverty Law Center 227-